The Prentice Hall Essentials Dictionary

of Culinary Arts

STEVEN LABENSKY

GAYE G. INGRAM

SARAH R. LABENSKY

ILLUSTRATIONS BY WILLIAM E. INGRAM

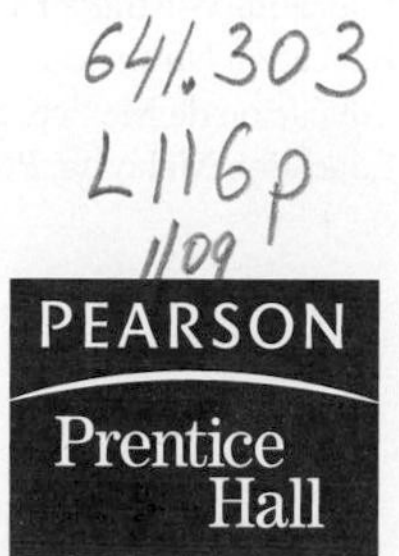

Upper Saddle River, NJ 07458

Library of Congress Cataloging-in-Publication Data

Labensky, Steven.
The Prentice Hall essentials dictionary of culinary arts/Steven Labensky, Gaye G. Ingram, Sarah R. Labensky; illustrations by William E. Ingram. — 1st ed.
p. cm.
ISBN 0-13-170463-X (alk. paper)
1. Food—Dictionaries. 2. Cookery—Dictionaries. I. Ingram, Gaye G. II. Labensky, Sarah R. III. Title.
TX349 . L34 2007
641. 303—dc22

2006101985

Editor-in-Chief: Vernon R. Anthony
Senior Editor: William Lawrensen
Managing Editor—Editorial: Judith Casillo
Managing Editor—Production: Mary Carnis
Production Liaison: Jane Bonnell
Production Editor: Amy Gehl, Carlisle Publishing Services
Manufacturing Manager: Ilene Sanford
Manufacturing Buyer: Cathleen Petersen
Senior Marketing Manager: Leigh Ann Sims
Marketing Coordinator: Alicia Dysert
Marketing Assistant: Les Roberts
Senior Design Coordinator: Miguel Ortiz
Cover Designer: Anthony Gemmellaro
Composition: Carlisle Publishing Services
Printer/Binder: RR Donnelley
Cover Printer: RR Donnelley

Pearson Education Ltd.
Pearson Education Singapore, Pte. Ltd.
Pearson Education Canada, Ltd.
Pearson Education—Japan
Pearson Education Australia PTY, Limited
Pearson Education North Asia Ltd.
Pearson Educación de Mexico, S.A. de C.V.
Pearson Education Malaysia, Pte. Ltd.

10 9 8 7 6 5 4 3 2 1
ISBN-13: 978-0-13-170463-3
ISBN-10: 0-13-170463-X

Contents

A Note from the Authors

One term not included in this dictionary is **culinary arts.** It is a phrase that means different things to different people and we could neither find nor devise any definition that captured all of its nuances. In the final analysis, however, we realized that it is this compendium on topics such as ingredients, preparation methods, restaurant management, cooking equipment, food history and sanitation, nutrition, prepared dishes and many more that truly defines culinary arts.

To assist you in using this dictionary, we note several rules that we followed in its preparation:

- If sources provided multiple, verified spellings for a term (including transliterations), we included alternative or variant spellings, listing the most commonly used one first.
- We tried to be faithful to the use of accent marks, characters and capitalization rules as found in the original (if written in the Latin alphabet) or most commonly approved source; often, other writers are not and many of the terms found here may appear elsewhere with the appropriate accents or capitalization omitted or altered.
- Pronunciations are given in a sounded-out phonetic form rather than with the standard phonetic alphabet with diacritical marks. This was done for the sake of practicality and usability. For languages that do not use the Latin alphabet, the transliteration is often the phonetic pronunciation as well (ex., Arabic).
- Where a geographic origin or time period is given, we did so with the understanding that such a designation identified the principal indigenous source of time period and that the specific ingredient, dish or the like may be available in other areas and eras.

Nothing found in this book, save this note, is the original creation of the authors. As with all reference books, it is a compilation derived from sources new and old, formally published and casually discussed. To paraphrase H. L. Mencken's preface to his *The American Language*, Supplement II (New York: Alfred A. Knopf, 1923):

> *We are not trained in linguistic science, and can thus claim no profundity for this book. It represents gatherings, not of experts in linguistics, but simply of teachers, cooks, and gourmets interested in language, and if there appears in it any virtue at all it is with the homely virtue of diligence.*

Errors and omissions are regrettable, but inevitable. We welcome comments and corrections, additions and explanations from users.

We wish to thank William Ingram, and his assistant James Ingram, for their superb illustrations and assistance throughout this project. We also wish to thank Maurizio Cristiani of *Another Language* and Barry Karrh for their assistance with translations and pronunciations. Finally, we are indebted to our families and friends for their input and support during this project.

STEVEN LABENSKY
GAYE G. INGRAM
SARAH R. LABENSKY

abaisse (ah-bess) French for a thin bottom crust; a rolled-out pastry or biscuit.

abalone (a-buh-LOH-nee) A group of gastropod mollusks found in warm seas worldwide, generally having a brownish-gray ear-shaped shell with an average length of 6 in. (17.7 cm), a large adductor muscle that fills the entire shell opening and an ivory flesh with a chewy texture and mild flavor; they are usually available canned or fresh; significant varieties include the black, ormer, pink, red and southern green abalones.

abbey beer A Belgian style of bottle-conditioned beer traditionally brewed in Trappist abbeys; generally, it is a strong, full-bodied, top-fermenting ale.

abóbora (ah-BAW-boh-rah) A large pumpkinlike squash with an orange flesh; used principally in Portuguese soups.

aboyeur (ah-boh-yer) At a food services operation following the brigade system, it is the person who accepts orders from the dining room, relays them to the various station chefs and reviews the dishes before service; also known as the expediter.

absinthe (AHB-senth) An alcoholic beverage distilled from oil of wormwood, balm, mint, hyssop, fennel, star anise and a high-proof brandy; it has a light yellow-green color, has a pronounced licorice flavor and is banned in many countries because of its high alcohol content and the toxic effects of wormwood; it is usually consumed diluted with water. *See* Pernod.

absolute alcohol Clinically pure ethyl alcohol (200 proof or 100%); it is used as a baseline for comparing the alcohol content of beverages.

absorption 1. The incorporation of a liquid into a solid or of a gas into a liquid or solid. 2. The process by which products of digestion such as monosaccharides are passed through the walls of the small intestines into the blood to be carried to other parts of the body.

Abyssinian gooseberry A small fruit native to East Africa; it has a delicate orange color, a minimal amount of flesh and a flavor reminiscent of apricots.

acacia honey A pale, clear honey with a delicate scent made principally from acacia blossoms in China, France, Canada, Hungary, Italy, Romania and elsewhere; it is one of the few honeys that does not crystallize with age.

acerola (ah-see-ROLL-ah) A bright red cherry-sized fruit that grows on shrubs (*Malpighia punicifolia*) in the West Indies; it has three pits, a juicy flesh, a moderately acidic, raspberry-like flavor and is eaten fresh or used in preserves and pies; also known as Barbados cherry and West Indian cherry.

acesulfame-K; acesulfame potassium (a-seh-SUHL-faym-K) A noncaloric artificial sweetener approximately 200 times sweeter than sugar; it is used in processed foods such as beverages, confections, sugar substitutes, dairy products and dry bases for puddings.

acetic acid (a-SEE-tik) 1. An organic acid naturally occurring in plant and animal tissues. 2. The essential constituent of vinegar.

achiote seeds (ah-chee-OH-tay) The seeds of the annatto tree, native to South America; the pulp surrounding the seeds is used as a yellow-to-red coloring agent for butter, cheese, margarine and smoked fish (it also adds a slightly musky flavor); also known as annatto and arnatto.

acid 1. Any substance that releases hydrogen ions in a watery solution; acids have a pH of less than 7, react with metals to form salts and neutralize bases. 2. A tasting term for a food or beverage with a pleasantly tart or tangy flavor; it can be a defect if too pronounced, however.

acid–base balance The mechanisms maintaining the proper equilibrium of acidity and alkalinity of the body's fluids (generally a pH of 7.35–7.45).

acidophilus milk Milk cultured with *Lactobacillus acidophilus,* bacteria that consume lactose and produce lactic acid in the process (which sometimes causes a sour flavor); acidophilus milk and products made from it are used by people who are lactose intolerant.

acidulated water Water mixed with a small amount of lemon juice or vinegar and used to prevent the discoloration of fruits and vegetables caused by acidulation.

acidulation The browning of cut fruit caused by the reaction of an enzyme (polyphenoloxidase) with the phenolic compounds present in these fruits; this browning is often mistakenly attributed to an exposure to oxygen; also known as enzymatic browning.

acorn The fruit of the oak tree (genus *Quercus*), it is shaped like a teardrop; some varieties are edible (but have a woody texture) and are eaten raw, roasted or roasted and ground into a flour or coffee substitute.

acorn squash A small- to medium-sized acorn-shaped winter squash with an orange-streaked dark green fluted shell (orange, yellow and creamy white varieties are also available), a pale orange flesh, a large seed cavity and a slightly sweet, nutty flavor.

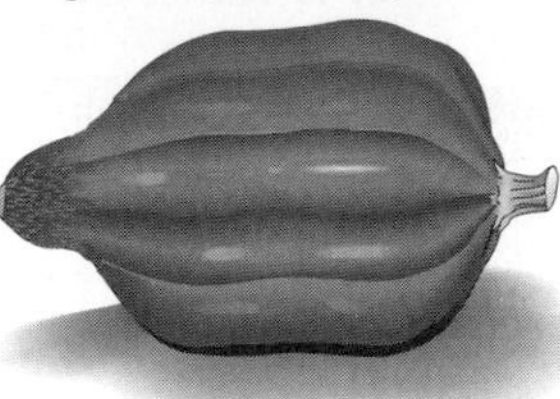
acorn squash

acrolein A bitter, volatile chemical produced from overheating fats.

active dry yeast A dehydrated granular form of yeast; a lack of moisture causes the yeast cells to become dormant, thus extending the product's shelf life. *See* yeast.

Acton, Eliza (Brit., 1799–1859) Author of *Modern Cookery for Private Families* (1845); intended as a text for British housewives during the first half of the 19th century, its recipes are clear with well-organized directions.

adductor A mollusk's single muscle, it extends from one valve (shell) through the flesh to the other valve; when it is relaxed, the shell is open; in many mollusks, such as abalone, it is the principal edible part.

ade A slightly tart beverage made of sugar (or other sweetener), water and a citrus juice such as lemon (for lemonade), lime (for limeade) or orange (for orangeade); it is served chilled in a tall glass, usually with ice.

adjust To taste a dish and add salt, freshly ground black pepper or other seasonings, if necessary.

adobado (ah-doh-BAA-doh) 1. A Mexican and Latin American chile, garlic and herb marinade used to season meat. 2. Spanish for marinated and generally used to describe marinated beef. 3. A Filipino cooking method in which pieces of meat and garlic are browned and then broth and vinegar are added as a sauce before serving.

adobe bread (ah-doh-bee) A yeast-leavened bread made by the Pueblo Indians of the American Southwest; it is traditionally flavored with nuts or seeds and baked in a beehive-shaped oven.

adobo sauce (ah-DOH-bo) A Mexican seasoning paste or sauce made from ground chiles, herbs and vinegar.

Adriatic fig A green-skinned, white-fleshed fig.

adulterate To make a substance impure by adding foreign, undesirous or inferior matter.

adzuki; azuki (ah-ZOO-kee; AH-zoo-kee) A small, somewhat square red bean of Asian origin (*Vigna angularis*); popular in Japanese cuisine either sugar coated or made into a sweet paste that is used to make sweets.

aebleskiver; ebleskiver (eh-bleh-SKEE-vor) 1. A Danish puffed cake or doughnut made in a specially designed pan with indentations for individually frying each cake; the cake is usually served as a breakfast treat with powdered sugar and strawberry jam. 2. Danish for doughnut.

aebleskiver pan (eh-bleh-SKEE-vor) A cast-iron pan with seven rounded 2.25-in.-wide indentations used for making aebleskiver.

aebleskiver pan

aegir, sauce (ahg-rah) A French compound sauce made from a hollandaise flavored with dry or prepared mustard.

ae mono (ah-e moh-noh) Japanese for dressed foods, usually saladlike dishes served chilled.

aerate 1. To dissolve air in a liquid or to expose a liquid to air. 2. To add air to a food (e.g., sifting flour or beating egg whites).

afifsuke-nori (af-fee-sue-kee-noh-ree) Japanese for sheets of nori brushed with soy sauce.

aflatoxin A toxin produced by molds and sometimes found on peanuts, cottonseed and corn.

aftertaste The sensation that remains in the mouth after swallowing or expectorating (spitting) a sampled food or beverage.

agave (ah-GAH-vee) A family of succulents native to the American Southwest, Central America and northern South America; the thick, pointed, flat leaves, which are sometimes poisonous if eaten raw, have a sweet, mild flavor when cooked.

agé (ah-gay) Japanese for deep-fry.

aged meat Meat stored under specific temperature and humidity conditions to increase tenderness and flavor. *See* dry aging *and* wet aging.

agemono (AH-gay-mo-no) Japanese for fried foods.

agglomerated cork A cork made from scraps of used corks glued together; also known as a composition cork or particle cork.

aging 1. The period during which freshly killed meat is allowed to rest so that the effects of rigor mortis dissipate. 2. The period during which freshly milled flour is allowed to rest so that it will whiten and produce less sticky doughs; this process can be accelerated chemically. 3. The period during which a cheese mellows and matures under specific temperature, humidity and other conditions; also known as curing. 4. The period during which wine, brandy, whiskey, certain beers and other alcoholic beverages are stored in oak barrels or stainless steel or glass tanks so that the slow, complex changes that add body, aroma and flavor characteristics can occur.

aglio e olio (AH-l'yoh a AW-loyh) Italian for garlic and oil, a dressing that is usually used on pasta.

ahi (ah hee) Hawaiian for yellowfin tuna.

ahole (ah-hoh lay) A saltwater fish found off Hawaii; it has large eyes and a silvery skin; the young fish is known as aholehole.

aigre-doux (ay-greh-DOO) French for the combined flavors of sour (aigre) and sweet (doux) (e.g., a sauce made with vinegar and sugar).

aiguillette (eh-gew-ee-ley) 1. A French cut of poultry (especially duck); it is a long, narrow slice of flesh taken from either side of the breastbone. 2. A French cut of the beef carcass; it is similar to rump round roast; also known as pièce de boeuf and pointe de culotte.

aïoli (ay-OH-lee) A garlic mayonnaise; it is used as a condiment or sauce.

aïoli à la Turque (ay-oh-LEE ah lah tewrk) A French sauce made from garlic and white bread soaked in milk, pressed through a sieve, blended with egg yolks and vinegar and then beaten with oil.

airline breast A boneless chicken breast with the first wing bone attached.

aitch bone (H bohn) Part of a quadruped's pelvic bone; also known as the edge bone.

aji (AH-khee) 1. A long, thin, tapering chile with thin flesh and a very hot, tropical fruit flavor; it has a green or red color when fresh and is yellow when dried and known as aji mirasol. 2. The common name used in Latin America to describe various members of the chile family *Capsicum baccatum*.

aji dulce (AH-khee DOOL-seh) A small, elongated, wide-shouldered, fresh chile with a green, yellow, orange or red skin and a very fruity, hot flavor.

akee (AH-kee) *See* genip.

akee and saltfish A Jamaican dish of sautéed salted fish, onions, bacon, sweet peppers and tomatoes mixed with akee and flavored with basil and oregano.

akule (ah-KOO-lay) A fish found off Hawaii; it is usually salted and dried; also known as bigeye scad.

al (ahl) Italian for to the, at the or on the; used in relation to a food, it generally designates a style of preparation or presentation.

à la (ah lah) French for in the manner or style of; used in relation to a food, it designates a style of preparation or presentation.

à la carte (ah lah kart) 1. A menu on which each food and beverage is listed and priced separately. 2. Foods cooked to order, as opposed to foods cooked in advance and held for later service.

à la king (ah lah KING) An American dish consisting of diced foods, usually chicken or turkey, in a cream sauce flavored with pimientos, mushrooms, green peppers and sometimes sherry.

à la mode (ah lah MOHD) 1. French for in the fashion or manner of. 2. In the United States, a dessert item topped with a scoop of ice cream.

albacore tuna (ahl-bah-kor) A variety of tuna found off Mexico and along the U.S. West Coast; it has a steely blue skin that becomes silvery on the belly, white flesh and an average market weight of 10–60 lb. (4.5–27 kg); it is often used for canning; also known as a longfin tuna.

albedo The fluffy white layer of a citrus rind; it has a bitter flavor. *See* zest.

Albert, sauce (al-BAIR) A French compound sauce made from a velouté flavored with horseradish and mustard; it is usually served with beef.

albóndiga (ahl-BON-dee-gah) 1. Spanish for meatball. 2. A Mexican and Spanish dish of spicy meatballs, usually in a tomato sauce.

Albuféra, sauce (ahl-bew-fay-rah) A French compound sauce made from a suprême sauce flavored with a meat glaze and finished with pimiento butter.

albumen (al-BYOO-mehn) The clear portion of the egg used as the nutrient source for the developing chick, constituting approximately two-thirds of its internal mass and containing most of its protein and riboflavin;

sometimes used in fresh or dried form as a fining or clarifying agent or whipped for general baking and cooking; also known as egg white.

albumin One of a group of simple proteins found in many plants and most animals; soluble in cold water and concentrated salt solutions and coagulates when heated; found in blood as serum albumin, in milk as lactalbumin and in egg whites as ovalbumin.

alcide sauce (ahl-seed) A French white wine sauce garnished with sweated shallots and horseradish.

alcohol 1. Popular term for ethyl alcohol. *See* ethyl alcohol. 2. An intoxicating beverage containing ethyl alcohol.

alcohol by volume The percentage of alcohol per metric volume of beer, wine or distilled spirits; also known as percentage of alcohol by volume.

alcohol by weight The percentage weight of alcohol per metric volume of beer, wine or distilled spirits (e.g., 6% alcohol by weight equals 6 g of alcohol per 100 cl of beer).

alcohol content The amount of alcohol in a beverage; federal regulations require that alcoholic beverages intended for retail sale be labeled with their alcohol content in proof and percentage of alcohol by volume.

alcoholic beverage control laws; ABC laws A general term for federal, state or local laws principally regulating the sale (as opposed to the manufacture) of alcoholic beverages.

al dente (al DEN-tay) Italian for to the tooth and used to describe a food, usually pasta, that is cooked only until it gives a slight resistance when one bites into it; the food is neither soft nor overdone.

alderman's walk A British cut of the venison or lamb carcass; it is the longest, finest slice from the haunch.

ale 1. A fermented malt beverage or style of beer made with a top-fermenting yeast and brewed at 60–70°F (16–20°C); it is often lower in carbonation and darker in color than lager beer. 2. Historically, any non-hopped malt beverage.

alembic (AH-lamb-bik) A large copper vessel with an onion-shaped top traditionally used for the double distillation of Cognac and other brandies.

alembic brandy A brandy such as Cognac or Armagnac made from grapes distilled in an alembic.

aleppo (a-leep-po) A coarsely ground red pepper used for its fragrance and flavor in Arabic cuisines.

alewife; ale wife A member of the herring family found in the Atlantic Ocean off North America; it has a silvery skin, a strong flavor and a market weight of 0.25–1 lb. (100–450 g); it is usually available smoked or pickled.

Alexandra, sauce A French compound sauce made from a suprême sauce flavored with truffle essence.

Alexandra mayonnaise A French mayonnaise sauce prepared with hard-cooked egg yolks, seasoned with dry mustard and garnished with chervil.

alfalfa (al-FAL-fuh) A plant (*Medicago sativa*) important for use as hay or animal fodder; also known as lucerne.

alfalfa honey A thick, creamy yellow honey principally made from alfalfa blossoms; popular in the United States, it is sometimes used for blending.

alfalfa sprouts Germinated alfalfa seeds; they have small, soft seeds and fine, slightly crunchy pale white to green sprouts and are used in sandwiches and salads.

al forno (ahl FOHR-no) Italian term for a food that is baked or roasted in an oven.

al fresco (al FREHS-koh) Italian for in the open and used to describe a meal or other social event taken outdoors.

algae; alga Any of numerous chlorophyll-containing plants of the phylum Thallophyta; ranging in size from single cells to large multicelled organisms, they grow in freshwater and saltwater, on or in other organisms or in soil and are generally rich in nutrients.

algérienne, sauce (al-JE-reh-en) A French compound sauce made from a tomato sauce garnished with julienne of sautéed green and red sweet peppers; also known as Algerian sauce.

Alhambra (a-lahn-bra) 1. A French garnish for meats; it consists of sautéed artichoke hearts, red or green bell peppers and tomatoes. 2. A French salad of beetroot, celery, artichoke hearts and lettuce dressed with mayonnaise.

alimentation The process of nourishing the body; it includes ingestion, mastication, swallowing, digestion, absorption and assimilation.

Alitame (AL-ih-taym) An artificial sweetener that is 2,000 times as sweet as sugar. At this time it is not FDA approved.

alkali A substance, such as baking soda, used in the bakeshop to neutralize acids and act as a leavening agent in cakes and breads. *See* base.

alkalized cocoa Cocoa powder ground from beans treated with an alkali solution (usually potassium carbonate) to raise their pH; this powder is milder, less acidic and darker than untreated cocoa; also known as Dutch-processed cocoa. *See* cocoa powder.

alkaloid A number of bitter organic substances with alkaline properties found in certain foods, principally plants.

alkanet (AL-kuh-neht) A member of the borage family, whose roots yield a red dye that is used to color various food products such as margarine.

allemande, sauce (ah-leh-MAHND) A French compound sauce made from a velouté thickened with egg yolks and heavy cream and flavored with lemon juice; also known as German sauce.

alliance, sauce (ah-leh-hanss) A French compound sauce made from a hollandaise flavored with tarragon vinegar, white wine, cayenne and white pepper and garnished with chervil.

allicin The odor-producing substance in garlic; some consider it effective in inhibiting bacterial growth and strengthening the immune system.

Allium (ahl-leh-uhm) Any of a variety of members of the genus *Allium* and members of the lily family; grown worldwide, they are usually highly aromatic and flavorful, with an edible bulbous base and edible flat, grasslike green leaves (e.g., onion, shallot, garlic and leek).

all-purpose flour White wheat flour blended to contain a moderate amount of protein; it is used for a wide range of general baking and cooking, especially in nonprofessional kitchens and is available bleached (either chemically or naturally) or unbleached (they may be used interchangeably).

allspice A member of the pimento family (*Pimenta officinalis*) and native to tropical regions in the Western Hemisphere; the plant has leathery leaves, white flowers and small, brown berries that are used as a spice; when ground, the berries have a flavor reminiscent of a mixture of cinnamon, clove, nutmeg, ginger and pepper; also known as Jamaican pepper.

allumette (al-yoo-MEHT) 1. A thin strip of puff pastry topped with a sweet or savory mixture (e.g., royal icing or flavored butter) and served as an hors d'oeuvre or petit four. 2. Foods (especially potatoes) cut into a matchstick shape of approximately 1/8 × 1/8 × 1–2 in. (0.3 × 0.3 × 2.5–5 cm).

almendrado (ahl-mehn-dray-doh) A Mexican almond-flavored dessert of beaten egg whites bound with gelatin and served with a creamy custard sauce; it is often tinted the colors of the Mexican flag.

almond The nut of the almond tree (*Prunus amygdalus*), native to the Mediterranean region and now cultivated in California; the nut has a pitted, lozenge-shaped, tan shell, a pale yellow–ivory center surrounded by a thin brown covering and a distinctive flavor and aroma; it is available blanched, variously sliced and/or flavored and in paste form; also known as the sweet almond. *See* bitter almond oil.

almond cream A mixture of finely ground almonds, butter, eggs, sugar and flour used primarily as a filling in tarts and pastries; also known as frangipane.

almond extract A concentrated flavoring made from bitter almond oil and alcohol that is widely used in pastries and baked goods.

almond meal; almond flour A fine powder made from ground almonds and sugar and used in desserts and pastries.

almond milk The almond-flavored liquid remaining after almonds are pounded to a paste with water and then strained.

almond oil A pale oil obtained by pressing sweet almonds; it has a clean, fairly neutral flavor and is used in baking and for confections, especially for oiling baking tins.

almond paste A pliable paste made of ground blanched almonds, sugar and glucose or egg whites and used in pastries as a flavoring and for decorative work; it is similar to marzipan but coarser, darker and less sweet.

almond syrup A syrup made from almonds and used as a sweetener and flavoring agent, especially in cocktails and desserts; also known as orgeat and sirop d'amandes.

Alpine strawberry A strawberry variety native to central Europe north of the Alps; the small fruit have a tapered, conical shape and an intense flavor. An imprecisely used term to describe any wild strawberry.

Alto Douro (AHL-toe DOO-roe) The classical region of port wine production in northern Portugal.

aluminum A metal used for cookware, cooking utensils, flatware, service items, storage items and other tools or equipment used in the kitchen; lightweight and a good conductor of heat, aluminum cookware is often coated with nickel, stainless steel or nonstick plastic.

amandine (AH-mahn-deen; ah-mahn-DEEN) French term for a dish garnished with almonds; also incorrectly known as almondine.

amaranth (AM-ah-ranth) 1. A vegetable (genus *Amaranthus*) with green- or maroon-centered purple leaves; the leaves have a slightly sweet flavor and are used like spinach in Caribbean and Chinese cuisines; also known as callaloo (especially in the Caribbean), Chinese spinach and een choy. 2. A flour ground from the seeds of the amaranth plant.

amaretti (am-ah-REHT-tee) Crisp, airy Italian macaroons made with bitter almond or apricot kernel paste.

Amaretto (am-ah-REHT-toh) An Italian amber-colored liqueur with an almondlike flavor, although it is actually flavored with apricot kernels; it was originally made in Saronno and called Amaretto di Saronno.

ambarella (ahm-bah-rehl-lah) A tree fruit (*Spondias dulcis*) native to the Society Islands in the South Pacific and related to the golden apple; the egg-sized fruit grows in clusters and has a grayish-orange skin, a yellowish pulp, several seeds, a pungent aroma and a slightly sour flavor reminiscent of an apple or pineapple.

ambassadrice, sauce (ahn-bas-sa-DRESSE) A French compound sauce made from a suprême sauce garnished with puréed poached chicken breast and finished with whipped cream.

amberjack A member of the jack family, this mild, lean fish is found along the South Atlantic coast and is usually sold whole.

ambrosia (am-BROH-ZHAH) 1. A 19th-century salad or dessert made of freshly grated coconut and fresh fruit, especially oranges; popular in the American South. 2. In Greek and Roman mythology, it refers to the food of the gods.

amchur; amchoor (AHM-choor) A powder made from dried, raw mangoes; it has a tangy flavor and is used as a spice, principally in Indian cuisines; also known as mango powder.

americainé, à l' (a-may-ree-KEHN) 1. A French dish (especially lobster) prepared with a spicy sauce of tomatoes, olive oil, onions, brandy and wine. 2. A French garnish for fish consisting of thin slices of lobster tail and americainé sauce.

americainé, sauce (a-may-ree-KEHN) A spicy French sauce made of tomatoes, olive oil, onions, brandy and wine.

American cheese An imprecisely used term for any of a group of natural cheeses made in the United States, including Cheddar, Cheddar-style cheeses, Colby, granular cheeses, washed-curd cheeses, Brick, Monterey Jack and others.

American service A style of service in which a waiter takes the order and brings the food to the table; the food is placed on dishes (i.e., plated) in the kitchen.

amino acids The building blocks of protein; every amino acid is composed of an amine group, an acid group and a distinctive side chain; approximately 20 are necessary for humans, approximately 8 of which are essential and must be obtained through diet.

amiral, sauce (a-me-herl) A French white wine sauce garnished with lemon zest and capers and finished with anchovy butter; also known as admiral sauce.

ammonium bicarbonate A leavener that is a precursor of baking powder and baking soda; it must be ground to a powder before use; also known as carbonate of ammonia, hartshorn and powdered baking ammonia.

amoricaine, à l' (ah-more-ree-cane, ah l') A French preparation for lobster in the Breton style (the ancient name for Brittany); the sliced lobster is sautéed in olive oil with tomatoes.

amuse-gueule (ah-muz-gull) French for appetizer.

anadama bread (ah-nah-dah-mah) A colonial American yeast bread flavored with cornmeal and molasses.

anadromous A fish that migrates from a saltwater habitat to spawn in freshwater.

Anaheim chile (AN-uh-hym) A long, tapered chile with a pale to medium bright green color, relatively thick flesh and mild, vegetal flavor; it is available fresh, canned or roasted but not dried and is named for the California city where it was first grown commercially; also known as the California chile and long green chile.

Anasazi (ah-nah-sah-zee) An heirloom variety of bean that was cultivated by the ancient peoples in what is now New Mexico and Arizona; it has a dark wine red color spotted with white.

ancho (ahn-cho) A dried poblano with broad shoulders tapering to a rounded end; the chile has a brick red to dark mahogany color, wrinkled flesh and relatively mild, fruity flavor with overtones of coffee, licorice, tobacco and raisin.

anchoïade (anh-shwah) A dish from France's Provence region made from puréed anchovies mixed with crushed garlic and olive oil; it is served on toast or with raw vegetables.

anchois, sauce aux (ahn-SHWAH) A French white wine sauce beaten with anchovy butter and garnished with diced anchovy fillets; also known as anchovy sauce.

anchovy A member of the herring family found in the Mediterranean Sea and off southern Europe; it has a long snout, a large mouth and a blue-green skin that becomes silvery on the sides and belly; it ranges in length from 5 to 9 in. (12 to 22 cm); usually available pickled or salted.

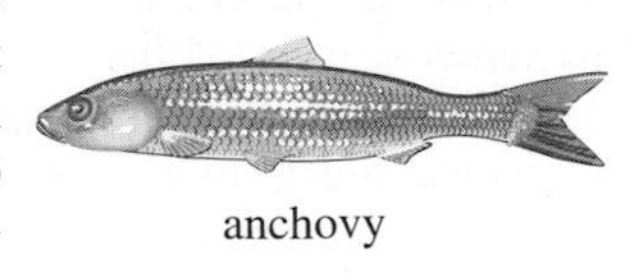
anchovy

ancienne, sauce (ahn-see-yen) A French compound sauce made from hollandaise and garnished with diced gherkins, sautéed mushrooms and truffles.

andalouse, à l' (ahn-dah-LOOZ, ah l') A French preparation method associated with the cuisine of Spain's Andalusia region; the dishes (usually large joints of meat) are characterized by a garnish of tomatoes, peppers, rice, eggplant and sometimes chipolatas.

andalouse, sauce (ahn-dah-LOOZ) A French compound sauce made from a velouté and tomato purée.

andouille sausage (an-DOO-ee; ahn-DWEE) A spicy smoked pork sausage (made with neck and stomach meat); originally from France, it is now a hallmark of Cajun cuisine.

angel biscuit A light, fluffy biscuit leavened with yeast, baking powder and baking soda; the dough must be refrigerated overnight before baking and can be kept refrigerated for several days and baked as needed.

angel food cake A light, airy cake made without egg yolks or other fats; its structure is based on the air whipped into the egg whites; it is typically baked in a tube pan.

angelica (an-JEHL-ih-cah) An herb of the parsley family (*Angelica archangelica*) with pale green, celerylike stalks; it is used to flavor liqueurs and sweet wines; the stalks are often candied and used to decorate desserts.

angel pie A cream pie, usually lemon, prepared in a baked meringue pie shell.

angels on horseback An hors d'oeuvre of shucked oysters wrapped in bacon, broiled and served on buttered toast points.

angel's share 1. The quantity of wine or distilled spirits lost through evaporation, seepage or other processes during aging or storage. 2. An amount of food, too small to keep, left on a plate after dining.

anglaise, à l' (ahn-GLEHZ, ah l') French preparation methods associated with English cuisine; the vegetables are poached or boiled and served plain or with chopped parsley and butter or the principal ingredient is coated in bread crumbs and pan-fried.

angler fish; anglerfish *See* monkfish.

anise (AN-ihs) A small annual member of the parsley family (*Pimpinella anisum*) native to the eastern Mediterranean region; it has bright green leaves with a mild licorice flavor that are sometimes used as an herb or in salads.

aniseeds; anise seeds The tiny, gray-green egg-shaped seeds of the anise plant; their distinctive, licorice flavor is used to flavor sweet and savory dishes as well as alcoholic and nonalcoholic beverages.

Antin, sauce d' (dahn-tahn) A French compound sauce made from a Madeira sauce flavored with dry white wine and garnished with mushrooms, truffles and fine herbs.

antipasto, antipasti (pl.) (ahn-tee-PAHS-toe) Italian for before pasta and used to describe hot or cold appetizers, usually simple foods such as cheeses, sausages, olives, marinated vegetables or the like.

aperitif (ah-pair-ee-TEEF) Any beverage, usually alcoholic, consumed before a meal to whet the appetite. *See* digestif.

aplet A firm but chewy confection made with reduced apple juice, gelatin and nuts. *See* cotlet.

à point (ah PWAH) 1. A steak cooked to medium-rare. 2. French for a food cooked to the perfect degree of doneness.

Appaloosa An heirloom variety of black and white or red and white bean native to the American Southwest.

appetite The psychologically compelling desire to eat; it is usually experienced as a pleasant sensation associated with seeing, smelling or thinking of food. *See* hunger.

appetizer 1. Finger food served before the meal to whet the appetite; the term is often used synonymously with the term hors d'oeuvre. 2. The first course of a meal, usually small portions of hot or cold foods intended to whet the appetite; also known as a starter.

apple A pome fruit (*Malus pumila*) with generally firm flesh that can range in flavor from sweet to tart; it is encased in a thin skin, which can range in color from yellow to green to red; apples can be eaten out of hand, cooked or used for juice and are grown in temperate regions worldwide and available all year, particularly during the fall.

apple brandy A brandy distilled from a mash of cider apples and usually aged in oak casks before blending and bottling. *See* applejack.

apple brown betty A colonial American baked pudding made with layers of fruit, spices, sugar and bread crumbs.

apple butter A thick brown spread made by slowly cooking apples, sugar, spices and cider.

apple charlotte A pastry made by lining a mold with buttered bread, then filling it with spiced, sautéed apples. *See* charlotte mold.

apple dumpling A dessert made by wrapping an apple in sweet pastry dough and baking it.

applejack 1. An alcoholic beverage made by grinding and pressing apples, fermenting the juice into cider and then distilling it; also known as apple brandy. 2. A sweet apple syrup. 3. An apple turnover.

apple juice The natural, unsweetened juice pressed from apples; it is pasteurized and may be partially or completely filtered.

apple pandowdy A deep-dish dessert made with a mixture of sliced apples, spices and sugar, topped with biscuit batter and baked.

applesauce A cooked purée of apples, sugar and sometimes spices; it can be smooth or chunky.

apricot A small stone fruit (*Prunus armeniaca*) with a thin, velvety, pale yellow to deep burnt orange skin, a meaty golden cream to bright orange flesh and an almond-shaped pit; it is highly perishable, with a peak season during June and July; the pit's kernel is used to flavor alcoholic beverages and confections.

apricot

aquafarming; aquaculture The business, science and practice of raising large quantities of fish and shellfish in tanks, ponds or ocean pens, usually for food.

aquavit; akvavit (ah-kar-VEET) A clear Scandinavian alcoholic beverage distilled from potatoes or grain and flavored with caraway seeds, cardamom and orange and lemon peels.

arabica coffee beans (ah-RAB-ie-kah) A species of coffee beans (*Coffea arabia*) grown around the world in high-altitude tropical and subtropical regions with plentiful rainfall; the most important species commercially, they are used for fine, richly flavored and aromatic beverages. *See* robusta coffee beans.

arak; arrack; arrak (ar-ruck) Any of various spirits distilled in the Middle East, Southeast Asia and the Far East from fermented coconut palm sap or a rice and molasses mash.

arame (ah-rah-meh) Dried, shredded seaweed with a greenish-brown color and a mild, delicate flavor; it is used as flavoring in Japanese cuisines.

aram sandwich (A-rhum; EHR-uhm) A sandwich made from softened lahvosh spread with a filling and rolled jelly-roll style, refrigerated and sliced into 1-in. pieces for service. Also known as levant.

arancini (ah-rahn-CHEE-nee) A Sicilian dish of rice and meat formed into balls.

arborio rice (ar-BOH-ree-oh) An ovoid, short-grain rice with a hard core, white color and mild flavor; it becomes creamy when cooked and is used for risotto.

archiduc, sauce (ahr-schwe-dehk) A French compound sauce made from a suprême sauce finished with a champagne reduction.

Arctic char A freshwater fish found in northern Europe, Canada and the northern United States; related to the brook trout (but not a true trout); it has an average market weight of 1 lb. (450 g) and a white to red flesh with a delicate flavor; also known as omble.

area chef At a large hotel, conference center or the like, the person responsible for a particular facility or function.

Argenteuil (ar-zhawn-TEW-ee) A French preparation method used to describe a dish with a sauce or garnish of asparagus tips or purée.

argol The tartar (potassium bitartrate) that a maturing wine deposits on the barrel staves; this precipitate is used to make cream of tartar.

aril The lacy outer covering of some seeds (e.g., nutmeg).

arlesienne, sauce (ahrl-ehs-yehng) A French compound sauce made from a béarnaise flavored with tomato purée and anchovy paste and garnished with diced tomatoes.

Armagnac (AR-manh-yak) A French brandy produced principally in Gers (southeast of Bordeaux) from white wine grapes; distilled and redistilled in one continuous operation and aged in black oak barrels, it has a dry, smooth flavor, a pungent bouquet and an amber color.

armand, d' (ar-mahnd, d') A French garnish consisting of soufflé potatoes, a red wine sauce, and chopped, sautéed goose liver and truffles; it is generally used for meats.

arm chops *See* blade chops.

Armenian cracker bread *See* lahvosh.

Armenian cucumber A very long, sometimes slightly coiled, ridged slicing cucumber with dark green skin, a pale green flesh, a mellow, sweet flavor and edible seeds.

Armenian wax pepper An elongated sweet pepper with a yellow skin and a mild, sweet flavor; used pickled or fresh.

arm roast 1. A subprimal cut from the beef primal chuck; somewhat tough, it is available with or without the bone. 2. A subprimal cut from the veal primal shoulder; usually available deboned, rolled and tied. 3. A subprimal cut of the pork primal shoulder; it is a moderately tender, flavorful roast.

arm steak A fabricated cut from the beef primal chuck; it is cut from the arm roast and available with or without the bone.

aromatic A food, usually an herb, spice or vegetable, added to a preparation primarily to enhance its aroma and secondarily its flavor.

arrabbiata (HAR-rah-bee-ah-tah) An Italian tomato sauce flavored with herbs, cayenne pepper, spicy sausage bits and bacon.

arracacha (ah-rah-cah-chah) A root vegetable (*Arracacia xanthoohiza*) native to northern South America; the brown-skinned cylindrical root has an off-white flesh with a potato-like texture and a vaguely sweet flavor.

arrowroot A starchy white powder made from the underground stems of a tropical plant, generally used as a thickener; it is flavorless and becomes clear when cooked.

artichoke, common The large flowerhead of a plant of the thistle family (*Cynara scolymus*); it has tough, gray-green, petal-shaped leaves with soft flesh (which is eaten cooked) underneath, a furry choke (that is discarded) and a tender center (called the heart and that is also eaten, usually cooked or pickled); also known as a globe artichoke.

artichoke

artificial sweetener A sugar substitute such as aspartame, cyclamate or saccharin; used as a food additive in processed foods or for individual use, has few if any calories and little if any nutritional value; also known as a synthetic sweetener.

artisanal (ar-TEE-shun-al) A craftsmanlike approach to bread making and cheese making in which the maker's skill and intuition and the quality of raw ingredients are given the highest priorities.

arugula (ah-ROO-guh-lah) A leaf vegetable (*Eruca sativa*) with dark green, spiky, dandelion-like leaves and a strong, spicy, peppery flavor; used in salads; also known as rocket, rucola and rugula.

asafetida; asafoetida (ah-sah-FEH-teh-dah) A pale brown resin made from the sap of a giant fennel-like plant native to India and Iran; it has a garlicky flavor and a fetid aroma; available powdered or in lump form, it is used (sparingly) as a flavoring in Indian and Middle Eastern cuisines; also known as devil's dung.

asakusa nori (ah-SAH-koo-sah NOH-ree) Thin dark sheets of dried seaweed; used as a flavoring and sushi wrapper in Japanese cuisine.

aseptic packaging (uh-SEHP-tihk) A means of packaging food and drink products so that they are exposed to a minimal amount of air; such products are usually vacuum-packed.

ash bread A cornbread, typically wrapped in cabbage leaves, baked in the ashes left in a fireplace; also known as corn pone. *See* hoecake.

Ashley bread A bread similar to spoon bread but made with rice flour; probably created in South Carolina.

Asiago (AH-zee-AH-go) A hard northern Italian grana cheese made from cow's milk; it has a pungent flavor and a grayish-white interior; when cured for 6 months or more, it is used for grating and cooking.

Asian pear A fruit ranging in size and color from large and golden brown to small and green; it has a juicy, crunchy, firm, granular texture and a sweet flavor; also known as a Chinese pear.

asparagus (ah-SPAR-ah-gus) A member of the lily family (*Asparagus officinalis*) with an erect stalk and small, scalelike leaves along the stalk, capped by a ruffle of small leaves; a young stalk is tender, with a slightly pungent, bitter flavor, an apple green color and a purple-tinged tip; it becomes tougher as it ages.

asparagus, white A very pale yellowish-green asparagus with a milder flavor than green asparagus; the asparagus is regularly reburied as the stalk grows, which retards the development of chlorophyll.

asparagus steamer An assemblage consisting of two tall pots; the inner pot has a perforated bottom and holds the asparagus upright; the assemblage is partially filled with water so that the stalks are simmered while the tips are steamed.

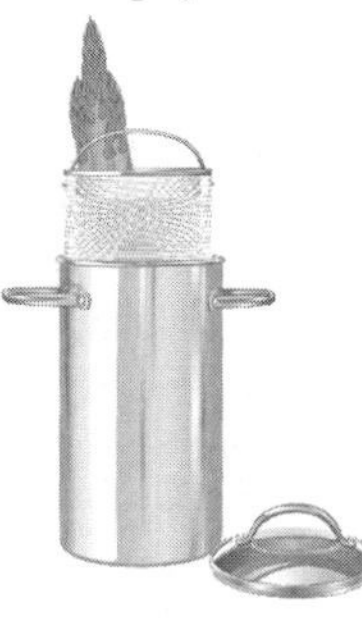

asparagus steamer

aspartame A food additive used as a synthetic sweetener in sugar substitutes and processed foods such as soft drinks, frozen desserts, refrigerated puddings and dried pudding bases; created by linking together two amino acids (aspartic acid and phenylalanine), it is 200 times sweeter than sucrose; it is registered under the name NutraSweet.

aspic A clear savory jelly made from clarified meat, fish or vegetable stock and gelatin; it is used to glaze cold foods. *See* hure.

aspic cutters Small metal cutters in various shapes (similar to cookie cutters); used to cut aspic, truffles, hard-boiled egg whites, tomato skins and the like into decorative designs.

aspic mold A $1\frac{1}{2}$-in.-(3.8-cm) deep, oval, flair-sided, stainless steel mold with a capacity of 4 fl. oz. (113.4 g); it is used for single servings of foods such as eggs in aspic; also known as an oval dariole. *See* timbale mold.

aspic mold

Asti Spumante (AH-stee spoo-MAHN-teh) A sweet, white sparkling wine made by the Charmat process in the town of Asti, Piedmont, Italy.

asure; ashure A sweet Middle Eastern soup made with whole grains, legumes, dried fruits and nuts; it is said to have been the last meal served on Noah's ark.

atemoya (a-teh-MOH-ee-yah) A hybrid fruit of the cherimoya and sweetsop and grown in Florida; it has a tough, sage green skin covered with short, petal-like configurations similar to those of a globe artichoke, a cream-colored pulp with large black seeds and a flavor reminiscent of mango and vanilla.

Atlantic clams Any of several varieties of clams found along the U.S. East Coast; they are generally classified as Atlantic hard-shell clams and Atlantic soft-shell clams.

Atlantic halibut A variety of halibut found off the East Coast of the United States and Canada; it has a lean white flesh with a sweet, mild flavor and a firm texture; also known as eastern halibut.

Atlantic hard-shell clams Atlantic clams with hard, blue-gray shells and a chewy meat that is not as sweet as that of other varieties; also known as quahogs; significant varieties include cherrystone clams, chowder clams, littleneck clams and topneck clams.

Atlantic mackerel A fish found in the Atlantic Ocean from the mid-Atlantic states of the United States to New England; it has a brilliant multihued coloration and two dozen or so wavy dark bands, a high fat content, a dark flesh, an average weight of 0.5–2.5 lb. (225–1140 g), and an assertive flavor; also known as Boston mackerel.

Atlantic oysters Any of several varieties of oysters found along the U.S. East Coast; generally, they have round, flat, dark gray shells, a grayish flesh with a soft texture and a briny flavor (the flavor and color often vary depending on the oyster's origin); many Atlantic oysters are named for their place of origin (e.g., Chesapeake Bay oysters and Long Island oysters); also known as American oysters, American cupped oysters and eastern oysters.

Atlantic salmon The most commercially important salmon species, aquafarmed extensively off Canada, Iceland, Ireland, Scotland and Norway (wild fish are rarely available); it has a grayish-brown skin with scattered black spots that becomes silvery and then white on the belly, a moist pink flesh, a high fat content, a delicate flavor and an average weight of 5–15 lb. (2.3–6.7 kg); it is often marketed with the fish's origin added to the name (e.g., Norwegian Atlantic salmon and Shetland Atlantic salmon).

Atlantic soft-shell clams Atlantic clams with thin, brittle shells that do not close completely because of the clam's protruding black-tipped siphon; they have a tender, sweet flesh; significant varieties include Ipswich clams, steamer clams and longneck clams.

atole (ah-TOH-leh) An ancient Mexican thick beverage consisting of masa, water or milk, crushed fruit and sugar or honey; it is served hot or at room temperature.

aubergine (oh-berr-yeen) British and French for eggplant.

au bleu (oh BLEUH) A French term indicating that the fish was prepared immediately after it was killed.

au gratin (oh GRAH-tan) A French term referring to a dish with a browned topping of bread crumbs and/or grated cheese; also known as gratinée.

au jus (oh zhew) A French term for roasted meats, poultry or game served with their natural, unthickened juices.

au naturel (oh nah-teur-EHL) A French term indicating that the food is served in its natural state; not cooked or altered in any fashion.

aurore, à la (oh-ROHR, ah lah) A name given to some French dishes containing tomato purée, especially egg and chicken dishes coated with sauce aurore.

aurore, sauce (oh-ROHR) A French compound sauce made from a velouté with tomato purée.

au sec (oh sek) A French term referring to something cooked until nearly dry.

avgolémono (ahv-goh-LEH-moh-noh) A Greek soup and sauce made from chicken broth, egg yolks and lemon juice (rice is added to the soup).

avignonnaise, sauce (ah-vee-nyon-aze) A French compound sauce made from a béchamel flavored with garlic, seasoned with grated Parmesan, finished with an egg yolk liaison and garnished with parsley.

avocado (a-voh-CAH-doh) A tropical fruit (*Persea americana*) with a single large pit, spherical to pear shaped; it has a smooth to rough-textured green to purplish skin and yellow to green flesh with a buttery texture and a high unsaturated fat content; it is generally used like a vegetable and consumed raw; also known as an alligator pear and vegetable marrow.

avocado

avocado oil A colorless, viscous oil obtained by pressing an avocado's pit; odorless, it has a neutral flavor and is principally used for salad dressings.

avoirdupois weight A system for measuring weight based on a pound of 16 oz. and an ounce of 16 drams.

Awenda bread (AH-wen-dah) A quick bread made with hominy grits and cornmeal; named for an Indian settlement near Charleston, South Carolina.

baba; baba au rhum (BAH-bah; BAH-bah oh rum) A light, rich Polish yeast cake studded with raisins and soaked in rum syrup; it is traditionally baked in individual cylindrical molds, giving the finished product a mushroom shape. *See* savarin.

babaco (BAH-bah-ko) A very long tropical fruit (*Carica pentagona*) native to South America with a star-shaped cross section, a soft, green skin that turns yellow when ripe, a juicy, pale apricot-colored flesh, few seeds and a slightly acidic flavor reminiscent of strawberries with hints of papaya and pineapple; also known as a chamburo.

baba ghanoush; baba ghanouj; baba ghannouj (bah-bah gha-NOOSH) A Middle Eastern dish of puréed eggplant, olive oil, tahini, lemon juice and garlic and garnished with chopped mint, pomegranate seeds or chopped pistachios; it is served as a dip or spread, usually with pita; also known as mutabbal.

babka (bahb-kah) A Jewish, Russian and Polish dessert consisting of a rich yeast dough made with many eggs and sweet butter, flavored with citrus peel and studded with raisins; sometimes cocoa or a cinnamon–sugar syrup is added.

baby back ribs A fabricated cut of the pork primal loin; it is a slab of ribs weighing 1.75 lb. (792 g) or less.

baby lamb The meat of a sheep slaughtered when it is 6–8 weeks old; the meat is very tender, with a mild, delicate flavor. *See* lamb, mutton *and* spring lamb.

bacalao (bah-kah-LAH-oh) Salt cod used in Spanish and South American cuisines.

Bacchus The Roman god of wine and of an orgiastic religion celebrating the power and fertility of nature. *See* Dionysus.

back 1. A portion of the veal carcass that contains the rib and loin primals in one piece. 2. A portion of the lamb carcass that contains the rack and loin primals in one piece.

back of the house The areas of a restaurant, hotel or the like not open to the public; they are generally office and work areas such as the kitchen and other food preparation areas, storerooms, receiving docks, laundries, and so on. *See* front of the house.

backribs A fabricated cut of the pork primal loin; it consists of the ribs cut from the anterior end; also known as country-style spareribs.

backstrap The elastic connective tissue found in the neck region of the beef, veal or lamb carcass; also known as yellow ligament.

back waiter The person at a restaurant responsible for clearing plates, refilling water and bread, crumbing the table and other tasks; also known as busperson, busser, commis de rang, demi-chef de rang and dining room attendant.

bacon A fabricated cut of the pork carcass, cut from the sides and belly; consisting of fat interspersed with strands of meat, it is salted and/or smoked and available sliced or in a slab.

bacon, Canadian A fabricated cut of the primal pork loin; it is a lean, boneless pork loin roast that is smoked; known as back bacon in Canada.

bacteria Any of the numerous species of microorganisms within the class Schizomycetes; there are three principal forms: spherical or ovoid (called cocci, which are incapable of movement), rod shaped (called bacilli) and spiral or corkscrew shaped (called spirilla if rigid and spirochetes if flexible); various bacteria play significant roles in putrefaction, fermentation, disease, digestion and so on, and they are generally very sensitive to temperature, moisture and pH levels. *See* lag phase, log phase *and* decline phase.

bacteria, aerobic Bacteria that need oxygen to survive; also known as aerobes.

bacteria, anaerobic Bacteria that can survive in the absence of oxygen; also known as anaerobes.

bacteria, facultative Bacteria that can survive with or without oxygen, although most show a preference for oxygen; most pathogenic bacteria are facultative; also known as facultative anaerobes.

bacteria, obligate anaerobic Bacteria that grow only in the absence of oxygen; also known as obligate anaerobes.

bael The fruit of a tree (*Aegle marmelos*) that grows wild in northern India and Southeast Asia; related to the citrus family, it resembles a grayish-yellow orange with a thin, hard rind and a gummy, yellow pulp with many seeds, a refreshing flavor and a strong, pleasant aroma.

bagatelle (bag-a-tel) A French strawberry cake composed of genoise cake split and filled with diplomat cream and fresh strawberries and topped with a thin layer of pale green marzipan; also known as le Fraisier.

bagel A dense, doughnut-shaped Jewish yeast roll; it is cooked in boiling water, then baked, which gives the rolls a shiny glaze and chewy texture.

bagna cauda (BAHN-yah COW-dah) Italian for hot bath and used to describe a dipping sauce made of olive oil, butter, garlic and anchovies and served with raw vegetables.

bagna cauda pot A tall glazed earthenware pot used for bagna cauda and often available with a burner.

baguette (bag-EHT) 1. A long, thin loaf of French bread with a hard, crisp crust and an airy, chewy interior. 2. An air-dried, salami-like French sausage shaped like a baguette. *See* French stick.

baguette pan A metal baking pan made of two or more long half-cylinders joined together side by side; the metal may be perforated to allow better air circulation; it is used for proofing and baking yeast breads; also known as a French bread pan.

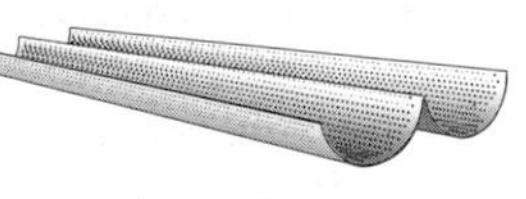
baguette pan

baharat (bah-hah-raht) Arabic for spice and used to describe a Middle Eastern flavoring blend that generally consists of peppercorns, coriander, cinnamon, cloves, cumin, cardamom, nutmeg and paprika.

bahmi goreng (bah-me go-rang) An Indonesian dish consisting of noodles cooked with foods such as shrimp or other shellfish, meat, chicken, eggs, onions, chiles, garlic, cucumber, peanuts and seasonings.

bain marie (bane mah-ree) 1. A hot water bath used to cook foods gently or to keep cooked foods hot; also known as a water bath. 2. A container for holding foods in a hot water bath.

bake A Caribbean breadlike biscuit made with coconut milk and cooked on a griddle or in a frying pan.

bake blind A technique for baking an unfilled pastry or tart shell; the shaped dough is weighted down with dry beans or pie weights, then baked completely before being filled.

bake cup A pleated paper or foil cup used to line a muffin or cupcake pan; the cup holds the batter, facilitating release of the baked product.

baked Alaska A dessert composed of liqueur-soaked sponge cake topped with a mound or half-sphere of ice cream, all of which is coated with sweetened meringue and browned just before service.

bake-off 1. To finish baking a frozen dough or partially baked product. 2. A bakeshop operation that relies on frozen doughs or partially baked products supplied from a central bakery or purchased from a manufacturer. 3. A contest, usually amateur, for making baked goods.

baker's knife A knife with a thin, 12-in. blade, a round, blunt tip and fine, closely spaced teeth; it is used for cutting delicate cakes and crisp pastries. *See* confectioners' knife.

baker's knife

baker's rack A portable metal rack designed to hold numerous sheet pans or hotel pans; it is used for moving pans of food quickly from one work area to another; also known as a speed rack.

bakewell tart; bakewell pudding A tart consisting of a layer of jam, preserved fruit or candied peel overlaid with a mixture of sugar, eggs and butter and baked with or without a pastry crust; also known as transparent pudding.

baking A dry-heat cooking method that heats food by surrounding it with hot, dry air in a closed environment; the term is usually used with reference to cooking breads, pastries, vegetables, fruits and fish. *See* roasting.

baking ammonia Ammonium bicarbonate; a chemical leavening agent sometimes used in cookies or crackers.

baking chocolate Pure chocolate liquor (although an emulsifier is sometimes added); also known as bitter or unsweetened chocolate.

baking powder A mixture of sodium bicarbonate and one or more acids, generally cream of tartar and/or sodium aluminum sulfate, used to leaven baked goods; it releases carbon dioxide gas if moisture is present in a formula.

baking powder, double-acting Baking powder that releases some carbon dioxide gas upon contact with moisture; more gas is released when heat is applied.

baking powder, single-acting Baking powder that releases carbon dioxide gas in the presence of moisture only.

baking sheet A firm, flat sheet of metal, usually aluminum, with low, straight sides, on which items are placed for baking.

baking soda Sodium bicarbonate, an alkaline compound that releases carbon dioxide gas when combined with an acid and moisture; it is used to leaven baked goods.

baking stone A heavy round or rectangular ceramic or stone plate used in lieu of a baking sheet for pizza and breads; also known as a pizza stone.

baking tile A thick, unglazed quarry tile, usually 8–12-in. square; used like a baking stone.

baking tile

baklava (BAAK-lah-vah) A Middle Eastern sweet pastry made with buttered phyllo dough layered with honey, nuts and spices, usually cut into diamond-shaped pieces after baking.

balance scale A scale with two trays; one holds the item to be weighed and weights are placed on the other until the two trays are counterbalanced; weights can be in the metric, U.S. or imperial system; also known as a baker's scale.

balloon whisk A large whisk used for whipping egg whites; its looped wires create a nearly spherical outline.

balloon whisk

ballotine (bahl-lo-teen) A charcuterie item similar to a galantine; it is usually made by stuffing a deboned poultry leg with a forcemeat and then poaching or braising it.

balsamic vinegar (bahl-sah-mek) A dark, mellow Italian vinegar with a sweet–sour flavor; it is made from concentrated grape juice fermented and aged for 15–20 years in a series of wooden casks.

balut (ba-loot) A Filipino delicacy consisting of a duck egg containing a partially developed embryo; it is usually dyed a bright fuchsia color.

bamboo shoots The ivory-colored edible shoots of a species of bamboo plant (*Bambusa vulgaris*); they are cut while the shoots are young and tender and have a woody appearance and fibrous texture; available fresh and canned and used in many Asian cuisines.

bamboo steamer An assemblage of two loosely slat-bottomed bamboo rounds with one lid; used to steam foods, the stacked baskets sit above boiling water in a wok and are available in diameters of 4–11 in.

banana The berry of a large tropical herb (especially *Musa paradisiaca sapientum*); the fruit grows in clusters (hands) and is long and curving with a brown-stained yellow skin (it is harvested while still green), a slightly sticky, floury, off-white pulp and a distinctive sweet flavor and aroma. *See* plantain.

banana chile A long, yellow-green chile with a mild flavor; used in salads, stuffed or pickled.

banana cream pie A single flaky pie crust filled with a mixture of custard and thinly sliced bananas, usually topped with meringue or whipped cream.

banana flowers The compact, purple, pointed heads at the tip of a forming bunch of bananas; they are used in Southeast Asian cuisines as a vegetable and garnish.

banana leaves The large, flat, dark green leaves of the banana plant; used in Central and South American, Mexican and African cuisines to wrap foods during cooking, they impart a delicate flavor to the foods and help keep them moist.

banana pudding A dessert from the American South consisting of vanilla custard layered with bananas and vanilla wafers and served chilled.

bananas Foster A dessert created by Brennan's Restaurant in New Orleans consisting of a sliced banana quickly sautéed in butter, rum, sugar and banana liqueur, then flambéed and served over vanilla ice cream.

Banbury cake; Banbury tart An oval-shaped British cake made of flaky pastry dough filled with dried fruit and spices; a speciality of Banbury, England.

banger A British sausage traditionally made from ground pork and bread crumbs; a beef banger is also available.

banh trang (ben train) Thin, round, semitransparent, hard, dry rice-paper crêpes used after moistening to wrap Vietnamese spring rolls.

banker's sauce *See* banquière sauce.

banneton (BAN-tahn) A French woven basket in which bread is allowed to rise before being baked; it is sometimes lined with cloth.

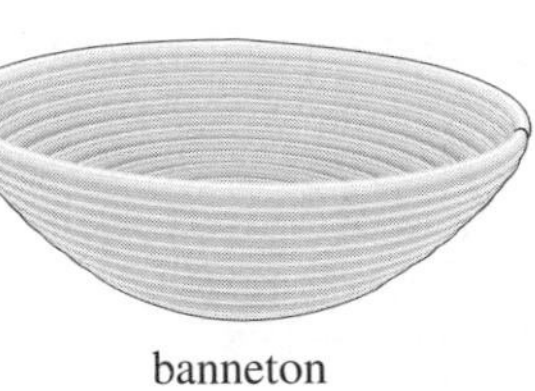
banneton

bannock (BAN-nuhk) A traditional Scottish sweet bread made with oats and barley and cooked on a griddle.

banquet event order (BEO) The written confirmation of details for a special meal or event.

banquière, sauce (bahn-kehr) A French compound sauce made from a suprême sauce blended with tomato purée and veal glaze, finished with Madeira and butter and garnished with truffles; also known as banker's sauce.

Banyuls (bahn-yulz) A French vin de liqueur comparable to a light, tawny port and used as an aperitif or dessert wine.

bao (bo) Slightly sweet, yeast-risen, steamed Chinese wheat buns with various fillings such as Chinese sausage, chicken with vegetables and salted duck egg, date and sweet bean paste and barbecued pork. *See* dim sum.

baobab (ba-OH-bahb) 1. The gourdlike fruit of a tree (*Adansonia digitata*) native to the tropical areas of central Africa; it has a whitish-yellow pulp that contains tartaric acid and is used as a food and flavoring ingredient; also known as monkey bread. 2. The leaves of this tree, which are eaten like a vegetable.

bap 1. A soft, white yeast roll traditionally eaten for breakfast in Scotland and England. 2. A soft, white yeast roll used for sandwiches, especially in Ireland.

bar back A bartender's apprentice or helper who replenishes ice and other supplies, prepares drink garnishes, cleans the bar area and generally assists in all but the final presentation of drinks and the collection of moneys.

barbacoa (bahr-bah-KOH-ah) A Mexican and Latin American dish of chile-marinated braised beef; it was originally cooked wrapped in maguey leaves, but now it is steamed in banana leaves or simply braised.

Barbados gooseberry The edible fruit of a cactus (*Pereskia aculeata*) native to the West Indies; it is small and spherical with a yellow to red color and a tart flavor.

Barbados sugar A moist, fine-textured raw sugar.

barbecue; barbeque; bar-b-q *v.* To cook foods over the dry heat created by this equipment. *n.* 1. A brazier fitted with a grill and sometimes a spit; it uses coals, hardwoods, gas or electricity as a heat source. 2. The foods, usually meat or poultry, cooked with this equipment and frequently coated with a tangy tomato- or vinegar-based sauce. 3. An informal meal or party, particularly in the United States, where such foods are cooked and served outdoors. *See* picnic.

barbecue sauce An American sauce traditionally made with tomatoes, onion, mustard, garlic, brown sugar and vinegar; it is used to baste barbecued meats and poultry.

barberry; berberis; berberry An ovoid berry (*Berberis vulgaris*) grown in Europe and New England; the unripened green berries are pickled and used like capers and the ripened berries, with a red skin and tart flavor, are used in preserves, syrups and baked goods; also known as a mahonias or Oregon grape.

bar brands The proprietary liquors (i.e., not generic or house brands) served at an establishment.

bar cookie A type of cookie made by baking the batter or dough in a sheet pan, then cutting it into individual serving–sized bars or squares.

barding fat A thin sheet of fatback used to wrap meats to be roasted or braised to keep them moist and prevent certain parts (such as the breasts of poultry) from overcooking.

bark A flat, irregularly shaped chocolate candy, usually containing nuts or fruit.

barley A small, spherical grain grown worldwide and usually pearled to remove its outer husk; the white grain has a slightly sweet, nutty, earthy flavor, chewy texture and high starch content; also known as pearl barley.

barley flour Ground barley; used for baking (principally scones) and as a thickener for milk-based soups and sauces.

barley sugar 1. A confection made by heating white sugar to the melting point, at which point it forms small grains resembling barley. 2. A hard lemon-flavored candy made from barley water.

barley water 1. A drink made by boiling barley in water and cooling it to room temperature; it is typically consumed with meals in Korea. 2. A British lemon- or orange-flavored drink similar to a lemon or orange squash. 3. A slightly fermented beverage made by steeping barley in water.

barm brack; barmbrack (BAHRM brak) An Irish yeast bread containing raisins and candied fruit peel.

barnyardy A tasting term for a food's (e.g., cheese) or beverage's (e.g., wine) earthy or goaty aromas or flavors reminiscent of a stable or barnyard; not necessarily intended to convey a negative impression.

baron 1. In the United States, a single section of the lamb carcass containing both hindquarters (legs and loin). 2. In the United States, an imprecisely used term to describe any of a variety of large subprimal cuts of beef used for roasting (e.g., steamship round). 3. In France, a single section of the lamb or mutton carcass containing the saddle and two legs. 4. In Great Britain, a single section of the beef carcass containing both primal sirloins.

barquette (bahr-KEHT) A small boat-shaped pastry shell used for appetizers or desserts; the dough may be sweet or savory.

barquette mold A boat-shaped tartlet mold with plain or fluted sides.

barquette mold

barracuda (bair-ah-COO-dah) *See* Pacific barracuda.

barrel 1. A cylindrical wooden container with slightly bulging sides made of staves hooped together with flat parallel ends; a standard barrel holds 31.5 U.S. gallons or 105 dry quarts. 2. The wooden, glass or stainless steel container in which wine, beer or a distilled spirit is stored, aged and sometimes shipped.

barrel aging The process of mellowing a wine or distilled spirit by storing it in a wooden barrel; over time, the product develops certain characteristics and also extracts components from the wood such as the tannin, which contributes to its body and flavor.

barrel fermentation A process used to make some white wines; the must ferments in an oak barrel instead of a temperature-controlled stainless steel vat to extract tannins, pigments, aromas and flavors from the wood.

barrique (bar-reek) A French oak barrel used to age wine; it holds approximately 230 l.

barrista (bar-RES-ta) A person who makes espresso and coffee drinks to order, especially at a coffee-house.

bar syrup *See* simple syrup.

base Any substance that combines with hydrogen ions; bases have a pH value above 7 and neutralize acids to form a salt; also known as an alkali.

basil (BAY-zihl; BA-zihl) An herb (*Ocimum basilicum*) and member of the mint family; it has soft, shiny light green leaves, small white flowers and a strong, pungent peppery flavor reminiscent of licorice and cloves (other varieties are available with flavors reminiscent of foods such as cinnamon, garlic, lemon and chocolate); available fresh and dried; also known as sweet basil. *See* opal basil.

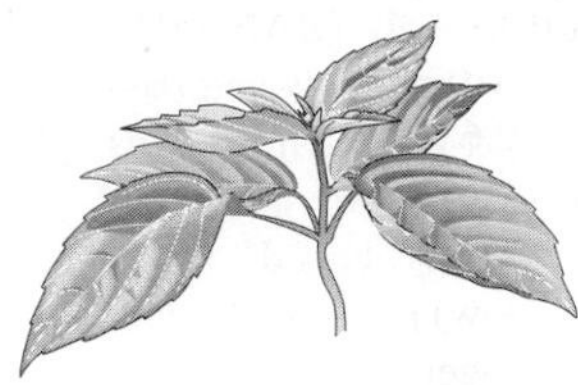
basil

basket weave A cake-decorating technique in which frosting is piped onto a cake to look as if it consists of interlaced double ribbons, a pattern similar to that of a woven basket.

basmati (bahs-MAT-tee) An aged, aromatic long-grain rice grown in the Himalayan foothills; it has a creamy yellow color, a distinctive sweet, nutty aroma and a delicate flavor.

basquaise, à la (bas-kaz, ah lah) 1. A French preparation method associated with the cuisine of the Basque; the dishes are characterized by the use of tomatoes, sweet peppers, garlic and often Bayonne ham. 2. A French garnish for large cuts of meat; it consists of Bayonne ham, mushrooms and pommes Anna.

bass 1. An imprecisely used term for several unrelated spiny-finned fish, including various freshwater sunfish such as the largemouth bass, saltwater corvina and aquafarmed hybrid striped bass. 2. A family of saltwater fish, including the black sea bass and striped bass.

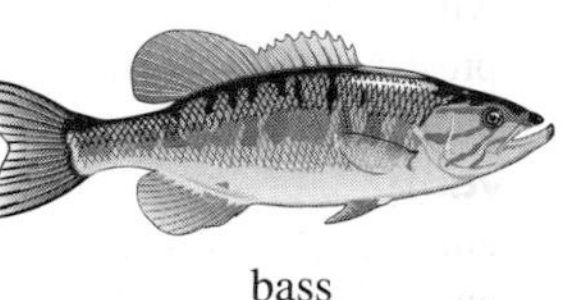
bass

bastard steak A fabricated cut of the beef carcass; it consists of the odd-shaped ends trimmed from other fabricated cuts, such as a T-bone.

basting Moistening foods during cooking (usually roasting, broiling or grilling) with melted fat, pan drippings, a sauce or other liquids to prevent drying and to add flavor.

bâtard (bah-tahr) An oval, uneven-shaped loaf of bread approximately 1 foot in length and weighing 10 oz. to 1 lb.

bâtarde (bah-tahr) A French white roux made with water bound with egg yolks and flavored with butter and lemon juice; also known as a butter sauce and usually served with vegetables and boiled fish.

Bath bun A sweet yeast bun filled with currants and candied fruit and coated with sugar; it originated in the town of Bath, England.

Bath chap A British dish consisting of the smoked or pickled lower portion of the cheeks of a long-jawed hog; it is usually boiled and then eaten cold.

batonnet (bah-toh-nah) Foods cut into a matchstick shape of approximately 1/4 × 1/4 × 2–2 1/2 in. (0.6 × 0.6 × 5–6 cm).

Battenberg A rectilinear cake popular during the Victorian era; it is composed of pink and white (or yellow) genoise arranged in a checkerboard pattern, held together with apricot jam and wrapped in marzipan.

batter *v.* To dip a food into a batter before cooking. *n.* 1. A semiliquid mixture containing flour or other starch used to make cakes and breads; gluten development is minimized and the liquid forms the continuous medium in which other ingredients are dispersed; it generally contains more fat, sugar and liquids than a dough. *See* dough. 2. A semiliquid mixture of liquid and starch used to coat foods for deep-frying.

batterie de cuisine (bat-TREE duh kwih-ZEEN) A French term for the cooking equipment and utensils necessary to equip a kitchen. *See* mise en place.

battuto (bah-TOO-toh) A mixture of pancetta, onion, garlic, parsley and other ingredients added raw to soups and stews; if lightly sautéed in olive oil, it is called soffritto.

Baumé (bo-may) 1. A hydrometer (saccharometer) used to measure the sugar content of grape juice or wine, especially sherry and port. 2. A scale for expressing the specific gravity of a liquid. 3. A method (scale) of measuring the density of sugar syrups.

Bavarian; Bavarian cream A molded, chilled dessert consisting of an egg custard thickened with gelatin and lightened with whipped cream; it can be flavored with fruit, liquor, chocolate and the like.

bavarois (bah-vah-wah) French for Bavarian.

bavaroise, sauce (bah-vah-wase) A French compound sauce made from a hollandaise beaten with crayfish butter and garnished with diced crayfish tails.

bay A small tree of the laurel family (*Laurus nobilis*), native to Asia; it produces firm leaves that are shiny on top and dull beneath; used as an herb, the leaves impart a lemon–nutmeg flavor and are usually removed from whatever food they are used to flavor before the item is eaten.

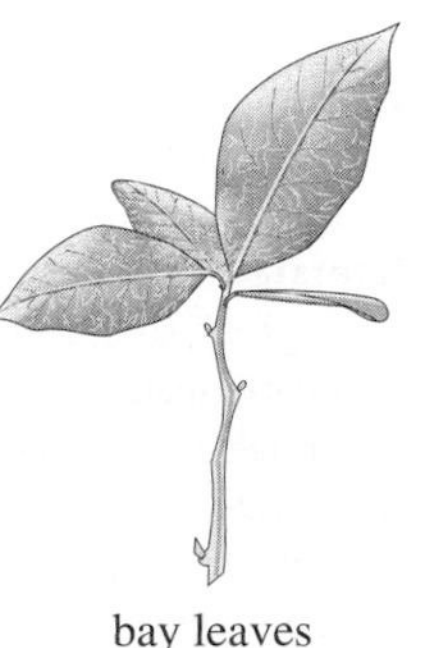
bay leaves

bay scallop A cold water scallop with a meat averaging 0.5 in. (1.27 cm) in diameter; its tender white meat is more succulent than that of the sea scallop.

bead border A border of piped frosting that resembles a string of beads; depending on application speed and pressure, the border can be a series of hemispherical beads or teardrops.

beam balance scale A scale with a removable tray to hold the item to be weighed; weights are adjusted along a bar connected to the tray until the weights and bar are counterbalanced by the tray and item; it can be calibrated in the metric, U.S. or imperial system.

bean curd A soft, cream-colored custard or gel-like product made from dried soybeans that have been soaked, puréed and boiled with water, then mixed with a coagulant, causing it to form curds; after the water is pressed out, it is usually cut into small squares and stored in cold water; it readily absorbs the flavors of other foods and sauces; also known as dòufù (China) and tofu (Japan).

bean curd, cotton A variety of bean curd with a firm texture and an irregular surface pattern achieved by straining the coagulated liquid through a semifine cloth and then pressing the curds; also known as aburage and momem tofu (Japan).

bean curd, silk A variety of bean curd with a soft, delicate texture and a smooth surface pattern achieved by straining the coagulated liquid through a fine mesh and allowing the strained curds to settle without pressing; also known as kinugoshi (Japan) and shui dòufù (China).

bean curd sheets *See* yuba.

bean flakes Beans that have been dried, steamed and flattened to hasten cooking times.

bean paste, red sweet A sweet purée of Chinese red beans, used as a pudding or a pastry filling.

bean paste, yellow A salty, pungent soybean paste used as a flavoring in Chinese cuisines.

bean pot An earthenware pot with a deep, bulbous body, a narrow mouth and a lid; the bowed sides expand the cooking surface and the narrow mouth minimizes moisture loss; available in 2- to 6-qt. capacities.

bean pot

beans 1. Any of various legumes (mostly from the genus *Phaseolus*) with a double-seamed pod containing a single row of seeds (sometimes also called beans); some are used for their edible pods, others for shelling fresh and still others for their dried seeds. 2. The ovoid or kidney-shaped dried seeds of legumes. *See* lentils, peas *and* pulses.

beans, dried Any of several varieties of seeds or peas left in the bean pod until mature and then shelled and dried.

bean sprouts The tender, young shoots of germinated beans (seeds) such as mung beans, alfalfa seeds, soybeans and wheat berries.

beard The hairy-looking gills of bivalves such as oysters and mussels; it is found at the open end of the shells opposite the hinge.

Beard, James (Am., 1903–1985) A highly esteemed food writer and respected cooking teacher; he authored numerous books, including *Theory and Practice of Good Cooking, Beard on Bread* and *James Beard's American Cookery;* his former home and cooking school in Greenwich Village, New York City, now houses the James Beard Foundation, which supports and promotes American cuisine.

béarnaise, sauce (bair-NAYZ) A French sauce made with a reduction of vinegar, wine, tarragon, peppercorns and shallots and finished with egg yolks and butter.

beat To mix by stirring rapidly and vigorously in a circular motion.

beaten biscuit A hard, crisp biscuit made by beating the dough vigorously for as long as half an hour; it originated in the American South during the 1800s.

beating A mixing method in which foods are agitated vigorously to incorporate air or develop gluten; a spoon or electric mixer with a paddle attachment is used.

Beauharnais, à la (boh-are-nay, ah-lah) A French garnish for tender cuts of beef (e.g., tournedos) consisting of stuffed mushrooms and quartered artichoke hearts.

beauty A fabricated cut of the beef primal rib; it is the first steak cut from the rib before the bone or with the bone removed.

béchamel sauce (bay-shah-mell) A French leading sauce made by thickening milk with a white roux and adding seasonings; also known as a cream sauce and a white sauce.

beechnut; beech nut A small, three-angled nut of the beech tree (genus *Fagus*); it has a slightly astringent flavor, similar to that of a chestnut or hazelnut, that improves with roasting; it is used roasted and ground like coffee or ground as animal feed.

beechwheat *See* buckwheat.

beef The meat of bovines (e.g., cows, steers and bulls) slaughtered when older than 1 year; generally, it has a dark red color, a rich flavor, interior marbling, external fat and a firm to tender texture. *See* veal.

beef, ground Beef ground from muscles found in various primals, but principally the chuck, short plate and sirloin; also known as hamburger and minced beef (especially in Europe).

beef, stewing A commercial standard for chunks of beef cut from any portion of the carcass except the heel and shank: 85% of it must be the equivalent of a 0.75- to 1.5-in. (19- to 38-mm) cube, and surface or seam fat shall not exceed 0.25 in. (6 mm) in thickness.

beef extract A strong beef stock reduced by evaporation to a thick, dark brown, salty paste and used as a flavoring.

beef forequarter Either bilateral half of the front portion of the beef carcass; it contains the chuck, brisket and shank, rib and short plate primals.

beef hindquarter Either bilateral half of the rear portion of the beef carcass; it contains the short loin, flank, sirloin and round primals.

beef jerky Thin strips of beef, traditionally dried in the sun and often lightly salted; they have a chewy, tough texture and a salty flavor.

beef primals The eight principal sections of the beef carcass: the chuck, brisket and shank, rib, short plate, short loin, flank, sirloin and round; each side of beef contains one of each primal.

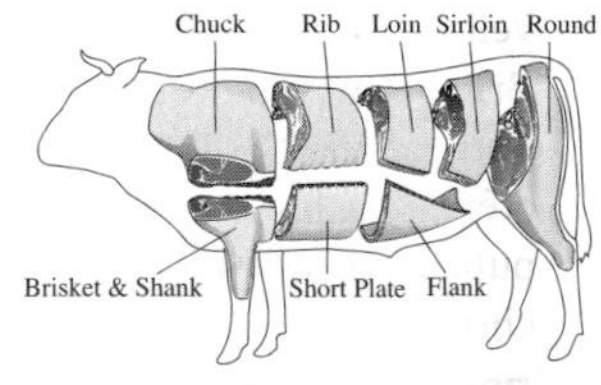

(American) beef primals

beef rib Any subprimal or fabricated cut from the beef primal rib with the bones intact.

beef short ribs A fabricated cut consisting of the ends of the rib bones from the beef primal rib (they are trimmed off to fabricate the rib roast).

beefsteak tomato 1. A large, bright red tomato with a slightly squat, elliptical shape and juicy flesh with many seeds; good for eating raw or cooked; also known as the common market tomato and slicing tomato. 2. An imprecisely used term for any of several varieties of large, slightly squat, red-skinned tomatoes.

beef tartare (tar-tar) Raw ground or chopped beef served with a raw egg yolk and garnished with chopped onions, capers and parsley.

Beef Wellington *See* filet de boeuf Wellington.

beer 1. Any of a large class of alcoholic beverages made by fermenting sugars derived from grains and often flavored with hops. 2. Any of various carbonated and/or slightly fermented alcoholic and nonalcoholic beverages flavored with roots. 3. The fermented mash of malted grains used to distill whiskey; also known as wash.

beer-brewing process The process by which beer is made; typically: (1) barley is malted and then cracked into grist; (2) the grist is mixed with hot water to form the mash; (3) the malt enzymes in the mash convert the grain starches into sugar, forming the liquid wort; (4) the draff or spent grains are sparged to recover any remaining extractable materials, which are added to the wort; (5) the wort is filtered and boiled with hops, which impart a bitter flavor and characteristic aroma; (6) yeast is added to the cooled wort to begin fermentation; (7) when the desired alcohol level is reached through fermentation, the wort is considered green beer; (8) the green beer is fined to increase clarity and conditioned to increase carbonation by either kraüsening or lagering (aging); and (9) the beer is bottled or kegged.

beet A large, bulbous edible root with an edible leafy green top (*Beta vulgaris*); its color is typically garnet red but can range from pinkish-white to deep red to yellow; also known as beetroot (especially in Great Britain), garden beet and red beet.

beggar's purse An appetizer consisting of a small crêpe topped with a savory filling; the edges are pulled up in pleats to form a sack and tied with a chive.

beignet (ben-YEA) French for fritter and used to describe a crisp, puffy, deep-fried, New Orleans pastry similar to a doughnut.

Belgian endive (EN-dyv; AHN-deev) A member of the chicory family grown in Belgium; it has a long, cigar-shaped head of compact, pointed leaves; the leaves have a creamy color with yellow tips and fringes (a purple-tipped variety is also available) and a slightly bitter flavor; also known as French endive (if grown in France) and witloof.

Belgian waffle A thick waffle made with very large, deep grids or pockets, usually served with fruit and whipped cream, especially for dessert.

belimbing (beh-lim-bing) A small ovoid fruit (*Averrhoa bilimbi*) related to the carambola with a light green, slightly rough skin and a sour flavor; used in Asian cuisines.

bell of knuckle A subprimal cut from the beef primal round; generally lean, flavorful and tough.

bell pepper A large fresh sweet pepper with a bell-like shape, thick juicy flesh, a mild sweet flavor and available in various colors, including green (the most common), red (a green bell pepper that has been allowed to ripen), white, brown, purple, yellow and orange; also known as green pepper, sweet bell pepper and sweet pepper.

belly 1. A primal cut of the pork carcass located just above the primal loin; consists of the spareribs and a large amount of fat with streaks of lean meat (the latter is usually cured and smoked for bacon); also known as pork belly and primal side belly. 2. The general name for the underside of a fish or quadruped.

belly of pork A British cut of the pork carcass; it is comparable to spareribs.

Belon (bay-lohn) 1. An oyster from France's Belon River region, it has a round, flat, brownish-green shell with a length of 1.5–3.5 in. (3.8–8.8 cm), a slim body and a slightly metallic flavor. 2. An imprecisely used marketing term for any of several European flat oyster varieties found along the New England coast.

Bel Paese (bell pah-AYZ-eh) A mild, soft, creamy Italian cheese made from cow's milk; it has an edible brownish-gray rind, a pale yellow interior and a fruity flavor; if made in Italy, the wrapper has a map of Italy; if made in the United States, it has a map of the Western Hemisphere.

beluga (buh-LOO-guh) Caviar harvested from the largest species of sturgeon; the large eggs are dark gray, well-separated and fragile.

bench A bakeshop term to describe the worktable, usually wooden, where products (bread doughs) are made.

bench scraper A handheld rectangular tool, typically 6 × 3 in., with a stainless steel blade and a rolled handle on one long side; used for cleaning and scraping surfaces.

bench scraper

bengali rice (ben-gah-lee) A short-grain white rice with a superior flavor, grown in the eastern India state of West Bengal.

benne seeds *See* sesame seeds.

benne seed wafers Thin, crisp wafers from the American South; they are made of flour, shortening, roasted benne seeds and cayenne pepper, usually served with cocktails.

bento; bento box (BEHN-to) A Japanese metal or lacquered wooden box divided into compartments used to store small dishes that hold all of the components of an individual meal, usually lunch.

berberé (behr-beh-ra) An Ethiopian spice blend generally consisting of garlic, red pepper, cardamom, coriander and fenugreek as well as other spices; often used in stews and soups.

Berchoux, sauce (bear-choh) A French compound sauce made from an allemande sauce with cream and finished with herb butter.

Bercy, sauce A French compound sauce made from a fish velouté with shallots, white wine, fish stock and seasonings; usually served with fish.

Bercy butter (bair-SEE; BUR-see) A French sauce made from white wine, shallots, butter, marrow, lemon juice, parsley, salt and pepper and served with broiled or grilled meats or fish; also known as shallot butter.

bergamot (BER-gah-mot) A member of the mint family (*Monarda didyma*); it has slightly toothed, dark green leaves with a citrusy flavor and the scent of bergamot oranges; the leaves are used in tisanes; also known as bee balm.

Berliner (behr-LEE-ner) A yeast-leavened doughnut without the center hole, it is usually filled with a fruit mixture. *See* Long John *and* bismarck.

Bermuda onion A large onion with a golden yellow outer layer, an ivory flesh and a moderately strong, pungent flavor.

berry 1. A cereal grain's seed. 2. An imprecisely used term to describe any small, juicy fruit that grows on a vine or bush and generally has a thin skin, multiple small to tiny seeds and a sweet flavor. 3. A fruit with seeds embedded in the pulp (e.g., banana, grape or tomato). 4. A crustacean's egg.

besan (bah-sahn) Channa dhal ground to a fine, pale yellow flour; it is used in Indian cuisines.

betel nut The small fruit of the areca palm (*Areca catechu*) native to the Philippines and Sumatra; it has a mottled brown skin and a pleasantly astringent flavor; the nut is chewed, but not swallowed, and is used as a breath sweetener and digestion aid.

betty A colonial American dessert consisting of a baked pudding made with layers of sweetened fruit and buttered bread crumbs; the most familiar is the apple brown betty, made with apples and brown sugar.

beurre blanc (burr BLANHK) French for white butter and used to describe an emulsified butter sauce made from shallots, white wine and butter; also known as butter sauce.

beurre Chivry (burr she-VREE) A compound butter made with shallots, tarragon, chives and burnet.

beurre Colbert; Colbert butter (kohl-BAIR) Unsalted butter mixed with a meat glaze and tarragon.

beurre composé (burr com-poh-ZAY) French for compound butter.

beurre manie (burr man-yay) French for kneaded butter and used to describe a mix of equal weights of flour and whole butter; it is whisked into a sauce just before service for quick thickening and added sheen and flavor.

beurre marchand de vin (burr mah-shon duh van) A French compound butter made by reducing red wine, shallots and demi-glaze au sec, then blending it into softened butter with parsley and lemon juice; usually served with steak. *See* marchand de vin, sauce.

beurre mâtre'd (burr may-traw-DEE) A French compound butter made with lemon juice and chopped parsley; served with grilled meats, either melted or in solid rounds or slices.

beurre noir (burr NWAR) French for black butter and used to describe whole butter cooked until dark brown (not black); it is sometimes flavored with vinegar or lemon juice, capers and parsley and served over fish, eggs and vegetables.

beurre noisette (burr nwah-ZEHT) French for brown butter and used to describe butter cooked until it is a light hazelnut (noisette) color; it is flavored and used in much the same manner as beurre noir.

beurre rouge (burr rooge) 1. An emulsified butter sauce made from red wine, butter and shallots. 2. A compound butter made with shellfish coral.

bharaat (bhur-aat) A sweet spice mix consisting of allspice, cinnamon, nutmeg and cloves; it is used to flavor rice dishes in Middle Eastern cuisines.

bharta (bhur-taa) An Indian cooking method that describes a dish, typically one made with vegetables, that has been cooked and puréed.

bialy (bee-AH-lee) A round, flat, chewy Jewish yeast roll similar to a bagel but with an indentation instead of a hole.

bibb lettuce A variety of butterhead lettuce with soft, pliable green leaves that have a buttery texture and flavor and are smaller and darker than Boston lettuce leaves; also known as limestone lettuce.

bicarbonate of soda *See* baking soda.

bien cuit (be-en KWEE) French for well done, usually referring to steak.

biga (BEE-gah) An aged dough made with yeast or sour dough; used in Italy; it is a type of sourdough starter.

bigarade, sauce (bee-gah-RAHD) A French compound sauce made with beef stock, duck drippings, orange juice, lemon juice, blanched orange peel and, sometimes, curaçao; traditionally made with bitter oranges but now made with sweet oranges, it is usually served with roast duck; also known as orange sauce.

bigarreau cherry A medium-sized, light to medium red cherry with a sweet flavor; also known as burlat cherry.

bignay A tree found in Southeast Asia and Australia; its large purple berries grow in clusters; too acidic to eat fresh, they are used for preserves; also known as Chinese laurel, currant tree and salamander tree.

billy by; billi-bi (bill-e bee) A French soup made from mussels cooked in white wine, onions, parsley and fish stock; the soup is served hot or cold with fresh cream, and the mussels are served separately.

biltong (BILL-tong) Strips of cured, air-dried beef or game; finer than beef jerky, it is used in South African cuisines.

bin 1. A storage rack on which wine bottles are laid on their side so that the wine is in contact with the cork; this prevents the cork from drying out, shrinking and allowing air to come into contact with the wine. 2. A box or enclosed space used to store dry goods such as grains.

bind 1. To thicken a hot liquid by stirring in eggs, flour and butter, cornstarch, cheese, cream or other ingredients. 2. To cause different foods to more or less adhere to one another, usually by mixing them with beaten eggs, milk, water, flour, oil, mayonnaise or other dressing.

Bing cherry A sweet cherry with a deep garnet, almost black color, smooth glossy skin, firm dark red flesh and sweet flavor.

bioengineered foods A process in which a gene or group of genes is extracted from the DNA of one plant or animal and spliced into that of another, generally to improve the appearance, texture and flavor of shipped and shelf-stable foods or to develop insect- and disease-resistant strains; also known as genetically engineered foods.

birch beer A sweetened, carbonated soft drink flavored with the sap of the black birch tree (genus *Betula*).

bird chile A small, dried, fiery hot chile used in Caribbean cuisines for pickles and condiments; the fresh version is known as Thai chile.

bird's beak knife A paring knife with a curved blade used for cutting curved surfaces or tournéeing vegetables; also known as a tournée knife.

bird's beak knife

Birdseye, Clarence (Am., 1886–1956) An American scientist who pioneered the use of freezing as a method of food preservation; his work led to quick deep-freezing as we know it today, and the company he founded remains one of the largest processors of frozen food.

bird's nest soup A Chinese soup made from the nest of a salangane, a type of swallow; the birds feed on a gelatinous seaweed, and their salivary glands secrete a gelatinous saliva used for their nests; the nests are soaked overnight until transparent and are then used for soup.

biriyani; biryani (beh-ree-YON-nee) An East Indian pilaf dish, usually made with chicken or lamb and flavored with cardamom, cloves, cinnamon and saffron and garnished with almonds and raisins.

biscotti (bee-skawt-tee) Italian for slices from a twice-baked, flattened cookie loaf.

biscuit (bees-kwee) 1. One of various types of French sponge cake, such as biscuit de Savoie or biscuit à la cuilliere. 2. French for cookie.

biscuit (BEHS-kitt) 1. A small, flaky quick bread leavened with baking soda or baking powder for a light, tender texture; the dough is rolled out and cut into circles or dropped from a spoon. 2. A thin, flat British cookie or cracker.

biscuit à la cuilliere (bees-kwee ah lah cwee-yehr) French for ladyfingers.

biscuit de Savoie (biss-kwee duh sah-wahr) A French sponge cake from Savoy; it is baked in a brioche pan.

biscuit method A mixing method used to make biscuits, scones and flaky doughs; involves cutting cold fat into flour and other dry ingredients before liquid is added.

bishop's bread A sweet quick bread made with dried fruit; created on the U.S. western frontier during the 19th century, where it was served to traveling clergy.

bismarck (BEHZ-mawrk) An elongated, jelly-filled and sugar-coated or frosted doughnut; it is fried or baked and sugar coated or frosted; also known as Long John and Berlin doughnut.

Bismarck herring A herring fillet cured in vinegar, salt, onions and sugar.

bisque (beesk) A thick French cream soup made of puréed fish, shellfish, poultry, meat or vegetables and traditionally thickened with rice.

bistro (BEES-troh) A small, casual cafe, usually serving relatively simple food and wine.

bitter 1. A harsh, relatively disagreeable acrid flavor. 2. A wine-tasting term for a sharp, unpleasant flavor caused by excessive tannin levels or other factors. 3. A British amber-colored, heavily hopped, dry (rather than bitter), cask-conditioned ale; usually served on draft. 4. A beer-tasting term for a sharp, slightly sour flavor caused by excessive hops.

bitter almond oil An oil extracted from bitter almond seeds that contains traces of lethal prussic acid; processed bitter almond oil is used as a flavoring ingredient in extracts, liqueurs and orgeat but is illegal in the United States.

bitter melon A long, cylindrical, bumpy-skinned fruit native to China and used like a vegetable; it has a yellow-green skin, a silvery-green flesh, brown seeds and a delicate, mild flavor; it becomes bitter and turns yellow-orange as it ages; also known as a balsam pear.

bitters A liquid made by distillation and infusion using herbs, spices and aromatics blended with a spirit base (usually rum); it is used as an aperitif, digestif, cocktail ingredient and home remedy for fevers and other ills.

bittersweet chocolate Chocolate containing minimal amounts of sugar and at least 35% chocolate liquor; eaten as a candy or used in pastries and confections. *See* chocolate-making process.

bivalves A general category of mollusks characterized by a soft body contained within two bilateral shells attached at a single hinge by a muscle; includes clams, cockles, mussels, oysters and scallops.

bizcochitos (bees-koh-chee-tohs) Mexican anise-flavored cookies topped with sugar and cinnamon.

black abalone A variety of abalone found along the U.S. West Coast; it has a large, smooth, ovoid blackish shell and an ivory flesh with a chewy texture and mild flavor.

Black and Tan A layered mixture of equal amounts of stout (on the top) and pale ale (on the bottom).

blackback flounder A member of the flounder family found in the Atlantic Ocean from Georgia to Canada; it has a dark brownish-black skin on top, a firm white flesh, a delicate flavor and an average weight of 1–2 lb. (450–900 g); also known as a winter flounder. *See* lemon sole.

black bean A relatively large, dried bean with black skin, a cream-colored flesh and a sweet flavor; also called a turtle bean and calypso bean.

blackberry A large shiny berry (*Rubus fruticosus*) with a deep purple, almost black color and a sweet flavor; also known as a bramble berry.

black bottom pie A rich custard pie made with a layer of dark chocolate custard on the bottom topped with a layer of white rum custard.

black bread A dark European-style peasant bread made with dark rye, molasses, cocoa, coffee and dark toasted bread crumbs.

black bun A traditional Scottish New Year's cake made of dried and candied fruit and spices enclosed in a rich pastry crust.

black butter *See* beurre noir.

black cake; black fruitcake A very dark, spicy fruitcake made with molasses; also known as English fruitcake.

black cow 1. Slang for an ice cream soda made with vanilla ice cream and some type of dark soda, such as root beer, chocolate soda or sarsaparilla. 2. Diner slang for chocolate milk.

black currant syrup A sweetened syrup made from black currants and used as a flavoring agent in beverages and desserts; also known as sirop de cassis.

blackened A Cajun cooking method in which food, usually meat or fish, is rubbed with a spice mixture and cooked in a very hot cast-iron skillet, giving the food an extra-crisp crust.

black-eyed pea The seed of a member of the pea family (*Vigna sinensis*) native to China; it is small and beige, with a black circular eye on the curved edge, and used in American southern and Chinese cuisines; also known as a cowpea (it was first planted in the United States as fodder). *See* yellow-eyed pea.

blackfish A fish found in the Pacific Ocean and used in Chinese cuisines; it has a lean flesh, a delicate flavor and many fine bones; also known as black trout and Chinese steelhead.

Black Forest ham A German smoked boneless ham with a blackened skin; traditionally, the color came from smoking the ham with resin-containing woods; also achieved by dipping the ham in cow's blood or soaking it in a caramel solution.

Black Forest torte A dessert made by layering Kirsch-soaked chocolate genoise with sour cherries and sweetened whipped cream.

black grouper A variety of Atlantic grouper found from Florida to Brazil; it has a blackish-brown skin with pale stripes, an average market weight of 10–20 lb. (4.3–8.6 kg) and a mild flavor.

black Mission fig A variety of fig with blue-black skin and crimson flesh.

black peppercorn *See* peppercorn, black.

black pudding An Irish blood sausage. *See* blood sausage.

black radish A large radish with a black skin and a crisp, white flesh; the flavor is often hot.

black raspberry *See* thimbleberry.

black rice 1. A rice, grown in Indonesia and the Philippines, with a long black grain and a nutty flavor; often used in puddings and cakes. 2. Unpolished rice.

black salt A salt with small quantities of other minerals; it has a reddish-gray color and a flavor similar to slightly sour, salty mineral water.

black sea bass A true bass found in the Atlantic Ocean from Cape Cod to North Carolina; it has a smoky gray to dusky brown skin, a firm, white, flaky flesh, a delicate, mild flavor and an average weight of 1.5 lb. (680 g); also known as a rock sea bass. *See* giant sea bass.

Black Tartarian cherry A variety of sweet cherry; the fruit has a dark red to purplish skin, a thick, tender flesh and a rich flavor.

black tea One of the three principal types of tea; the leaves are rolled and fully fermented before being heated and dried; the beverage is generally a dark reddish-brown color with a strong, full flavor. *See* green tea *and* oolong tea.

black vinegar A dark, mild, slightly sweet vinegar made from glutinous rice or sorghum; its flavor ranges from smoky to wine-yeasty.

black walnut A native American nut (*Juglans nigra*) with a very hard black shell, a strong, slightly bitter flavor and a high fat content; it is not as popular as the English walnut. *See* white walnut.

blade chops A fabricated cut of the pork primal Boston butt and the lamb primal shoulder; it is tough and contains a large percentage of bone; also known as arm chops.

blade meat A subprimal cut of the beef primal rib; it is the lean flesh overlying the rib eye and ribs; also known as cap meat, deckle meat, false meat, rib lifter meat and wedge meat.

blade roast; blade pot roast A subprimal cut of the beef primal chuck; generally lean, tough and flavorful.

blade steak 1. A fabricated cut of the beef primal chuck; it is a relatively tough steak. 2. A fabricated cut of the pork primal Boston butt; it is a relatively tender steak.

blanching Cooking a food very briefly and partially in boiling water or hot fat; generally used to assist preparation (e.g., loosen peels), as part of a combination cooking method, to remove undesirable flavors or to prepare food for freezing.

blanching pot An assemblage of two pots: a smaller pot with perforated sides and bottom and a larger pot that holds the cooking liquid; food is placed in the smaller pot, which is submerged in the larger one; once the food is cooked, the inner pot is removed and the liquid drains away.

blancmange (BLAHNG-mahnzh) A French milk pudding or custard, usually flavored with almonds.

bland A tasting term for a food that is flat, dull and lacks flavor and/or finesse.

blanquette (blahn-KEHT) A French white stew made with veal, lamb or chicken, mushrooms and small white onions; the meat is not browned and is cooked in a white stock; the dish is finished with egg yolk and cream.

blanquette de veau (blahn-KEHT duh voh) A French stew of veal; it is garnished with mushrooms and onions and served in a cream sauce.

blast frozen Food frozen rapidly at extremely low temperatures (−10°F [−23.3°C] or lower) while air circulates around the item at high velocity.

bleached flour Flour that has been whitened by removing the yellow pigment; flour can be bleached through aging or by adding bleaching and oxidizing agents.

bleeding A bakeshop term used to describe a dough (unbaked) that has been cut and left unsealed at the cut, thus permitting air and gas to escape.

blend *v.* 1. To mix two or more ingredients together until uniformly combined. 2. To combine different varieties or grades of an item to obtain a mixture of a particular character, quality and/or consistancy. *n.* A mixture of two or more flavors or other attributes.

blender An appliance used to chop, blend, purée or liquefy foods; has a tall narrow container, usually with a lid and handle, that sits on top of a driveshaft and has a four-pronged rotating blade at its bottom. *See* immersion blender *and* vertical cutter/mixer (VCM).

blender

blending A mixing method in which two or more ingredients are combined just until they are evenly distributed; a spoon, rubber spatula, whisk or electric mixer with its paddle attachment is used.

blending fork A large fork with sharp blades on the backs of the tines; used for incorporating fat into flour.

blending fork

blenny (BLEN-ee) A group of scaleless freshwater or saltwater fish (the body is covered with a mucous membrane); it has an average market length of 4–6 in. (10–15 cm) and white flesh with a mild flavor.

bleu (bluh) *See* very rare.

Bleu; Fromage Bleu (bluh; froh-MAHZ bluh) 1. A French term for a group of Roquefort-style blue-veined cheeses made in France's Roquefort region from milk other than ewe's milk. 2. A French term for blue-veined cheeses made elsewhere in France regardless of the kind of milk used. *See* blue cheese.

bleu cheese *See* blue cheese.

blind tasting A method of evaluating foods or beverages (both alcoholic and nonalcoholic) without knowing the product's name, place of origin, principal or distinguishing ingredients or other identifying information.

blini (blee-nee) Leavened Russian pancakes made from a buckwheat and wheat flour batter; they are usually served as hors d'oeuvre with sour cream and caviar or smoked fish; singular is blin.

blini pan A shallow pan with a heavy bottom, sloping sides and a smooth surface; used to make blini with a 3.75-in. diameter. *See* crêpe pan.

blini pan

blintz A very thin, tender Jewish pancake filled with fruit and/or cheese, then baked or sautéed.

bloater A salted and smoked herring.

blond de veau (blon duh voh) A concentrated veal broth used in French cuisine for soups and sauces; it forms a jelly when cold and is used for a chaud froid or any sauce that should set when chilled.

blond de volaille (blon duh voh-LIE) A concentrated chicken broth used in French cuisine for soups and sauces and for braising vegetables; it forms a jelly when cold and is used for a chaud froid or any sauce that should set when chilled.

blondie A cakelike bar cookie made with butterscotch and vanilla.

blood 1. The fluid that circulates through the heart, arteries, veins and capillaries of mammals, birds and fish, carrying nourishment, oxygen, heat, vitamins and other essential chemical substances; principally composed of a fluid medium (plasma) with red and white corpuscles (blood cells) and platelets. 2. The blood of certain animals is used to make black pudding and to thicken dishes called civet.

blood alcohol level The amount of alcohol found in the human body at a given time; it reflects the amount of alcohol a person has consumed and is expressed as a percentage of the alcohol in the blood by volume.

blood cholesterol Cholesterol found in the bloodstream; the measure of blood cholesterol level is used as an indicator of a person's risk for cardiovascular disease.

blood orange A medium-sized orange with a red or red-streaked white flesh (the color reflects a pigment, anthocyanin, not normally present in citrus); it has a sweet flavor that is less tart than that of a typical orange.

blood sausage; blood pudding A black-colored sausage generally made from hog's blood, bread crumbs, suet and oatmeal; sometimes rice is added; usually available as large links; also known as black pudding.

bloom 1. A dull gray film or grayish-whitish streaks that sometimes appear on chocolate if the cocoa butter separates; the chocolate's flavor and cooking properties are not affected; also known as chocolate bloom and fat bloom. 2. A measure of gelatin's strength. 3. The process of softening gelatin in a cool liquid before it is dissolved.

blown sugar A boiled mixture of sucrose, glucose and tartaric acid colored and shaped using an air pump; used to make decorative objects (e.g., fruits) and containers.

blueberry A small berry (*Vaccinium corymbosum*) native to North America; it has a smooth skin, a blue to blue-black color, a juicy light gray-blue flesh and a sweet flavor; it is eaten raw, used in baked goods or made into jams and jellies.

blue cheese 1. A generic term for any cheese containing visible blue-green molds that contribute a characteristic tart, sharp flavor and aroma; also known as a blue-veined cheese or bleu cheese. 2. A group of Roquefort-style cheeses made in the United States and Canada from cow's or goat's milk rather than ewe's milk and injected with molds that form blue-green veins; also known as blue mold cheese or blue-veined cheese.

blue cheese dressing A salad dressing made with a blue-veined cheese (other than Roquefort), heavy cream or sour cream, lemon juice, chives, Worcestershire sauce and Tabasco sauce. *See* Roquefort dressing.

blue crab A variety of crab found in the Atlantic Ocean off the U.S. East Coast and the coast of Europe from

France to Denmark as well as in the Gulf of Mexico; it has blue claws and an oval, dark blue-green hard shell, an average market diameter of 4–7 in. (10–18 cm) and a rich, sweet flavor; available in hard and soft shells, it accounts for most of the crab consumed in the United States and is sometimes referred to simply as crab. *See* buckram, peeler crab *and* various listings under crab.

bluefin tuna A variety of tuna found in the Pacific and Atlantic Oceans off North America; it has a deep blue-green skin, an ivory pink flesh, a rich flavor and an average market weight of 15–80 lb. (6.8–36 kg); used for sashimi.

bluefish A saltwater fish; it has a blue-green skin on top that fades to silver on the belly, an average market weight of 3–6 lb. (1.4–2.7 kg), high fat content and dark flesh with a delicate flavor; also known as a blue runner.

bluegill; bluegill crappie A freshwater fish and member of the sunfish family found throughout the United States; it has a black spot on the dorsal fin, a blue-black ear flap and an average market weight of 0.5 lb. (225 g).

blue mussel A variety of mussels found wild along the U.S. East Coast and aquafarmed on both coasts; it has a dark blue, elongated ovoid shell, orangish-yellow plump meat with a firm texture and a sweet flavor (the meat of a wild blue mussel is much smaller than that of a cultivated blue mussel).

blue plate special A menu term, generally at an inexpensive restaurant, for the day's special; it is usually an entire meal (appetizer or soup, entrée, dessert and beverage).

bluepoint oyster; blue point oyster 1. An Atlantic oyster found in Long Island's Great South Bay; it has a squarish shell with a length of 5–6 in. (12–15 cm) and a plump flesh. 2. An imprecisely used term for any medium-sized Atlantic oyster.

bluggoe fig (blue-goh-ah) A variety of bananas grown in the Caribbean; the fruit has a reddish-purple color and is used like a vegetable; also known as a bird fig.

blush wine 1. A slightly sweet, light-bodied white wine made from black grapes such as Zinfandel, Pinot Noir or Cabernet Sauvignon; its color ranges from pale salmon to pink. 2. A wine blended from red and white wines; also known as a light rosé.

boar An uncastrated male swine. *See* pig *and* sow.

bobotee An American puddinglike dish of milk, bread crumbs, onions, almonds and hot sauce.

bocconcini (buh-CON-chee-ny) Fresh mozzarella cheese shaped into small balls, about 1 in. in diameter.

bock beer (bok) A dark, sweet, full-bodied lager beer traditionally brewed during the spring in Germany.

body 1. A tasting term used to describe the feel or weight of a food on the palate or the feel of a food to the touch; it can be firm, springy, supple, elastic, runny, grainy and so on. 2. A tasting term used to describe the feel and weight of a beverage on the palate; it can range from a full body to a light body (watery). 3. The consistency of something. 4. The entire physical structure of an organism. 5. The torso or trunk of an animal.

boeuf à la mode (buhf ah lah mod) A French beef stew with vegetables.

boeuf bourguignon (buhf bor-geen-yohn) A French dish of beef braised in red wine and garnished with onions and mushrooms.

boil; boiling *v.* To cook by boiling. *n.* A moist-heat cooking method that uses convection to transfer heat from a hot (approximately 212°F [100°C]) liquid to the food submerged in it; the turbulent waters and higher temperatures cook foods more quickly than do poaching and simmering.

boiled candy A candy made by boiling sugar, butter and a flavoring, usually peppermint.

boiled custard 1. An egg and milk custard cooked on the stove top rather than baked in the oven. 2. A beverage from the American South made from an egg and milk custard, similar to eggnog.

boiled dressing A type of mayonnaise made by cooking salt, mustard, sugar, cayenne, flour, egg, milk, butter and vinegar until thickened; it is then strained and cooled.

boiled icing *See* Italian meringue.

boiler onion A small, tender onion with a white outer layer, a white flesh and a mild flavor; usually creamed or used in casseroles, soups and stews.

boiling point The temperature at which a liquid reaches a boil; the boiling point varies depending on the specific gravity of the substance and the altitude.

ALTITUDE	**BOILING POINT OF WATER**	
Sea level	212°F	100°C
2,000 feet	208°F	98°C
5,000 feet	203°F	95°C
7,500 feet	198°F	92°C
10,000 feet	194°F	90°C

bok choy A member of the cabbage family native to southern China; it has long, wide, white, crunchy stalks with tender, smooth-edged, dark green leaves; it is used raw, pickled or cooked; also known as baak choy, Chinese mustard, Chinese white mustard cabbage, celery mustard, pak choi and white mustard cabbage.

bolar A subprimal cut of the beef primal chuck; it is a tough, very lean roast.

bolete A wild mushroom (*Boletus edulis*) with a large bulbous stem, a broad bun-shaped cap, a brownish-tan color, a smooth, meaty texture and a pungent, woodsy flavor and aroma; more commonly available dried in the United States.

boletus (boh-le-tus) A genus of wild mushrooms with fleshy caps and stems, ranging in color from white to dark brown; significant varieties include the bolete, cèpe and porcini.

bollito (bo-lee-to) A variety of bean; it is related to the pinto bean, but smaller.

bollito misto An Italian dish consisting of a variety of boiled meats, such as calf's head, chicken, beef, veal, tongue and/or pork sausages served with green beans and other vegetables.

bologna (bah-LOW-nyah; bah-LOW-nee) A large, highly seasoned sausage made from pork, beef and veal; named for Bologna, Italy (although the Italian sausage associated with that city is mortadella), it is available cooked and usually served cold; also known as baloney.

bolognese (boh-loh-nay-see) An Italian meat sauce for pasta made from ground meat, tomatoes, celery, carrots and bacon and seasoned with garlic, herbs and olive oil; also known as ragù and sugo.

bolster The thick band of steel on a forged knife blade; part of the blade, it runs along the heel and up onto the spine; also known as the shoulder.

bomba (bom-bha) A variety of rice grown in the Mediterranean region; particularly Spain; it is nearly round, with a creamy texture after cooking and is generally used for paella.

bombe; bombe glacée (baum) A French dessert consisting of layers of ice cream and sherbet packed into a round or spherical mold, frozen, then unmolded and decorated for service.

bonbon (bohn-bohn) 1. A small piece of candy, usually chocolate-coated fondant. 2. French for any bite-sized candy, confection or sweetmeat.

bone *v.* To remove a bone from a cut of meat, poultry or fish. *n.* Any of numerous structures forming a vertebrate's skeleton; they are composed of cartilaginous substances and calcareous salts; larger bones have a soft, fatty substance in their center known as marrow.

bone china A white translucent ceramic ware developed in England and made from kaolin, china stone and bone ash fired at an intermediate temperature; can be decorated and is used for fine dishes and serving pieces.

bonefish A game fish found off Florida; it has a silvery color; also known as banana fish and ladyfish.

bone-in brisket A subprimal cut of the beef primal brisket and shank; part of the animal's breast, it is quite fatty.

boneless rib roast A subprimal cut of the beef primal short loin; it is tender and flavorful and can be fabricated into strip loin steaks.

boneless shoulder roast A subprimal cut of the beef primal chuck; it is tough and flavorful and is sometimes fabricated into boneless shoulder steaks.

boniato (bou-nee-AH-toh) *See* sweet potato, white.

boning knife A knife used to separate meat from bones; there are two types: one has a rigid blade 5–7-in. long, and the other has a longer, thinner blade that can be rigid or flexible.

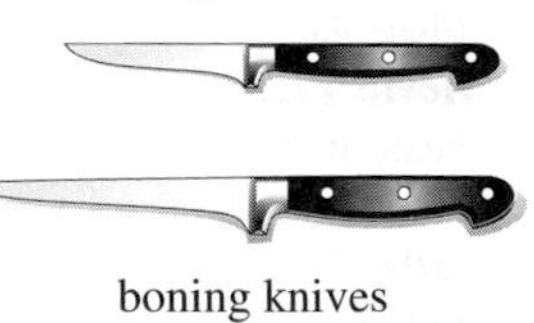

boning knives

bonito (boh-NEE-to) A variety of tuna found in the western Pacific Ocean; it has a moderate to high fat content, a strong flavor and a weight that generally does not exceed 25 lb. (11.3 kg); often used in Japanese cuisine.

bonne femme; bonne-femme, à la (bun fam) French for good wife and used to describe dishes prepared in a simple, homey, rustic manner and usually served in the dish in which they were cooked (e.g., a casserole).

bontemps, sauce (bohn-tahn) A French compound sauce made from a velouté flavored with a reduction of onion, paprika, mustard and cider and finished with butter.

borage (BOHR-ihj) An herb (*Borago officinalis*) native to Europe, with downy blue-green leaves and blue flowers; the leaves have a slight cucumber flavor and are used for tisanes and as a flavoring for vegetables, and the flowers are used in salads and for tisanes.

Bordeaux, red Red wines from Bordeaux; the principal grapes used are Cabernet Sauvignon, Cabernet Franc and Merlot and to a lesser extent Malbec and Petit Verdot.

Bordeaux, white White wines from Bordeaux; the principal grapes used are Sauvignon Blanc and Sémillon and to a lesser extent Muscadelle, Colombard and Ugni Blanc.

bordelaise, à la (bohr-dl-AYZ, ah lah) French for in the style of Bordeaux and used to describe dishes using ingredients such as bone marrow, shallots and wine (both red and white).

bordelaise, sauce A French compound sauce made from a demi-glaze flavored with red wine, herbs and shallots; cooked, diced marrow is added before serving; also known as Bordeaux sauce.

border mold A doughnut-shaped mold with a large interior void; it is used to mold food that will be used as a border around a second food that will sit in the interior well.

borecole A variety of kale that grows to 6 ft. (2 m) or more in height; also known as palm tree cabbage.

borek; bourek, burek (BOOR-ehk) Any of various Turkish fried or baked appetizers made from layers of very thin wheat dough filled with a sweet or savory (especially cheese) mixture.

borlotto (boar-LOT-to) A plump, oval-shaped dried bean native to Italy; it has a thin, pink to pale brown maroon-streaked skin and a bitter flavor.

borscht; borsch; borschok (BOHR-sht; BOHR-sh) A Polish and Russian soup made with fresh beets, shredded cabbage and/or other vegetables, with or without meat; it is served hot or cold and garnished with sour cream.

boscaiolo, alla (boss-kye-OH-loh, AH-lah) Italian for woodsman's style and used to describe a pasta sauce made with mushrooms, tomatoes and sometimes fried eggplant.

Boston baked beans An American dish of navy or pea beans, salt pork, molasses and brown sugar baked in a beanpot or casserole.

Boston brown bread A dark, sweet steamed bread made with rye and wheat flour, cornmeal and molasses.

Boston butt A primal cut of the pork carcass; located just above the primal pork shoulder, it consists of a portion of the bladebone and is very meaty and tender; used for roasts and steaks; also known as butt and shoulder butt. *See* cottage ham.

Boston clam chowder *See* chowder; also known as New England clam chowder.

Boston cracker A large, thin biscuit or cracker with a plain but slightly sweet flavor; served with cheese.

Boston cream pie A traditional American cake made of two layers of sponge cake filled with vanilla custard and topped with chocolate glaze.

Boston cut A subprimal cut of the beef primal chuck; it is a tough, flavorful roast with a bone.

Boston fish chowder A soup associated with Boston and consisting of onions, green pepper, celery, fish and potatoes cooked in fish stock and milk, flavored with cayenne and herbs and garnished with flaked cod or other fish.

Boston lettuce A variety of butterhead lettuce with soft, pliable pale green leaves that have a buttery texture and flavor and are larger and paler than bibb lettuce leaves.

botano (bow-tah-noh) Mexican and Latin American appetizers or foods usually consumed with alcoholic beverages.

bottle *v.* To place a liquid in a bottle. *n.* 1. A container of various shapes and capacities, usually made of glass or plastic, without handles and with a narrow neck that is closed with a plug (cork), screw top or cap; principally used to hold liquids. 2. The quantity that a bottle holds. 3. Slang for a drinking problem (i.e., his problem is the bottle).

bottle aging The development of a beer or still wine while in its bottle; during this period, the products become softer and richer, and complex aromas and flavors are created.

bottled in bond A whiskey labeling term indicating that the contents are 100 proof, at least 4 years old, produced by a single distiller in one distilling season and stored in a bonded warehouse under government supervision until taxed and shipped to the retailer; it is a means of aging whiskey without having to pay tax on it until it is ready for sale.

bottom round A subprimal cut of the beef primal round; it is the muscle found along the leg bone on the outside side of the animal's leg and sometimes includes the eye round; fairly tender and flavorful, it is sometimes fabricated into steaks; also known as the outside round.

bottom sirloin A subprimal cut of the beef primal round; it is the end of the sirloin tip muscle.

bottom sirloin butt steak; bottom butt steak A fabricated cut of the beef primal sirloin nearest the round; it is somewhat tough.

botulism An extremely severe form of food poisoning that can lead to paralysis and even death; it is caused by ingesting toxins created by the bacteria *Clostridium botulinum*. *See* Clostridium botulinum.

bouchée (boo-SHAY) French for mouthful and used to describe a small round puff pastry container usually filled with a hot savory mixture.

boucherie (boo-cher-ree) 1. French for butcher shop. 2. A daylong Cajun event held when hogs are slaughtered and every edible part is prepared for use.

boudin blanc (boo-dahn blahnk) 1. French for white sausage and used to describe a sausage made with poultry, veal, pork or rabbit mixed with bread crumbs. 2. A Louisianian sausage made from pork shoulder, rice and onions.

boudin noir (boo-dahn nwahr) French for black sausage and used to describe a sausage made with blood and pork fat, onions and cream; also known as black pudding.

bouillabaisse (BOOL-yuh-BAYZ) A thin stew traditionally made in France's Provence region from a variety of fish and shellfish, olive oil and tomatoes, flavored with white wine, garlic, herbs and saffron and served over thick slices of bread.

bouillon (BOOL-yahn) French for broth and used to describe a stock made by cooking meat, poultry, fish or vegetables in water; the solids are removed before the broth is used in soups or sauces or as a poaching medium.

bouillon cube A concentrated cube of dehydrated beef, chicken or vegetable stock; it is also available in granular form; both must be dissolved in a hot liquid.

boulanger (bu-layn-jhaj) At a food services operation following the brigade system, it is the person responsible for all breads and baked dough containers for other menu items; also known as the bread baker.

boulangère, à la (bu-lahn-jehr, ah lah) A French preparation method for meat (especially lamb) in which the meat is roasted in a pan on a bed of potatoes and onions.

boule (bool) French for ball and used to describe a round loaf of white bread.

bound salad A salad composed of cooked meats, poultry, fish, shellfish, pasta or potatoes combined with a dressing.

bouquet garni (boo-kay gar-nee) A French seasoning blend of fresh herbs and vegetables tied in a bundle with twine and used to flavor stocks, sauces, soups and stews; a standard bouquet garni consists of parsley stems, celery, thyme, leeks and carrots. *See* nouet, sachet *and* touffe.

bouquetière (boo-kuh-tyehr) French for a garnish (bouquet) of carefully cut and arranged fresh vegetables.

bouquetière, à la (boo-kuh-tyehr, ah lah) 1. A dish that is garnished with bouquets of vegetables of different colors. 2. A dish garnished with a macédoine of vegetables bound with a béchamel sauce.

bourbon An American straight whiskey distilled from a fermented grain mash made with a minimum of 51% corn; it is aged in new charred white oak barrels (which impart color, flavor and aroma) for at least 2 years and bottled between 80 and 125 proof; also known as straight bourbon.

bourbon ball A small, round uncooked candy made with bourbon whiskey; the alcohol content remains in the finished product.

bourguignonne, à la (bohr-ghee-n'yohn, ah lah) A French preparation method associated with the cuisine of the Burgundy region; the dishes are characterized by braising meats with red wine and usually garnishing them with mushrooms, small onions and bacon.

bourguignonne, sauce A French compound sauce made from a demi-glaze cooked with red wine and bacon and flavored with onions, shallots, parsley, thyme and bay leaf; also known as Burgundy sauce.

bourride (boo-REED) A fish stew made in France's Provence region; after cooking, the liquid is removed and the stew is bound with aïoli.

Boursin (boor-SAHN) A triple cream cheese made from cow's milk in factories worldwide; it has a white color, no rind and a spreadable texture; it is often flavored with pepper, herbs or garlic and packaged in foil-wrapped cylinders.

bovine Pertaining to members of the oxen family, including bulls, calves, cows, heifers, stags and steers.

bowl 1. A round vessel used for preparing and serving foods, especially those with a liquid or semiliquid texture. 2. The concave (from the front) portion of a spoon attached to the handle. 3. The part of a glass or goblet that rests on a stem or foot and holds the liquid.

bowl scraper A palm-sized, wedge-like plastic tool with a curved edge to help it conform to concave surfaces; it is used to remove and transfer the last bits of food from a bowl or board to a bowl, board, pastry bag or other receptacle; also known as a scraper.

box grater Four flat graters, generally of different degrees of coarseness, joined to form a box, usually with a handle on top.

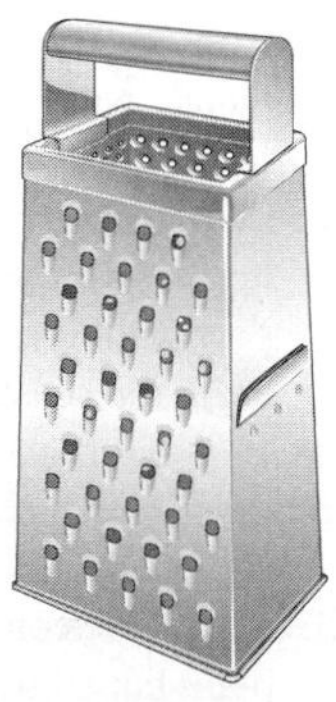

box grater

box oyster An Atlantic oyster found in Long Island's Gardiner's Bay; it has a squarish shell with a length of 5–6 in. (12.7–15.2 cm) and a large body.

boxty; broxty (BOX-tee) An Irish dish consisting of a thick potato and wheat flour pancake cut into wedges and cooked on a griddle.

boysenberry A blackberry and raspberry hybrid named for its progenitor, Rudolph Boysen; shaped like a raspberry, it has a purple-red color and a rich, sweet, tart flavor.

bracelet A cut of the lamb carcass that contains the primal rack with the connecting breast section.

braciola (brah-chee-OHL-lah) 1. Italian for escallop. 2. Italian for a slice or chop of meat, often stuffed.

brains The soft, convoluted mass of gray and white matter found in the cranium of vertebrates that controls mental and physical activities; as a variety meat, sheep and pig brains are best.

braising (bray-zeng) A combination cooking method in which foods are first browned in hot fat, then covered and slowly cooked in a small amount of liquid over low heat; braising uses a combination of simmering and steaming to transfer heat from a liquid (conduction) and the air (convection) to the foods.

bramble jelly An English jelly made from crab apples and blackberries.

bran The tough, outer covering of the endosperm of various types of grain kernels; it has a high fiber and vitamin B content and is usually removed during milling; used to enrich baked goods and as a cereal and nutrient supplement.

brandy A spirit distilled from grape wine or the fermented juice of other fruits with a minimum proof of 60 and usually aged in an oak cask; its color, flavor and aroma depend on the wine or fermented juice used and the length of time it ages in the cask. *See* Cognac.

brandy butter An English hard sauce made with butter, sugar and brandy; served cold with hot Christmas pudding and other steamed puddings. *See* hard sauce.

brandy snap A thin, crisp cookie usually flavored with brandy, spices and molasses.

Branston Pickle Relish The proprietary name of an English condiment made of carrots, rutabaga, cauliflower, zucchini, dates and tomatoes; usually served with cheese, cold meats and open-faced sandwiches.

brasserie (BRAHS-uhr-ee) A restaurant where beer, wine, cider and other drinks are served; the limited menu usually offers simple, hardy foods.

Bratwurst (BRAHT-wurst; BRAHT-vurst) A fresh German sausage made from pork and veal, seasoned with ginger, nutmeg and coriander or caraway seeds.

Braunschweiger (BROWN-shwi-ger) A soft, spreadable German smoked sausage made from pork liver enriched with eggs and milk.

brawn 1. A charcuterie item made from simmered meats packed into a terrine and covered with aspic; also known as an aspic terrine. 2. An English dish of boiled, boned, jellied and potted pig's head; served cold; also known as headcheese.

brazier; braiser A pan designed for braising; it is usually round with two handles and a tight-fitting lid; also known as a rondeau.

Brazilian Robusta coffee beans grown in Brazil and usually used to make instant coffee.

Brazilian malagueta (mah-lah-gwee-tah) A small, tapered fresh chile with a thin, light to medium green flesh and a very hot, vegetal flavor.

Brazil nut A seed of an Amazon jungle tree (*Bertholettia excelsa*); the white, richly flavored and high-fat nut is encased in a very hard, dark brown triangular shell; the seeds grow in a cluster inside a hard, globular pod; also known as a creamnut, para, paranut and savory nut.

bread *v.* To coat a food with flour, beaten eggs and bread crumbs or cracker crumbs before cooking. *n.* A food baked from a dough or batter made with flour or meal, water or other liquids and a leavener.

bread-and-butter pickles Sweet pickles made from sliced cucumbers cured with onions, mustard seeds and celery seeds.

bread and butter plate A plate, 5–6 in. in diameter, used for individual servings of bread and butter; also known as a butter plate.

bread bowl A round loaf of bread; the top is sliced off, the center hollowed out and the crust and remaining interior is used as a bowl for soups, stews or the like, with the bowl being consumed as part of the meal.

bread crumbs Small bits of bread used as a coating for fried foods or as a topping; they can be made from most breads and are sometimes seasoned with herbs and/or spices.

bread crumbs, dry Commercially prepared bread crumbs or oven-dried fresh bread crumbs; they are more uniform and crisper than fresh bread crumbs and provide a smoother, denser coating.

bread crumbs, fresh Crumbs obtained by processing fresh bread in a food processor; they are softer and give more texture to breaded foods than do dry bread crumbs.

bread flour A strong flour, usually made from hard winter wheat and containing 11–13% protein; used for making yeast-leavened breads.

breadfruit A large spherical fruit of a tropical tree related to the fig family (*Artocarpus communis*) and grown in the South Pacific, India and West Indies; it has a bumpy green skin, a cream-colored flesh with the texture of fresh bread, and a bland flavor; baked, grilled, fried or boiled, it is served as a sweet or savory dish.

breading 1. A coating of bread or cracker crumbs, cornmeal or other dry meal applied to foods that will typically be deep-fried or pan-fried. 2. The process of applying this coating.

bread knife A long, moderately rigid knife with a wave-cut edge similar to a serrated edge; used to slice baked goods; its blade ranges in length from 8 to 10 in. and has a blunt tip.

bread knife

bread machine An electrical, computer-driven machine that mixes, kneads, proofs and bakes bread; a blade in the cannister base mixes and kneads the dough and a heating coil bakes the bread.

bread-making process The process by which most yeast breads are made; typically (1) the ingredients are scaled or weighed; (2) the dough is mixed and kneaded; (3) the dough is allowed to ferment; (4) the dough is punched down; (5) the dough is divided into portions; (6) the portions are rounded and shaped; (7) the shaped portions of dough are proofed; and (8) the products are baked, cooled and stored.

breadnut The fruit of a tree (*Brosimum alicastrum*) grown in the Caribbean and Central America; it is generally roasted and ground for flour; also known as Maya breadnut.

bread pudding A baked dessert made with cubes or slices of bread soaked in a mixture of eggs, milk, sugar and flavorings.

bread salad *See* panzanella alla marinna.

bread sauce An English sauce of bread crumbs and onion-flavored milk seasoned with cayenne and nutmeg and finished with cream; traditionally served with boiled beef, game, roasted poultry and large joints of meat.

bread stick A long, thin stick of yeast bread, usually crispy and garnished with seeds or herbs.

breakfast steak A fabricated cut of the beef primal chuck; a thin, moderately tender steak.

bream 1. In Europe, a common freshwater fish and member of the carp family. 2. An imprecisely used name for a variety of freshwater sunfish caught in the United States for sport. *See* sea bream.

breast 1. The portion of the beef carcass containing the primal short plate and brisket (with or without the shank). 2. A subprimal section of the veal primal foreshank and breast; it is the flavorful breast, which has a high percentage of connective tissue and is often ground, cubed or rolled and stuffed. 3. A primal section of the lamb carcass; it is located beneath the primal rack and contains the rib tips, breast and foreshank. 4. The fleshy white meat part of the body between the neck and abdomen on poultry.

brek; brik (brehk) A Tunisian deep-fried turnover filled with a spicy meat or fish mixture often bound with egg; served with harissa.

bresaola (brehsh-ay-OH-lah) An Italian dried, salted beef filet that has aged for 2 months; it is usually sliced thin and served as antipasto.

Bresse mayonnaise A French sauce made from a Spanish mayonnaise flavored with Madeira and orange juice, seasoned with cayenne pepper and finished with puréed, sautéed chicken livers.

bretonne, à la (breh-TAWN, ah lah) A French garnish (for mutton and lamb) of puréed white haricot (navy) beans with a sauce bretonne.

bretonne, sauce 1. A French sauce for fish or chicken: a white wine sauce finished with cream and garnished with julienne of celery, leeks, mushrooms and onions. 2. For meat: a French compound sauce of demi-glaze flavored with a reduction of white wine and shallots, tomato purée, butter and parsley.

brew *v.* 1. To make tea or coffee by boiling or steeping the tea leaves or coffee grounds in water. 2. To make beer. *See* beer-brewing process. *n.* Slang for beer, especially draught.

brewers' yeast *Saccharomyces cerevisiae;* a cultured yeast used for brewing beer; also used as a nutritional supplement.

brew pub A commercial establishment that brews its own beer for sales on and off premises; it typically also serves food.

brick tea Tea leaves that are steamed and pressed into a brick; originally made for easy transportation, now prized for their attractive embossed designs.

bridge mix An assortment of candies or nuts, often coated with chocolate, served at social events such as bridge parties.

Brie (bree) A soft, creamy French cheese made from cow's milk; it has a pale ivory-gold color, a soft, leathery white rind and a delicate, somewhat nutty flavor; rind-ripened, it can develop an ammonia odor if overly ripe; traditionally named after its place of origin.

brigade A system of staffing a kitchen so that each worker is assigned a set of specific tasks; these tasks are often related by cooking method, equipment or type of foods being produced; also known as a kitchen brigade.

Brillat-Savarin, Jean-Anthelme (Fr., 1755–1826) A magistrate and gastronome and the author of *Physiologie du goût* (*Physiology of Taste,* 1825), which contains his observations on dining, food preparation and the science of cuisine; several classical French preparations carry his name.

brine A salt and water solution.

brining A method of curing, preserving and/or flavoring certain foods such as meats, fish, vegetables and cheese by immersing them in brine or injecting brine into them; also known as pickling. *See* pickle.

brining solution A very salty marinade (generally 20% salinity) used to preserve and/or flavor certain foods; it can be flavored with sugar, herbs and spices.

brioche (bree-ohsh) A light, tender French yeast bread enriched with eggs and butter.

brioche a tête (bree-ohsh ah tet) Brioche shaped in a round, fluted mold and topped with a small ball of dough, which creates a topknot or head after baking.

brioche pan A round, fluted metal baking pan with flared sides, available in many sizes; used for baking traditionally shaped brioche and for molding custards and Bavarians.

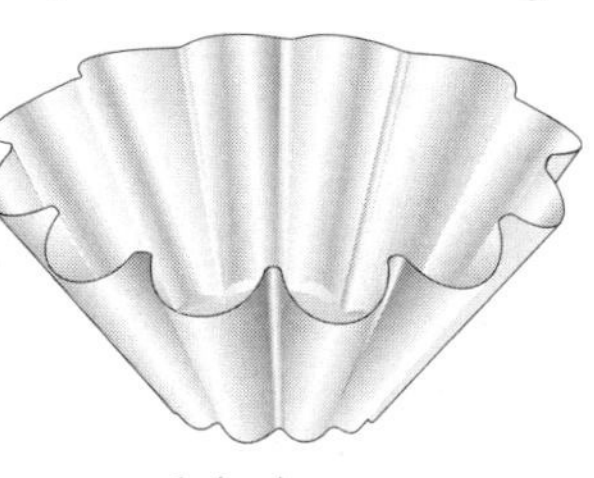
brioche pan

brisket (bres-khet) A fabricated cut of the beef primal brisket and foreshank; it is the animal's breast; available boneless, it is tough and flavorful.

brisket, flat cut A very flavorful brisket with minimal fat.

brisket, point cut A fattier and less flavorful brisket.

brisket and shank A primal section of the beef carcass; it is under the primal chuck and includes such flavorful, moderately tough subprimal or fabricated cuts as the brisket and foreshank.

Bristol Cream A blended sherry marketed by a British firm, Harveys of Bristol; the most popular sherry sold in the United States.

Bristol oyster An Atlantic oyster found off South Bristol, Maine; it has a round shell with an average length of 2.5 in. (6.3 cm) and a plump body.

British gallon A unit of measurement for volume in the imperial system; it is 160 fl. oz.; also known as an imperial gallon.

brittle A flat, irregularly shaped candy made by mixing nuts into caramelized sugar.

broad bean *See* fava bean.

broccoflower (BROH-koh-flowr) A light green cauliflower that is a cross between broccoli and cauliflower, with a milder flavor than either vegetable.

broccoli (BROH-klee) Italian for cabbage sprout and used to describe a member of the cabbage family (*Brassica oleracea*) with a tight cluster (called a curd) of emerald green florets on top of a stout, paler green edible stalk with dark green leaves.

broccoli raab (BROH-klee RAH-ahb) *See* rape.

brochettes (bro-shettz) Skewers, either small hors d'oeuvre or large entrée size, threaded with meat, poultry, fish, shellfish and/or vegetables and grilled, broiled or baked; sometimes served with a dipping sauce.

Broglie, sauce (bro-glee) A French compound sauce made from a Madeira sauce flavored with mushrooms and garnished with diced ham.

broiler Cooking equipment in which the heat source (gas or electric) is located above the rack used to hold the food; it is generally enclosed and can be combined with an oven.

broiler pan An assemblage consisting of a 1.5-in.-deep drip pan with a slotted tray insert; the slots channel rendered fats to the drip pan to reduce smoking and splattering.

broiling A dry-heat cooking method in which foods are cooked by heat radiating from an overhead source. *See* grilling.

broken pekoe Broken pekoe tea leaves, generally used for quick brewing. *See* pekoe.

bromated flour A white flour to which potassium bromate has been added.

bromelin (BROH-meh-lin) An enzyme found in pineapples and used as a meat tenderizer.

brooklime A wild green with a slightly bitter flavor found near North American and northern European streams and marshes.

Brooklyn cake A light, white cake made with beaten egg whites, sugar, lemon juice and cornstarch; popular in the late 19th century.

brook trout A freshwater trout found in eastern North America, Argentina and Europe; it has a dark olive skin that pales on the sides and becomes reddish on the belly, with red spots outlined in pale blue, a white flaky flesh (wild brook trout has a pale yellow or orange flesh), a delicate flavor and an average weight of 1 lb. (450 g); also known as a speckled trout.

broth A flavorful liquid obtained from the long simmering of meats and/or vegetables.

brown To caramelize the surface sugars of a food by applying heat, invariably through a dry-heat cooking method.

brown ale A dark brown ale with a malty bouquet, a bittersweet flavor, a light to medium body and a relatively low alcohol content; made in the United States, Great Britain, Belgium and Canada; also known as American brown ale.

brown and serve A term used to describe a product (usually bread) that is cooked to doneness but not browned; browning is done just before service.

brown bean A plump ovoid-shaped bean with a brown skin and lighter brown flesh; used in northern European and Scandinavian cuisines; also known as the Dutch brown bean.

brownie A cakelike bar cookie, usually made with chocolate and garnished with nuts.

browning 1. The change in a red wine's color from ruby-purple to ruby with brown edges, caused by aging; once the wine has completed browning, it is fully mature and not likely to improve. 2. The change in a food's appearance as its surface sugars caramelize through the application of heat, invariably through a dry-heat cooking method. *See* caramelization.

brown rice A form of processed rice with only the tough outer husk removed; the retained bran gives the rice a light tan color, a nutlike flavor and a chewy texture; it is available in long-, medium- and short-grain forms.

brown sauce A French leading sauce made with a rich, brown meat stock to which a brown roux and mirepoix are added, followed by a tomato purée; also known as espagnole sauce and Spanish sauce.

brown stew A stew in which the meat is first browned in hot fat.

brown stock A richly colored stock made of chicken, veal, beef or game bones and vegetables, all of which are caramelized before they are simmered in water with seasonings.

brown sugar Soft, refined sugar with a coating of molasses; can be dark or light, coarse or fine.

brown trout A freshwater trout found in North America and Europe; it has a golden-brown to olive skin with large black or brown spots and small orange-red spots, an average market weight of 1–2 lb. (450–900 g), a white to pale orange flaky flesh and a delicate flavor.

brown Turkey fig A particularly meaty and flavorful pear-shaped fig with a skin color that ranges from violet to brown.

brown venus clams Any of several varieties of venus clams found off western Europe and in the Mediterranean Sea; they have a thick, brown, smooth, shiny shell with an average length of 3–5 in. (7.6–12.7 cm) and sweet meat; also known as smooth venus clams.

bruise 1. To crush a food partially, especially an herb, to release its flavor. 2. To crush or injure a food, causing discoloration or softening.

brûlé (broo-LAY) French for burned and used to describe the browning of a food by means of direct, intense heat.

brunch A meal taken, usually leisurely, between 11 A.M. and 3 P.M.; a combination of breakfast and lunch, it usually offers breakfast foods and almost anything else.

brunoise (broo-nwaz) 1. Foods cut into approximately 1/8-in. (3-mm) cubes. *See* paysanne. 2. Foods garnished with vegetables cut in this manner.

Brunswick stew A stew associated with Brunswick County, Virginia; originally made with squirrel and onions; today, it is generally made with rabbit or chicken and vegetables such as corn, okra, lima beans, tomatoes and onions.

bruschetta (broo-SKEH-tah) 1. An Italian appetizer of toasted bread slices rubbed with garlic and drizzled with olive oil and sometimes topped with tomatoes and basil; served warm. 2. In the United States, any of a variety of appetizers made from toasted bread drizzled with olive oil and topped with olives, tomatoes, cheese or other ingredients.

brush To apply a liquid with a pastry brush to the surface of a food to baste or glaze the item.

Brussels sprouts A member of the cabbage family (*Brassica oleracea*) developed in Belgium; the small, spherical heads of tightly packed yellow-green leaves grow along a long, tapering stalk.

bruxelloise, à la (broo-csa'-l'wahz) A French garnish for small joints of meat consisting of stewed Brussels sprouts, chicory and potatoes.

b'steeya; bisteeya; bastela, bastila and pastilla (bs-TEE-yah) A Moroccan dish of phyllo dough filled with shredded pigeon or chicken, almonds and spices;

baked and sprinkled with confectioners' sugar and cinnamon.

bubble and squeak A British dish of mashed potatoes, chopped cabbage and, traditionally, boiled beef, mixed together and fried.

buccellato (boo-che-LAH-toh) 1. A Sicilian ring-shaped cake containing dried fruit and spices. 2. A raisin and anise-flavored cake typically presented to children on their confirmation day in Italy's Tuscany region.

bûche de Noël (boosh dah noh-ehl) French for Yule log and used to describe a traditional Christmas cake made with genoise and buttercream, shaped and decorated to resemble a log.

Bucheron (BOOSH-rawn) A tangy but mild French goat's milk cheese; it has a soft, white interior and usually comes in logs with a white rind or covered in black ash.

bucket steak A fabricated cut of the beef primal round; cut from the side of the round, it has an oval shape and is moderately tender; also known as a baseball steak.

buckeye A candy made by dipping small balls of a creamy peanut butter mixture in melted chocolate; popular in Ohio, the Buckeye State.

buckle An old-fashioned, deep-dish, fruit dessert made with a layer of cake batter that rises to the top as the dish bakes, forming a crisp crust.

buckram A blue crab whose soft shell has toughened but has not yet become hard.

buckwheat; buckwheat groat (BUHK-wheht grot) Neither a wheat nor a grain, it is the hulled and slightly crushed triangular seed (called a groat) of a plant related to the rhubarb; used like rice; also known as beechwheat, saracen corn, sarrasin and sarrazin. *See* kasha.

buckwheat flour Ground buckwheat; it has a dark color with darker speckles and a strong flavor.

buckwheat honey A thick, reddish-brown, strongly flavored honey, traditionally coarse and granulated; made principally from buckwheat blossoms in North America and Europe; also available in a clear form.

bucky dough A bakeshop term used to describe dough that is hard to handle.

bufala (BOO-fah-lah) Italian for water buffalo; it is used as a work animal and for producing the milk used in mozzarella.

buffalo The meat of the American bison (also known as buffalo); it has a deep red color, coarse texture and strong, sweet flavor.

buffalo chopper An appliance used to process moderate to large amounts of food such as bread crumbs or onions; food is placed in a large bowl that rotates beneath a hood where curved blades chop it; can also be fitted as a slicer/shredder or meat grinder; also known as a food chopper.

buffalo fish A fish found in the Mississippi River and Great Lakes; it has a dull brown to olive skin with a white ventral side, an average market weight of 8–10 lb. (3.6–4.5 kg), a moderate amount of fat and a firm texture; significant varieties include the black, prairie, rooter, smallmouth and suckermouth buffalo fish.

Buffalo wings 1. Deep-fried chicken wings served with a spicy red sauce and blue cheese dressing as an appetizer or finger food; they originated in the Anchor Bar in Buffalo, New York. 2. A term used imprecisely to describe any variety of seasoned chicken wings (e.g., teriyaki) served as an appetizer or finger food.

buffet 1. A meal or social event at which persons help themselves to foods arranged on a table or other surface; seating is not always provided. 2. A sideboard table from which foods are served or kept during a meal.

bulb baster A tool used to baste meat, poultry and fish; the basting liquid is drawn into the hollow body by suction created by squeezing the bulb at the other end; available with a hollow, needlelike attachment for injecting the basting liquid into food.

Bulgarian mayonnaise; mayonnaise Bulgare (bul-gahr) A French mayonnaise sauce blended with puréed tomato sauce and garnished with diced celery root that was poached in lemon and white wine.

bulgur; bulgar; bulghur; bulghur wheat (BUHL-guhr) A wheat berry that has had the bran removed; it is then steamed, dried and ground into various degrees of coarseness; it has a nutlike flavor and texture and a uniform golden-brown color; it is used for salads, stews or cooked like rice. *See* tabbouli.

bullet A lobster (usually a Maine lobster) with no claws.

bullhorn pepper A long, curved fresh yellow pepper with a mild flavor.

bun Any of a variety of small, round yeast rolls; can be sweet or savory.

Bündenfleisch (BEWND-ner-flysh) A Swiss method of serving air-dried beef; it is scraped into very thin wafers and dressed with oil and vinegar and served as an hors d'oeuvre; also known as Bindnerfleisch or Bündnerteller.

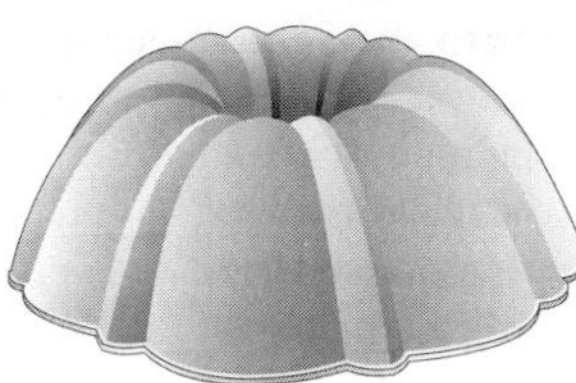
bundt pan

Bundt pan A tube pan with curved, fluted sides and used for baking cakes and quick breads.

buñuelo (boo-NWAT-loh) A light, hollow Spanish pastry that is deep-fried and dusted with cinnamon sugar.

burbot A freshwater cod found in the United States and Europe; it has a mottled brown skin with a white underbelly, a white, tender flesh that is slightly fattier than the saltwater varieties and a delicate flavor.

burdock A slender root vegetable (*Arctium lappa*) with a rusty brown skin, grayish-white flesh, crisp texture and sweet, earthy flavor; it grows wild in the United States and Europe and is cultivated in Japan, where it is known as gobo.

burgoo 1. A thick stew from the American South; it is made from pork, chicken, lamb, veal, beef, potatoes, onions, cabbage, carrots, corn, lima beans and okra. 2. An oatmeal porridge served to English sailors as early as 1750.

Burgundy (boor-guhn-dee) 1. One of France's six principal grape-growing and wine-producing regions, located in southeast France. 2. The red or white wine produced in this region.

Burgundy snail *See* escargot de Bourgogne.

burner A device that produces heat from gas, electricity or other fuels; it can be arranged with other burners on a stove top or be portable, sometimes with a built-in fuel source such as propane.

burnet (BUR-niht) An herb (*Poterium sanguisorba*) with tiny-toothed, bright green leaves and a sharp, nutty, cucumber-like flavor; the leaves are used in salads and soups or cooked as a vegetable; also known as salad burnet.

burnt cream The English name for crème brûlée.

burrito; burro (bur-EE-toh) A Mexican and American Southwest dish consisting of a large flour tortilla folded and rolled around a savory filling of chorizo, chicken, machaca, refried beans or the like and garnished with lettuce, sour cream, cheese, tomato, guacamole and so on. *See* wrap.

burro banana A variety of banana grown in Mexico; it has a flat, boxy shape and a tangy lemon–banana flavor; also known as a chunky banana.

bushel A unit of volume measurement in the American and imperial systems; approximately 2150 cu. in. or 4 pecks.

bush pumpkin A variety of small, flat, ribbed squash with a bright white skin, a yellow flesh and a flavor reminiscent of artichoke hearts.

butcher *v.* To slaughter and dress or fabricate animals for consumption. *n.* The person who does one and/or the other.

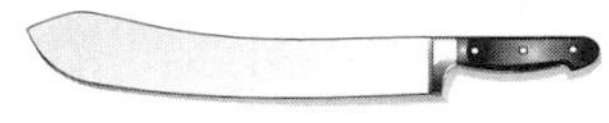
butcher knife

butcher knife A knife with a rigid 6- to 14-in. blade that curves upward in a 25-degree angle at the tip; it is used for fabricating raw meat; also known as a scimitar.

butcher's twine A narrow, strong string generally made of cotton or linen, used to truss poultry, tie roasts and so on.

butler service; butlered hors d'oeuvre The presentation by service staff of hors d'oeuvre, carried on trays, to guests; also known as passed hors d'oeuvre.

butler's pantry A small room or pantry located between the dining room and the kitchen; used for serving and storing china, crystal and the like.

butt 1. The sirloin end (as opposed to the short loin end) of a beef primal loin. *See* Boston butt. 2. The upper end of a ham (opposite the narrow shank end); also known as the rump. 3. The traditional standard cask or barrel used for aging and shipping sherry; it holds 500 l (approximately 132 U.S. gallons). 4. The rear end of a knife handle.

butter A fatty substance produced by agitating or churning cream; it contains at least 80% milkfat, not more than 16% water and 2–4% milk solids; it melts into a liquid at approximately 98°F (38°C) and reaches the smoke point at 260°F (127°C); used as a cooking medium, ingredient and topping.

butter, clarified Purified butterfat; the butter is melted and the water and milk solids are removed; also known as drawn butter.

butter, drawn *See* butter, clarified.

butter, salted Butter with up to 2.5% salt added; salt changes the flavor and extends the keeping qualities.

butter, sweet cream Butter made from pasteurized cream and usually lightly salted; this is the type of butter principally sold in the United States.

butter, whipped Butter with air incorporated into it to increase volume and spreadability (it also becomes rancid more quickly).

butter bean *See* lima bean.

butter clam A small Pacific hard-shell clam found in Puget Sound; it has a sweet, buttery flavor.

buttercream A light, smooth, fluffy frosting of sugar, fat and flavorings with egg yolks or whipped egg whites sometimes added; there are three principal kinds: simple, Italian and French.

buttercup squash A moderately large, wide, squat turban squash with a blue-gray turban and a dark green shell; it has an orange-colored flesh and a flavor reminiscent of a sweet potato.

butter curler A tool with a curved serrated blade; used to produce a shell-like curl of butter by dragging the knife across the butter.

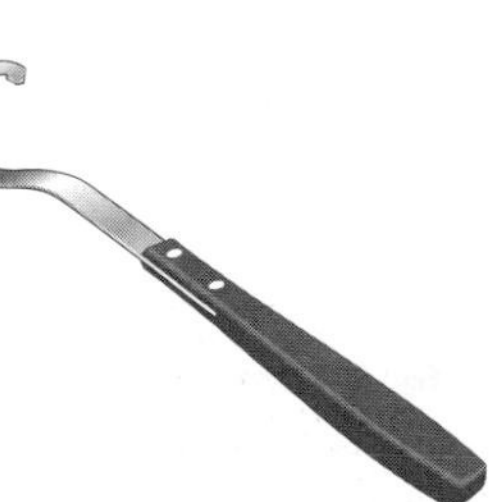

butter curler

butterfat *See* milkfat.

butterfish A fish found off the northeast coast of the United States; it has a silvery skin, average market weight of 1.5 lb. (675 g), high fat content, rich, sweet flavor and fine texture; also known as dollarfish and harvest fish.

butter-flavored granules A low-calorie product made by removing the fat and water from butter extract; it is reconstituted by blending with a liquid or being sprinkled directly on food.

butterflied A market form for fish; the fish is pan dressed, boned and opened flat like a book; the two sides remain attached by the back or belly skin.

butterfly To split food, such as boneless meat, fish or shrimp, nearly in half lengthwise, leaving the halves hinged on one side so that the item spreads open like a book; used to increase surface area and speed cooking.

butter knife A small knife used to serve butter at the table.

butter lettuce *See* lettuce, butterhead.

butter melter A short, round, tin-lined copper pot with a spout and available in 2- to 9-oz. capacities; used for melting butter; also known as a spouted saucepan.

buttermilk 1. Fresh, pasteurized skim or low-fat cow's milk cultured (soured) with *Streptococcus lactis* bacteria; also known as cultured buttermilk. 2. Traditionally, the liquid remaining after the cream was churned into butter.

buttermilk, dried The powder form of buttermilk; often used as a food additive in dry mixes, desserts, soups and sauces.

buttermilk pie A pie from the American South with a filling of buttermilk, sugar, butter, eggs and flour and flavored with lemon juice, nutmeg and vanilla.

butter mold A mold used to form softened butter into an attractive shape or to imprint a design on its surface.

butternut squash A large, elongated pear-shaped squash (*Caryoka nuciferum*) with a smooth yellow to butterscotch-colored shell, an orange flesh and a sweet, nutty flavor.

butter oil The clarified fat portion of milk, cream or butter obtained by removing the product's nonfat constituents; also known as anhydrous milkfat.

butter paddles Two ridged wooden paddles used to make decorative butter balls; the butter is placed between the paddles and rotated lightly until it forms a small ball.

butter pat 1. A small piece of butter intended as an individual serving. 2. A small dish, 2–3-in. in diameter, designed to hold butter at the dinner table; it is part of each place setting.

butter sauce *See* bâtarde *and* beurre blanc.

butterscotch 1. A flavor derived from brown sugar and butter, used for cookies, candies, sauces and the like. 2. A hard candy with the flavor of butterscotch.

butter spreader A small dull-edged knife with a moderately broad blade used by a diner to spread butter; it is often placed on the bread plate at each setting.

butter steak A fabricated cut of the beef primal chuck; it has a grainy texture and is relatively tender.

butter steam A method of cooking in butter or margarine in a closed container; also known as sweating.

butter tart A Canadian dessert made with a sweet pastry shell and filled with a vanilla-flavored buttery filling sweetened with brown sugar and raisins.

butter the size of an egg A traditional measure of volume for butter; approximately 1/4 cup (2 oz.).

butter the size of a walnut A traditional measure of volume for butter; approximately 2 tablespoons (1 oz.).

button An immature stage of growth of a capped mushroom when the cap has not yet expanded.

button mushroom *See* common store mushroom.

butt tenderloin The larger portion of the tenderloin found in the beef primal sirloin; it is used to fabricate châteaubriand. *See* short tenderloin.

BYOB Slang abbreviation for bring your own bottle, beer, or booze, meaning that guests should bring their own beverages, usually alcoholic.

Byrrh (bihr) A French aromatized red wine flavored with herbs and quinine.

bzar (bz-ahr) A North African masala with sweet and hot spices such as cinnamon, red pepper, cloves, turmeric, ginger, black pepper and cumin.

cabbage, green The common market cabbage (*Brassica oleracea*) with a large, firm, spherical head of tightly packed pale green waxy leaves; flat and conical heads are also available; also known as the common cabbage.

cabbage, red A variety of the green cabbage with dark red-purple waxy leaves; a red cabbage is usually smaller than a green cabbage, with tougher, slightly more bitter leaves.

cabbage, white A variety of the green cabbage with creamy white waxy leaves; also known as a drumhead cabbage and Dutch cabbage.

cabbages 1. Vegetables of the *Brassica* family; generally quick-growing, cool-weather crops used for their heads (e.g., red cabbage), flowers (e.g., cauliflower), stalks and leaves (e.g., bok choy), and leaves (e.g., kale). 2. More specifically, various members of the *Brassica* family used for their heads.

cabinet pudding An English dessert made with layers of bread, cake or ladyfingers, dried fruit and custard; sometimes flavored with liqueurs and served with crème anglais.

cacao (kah-KAH-oh) The dried and partly fermented seed of the cacao tree (*Theobroma cacao*) grown in tropical regions of the Western Hemisphere; it is used principally in the preparation of cocoa, chocolate and cocoa butter.

caca-poule (cau-cau-poo-la) A small spherical fruit (*Diospyros digina*) native to the Caribbean region; it has a yellowish-brown skin and a sweet, brownish flesh; also imprecisely known as sapote.

cacciatore, à la (ka-cha-TOH-reh) An Italian preparation method for meats, usually chicken, stewed with tomatoes, onions, mushrooms and various herbs and spices and sometimes wine (e.g., chicken cacciatore).

cactus pear *See* prickly pear.

café au lait (ka-FAY oh LAY) A French beverage of equal parts hot, strong coffee and hot milk.

café brûlot (ka-FAY broo-LOW) A traditional New Orleans drink of dark coffee and brandy; it is flavored with citrus rind and usually served flaming.

café complet (ka-FAY kom-play) A traditional French breakfast consisting of a croissant, butter, jam and coffee or café au lait.

Café Diable (ka-FAY dee-ah-blae) A hot beverage made of black coffee, Cognac, Cointreau, curaçao, cloves, coffee beans and cinnamon sticks.

café filtre (ka-FAY filt'r) Coffee made by pouring hot water through ground coffee beans held in a filtering device fitted over a cup or pot.

cafeteria round Any of a variety of subprimal cuts of the beef primal round; they are large roasts, with or without bones, generally carved on a buffet line.

caffè Americano (kahf-AY a-mer-i-CAH-no) An Italian beverage made from approximately one-fourth espresso and three-fourths hot water.

caffeine (kaf-feen) An odorless, bitter-tasting alkaloid found in cacao beans, coffee beans, cola nuts, tea leaves and other plants; acts as a stimulant on the central nervous system and as a diuretic.

caffè latte (kahf-AY LAH-tay) 1. An Italian beverage made from one-third or less espresso and two-thirds or more steamed milk, sometimes served with a dollop of foam on top; usually served in a tall glass. 2. Italian for coffee with milk.

caffè mocha (kahf-AY MO-kah) A beverage made from chocolate syrup, one-third espresso and approximately two-thirds steamed milk; it is topped with whipped cream sprinkled with cocoa powder; usually served in a tall glass.

Caipirinha (Cah-e-pee-ree-nya) A South American (particularly Brazilian) cocktail made of cachaça, lime chunks and confectioners' sugar.

cajeta (kah-HEH-tah) A Mexican caramel sauce made from goat's milk.

Cajun cooking A style of cooking associated with the descendants of French Acadians from Nova Scotia now living in Louisiana; it combines the cuisines of France and the American South, producing hardy dishes typically containing spices, filé powder, onions, green pepper, celery and a dark roux. *See* Creole cooking.

Cajun popcorn An appetizer of spicy shelled, battered and deep-fried crawfish or shrimp.

cake In the United States, it includes a broad range of pastries, including layer cakes, coffee cakes and gateaux; it can refer to almost anything that is baked, tender, sweet and sometimes frosted.

cake breaker A long-toothed metal comb with 3.5-in.-long (8.8-cm-long) metal teeth attached to an offset handle; used to cut angel food and chiffon cakes.

cake circle Variously sized circles of corrugated cardboard placed underneath a cake or cake layer for support and stability.

cake comb A small, flat triangle or rectangle of hard plastic or stainless steel with dull serrated edges used for marking a design or pattern into the frosting on a cake; also known as an icing comb or a pastry comb.

cake decorating combs

cake flour A low-protein wheat flour used for making cakes, pastry doughs and other tender baked goods.

cake knife A knife with a flat, spadelike 6-in.-long (15.2-cm-long) blade with fine cutting teeth; used to portion and serve cakes and pies and also for lifting and serving the portions.

cake knife

cake pans Variously shaped and sized containers for baking cake batter.

cake strip A heat-resistant strip of metallic fabric wrapped around the outside of a cake pan to maintain an even temperature during baking.

cake tester A long, thin metal wire with a small ring or handle; it (or a clean broom straw) is used to test a cake for doneness.

calabash (KAH-lah-bahsh) 1. A variety of passion fruit (*Passiflora maliformis*) native to Central America and the Caribbean region; it has an apple shape, a thin yellowish-brown skin that can be leathery and flexible or hard and brittle, a grayish or orange-yellow juicy flesh and a pleasant, fragrant flavor. 2. In American southern cuisine, a style of breaded or battered fried fish; named for the seacoast town of Calabash, North Carolina.

calabaza (kah-lah-BAH-tha) A very large, spherical or slightly pear-shaped squash with a fine-grained orange-colored flesh and a flavor similar to that of a pumpkin but moister and sweeter; also known as abobora, ahuyama, crapaudback, Cuban squash, giraumon, toad-back, West Indian pumpkin and zapallo.

calamari (kal-uh-MAIR-ee) *See* squid.

calas (KAH-lahs) A New Orleans pastry made by frying patties of a sweet batter containing cooked rice.

calasparra (cah-las-par-rah) A fine Spanish rice; it is the only controlled denomination of origin rice in Europe and is sold in small cotton sacks.

calcium 1. A major mineral used principally to form bones and teeth and to ensure proper nerve conduction, blood clotting and muscle contraction and relaxation; significant sources include dairy products, sardines, beans and bean curd, cauliflower, chard, kale, some citrus fruits, legumes and calcium-fortified foods. 2. A food additive used as a nutrient supplement.

caldron; cauldron A heavy cast-iron or cast-aluminum casserole or kettle with a rounded bottom and straight sides.

calendula (cah-len-duh-lah) A plant (*Calendula officinalis*) with bright yellow-orange flowers that are used as a garnish or as a yellow food coloring; also known as pot marigold.

calf Meat from cattle slaughtered when 5–10 months old; it has a grayish-red color, some marbling and external fat and a less delicate flavor than that of veal. *See* beef *and* veal.

Calia ham A subprimal cut of the pork primal shoulder; it is a relatively tender roast.

calico scallop A variety of very small scallops found in warm waters off the U.S. East Coast and Gulf coast; it has a red and white speckled shell and tender, sweet white meat.

California chile, dried *See* New Mexico green chile, dried *and* New Mexico red chile, dried.

California mayonnaise Heavy cream blended with ketchup and seasoned with Worcestershire sauce, Tabasco, paprika and lemon juice.

California menu A single menu listing breakfast, lunch and dinner foods, all of which are available all day.

California roll A form of sushi made for the American palate; it consists of avocado, crabmeat, cucumber and other ingredients wrapped in vinegared rice and bound by nori.

calimyrna fig (kahl-eh-MURN-a) A large squat fig with a green skin, white flesh and sweet flavor.

callaloo; calaloo; calalou; calalu; callilu (CAH-la-lu) 1. The very large leaves of plants native to the Caribbean region; they have a flavor similar to that of spinach. *See* dasheen. 2. A Caribbean stew made with callaloo, crab, pork and okra.

calliope coffee A simple gelatin dessert made with strong coffee; it is molded in individual servings and garnished with whipped cream; popular on Mississippi River showboats in the early 20th century.

Calorie; calorie 1. A Calorie or kilocalorie (also written as kcalorie, kcal or Cal.) is the amount of heat necessary to raise the temperature of 1 kg of water 1°C. 2. A calorie is a unit of heat used to measure the energy-producing value of foods (1 g of pure carbohydrate or 1 g of pure protein has 4 kcal; 1 g of pure fat has 9 kcal, and 1 g of alcohol has approximately 7 kcal); calorie is frequently and inappropriately used instead of Calorie. *See* joule.

calrose rice A white rice with a high starch content; it becomes slightly sticky when cooked.

Calvados (KAL-vah-dohs) An apple brandy made in Calvados, Normandy, France; distilled from a mash of cider apples, it is aged in oak casks for 3–10 years before blending and bottling.

calves Young cows or bulls. *See* veal *and* calf.

calves' liver; calf's liver The large-lobed organ of a calf; it has a dark reddish-brown color, a tender texture and a strong flavor.

calzone (kal-ZOH-nay) 1. An Italian–American dish made with pizza dough shaped like a large turnover and stuffed with various meats, vegetables and cheeses; it is deep-fried or baked. 2. A Mexican sugar cookie.

Cambozola (kam-boh-ZOH-lah) A soft German cheese; it has a downy rind, a creamy texture and a pale ivory-gold color streaked with blue veins.

cambric tea A beverage of hot water, milk, sugar and a dash of tea, given to children to make them feel like a part of a social gathering.

Cambridge sauce; Cambridge mayonnaise An English sauce similar to mayonnaise and used as a cold sauce for cold meat or fish dishes; it is made from oil and vinegar dripped into pounded hard-cooked egg yolks, capers, anchovies, chervil, tarragon, chives and cayenne.

Camellia sinensis A woody plant, usually pruned to a flat-topped shrub, whose young shoots, unopened leaf buds and leaves are used to make tea; it is grown in warm, wet, subtropical and tropical climates at various elevations worldwide; the finer teas tend to come from plants grown at higher altitudes, and the choicest selections are the terminal bud with its two adjacent leaves.

Camembert (kam-uhn-BAIR) A soft, creamy French cheese made from cow's milk; it has a creamy texture, a pale ivory-gold color and a whitish-gray, yellow-flecked rind; when perfectly ripe, it oozes thickly, and when overly ripe, it is runny and bitter, with a strong ammonia odor.

Camerani, sauce (cah-mae-rah-nee) A French compound sauce made from a Madeira sauce garnished with minced black truffle.

campagnola, alla (kahm-pah-N'YOH-lah, AH-lah) Italian for country style and used to describe a preparation method in which the principal ingredient is served with tomatoes and onions.

Campari (kahm-PAH-ree) An Italian bitters with an astringent, bittersweet flavor and red color; a sweet variety is also available.

Campylobacter jejuni A species of bacteria that causes gastroenteritis (called campylobacteriosis); the bacteria is transmitted through contaminated raw milk.

caña (CAHN-yah) The sugarcane from which molasses is derived.

Canadian whisky Made in Canada, a whisky distilled from a mash of corn, rye, wheat and barley and aged for 6–8 years in oak casks; it has a light body, a slightly pale color and a mellow flavor.

canaigre (kahn-neh-gruh) An herb (*Rumex hymenosepalus*) native to the American Southwest with long green leaves and a reddish stem; its tuberous roots are roasted and ground into flour in Native American cuisines.

canapé (KAN-uh-pay; KAN-uh-pee) An hors d'oeuvre consisting of toasted or untoasted bread cut into a shape (sliced vegetables such as cucumbers are also used) and typically topped with a spread (e.g., butter or cream cheese) and one or more savory garnishes (e.g., foie gras or sausage).

canard à la presse (kah-nar ah lah press) A French dish consisting of a roasted duck served with a sauce made from the mashed liver, juices extracted from the carcass in a duck press, Cognac and wine; the legs are grilled and served as a second course; also known as pressed duck.

Canary Island banana A variety of banana; it is shorter, more flavorful and more delicate than the common banana; also known as the Chinese banana and dwarf banana.

candied fruit Fruit that is crystallized in sugar.

candlenut A spherical, oily nut (*Aleurites moluccana*) with a creamy yellow color and similar in texture and flavor to the macadamia; cultivated in Indonesia, the Philippines and other Pacific Islands and generally used crushed to provide flavor and texture to savory dishes.

candy *v.* 1. To preserve or coat a fruit, flower or other food with sugar or heavy sugar syrup. 2. To cook a food such as carrots or sweet potatoes in sugar and butter, or in syrup, so as to give it a sweet, glossy coating. *n.* Any of a large variety of sweet confections made principally from sugar and flavorings.

canelle knife *See* stripper.

cane syrup A thick, sweet syrup; it is the result of an intermediate step in the sugarcane-refining process when the syrup is reduced.

caneton à l'orange (ka-nuh-tohn ah lo-rahnzh) A French dish consisting of a roast duckling served with an orange-flavored sauce and garnished with fresh orange slices; also known as caneton à la bigrade and duck à l'orange.

canistel (kah-NEHS-stuhl) A long, egg-shaped fruit (*Pouteria campechiana*) native to Central America and the Caribbean region; it has a shiny lemon to orange-yellow skin when ripe, a firm orange flesh that becomes softer toward the center and a flavor reminiscent of a baked sweet potato.

canna The tuber of this popular flower (genus *Canna*) is ground and used as a flour and thickening agent in West Indian soups and sauces; also known as Indian shot.

canneler (can-lay) French for to flute and used to indicate that the edges of a pastry shell or similar item should be fluted or that a fruit or vegetable should be cut with an implement that leaves a fluted edge.

cannellini (kan-eh-LEE-nee) Large, elongated kidney-shaped beans grown in Italy; they have a creamy white color and are used in soups and salads; also known as white kidney beans.

canner The lowest USDA quality grade for beef; the meat is not for retail sale and is used primarily in processed or canned products.

canning A food preservation method; a food is sealed in a metal or glass container that is then subjected to high temperatures to destroy microorganisms that cause spoilage (it also cooks the foods slightly); the sealed environment also eliminates oxidation and retards decomposition.

canning, open-kettle Preserving food by cooking it in an uncovered saucepan and packing it, usually while hot, in a hot, sterilized jar, which is then sealed, cooled and stored.

canning, pressure Processing sealed jars of food under pressure at 240°F (115°C) (at sea level to 2000 ft. [600 m] above; adjustments must be made at higher altitudes); this method is necessary for low-acid food to destroy bacteria that can cause spoilage and food poisoning, including botulism.

canning, water bath Processing certain acidic and/or sweet foods to destroy bacteria, enzymes, molds and yeasts that can cause spoilage; filled, sealed jars are boiled (or simmered) for specific lengths of time in water deep enough to cover them by an inch or so at top and bottom.

cannoli (kan-OH-lee) An Italian pastry composed of a deep-fried tube of sweet pastry dough filled with sweetened ricotta studded with candied fruit, chocolate or pistachio nuts.

cannoli form (kan-OH-lee forhm) A 4- to 6-in.-long aluminum or tinned steel tube with a diameter of 5/8 to 1 in.; it is used to shape cannoli by wrapping the dough around the form before frying it.

cannonball guava A large green guava with a dark ring around it; its yellow-pink flesh is sweet and its seeds are edible.

canola oil (kan-OH-luh) An oil made in Canada from rapeseeds; it is relatively low in saturated fats, contains omega-3 fatty acids and has a bland, neutral flavor suitable for cooking and other uses.

can opener, crank A hand tool used to open tin cans; a sharp cutting wheel is clamped over the rim of the can, then a hand crank is turned, causing the wheel to puncture the can and bend down the cut edge around the perimeter of the lid.

can opener, manual A tool used to open tin cans, lift off crown caps, and uncork bottles; the tip of the short blade punctures the can; then, with a rocking motion, it rips around the perimeter of the lid; it usually has a hook that lifts crown caps and a coiled wire worm to uncork bottles.

can opener, table-mounted A table-mounted tool with a long arm to which is attached a sharp blade that pierces the can; a hand crank turned against the blade cuts the can lid.

cantaloupe (KAN-teh-lohp) Named for Cantalupo, Italy, where it was first grown in Europe; it is a small, spherical melon (*Cucumis melo*) with a rough surface that is fissured into segments, it has a pale green to orange flesh with a sweet flavor and a central cavity with many small seeds. *See* Charentais melon *and* Ogen.

cantucci (kahn-TOO-chee) Almond-flavored cookies from Italy's Tuscany region; they are usually eaten with wine.

canvasback duck A wild duck found in North America; it has a distinctive, rich flavor.

cape gooseberry A cherry-sized fruit (*Physalis peruviana*) native to South America; enclosed in a thin, papery, cream-colored husk, it has a thin, waxy yellow-green to orange skin, many seeds and a pleasant, distinctive flavor; eaten raw or used in baked goods and jams; also imprecisely known as a ground-cherry or winter cherry.

capers The unopened flower buds of a shrub (*Capparis spinosa*) native to the Mediterranean region; after curing in salted white vinegar, the buds develop a sharp, salty–sour flavor and are used as a flavoring and condiment. *See* nonpareils.

caper sauce An English sauce made from capers, butter, flour and the juices from the roasted meat with which it is served.

capirotada (kahpeh-roh-tah-dah) A Mexican bread pudding made with raisins, caramelized sugar and cheese; it is typically served during Lent.

capital cut steak A fabricated cut of the beef primal rib; it is a bone-in rib steak.

capon A rooster castrated before it is 8 weeks old and fattened and slaughtered before it is 10 months old; it has a market weight of 4–10 lb. (1.8–4.5 kg), a soft, smooth skin, a high proportion of light to dark meat, a relatively high fat content and juicy, tender, well-flavored flesh.

caponata (kap-oh-NAH-tah) A Sicilian dish of cooked eggplant, onions, tomatoes, anchovies, olives and pine nuts flavored with capers and vinegar and served at room temperature as a salad, side dish or relish.

cappuccino (kahp-uh-CHEE-noh) An Italian beverage made from equal parts espresso, steamed milk and foamed milk, sometimes dusted with sweetened cocoa powder or cinnamon; usually served in a large cup.

capsaicin (kap-say-ee-zin) A compound found in the placental ribs (the interior white veining to which the seeds are attached) of a chile (genus *Capsicum*) and responsible for the chile's hot flavor.

captain The person at a fine dining restaurant responsible for explaining the menu to guests and taking their orders as well as any table-side preparations; also known as chef d'étage.

carafe (kah-RAHF) A glass container used to serve wine (generally young, inexpensive wine), coffee, water or other beverages at the table; usually in liter and half-liter sizes and generally without a lid, cork or other stopper. *See* decanter.

carambola (kair-ahm-BOH-lah) A fruit (*Averrhoea corambola*) native to Asia; it has a moderately long body with five prominent ridges running its length that create a star-shaped cross section; the fruit has a waxy orange-yellow skin, a crisp, juicy, yellow flesh and a sweet to tart flavor; used in sweet and savory dishes, as a garnish, or in chutneys; also known as star fruit and Chinese star fruit.

caramel 1. A substance produced by cooking sugar until it becomes a thick, dark liquid; its color ranges from golden to dark brown, and it is used for coloring and flavoring desserts, candies, sweet and savory sauces, and other foods. 2. A firm, chewy candy made with sugar, butter, corn syrup and milk or cream.

caramelization The process of cooking sugars; the browning of sugar enhances the flavor and appearance of foods.

caramelize To heat sugar to very high temperatures, usually 310–360°F (153–182°C); this causes the sugar to brown and develop a full, rich, intense flavor.

caramel ruler; caramel bar A stainless steel or chromed steel bar (0.5 × 0.5 × 20–30 in.) used to hold a caramel, chocolate or fondant mixture while it cools; also known as a chocolate ruler or chocolate bar.

caramel sauce A dessert sauce made from caramelized sugar diluted with water, milk or cream.

carapace The hard outer covering of a shellfish.

caraway An herb and member of the parsley family (*Carum carvi*); the fleshy root is eaten as a vegetable, and the feathery leaves are used in salads or as garnish.

caraway seeds The small, crescent-shaped brown seeds of the caraway plant; they have a nutty, peppery, aniselike flavor and are used to flavor baked goods, savory dishes and the liqueur Kümmel.

carbohydrates A class of organic nutrients, including sugars, glycogen, starches, dextrin and cellulose, that contain only carbon, hydrogen and oxygen; occurring naturally in plants and milk, they are used by the body principally for energy.

carbon A nonmetallic element that, along with oxygen and hydrogen, is the characteristic constituent of organic matter; it occurs in pure form as diamonds and graphite and in impure form as charcoal.

carbonada (kahr-boh-NAH-doh) Any of several South American stewlike dishes baked in a casserole.

carbonade (car-bohn-ahd) Meat that has been browned until it has a crust and is then cooked in a liquid (braised).

carbonara, alla (kar-boh-NAH-rah, ah-la) An Italian dish of pasta, usually spaghetti, with a sauce of eggs, cream, Parmesan and bits of cooked bacon.

carbonated beverage A beverage that does not contain alcohol; it is effervescent (mechanically induced) and usually flavored, sweetened and/or colored; also known imprecisely as a soft drink.

carbonation The process or effect of dissolving carbon dioxide in a liquid to create or increase effervescence.

carbon dioxide A colorless, odorless gas formed from the combustion of carbonaceous materials, the fermentation process or found in natural springs. *See* fermentation *and* carbonation.

carbonnade à la flamande (kar-bohn-AHD ah lah flah MAHND) A thick Belgian beef stew flavored with beer, bacon, onions and brown sugar.

carbon steel An alloy of carbon and iron used for knife blades; easily sharpened, it corrodes and discolors easily. *See* stainless steel *and* high-carbon stainless steel.

carcass The cleaned, dressed body of a slaughtered animal; it contains both forequarters and hindquarters.

cardamom (KAR-duh-muhm) A member of the ginger family (*Elettaria cardamomum*); its long, light green or brown pods contain a seed that has a strong, lemony flavor with notes of camphor and a pleasantly pungent aroma; available in the pod, whole or ground and used principally in Indian and Middle Eastern cuisines.

cardinale, sauce (kahr-dee-NAHL) A French compound sauce made from a béchamel flavored with fish stock and truffle essence, seasoned with cayenne pepper, and finished with lobster butter.

cardoon (kahr-DOON) Closely related to the globe artichoke, this vegetable (*Cynara cardunculu*) is composed of stalks that grow in bunches; the silver-gray stalks are long, flat and wide with notched sides and a fuzzy texture; they are boiled, baked and braised in French, Italian and Spanish cuisines.

Carême, Marie-Antoine (Antonin) (Fr., 1783–1833) A chef and pastry cook acknowledged as the master of French grande cuisine. He worked his way up from the streets of Paris to become one of the most famous chefs of all time, ultimately employed by Tsar Alexander I of Russia, the Prince Regent of England, Talleyrand and Baron de Rothschild. He authored several texts on the culinary arts, primarily *L'Art de la Cuisine,* and instituted the system for sauce classification still in use today.

caribou A large antlered member of the reindeer family; a game animal, its fatty meat, known as venison, is not particularly flavorful.

Carignan, sauce A French compound sauce made from a demi-glaze flavored with tomatoes and finished with Málaga or port.

carissa A fruit from a low, thorny bush native to southern Africa (*Carissa macrocarpa*); the small spherical fruit has a scarlet skin with dark red streaks, white-flecked red flesh, thin brown seeds, a granular texture, and a slightly sharp, acidic flavor; also known as a natal plum.

carne seca (KAHR-neh seh-kah) Sun-dried and salted beef used in Mexican and Latin American cuisines.

carnitas (kahr-NEE-tahz) Mexican for little meats and used to describe a dish of small shreds of browned pork, usually eaten with salsa or used as a filling for tacos and burritos.

carob (KAIR-uhb) The edible pulp of the long, leathery pods of an evergreen tree of the pea family (*Ceratonia siliqua*) native to the Middle East; the pulp has a chocolate-like flavor and is usually dried, roasted and ground to a powder and used to flavor candy and baked goods or as a chocolate substitute, also known as St. John's bread and locust bean.

Carolina rice A long-grain rice originally planted in North Carolina, but now cultivated in California, Texas, Louisiana and Arkansas.

carotene, alpha-, beta- and gamma- 1. A substance found in plants and used by the body as a vitamin A provitamin. 2. A group of yellow to orange pigments found in plants. 3. A food additive used as a yellow or orange food coloring. 4. Especially beta-carotene, a nutrient supplement and food additive that, as an antioxidant, is believed to lower the risk of cancer.

carotenoid A naturally occurring pigment that predominates in red and yellow vegetables such as carrots and red peppers.

carp A freshwater fish found in Asia, Europe and North America; generally has an olive green skin that becomes more yellow on the belly, an average market weight of 2–8 lb. (0.9–3.6 kg), and a lean, firm flesh that sometimes has a muddy flavor.

carpaccio (kahr-PAH-chee-oh) An Italian dish of thinly sliced raw beef drizzled with olive oil and lemon juice, garnished with capers and sometimes onions, and served as an appetizer.

carpetbag steak A thick beef steak with a pocket cut into it; the pocket is stuffed with seasoned oysters and the meat is grilled.

carré d'agneau (kar-ray dahn-yo) French for rack of lamb.

carrier A person (or other animal) who harbors a pathogenic organism and is potentially capable of spreading it to other humans or animals; a carrier usually appears not to have any discernible signs or symptoms of the disease.

carrot A member of the parsley family (*Daucus carota*); it has lacy green foliage, an edible orange taproot with a mild, sweet flavor and crisp texture, and a tapering shape; it comes in a variety of sizes; also known as an underground cherry.

carryover cooking The cooking that occurs after a food is removed from a heat source; it is accomplished by the residual heat remaining in the food.

cartilage A tough, whitish elastic connective tissue that helps give structure to an animal's body; also known as gristle.

carving fork A two-pronged fork with a hand guard. *See* two-pronged fork.

carving fork

carving knife A knife with a long slender blade used to slice cooked meat; it can have a beveled edge (used for carving a ham) or be more rounded (which adds strength); also known as a meat carver.

carving station The area of a buffet where freshly roasted meats are carved to order; the station is usually a freestanding table with a heat lamp to keep the meats warm.

casaba (kah-SAH-bah) A large, spherical winter melon (a muskmelon) native to Turkey; it has a thick yellow rind with deep, rough furrows that wrinkle at the pointed end, an ivory-colored flesh, and a mild cucumber-like flavor.

casalinga, alla (kah-sah-LEEN-'gah, AH-lah) Italian for housewife style or homemade and used to generally describe peasant or country cooking.

Casanova, à la (cah-sah-noh-vah, ah lah) A French garnish for fish consisting of oysters and mussels in a white wine sauce sprinkled with truffle slices.

cascabel (KAHS-kah-behl) A small, dried, spherical chile with a thick reddish-brown flesh and a medium hot, slightly acidic flavor.

casein (kay-seen) 1. A milk protein containing all essential amino acids. 2. The principal milk protein that solidifies milk into cheese; this solidification is facilitated by the action of rennet.

cashew A sweet, butter-flavored, kidney-shaped nut with a high fat content; it grows at the end of the cashew apple in three layers of shell, one of which contains a toxic brown oil.

cashew apple A pear-shaped fruit (actually a stalk) from a tree (*Anacardium occidentale*) native to Central and South America; it has a yellow-orange skin and tart, astringent flavor and is used for making vinegar, liqueurs and wine; the cashew nut grows on the outside of the apple at its base; also known as darkassou.

casing The outer covering or membrane of a sausage; it holds the forcemeat or other fillings; a casing can be made from animal intestines, collagen or artificial materials.

cassata (kas-SAA-tah) A Sicilian dessert for which a mold is lined with liqueur-soaked chocolate sponge cake, then filled with ricotta, candied fruit and chocolate shavings; the dessert is chilled, unmolded and decorated with marzipan and whipped cream.

cassava; cassava root (cah-SAH-vah) A large, long starchy root (*Manihot utilissima*) with a tough brown skin and crisp white flesh; a staple of South American and African cuisines and used to make tapioca; also known as Brazilian arrowroot, manioc and yuca.

cassava flour *See* tapioca.

casserole 1. Any of a variety of baked dishes made with meat, poultry, fish, shellfish, pasta and/or vegetables, bound with a sauce and often topped with bread crumbs, cheese or the like. 2. The deep dish, usually with two handles and a tight-fitting lid and made of ceramic or glass, used to bake and serve these foods.

casserole braising A method for cooking poultry and meats in a close-fitting covered casserole; also known as en cocotte; casserole braising can be carried out with fat alone (poêler) or with a small amount of liquid (étuver).

cassia (KAH-see-uh; KASH-uh) A spice that is the inner bark of the branches of a small evergreen tree (*Cinnamomum cassia*); it has a darker red-brown color, coarser texture and stronger, less subtle and slightly more bitter flavor than its close relative, cinnamon, and is often sold as cinnamon; it is also known as Chinese cinnamon. *See* cinnamon.

cassoulet (ka-soo-LAY) A French stew of white beans, sausages, pork or lamb and preserved goose or duck flavored with a bouquet garni and an onion studded with cloves and garlic.

Castelan sauce; castellane, sauce (cas-tay-lan) A French compound sauce made from a Madeira sauce flavored with tomatoes and garnished with diced bell peppers and ham; usually served with lamb or beef medallions, garnished with diced, sautéed tomatoes, potato croquettes and fried onion rings.

caster A small glass, ceramic or metal bottle with a perforated top used for sprinkling sugar, pepper, dry mustard or other dry seasonings or ingredients on food.

cast iron An alloy of iron, carbon, and other elements; depending on the composition, it can be soft and strong or hard and brittle. *See* ironware.

castor sugar; caster sugar *See* superfine sugar.

Catalane, sauce (kah-tahl-ahn) A French compound sauce made from a Madeira sauce, seasoned with garlic, mustard, tomato and cayenne; it is typically served with sautéed beef medallions on a base of sliced, sautéed eggplant and garnished with large mushroom caps stuffed with risotto.

cataplana (kah-tah-plah-nah) A Portuguese copper pan with two handles and a hinged lid; used to steam and serve shellfish and vegetables.

cataplana

catarina (cah-tah-reh-nah) A small, dried, garnet-colored chile shaped like a teardrop or bullet; it has a medium hot, crisp flavor.

catchup; catsup *See* ketchup.

caterer A person or entity that supplies foods, beverages, service items, personnel and/or almost anything else necessary for a social event at the caterer's own facility or elsewhere.

catfish A freshwater fish found in southern and midwestern American lakes and rivers and extensively aquafarmed; it has long barbels, a scaleless brownish skin, a pure white, slightly fatty flesh, a firm texture, and a mild, sweet flavor. *See* hogfish.

catfish, channel The common catfish; it has a deeply forked tail, a relatively small head, small irregular spots on a tough, inedible skin, and an average weight of 2–5 lb. (1–2.2 kg). *See* fiddler.

catfish tender A subprimal cut of the beef primal chuck; it is a somewhat tough, front-cut chuck roast.

cats' tongues Long, thin, slightly sweet cookies; also known as langues de chat.

cattle The collective name for all domesticated oxen (genus *Bos*), including bulls, calves, cows, heifers, stags and steers.

caudière; caudrée (koh-DYEHR; koh-DRAY) A French seafood soup or stew based on mussels and onions.

caudle (KAUH-dahl) A hot drink made of wine or beer mixed with eggs, bread, sugar and spices; usually consumed for alleged medicinal purposes.

caul fat The fatty membrane that lines the abdominal cavity of hogs and sheep; this thin, lacy, weblike net is used to wrap forcemeats and melts rapidly when cooked, thereby basting the item.

cauliflower A member of the cabbage family (*Brassica oleracea*); it has a head (called a curd) of tightly packed white florets (a purple variety is also available) partially covered with large, waxy, pale green leaves on a white-green stalk; some varieties have a purple or greenish tinge.

cavaliére, sauce (cah-vah-lee-yair) A French compound sauce made from a demi-glaze flavored with tomatoes, seasoned with mustard and tarragon vinegar, and garnished with capers and diced sour gherkins.

caviar (kav-ee-AHR) 1. The salted roe of the sturgeon; the small spheres have a crisp texture that should pop in the mouth and have a pleasantly salty flavor; available fresh or pasteurized in tins and jars. *See* beluga, malossol, osetra *and* sevruga. 2. An improperly and imprecisely used term to describe the roe of fish such as whitefish, lumpfish, salmon, herring, pike and perch.

caviar, pasteurized Caviar that is heated and placed in airtight jars; it has a long shelf life, although some flavor is lost.

caviar, pressed A processed caviar made from osetra and sevruga roes; it has a spreadable, jamlike consistency.

cayenne; cayenne pepper (KI-yen; KAY-yen) 1. A hot, pungent, peppery powder blended from various ground, dried hot chiles and salt; it has a bright orange-red color and fine texture; also known as red pepper. 2. A dried, thin, short chile with a bright red color, thin flesh and hot, tart, acidic flavor; usually used ground.

cazuela (kah-SWEH-lah) 1. A shallow, rustic unglazed earthenware casserole with a glazed interior and no cover; used in traditional and rural Spanish cuisines. 2. The stew cooked in such a dish.

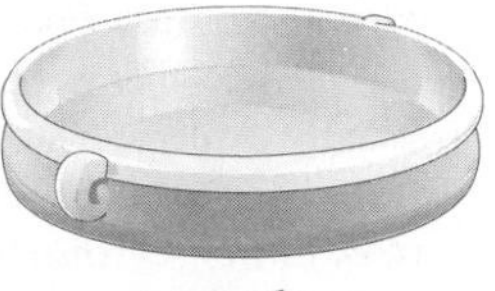
cazuela

celeriac (seh-LER-ee-ak) A small to medium-sized, brown, knobby vegetable (*Apium graveolens*) that is the root of a specially bred celery plant; it has a flavor reminiscent of celery and parsley and is eaten raw or cooked; also known as celery knob and celery root.

celery (SELL-ree) Developed in 16th-century Italy, this vegetable (*Apium graveolens*) grows in bunches of long, stringy, curved stalks or ribs surrounding a tender heart; it can be eaten raw, cooked or used as a flavoring; there are two principal celery varieties: Pascal (which is pale green) and golden (which is creamy white); also known as branch celery.

celery root *See* celeriac.

celery salt A seasoning blend of ground celery seeds (lovage) and salt.

celery seeds The seeds of the herb lovage; they are small and brown and are used in pickling and as a flavoring.

cellar 1. A place to store wine; although not necessarily underground, it should be cool, dark and vibration free; also known as a wine cellar. 2. A wine collection.

cellophane noodles Relatively clear Asian noodles made from a dough of mung bean flour and water; they have a slippery-soft texture when cooked; also known as glass noodles, translucent noodles, transparent noodles, shining noodles, silver noodles, bean threads and bean vermicelli.

cellulose A polysaccharide occurring naturally in the cell walls of plants; as dietary fiber, it provides no nutritional value, because it is not absorbed during digestion.

Celsius A temperature scale with 0° as the freezing point of water and 100° as its boiling point; to convert to Fahrenheit, multiply the Celsius figure by 9, divide by 5, and add 32; also known as centigrade.

celtuce (cehl-TUSS) A hybrid lettuce with celerylike stalks and moderate-sized tender leaves with a celery-like flavor.

cenci (CHEN-chee) Italian for rags and tatters and used to describe pastries made from thinly rolled strips of sweet rum- or brandy-flavored dough tied into knots, deep-fried and sprinkled with confectioners' sugar while still warm.

cendré (sun-drae) French term for cheeses ripened in ashes (vegetable ash gives them a bluish hue); they are usually made in wine-producing regions.

centaury, common An annual or biennial herb (*Cenaurium erythraea*) with an erect stem, slender, narrow leaves and bright rose-red, funnel-shaped flowers; the stems are used medicinally and to make bitter herbal wines and liqueurs.

center cut 1. A fabricated or subprimal cut of beef, veal, lamb or pork taken from the interior of a subprimal or primal cut; the outer edges or ends of the larger cut are removed to create a more desirable portion from which more uniform and attractive smaller cuts are produced. 2. The cut that divides a ham into the rump (butt) and shank halves. *See* wheel.

center-cut chuck steaks Fabricated cuts of the beef primal chuck; they are steaks cut from the center of the primal chuck and are flavorful and meaty.

center-cut steak A fabricated cut of the beef primal round; it is a tender, very lean round steak.

center loin chop; center-cut rib chop A fabricated cut of the pork primal loin; a chop cut from the center of the loin.

center slice ham A fabricated cut of the pork primal fresh ham; it is an oval slice of ham containing a small round bone and cut from an area approximately 1 in. (2.54 cm) on either side of the center cut.

centi- *See* metric system.

centigrade *See* Celsius.

cephalopods (SEHF-uh-luh-pods) A general category of mollusks characterized by elongated muscular arms, often with suckers, a distinct head with well-developed eyes and a beak-shaped jaw, a saclike, fin-bearing mantle, an ink sac, and a thin internal shell called a pen or cuttlebone; significant varieties include the cuttlefish, octopus and squid.

ceramics Hard, sometimes brittle, materials made from clay and similar materials treated by heat and often glazed; ceramics, which include earthenware, porcelain and stoneware and are used for cookware, bakeware, dinnerware and serviceware, conduct heat evenly, retain temperatures well and, depending on the glaze, if any, are generally nonreactive with acids and bases.

cereal 1. Any gramineous plant yielding an edible grain such as wheat, rye, oats, rice or corn. 2. A term used imprecisely to describe any such plant, as well as a plant yielding an edible seed such as buckwheat. 3. These grains and seeds. 4. Processed foods such as breakfast cereals made from these grains and seeds.

ceriman (SEHR-uh-muhn) *See* monstera.

cervelas (sehr-veh-la) A French sausage available in large and small sizes; traditionally made with hog brains, now made from pork meat and fat, seasoned with garlic; also known as saucisse de Paris or saucisson de Paris.

cervelat (Sehr-vuh-la) A style of French sausages made from chopped pork and/or beef, seasoned with herbs, spices and other flavorings such as garlic or mustard; they are preserved by curing, drying and smoking and have a semidry to moist, soft texture.

Ceylon A Sri Lankan black pekoe tea; the beverage has a golden color, full flavor, and delicate fragrance; ideal for serving iced, because it does not become cloudy when cold.

chafing dish A dish used to warm or cook foods; it consists of a container with a heat source (candle, solid fuel or electric element) directly beneath it; the container can be an assemblage similar to a bain marie; also known as réchaud, which is French for reheat.

chafing dish

chain The side muscle of a tenderloin.

chakin (cha-ken) A Japanese form of sushi; thin sheets of omelet are filled with a seasoned rice mixture and shaped into rolls or balls.

chalaza; chalaza cord (kuh-LAY-zah) *pl.* chalazae. A thick, twisted strand of egg white anchoring the yolk in place; neither an imperfection nor part of an embryo; the more prominent the cord, the fresher the egg.

challah; hallah (HKAH-lah; HAH-la) A tender, rich Jewish yeast bread usually made with butter and honey and shaped into a braided loaf.

challah knaidel (khah-la knayd-dhul) A Jewish dumpling made from dried challah crumbs.

chalupa (chah-LOO-pah) Corn tortilla dough formed into the shape of a boat and fried; it is used in Mexican cuisine filled with shredded beef, pork, chicken, vegetables or cheese.

chambering The process by which a pocket inside an oyster's shell that is started by water, a worm or a grain of sand is sealed off with a chalky substance the oyster produces; the foreign substance putrefies and releases a strong odor, indicating that the oyster may be bad.

Chambord (sham-bor) A plum-colored, sweet French liqueur with a black raspberry flavor.

chamomile; camomile (KAM-uh-meel) A perennial plant (*Chamaemelum nobile*) with daisylike flower heads that are used for a tisane that calms the stomach and has a faint aroma reminiscent of lemon and pineapple.

Champagne (cham-PANE-ya) 1. A sparkling wine from France's Champagne region made by the méthode champenoise using only three grape varieties: Chardonnay, Pinot Noir and Pinot Meunier. 2. The district in northeast France where this sparkling wine is made. 3. A term inappropriately applied to any sparkling wine other than that produced in Champagne.

champagne, sauce au 1. A French compound sauce made from a béchamel flavored with shallots and Champagne and finished with butter. 2. A French compound sauce made from a demi-glaze flavored with shallots, herbs and wine and finished with butter and Cognac.

champagne grapes A variety of very small, purplish-black or reddish-brown grapes with a very sweet flavor; used for garnish and snacking and not for wine.

champagne saucer A stemmed glass with a flattened, shallow bowl ranging in size from 3 to 10 fl. oz.; traditionally used to serve sparkling wine, it is no longer generally used, because too great a surface area of wine is exposed to the air, thus allowing the effervescence to escape too rapidly; also known as a saucer, saucer glass or coupe.

champagne tulip A stemmed glass with an elongated V-shaped or tulip-shaped bowl ranging in size from 6 to 10 fl. oz.; developed by French Champagne producers, it is recommended for serving sparkling wines because it helps trap the effervescence.

champagne vinegar A vinegar with a pale color and a mild flavor; it is used for making salad dressings.

champignon (sham-peen-yawn) A domed hand tool usually made of wood and resembling a mushroom; it is used to purée fruit, vegetables, fish and poultry through a tamis.

champignon

channa dal (chaa-naa dahl) Yellow split peas used in Indian cuisines. *See* besan *and* pigeon pea.

channeled whelk A variety of whelk found in the Gulf of Mexico and along the U.S. East Coast; it has a thin, irregularly channeled, brownish shell with an average size of 6 in. (15.2 cm) and a lean, very tough, and flavorful flesh; also known as the pear whelk.

channel fat Fat located over the vertebrae on the inside of the pork primal loin and the beef chuck and rib primals.

chanterelle (shan-tuh-REHL) A trumpet-shaped wild mushroom (*Cantharellus cibarius*) found in North America and Europe; it has a ruffled-edge cap, a yellow-orange color, a smooth, slightly chewy texture, a distinctive fruity, nutty flavor, and a clean, earthy aroma; several closely related species are sold under the same name.

Chantilly (shan-TIHL-lee; shahn-tee-YEE) 1. A general category of hot and cold emulsified French sauces to which whipped cream is added; the sauces are also known as mousselines. 2. Lightly sweetened whipped cream sometimes flavored with vanilla and used as a dessert topping.

Chantilly, sauce (shahn-tee-YEE) A French compound sauce made from a suprême with unsweetened whipped heavy cream folded in; usually served with poached chicken or veal sweetbreads.

chapati; chapatti (chah-PAH-tee) An Indian pancake-like unleavened bread made from whole wheat dough and cooked on a griddle.

chapon (shah-POHN) A bread crust rubbed with garlic and used to garnish a salad or a thin soup or to rub inside a bowl to impart a slight garlic flavor to its contents (e.g., salad greens).

charcoal A porous black residue of partially burned organic matter, particularly wood; once ignited, it puts forth a steady heat and is used for cooking, especially grilling.

charcuterie (shahr-COO-tuhr-ree; shar-coo-tuhr-EE) 1. The production of pâtés, terrines, galantines, sausages, crépinettes and similar foods. 2. The shop where such foods are made and/or sold. 3. Originally referred only to products produced from pork.

charcutière, sauce (shahr-COO-tee-aihr) A French compound sauce made from a sauce Robert garnished with a julienne of sour gherkins.

chard 1. A general term for the leafstalk of leafy green vegetables; also known as midrib. 2. A member of the beet family (*Beta vulgaris,* var. *cicla*); it has crinkly dark green leaves and silvery, celerylike stalks; the leaves are prepared like spinach and have a similar tart flavor, and the stalks are prepared like asparagus and have a tart, somewhat bitter flavor; also known as Swiss chard. *See* rhubarb chard.

Chardonnay (shar-doh-nay) 1. Considered by some the finest white wine grape, it is planted worldwide and used for the great French white Burgundies and sparkling wines; sometimes called Pinot Chardonnay, even though not a member of the Pinot family. 2. White wines made from this grape; they range from clean, crisp and with a hint of fruit to rich and complex. 3. A sparkling white wine made from this grape.

Charentais melon (shahr-ahng-tehs) A French variety of cantaloupe; it has a yellow-green ribbed skin and a sweet, fragrant, orange flesh; it is spherical rather than ovoid.

charger 1. A large flat plate placed under a dinner plate on which foods are rarely placed; also known as a service plate. 2. A large flat plate used for food, usually carefully composed presentations and architectural foods. 3. A large flat platter used for carrying and serving meats.

charlotte (SHAR-loht) A French dessert in which a mold is lined with ladyfingers, sponge cake or bread, then filled with Bavarian cream and/or fruit, chilled, and unmolded for service.

charlotte mold A deep, pail-shaped cylindrical mold with a small handle on each side, usually made of tinned steel; used for molding desserts.

charlotte mold

charlotte russe A French dessert consisting of a charlotte made with strawberries and whipped cream.

Charmat process A sparkling wine-making process during which the second fermentation takes place in a tank rather than in the bottle; also known as bulk process, tank fermentation, cuvé close, autoclave and granvas.

charmoula; chermoula (skar-moo-lah) A thick, spicy ragoût of onions, raisins, carrots and celery flavored with ras al-hanout, bay leaf, dried rose petals, vinegar and shallots; served hot or cold as a sauce for grilled meats in various Arabic cuisines.

charoset (ha-row-set) A Jewish dish made from apples, nuts and raisins flavored with cinnamon and bound with red wine; part of the Passover seder.

charred A food prepared on a hot grill or cooking surface; the food's surface is usually well cooked, with a roasted, caramelized flavor, while the interior is rare.

charring 1. The process of searing the outside of a food, usually on a hot grill or cooking surface. 2. The process of burning the inside of a barrel that will be used for wine, whiskey, brandy, or other distilled spirits; this helps color, mellow and age the barrel's contents.

charro beans Pinto beans that are cooked with pork shank or bacon, garlic, green chiles, tomatoes and cilantro.

chasoba (CHA-so-bah) Japanese soba noodles made with green tea.

chasseur (shah-SUR) French for hunter and used to describe a dish of sautéed chicken, veal, beef or game served with a brown sauce flavored with shallots and white wine and garnished with mushrooms.

chat (chaat) 1. An Indian dish made with vegetables, fruits and spices, eaten cold as a snack or appetizer. 2. General term for India's many and varied snack foods.

châteaubriand (sha-toh-bree-AHN) 1. A fabricated cut of the tenderloin muscle from the beef short loin and sirloin primals; it is cut from the thick end of the muscle generally found in the sirloin primal and is very tender and flavorful. 2. A thick slice of filet of beef tenderloin grilled and traditionally served with château potatoes or soufflé potatoes and béarnaise sauce.

châteaubriand, sauce A French sauce traditionally used for a grilled châteaubriand aux pommes (now sauce béarnaise is more frequently used); a compound sauce made from a demi-glaze flavored with white wine, shallots and tarragon and finished with cayenne and lemon juice.

château potatoes *See* pommes château.

cha thai A Thai iced tea made of ground tea leaves, vanilla, roasted corn and orange food coloring; it is brewed several times and then mixed with sugar and milk.

Chatham oyster An Atlantic oyster found off Chatham, Cape Cod; it has a fat body and bland flavor.

chat masala (chaat ma-sa-la) A masala consisting of ground asafetida, mint, ginger, ajowan, cayenne, black salt, mango powder, cumin and dried pomegranate seeds and used to season Indian vegetable salads.

chaud-froid (shoh-FRWAH) French for a dish prepared hot and served cold; usually refers to meat, poultry or game covered with a brown or white sauce, glazed with aspic, and garnished with cut vegetables set in the aspic.

chaudin A Cajun dish of ground pork combined with vegetables and seasoned rice and packed into a pig's stomach and baked or steamed; it is sliced and eaten warm or cold.

chaurice (shoh-reeze) A Cajun and Creole pork sausage containing fresh vegetables and seasoned with powdered chiles.

chayote (chy-OH-tay) A squashlike, pear-shaped fruit (*Sechium edule*) native to Central America; used like a vegetable, it has a pale green furrowed or slightly lumpy skin, a white-green flesh, a single seed, and a bland, somewhat starchy, cucumber-like flavor; also known as mirliton (especially in Louisiana) and vegetable pear.

Cheddar, American A firm cheese made from whole cow's milk (generally pasteurized) produced principally in Wisconsin, New York and Vermont; its color ranges from white to orange and its flavor from mild to very sharp.

Cheddar, English A firm cheese made from whole cow's milk (raw or pasteurized) and named for the village of Cheddar in Somersetshire, England; its color ranges from nearly white to yellow or orange and its flavor from mild to sharp.

Cheddar, Vermont A Cheddar cheese made in Vermont; it has a light yellow to yellow-orange color and a rich, sharp, assertive flavor.

cheddaring process An alternative to the milling step in cheese making; the dense curds are stacked on top of each other to squeeze out the whey and force the fine filaments of milk protein closer together, giving the final cheese (usually called Cheddar) a more solid texture. *See* cheese-making process.

cheeks The tender fleshy muscles located beneath the eyes and between the ears and nose (or snout) of a mammal; veal and hog cheeks are often consumed; also known as jowls.

cheese Dairy products made from milk curds separated from the whey; numerous varieties are found worldwide.

cheese balls Mashed cheese mixed with herbs and/or other flavorings and reshaped into balls; the balls are then sometimes coated in herbs, nuts or other garnishes; usually served as an hors d'oeuvre.

cheesecake A rich, smooth dessert made by blending cream cheese, cottage cheese or ricotta with sugar, eggs and other flavorings, then baking; usually prepared in a springform pan dusted with cookie crumbs or ground nuts; the baked dessert is often topped with sour cream or fruit.

cheesecloth A loosely woven cotton gauze used for straining stocks and sauces and wrapping poultry and fish for poaching.

cheese grater A grater with a slightly convex, relatively fine grating surface attached to a handle; used for grating hard cheeses such as Parmesan directly over food.

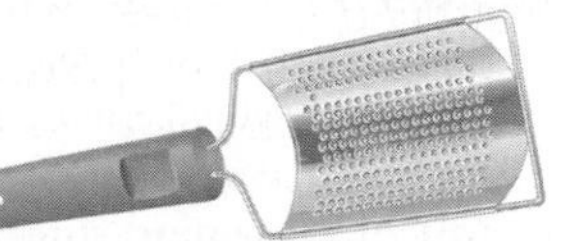
cheese grater

cheese knife *See* Gorgonzola knife, hard cheese knife, Parmesan knife *and* tomato knife.

cheese-making process The process by which cheese is made; typically (1) milk is warmed and a lactic starter bacteria added to alter the milk's acidity; (2) rennet is added to coagulate the milk into curds and whey; (3) the whey is drained away and the curds are cut and cooked, resulting in dense curds; (4) the dense curds are milled into curd granules; (5) the curds are salted and pressed to remove any additional whey, the resulting product being called green cheese; (6) mold or bacteria is added and the cheese is allowed to ripen and age. *See* cheddaring process *and* ripening.

cheese plane A spade-shaped utensil with a single slot; the cutting edge, on the front side of the slot, is parallel to and just below the flat blade and tilts upward at a 25-degree angle; cheese is sliced by pulling the plane across it; the edge cuts the cheese, and the slice is lifted through the slot to rest on the plane's top.

cheese plane

chef 1. French for chief. 2. Short for chef de cuisine. 3. A title of respect given to a person skilled in food preparation and usually in charge of a professional kitchen; he or she is generally responsible for planning menus, ordering foodstuffs, training and supervising cooks and other personnel, and preparing food.

chef du cuisine At a food services operation, the person responsible for all kitchen operations, developing menu items, and setting the kitchen's tone and tempo. *See* chef *and* executive chef.

chef's knife An all-purpose knife used for slicing, chopping and mincing; its rigid 8- to 14-in.-long blade is wide at the heel, tapering to a point; also known as a French knife.

chef's knife

chef's salad A salad of tossed greens topped with julienne of cold meat (usually ham, chicken and/or turkey) and cheese and sliced vegetables and hard-boiled eggs; it is topped with a dressing; often served as an entrée.

Chelsea buns Square, spicy yeast rolls filled with fruit and coated with sugar; created at the Chelsea Bun House and popular in London during the late 17th and early 18th centuries.

chemical leavening agents Chemicals added to batters and doughs to assist leavening through the production of carbon dioxide released as the result of chemical reactions between acids and bases. *See* baking powder *and* baking soda.

Chenin Blanc (sheh-nan blahn) 1. A white wine grape grown predominantly in California, France's Loire Valley and South Africa; also known as Steen (in South Africa). 2. A white wine made from this grape; it can range from clean, crisp and fruity to rich, sweet and honeyed.

cherbourg (shehr-borg) A French beef consommé flavored with Madeira wine and garnished with julienne of mushrooms and truffles, poached egg and ham quenelles.

cherbourg, sauce (shehr-borg) A French compound sauce made from a béchamel finished with crayfish butter and garnished with crayfish tails.

cherimoya (chair-uh-MOY-ah) The egg-shaped fruit of a small tropical tree (*Annona cherimola*); it has a rough green skin that turns blackish-brown when the fruit is ripe, a yellowish-white segmented flesh, a custardlike though somewhat granular texture, and a flavor reminiscent of pineapple, mango and strawberry; also imprecisely known as a custard apple or sweetsop.

cherries jubilee A dessert made by topping vanilla ice cream with dark, pitted cherries that were sautéed with sugar and Kirsch or brandy; the cherry mixture is often flamed table side.

cherry 1. A small stone fruit from a tree (genus *Prunus*) grown in temperate climates worldwide; there are two principal types: sour and sweet; both types are generally available fresh, dried, canned and frozen. 2. The ripe red berry of the coffee plant; a coffee bean is the seed within the cherry.

cherry, sour Any of a variety of cherries (*Prunus cerasus*) with a skin and flesh color varying from light to dark red and an acidic, tart flavor; they are usually cooked with sugar and used as a pie or pastry filling; also known as a tart cherry.

cherry, sweet Any of a variety of cherries (*Prunus avium*) that are spherical to heart shaped, with a skin and flesh color varying from pale yellow to dark red, a juicy flesh and a sweet flavor; they are eaten fresh, candied or in baked goods.

cherrystone clam; cherrystone quahog An Atlantic hard-shell clam that is under 3 in. (7.6 cm) across the shell; the shells are tannish gray, and the chewy meat has a mild flavor.

cherry tomato 1. A small spherical tomato with a bright red or yellow skin; the yellow-skinned variety has a less acidic and blander flavor than the red-skinned variety. 2. An imprecisely used term for any of several varieties of small, spherical tomatoes.

chervil (cher-vil) An herb and member of the parsley family (*Anthriscus cerefolium*) native to Russia; it has dark green, curly leaves that have a parsleylike flavor with overtones of anise and are generally used fresh.

chess pie A dessert from the American South consisting of a flaky pie shell filled with a sweet custard made from sugar, eggs, butter and small amounts of vinegar and cornmeal or flour; when baked, the filling becomes dense and translucent, with a thin, crisp, crusty top.

chestnut The nut of the sweet chestnut tree (*Castanea sativa*); edible when cooked, it has a dark brown outer shell, a bitter inner skin, and a high starch content; it is used in savory and sweet dishes.

chestnut pan A shallow frying pan with a perforated bottom used to roast chestnuts; designed to permit some contact between the food and the heat source (usually a flame).

chestnut pan

chestnut pumpkin A variety of medium-sized spherical squash with a bumpy, yellow-orange skin, a slightly flattened appearance, and a flavor reminiscent of chestnuts.

chèvre (SHEHV-ruh) 1. French for goat. 2. Any French goat's milk cheese; usually pure white with a tart flavor, their textures can range from soft, moist and creamy to dry, firm and crumbly and their shapes from small to medium-sized cones, cylinders, disks or pyramids left ungarnished or covered with black ash, leaves, herbs or pepper.

chevrotin (sheh-vroh-teen) A category of cheeses made in France's Alpine region from goat's milk; the cheeses are generally dried and firm with a smooth surface and a tangy flavor.

chewing gum A flavored, rubbery substance often made from chicle; it is chewed and should not be swallowed.

chewy 1. A food that is difficult to chew completely because it is tough, sticky or gummy. 2. A wine-tasting term for a rich, full-bodied, slightly alcoholic, and very strongly flavored wine.

Chianti (k'yahn-tee) A red wine made in Tuscany, Italy, principally from Sangiovese grapes mixed with small amounts of Canaiolo grapes and the white Malvasia grapes; the young wines are refreshing and tart, and the older wines aged in wooden casks are richer and more complex.

Chiboust cream (she-boo) A vanilla pastry cream lightened with Italian meringue; gelatin is sometimes added to the cream for stability; used in French pastries as a filling (e.g., gâteau St. Honoré).

chicken One of the principal kinds of poultry recognized by the USDA includes any of several varieties of common domestic fowl used for food as well as egg production; it has both light and dark meat and relatively little fat.

chicken, broiler-fryer A chicken slaughtered when 13 weeks old; it has a soft, smooth-textured skin, a relatively lean flesh, a flexible breastbone, and an average market weight of 3.5 lb. (1.5 kg).

chicken, free-range A chicken allowed greater access to the area outside the coop and usually raised on a special diet made without additives; it is generally slaughtered when 9–10 weeks old and marketed with head and feet attached; the average market weight is 4.5–5 lb. (2–2.3 kg).

chicken, roaster A chicken slaughtered when 3–5 months old; it has a smooth-textured skin, tender flesh, a less flexible breastbone than that of a broiler, and an average market weight of 3.5–5 lb. (1.5–2 kg).

chicken, stewing A chicken slaughtered when 10–18 months old; a mature bird, it has a nonflexible breastbone, a flavorful but less tender flesh, and an average market weight of 2.5–8 lb. (1.1–3.6 kg); also known as a stewing hen and boiling fowl.

chicken à la king An American dish of diced chicken (or turkey) in a cream sauce with pimientos, mushrooms, green peppers and sometimes sherry.

chicken cacciatore *See* cacciatore, à la.

chicken classes Significant chicken classes are the game hen, broiler-fryer chicken, roaster chicken, capon and stewing chicken.

chicken-fried steak A dish from the American South and Midwest; it consists of a thin, tenderized steak dipped into a milk–egg mixture and seasoned flour, then pan-fried; it is usually served with country gravy.

chicken fry steak A fabricated cut of the beef primal round; it is cut from the top round and somewhat tough.

chicken Kiev (kee-EHV) A dish consisting of a boned chicken breast wrapped around a piece of herbed butter, breaded, and deep-fried.

chicken liver The small twin-lobed liver of a chicken; it has a reddish-brown color, a soft, crumbly texture and a delicate flavor.

chicken lobster A marketing term for a 1-lb. (455-g) lobster.

chicken long rice A Hawaiian souplike preparation consisting of mung bean threads and chicken flavored with ginger and green onions; it is often served at a luau.

chicken of the wood mushroom A wild mushroom (*Laetiporus sulphureus*) with a red-orange cap that is bright yellow underneath; it has a somewhat stringy, chewy texture and a mild flavor.

chicken Tetrazzini (teh-trah-ZEE-nee) An Italian dish consisting of spaghetti and julienne of chicken bound with a sherry and Parmesan sauce, topped with bread crumbs and/or Parmesan and baked; originally made with swan; turkey can be substituted for the chicken.

chickpea; chick-pea A somewhat spherical, irregular-shaped, pealike seed of a plant (*Licer arieinum*) native to the Mediterranean region; it has a buff color, a firm texture, and a nutty flavor; used in Mediterranean and Middle Eastern cuisines in soups, stews and salads, it is also roasted and eaten as a snack; also known as ceci and garbanzo bean.

chickweed A wild green that grows in temperate climates worldwide; it is a tender vegetable that goes well with rich meats.

chicory A plant (*Cichorium intybus*) with long silvery white, tightly folded leaves and a slightly bitter flavor; also imprecisely known as endive (especially in France and the United States). *See* Belgian endive, endive, radicchio *and* succory.

chicos Dried kernels of corn used in Native American and Southwestern stews; also known as parched corn.

chiffon A sweet cream or custard thickened with gelatin and lightened with stiffly whipped egg whites.

chiffonade (chef-foh-nahd) *v.* To finely slice or shred leafy vegetables or herbs. *n.* Finely cut leafy vegetables or herbs often used as a garnish or bedding.

chiffon cake A light, moist, airy cake made with oil, usually flavored with lemon or orange, and baked in a large tube pan.

chiffon pie A dessert traditionally made with a crumb crust and filled with a fluffy, delicately flavored filling made by adding flavorings and whipped egg whites to an egg yolk base (sometimes gelatin is added as a stabilizer).

chilaca (chee-LAH-kah) A thin, long, curved fresh chile with a dark brown color and and medium hot flavor; usually available dried and called pasilla or negro.

chilaquiles (chee-lah-KEE-lehs) A Mexican dish consisting of tortilla strips sautéed with foods such as chiles, chorizo, beef or chicken and cheese; sometimes layered like lasagna and baked.

chilcostle A thin, elongated, tapering dried chile with a splotchy red-orange skin, a thin flesh, and a dry, citrusy, medium hot flavor.

Child, Julia (Am., 1912–2004) An American trained in French cooking; she is best known for teaching Americans about French cuisine through her public television show, *The French Chef,* begun in 1963, and her many books, including *Mastering the Art of French Cooking, Volumes I and II* (1961, 1970), *From Julia Child's Kitchen* (1975), and *The Way to Cook* (1989).

chile; chile pepper; hot pepper The fruit of various plants of the Capsicum family; a chile can have a mild to fiery hot flavor (caused by the capsaicin in the pepper's placental ribs) with undertones of various fruits or spices; a fresh chile is usually yellow, orange, green or red, and its shape can range from thin, elongated and tapering to conical to nearly spherical; a dried chile, which is sometimes referred to by a different name than its fresh version, is usually more strongly flavored and darker colored. *See* pepper *and* sweet pepper.

chile Colorado *See* New Mexico red chile, dried.

chile con queso (CHIH-lee kon KAY-soh) A Mexican dip of melted cheese flavored with green chiles and served with tortilla chips or raw vegetables.

chile flakes Coarsely crushed dried chiles whose flavor and color depend on the chiles used; also known as crushed chiles.

chile oil A vegetable oil in which hot red chiles have been steeped to impart flavor and color; used as a cooking medium and flavoring in Asian cuisines.

chile paste; chile paste with garlic A paste made from fermented fava beans, flour, red chiles and sometimes garlic; used as a flavoring in Chinese cuisines.

chile powder Pure ground dried chiles; depending on the variety used, its flavor can range from sweet and mild to pungent and extremely hot and its color from yellow-orange to red to dark brown; used as a flavoring. *See* chilli.

chile rellenos (CHEE-leh rreh-YEH-nohs) A Mexican dish of mild roasted chiles stuffed with cheese, dipped in an egg batter and fried.

chili A stewlike dish flavored with chiles. *See* chile *and* chilli.

chili con carne (CHIL-ee kohn KAHR-nay) A Mexican stewlike dish of ground or diced meat, usually beef, flavored with onions, tomatoes, chiles and chilli powder; if beans are added, it is known as chili con carne with beans; also known as chili or a bowl of red.

chilli; chilli powder A commercial blend of herbs and spices such as oregano, cumin, garlic, dried chiles and other ingredients; its flavor and color vary depending on the manufacturer; it is used in American southwestern and Mexican cuisines.

chilli sauce; chili sauce A spicy, ketchuplike sauce made from tomatoes, chiles or chile powder, onions, green peppers, vinegar, sugar and spices.

chiltepe A short, curved, tapering dried chile with a thin flesh, a bright orange-red color, and a searingly hot flavor.

chimichanga (chee-mee-CHAN-gah) A dish from the American Southwest consisting of a deep-fried burrito, which can be filled with a sweet or savory mixture such as apples or shredded pork; depending on the filling, it can be garnished with confectioners' sugar or sour cream, salsa, pico de gallo, guacamole and shredded cheese.

chimichurri (chee-mee-choo-rree) A thick Argentinean herb sauce made with olive oil, vinegar and finely chopped parsley, oregano, onion and garlic, it is usually served with grilled meats.

china 1. Plates, bowls and cups made of porcelain. 2. An imprecisely used term to describe plates, bowls and cups made from materials other than porcelain, such as plastic, earthenware, metal and the like.

china cap A conical metal strainer with a perforated metal body; used for straining stocks and sauces and, with a pestle, to purée soft foods. *See* chinois.

chine (chyn) *v.* To sever the backbone during butchering. *n.* 1. The backbone or spine of an animal. 2. A subprimal cut of a beef, veal, lamb, pork or game carcass containing a portion of the backbone with some adjoining flesh.

Chinese cleaver A smaller, medium-weight cleaver used to chop and trim foods; also known as a kitchen cleaver. *See* cleaver.

Chinese cleaver

Chinese cucumber *See* tea melon.

Chinese date An olive-sized fruit (*Zizyphus jujuba*) with a leathery red, off-white or black skin, a yellow flesh and a prunelike flavor; it is usually stewed with a sweetener and used in sweet and savory dishes or eaten as a snack; also known as Chinese jujube, jujube and red date.

Chinese dumplings *See* pot stickers.

Chinese five-spice powder A spice blend generally consisting of ground cloves, fennel seeds, star anise, cinnamon and Szechwan pepper; used in Chinese and Vietnamese cuisines.

Chinese ladle A ladle with a broad, shallow, 4-oz. bowl and a long handle; the disklike face of the bowl is used for turning or transferring food in and from a wok.

Chinese mixed pickle Vegetables such as carrots, green peppers and cucumbers flavored with ginger, mustards and chiles and pickled in vinegar, sugar and salt; used as a condiment in Chinese cuisines for cold meats, fried foods and fermented eggs and as an ingredient in sweet-and-sour dishes.

Chinese pear *See* Asian pear.

Chinese pepper *See* Szechwan pepper.

Chinese plum A fruit (*Prunus armeniaca, P. mume*) native to China; it is similar to an apricot, with a reddish-gold skin and a sweet flavor.

Chinese restaurant syndrome A medical condition characterized by headaches, neck or chest pains, hot flashes and/or heart palpitations; thought by victims to be caused by consuming foods containing the flavor enhancer monosodium glutamate (MSG).

chinois (sheen-WAH) A conical metal strainer with a very fine mesh; it is used for straining stocks and sauces. *See* china cap.

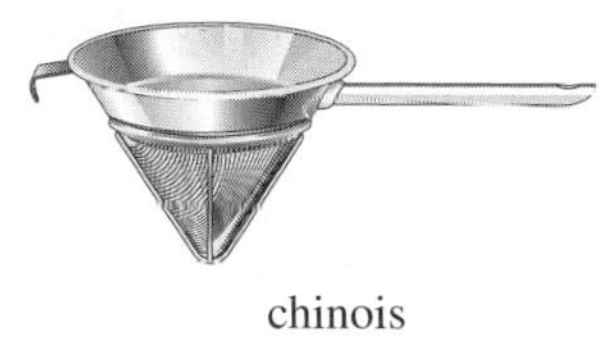
chinois

chinook salmon Salmon found in the Pacific Ocean from northern California to Alaska; it has a greenish skin that becomes silvery on the sides and belly, a mouth with a black interior, a high fat content, a red-orange to pale pink, large-flaked flesh, a rich flavor and an average weight of 5–30 lb. (2.3–13.6 kg); it is often marketed with the fish's spawning river added to the name (e.g., Columbia chinook salmon, Yukon chinook salmon); also known as blackmouth salmon and king salmon.

chiogga A beet with concentric red and white rings; also known as a candy cane beet.

chipolata (shee-po-LAH-tah) A small Italian sausage made from pork flavored with thyme, chives, coriander, cloves and sometimes red pepper.

chipolatas, à la (shee-po-lah-tahs, ah-lah) A French method of garnishing foods with small pork sausages.

chipotle (chih-POHT-lay) A dried, smoked jalapeño; this medium-sized chile has a dull tan to dark brown color with a wrinkled skin and a smoky, slightly sweet, relatively mild flavor with undertones of tobacco and chocolate.

chipped beef Wafer-thin slices of beef that is smoked, salted and dried; also known as dried beef.

chipped beef on toast Chipped beef served in a white sauce over toast.

chips 1. Any of a variety of small, thinly sliced deep-fried foods such as potatoes or tortillas; usually eaten as snacks, often with a dip. 2. British for French fries.

chirashi-zushi (chee-RAH-shee ZOO-shee) Japanese for scattered sushi and used to describe a type of sushi made by arranging cooked or raw fish, shellfish and sometimes vegetables on loosely packed zushi; it is often served in a bowl.

chirinabe (chree-ree-NAH-beh) A Japanese dish consisting of pieces of fish (cod or sea bass), tofu and vegetables that are cooked in a simmering broth by an individual diner at the table.

chirorija An orange and pomelo citrus hybrid.

chitarra (key-tah-rah) A guitarlike Italian tool used to cut pasta by rolling the dough against (or over) the tool's steel wires.

chitterlings; chitlins; chitlings The small intestines of freshly slaughtered hogs; cleaned and simmered for soups, battered and fried, or used as sausage casings.

chives An herb and member of the onion family (*Allium schoenprasum*), with long, slender, hollow, green stems and purple flowers; the stems have a mild, onionlike flavor and are generally used fresh, although dried, chopped chives are available.

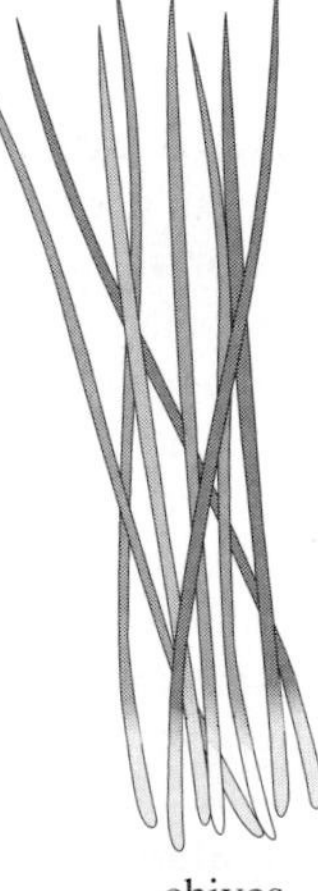
chives

chives, garlic An herb and member of the onion family (*Allium tuberosum*), with solid stems that have a garliclike flavor and are broader, coarser and flatter than regular chives; generally used fresh, although dried garlic chives are available; also known as Chinese chives, flowering chives, kuchai and oriental garlic.

Chivry, sauce (she-VREE) A French compound sauce made from a chicken velouté flavored with white wine, shallots, tarragon and chervil and finished with Chivry butter; usually served with eggs and poached or sautéed poultry. *See* beurre Chivry.

chix A lobster (usually a Maine lobster) weighing less than 1 lb. (450 g).

chocolate Roasted, ground, refined cacao beans used as a flavoring, confection or beverage. *See* chocolate-making process.

chocolate, white A confection made of cocoa butter, sugar and flavorings; it does not contain cocoa solids.

chocolate bloom *See* bloom.

chocolate dipping fork A wooden-handled utensil with a stainless steel oval or round bowl, a wire spiral or grid, or long tines; each shape is used for dipping a particular shape or type of candy into melted chocolate; also known as a candy dipper or truffle dipper.

chocolate liquor; chocolate mass The product formed during the first stage of the chocolate-making process; it results from crushing or grinding cocoa nibs before the sugar or flavorings are added; also known as cocoa liquor. *See* chocolate-making process.

chocolate-making process The process by which chocolate is made; typically (1) large pods containing cocoa beans are harvested from the tropical cacao tree; (2) the beans are scraped out of the pods and allowed to ferment; (3) the fermented beans are dried in the sun and then packed and shipped to manufacturers; (4) at the factory, the beans are blended and roasted to create the desired flavors and aromas; (5) they are crushed and the shells (husks) are removed; (6) the cleaned cocoa kernels, known as nibs, are milled into a thick paste, known as chocolate liquor or mass, which is distributed as unsweetened chocolate; (7) the chocolate mass may be refined further by pressing it to remove the cocoa butter, leaving dry cocoa powder; (8) cocoa butter, sugar, milk solids, vanilla and other flavorings can be added to the chocolate mass to produce various types of chocolate: bittersweet, semisweet or milk (white chocolate is produced from cocoa butter, sugar and flavorings, without cocoa solids); (9) after the flavorings are added, the mixture is blended and milled until smooth; (10) some manufacturers refine the blended chocolate further through conching, which results in a velvetlike texture and added stability; (11) the finished chocolate is poured into molds to harden, then wrapped and shipped to purchasers.

chocolate milk A beverage generally made of whole, pasteurized, homogenized milk with 1.5–2% liquid chocolate and sometimes a sweetener.

chocolate mill A wooden stick with an enlarged end used to whip or beat chocolate to a froth.

chocolate mold A plastic or metal mold, available in a variety of shapes and sizes, used for molding chocolate candies; a shallow mold is used for solid molding and a two-part mold is used for hollow molding and filled chocolates.

chocolate plastic; chocolate modeling paste A pliable decorating paste with the texture of marzipan; made from a mixture of chocolate and corn syrup.

chocolate ruler; chocolate bar *See* caramel ruler.

chocolate syrup A pourable mixture of chocolate and cream or butter; it is often sweetened and flavored with an extract or liqueur and used to garnish pastries and desserts.

chocolate truffle A rich, creamy candy made by coating a ball of chocolate ganache with tempered chocolate, cocoa powder, confectioners' sugar, chopped nuts or the like.

chocolate velvet cake A very rich, dense, fudgelike chocolate cake created by pastry chef Albert Kumin at the Four Seasons restaurant in 1959.

choice The second-highest (USDA) quality grade designation for beef, veal and lamb; the most commonly used grade; it is well marbled (but less so than prime) and will produce a tender and juicy product.

chokeberry The fruit of an ornamental shrub (genus *Aronia*); inedible raw, it can be cooked with sugar for preserves.

chokecherry Any of several varieties of wild sour cherries (*Prunus virginiana*) native to North America; the skin, which is red when immature, blackens as it ripens, and the dark red flesh has an astringent flavor; used for making preserves.

cholent; cholend (chkoll-ent) A Jewish one-dish braised meal consisting of meat (usually beef or tongue), a grain (typically pearl barley) and vegetables (carrots, onions, potatoes and the like) flavored with schmaltz, garlic, thyme and paprika.

cholesterol (koh-LESS-ter-all) A sterol found in animal foods and manufactured by the body to assist in the formation of certain hormones, vitamin D and cell membranes; excess cholesterol in the blood has been linked to cardiovascular disease.

chop *v.* To cut food into small pieces; uniformity of size and shape is neither necessary nor feasible. *n.* A fabricated cut of meat including part of the rib.

chop che (jop chee) A Korean stir-fry of clear noodles, beef and assorted vegetables; the Korean version of chow mein.

chopsticks A pair of slender sticks, usually cylindrical and sometimes slightly pointed, made of metal, ivory, plastic, wood or other materials that are held between the thumb and fingers of one hand and used to move food during cooking or from a service item to the mouth; used principally in Asian countries such as China, Japan and Korea.

chop suey (chop soo-ee) A Chinese–American dish of stir-fried beef, pork, chicken and/or shrimp and vegetables such as bean sprouts, mushrooms, water chestnuts, bamboo shoots and onions in a starchy sauce served over rice.

chorizo (chor-EE-zoh; chor-EE-soh) 1. A Mexican sausage made from fresh pork, seasoned with garlic and powdered chiles; usually cooked without the casing. 2. A Spanish sausage made from smoked pork, seasoned with garlic and powdered chiles; it is usually cooked without the casing.

Choron, sauce (show-RAWHN) A French compound sauce made from a béarnaise tinted red with tomato purée.

choucroute (shoo-CROOT) A dish made in France's Alsace region from cabbage cooked with goose fat, onions, juniper berries and white wine.

choucroute à l'ancienne (shoo-CROOT ah lan-see-ahn) A French dish consisting of sauerkraut prepared in the traditional way with carrots and onions; it is flavored with peppercorns, caraway seeds, garlic, cloves, juniper berries, bay leaves and thyme and served with sausages and smoked loin of pork; a specialty of Alsace.

choucroute fork A 2.5-in.-wide fork with four sharp tines and a slight dip at the prong–handle juncture to prevent juices from being transferred from the pot to the platter; the tines are used to separate strands from their mass.

choucroute garni Choucroute garnished with potatoes and smoked pork, pork sausages, ham or goose.

choux pastry (shoo paste-re) A classic French pastry dough used for making éclairs, cream puffs and the like; this sticky, pastelike dough is made with boiling water and/or milk, butter, flour and eggs, first cooked on the stove top, then baked in an oven; the resulting products have a hard, crisp exterior and a nearly hollow interior; also known as pâte à choux.

chow-chow; chowchow 1. A mixed vegetable and pickle relish flavored with mustard. 2. Originally, orange peel and ginger in a heavy syrup; used as a condiment in Chinese cuisines.

chowder A hearty soup made from fish, shellfish and/or vegetables, usually containing milk and potatoes and often thickened with roux.

chowder clam; chowder quahog An Atlantic hard-shell clam; it usually measures more than 4 in. (7.6 cm) across the tannish-gray shell and has a very chewy and tough, pinkish-tan meat; usually minced for chowders and soups.

chow mein; chao mein 1. Chinese for fried noodles. 2. A Chinese–American stir-fry dish of poultry, shrimp and/or meat with vegetables such as bean sprouts, mushrooms, water chestnuts, bamboo shoots and green onions served over fried noodles.

choy sum; choysum A member of the cabbage family; it has yellow flowers and dark green leaves; when steamed it is crisp and tender with a delicate flavor; also known as Chinese flowering cabbage.

chrane (kra-nay) A Jewish preserve made from cooked beets flavored with horseradish, malt vinegar and sugar.

Christmas pudding An English steamed pudding made of suet, dried fruits and spices, usually flamed with brandy and decorated with holly.

chrysanthemum greens The green leafy portions of a chrysanthemum variety; they are generally picked before the plant blooms and have a slightly bitter flavor.

chub A member of the whitefish family found in American midwestern lakes; it has a very soft flesh and an average market weight of 0.6–2.5 lb. (0.15–1.1 kg); often smoked.

chuck A primal section of the beef carcass; it is the shoulder and contains some of the backbone, five rib bones, bladebone, arm bone and much connective tissue; it includes such flavorful but often tough subprimal or fabricated cuts as the clod, cross-rib pot roast and chuck short ribs and is used for cubed steaks and ground beef; also known as the bladebone (especially in Great Britain) and shoulder.

chuck, ground Beef ground from the various small muscles found in the primal chuck.

chuck filet A subprimal cut of the beef primal chuck; cut from the center, it is somewhat tough.

chuck roast A fabricated cut of the beef primal chuck; it is a somewhat tough but flavorful roast cut from the shoulder.

chuck short ribs A fabricated cut of the beef primal chuck; they are the tips of the first five ribs.

chuck tender A subprimal cut of the beef primal chuck; somewhat tough and lean with a streak of gristle in its center; it is fabricated into small steaks (with the gristle left in) or the gristle is removed for a tied roast; also known as chicken steak, Jewish tender, mock tender and Scotch tender.

chuck wagon steak A fabricated cut of the beef primal chuck; it is somewhat tough, flavorful, boneless and round.

chuka soba (CHOO-koo soh-bah) Thin yellow Japanese soba noodles; generally used for soups and salads.

chump A British cut of the lamb, pork and veal carcass; it is the hind end of the loin before it becomes the top of the leg.

chum salmon A variety of salmon found in Washington's Puget Sound and off the west coasts of Canada and southern Alaska; it has a metallic blue skin with a slight purplish sheen that becomes silvery on the sides and belly, a lean, yellow to white flesh, a poor flavor, and an average market weight of 5–10 lb. (2.3–4.5 kg); also known as dog salmon and keta salmon.

chunked and formed A meat product consisting of chunks of beef, veal, lamb or pork that have been massaged, ground or diced and then formed into the desired shape.

chunk-style honey Honey with pieces of the honeycomb included; also known as comb honey.

chupe (choo-pay) A South American term for a thick, savory stew made with ingredients such as potatoes, tomatoes, corn, milk or a soft cheese, eggs and other ingredients.

churn *v.* To agitate cream or milk so that the fat separates from the liquid, forming a solid (butter). *n.* The vessel in which milk or cream is agitated to make butter or ice cream.

churn beater A tool with a spring tightly coiled into a conical shape; it is used to agitate thin batters in a small container.

churn beater

churro (choo-roa) A deep-fried Mexican pastry similar to a doughnut; it is flavored with cinnamon and rolled in a cinnamon–sugar mixture while hot.

chutney From the Hindi chatni, it is a condiment made from fruit, vinegar, sugar and spices; its texture can range from smooth to chunky and its flavor from mild to hot.

chutoro (choo-toh-roh) Japanese for the somewhat fatty flesh found at the belly near the tail and back of a tuna (maguro); it is used for sushi and sashimi.

ciabatta (ch'yah-BAH-tah) Italian for slipper and used to describe a slipper-shaped loaf of bread.

cicely, sweet cicely A fragrant herb of the parsley family; it has anise-flavored leaves and seeds.

cider Pressed apple juice; it is used to make sweet cider, hard cider, vinegar and applejack.

cider apple Any of a variety of apples whose fruit have a somewhat bitter, astringent flavor; generally used to make cider.

cider mill 1. A machine that releases the juice from an apple by applying pressure. 2. The building where cider is made.

cider vinegar A vinegar made by fermenting pure apple juice into hard cider and then exposing it to the air; clear, it has a pale brown color and a strong, somewhat harsh flavor.

cilantro (si-LAHN-troh) The dark green, lacy leaves of the cilantro plant (*Coriandrum sativum*); used as an herb, they have a sharp, tangy, fresh flavor and aroma and are used fresh in Mexican, South American and Asian cuisines; also known as Chinese parsley. *See* coriander.

cilindrati (chee-leen-drah-tee) Italian croissants made from a very thin bread dough that has been rolled out repeatedly before being formed into rolls.

cinnamon A spice that is the inner bark of the branches of a small evergreen tree (*Cinnamomum zeylanicum*) native to Sri Lanka and India; it has an orange-brown color and a sweet, distinctive flavor and aroma; usually sold in rolled-up sticks (quills) or ground, it is used for sweet and savory dishes and as a garnish; also known as Ceylon cinnamon. *See* cassia.

cioppino (chuh-PEE-noh) An Italian or Italian–American stew made with tomatoes and a variety of fish and shellfish.

cipollini (chee-poh-LEE-nee) The bulbs of the grape hyacinth (genus *Muscari*); they resemble small onions and have a mild, onionlike flavor; cooked like a vegetable in Italian cuisine.

ciseler (see-sah-lay) 1. French for to cut, specifically to cut foods into julienne. 2. French for to score, as in slashing a whole fish to speed cooking.

citron (SIHT-ron) A citrus fruit (*Citrus medica*) native to China; approximately the size of a lemon, it has a dry pulp and a thick, lumpy, yellow-green skin that is candied and used in baking.

citronella A tropical perennial grass (*Cymbopogon nardus*); it has a strong, lemony aroma and is used as a flavoring and in salads; the oil is used as an insect repellent.

citrus; citrus fruits Members of the genus *Citrus;* grown on trees and shrubs in tropical and temperate climates worldwide, these fruits generally have a thick rind, most of which is a fluffy, bitter white layer (albedo) with a thin exterior layer of skin (zest) that can be green, yellow, orange or pinkish; the flesh is segmented and has an acidic flavor ranging from sweet to very tart.

citrus zester *See* zester.

city chicken Veal cubes served on kabobs.

civet (SIHV-iht) 1. A French stew of any furred animal, especially rabbit, squirrel or hare, with onions and larding bacon, cooked with red wine and thickened with the animal's blood. 2. A fixative derived from glandular secretions of the African civet cat.

clabber Naturally soured and curdled unpasteurized whole milk that is thin enough to drink; it can separate into a very white semifirm liquid on the bottom and a layer of yellow cream on top; very sour, it is often eaten in the American South with sugar or black pepper and cream.

clafouti (kla-foo-tee) A rustic French dessert tart made with fruit, usually dark sweet cherries, baked in an egg custard.

Claiborne, Craig (Am., 1920–2000) Food writer and restaurant reviewer for the *New York Times* and author of *The New York Times Cookbook;* his recipes introduced international fare to novice cooks, and his reviews taught readers how to respect and critique every kind of dining establishment.

clairet (cleh ray) 1. An old French term for a rather light red wine of Bordeaux. 2. A light red wine made in France's Bordeaux region; the wine, which has little tannin and a deep rose color, resembles a full-bodied rosé and is usually served chilled.

Clamart, à la (clah-mahr, ah lah) A French garnish consisting of whole or puréed green peas.

clambake A social gatheing where the food, usually clams, lobsters, crabs, chicken, corn, potatoes and sweet potatoes, is cooked in a pit lined wth heated rocks and covered with seaweed.

clam chowder, Manhattan A clam chowder made with tomatoes.

clam chowder, New England A clam chowder made with cream or milk; also known as Boston clam chowder.

clam knife A small knife used to open clams; it has a rigid blade and a round tip.

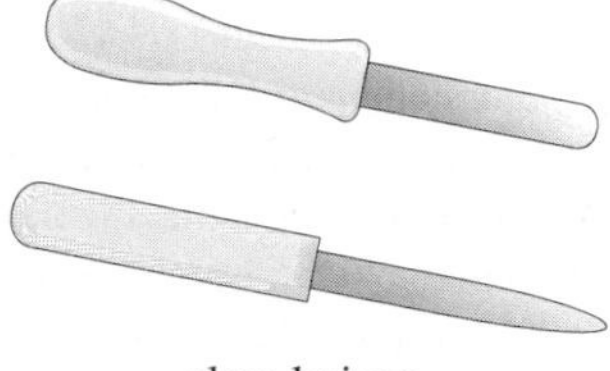

clam knives

clams A large group of bivalve mollusks found in coastal saltwaters worldwide; they have hard or soft, beige, gray, blue or brown shells and juicy, often chewy, pinkish-tan to gray meat with a mild to sweet flavor. *See* Atlantic clams *and* Pacific clams.

clams casino An American dish of clams served hot on the half shell with a topping of seasoned butter and crisp bacon.

claret (KLAR-eht) 1. In the United States and continental Europe, a light, red table wine made from any red wine grapes grown anywhere. 2. In England, a red wine from France's Bordeaux region.

clarification The process of transforming a broth into a clear consommé by trapping impurities with a clearmeat.

clarified butter *See* butter, clarified.

clarify To clear a cloudy liquid by removing the suspended particles and sediment.

clary sage The essential oil of clary; it is used to flavor vermouth and liqueurs; also known as Muscatel oil.

classes The subdivision of poultry kinds based on the bird's age and tenderness.

classic cuisine; classical cuisine A late-19th- and early-20th-century refinement and simplification of French grande cuisine; it relies on the thorough exploration of culinary principles and techniques and emphasizes the refined preparation and presentation of superb ingredients.

clay chicken pot An unglazed clay casserole with a lid; it is soaked in cold water before use; when heated, the steam from the wet clay helps cook the food.

clean In a food safety context, to remove visible dirt and soil from an object or environment. *See* sanitize *and* sterilize.

clearmeat A mixture of egg whites, ground meat, an acidic product and other ingredients; used to clarify a broth.

clear soups Unthickened soups, including broths, consommés and broth-based soups.

cleaver A large, heavy, almost rectangular knife with a relatively flat cutting edge; unbalanced to add momentum to the stroke, it is used to split cartilage and bone; also known as a butcher's cleaver. *See* Chinese cleaver.

clementine A small, spherical citrus fruit that is a hybrid of the tangerine and the Seville orange; it has an orange-red rind, a seedless, juicy flesh, and a sweet flavor.

clingstone A general description for a fruit that has flesh that adheres to its pit. *See* freestone.

cloche (klosh) 1. A convex dish cover with a knob or handle on top, usually of stainless steel or silver-plated metal; used to keep food hot, especially in restaurants. 2. An unglazed ceramic baking dish with a high domed cover used for baking crisp, crusty breads.

clod A subprimal cut of the beef primal chuck; it contains the large outside muscle system above the elbow; lean, tough and flavorful, it is often fabricated into steaks and roasts; also known as the shoulder clod.

closed pit A barbecue cooking pit or style of cooking in which the meat is cooked in an enclosed space using heat and smoke from a fire. *See* open pit.

closed side The right side of a beef carcass. *See* open side.

Clostridium botulinum A species of bacteria that causes botulism; common sources include cooked foods (e.g., rice, smoked fish and canned foods, especially vegetables) held for an extended period at warm temperatures with limited oxygen.

Clostridium perfringens A species of bacteria that causes food poisoning; common sources include reheated meats, sauces, stews and casseroles.

clotted cream A thickened cream made from unpasteurized milk that is gently heated until a semisolid layer of cream forms on the surface; after cooling the thickened cream is removed and can be spread or spooned, often onto a scone or other baked good; also known as Devonshire cream or Devon cream.

cloudberry A wild berry (*Rubus chamaemorous*) found in Scandinavia, Canada and New England; resembling a raspberry, it has an amber color and a tart flavor and is used principally for jams; also known as bake-apple berry, mountain berry and yellow berry.

cloud ear mushroom A mushroom (*Auricularia polytricha* and *A. auricula*) that grows on tree stumps in China; it has a shallow oval cup, a slightly crunchy texture and a bland flavor and is generally available only in dried form; also known as Jew's ear mushroom, tree ear mushroom and wood ear mushroom.

clove 1. A spice that is the dried, unopened flower bud of a tropical evergreen tree (*Eugenia aromatica*); it has a reddish-brown color, a nail shape and an extremely pungent, sweet, astringent flavor; available whole or powdered. 2. A segment of a bulb, such as garlic. 3. A British unit of weight for goods such as cheese; equal to 8 lb. (3.5 kg).

clover honey A thick, light-colored, full-flavored, all-purpose honey principally made from clover blossoms and popular in North America and Europe.

cloverleaf roll A soft yeast roll made by placing three small balls of dough in a muffin cup to rise together, resulting in a roll shaped like a three-leaf clover.

club sandwich; clubhouse sandwich A double-layer sandwich of toasted or untoasted bread, chicken or turkey, lettuce, tomato and bacon.

club steak A fabricated cut of the beef primal short loin; this tender cut contains an L-shaped section of the backbone and a portion of loin eye muscle but none of the tenderloin. *See* shell steak, T-bone steak *and* porterhouse steak.

coagulation The irreversible transformation of proteins from a liquid or semiliquid state to a drier, solid state; usually accomplished through the application of heat.

coalpot A piece of cooking equipment used in the Caribbean region; it consists of a large brown clay pot up to 18 in. (45 cm) high and 10–12 in. (25–30 cm) in diameter; the wide, deep bowl with holes bored in the bottom forms the top of a broad, hollow column, partly open on one side near the base and broadened at the bottom to provide stability; a fire is started in the bowl, and cooking takes place inside on pans or a grill.

coarse 1. Composed of relatively large parts or particles; not fine in texture. 2. A wine-tasting term for a rough-textured wine that may have too high an alcohol content or a wine lacking finesse. 3. A beer-tasting term for an overly hopped, bitter beer.

coarsely chop To cut food into small pieces, about 3/16-in. (0.5-cm) square.

coarse salt *See* kosher salt.

coat To cover a food (sometimes first dipped in a liquid such as eggs or milk) with an outer covering (coating) of bread crumbs, flour, dry seasonings or the like.

coat a spoon A technique used to determine if a mixture such as a custard is done; it is done if the mixture clings to a spoon when held aloft and a line drawn across it does not disappear.

coating A layer of foods (e.g., flour, bread crumbs, batter or cornmeal) covering a principal ingredient; a coating is used to produce a crispy or caramelized surface, to protect the principal ingredient from a cooking medium, or to add flavors and texture.

coban (koh-bahn) A dried, smoked pequin; this chile has a fiery hot flavor.

cobbler A deep-dish fruit tart with a rich, sweet, biscuit-type dough covering the fruit.

cobb salad A salad of chopped chicken or turkey, tomatoes, avocado, bacon, hard-boiled eggs, scallions, Cheddar and lettuce dressed with a vinaigrette and garnished with a blue cheese.

cock 1. The male of any bird. 2. A rooster.

cock-a-leekie; cockie leekie (kock-ah-LEE-ke) A Scottish soup made from an old cock or hen flavored with leeks, bacon, parsley, thyme, bay leaf and other seasonings and garnished with cooked prunes and leeks.

cockles A family of bivalves with heart-shaped shells that measure 1 in. (2.5 cm) across; they have a long, finger-shaped foot, a gritty, chewy texture, and a mild flavor; also known as heart clams.

cockscomb; cock's comb The red, fleshy crest found on the head of male poultry; used in French cuisine as a garnish or as a savory tart filling.

cocktail 1. A drink made of one or more alcoholic beverages mixed with juice, soda or other ingredients and sometimes garnished with fruit; it is usually consumed before a meal or at a party; also known as a mixed drink. 2. A dish of cold foods, often bound or served with a dressing or sauce and generally served as an appetizer or dessert (e.g., shrimp cocktail and fruit cocktail).

cocktail sauce A sauce used for shellfish and as a condiment; made from ketchup or chile sauce mixed with horseradish, lemon juice and a hot red pepper sauce.

cocktail strainer A perforated stainless steel spoon or round strainer often surrounded by a flexible metal coil or wire spring; it has ears or grips that fit over the rim of a shaking glass and is used for straining cocktails containing fruit, pulp or ice.

cocoa 1. A hot beverage made with cocoa, a sweetener and milk; also known as hot chocolate. 2. Chocolate that has had most of its fat removed, then is pulverized into a powder; used to flavor baked goods and sauces.

cocoa beans Seeds of the cacao tree. *See* cacao *and* chocolate-making process.

cocoa butter The cream-colored fat extracted from cocoa beans during the process of making cocoa powder; used to make bar chocolate, white chocolate and cosmetics. *See* chocolate-making process.

cocoa mix A mixture of cocoa powder, dry milk and a sweetener; mixed with hot or cold water to make a chocolate-flavored beverage; also known as instant cocoa.

cocoa nibs Roasted, shelled cocoa bean kernels. *See* chocolate-making process.

cocoa powder A brown, unsweetened powder produced by crushing cocoa nibs and extracting most of the fat (cocoa butter); it is used as a flavoring; also known as unsweetened cocoa. *See* alkalized cocoa *and* chocolate-making process.

cocoa powder, Dutch process Cocoa powder that has been treated with an alkali to neutralize its natural acidity; it is darker and milder than a nonalkalized powder.

coconut The fruit of a tropical palm tree (*Cocos nucifera*); it has a hard, woody shell enclosed in a thick fibrous husk; the shell is lined with a hard white flesh, and the hollow center is filled with a sweet milky-white liquid.

coconut, dried The shredded or flaked flesh of the coconut; often sweetened; also known as copra.

coconut cream A coconut-flavored liquid made like coconut milk but with less water; the resulting liquid is thicker, creamier and more flavorful. *See* cream of coconut.

coconut juice; coconut water The slightly opaque liquid from a fresh coconut; sometimes known imprecisely as coconut milk.

coconut milk A coconut-flavored liquid made by pouring boiling water over shredded coconut; the mixture is cooled and the white liquid is strained.

coconut oil An oil obtained from the dried coconut; dense, white, buttery and high in saturated fats; it is used for cooking and in processed products such as candies, margarine, baked goods, soaps and cosmetics.

coconut syrup A nonalcoholic, sweetened syrup made from coconut meat and milk; used for preparing cocktails and as a flavoring agent in desserts.

cocotte (koh-KOT) French for casserole and used to describe a round or oval cooking pan with two handles and a tight-fitting lid; used for slow-cooking dishes such as daubes and other braised dishes; it is available in a variety of materials and sizes. *See* en cocotte.

cod; codfish A large family of saltwater fish, including Atlantic cod, Pacific cod, pollock, haddock, whiting and hake; generally, they have a mild, delicate flavor, a lean, white flesh and a firm texture; they are available fresh, sun-dried, salted or smoked.

cod, Atlantic Cod found in the northern Atlantic Ocean; they have a silvery skin with rust-colored spots and an average market weight of 10 lb. (4.4 kg). *See* scrod.

cod, Atlantic

cod, Pacific Cod found in the northern Pacific Ocean; they have a dark gray or brown skin that fades to grayish-white on the belly, a very soft texture, and an average market weight of 5–10 lb. (2.2–4.5 kg); they are sometimes mistaken for rock cod or black cod, which are unrelated; also known as gray cod.

coddle To cook foods, usually eggs, slowly in a container set in a water bath.

coeur à la crème (kurr ah lah krehm) French for heart with cream and used to describe a dessert made by combining cream cheese with whipping cream or sour cream and molding the mixture in a wicker or cheesecloth-lined mold (usually heart shaped) to remove the whey or liquid; the cheese is unmolded and garnished with berries.

coeur à la crème mold A heart-shaped wicker basket or heart-shaped porcelain mold with holes in the bottom used to mold the dessert coeur à la crème; it is approximately 1 in. high and 3–7 in. in length and diameter.

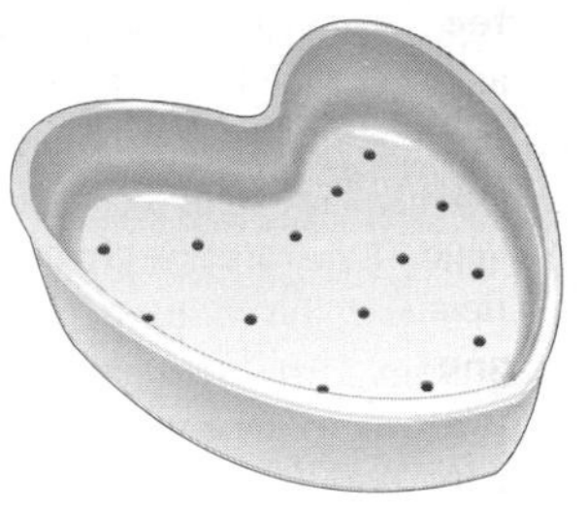

coeur à la crème mold

coeur de filet (cou-ere day fee-lay) A French cut of the beef carcass from the heart of the tenderloin; it is a porterhouse steak.

coffee 1. A dark brown, aromatic beverage made by brewing roasted and ground beans of the coffee plant (genus *Coffea*). 2. The beans of the coffee plant; of two general varieties, they are usually named for the geographical location where they are grown. *See* arabica coffee beans *and* robusta coffee beans. 3. A term used imprecisely to describe the beverage as generally consumed in the United States and made from approximately 2 level tablespoons of ground coffee per 6 fl. oz. of water.

coffee, decaffeinated 1. Coffee beans that have had the caffeine removed by the direct contact method or the Swiss water process. 2. The beverage made from such beans.

coffee, flavored A coffee that has acquired a particular flavor or aroma by tumbling the beans with one or more flavoring or aromatic oils; flavors include vanilla, chocolate, liqueurs, spices and nuts.

coffee beans, green Coffee beans (both arabica and robusta) in their raw state; when fresh from the berry, they are a light olive-tan; as they dry, they become pale yellow-orange.

coffee cake; coffeecake A sweet, leavened, breadlike cake usually flavored with nuts, fruit or spices and topped with frosting, glaze or streusel; traditionally served for breakfast or brunch.

coffee cream *See* cream, light.

coffee-cup-full A traditional measure of volume; it is approximately 6 fl. oz.

coffee grinder A machine that grinds roasted coffee beans before brewing; it can be electric or manual, with the fineness of the grind usually dependent on the length of time the grinder operates; also known as a coffee mill.

coffee milk 1. Coffee with hot milk. 2. A little coffee in a glass of milk.

coffee syrup A coffee-flavored sweetened syrup used as a flavoring agent, principally in beverages.

coffee whitener A nondairy product used to whiten coffee; usually made from corn syrup, emulsifiers, vegetable fats, coloring agents, preservatives and artificial flavorings.

Cognac (kohn-yahk) A brandy distilled from wines made from Folle Blanche, Saint-Emilion and Colombard grapes grown within France's Charente and Charente-Martime departments; it is distilled in a two-step process and aged in Limousin oak barrels, sometimes for as long as 50–55 years. *See* brandy.

coho salmon (koh-ho) A variety of salmon found in the Pacific Ocean from Oregon to Alaska; it has a metallic blue skin that fades to silver on the sides and belly with irregular black spotting, a black mouth with a white gum, a light to dark pink flesh, high fat content, a mild flavor, and an average market weight of 3–12 lb. (1.4–5.4 kg), although aquafarmed coho are usually 1 lb. (450 g); also known as a silver salmon.

Cointreau (KWAHN-troh) A clear, colorless, orange-flavored French liqueur.

cola A sweet, carbonated soft drink flavored with a syrup made from an extract of coca leaves and cola (kola) nuts, caramel, sugar, acids and aromatic substances.

colander A bowl-shaped utensil with many perforations and usually short legs; it is used to drain liquids from solids.

colander

cola nuts; kola nuts The reddish, fragrant, nutlike seeds of the kola tree (*Cola acuminata* and *C. nitida*), native to tropical Africa and grown in the West Indies and South America; they contain caffeine and theobromine and are used as a principal flavoring ingredient in carbonated soft drinks.

Colbert, sauce (kohl-bair) A French compound sauce made from a demi-glaze flavored with butter, wine, shallots, lemon juice, nutmeg, tarragon, parsley and Madeira; often used for meats or game.

colcannon (kuhl-CAN-uhn) An Irish dish of mashed potatoes and cooked cabbage mixed with butter and milk and flavored with chives and parsley.

Colchester oyster (KOAL-chuh-str) A variety of common European oyster found off Colchester, England; known as a Walflete oyster during Elizabethan times.

cold box 1. A large walk-in storage room for foods and beverages, kept at a temperature of 34–40°F (1.1–4.4°C). 2. A chilled room where Champagne and sparkling wines are disgorged.

cold cuts Thin slices of various meats, such as ham, roast beef, salami and turkey, and sometimes cheeses, sliced and served cold, usually for a sandwich or salad.

cold-pack cheese A cheese product made from one or more cheeses of the same or different varieties (typically Cheddar-style or Roquefort-style cheeses) finely ground and mixed without heating to a spreadable consistency; flavorings are sometimes added; also known as club cheese. *See* processed cheese.

cold smoker A smoker used to cold smoke foods; the heat source is separate from the food, with the smoke channeled to the food through a pipe to dissipate heat.

cold smoking A method of curing, preserving and/or flavoring certain foods by exposing them to smoke at temperatures of 50–85°F (10–29°C) for a prolonged period; such foods are usually not fully cooked, and many must be cooked before eating; most cold-smoked meats, fish, shellfish and poultry are first salt cured or brined and often are drier than hot smoked foods and have more concentrated flavors. *See* hot smoking.

cold-water tails Tails harvested from spiny lobsters caught off South Africa, Australia and New Zealand; available frozen, their flavor is superior to that of warm-water tails.

coleslaw; cole slaw A salad of Dutch origin made from shredded cabbage and sometimes onions, sweet peppers, pickles and/or bacon bound with a mayonnaise, vinaigrette or other dressing and sometimes flavored with herbs.

collagen A water-insoluble protein found in connective tissues such as skin, ligaments, tendons and cartilage; it yields gelatin when cooked with moist heat.

collard; collard greens; collards A member of the kale family, with dark green, paddlelike leaves that grow on tall, tough stalks; the leaves have a flavor reminiscent of cabbage and kale.

collée, mayonnaise (koh-lee) A French mayonnaise sauce blended with liquefied meat aspic and used as a coating for cold foods.

Colombian Arabica coffee beans grown in the foothills of the Andes Mountains in Colombia; the beverage has a rich, mellow flavor.

coloring agent One of three dozen or so naturally occurring or synthetic food additives used to add, change or intensify color in a processed food; most coloring agents are known by their color and number (e.g., blue no.1, yellow no. 5 and red nos. 3 and 40); also known as artificial color and food coloring. *See* pigment.

columba; columba pasquale (koh-LOHM-bah pas-KWAH-leh) An Italian Easter cake in the shape of a dove made with a yeast-risen dough filled with candied fruit and topped with crystallized sugar and toasted almonds.

Columbia River smelt *See* eulachon.

comal (koh-MAHL) A round, flat griddle used for cooking tortillas; made of unglazed earthenware (to be used over a fire) or metal (to be used on a stove top).

comb honey Liquid honey still in the comb, both of which are edible; also known as chunk-style honey.

combination cooking methods Cooking methods, principally braising and stewing, that employ both dry-heat and moist-heat procedures.

combination menu A menu that combines the pricing techniques of table d'hôte and à la carte menus; that is, some items are grouped together for a set price and other items are priced individually.

combine To mix two or more ingredients together until they do not separate.

comfits (kohm-fees) Pieces of fruit, nuts, seeds or spices dipped in a sugar syrup and then rolled in finely pounded granulated sugar.

comfrey (KOHM-free) An herb of the borage family (*Symphytum officinale*) with coarse stems and leaves and bell-shaped white, yellow or pinkish flowers; the leaves can be battered and fried and the flowers added to salads as garnish; also known as consound.

commercial The best of the lower USDA quality grades for beef; it is usually sold as ground beef.

commis (kohm-ee) The apprentice at a food services operation following the brigade system.

common European oyster Any of several varieties of oysters; generally, they have a flat, smooth, almost circular shell with an average length of 2–5 in. (5.08–12.7 cm) and pale gray or green to tan flesh; their flavor varies depending on their origin, and many are named for their place of origin.

common field mushroom A wild mushroom (*Agaricus campetris*) found in open grassy areas during the summer and fall; closely related to the common store mushroom; also known as field mushroom and meadow mushroom.

common meringue A mixture of stiffly beaten egg whites and granulated sugar; depending on its intended use, it may be soft (made with equal parts egg white and sugar) or hard (made with at least twice as much sugar as egg white).

common store mushroom The common, all-purpose market mushroom (*Agaricus brunnescens* and *A. bisporus*) cultivated worldwide; it has a pale, off-white, thick stem, a gently rounded, small- to medium-sized cap that is pale off-white when fresh and turns brown when bruised and gray with age, a mild, earthy flavor, and a dense, firm texture that softens when cooked; also known as button mushroom, white button mushroom, market mushroom, cream mushroom, Italian brown mushroom and Paris brown mushroom.

complementary proteins Two or more plant foods that lack different essential amino acids, but paired together, they are the equivalent of a complete protein (e.g., soybeans and rice; legumes and cereal).

complete protein A protein containing all of the essential amino acids in the correct proportions for human use; found in only a few animal foods (e.g., chicken eggs and milk) and generally lacking in plant foods.

complex carbohydrates A group of carbohydrates with little to no flavor and various levels of solubility and digestibility; includes polysaccharides such as starches, dextrin, cellulose and glycogen, all of which are composed of long chains of sugars; generally found in vegetables, grains and some fruits.

compote 1. Fresh or dried fruit cooked in a sugar syrup. 2. A deep, stemmed dish (usually glass or silver) used to hold candy, nuts or fruit; also known as a compotier.

compound butter A mixture of softened whole butter and flavorings used as sauce or to flavor and color other sauces; also known as beurre composé.

compressed yeast A mixture of yeast and starch with a moisture content of approximately 70%; also referred to as fresh yeast. *See* yeast.

concassée (kon-kaas-SAY) Peeled, seeded and diced tomatoes.

concentrate *v.* To remove moisture from a food, principally by boiling, drying or freeze-drying. *n.* The resulting product; it can be dry or syrupy and usually has a rich, very full flavor and is used as a flavoring (e.g., demi-glaze) or is rehydrated (e.g., coffee).

conch A medium-sized to large gastropod mollusk found in the Caribbean Sea and off Florida; it has a peachy-pink spiral shell and a lean, smooth, and very firm, chewy flesh with a sweet–smoky flavor; also known as lambi (especially in the Caribbean).

conching (KONCH-eng) One of the final stages in chocolate production; a process in which huge vats of melted chocolate are slowly stirred with rotating blades; this gives the chocolate a very smooth texture and removes excess moisture and volatile acids. *See* chocolate-making process.

concombres, sauce aux (koh-kawng-br) A French compound sauce made from a velouté flavored with aniseed and garnished with parsley and julienne of fresh or pickled cucumbers.

Concord grape A grape native to North America (*Vitis labrusca*); it has a loose, blue-black skin, a pale green flesh and seeds, and a mild, sweet flavor; used principally for preserves and juice.

condiment 1. Traditionally, any item added to a dish for flavor, including herbs, spices and vinegars; now also refers to cooked or prepared flavorings or accompaniments such as relishes, prepared mustards, ketchup, bottled sauces and pickles; unlike seasonings, condiments are typically added to a dish by the diner. *See* seasoning. 2. (kohn-day-mohn) French for chutney.

conduction The transfer of heat from one item to another through direct contact (e.g., from a pot to a food).

Coney Island 1. A hot dog covered with relish, mustard, ketchup and sauerkraut; more rarely, a hamburger garnished in the same fashion. 2. A white pork sausage.

confection A general term for any kind of candy or other sweet preparation (e.g., ice cream or fruit preserves).

confectioner The person who makes or sells confections.

confectioners' foil Brightly colored, pliable foil used to wrap candies, individual pastries or pieces of cake for an attractive presentation.

confectioners' knife A knife with a 10-in. blade, a round, blunt tip and a widely spaced wave cut edge; the blade cants upward 5°, making it more comfortable for slicing; used for cutting candies, fruit jellies or baked meringues.

confectioners' knife

confectioners' sugar Refined sugar ground into a fine, white, easily dissolved powder; also known as powdered sugar and 10X sugar.

confectionery; confectionary 1. A general category of candies, sweets and other food products based on sugar. 2. The art, techniques and processes for producing them as well as the place where they are produced or sold. 3. The place where they are produced or sold.

confectionery fat A fat that is hard at room temperature and soft at body temperature, such as hydrogenated coconut oil or cocoa butter; it is used primarily in baked goods.

confiseur (kawng-fee sewr) At a food services operation following the brigade system, the person responsible for all candies, petit fours and similar items.

confit (kohn-FEE) A method of preserving meats, especially poultry, associated with southwestern France; the meat is cooked in its own fat and stored in a pot covered with the same fat.

conformation The proportion of meat to bone and the general shape of the carcass; a basis for determining quality and yield.

congeal To change from a liquid to a solid state; to become set, firm or rigid, usually by chilling.

congee (kohn-gee) An Asian (particularly Chinese) watery rice porridge.

conger eel A very large scaleless, saltwater, eel-shaped fish; it has little culinary significance.

conical pestle A snub-nosed wooden cone with a short handle used to press cooked or partially cooked foods through a chinois.

connective tissues Tissues found throughout an animal's body that hold together and support other tissues such as muscles.

conserve A spread for baked goods made from fruits, nuts and sugar cooked until thick.

consommé (kwang-soh-may) 1. A rich stock or broth that has been clarified with a clearmeat. 2. French for soup and used to describe a clear, thin, flavorful broth. *See* potage.

contaminate In the food safety context, to render an object or environment impure or unsuitable by contact or mixture with unclean or unwanted matter.

contamination In the food safety context, the presence, generally unintentional, of harmful organisms or substances in food; the contamination hazards can be biological, chemical or physical. *See* direct contamination *and* cross-contamination.

continental breakfast A breakfast of bread (e.g., toast, croissants, pastries or the like) and a beverage (e.g., coffee, tea, milk or juice).

convection The transfer of heat caused by the natural movement of molecules in a fluid (air, water or fat) from a warmer area to a cooler one.

convection oven An oven in which the heat is circulated by an interior fan.

convenience food A processed food product; generally of three types: an item that is completely prepared and needs only to be used (e.g., peanut butter), an item that is completely prepared and needs only to be heated (e.g., a frozen pizza) or an item that requires some preparation but far less than that needed if made from scratch (e.g., a cake mix).

converted rice Rice that is pressure-steamed and dried before milling to remove surface starch and help retain nutrients; it has a pale beige color and the same flavor as white rice; also known as parboiled rice.

cook *v.* To prepare foods. *n.* One who prepares foods for consumption by others.

cooked cheese A cheese that is made by heating the milk to help solidify the curds.

cooker 1. A stove. 2. An apple used for cooking purposes (as opposed to being eaten raw).

cookery The art, practice or work of cooking.

cookie cutter A metal or plastic tool used to cut rolled-out doughs into various shapes.

cookie molds Wood, plastic, metal or ceramic molds, available in a huge variety of shapes and sizes, used to make decorative designs from cookie dough.

cookie press; cookie gun A tool consisting of a hollow tube fitted at one end with a decorative template or nozzle and at the other with a trigger for forcing soft cookie dough through the template to create the desired shape.

cookies Small, sweet, flat pastries, usually classified by preparation or makeup techniques as drop, icebox, bar, cutout, pressed and wafer.

cookie sheet A flat, firm sheet of metal, usually aluminum, with very low or open sides on which cookies, biscuits and other items are baked.

cookie stamp A small glass, plastic, wood or ceramic tool for pressing a pattern or design into the dough of individual cookies before baking.

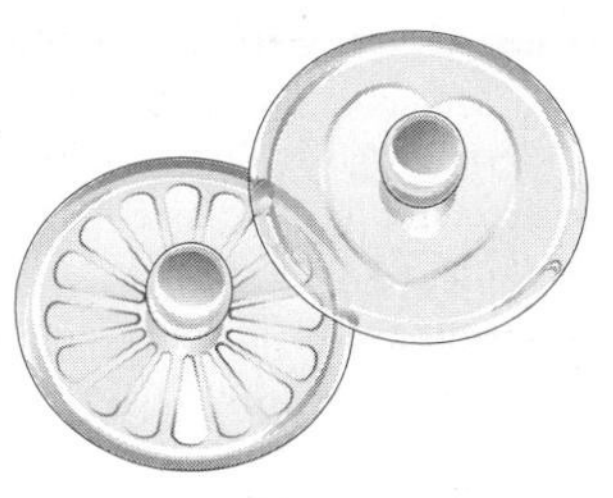

cookie stamps

cooking The transfer of energy from a heat source to a food; this energy alters the food's molecular structure, changing its texture, flavor, aroma and appearance.

cooking banana *See* plantain.

cooking oil Any oil used as a cooking medium. *See* salad oil.

cooking surface The burners, griddle or other heated areas or platforms used for stove-top cooking.

cooking wine An inexpensive red, white or rosé wine, often with salt added, used for cooking and not as a beverage.

cookware Any of a large variety of vessels and containers used on the stove top or in an oven to cook food or store it; they can be made of metal (e.g., copper, aluminum, stainless steel and cast iron), glass, ceramics or the like and include pots, pans, hotel pans and molds.

cool To allow a food to sit until it is no longer warm to the touch.

cooler 1. A long drink, usually based on fruit juices, with a low alcohol content. 2. A long drink, usually a mixture of white wine and fruit juice. 3. A device, container or room that cools or keeps food cool. *See* ice chest.

cooling rack A flat grid of closely spaced metal wires resting on small feet; used for cooling baked goods by allowing air to circulate around the food.

coppa (KOAP-pah) An Italian sausage made from pork loin marinated in garlic and red wine; it is braised, dried and eaten before it hardens.

copper 1. A trace element used principally as an enzyme component and to assist the formation of collagen and hemoglobin; significant sources include meat and drinking water. 2. A metal used for cookware and an excellent conductor of heat; the cookware can be solid copper, copper lined with tin or copper sandwiched between layers of aluminum or stainless steel; also used for flatware and serviceware.

copper bowl A round-bottomed, unlined copper bowl available in various sizes and usually used for whisking egg whites.

copra *See* coconut, dried.

coq au vin (kohk oh VAHN) A French dish of chicken, mushrooms, onions and bacon or salt pork cooked in red wine.

coquilles (koh-KEE) French for shells and used to describe a shell-shaped dish used for baking and serving foods such as fish in a white sauce.

coquilles Saint Jacques (koh-kee san zhahk) A French dish of scallops in a creamy wine sauce (sauce Mornay), topped with bread crumbs or cheese and browned; usually served in a scallop shell.

coral The roe (eggs) of a mollusk such as a scallop or a crustacean such as a lobster.

Cordelier, sauce (kor-duh-lee-ay) A French compound sauce made from a Madeira sauce finished with goose liver purée and garnished with sliced black truffles; also known as Franciscan sauce.

cordon bleu (kor-dohn BLUH) 1. French for blue ribbon and used to describe the honor afforded chefs of great distinction. 2. A French dish consisting of thin boneless chicken breasts or veal scallops sandwiched around a thin slice of prosciutto or other ham and an emmenthal-style cheese, then breaded and sautéed.

core *v.* To remove the central seeded area from a fruit. *n.* The center part of pomes (fruits from the family Rosaceae such as apples, pears and quince); sometimes tough and woody, it contains the fruit's small seeds (called pips).

corer A short, sharp-ended metal cylinder set on a shaft attached to a handle; used to remove the core from fruits such as apples or to hollow vegetables for stuffing.

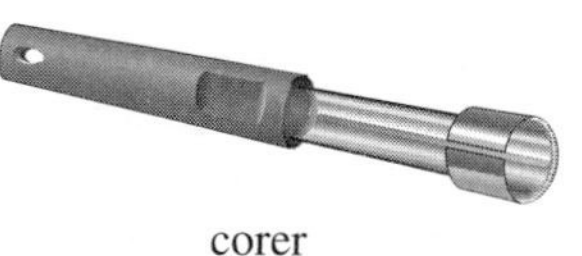
corer

coriander (KOR-ee-an-der) The tiny yellow-tan ridged seeds of the cilantro plant (*Coriandrum sativum*); used as a spice, they have a flavor reminiscent of lemon, sage and caraway; they are available whole or ground and are used in Middle Eastern, Indian and Asian cuisines and pickling spice blends. *See* cilantro.

cork 1. The spongy tan bark of the *Quercus suber* (cork oak). 2. A bottle stopper carved from this material or formed from such bark granules bound with an adhesive.

corkage A restaurant's charge for opening, cooling (if necessary) and pouring a bottle of wine brought by a customer to the restaurant for his or her use.

corkscrew A tool used to remove a cork from a bottle; the simplest is a spiral wire attached to a handle.

corn 1. A tall, annual plant native to the Western Hemisphere and producing white, yellow, blue or multicolored grains arranged on a cob; the grains (called kernels) are consumed as a vegetable when young and are available fresh, canned, frozen or dried and ground into cornmeal; also known as maize (especially in Great Britain), sweet corn and common corn. *See* hominy. 2. The edible seeds of other plants, especially wheat in England and oats in Scotland.

corn, dent Any of a variety of hardy, high-yield corn grown principally for fodder in the United States, although starch and oil are also extracted from it.

corn, flint Any of a variety of fast-ripening corn; this hardy corn is most similar to wild corn.

corn, flour Any of a variety of corn grown in Central and North America principally for flour.

corn, sweet Any of a variety of corn grown worldwide principally to be eaten on the cob or in loose form; the kernels can be white or yellow and are sweet and tender.

corn, waxy Any of a variety of corn whose kernels are covered with a waxy substance; it has a low starch and high sugar content and is used as a food additive in puddings and sauces; grown in Asia principally for flour.

corn bran A dry-milled product of high fiber content obtained from corn; used to increase the fiber content of baked goods or to thicken sauces and soups.

corn bread A quick bread made with cornmeal.

corn bread, hot water A batter of cornmeal and hot water dropped into deep hot fat and fried.

corn bread, light Traditional corn bread batter with a small amount of yeast to give the finished product rise; it is usually cooked on a griddle.

corn bread dressing A poultry stuffing made with crumbled corn bread, sausage, onions, celery and herbs.

corn cakes Small pancakelike cakes made from a batter of cornmeal and water or milk; also known as batter cakes.

corn dodgers; dodgers Deep-fried, boiled or baked corn cakes made from corn pone.

corn dog A frankfurter dipped in cornmeal batter and fried or baked; usually served on a stick.

corned beef Beef, usually a cut from the brisket or round, cured in a seasoned brine; it has a grayish-pink to rosy red color and a salty flavor; also known as salt beef.

cornelian cherry; cornel A small, olive-shaped fruit (*Cornus mas*) with a long stone, a bright red color and a tart, slightly bitter flavor; used for preserves or pickled like olives; also known as dog cherry and Siberian cherry.

Cornell bread An enriched bread made with a high-protein flour; the formula, developed at Cornell University in the 1930s, adds small amounts of soy flour, nonfat dry milk powder and wheat germ to unbleached white flour.

corner plate A subprimal cut of the beef primal short plate; it includes portions of ribs numbers 6–8.

cornet (kohr-nay) 1. A French horn-shaped pastry filled with sweetened whipped cream. 2. An hors d'oeuvre or garnish consisting of a slice of meat rolled into a cone and filled, usually with a cream cheese– or butter-based spread.

corn flour 1. Finely ground cornmeal; it has a white or yellow color and is used as a breading or in combination with other flours. 2. In Great Britain, refers to both finely ground cornmeal and cornstarch. *See* cornstarch.

cornichon (KOR-nih-shohn; kor-nee-SHOHN) French for a tiny pickled gherkin cucumber; it is the traditional accompaniment to a meat pâté.

cornmeal Dried, ground corn kernels (typically of a variety known as dent); it has a white, yellow or blue color, a gritty texture and a slightly sweet, starchy flavor and is available in three grinds (fine, medium and coarse); used in baking, as a coating for fried foods or cooked as polenta.

cornmeal, steel-ground Cornmeal ground by a process that removes the hull and germ.

cornmeal, water-ground Cornmeal ground by a process that preserves some of the hull and germ.

corn oil A pale yellow oil obtained from corn endosperms; it is odorless, almost flavorless and high in polyunsaturated fats and has a high smoke point; a good medium for frying and also used in baking, dressings and to make margarine.

corn pone An eggless cornmeal batter shaped into small ovals and fried or baked.

corn salad *See* mâche.

corn smut A bulb-shaped fungus (*Ustilago maydis*) that grows on ears of corn, causing them to swell and turn black; considered a delicacy, it has a sweet, smoky flavor similar to a cross between corn and mushrooms; also known as cuitlacoche.

cornstarch A dense, very fine, powdery flour made from ground corn endosperm and used as a thickening agent; also known as corn flour (especially in Great Britain).

corn syrup A thick, sweet syrup derived from cornstarch and composed of dextrose and glucose; available as clear (light) or brown (dark), which has caramel flavor and color added.

corn whiskey An American whiskey distilled from a mash made from a minimum of 80% corn; aged for at least 2 years in new or used charred oak barrels.

correct seasonings 1. To taste a food just before service and add seasonings, especially salt and freshly ground black pepper, if necessary. 2. To reduce a strong flavor by adding a liquid.

cos lettuce *See* romaine lettuce.

Cosmopolitan A cocktail made of vodka, Triple Sec, Rose's Lime Juice and cranberry juice and served in a martini glass.

costmary (KOHS-mah-ree) An herb (*Chrysanthemum balsamita*) with a strong camphor, minty flavor and aroma; used to clear and preserve home-brewed ale and occasionally as a salad ingredient or garnish; also known as alecost and mint geranium.

cosy A fabric cover, usually knitted or quilted, used to cover a teapot to keep it warm.

côte (koat) French for rib and used to describe a cut from the ribs of a veal carcass; côtelettes premières are the four cutlets from the more desirable end of the neck nearest the loin, and côtelettes sécondes or découvertes are the four cutlets from the area nearest the shoulder.

Côtes-du-Rhône (koat doo rone) A general name given to all red, white and rosé wine produced in the Rhône Valley; the wines, generally red, produced in the north are made from the Syrah grape and the red wines produced in the south are primarily made from Grenache, plus Syrah, Mourvèdre and Cinsault.

cotlet A firm but chewy confection made with cooked apricots, gelatin and nuts. *See* aplet.

cottage cheese A soft, fresh cheese made from skimmed cow's milk or reconstituted skimmed or nonfat dry cow's milk powders; it has a white color, a moist, large grain texture and a mild, slightly tart flavor; it cannot contain more than 80% moisture; available flavored or unflavored in three forms: small curd, medium curd and large curd; also known as curd cheese.

cottage cheese, creamed Cottage cheese with 4–8% added cream; available plain or flavored, it is highly perishable.

cottage ham A fabricated cut of the Boston butt; it is smoked and usually boneless.

cottage pudding A plain cake topped with a warm, sweet, puddinglike sauce.

cottonseed oil A thick, colorless oil obtained from the seeds of the cotton plant (genus *Gossypium*); it is usually blended with other oils to make highly refined products sold as vegetable or cooking oil.

cotto salami (kot-TOE suh-LAH-mee) A large Italian sausage made from pork and beef, highly seasoned with garlic, black peppercorns and other spices; it is cured and air-dried.

Cotuit oyster An Atlantic oyster found off Cotuit, Cape Cod; it has a shell with an average length of 3 in. (7.6 cm), a plump body and a moderately salty flavor.

couche (koosh) French for a large piece of heavy linen or canvas that is dusted with flour and wrapped around yeast bread dough to help hold its shape during proofing.

coulibiac (koo-lee-BYAHK) The French adaptation of a Russian dish, kulebiaka, which consists of a creamy mixture of salmon, rice, hard-cooked eggs, mushrooms, shallots and dill enclosed in a pastry envelope usually made with brioche dough; it can be large or small and served as a first course or a main course.

coulis (koo-lee) 1. A sauce made from a purée of vegetables or fruit; it may be hot or cold. 2. Traditionally, thickened meat juices used as a sauce.

country captain A dish of chicken, onions, tomatoes, green pepper, celery, currants, parsley, curry powder and seasonings cooked in a covered skillet, served over rice and garnished with toasted almonds.

country gravy A gravy made from pan drippings, flour and milk; consistency can vary from thick to thin.

country ham *See* ham, country.

country-style forcemeat *See* forcemeat, country-style.

coupe (koop) 1. A glass or metal bowl sitting on a short stem and used to serve ice cream, fruit salad or similar foods. 2. A dessert of ice cream topped with fruit and whipped cream, usually served in a coupe dish.

coupler A plastic conical tube with a screw-on cover or nut; the conical piece is placed inside a pastry bag and a pastry tip is attached to the bag with the nut; used to allow pastry tips to be changed during decorating without emptying the pastry bag. *See* pastry bag *and* pastry tip.

courgette (koor-jhet) French for zucchini and the name used for it throughout Europe. *See* marrow squash.

court bouillon (kort boo-yon) Water simmered with vegetables, seasonings and an acidic product such as vinegar or wine; used for simmering or poaching fish, shellfish or vegetables.

couscous (KOOS-koos) 1. Small, spherical bits of semolina dough that are rolled, dampened and coated with a finer wheat flour; a staple of the North African diet. 2. A North African dish composed of a meat and/or vegetable stew flavored with cumin and served over the cooked semolina.

couscousière (koos-koos-yair) A metal or earthenware assemblage of two bulbous pots; the top pot, which holds the couscous, has a perforated bottom and lid and sits on the lower pot, which holds the stew; the steam from the stew cooks the couscous.

couscoussière

couverture (koo-vay-tyoor) A high-quality chocolate with a minimum of 32% cocoa butter; very smooth and glossy, it is used for coating candies and truffles, molding and pastry making. *See* chocolate-making process.

cover count The number of customers at a food services facility over a specific time period.

covered chicken fryer A deep frying pan, usually made of cast iron, with a short stubby handle and a domed lid; used for frying and braising.

cowberry A member of the cranberry family (*Vaccinium vitis-ideae*); a red berry with a tart flavor, it grows wild in pastures in the northern United States and Canada; used for preserves; also known as a mountain cranberry and red whortleberry.

cows Female cattle after their first calving; raised in the United States principally for milk; in France, they are used for beef when no longer needed for milk.

cowslip A sweetly scented spring flower (*Primula veris*); it can be eaten fresh (usually with cream), crystallized in sugar as a confection or used to flavor wine, vinegar, mead or syrup.

crab Any of a large variety of crustaceans found in freshwaters and saltwaters worldwide; generally, they have a flat, round body with 10 legs, the front 2 being pinchers, and a pink-tinged white flesh with a sweet, succulent flavor; significant varieties include the blue, dungeness, king, snow and stone crabs. *See* blue crab.

crab, claw meat A market form of the blue crab; it consists of the brownish claw meat.

crab, flake and lump meat A market form of the blue crab; it is a combination of flake and lump meat.

crab, flake meat A market form of the blue crab; it consists of small pieces of meat from the body muscles.

crab, lump meat A market form of the blue crab; it consists of whole, relatively large chunks of meat from the large body muscles.

crab, soft-shell A blue crab harvested within 6 hours after molting; it has a soft, pliable, brownish-green shell and an average market width of 3.5 in. (8.75 cm); once cooked, the entire crab is eaten; it has a crunchy texture and a mild flavor; available fresh or frozen. *See* buckram *and* peeler crab.

crab apple; crabapple Any of a variety of small, hard apples (*Malus sylvestris*) with a deep red skin and a very tart flavor; used principally for preserves or spiced and canned for use as a condiment for pork and poultry or as a garnish.

crab boil A commercial spice blend used to flavor the liquid in which shellfish will be cooked; generally contains mustard seeds, peppercorns, bay leaves, allspice, ginger and chile flakes; also known as shrimp boil.

crab cake A mixture of lump crabmeat, bread crumbs, milk, egg, scallions and seasonings formed into small cakes and fried.

crab imperial An American dish of crabmeat bound with mayonnaise or a sherried cream sauce and placed in blue crab shells or scallop shells, sprinkled with bread crumbs or Parmesan and baked.

crab Louis (LOO-ee) A cold dish of crabmeat on a shredded lettuce bed, dressed with mayonnaise, chiles, cream, scallions, green pepper, lemon juice and seasonings and garnished with tomatoes and hard-boiled eggs.

cracked 1. A food broken into small pieces, usually not of uniform size and shape (e.g., cracked wheat or cracked ice). 2. An olive that has been lightly crushed but not pitted.

cracked wheat The whole wheat berry broken into coarse, medium or fine particles.

cracker A dry, thin, crisp baked product, usually savory.

cracker flour A soft wheat flour that does not absorb much moisture and does not need prolonged mixing.

cracker meal Finely crushed crackers used to coat meat or fish.

cracklin' bread Cornbread with bits of cracklings scattered throughout.

crackling rice A Chinese dish made from the scrapings of rice from the bottom of the rice cooker or pot; the scrapings are dried, then deep-fried, and often served with soup or a sauce.

cracklings; cracklin's The crisp pork rind after the fat has been rendered.

Cracow sausages Polish sausages containing 80% pork, 10% bacon and 10% beef and flavored with garlic, pepper and caraway seeds.

cranberry; craneberry A small red berry of a plant (genus *Viburnum*) with low, trailing vines that grows in American bogs; it has a tart flavor and is used for sauces, preserves, beverages and baked goods; also known as American cranberry, bounceberry and bearberry.

cranberry bean A kidney-shaped bean with a red-streaked, cream-colored skin and a nutty flavor; available fresh and dried; also known as a shell bean and shellout.

cranberry juice The juice made from the liquid constituent of cranberries; it can be sweetened or unsweetened.

crappie (CRAW-pee) A member of the sunfish family found in the Mississippi River and Great Lakes; it has an average market weight of 2–5 lb. (0.9–2.3 kg) and a soft, lean, white flesh with a bland flavor; principal varieties are the black crappie and white crappie; also known as calico bass, papermouth, speckled perch (especially in the American South) and strawberry bass.

C-ration A canned field ration used by the U.S. army.

crawdad *See* crayfish.

crawfish *See* crayfish.

crayfish Any of several freshwater crustaceans found in North America; generally, they resemble small lobsters, with a brilliant red shell when cooked; they range in size from 3.5 to 7 in. (8 to 17.5 cm) and have lean, tender flesh (mostly in the tail) with a sweet flavor; also known as crawfish and crawdad (particularly in the American South).

crayfish

cream 1. A component of milk with a milkfat content of at least 18%; it has a slight yellow to ivory color, is more viscous and richer tasting than milk, and can be whipped to a foam; it rises to the top of raw milk; as a commercial product, it must be pasteurized or ultrapasteurized and may be homogenized. 2. *See* creaming.

cream, heavy whipping Cream with a milkfat content of 36–40%; pasteurized but rarely homogenized; it is used for thickening and enriching sauces and making ice cream; can be whipped to a foam and used as a dessert topping or folded into custards or mousses for flavor and lightness.

cream, light Cream with a milkfat content of 18–30% and typically used for coffee, baked goods and soups; also known as breakfast cream, coffee cream and table cream.

cream, light whipping Cream with a milkfat content of 30–36%; used for thickening and enriching sauces and making ice cream; it can be whipped to a foam and used as a dessert topping or folded into custards or mousses for flavor and lightness.

cream, manufacturing; cream, manufacturers' A heavy cream packaged without pastuerization; it contains 40% milkfat and is thicker than regular cream; it is used in sauces and can attain a greater, more stable volume when whipped.

cream, pressurized whipping Cream with sugar, stabilizers, emulsifiers and other food additives added and sold under pressure in an aerosol can; used principally as a decorative topping.

cream, single The English term for light cream with a milkfat content of at least 18%; it is often poured over fruit, flans and puddings.

cream ale A sweet, honey- to golden-colored ale brewed in the United States; highly carbonated, with a rich foam and strong effervescence.

cream cheese A fresh, soft, mild, white cheese made from cow's cream or a mixture of cow's cream and milk (some goat's milk cream cheeses are available); used for baking, dips, dressings, confections and spreading on bread products; it must contain 33% milkfat and not more than 55% moisture and is available, sometimes flavored, in various-sized blocks or whipped.

cream cracker A crisp, unsweetened English biscuit usually eaten with cheese.

creamery 1. A room, building or establishment where milk and cream are processed and butter and cheese are produced. 2. A place where dairy products are sold.

cream filling A pie filling made of flavored pastry cream thickened with cornstarch.

cream horn A small pastry made by wrapping thin strips of puff pastry around a cone-shaped metal form and baking; the baked horn is then removed from the form and filled with whipped cream or custard.

cream horn mold A tapered, tinned-steel tube 6 in. long with a base diameter of 1–1 1/4 in.; used for making cream horns.

creaming A mixing method in which softened fat and sugar are combined vigorously to incorporate air; used for making some quick breads, cookies and high-fat cakes.

cream of coconut The thicker, more flavorful liquid that rises to the top of coconut milk; it is available sweetened.

cream of tartar Tartaric acid; a fine white powder derived from an acid found on the inside of wine barrels after fermentation; it is used to give volume and stability to beaten egg whites and to prevent sugar from crystallizing when making candy or frosting.

cream puff A small round shell made from choux pastry and filled with custard or whipped cream; served alone or as part of another dessert (e.g., gâteau St. Honore or croquembouche).

cream puff pastry *See* choux pastry.

creams Light, fluffy or creamy-textured desserts or dessert ingredients made with whipped cream or whipped egg whites (e.g., Bavarian creams, chiffons, mousses and crème Chantilly); also known as crèmes.

cream sauce *See* béchamel sauce.

cream sherry A type of sherry; it is sweet, with a rich, nutty flavor, a deep golden color and a full body.

cream soda A sweet, carbonated drink flavored with vanilla; originally made with soda water.

cream soups Thickened soups made from vegetables, poultry, fish and/or shellfish but not necessarily cream; the ingredients are often puréed.

Crécy, à la (kray-cee, ah lah) 1. A French garnish consisting of julienne of carrots. 2. A French preparation method characterized by dishes containing carrots.

crema (KRAI-mah) 1. Spanish and Italian for cream (especially in northern Italy). 2. An Italian custard, creamed soup or flavor of ice cream. 3. The soft, golden froth that appears on a cup of freshly brewed espresso. 4. A Greek corn flour (cornstarch) pudding sometimes flavored with vanilla or tangerine peel and served chilled, garnished with cinnamon or nuts.

crème anglaise; crème a l'anglaise (krehm ahn-GLEHZ; khrem ah lahn-GLEHZ) A rich, sweet French custard sauce made with eggs, sugar, vanilla and milk or cream; also known as vanilla custard sauce.

crème au beurre au lait (oh burr oh lay) A French buttercream made with pastry cream.

crème brûlée (broo-lay) French for burned cream and used to describe a rich custard topped with a crust of caramelized sugar.

crème caramel (kair-ah-MEHL) A French egg custard baked in a caramel-lined mold; the chilled custard is inverted and unmolded for service, creating its own caramel glaze and sauce; also known as flan in Spanish, crema caramella in Italian and crème renversée in French.

crème Chantilly; Chantilly cream (shahn-tee-yee) Heavy cream whipped to soft peaks and flavored with sugar and vanilla; used to garnish pastries or desserts or folded into cooled custard or pastry cream for fillings.

crème Chiboust (chee-boos) A pastry cream lightened by folding in Italian meringue.

crème de (krehm duh) French for cream of and used as part of the name of intensely sweet liqueurs; usually followed by the name of the principal flavoring ingredient.

crème pâtissière (pah-tees-syehr) French for pastry cream. *See* pastry cream.

crème renversée (rehn-vehr-seh) A French custard baked over a layer of caramelized sugar and inverted for service.

crenshaw melon; cranshaw melon A large ovoid to pear-shaped hybrid muskmelon with a netless, lightly ribbed rind, a golden-green color, a salmon-orange flesh and a strong spicy aroma.

Creole, à la (cree-ohl, ah lah) A French preparation method associated with Creole cuisine; the savory dishes are characterized by the use of rice, tomatoes, green pepper, onions and spices, and the sweet dishes are characterized by the use of rum, pineapples and vanilla.

Creole coffee Coffee brewed from ground coffee beans and chicory root; also known as New Orleans coffee.

Creole cooking A cuisine combining elements of French, Spanish and African cuisines and native to New Orleans, Louisiana; it is characterized by the use of butter, cream, green peppers, onions, celery, filé powder and tomatoes. *See* Cajun cooking.

Creole cream cheese A homemade soft cow's milk cheese; it is made by clabbering buttermilk with skim milk; after the mixture is drained, cream is poured over the curds; when ready to eat, the cream is mixed with the curds and topped with sugar and fruit or salt and pepper.

Creole mustard A hot, spicy mustard flavored with horseradish and made from brown mustard seeds that have been marinated in vinegar.

Creole sauce An American sauce consisting of onions, green and red peppers, celery, tomatoes and tomato paste, flavored with bay leaves.

crêpe (krayp) A thin, delicate, unleavened griddle cake made with a very thin egg batter cooked in a very hot sauté pan; used in sweet and savory preparations.

crêpe pan A low pan with a heavy bottom, sloping sides and a smooth surface; it is sized by diameter of the crêpe made: 5–6 in. for dessert crêpes and 6–7 in. for entrée crêpes. *See* blini pan.

crêpe pan

crêpes Suzette (kraypz sue-zeht) A dessert consisting of sweet crêpes sautéed in orange butter, then flamed with an orange liquor or brandy.

crépinette (kray-pee-NEHT) A small, slightly flattened French sausage made from pork, lamb, veal or chicken; sometimes flavored with truffles; it is wrapped in caul rather than a casing.

crespelle (krehs-PEHL-lay) Thin Italian pancakes; they are either stacked with different savory or sweet fillings between the layers or filled and rolled like crêpes.

cress Any of a variety of plants (*Lepidium sativum*) related to the cabbage family with small dark green leaves, thin stems and a delicate, slightly peppery flavor (e.g., watercress); used for salads.

crimini; cremini (kree-MEE-nee) Italian for various common store mushrooms.

crimp 1. To pinch or press together the edges of pastry dough using fingers, a fork or other utensil; the decorative edge seals the dough. 2. To cut gashes along both sides of a fresh fish; the fish is then soaked in ice water to firm the flesh and help the skin crisp when cooked.

crimper/cutter A hand tool with two crimping disks axle-set flush against either side of a cutting wheel; it can press, crimp and cut dough simultaneously; used for ravioli, empañadas, turnovers and other pastry doughs; also known as a doughspur.

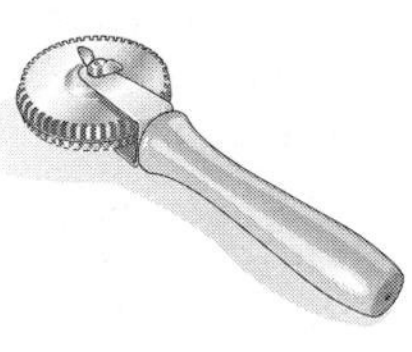
crimper/cutter

crisp *v.* To refresh vegetables such as carrots or celery by soaking them in ice water or baked goods such as crackers by heating them. *adj.* A description of produce that is firm and fresh and not soft or wilted (e.g., an apple or lettuce leaf) or a baked good that is hard and brittle and not soft (e.g., a cracker). *n.* A baked deep-dish fruit dessert made with a crumb or struesel topping; similar to a cobbler.

crispbread A thin, crisp, rectangular Scandinavian-style crackerlike bread traditionally made with rye flour but now often containing some wheat flour.

croaker A member of the drum family found off the U.S. East Coast and in the Gulf of Mexico; it has a dark speckled skin, an average market weight of 0.5–2 lb. (225–900 g), and a lean flesh with a mild flavor; also known as Atlantic croaker, crocus, hardhead and king billy.

crockpot An electrical appliance that simmers food slowly for extended periods of time in a covered glass or ceramic pot.

croissant (kwah-SAHN; kwah-SAHNT) A rich, buttery, crescent-shaped roll made with flaky yeast dough.

croissant cutter A hollow, rolling pin–shaped utensil with stainless steel triangular blades; when rolled across dough, it cuts out triangular shapes that are then rolled into croissants.

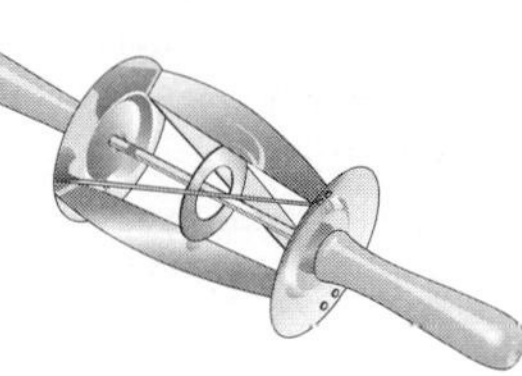
croissant cutter

croissant dough A rolled-in or laminated dough made with yeast and large quantities of butter; used for making croissants and other pastries.

crookneck squash A summer squash with a long slender neck and bulbous body, a pale to deep yellow skin with a smooth to bumpy texture, a creamy yellow flesh, and a mild, delicate flavor; also known as yellow squash.

crop The gullet of birds; in grain-eating birds, it forms a pouch that can be stuffed.

croquante (krow-kahn't) 1. An elaborate centerpiece for a traditional grand French buffet; made with trellised bands of marzipan set on a pastry base; the marzipan top is filled with small rounds of pâte feuilletée, each with a preserved cherry in the middle. 2. A French confection consisting of a basket made of marzipan filled with ice cream.

croque madame (krohk mah-dahm) A croque monsieur with a fried egg on top.

croquembouche (kroh-kuhm-BOOSH) French for crisp in the mouth and used to describe an elaborate dessert composed of small, custard-filled cream puffs that are coated with caramel and stacked into a tall pyramid; the outside is then decorated with spun sugar and sugar flowers; traditionally served at weddings.

croque monsieur (krohk muhs-yur) A French ham and cheese sandwich cooked in a sandwich grilling iron.

croquette (kroh-keht) A food such as salmon or potatoes that has been puréed and/or bound with a thick sauce (e.g., béchamel), formed into small shapes, breaded and deep-fried.

cross-contamination In the food safety context, the transfer, typically by food handlers, of biological, chemical or physical contaminants to food while processing, preparing, cooking or serving it. *See* direct contamination.

cross-cut A fabricated cut of meat cut across the muscle grain or on the bias.

crostini (kroh-STEE-nee) 1. Italian for little toasts and used to describe small, thin slices of toasted bread, usually brushed with olive oil. 2. Canapés of thin toasted bread with a savory topping. 3. Croutons used for soups or salads.

crottin (kroh-tinh) Any French goat's milk cheese shaped like a small flattened ball.

croustade (kroo-STAHD) An edible container used to hold creamed meat or vegetable mixtures (e.g., a thick stew); it can be a hollowed-out bread loaf or made from shaped and deep-fried pastry dough or puréed potatoes.

croûte, en (KROOT, ahn) A food (usually meat, poultry, fish or pâté) wrapped in pastry and baked.

crouton (KROO-tawn) 1. A small piece of bread, often seasoned, that has been toasted, grilled or fried; it is used as a garnish for soups or salads. 2. A small piece of aspic, usually in a decorative shape, used to garnish a cold dish.

crown roast 1. A fabricated cut of the lamb primal rack; it is formed by tying the ribs in a circle (ribs up and fat inside); after roasting, the tips can be decorated with paper frills and the hollow center section filled with a stuffing. 2. A fabricated cut of the pork primal loin; similar to the lamb cut.

cruciferous vegetables (krew-SIH-fer-uhs) Vegetables such as broccoli, Brussels sprouts, cabbage, cauliflower, chard, kale, mustard greens, rutabagas and turnips that contain antioxidants and are high in fiber, vitamins and minerals.

crudités (kroo-dee-TAY) Raw vegetables usually served as hors d'oeuvres accompanied by a dipping sauce.

cruet (krew-ay) French for a small jar with a lid used for making and storing vinaigrette dressing, vinegar or other liquids.

cruller (KRUHL-uhr) A Dutch doughnut-type pastry made from a twisted strip of deep-fried dough topped with sugar or a sugar glaze.

crumb *v.* To remove crumbs and other food debris from the table, usually between courses. *n.* 1. A small piece, especially of a bread or other food. 2. The texture of a food, especially breads or baked goods.

crumble A dessert made of fresh fruit topped with a crumbly pastry mixture and baked.

crumbly A tasting term for a food that has a tendency to fall apart or break into small pieces.

crumpet A small, thin, round, yeast-leavened British batter bread cooked on a griddle or stove top, similar to an English muffin.

crush *v.* 1. To reduce a food to its finest form (e.g., crumbs, paste or powder); it is often done with a mortar and pestle. 2. To smash an ingredient such as garlic or ginger with the side of a knife or cleaver to release their flavors or facilitate cooking. *n.* 1. The harvest of the grapes used for a wine; a term synonymous with harvest or vintage. 2. A type of soft drink, usually citrus flavored.

crust 1. The hardened outer layer of a food such as a bread or a casserole. 2. A pie or tart shell. 3. The sediment a wine (usually a red wine and especially a vintage port) deposits during bottle aging; sometimes referred to as deposit.

crustacean One of the principal classes of shellfish; they are characterized by a hard outer shell and jointed appendages; includes crabs, lobsters and shrimp. *See* mollusks.

crystallization The process of forming sugar crystals.

crystallized flowers Flowers such as violets soaked in a thick sugar syrup heated to 220–224°F (32–36°C), drained and dried; sugar crystals are left on the flowers, and they are used to decorate baked goods and candies.

crystallized fruits Small fruits or segments of larger ones soaked in a thick sugar syrup heated to 220–224°F (32–36°C), drained and dried; sugar crystals are left on the fruits.

crystal sugar Refined sugar processed into grains that are several times larger than those of granulated sugar; used for decorating cookies and other baked goods; also known as sanding sugar and pearl sugar.

csipetke (chi-pet-ke) Small pieces of thinly rolled egg noodle dough used for sweet and savory Hungarian dishes; also known as pinched noodles.

Cuban bread A hard-crusted white bread made with only flour, water, yeast, salt and sugar; slightly sweeter than traditional French bread, which it otherwise resembles.

Cubanelle pepper A long, tapered sweet pepper with a yellow or red color.

cube To cut food into 0.5-in. (1.27-cm) squares; these chunks are generally larger than foods that are diced.

cubed steak A fabricated cut, typically from the beef chuck, round or flank primals; they are tough slices of meat that are tenderized by pounding and scoring the surface in a pattern of squares; also known as tenderized steak.

cucumber The edible fleshy fruit of several varieties of a creeping plant (*Cucumis sativus*); most have a dark green skin and a creamy white to pale green flesh; generally divided into two categories: pickling and slicing.

cucumber

cucumbers, pickling Cucumbers such as the dill and gherkin; they have sharp black or white spines and a bitter, astringent flavor when raw; used for pickling.

cucumbers, slicing Cucumbers such as the burpless, English, lemon and common green market variety; they have a relatively thin skin, a juicy flesh, many soft, whitish seeds and a cool, astringent flavor.

cuillère, à la (kwee-yair, ah lah) French for a method of brown-braising meats for a long period until they are so soft they can be served with a spoon.

cuisine (kwih-ZEEN) 1. French for the art of cookery. 2. French for kitchen. 3. The ingredients, seasonings, cooking procedures and styles attributable to a particular group of people; the group can be defined by geography, history, ethnicity, politics, culture or religion.

cuisine minceur (kwee-ZEEN man-SEUR) A style of cooking pioneered by the French chef Michel Guerard; it emphasizes healthful foods prepared in a light style without added cream or fats.

cuisseau (kwee-so) A French cut of the veal carcass; it is the cushion of veal; also known as noix.

cuisson (kwee-sohn) 1. French for cooking and used to connote culinary processes and details, especially cooking time. 2. The liquid used for shallow poaching.

cuitlacoche; huitlacoche (hweet-la-KO-chay) *See* corn smut.

culatello (koo-lah-TEHL-oh) An Italian ham that has been cured and soaked in wine during aging; it is lean, with a rosy red color and a delicate flavor.

culinary (KUL-ah-nair-e; QUE-lynn-air-e) Of or relating to a kitchen or the activity of cooking.

cull *v.* To examine a group of fungible or nonfungible goods and select appropriate units. *n.* 1. A lobster, usually a Maine lobster, with only one claw. 2. The lowest USDA quality grade for lamb and veal; the meat is usually used for ground, canned or other processed products.

culotte de boeuf (koo-loht duh buff) 1. A fabricated cut of the beef primal sirloin; also known as a sirloin steak. 2. A French cut of the beef carcass; it is the end of the loin near the hipbone and usually cooked as a roast. 3. A British cut of the beef carcass; it is part of the rump (round) and is used for a rump roast or further fabricated into rump steaks.

cultured Used to describe any dairy product made from milk inoculated with certain bacteria or molds to achieve flavor, aroma and texture characteristics in the final product (e.g., buttermilk and blue cheese).

Cumberland sauce An English sweet-and-sour sauce made from port, lemon and orange juice and zest and red currant jelly; usually served with duck, venison or other game.

cumin (KUH-mihn; KYOO-mihn) A spice that is the dried fruit (seed) of a plant in the parsley family (*Cuminum cyminum*), native to the Middle East and North Africa; the small crescent-shaped seeds have a powerful, earthy, nutty flavor and aroma and are available whole or ground in three colors (amber, white and black); used in Indian, Middle Eastern and Mexican cuisines; also known as comino.

cup 1. A vessel with a handle; it rests on a saucer and is generally used for coffee or tea. 2. A unit of measurement in the U.S. system equal to 8 fl. oz. *See* measuring cups, dry; *and* measuring cups, liquid. 3. A punch-type beverage such as Sangria made of wine flavored with brandy, liqueurs, fresh fruits and/or herbs mixed in a pitcher with ice and served in a cup or glass.

cupcake A small individual-sized cake baked in a mold such as a muffin pan; usually frosted and decorated.

curd 1. The edible flower head of various members of the cabbage family (e.g., broccoli and cauliflower). 2. A creamy mixture of citrus juice, sugar, butter and egg yolks; used as a topping for baked goods as in lemon, lime and orange curd.

curdle The separation of milk or egg mixtures into liquid and solid components; generally caused by excessive heat, overcooking or the presence of acids.

curds The semisolid portion of coagulated milk (whey is the liquid portion); generally used for making cheese.

cure To preserve foods by drying, salting, pickling or smoking.

curing Any of several methods of processing foods, particularly meats and fish, to retard spoilage. *See* aging, drying, pickle, salt curing *and* smoking.

curing salt A mixture of salt and sodium nitrite that inhibits bacterial growth; used as a preservative, often for charcuterie items.

currants 1. Dried Zante grapes; seedless, they resemble very small, dark raisins and are used in baked goods and for snacking. 2. The small berries of a prickly shrub (genus *Ribes*); grown in clusters like grapes, they have a tart flavor and can be black, red or golden (also known as white); black currants are used to make syrups, preserves and liqueurs (e.g., crème de cassis); red and golden currants are used in sauces, desserts, preserves (e.g., bar-le-duc) and sweet dishes.

curry 1. Any of several hot, spicy Indian meat and/or vegetable stewlike dishes; usually served with rice and side dishes such as chutney, nuts and coconut. 2. A general term used to imprecisely describe any of a wide variety of spicy, Asian, stewlike dishes.

curry leaf An herb (*Chalcas koenigii*) with bright, shiny green leaves resembling bay leaves (it should not be confused with the ornamental gray-leaved curry plant); the leaves, which impart a spicy, curry-like flavor, are used in Indian and Southeast Asian cuisines.

curry powder An American or European blend of spices associated with Indian cuisines; the flavor and color vary depending on the exact blend; typical ingredients include black pepper, cinnamon, cloves, coriander, cumin, ginger, mace and turmeric, with cardamom, tamarind, fennel seeds, fenugreek and/or chile powder sometimes added.

curry powder, Bombay style A distinctively sweet, moderately hot style of curry powder.

curry powder, Chinese style A distinctively hot, peppery style of curry powder.

curry powder, Madras style A distinctively pungent, hot style of curry powder.

cush (koosh; kuhsh) 1. A sweetened, mushy cornmeal mixture that is fried in lard and served as a cereal with cream and sugar or cane syrup. 2. A cornmeal pancake from the American South. 3. A soup of cornmeal, milk, onions and seasonings popular in the American South. 4. The Gullah term for cornmeal mush.

cushaw (koo-SHAH) A large, ivory-colored crookneck squash with yellow-orange flesh and a bland flavor.

custard Any liquid thickened by the coagulation of egg proteins; its consistency depends on the ratio of eggs to liquid and the type of liquid used; it can be baked in the oven in a bain marie, or on the stove top.

custard cup A small handleless ceramic cup with a 4- to 5-oz. capacity.

custard cup

cut *v.* To separate into pieces using a knife or scissors. *n.* An imprecise term for a piece of meat (usually a fabricated cut).

cut in A technique for combining solid fat with dry ingredients until the mixture resembles small crumbs; it is done with a pastry fork, pastry blender, two knives, fingers, a food processor or an electric mixer.

cutlet 1. A thin, tender cut of meat, usually lamb, pork or veal, taken from the leg or rib section. 2. Finely chopped meat, fish or poultry bound with a sauce or egg and formed into the shape of a cutlet; usually breaded and fried.

cutter The second lowest USDA quality grade for beef; it is generally used in canned meat products, sausages and ground beef.

cutting *v.* 1. Reducing a food to smaller pieces. 2. A mixing method in which solid fat is incorporated into dry ingredients until only lumps of the desired size remain. *n.* A root, stem or leaf removed from a plant and used for propagation.

cutting and folding The process of repeatedly moving a spatula or spoon vertically through a mixture, lifting the ingredients and turning the ingredients over to achieve a uniform disbursement; often used in the context of adding beaten egg whites; also known as folding.

cuttlebone *See* cephalopods.

cuttlefish A cephalopod mollusk found in the Atlantic Ocean; it has a flattened, ovoid body extending into thin fins at the sides, black and white stripes on the top and a lighter coloring beneath; it can reach 25 in. (63.5 cm) in length and 12 in. (30.4 cm) in diameter; it has a tough, chewy texture and a mild flavor.

cyclamate A nonnutritive (zero calories) artificial sweetener approximately 30 times as sweet as sugar; available in Canada, its use is restricted in the United States because of its possible carcinogenic properties.

D

dab (dahb) 1. A small flatfish found in the Pacific Ocean from California to Alaska; it has an average market weight of 4–12 oz. (110–340 g), low fat content, and moist flesh with a delicate, sweet flavor; also known as a sanddab. *See* plaice, American. 2. A term used imprecisely to describe various flounders and other small flatfish.

dacquoise (dah-kwahz) 1. A baked meringue made with ground nuts. 2. A French pastry made with layers of baked meringue filled with whipped cream or buttercream.

daikon (DI-kon) A long, large cylindrical radish native to Asia; it has a creamy white or black skin, a juicy, crisp, white flesh and a sweet, slightly spicy, fresh flavor; it can be eaten raw or cooked; also known as Asian radish, rettiche and winter radish. *See* radish, white.

dairy A room, building or establishment where milk is kept and butter and/or other dairy products such as cheese are made and sometimes sold.

dairy products Cow's milk and foods made from cow's milk, such as butter, yogurt, sour cream and cheese; sometimes, other milks and products made from them are included (e.g., goat's milk cheese).

dal *See* dhal.

Dallas cut chuck roast A subprimal cut of the beef primal chuck; it is a roast with the fat and bone removed.

dancy orange A variety of mandarin orange; it is relatively small with a medium to dark orange rind.

dandelion A plant (*Taraxacum officinale*) with bright green jagged-edged leaves that have a slightly bitter, tangy flavor and are used in salads or cooked like spinach.

dandelion wine A wine made from the fresh yellow flowers of the wild dandelion plant, citrus fruits and raisins.

Danish dough whip A tool with a long wooden handle attached to a flat coiled wire whisk; used for combining batters and bread doughs.

Danish pastry A breakfast pastry made with a sweet, buttery, flaky yeast dough filled with fruit, nuts or cheese and sometimes glazed.

Danish pastry dough; Danish dough A sweet rolled-in or laminated dough made with yeast and eggs; it is used for Danish pastries and sweet rolls.

Danoise, sauce; Danish sauce (dan-whaz) A French compound sauce made from a béchamel blended with poached chicken purée, flavored with mushroom essence and garnished with chopped herbs.

dariole (DAIR-ee-ohl; dah-ree-OHL) 1. A small, deep-sided mold used for pastries, cheese flans, babas, vegetable custards and rice pudding. 2. An item made in such a mold.

Darjeeling (dahr-jee-lehng) A large-leaf black tea grown on the Indian foothills of the Himalayas; the beverage has a rich flavor and a bouquet reminiscent of muscat grapes.

dark beer A full-bodied, deep-colored and creamy-tasting beer usually produced by adding roasted barley to the mash during the initial brewing stages.

dark meat The leg and thigh flesh of a chicken or turkey; it has a dark grayish-brown color when cooked and more connective tissue and fat than light meat; the darker color is the result of the increased myoglobin content in these frequently used muscles; other birds, such as duck or goose, are all dark meat.

darne (dahrn) A French cut of fish, especially of a large roundfish such as salmon; it is a thick slice cut perpendicular to the backbone; also known as a dalle.

dartois (dahr-twah) A French pastry or hors d'oeuvre consisting of two sheets of puff pastry enclosing a sweet or savory filling; it is baked and cut crosswise into individual pieces.

dash A traditional measure of volume; it refers to a small amount of a seasoning that is added to a dish by a quick, downward stroke of the hand and is approximately 1/16 or 1/8 teaspoon.

dasheen (da-SHEEN) A large, spherical root vegetable related to taro and grown in the southern United States and Caribbean region; the tuber has a brown skin, a gray-white starchy flesh and a nutty flavor when cooked; its large leaves, known as callaloo, have a delicate flavor and are cooked like spinach or used to wrap foods for cooking.

dashi (DAH-shee) A Japanese stock made with katsuobushi and dried kelp; it is used as a soup or flavoring.

date The fruit of a palm tree (*Phoenix dactylifera*) native to the Middle East and Mediterranean region; most varieties are long and ovoid (some are more spherical) with a thin, papery skin that is green and becomes yellow, golden brown, black or mahogany red when ripe; it has an extremely sweet flesh with a light brown color, a chewy texture and a single, long, narrow seed; eaten fresh or dried.

date plum A cherry-sized fruit (*Diospyros lotus*) related to the American persimmon; it has a yellowish-brown to blue-black skin color and a datelike flavor.

date sugar The coarse brown crystals obtained by pulverizing dehydrated dates.

daube (doab) A French dish consisting of beef, red wine, vegetables and seasonings braised in a daubiére.

daubiére (doh-beh-yay) A medium-sized French covered pot with a deep, bulbous ceramic or metal body and a high-angled handle; used for daubes and other braised dishes; also known as a toupin.

daubiére

Daumont, sauce (doe-MON) A French compound sauce made from a hollandaise flavored with oyster liqueur and garnished with diced mushrooms, truffles and oysters.

dauphine, à la (doh-FEEN) 1. French for in the style of Dauphine and used to describe a method of preparing vegetables in the same manner as dauphine potatoes. 2. A joint of meat garnished with dauphine potatoes.

dauphine potatoes; pommes dauphine A French dish of puréed potatoes mixed with choux pastry, shaped into balls, and deep-fried.

dauphinoise, pommes à la (doh-feen-wahz) 1. A French method of preparing potatoes; the potatoes are cut into thin, round slices and placed in a gratin dish with garlic, butter and cream and baked. 2. A French method of preparing sliced potatoes by covering them with a mixture of eggs, milk and cream in a gratin dish and then topping them with grated cheese and baking.

Davis, Adelle (Am., 1904–1974) A dietitian and nutritionist, she popularized current concepts of nutrition; promoted vitamin supplements, organic produce, fertilized eggs, raw milk, whole grain breads, preservative-free foods, exercise and psychotherapy, and wrote *Let's Cook It Right, Let's Eat Right to Keep Fit, Let's Get Well,* and *Let's Have Healthy Children.*

de agua (day ahg-wah) A long, thin, tapering chile with a thin red and green flesh and mild, vegetable flavor; often stuffed or used in soups and mole sauces.

de árbol (day ahr-bohl) An elongated, pointed, brick red, dried chile with a thin flesh and a very hot, smoky, tannic, and grassy flavor.

debone To remove the bones from a cut of meat, fish or poultry.

decanter The glass container into which wine is decanted before serving; it usually has a stopper and a capacity of 750 or 1500 ml. *See* carafe.

deci- *See* metric system.

deckle meat *See* blade meat.

deck oven An oven containing separate shelves; the product can be baked in pans or directly on the solid shelves.

decline phase A period during which bacteria in a colony or culture die at an accelerated rate because of overcrowding and competition for food, space and moisture; also known as negative growth phase. *See* lag phase *and* log phase.

decoction The process and result of extracting flavors or essences by boiling and reducing a liquid and food.

decompose To separate into constituent parts; to disintegrate; to rot. *See* putrefaction.

decorateur (deck-koh-rah-tuhr) At a food services operation following the brigade system, it is the person responsible for all showpieces and special cakes.

decoration The ornamenting of food for presentation; unlike a garnish, a decoration does not form an integral part of the dish; a decoration (e.g., sprigs of herbs or pieces of fruit) should echo flavors in the food itself.

decorator's icing *See* royal icing.

deep-dish A sweet or savory pie made in a deep pie dish or a shallow casserole and having only a top crust.

deep-dish pizza A pizza baked in a 1 to 2 in. deep, straight-sided pan; the crust is usually thick and chewy.

deep-freezing A method of preserving food by storing it at a temperature of −10 to 0°F (−40 to 18°C); flavors generally remain unimpaired even after several months of storage.

deep fryer; deep-fat fryer 1. An appliance used to cook foods in hot fat; the fat is heated by an internal source controlled by a thermostat; it has a deep well to hold the fat and usually comes with baskets to hold and drain the foods. 2. A deep pot with two handles and slightly curving or sloping sides and a wide surface area; it is used to cook foods in hot fat, which is heated by the stove top on which the pot sits; it usually has a basket to hold and drain the foods.

deep-frying A dry-heat cooking method using convection to transfer heat to a food submerged in hot fat; foods to be deep-fried are usually first coated in a batter or breading.

deglaze To swirl or stir a liquid (usually wine or stock) in a pan to dissolve cooked food particles remaining on the bottom; the resulting mixture often becomes the base for a sauce.

degrease To skim the fat from the top of a liquid such as a sauce or stock.

dégustation menu (deh-gys-tah-ssyohn mehn-hu) A prix fixe menu consisting of numerous small courses specially chosen and prepared by the chef; also known as a tasting menu.

dehydrate To remove or lose water.

delicata squash (dehl-ih-CAH-tah) A long, cylindrical winter squash; it has a pale yellow skin with green striations, yellow flesh, and a flavor reminiscent of sweet potato and butternut squash; also known as a sweet potato squash.

delicatessen; deli 1. A grocery store that specializes in cooked meats (e.g., pastrami and corned beef) and prepared foods (e.g., potato salads and pickles); traditionally, the foods were of Jewish cuisines, but other ethnic foods, especially Italian, are now included. 2. Such foods.

della casa (DEH-lah KAH-sah) Italian for of the house and used to describe the dishes that are a restaurant's specialty.

Delmonico family (active 1835–1881) A Swiss-born family that built the first luxurious restaurant in New York; the menu was written in both French and English, and the original cuisine—part French and part regional American—was labeled Continental and included the Delmonico steak, avocado salad, lobster Newburg and baked Alaska.

Delmonico potatoes A 19th-century American dish of boiled, buttered potato balls sprinkled with lemon juice, parsley, salt and pepper.

Delmonico steak *See* strip loin steak.

Demerara sugar A dry, coarse-textured raw cane sugar from Guyana.

demi-chef At a food services operation following the brigade system, it is the person responsible for assisting a chef de partie (station chef); also known as an assistant.

demi-glace (deh-me-glass) French for half-glaze and used to describe a mixture of half brown stock and half brown sauce reduced by half.

demi-glaze (deh-me-glaz) The English spelling of demi-glace.

demi-tasse (dehm-ee-tahs) 1. Strong, black coffee served after dinner; especially in France. 2. A small cup with a single handle; used for coffee.

denatured protein A protein that has been treated with heat, acid, base, alcohol, heavy metal or other agent, causing it to lose some of its physical and/or chemical properties.

Denver omelet *See* western omelet.

Denver pot roast A subprimal cut of the beef primal round; it is the tough, well-trimmed heel of the round.

Denver ribs *See* lamb riblets.

Denver sandwich *See* western sandwich.

depression cake A cake made with shortening, water and brown sugar instead of butter, eggs and milk; also known as a war cake.

Derby Pie The proprietary name of a very rich, single crust, chocolate chip–pecan pie flavored with bourbon.

Desdemona A pastry named for the Shakespearean character, it consists of small round biscuits similar to ladyfingers sandwiched together with a vanilla-flavored whipped cream, brushed with apricot glaze, and covered with a Kirsch-flavored fondant.

desem (DAY-zum) A type of sourdough made by storing a small ball of unleavened dough in a sack of flour for several days to develop natural yeasts.

desiccate 1. To dry thoroughly. 2. To preserve foods by removing virtually all moisture.

dessert (dess-ahrt) The last course of a meal; a sweet preparation, fruit or cheese is usually served.

dessert spoonful A traditional measure of volume; it is approximately 1 $^1/_2$ teaspoons.

dessert wine A sweet wine served with dessert or after a meal; it includes those whose grapes were affected by the noble rot (e.g., Sauternes or Beerenauslese), wines made from dried or partially dried grapes and fortified wines (e.g., sherry or port).

détendre (deh-tahn-druh) A French culinary term meaning to soften a paste or mixture by adding an appropriate substance such as milk, stock or beaten eggs.

detergent 1. Any of a group of synthetic or organic liquid- or water-soluble cleaning agents that, unlike soap, are not prepared from fats. 2. A term used imprecisely for any cleaning agent, including soap.

detrempe (day-trup-eh) A paste made with flour and water during the first stage of preparing a pastry dough, especially rolled-in doughs.

deuce 1. Restaurant industry slang for a table for two; also known as a two-top. 2. A marketing term for a $1\frac{3}{4}$- to 2- lb. (794- to 907-g) lobster; also known as a 2 pounder.

deveining The process of removing a shrimp's digestive tract.

developing dough Mixing a dough to make it smoother (i.e., the proteins are properly hydrated and the gluten is stretched and relaxed); the dough is developed when it pulls away from the sides of the bowl.

devil To combine food with hot and spicy seasonings such as mustard, Tabasco sauce or red pepper.

deviled egg plate A plate with several egg-shaped indentations and used for serving deviled eggs.

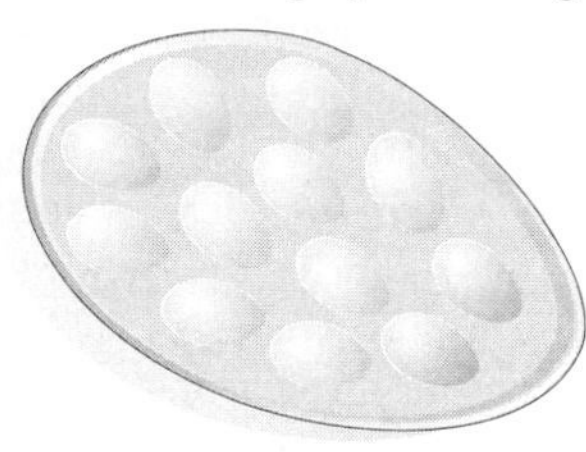

deviled egg plate

deviled eggs Hard-boiled eggs whose yolks are removed from the white, mashed, seasoned and bound with mayonnaise; the mixture is then returned to the white using a pastry tube or spoon.

devil's dung *See* asafetida.

devil's food cake A very rich, moist chocolate cake leavened with baking soda, which gives the cake a reddish-brown color.

devils on horseback 1. In the United States, an appetizer of oysters wrapped in bacon, seasoned with red pepper or Tabasco sauce, broiled, and served on toast points. 2. In Great Britain, an appetizer of wine-poached prunes stuffed with a whole almond and mango chutney, wrapped in bacon, broiled, and served on toast points.

Devonshire cream; Devon cream *See* clotted cream.

dewberry Any of a variety of blackberries (*Rubus caesius*) grown on trailing vines; the berry is smaller than an ordinary blackberry and has fewer and larger drupelets.

dhal; dhall; dal (d'hahl) 1. Hindi for any of a large variety of dried and split pulses used in Indian cuisines. 2. An Indian dish made with such legumes, onions and spices. *See* pigeon pea *and* gram.

Diable, sauce (dee-AHB-luh) A French compound sauce made from a demi-glaze flavored with shallots, white wine, vinegar, herbs, dry mustard, black pepper and cayenne and garnished with parsley.

diagonals Elongated or oval-shaped slices of cylindrical vegetables or fruits.

diagonal slicing A cutting method in which the food (often tough meat or hard vegetables) is sliced at an angle of approximately 60 degrees (i.e., not perpendicular to the cutting surface).

diamond roast A subprimal cut of the beef primal round; it is a very lean, somewhat tender roast cut from the side of the round.

Diane, à la (dee-EHN, ah lah) A French preparation method for sautéed or broiled steak; the steak is garnished with Worcestershire sauce, cream and butter; variations include the addition of sherry, shallots, brandy and/or pâté.

Diane, sauce (dee-EHN) A French compound sauce made from a pepper sauce flavored with a game glaze, finished with heavy cream, and garnished with hard-cooked egg whites and black truffle; usually served with venison.

diavola (dee-A-vuh-lah) An Italian tomato sauce seasoned with paprika and cayenne pepper.

dice *v.* To cut food into cubes. *n.* The cubes of cut food.

dice, large Cubes of approximately 5/8 in. (1.5 cm).

dice, medium Cubes of approximately 3/8 in. (9 mm).

dice, small Cubes of approximately 1/4 in. (6 mm).

dieppoise, sauce (dee-ep-WAHZ) A French compound sauce made from a fish velouté finished with shrimp butter.

diet 1. The liquid and solid foods regularly consumed during the course of normal living. 2. A prescribed or planned allowance of certain foods for a particular purpose, such as a low-sodium diet for a person prone to high blood pressure. 3. A prescribed or planned program of eating and drinking sparingly in order to lose weight.

diet, balanced A diet with adequate energy-providing nutrients (carbohydrates and fats), tissue-building nutrients (proteins), inorganic chemicals (water and minerals), regulators and catalysts (vitamins), and other foods (dietary fiber) necessary to promote health.

dietary fiber Carbohydrates such as cellulose, lignin and pectin that are resistant to digestion but nutritionally significant because they add bulk to the diet by absorbing large amounts of water and facilitate elimination by producing large stools; also known as roughage.

dietitian A person trained in nutrition, food science and diet planning who applies that knowledge and experience to regulating or advising on the dietary needs of the healthy and sick; a registered dietitian (R.D.) has met certain minimal educational standards and passed the American Dietetic Association's professional examination. *See* nutritionist.

diet spread A margarine product with 40% less fat and approximately half the calories of regular margarine; available whipped or in a squeeze bottle, it is generally used as a spread and not for cooking or baking.

digestif (dee-jess-teef) A beverage (usually a brandy or liqueur) consumed at the end of a meal and thought to aid digestion. *See* aperitif.

digestion The process by which food is mechanically and chemically broken down in the alimentary tract and converted into either absorbable substances used to sustain life (e.g., monosaccharides) or waste.

digestive biscuit A slightly sweet English biscuit made from wholemeal flour and sometimes covered with chocolate; also known as a sweetmeal biscuit.

digestive system All of the organs and glands directly associated with the ingestion and digestion of food; the principal units are the mouth, salivary glands, esophagus, stomach, liver, gallbladder, bile duct, pancreas, pancreatic duct, small intestine (including the duodenum, jejunum and ileum), large intestine (including the cecum, colon and rectum) and anus.

Dijon (deh-zjohn) A French prepared mustard made in the Dijon region from black or brown mustard seeds blended with salt, spices and white wine or verjuice; it has a clean, sharp, medium-hot flavor, a yellow-gray color and a creamy texture.

Dijon-style mustard; dijon mustard Any prepared mustard similar to Dijon but not made in that region.

dill An annual plant and a member of the parsley family (*Anethum graveolens*); the feathery leaves have a parsleylike flavor with overtones of anise and are used fresh or dried as an herb; the flat, oval, brown seeds have a slightly bitter, caraway-like flavor, also with overtones of anise, and are used as a spice.

dill

dill pickles Preserved cucumbers; the preserving medium is usually strongly flavored with dill.

dill pickles, sour The cucumbers are prepared in a fermented salt stock, then placed in a seasoned vinegar solution.

dill pickles, sweet The cucumbers are packed in brine, then drained and packed in a sugar syrup with vinegar.

dilute To reduce a mixture's strength or flavor by adding a liquid, usually water.

dim sum; dem sum (dihm suhm) Cantonese for heart's delight and used to describe a variety of snacks such as steamed or fried dumplings, shrimp balls, spring rolls, steamed buns and Chinese pastries; they can be served any time of day.

dining room manager The person responsible for running the front of the house; duties include training service personnel, overseeing wine selections, working with the chef to design the menu, and arranging guest seating; also known as maître d'hotel or maître d'.

dinner 1. Traditionally, in the United States, the main meal of the day, which was served at noon. *See* supper. 2. The main meal of the day, usually served in the evening.

dinnerware The china, flatware and glassware used at the table for eating. *See* serviceware.

Dionysus The Greek god of wine and of an orgiastic religion celebrating the power and fertility of nature. *See* Bacchus.

dip 1. A thick creamy sauce or condiment (served hot or cold) to accompany raw vegetables, crackers, processed snack foods such as potato chips or the like, especially as an hors d'oeuvre; usually made with a mayonnaise, sour cream or cream cheese base and flavorings. 2. Thai for raw, half cooked.

diplomat, sauce (de-plo-mah) A French compound sauce made with lobster butter and a sauce normandy, garnished with diced truffles and lobster.

diplomat cream A mixture of equal parts vanilla pastry cream and sweetened whipped cream.

diplomat pudding A British dessert made of liqueur-soaked ladyfingers or sponge cake layered with candied fruit, jam and custard.

dipping fork A fork with two long thin tines used for spearing foods to be dipped in sugar, chocolate or the like.

direct contact method A method of removing caffeine from coffee beans by applying a chemical solvent (e.g., methylene chloride) or carbon dioxide gas (under high pressure and at a high temperature) to the beans; this removes the caffeine and the wax but not the flavoring agents; the chemical solvent is burned off during the roasting. *See* Swiss water method.

direct contamination In the food safety context, contamination of raw foods, or the plants or animals from which they come, in their natural settings or habitats by contaminants in the air, soil or water. *See* cross-contamination.

Dirty Martini A cocktail made of gin, dry vermouth and a splash of brine from bottled olives, served straight-up or on the rocks, and garnished with an olive.

dirty rice A Cajun dish of rice cooked with chicken livers or gizzards and onions and flavored with bacon fat.

disaccharide A carbohydrate such as sucrose, lactose or maltose that is crystalline, sweet, soluble and digestible; composed of two sugar units, it will hydrolyze into its component simple sugars (monosaccharides); also known as a double sugar.

disjoint To divide two bones (with flesh attached) at their joint (e.g., separating a chicken leg from the thigh).

distillation The separation of alcohol from a liquid (or, during the production of alcoholic beverages, from a fermented mash); it is accomplished by heating the liquid (the mash) to a gas that contains alcohol vapors; this steam is then condensed into the desired alcoholic liquid (beverage).

distilled spirits Whiskey, rum, brandy, gin and other liquids created through the distillation process and containing ethyl alcohol; also known as spirits and more imprecisely and commonly known as liquor.

distilled white vinegar A vinegar made from a grain alcohol mixture; clear and colorless, it has a rather harsh, biting flavor.

distributor A business that purchases goods wholesale directly from suppliers or other middlemen and then sells the goods to retailers; a distributor sometimes repackages or relabels the goods.

Divine, sauce (de-vee-nay) A French compound sauce made from a hollandaise flavored with poultry glaze and finished with unsweetened whipped cream.

divinity A white, fudgelike candy made with whipped egg whites, sugar and chopped nuts or other flavorings. *See* seven-minute frosting.

Dobostorte; Dobos torte (DOH-bohs-TOR-te) A German pastry composed of several very thin layers of sponge cake filled with chocolate or mocha buttercream and topped with caramel glaze.

docker A tool used to pierce small holes in pastry dough; it resembles a small paint roller, with numerous short spikes.

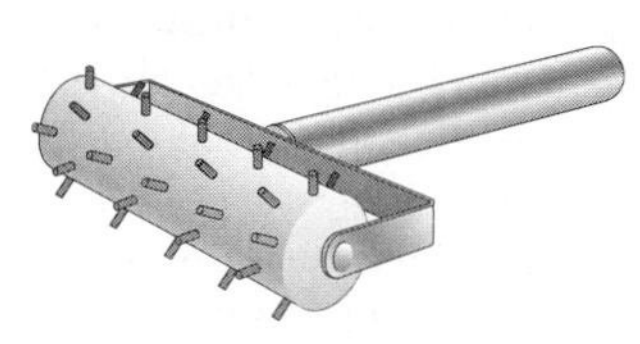

docker

docking Pricking small holes in an unbaked dough or crust to allow steam to escape and prevent the dough from rising when baked.

dog cherry *See* cornelian cherry.

doily An ornamental paper or fine fabric napkin used to decorate plates, especially for desserts, or to distinguish different items (e.g., decaffeinated coffee from regular coffee).

dollarfish *See* butterfish.

dollop An imprecise measure of volume for a soft food such as whipped cream or mashed potatoes; it can be approximately the mounded amount contained on a teaspoon or tablespoon.

dolly mix An English assortment of small sweets in various shapes, colors and flavors.

Dolly Varden An anadromous trout found in the northern Pacific Ocean from California to Alaska and Japan to Korea; it has an olive skin with pink, orange or yellow spots, a yellow to orange, flaky flesh, and a delicate flavor and can weigh up to 20 lb. (9 kg).

dolma (dol-MAH) Any of a variety of fruits (e.g., apples), vegetables (e.g., squashes and peppers) or leaves (e.g., grape and cabbage) stuffed with a savory filling and braised or baked; served hot or cold, as an appetizer or entrée, in Mediterranean cuisines.

dolphin 1. A marine mammal; it is illegal to catch or sell a dolphin for food. 2. An imprecisely used term for the saltwater fish known as a dolphinfish.

dolphinfish A saltwater fish found in tropical waters; it has a silvery, iridescent skin, an off-white to pink flesh, a firm texture, a moderately high fat content, a sweet flavor, and an average market weight of 5–15 lb. (2.7–6.8 kg); also known as mahi mahi (Hawaiian) and dorado (Spanish). *See* pampano.

domestic Dover sole A member of the flounder family found off the U.S. West Coast; it is often afflicted with a parasite that causes the flesh to become slimy and gelatinous.

Dom Perignon (dom peh-ree-n'yawn) 1. The 17th-century cellar master at the Abbey d'Hautviller, popularly credited with inventing Champagne (all he actually discovered was that blending grapes from different vineyards improved the quality of the sparkling wine produced the following spring). 2. The finest and most expensive sparkling wine produced by Moët and Chandon.

donburi (don-boor-ree) A Japanese meal in a bowl consisting of rice with a wide range of topping choices.

donut *See* doughnut.

doogh (dooke) Persian for a palate-cleansing yogurt and soda water drink flavored with dried mint.

Doppltes Beefsteak (dopple-tess bif-stek) A German cut of the beef carcass; it is comparable to châteaubriand.

dorado (doh-rah-doh) *See* dolphinfish.

dorato (doh-RAH-toh) Italian for an ingredient that has been dipped in egg batter and fried to a golden color.

doro wat; doro wot' (doe-roe oo-at) An Ethiopian chicken stew flavored with garlic, berberé, nit'rk'ibé and tomatoes, served with hard-boiled eggs and eaten with injera.

dosa (do-sah) A pancakelike bread made in southern India from ground lentils and flavored with coriander, cumin, black peppercorns and fenugreek; traditionally served with a thin vegetable curry flavored with sambar masala.

dot To place small pieces of an ingredient, usually butter, over the surface of a food.

double-acting baking powder A chemical leavening agent that releases carbon dioxide gas when moistened and again when heated. *See* baking powder.

double boiler An assemblage used to cook heat-sensitive foods such as sauces, chocolate or custards; one pot sits partway down a second pot; simmering water in the bottom pot gently heats the top pot's contents; also known as a double saucepan.

double crust A pie, cobbler or other pastry prepared with both a top and bottom layer of dough. *See* crust.

double-frying process A moist-heat cooking method in which a food (e.g., potatoes) is first deep-fried at one temperature and then deep-fried again at a higher temperature, causing the food to puff up.

dòufù (doh-foo) Firmly pressed Chinese-style tofu; also known as bean cake.

dòufù-bok (doh-foo-bock) Deep-fried hollow cubes of Chinese-style tofu; also known as hollow agé cubes.

dough A mixture of flour and other ingredients used in baking and often stiff enough to cut into shapes; it has a low moisture content and gluten forms the continuous medium into which other ingredients are embedded; it generally has less fat, sugar and liquid than a batter. *See* batter.

dough conditioner; dough strengthener A type of food additive used to modify a dough's starch and gluten content to produce a more stable product, increase loaf volume and/or prevent loss of leavening.

dough cutter; dough scraper A thin, rectangular piece of unsharpened stainless steel topped with a wooden or plastic handle; used to cut portions of dough, to clean wooden worktables, and to lift or move foods; also known as a bench scraper.

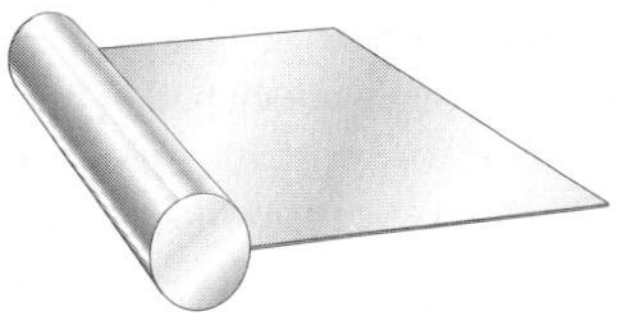
dough cutter/scraper

dough divider A stainless steel tool composed of several cutting wheels attached to metal bars on an expandable, accordion-like frame; used to cut several evenly sized strips of dough at once; also known as a Danish cutter or an expandable pastry cutter.

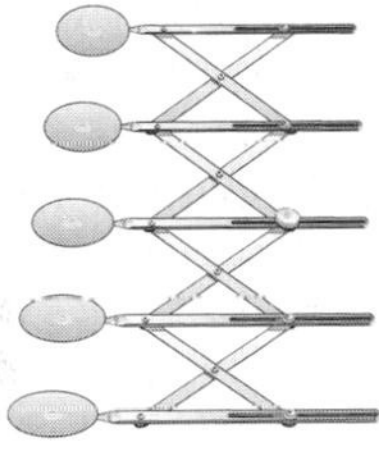
dough divider

doughnut; donut A small round or ring-shaped cake of sweet, leavened dough that is deep-fried, often coated with glaze, sugar or frosting and sometimes filled.

doughnut cutter A utensil made of two 1-in.-high rings; the smaller one is centered inside the larger one, and the utensil is held together with a U-shaped handle; sometimes the inner ring is detachable; it is used to cut doughnuts from dough.

doughnut peach A variety of squat, round peach with a concave center.

doughnut screen A screenlike or gridded utensil used to lift doughnuts from the cooking fat or to keep them under the fat's surface during cooking.

doughspur A scalloped wheel with a handle, used for decorating pastry; also known as a crimper/cutter.

draft beer; draught beer Unpasteurized beer sold in a 1-gallon or larger container; the beer is drawn off for service through a tap or spigot.

dragées (dra-zhay) 1. Tiny silver or gold balls made of sugar and used to decorate cookies and pastries. 2. Candied almonds with a hard sugar coating.

dragon's eye *See* longan.

Dragoon Punch A punch made of sparkling wine, ale, porter, amontillado sherry, brandy, sugar and lemon slices.

drain *v.* 1. To allow a liquid to withdraw from, pour out of or pour off an item, sometimes with the use of a strainer or colander. 2. To blot fat from a food. *n.* A device facilitating or channeling the withdrawing liquid.

draw 1. To eviscerate (i.e., remove the entrails from) game, poultry, fish or the like. 2. To clarify a mixture, as in drawn butter.

drawn A market form for fish in which the viscera is removed.

drawn butter *See* butter, clarified.

dredger A can-shaped container with a perforated top used for sprinkling dry condiments at the table or for sifting cocoa powder or confectioners' sugar onto pasteries or confections in the kitchen.

dredging Coating a food with flour or finely ground crumbs; usually done before sautéing or frying or as the first step of the standardized breading procedure.

dress 1. To prepare game, foul or fish for cooking by eviscerating, plucking, trussing, cleaning, scaling and so on. 2. To add a vinaigrette or other salad dressing to a salad. 3. To set and decorate a table or room for a festive occasion. 4. To add an unexpected touch to a dish or meal.

dressing 1. A sauce, usually cold, used on salads. 2. Another name for poultry stuffing. *See* stuffing.

dried beef *See* chipped beef.

dried fruit Fruit from which most of the moisture has been removed through a natural or artificial dehydration process (final moisture content is 15–20%); this concentrates sweetness and alters (usually strengthening) the flavor; dried fruit usually has four to five times the calories by weight as fresh fruit and can be stored for 1 year; eaten as a snack or used in baked goods, sweet dishes and savory dishes, either as is or reconstituted with a liquid.

dried milk; dry milk powder A product made from whole milk from which the water has been extracted, leaving the milkfat and milk solids in a dried, powdery form.

dried milk, nonfat; dry milk powder, nonfat A product made from skim milk from which the water has been extracted, leaving the milk solids in a dried, powdery form.

drink *v.* 1. To consume a liquid. 2. To consume an alcoholic beverage. *n.* 1. Any liquid that is swallowed to quench thirst, for nourishment or for enjoyment. 2. A beverage containing alcohol.

drink box The plastic or waxed-cardboard container in which a beverage, usually a juice product, is sold; also known as a juice box.

drinking water *See* water, drinking.

drippings The melted fat and juices released when meat is roasted; used as a flavoring, a sauce, a gravy base or a cooking medium; also known as pan drippings.

drizzle To pour a liquid in a very fine stream over a food or plate.

drop batter A batter that is too thick to pour; it is dropped from a spoon in portions or mounds.

drop cookie A cookie made by dropping spoonfuls of soft dough onto a baking sheet.

drop lid A lid that is smaller than the pot; it is placed directly on the food being cooked to help prevent delicate foods from losing their shape or falling apart.

drum Any of a large variety of fish named because of the drumming or croaking sounds they make during mating; found in temperate Atlantic and Pacific Ocean waters, principally off North America; they generally have a low fat content, a firm white flesh, and a market weight of 1–30 lb. (0.9–13.5 kg); significant varieties include the Atlantic croaker, black croaker, black drum, California corvina, hardhead, kingfish, redfish, sea trout, spot and white sea bass.

drum sieve A utensil used for puréeing foods; a mushroom-shaped pestle pushes food through the sieve's mesh, which is held in a wooden ring and can be fine or coarse and made from wire, horsehair or nylon; also known as a tamis.

drum sieve

drumstick 1. The lower portion of a poultry leg, including the bone, meat, fat layer and skin. 2. *See* winged bean.

drupelets Small, individual sections of a fruit, each with its own seed; as a group, they comprise the entire fruit (e.g., a raspberry).

drupes Members of the genus *Prunus,* many of which are native to China but now grow in temperate climates worldwide; these fruits (e.g., apricots and peaches) generally have a thin skin (called an epicarp), a soft, juicy, sweet flesh (called a mesocarp), and a single woody pit (called a stone); also known as stone fruits.

dry aging The process of storing meat under specific temperature and humidity conditions for up to 6 weeks to increase tenderness and flavor; it is the start of the natural decomposition process and can result in significant moisture loss. *See* wet aging.

dry beer A beer that is drier to the taste than most other beers and leaves little to no aftertaste; it is usually made by extracting as much sugar as possible from the mash during the cooking process and then fermenting it for an additional 7 days.

dry cured Meat or fish preserved by rubbing the food with salt (seasonings are often also applied); also known as salted.

dry curing A method of curing meat or fish by packing it in salt and seasonings.

dry-heat cooking methods Cooking methods, principally broiling, grilling, roasting or baking, sautéing, pan-frying and deep-frying, that use air or fat to transfer heat through conduction and convection; dry-heat cooking methods allow surface sugars to caramelize. *See* moist-heat cooking methods.

dry ice The proprietary name of a form of crystallized carbon dioxide used as a coolant; it passes directly from a solid to a gas at −109.3°F (−78.5°C), absorbing a great deal of energy.

drying A method of preserving foods by dramatically reducing their moisture content, either naturally or by mechanical means; drying usually changes the food's texture, appearance and flavor; also known as dehydrating.

dry mustard *See* mustard, ground.

dry quart A unit of volume measurement in the American and imperial systems; approximately 67.2 cu. in.

dry roasting A dry-heat cooking method that heats food by surrounding it with hot air, usually in a closed environment and with little or no moisture or fat added.

dry storage A storeroom or storage area where nonrefrigerated goods are stored; it can be an environment offering some control over temperature, humidity and/or light.

Dubarry, à la; du Barry, à la (doo-bah-ree) A French dish prepared or garnished with cauliflower.

Dubonnet; Dubonnet rouge (doo-bo-nay) A French aperitif made from red wine and flavored with quinine and bitter herbs, usually served over ice with a squeeze of lemon.

Dubonnet blanc A drier white version made from white wine.

duchesse, à la (duh-shees, ah lah) 1. A French preparation method in which various dishes are garnished, surrounded or served with duchess potatoes. 2. In pastry, refers to certain preparations containing almonds.

duchesse, sauce; duchess, sauce (duh-shees) A French compound sauce made from a béchamel finished with butter and garnished with julienne of pickled tongue and mushrooms.

duchess potatoes; pommes duchesse (duh-shees) A purée of cooked potatoes, butter and egg yolks, seasoned with salt, pepper and nutmeg; it can be eaten as is or used to prepare several classic potato dishes.

duck 1. One of the principal kinds of poultry recognized by the USDA; any of several varieties of domesticated web-footed swimming birds used for food; it has a high percentage of bone and fat to meat, a fatty skin, no light meat, and a rich flavor; significant varieties include the Long Island duck and muscovy duck. 2. African-American slang for an alcoholic beverage.

duck, broiler-fryer; duckling, broiler-fryer A duck slaughtered before it is 8 weeks old; it has a soft bill and windpipe, an average market weight of 3.5–5 lb. (1.5–1.8 kg) and very tender flesh.

duck, mature A duck slaughtered at 6 months or older; it has a hard bill and windpipe, an average market weight of 4–6 lb. (1.8–2.5 kg) and tough flesh.

duck, roaster; duckling, roaster A duck slaughtered before it is 16 weeks old; it has an easily dented windpipe, an average market weight of 4–6 lb. (1.8–2.5 kg) and a tender flesh with a rich flavor.

duck, wild Any of several varieties of duck that have not been domesticated; generally, their flesh is darker than that of a domesticated duck and has a denser texture and a nuttier, gamier flavor; significant varieties include the mallard, teal and widgeon.

duck à l'orange *See* caneton à l'orange.

duck classes Significant duck classes are the broiler-fryer duckling, roaster duckling and mature duck.

duck press A device used to extract the juices from a cooked duck carcass; used in French cuisine for preparations such as pressed duck.

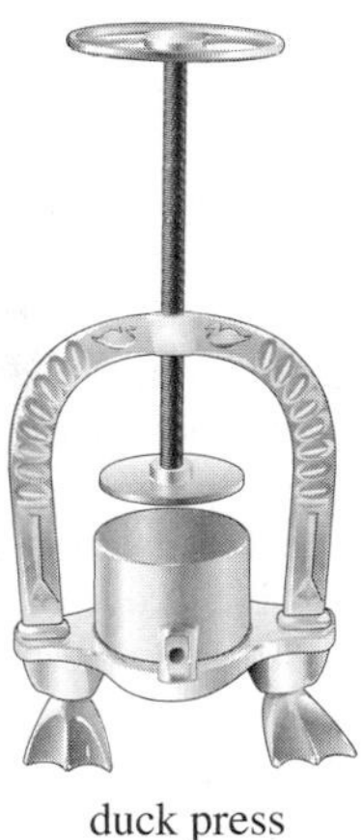

duck press

duck sauce A thick, sweet-and-sour Chinese sauce made from plums, apricots, sugar and seasonings; served with duck, pork or spareribs; also known as plum sauce.

dudi (doo-dee) A variety of edible gourds with a pale green hard shell that is sometimes slightly fluted, a creamy yellow-green flesh, and a mild flavor reminiscent of cucumbers; also known as bottle gourd, doodhi lokhi, lokhi and woo lo gwa.

duff 1. A steamed pudding containing fruit; traditionally boiled in a cloth bag. 2. Archaic English for dough.

du jour (doo zhoor) French for of the day and used to introduce a menu item that is a special for a particular day, such as a soup.

dulce (DOOL'th-eh) 1. Spanish for sweet. 2. A sweetening agent added to certain sherries at bottling. 3. A very sweet Spanish confection made with sugar and cream.

dulse A coarse, red seaweed found on the rocky coasts of the North Atlantic; it is dried and eaten as is or fried or toasted in Scottish cuisine; it has a salty, tangy flavor.

Dumas, Alexandre (Fr., 1802–1870) A prolific dramatist and novelist and the author of the *Grand Dictionaire de Cuisine,* which is considered to be more picturesque than accurate.

dump cake A cake made by combining and mixing all the ingredients in the pan in which the batter is baked.

dumpling 1. A dessert made by covering a piece of fruit or fruit mixture with sweet dough and baking. 2. A dessert consisting of a small mound of sweet dough poached in a sweet sauce, usually served with cream. 3. Any of a variety of small starchy products made from doughs or batters; they can be plain or filled with a savory mixture and simmered, steamed or fried.

dùn (dang) A Chinese cooking method in which foods are braised in their own juices (seasoned or plain) over high heat or slowly over low heat in a tightly covered casserole; also known as wei.

Dunant, sauce; Dunand, sauce (dew-nahn) A French compound sauce made from a hollandaise flavored with truffle essence and langoustine (or lobster) butter and finished with unsweetened whipped cream.

Dundee cake A Scottish fruitcake made with candied citrus, currants, almonds and spices; the top is completely covered with blanched almonds.

Dundee Marmalade The proprietary name of a dark, rich orange marmalade, originally made in Dundee, Scotland.

dungeness crab A variety of crab found in the Pacific Ocean from Alaska to Mexico; only males can be sold legally; it has a flattened body, a reddish-brown, spotted, hard shell, small, short legs, an average market width of 5.25–6.5 in. (14.3–16 cm), and a white flesh with a delicate, sweet flavor.

duodenum The first portion of the small intestine, extending from the stomach to the jejunum; the site where bile, pancreatic juice and intestinal juices mix with the acid and food that have just passed through the stomach (known as chyme).

durian (DOOR-ee-uhn) A very large fruit (*Durio zibethinus*) native to Southeast Asia; it has a brown-green spiked shell, a yellow-white flesh, a rich, custardlike texture, a slightly sweet flavor, and an overwhelmingly foul aroma; also known as civet fruit.

durum wheat A very hard wheat with high glutenin and gliadin contents; usually ground into semolina, which is used to make pasta.

dust *v.* To coat a food or utensil lightly with a powdery substance such as flour or confectioners' sugar. *n.* The smallest size of broken tea leaves or tea particles; generally used in tea bags. *See* orange fannings *and* fannings.

dusting flour Flour sprinkled on a workbench or other surface to prevent dough from sticking to the surface when being rolled or formed.

Dutch chile; Dutch pepper A long, slightly curved, tapering fresh chile with a bright red color, a thick flesh, and a sweet, hot flavor.

Dutch oven A large kettle, typically made of cast iron, with a tight-fitting lid; used for stewing or braising.

Dutch-processed cocoa *See* alkalized cocoa.

duxelles (dook-SEHL; deu-SEHL) A French garnish or stuffing mixture made from chopped mushrooms, onions and shallots sautéed in butter.

duxelles, sauce à la (dook-SEHL) A French compound sauce made from a demi-glaze flavored with puréed mushrooms, shallots and onions simmered in white wine; tomato purée is then added, and it is finished with butter and parsley.

dyspepsia coffee A mixture of equal parts ground coffee and cornmeal moistened with molasses, browned in the oven and used as one would use ground coffee; considered a cure for indigestion.

Earl Grey A mixture of Indian and Sri Lankan black teas, flavored with oil of bergamot; the beverage has a delicate flavor and is served without milk or lemon.

eau-de-vie (oh-duh-VEE) French for water of life and used to generally describe distilled spirits made from grape wine or fermented fruits.

Eccles cake An individual-sized, dome-shaped British cake made with puff pastry or short crust pastry and filled with currants, dried fruit, sugar and spices; traditionally served for afternoon tea.

éclair (ay-clahr) An oblong, finger-shaped French pastry made with choux dough, filled with pastry cream and topped with icing or glaze.

éclair paste A soft dough that produces hollow baked products with crisp exteriors (e.g., éclairs, cream puffs and savory products); also known as pâte à choux.

éclair plaque A flat rectangular metal pan with 12 1- × 3-in. shallow indentations used to form éclairs, ladyfingers and langues de chat.

écossaise, sauce (a-koss-saze) A French compound sauce made from a béchamel blended with hard-boiled egg yolks and garnished with julienne of hard-boiled eggs; also known as Scotch sauce.

edamame (eh-DAH-mah-meh) Japanese for fresh soybeans.

eel A variety of anadromous fish with an elongated, snakelike shape, pointed snout, and large mouth; colors range from gray to olive to black; generally, it has a fatty flesh with a firm texture and a rich, sweet flavor.

eel, American An eel found in rivers and bays along North America's northern East Coast; also known as a silver eel.

eel, European An eel found in European waters; it has a dark gray to olive skin and gelatinous flesh.

effervescence Small bubbles released in a liquid, creating a sparkling sensation on the palate.

e-fu Relatively flat, yellow-colored Chinese noodles made from eggs and wheat flour.

egg The ovoid, hard-shelled reproductive body produced by a bird, consisting principally of a yolk and albumen; it is a good source of protein, iron, sulfur and vitamins A, B, D and E, but also relatively high in cholesterol.

egg-and-bread-crumb A method of dipping food into beaten egg and then into bread crumbs before frying it to give it a crisp coating.

egg bread A yeast bread enriched with eggs, such as brioche or challah. *See* spoon bread.

egg coffee Coffee to which an egg had been added during preparation (boiling); the egg helps precipitate the coffee grounds.

egg cream A soda fountain concoction consisting of chocolate syrup, milk and seltzer; there is no egg or cream in an egg cream, but if properly made, a foamy, egg white–like head forms on top of the drink.

egg custard A dessert made with eggs, sugar and vanilla, usually baked in individual molds or cups.

egg foo yong; egg foo yung A Chinese–American dish of eggs mixed with garnishes (e.g., bean sprouts, scallions, water chestnuts, pork, chicken and/or shrimp) and pan-fried; usually served with a thick sauce.

egg grades A grading system developed by the U.S. Department of Agriculture (USDA) and based on a chicken egg's exterior and interior qualities, not size; grade AA is the highest, followed by grades A and B.

eggnog A rich beverage made of eggs, cream or milk, sugar, spices and spirits (usually rum, brandy or whiskey).

eggplant A member of the nightshade family (*Solanum melongena*), its fruit is used like a vegetable; the fruit has a dense, khaki-colored flesh with a rather bland but sometimes bitter flavor that absorbs other flavors during cooking; also known as a guinea squash.

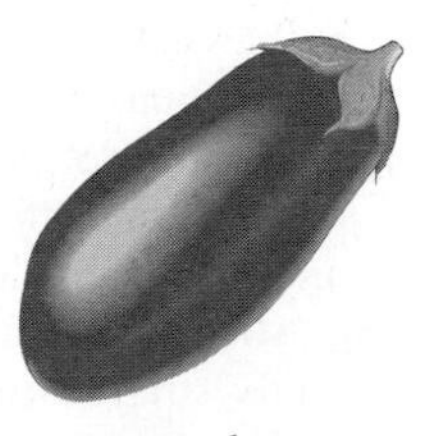

eggplant

eggplant, Asian Any of a variety of eggplants that are generally small with soft flesh and are either spherical or long and thin, with skin colors ranging from creamy white to yellow to deep purple; also known as a garden egg (especially in Africa), oriental eggplant and Japanese eggplant.

eggplant, Italian A variety of eggplant that looks like a miniature Western eggplant; also known as a baby eggplant.

eggplant, Western A variety of eggplant shaped like a large plump pear with a shiny lavender to purple-black skin.

eggplant caviar A dip or spread of thick, puréed roasted eggplant, onion, olive oil and seasonings.

egg poacher, immersible A small, footed utensil with a long handle and perforated oval bowl used to hold an egg while it is immersed in lightly vinegared simmering water.

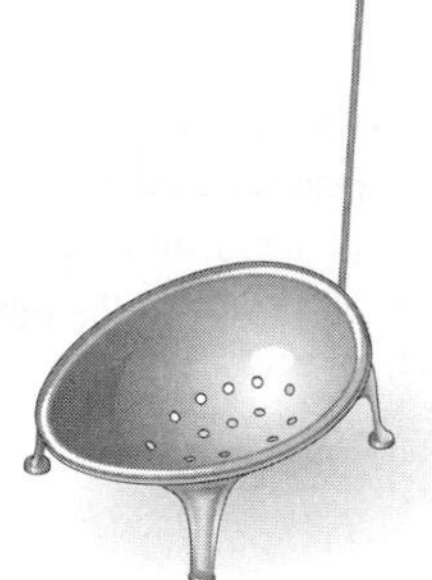
egg poacher

egg roll A deep-fried Chinese pastry made from a thin flour and water dough wrapper folded around a savory filling of vegetables and sometimes meat. *See* spring roll.

egg roll skins Wafer-thin sheets of dough made from flour, eggs and salt and used to wrap fillings; available in squares or circles and used in Chinese and other Asian cuisines. *See* lumpia wrappers.

eggs Benedict A brunch dish consisting of an English muffin topped with ham or Canadian bacon, a poached egg and hollandaise sauce.

egg separator A small cuplike vessel with a slot running midway around the perimeter; the egg white slides through the slot, leaving the yolk in the cup.

eggshell An egg's hard, brittle outer covering; composed of calcium carbonate, its color is determined by species and breed and has no effect on quality, flavor or nutrition.

eggs Hussarde (oo-sard) A brunch dish consisting of an English muffin topped with ham, a poached egg and a red wine sauce.

egg slicer A utensil with a hinged upper portion tautly strung with stainless steel wires and a base with an oval depression with slats that correspond to the wires; an egg is placed in the base and the top portion is brought down, cutting the egg into even slices.

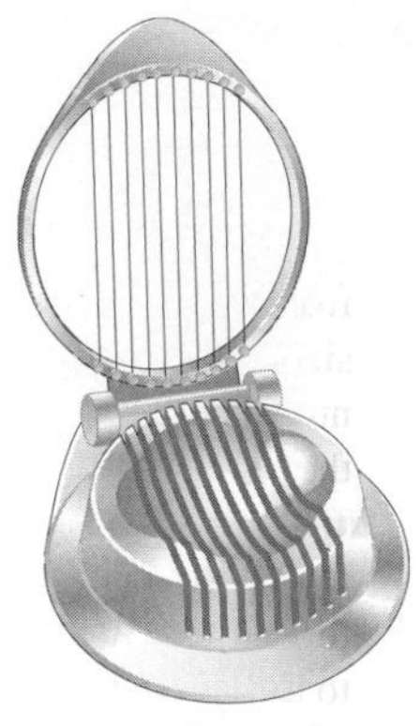
egg slicer

eggs Sardou (sahr-DOO) A brunch dish consisting of an artichoke heart topped with anchovy fillets, a poached egg and hollandaise sauce, sprinkled with chopped ham and garnished with a truffle slice.

egg substitute A liquid product usually made of egg white, food starch, corn oil, skim milk powder, artificial coloring and other additives; it does not contain cholesterol and is generally used like real eggs.

egg timer An hourglass that drains in 3 minutes, the time necessary to soft boil an egg.

egg wash A mixture of beaten eggs (whole eggs, yolks or whites) and a liquid, usually milk or water, used to coat doughs before baking to add sheen.

egg white *See* albumen.

egg yolk *See* yolk.

Egyptian rice A short-grain, round, semiglutinous rice used for puddings and stuffed vegetables in North African cuisines.

elastin A protein found in connective tissues, particularly ligaments and tendons, that does not dissolve when cooked; it often appears as the white or silver covering on meats known as silverskin.

elderberry The fruit of the elder tree (*Sambucus canadensis*), which grows throughout the Northern Hemisphere; it has a purple-black skin and a very tart flavor; used for preserves, pies and wine; the berry contains a poisonous alkaloid that is destroyed during cooking.

election cake A leavened fruitcake flavored with spices and sherry; traditionally baked to celebrate election day, especially in New England.

electronic scale A scale that weighs objects according to the degree an internal spring is depressed when the object is placed on a tray above the spring; the weight is displayed on a digital readout that can be finely calibrated in the metric, U.S., or imperial system; electronic scales are often used as portion scales. *See* spring scale.

elephant ear 1. A Midwest American deep-fried yeast dough confection; the dough is shaped into a large disk, deep-fried, and sprinkled with confectioners' sugar or cinnamon sugar while hot. 2. *See* palmier.

elephant garlic A member of the leek family; the very large cloves have a white outer layer, a pinkish-white interior and a mild garlicky flavor.

Emmental; Emmentaler (EM-en-tahler) A firm cheese made in Switzerland's Emme River Valley from cow's milk; it has an ivory-gold color, medium-sized to large eyes, a natural light brown rind and a nutty, sweet flavor; also commonly know as Swiss in the United States and Emmenthaler in France.

emu A large flightless bird native to Australia; smaller than an ostrich, its meat is similar: lean and purple, turning brown when cooked and with a flavor similar to that of lean beef. *See* ostrich *and* rhea.

emulsification The process by which generally unmixable liquids, such as oil and water, are forced into a uniform distribution.

emulsifier; emulsifying agent A type of food additive used to aid emulsification (i.e., to create a uniform dispersion) as well as improve and/or preserve homogeneity and stability in processed foods.

emulsion 1. A uniform mixture of two unmixable liquids, often temporary (e.g., oil in water). 2. A flavoring oil, such as those from citrus fruits, mixed into water with the aid of emulsifiers.

en bordure (ahn bohr-dur') French for in a border and used to describe food prepared with a border of duchesse potatoes.

enchilada (en-chuh-LAH-dah; en-chee-LAH-tha) A Mexican dish consisting of a soft corn tortilla wrapped around fish, shellfish, poultry, meat or cheese and topped with a tomato-based salsa, cheese, guacamole and/or sour cream; enchiladas are also served stacked, topped with a fried egg.

enchilada style A manner of garnishing Mexican foods such as burritos with a tomato-based salsa, cheese, guacamole and/or sour cream.

en cocotte (ahn koh-KOT) French for cooked in a casserole.

en croûte *See* croûte, en.

endive (ehn-deeve; ahn-deeve) 1. A plant (*Cichorium endivia*) with curly dark green leaves and a slightly bitter flavor; also known as curly endive and imprecisely known as chicory (especially in France and the United States). *See* chicory, escarole *and* frisée. 2. A term used imprecisely in the United States to describe Belgian endive.

end-to-end A meat-purchasing specification requesting that the butcher provide all the cuts made from the primal or subprimal.

English breakfast A hearty breakfast consisting of eggs, meat (sausage, bacon, ham and/or fish), broiled tomatoes, mushrooms, baked goods, jam, fruit or juice and tea or coffee.

English breakfast tea A blend of several Indian and Sri Lankan black teas; the robust beverage is more full flavored and richly colored than one made from any single black tea.

English chop A fabricated cut of the veal primal loin and the lamb primal loin; it contains part of the kidney; also known as a kidney chop.

English cucumber; English seedless cucumber A long, virtually seedless cucumber with a mild flavor and dark green skin; also known as a hothouse cucumber.

English monkey An American dish made from bread crumbs, milk, butter, tomatoes and cheese poured over crackers.

English muffin A thin, round bread made with yeast dough and baked on a griddle, usually split and toasted for service.

English sole A member of the flounder family found off the U.S. West Coast; it has a brownish-gray skin, a white flesh, a mild flavor, and an average market weight of 0.75 lb. (340 g); also known as lemon sole and California Dover sole.

English walnut A nut (*Juglans regia*) with a hard, wrinkled, tan shell enclosing two double-lobed sections; it has a sweet flavor and is used for snacking, in sweet and savory dishes, and for obtaining oil; also known as the Persian walnut. *See* black walnut.

English whole grain mustard A hot, pungent mustard made from whole mustard seeds, white wine, allspice and black pepper.

enoki; enokitake; enokidake (en-oh-kee; en-oh-kee-TAH-kee) A mushroom (*Flammulina velutipes*) native to Japan but now cultivated in the United States; grown in clumps, the mushroom has a long, thin stem, a tiny white or pale orange cap, a crunchy texture and a mild, almost fruity flavor; it is usually eaten raw or used as a garnish (heat tends to toughen it); also known as Christmas mushroom, velvet stem mushroom and winter mushroom.

enology; oenology (ee-NAHL-uh-jee) The art and science of wine production from harvest to vinification to bottling.

enrich To thicken or enhance a sauce by adding butter, egg yolks or cream just before service.

enriched Subject to U.S. Food and Drug Administration (FDA) regulations, a processed grain or cereal product such as bread, flour or rice to which specific vitamins (riboflavin, niacin and thiamine) and iron have been added during processing, either to replace nutrients lost during processing or to supplement naturally occurring ones. *See* fortified.

enriched bleached flour Flour that has been whitened to remove yellow pigments and fortified with vitamins and minerals.

enrobe To coat a candy or pastry with chocolate, sugar or fondant, usually by pouring rather than dipping.

entrails The internal organs contained within the trunk of an animal; includes the liver, intestines, stomach, kidneys and so on.

entrecôte (ahn-treh-KOHT) French for between the ribs and used to describe a French cut of the beef carcass that is the flesh between the 9th and 11th ribs; it is the classic French steak.

entrée (ahng-tray) 1. In the United States, the main dish of a meal and often consisting of meat, poultry, fish or shellfish accompanied by a starch and/or vegetable. 2. In many European countries, the first course.

entremetier (ehm-tray-mee-tee-ay) At a food services operation following the brigade system, the person responsible for the combined functions of the potager and legumier.

entremets (ehm-tray-mais) The course served after the roast at a classic cuisine-style banquet; usually composed of vegetables, fruits, fritters or sweets.

epazote (eh-pah-soh-teh) An herb (*Chenopodium ambrosiodes*) native to the Americas with a kerosene-like aroma and a wild, strong flavor; it is used fresh in Mexican and American Southwestern cuisines and used dried for a beverage; also known as stinkweed and wormweed.

epi (ay-pee) 1. French for an ear of wheat. 2. A yeast dough baguette that is shaped to resemble a stalk of wheat.

épices fines (ay-pis feen) French for fine spices and used to describe a spice and herb blend that generally includes white pepper, allspice, mace, nutmeg, rosemary, sage, bay leaves, cloves, cinnamon and marjoram.

epicure (EHP-ih-kyoor) One who cultivates the knowledge and appreciation of fine foods and wines.

Epicurus A Greek philosopher who espoused the pursuit of happiness (or the avoidance of pain and disturbance); this philosophy has often been interpreted as praising an indulgence in luxury and sensual pleasures.

Époisses (ay-pwass) A soft cheese made in Burgundy, France, from cow's milk; it has a smooth, creamy interior, a pleasant flavor and a slightly orange crust that is washed with the local white wine or marc.

ersatz food A substitute food; a food product created to resemble or substitute for a natural food (e.g., a hamburger made from textured plant protein).

escallop (eh-SKAH-laph) To bake foods (e.g., potatoes or fish) with a sauce topped with bread crumbs.

escalope (eh-SKAL-oph) A French term for a thin scallop of meat.

escargot de Bourgogne (ays-skahr-go day boor-gone-yay) A land snail from France's Burgundy region; it has a dull, yellowish-brown shell, a market length of 1.75 in. (4.1 cm), and a mottled grayish-tan flesh with a rich flavor and firm, tender texture; also known as the Burgundy snail.

escargot petit-gris (ays-skahr-go peh-te-GREE) A snail found in southern Europe; it has a yellow-flecked white shell, an average market length of less than 1 in. (2.5 cm), and a brownish-gray flesh with a more delicate flavor than that of the larger escargot de Bourgogne.

escargots bourguignonne (eays-skahr-go boorg-ee-nyun) A French dish of snails served hot in their shells or ceramic cups and cooked in butter flavored with shallots, garlic and parsley.

escarole (es-kah-roll) An endive with broader, paler, less curly leaves and a less bitter flavor; also known as Batavian endive.

Escherichia coli (E. coli) A species of bacteria that causes acute diarrheal disease; the bacteria are transmitted by infected food handlers and through ingestion of contaminated foods (especially milk) or water.

Escoffier, Auguste (Fr., 1846–1935) A chef known for refining and defining French cuisine and dining during the late 19th century; he operated dining rooms for the finest hotels in Europe, including the Savoy and the Carlton in London and the Place Vendôme in Paris, and authored several culinary texts, including *Ma Cuisine* (1934) and a treatise for professional chefs, *Le Guide Culinaire* (1903).

espagnole, à l' A French term for prepared in the Spanish style, usually with tomatoes, onion, garlic and sweet peppers.

espagnole, mayonnaise à l' (ess-spah-noyl) A French mayonnaise sauce flavored with garlic, mustard and paprika and garnished with ham; also known as Spanish mayonnaise.

espagnole, sauce (ess-spah-noyl) A French leading sauce made of brown stock, mirepoix and tomatoes and thickened by brown roux; it is often used to produce a demi-glaze; also known as brown sauce and Spanish sauce.

espresso (ess-PRESS-o) 1. An Italian coffee-brewing method in which hot water is forced through finely ground and packed coffee (usually very dark roasted beans) under high pressure; the resulting beverage is thick, strong, rich and smooth, not bitter or acidic. 2. The resulting beverage; it is usually served in a small cup or used as an ingredient in other coffee drinks.

espresso macchiatto (ess-PRESS-o mock-e-AH-toe) An Italian beverage of espresso marked with a dollop of steamed milk; usually served in a small cup.

espresso maker An hourglass-shaped assemblage used to make espresso; the base is filled with water and the center basket with finely ground coffee; heat forces the steam and boiling water through a central vent and across the coffee grounds; the finished espresso is then received in the top container.

espresso maker

essence 1. A concentrated liquid usually made from an herb, spice or flower and used as a flavoring or aromatic. 2. French for the concentrated stock or extract of a flavorful ingredient (e.g., mushroom, truffle, celery or leek); it can be used as a sauce (sometimes either finished with butter or emulsified as a vinaigrette) or as a flavoring ingredient for classic sauces.

essential amino acids Amino acids that cannot be synthesized in the body at all or in amounts sufficient to maintain health and must be supplied by the diet; generally recognized as essential for a normal adult are histidine, isoleucine, leucine, lysine, methionine, cysteine, phenylalanine, tyrosine, threonine, tryptophan and valine; arginine is considered essential for infants and children but not adults, and some nutritionists consider tyrosine and cysteine nonessential. *See* complete protein.

essential nutrients Nutrients such as minerals, many vitamins and certain amino acids the body cannot synthesize at all or in amounts sufficient to meet its needs; necessary for growth and health, they must be obtained through the diet.

essential oils The volatile oils that give plants their distinctive fragrances; these oils, usually composed of esters, can be extracted or distilled from some flowers, leaves, seeds, resins or roots and used as aromatics and flavorings in cooking (e.g., peppermint oil and citrus oil) and the production of alcoholic beverages.

estouffade (ehs-toh-fhad) 1. A French stew in which the pieces of meat are first browned in fat before moistening, usually with white or red wine. 2. A concentrated brown stock made with both beef and veal; the term is rarely used in this sense in modern kitchens.

estragon, sauce à l' (ess-trah-GON, ah-l') A French compound sauce made from a demi-glaze flavored with shallots and tarragon and garnished with tarragon; also known as tarragon sauce.

étamine (eh-tay-meen) A French cloth used for straining stocks, sauces and the like.

ethnic cuisine Generally, the cuisine of a group of people having a common cultural heritage, as opposed to the cuisine of a group of people bound together by geographical or political factors.

ethyl alcohol (ETH-OHL) A colorless, volatile, flammable, water-miscible liquid with an etherlike aroma and a burning flavor produced by the yeast fermentation of certain carbohydrates; the intoxicating component of alcoholic beverages; also known as alcohol, fermentation alcohol, grain alcohol, pure alcohol, spirits and spirits of wine.

ethylene gas A colorless, odorless hydrocarbon gas naturally emitted from fruits and fruit-vegetables; it encourages ripening.

étouffée (eh-too-fay) French for smothered and used to describe a stewed dish cooked with little or no liquid in a tightly closed pot; usually served over white rice.

étuver; étouffer (eh-too-vay) A French term describing how a food is to be covered while it is being cooked; in most recipes, the term implies that the food is to be cooked in a very small amount of liquid, but it could also mean that the food is to be cooked in a covered container. *See* casserole braising.

eulachon A variety of smelt found in the Pacific Ocean from Alaska to California; it has a silvery body with olive green markings, an average market length of 12 in. (30.4 cm), a very high fat content, and a rich flavor; a significant market variety is the Columbia River smelt; also known as candlefish or candlelight fish (Native Americans used dried smelts with a bark wick as a source of light).

evaporated milk *See* milk, evaporated.

evaporation The process by which heated water molecules move faster and faster until the water turns to gas (steam) and vaporizes; evaporation is responsible for the drying of foods during cooking.

executive chef At a large food services operation, the person responsible for coordinating and directing kitchen activities, developing menu items, educating dining room staff, purchasing food and equipment and so on.

expiration date A date stamped by a manufacturer, distributor or retailer on a food product's label indicating the last date on which the consumer should use it; the date is usually preceded by the phrase "use by."

Explorateur (ex-ploh-rah-tuhr) A triple cream cheese made in La Tretoire, France, from cow's milk; it contains 75% milkfat and has a bloomy white rind, an ivory interior and a delicate, rich flavor.

extracts 1. Concentrated mixtures of ethyl alcohol and flavoring oils such as vanilla, lemon and almond. 2. Concentrated flavors obtained by distilling, steeping and/or pressing foods. 3. Sugars derived from malt during the mashing process in brewing and distillation. 4. Nonvolatile and nonsoluble substances in wine such as acids, tannins and pigments; to the taster, they indicate the presence of elements that add flavor and character.

extrusion The process of forcing dough (e.g., pasta) through perforated plates to create various shapes.

eye round; eye of round A subprimal cut of the beef primal round; it is not attached to the leg bone and is flavorful and somewhat tough; it is sometimes combined with the bottom round for a roast or fabricated into steaks.

Ezekiel mix A mixture of flours and grains based on a biblical formula found in Ezekiel 4:9; it usually contains wheat flour, barley, spelt, millet and ground lentils.

fabricate To cut a large item into smaller portions; it often refers to the butchering of meat, poultry or fish.

fabricated product A food item after trimming, boning, portioning and so on.

faire tomber à glace (fare thom-bay ah glass) French for the process of reducing a liquid, such as a stock or a sauce, until the sugars caramelize and separate from any fat contained in the liquid.

fairy bread A British snack consisting of slices of fresh bread spread with butter and coated with hundreds and thousands.

fairy ring mushroom A mushroom (*Marasimus oreades*) that grows in a ring on areas of short-cropped grass, especially in Europe, and has a mild flavor; with a slender stem and a round, flat cap, it appears similar to certain poisonous mushrooms; also known as faux mousseron.

fait tout (fay too) French for do all and used to describe a flare-sided saucepan.

fajitas (fah-HEE-tuhs) A Mexican–American dish consisting of strips of skirt steak marinated in lime juice, oil, garlic and red pepper, and then grilled; the diner wraps the meat in a flour tortilla and garnishes it with items such as grilled onions and peppers, guacamole, pico de gallo, refried beans, sour cream and salsa; chicken, pork, fish and shellfish (usually shrimp) can be substituted.

falafel; felafel (feh-LAH-fehl) Middle Eastern deep-fried balls of highly spiced, ground chickpeas; usually served in pita bread with a yogurt sauce or tahini.

falernum (fah-LEHR-noom) A flavoring syrup made from a simple syrup, lime juice, almonds, ginger and spices; used as a sweetener and flavoring ingredient for rum drinks.

fancy 1. Fish that has been frozen previously. 2. A quality grade of fruits, especially canned or frozen.

fannings Moderate-sized particles of broken tea leaves. *See* orange fannings *and* dust.

fan shell scallop A variety of scallop found in the Mediterranean Sea; it has a white shell with a diameter of 4–5 in. (10.1–12.7 cm) and a tender, sweet, white meat.

farce (faahrs) French for stuffing and used to describe a forcemeat.

farci (far-SEE) 1. French for stuffed. 2. A French dish of cabbage stuffed with sausage meat, wrapped in cheesecloth and cooked in stock.

farfel (FAHR-fuhl) 1. Fresh egg noodle dough that is grated or minced and used in soups; also known as egg barley. 2. In Jewish cuisine, a food that is broken into small pieces (e.g., dried noodles). 3. A Jewish dish of small pieces or balls of lokshen dough; they are cooked like rice or noodles, or toasted.

farina (fah-REE-nah) 1. A fine flour made from a grain, roots or nuts; used chiefly for puddings or as a breakfast cereal. 2. A porridge made from such flour. 3. The purified middlings of hard wheat other than durum. 4. A fine wheat flour used like arrowroot or semolina. 5. A fine powder made from potatoes and used as a thickener. 6. Italian for flour.

farinaceous (fah-ree-nank-chay-ooz) A food consisting of or made from flour or meal.

Farmer, Fannie (Am., 1857–1915) The author of *The Boston Cooking-School Cookbook* (1896), which later became known as *The Fannie Farmer Cookbook,* and culinary arts instructor; as an educator and author she stressed the accurate use of measurements and strived for a uniformity of results, thereby making cooking a science rather than a hit-or-miss affair.

farmer cheese; farmer's cheese 1. An American cottage cheese–style cheese made from whole or partly skimmed cow's milk; generally eaten fresh, it has a soft texture (but is firm enough to slice or crumble), a milky white appearance and a slightly tangy flavor; also known as pressed cheese. 2. A term used imprecisely to describe a basic, fresh cheese such as cottage cheese.

Fasnacht; Fastnacht (FAAS-nakht) A Pennsylvania German diamond-shaped potato yeast dough that is deep-fried in pork fat; traditionally served with jam or molasses for breakfast on Shrove Tuesday.

fast food 1. Food dispensed quickly at a restaurant generally offering a limited menu of inexpensive items, many of which may not be particularly nutritious; the food can be eaten on premises, taken out or sometimes delivered. 2. Precooked or other processed food requiring minimal preparation at home. 3. *See* slow food.

fatback The layer of fat that runs along a hog's back just below the skin and above the eye muscle; usually available unsmoked and unsalted; used for lard and lardons and to prepare charcuterie items. *See* salt pork.

fat rascal A large scone, about 6 in. in diameter, made with candied citrus peel, candied cherries, spices and almonds and served split in half and buttered; a specialty of Yorkshire, England.

fats 1. A general term used to describe a class of organic nutrients that includes the lipid family of compounds: triglycerides (fats and oils), phospholipids and sterols. 2. Nutrients composed of glycerol and 3 units of fatty acid; they occur naturally in animals and some plants and are used principally in the body to store energy from food eaten in excess of need (1 g of fat delivers 2.25 times the calories delivered by 1 g of carbohydrates or protein). 3. Lipids that are solid at room temperature. 4. A general term for butter, lard, shortening, oil and margarine used as cooking media or ingredients.

fattoush (fah-TOOSH) A Middle Eastern meza salad made with toasted bread, lettuce, spinach, scallions, cucumbers, tomatoes and bell peppers flavored with parsley and mint and dressed with lemon juice, olive oil, garlic and sumac.

faux filet (foh fee-LAY) A French cut of the beef carcass; it is the eye of sirloin; also known as contre filet.

fava bean (FAH-vuh) A large, flat, kidney-shaped bean (*Vicia faba*) with a tough pale green skin when fresh that turns brown when dried; the skin is usually removed before cooking; the interior is light green when fresh and cream colored when dried; available fresh, dried or canned and used in Mediterranean and Middle Eastern cuisines; also known as a broad bean.

feijoa (fay-YOH-ah; fay-JOH-ah) A small- to medium-sized fruit (genus *Psidium*) native to South America; it has an ovoid shape, a thin, green, bloom-covered skin sometimes blushed with red, a cream-colored, somewhat grainy flesh encasing a jellylike center with many tiny seeds, and a flavor reminiscent of pineapple and strawberry; also known as a guavasteen and pineapple guava.

feijoada (fay-JOH-dah) A Brazilian stew of smoked meats (especially pork), dried beef, chorizo and/or tongue with black beans and flavored with onions, garlic, tomatoes, chiles, oranges and herbs; it is served with rice and a hot pepper sauce with lime.

Felix, sauce A French compound sauce made from a demi-glaze flavored with lobster butter and finished with lemon juice.

fell The tough, thin membrane covering a carcass; it is just below the hide and consists of intermingled connective and fatty tissues.

fennel, common A perennial plant (*Foeniculum vulgare*) with feathery foliage and tiny flowers; the plant's oval, green-brown seeds have prominent ridges, short, hairlike fibers and a weak, aniselike flavor and aroma and are available whole and ground; used in baked goods and savory dishes in Italian and central European cuisines and to flavor alcoholic beverages.

fennel, Florence A perennial plant (*Foeniculum vulgare* var. *dulce*) with a broad, bulbous root, white to pale green celery-like stalks and bright green, feathery foliage; it has a flavor similar to but sweeter and more delicate than that of anise; the root is cooked like a vegetable, the foliage is used as a garnish or flavor enhancer and the stalks are used in salads or cooked; also known as finocchio and sweet fennel and known imprecisely as sweet anise.

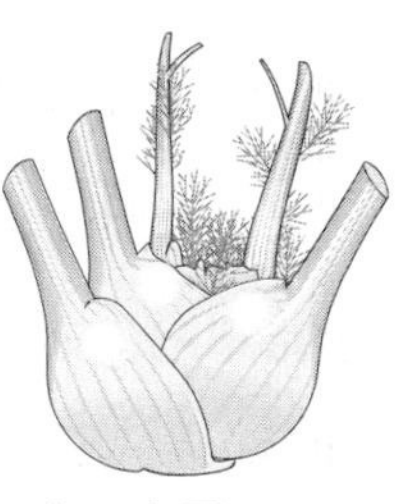

fennel, Florence

fenugreek (FEHN-yoo-greek) A spice that is the seed of an aromatic plant of the pea family (*Trigonella foenum-gracum*) native to the Mediterranean region; the pebble-shaped seeds have a pale orange color and a bittersweet, burned-sugar flavor and aftertaste; the seeds are available whole and ground and are used in Indian and Middle Eastern cuisines.

fermentation 1. The process by which yeast converts sugars to alcohol and carbon dioxide; this process is fundamental to the making of leavened breads, beers, wines and spirits. 2. The period that yeast bread dough is left to rise. 3. The process of souring milk with certain bacteria to create a specific dairy product (e.g., yogurt and sour cream).

fermented black beans Small black soybeans preserved in salt; they have a very salty, pungent flavor and are used in Chinese cuisines as a flavoring for meat and fish dishes; also known as Chinese black beans and salty black beans.

fermière, à la (fayr-myayr, ah lah) 1. A French garnish for poultry and braised meats consisting of carrots, turnips, onions, potatoes and celery braised in butter and the meat's natural juices. 2. A French garnish consisting of small half-moon slices of carrots, celeriac, turnips and leeks simmered in butter and mixed with either a veal velouté or a white wine sauce.

Feta (FEH-tah) 1. A soft Greek cheese made from ewe's milk (or occasionally goat's milk) and pickled in brine; it has a white color, a crumbly texture, and a salty, sour, tangy flavor. 2. A soft, white, flaky American feta-style cheese made from cow's milk and stored in brine.

fettuccine Alfredo (feht-tuh-CHEE-nee al-FRAY-doh) An Italian dish of fettuccine mixed with a rich sauce of butter, cream and Parmesan and sprinkled with black pepper.

feu doux (fer doo) French for gentle heat and used to describe an enameled cast-iron oval pot with a deeply indented lid used for braising and available in capacities of 2.5–6 qt.; the lid's large encircling groove once held hot coals but now is used for iced water to condense internal steam quickly, causing the droplets to drip into the pot; also known as doufeu.

feuilletage (fuh-yuh-TAHZH) French for flaky and used to describe puff pastry or the process of making puff pastry. *See* mille-feuille *and* puff pastry.

few A food-labeling term approved by the U.S. Food and Drug Administration (FDA) to describe a food that can be eaten frequently without exceeding dietary guidelines for fat, saturated fat, cholesterol, sodium or calories.

fewer A food-labeling term approved by the U.S. Food and Drug Administration (FDA) to describe a nutritionally altered food that contains at least 25% fewer calories than the regular or reference (i.e., FDA standard) food.

fiasco (vee-ASK-co) The hand-blown, round-bottomed bottle with a woven straw covering associated with Chianti; these bottles are now rarely used because of their expense.

fiasco

fiber A slender, threadlike structure or cell that combines with others to form animal tissues (such as muscles) or plant tissues (such as membranes). *See* dietary fiber.

ficelle (feh-cell) French for string and used to describe a very long, thin loaf of French bread with a high ratio of crust to interior.

ficelle, à la (feh-cell, ah lah) A French preparation method for a filet of beef; it is bound with twine, browned in the oven, and boiled in consommé.

fiddlehead fern An edible fern (*Pteridium aquilinium*); the young, tightly coiled, deep green fronds have a flavor reminiscent of asparagus and green beans; cooked like a vegetable or used in a salad; also known as bracken and ostrich fern.

fiddler A small channel catfish; it has an average weight of 1 lb. (450 g).

field pea A variety of pea, either green or yellow, cultivated to be dried and not to require soaking before it is cooked; it usually splits into two small hemispherical disks along a natural seam; also known as a split pea.

field salad *See* mâche.

FIFO First in–first out; a system for using and valuing inventory, particularly perishable and semiperishable goods, in which the items are used in the order of their receipt; that is, items that are received first are used before subsequently received ones; also known as rotating stock.

fig A variety of oblong or pear-shaped fruits (*Ficus carica*) that grow in warm climates; generally, they have a thick, soft skin that is green, yellow, orange or purple, a tannish-purple flesh, a sweet flavor, and many tiny edible seeds; available fresh or dried.

figaro, sauce (fee-gah-roh) A French compound sauce made from a hollandaise flavored with tomato purée and parsley; usually served with fish or poultry.

figgy pudding An English dish made of dried figs stewed in wine and often served with a fish course during Lent.

filbert The nut of the cultivated hazel tree (genus *Corylus*); shaped like a smooth brown marble, it is a bit larger and less flavorful than its wild cousin, the hazelnut, and its bitter skin should be removed before using; a similar type of cultivated hazel tree nut is known in England as a cob, cobnut or Kentish cob. *See* hazelnut.

filé powder (fih-LAY; FEE-lay) The ground leaves of the sassafras tree; used in Cajun and Creole cuisines as a seasoning and thickener.

filet (fee-lay) *v.* To fabricate a boneless cut of meat. *n.* 1. A general term for a boneless cut of meat, usually one that is tender and flavorful; sometimes imprecisely spelled fillet. See fillet. 2. A French cut of the lamb carcass; it is the entire loin and is usually fabricated into chops known as côte de filet or côtelettes dans le filet. 3. A French cut of the pork carcass; it is cut from the center of the loin and has the kidney attached.

filet de boeuf rôti (fee-lay duh buff roe-TEE) French for roast filet of beef.

filet de boeuf Wellington (fee-lay duh buff well-eng-tohn) A dish of a roasted filet of beef coated with foie gras or duxelles and wrapped in pastry and baked.

filet mignon (fee-lay me-NYON) A fabricated cut of the short end of the tenderloin found in the beef short loin and sirloin primals; it is cut from the center of the tenderloin and is lean, very tender, flavorful and larger than a tournedo; also known as a beef filet.

fillet (FILL-eh) *v.* To fabricate a boneless cut of fish. *n.* The side of a fish removed intact, boneless or semiboneless, with or without skin. *See* filet.

filleting knife A knife used to bone fish or thinly slice produce; its flexible blade is 6–7 in. long.

filleting knife

filo (PHE-lo) *See* phyllo.

filter method A coffee-brewing method; finely ground coffee is measured into a paper filter fitted into a plastic or china cone sitting on a pot or mug, hot water is slowly poured over the grounds, and the coffee drips into the receptacle, which can be kept warm over a low flame or on a hot plate.

financier (fee-nahng-syehr) A French sponge cake made with ground almonds; traditionally rectangular and coated with sliced almonds; served as a petit four or individual pastry or used as part of a more elaborate pastry.

financière, sauce (fin-ahn-see-AIR) A French compound sauce made from a demi-glaze flavored with chicken stock, truffle essence and Sauternes or Madeira and garnished with truffles and mushrooms.

fines herbes (FEENZ erb) A seasoning blend used in French cuisine; it typically includes chervil, chives, parsley, tarragon and other herbs.

finish *v.* 1. To add butter to a sauce nearing completion to impart shine, flavor and richness. 2. To brown a food (often, one with bread crumbs, grated cheese or other topping) under an overhead heat source. 3. To complete the cooking of a food begun on the stove top by putting it in the oven. *n.* 1. The proportion of fat to lean meat on a carcass or in a particular cut; a basis for determining yield and quality.

finnan haddie; finnan haddock (FIHN-uhn HAD-ee) A partially boned, lightly salted, smoked haddock; named after the Scottish fishing village of Findon.

Finnoise, sauce; Finnish sauce (fenn-wahz) A French compound sauce made from a chicken velouté seasoned with paprika and garnished with a julienne of green peppers and herbs.

firm-ball stage A test for the density of sugar syrup: the point at which a drop of boiling sugar will form a firm but pliable ball when dropped in cold water; equivalent to approximately 248°F (120°C) on a candy thermometer.

fish Any of thousands of species of aquatic vertebrates with fins for swimming and gills for breathing found in salt-water and freshwater worldwide; most are edible; fish are classified by bone structure as flatfish or round fish. *See* flatfish, round fish *and* shellfish.

Fisher, M. F. K. (Am., 1908–1992) One of America's greatest food writers and the author of *Serve It Forth, Consider the Oyster, How to Cook a Wolf, The Gastronomical Me* and *An Alphabet for Gourmets,* as well as the translation of *The Physiology of Taste,* or *Meditations on Transcendental Gastronomy,* by Jean Anthelme Brillat-Savarin.

Fish House Punch A punch made of brandy, peach liqueur, rum, sugar, lemon juice and water.

fish knife A knife with a short, very broad, saber-shaped blade with a notch near the handle (for removing bones) and a slightly angled top edge; used for eating fish.

fish paste A thick, dark brown paste made from mashed, dried fish and/or shellfish; sometimes chiles are added; used as a flavoring, it has a very salty flavor and a strong, pungent aroma.

fish poacher A long, narrow, metal pan with a perforated rack used to raise and lower the fish in one piece.

fish poacher

fish quality grades U.S. Department of Commerce (USDC) grades for common fish packed under federal inspection; each species has its own grading criteria.

fish sauce A thin, dark brown liquid made from anchovy extract and salt; used as a flavoring, it has a very salty flavor and a strong, pungent aroma.

fish shears A pair of strong scissors with straight blades (one is thin, tapering and serrated, and the other is broad and has a rounded point); used to cut through fish fins, flesh and bones. *See* kitchen shears.

fish shears

five-spice powder *See* Chinese five-spice powder.

fixed price *See* table d'hôte.

flageolet (fla-zhoh-LAY) A small kidney-shaped bean cultivated in France; it has a pale green to creamy white color, is generally available dried or canned and is used as an accompaniment to lamb.

flake *v.* To separate pieces of food (e.g., cooked fish) into small slivers. *n.* A small sliver.

flamande, à la (flamanhd, ah lah) 1. A French term indicating that beer is an ingredient in the dish. 2. A French preparation method associated with Belgian cuisine; the dishes are characterized by a garnish of stuffed braised balls of green cabbage, glazed carrots and turnips, potatoes and sometimes diced salt pork and slices of sausages.

flamande, sauce; Flemish sauce (flamanhd) A French compound sauce made from a hollandaise seasoned with dry mustard and garnished with parsley.

flambé (flahm-bay) Foods served flaming; the flame is produced by igniting the brandy, rum or other alcoholic beverage poured on or incorporated into the item; also known as flamed.

flambé trolley A small table on casters fitted with one or two burners (butane or spirit) and used in restaurants for flaming dishes table side. *See* guéridon.

flamed The American word for flambé.

flame seedless grapes A popular variety of red-skinned table grapes; the fruit have a crisp flesh and a sweet flavor; also known as red flame seedless grapes.

flan (flahn) 1. A shallow, open-faced French tart, usually filled with fruit or custard. 2. A custard baked over a layer of caramelized sugar and inverted for service. 3. Spanish for crème caramel.

flan de queso (flahn dee quee-soh) A Peruvian custard dessert made of cottage cheese, condensed milk, water and eggs, served with fresh or stewed fruit.

flank A primal section of the beef carcass; located beneath the loin and behind the short plate, it contains no bones, and the meat is flavorful but tough, with a good deal of fat and connective tissue; it produces fabricated cuts such as flank steak, London broil, the hanging tenderloin and ground beef.

flank steak A fabricated cut of the beef primal flank; this tough, somewhat stringy cut is very flavorful.

flan ring A bottomless metal mold with straight sides; it is used for shaping pastry shells and tarts and is available in several shapes and sizes.

flan ring

flan tin A tart pan with a removable bottom.

flapjack Slang for pancake.

flash frozen Food that has been frozen very rapidly using metal plates, extremely low temperatures or chemical solutions.

flatbread; flat bread A category of thin breads that may or may not be leavened, with textures ranging from chewy to crisp; these products tend to be more common in regional or ethnic cuisines (e.g., tortilla, pita bread, naan and focaccia).

flatbrød (FLAHT-brur) Scandinavian cracker breads; they are very thin and crisp and usually made with rye, barley and/or wheat flour.

flatfish A general category of fish characterized by asymmetrical, compressed bodies with both eyes on top of the heads and a dark top skin; they swim in a horizontal position and are generally found in deeper ocean waters (e.g., flounder, halibut and turbot). *See* round fish.

flat icing A simple icing made of water, confectioners' sugar and corn syrup and usually flavored with vanilla or lemon; it is white and glossy and is usually used as a glaze on baked goods such as Danish pastries; also known as plain water icing.

flatiron A subprimal cut of the beef primal chuck; it is a boneless roast divided in the middle.

flat-leaf parsley *See* Italian parsley.

flat slicing A cutting method in which the knife blade is held parallel to the ingredient (and the cutting surface) and the food is sliced horizontally from right to left; generally used with soft foods such as tofu and cold jellied meats.

flat top A cooking surface that is a single steel plate; it supplies even but less intensive heat than an open burner but is able to support heavier weights and makes a larger surface available for cooking. *See* griddle.

flatware Eating utensils such as forks, knives and spoons.

flat whisk A long whisk used for quickly incorporating flour into melted butter; its looped wires lay in near parallel planes; also known as a roux whisk.

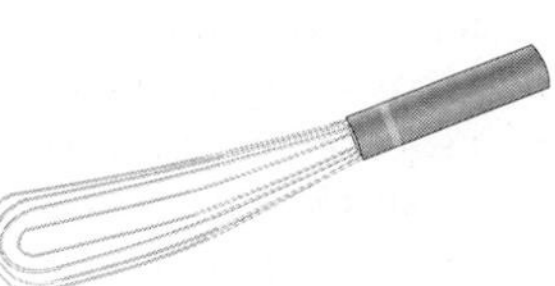
flat whisk

flauta (FLAUW-tah) A Mexican dish consisting of a corn tortilla rolled around a savory filling and deep-fried; often garnished with guacamole, sour cream and salsa.

flavonoids A group of more than 200 naturally occurring compounds (pigments) found in produce such as citrus, leafy vegetables (e.g., red cabbage), red onions, red beets and soybeans; they may have antioxidant capabilities.

flavor *v.* To add seasonings or other ingredients to a food or beverage to improve, change or add to the taste. *n.* 1. The distinctive taste of a food or beverage. 2. A quality of something that affects the sense of taste.

flavoring An item that adds a new flavor to a food and alters its natural flavors; flavorings include herbs, spices, vinegars and other condiments.

flax seeds The seeds of the flax plant (*Linum usitatissium*), an annual herb; the seeds are used for linseed oil and as a flavoring and garnish in Asian cuisines.

flead The inner membrane of a pig's stomach; it is a fine, thin lining full of pieces of pure lard; lard must be purified if taken from areas other than the flead.

fleischig (fly-schigg) Yiddish for meat, foods made of meat and meat products; one of the three categories of food under Jewish dietary laws (kosher). *See* kosher, milchig *and* pareve.

flesh 1. When referring to fruits and vegetables, it is typically the edible area under the skin or other outer covering; also known as the pulp. 2. The muscles, fat and related tissues of an animal.

fleur de sel de Guerande Very rare and expensive sea salt from French salt basins just south of Brittany; its grey, mineral-laden crystals have a complex flavor, so it is used mainly as a garnish.

fleuron (flew-rawng) A half-moon shape of puff pastry used to garnish entrées.

flitch 1. A side of a hog, salted and cured. 2. A strip or steak cut from a fish, especially halibut.

floating island A dessert consisting of mounds of poached meringue floating in vanilla custard sauce; also known as oeufs à la neige and snow eggs.

florentine (FLOOR-en-teen) A very thin, crisp cookie or candy made with honey, sugar, nuts and candied fruit; the underside of the cooled confection is usually coated with chocolate.

florentine, à la (FLOOR-en-teen, ah lah) A French preparation method associated with the cuisine of Florence, Italy; the dishes are characterized by a bed of spinach on which the principal ingredient, topped with a Mornay sauce and sometimes sprinkled with cheese and browned, is laid.

floret One of the closely clustered small flowers that comprise a composite flower or curd (e.g., broccoli or cauliflower).

flounder A large family of flatfish found in the coastal waters of the Atlantic Ocean, Gulf of Mexico and Pacific Ocean; generally, they have a brownish-gray skin, a lean, firm, pearly or pinkish-white flesh and a mild flavor; some are marketed as sole, and sometimes different varieties of flounder and sole are marketed under the same name; significant varieties include blackback flounder, English sole, fluke, gray sole, plaice, starry flounder and yellowfin flounder. *See* sole.

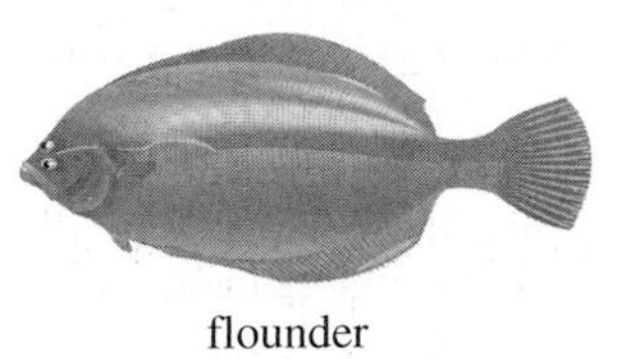
flounder

flour *v.* To cover or dust a food or utensil with flour. *n.* A powdery substance of varying degrees of fineness made by milling wheat, corn, rye or other grains or grinding dried vegetables (e.g., mushrooms), fruits (e.g., plantains) or nuts (e.g., chestnuts).

flour, strong Flour with a high protein content.

flour, weak Flour with a low protein content.

flower nail A small tool that consists of a metal or plastic nail-like stem topped with a platform; used in cake decorating to form three-dimensional flowers, arches or scrolls.

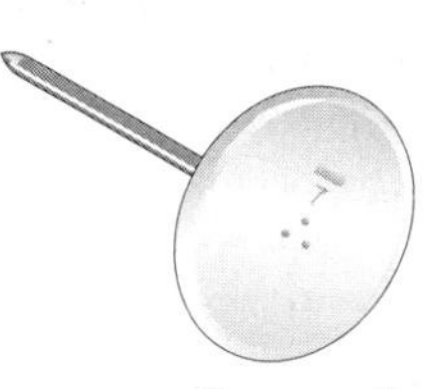
flower nail

fluid ounce (fl. oz.) A measure of liquid volume used in the U.S. system; 128 fl. oz. equals 1 U.S. gallon.

fluke 1. A member of the flounder family found in the Atlantic Ocean from the mid-Atlantic states to New England; it has a dark, spotted skin, a lean, white flesh, a sweet, mild flavor and an average market weight of 2–4 lb. (0.9–1.8 kg); also known as summer flounder. 2. A term used imprecisely to describe any young or small flounder found in the Atlantic Ocean.

flummery (FLUHM-muh-ree) 1. A British dessert that traditionally was a molded oatmeal or custard pudding. 2. In the United States, a dessert of simmered berries thickened with cornstarch and served cold with cream.

flute *v.* 1. To make a decorative pattern on the raised edge of a pie crust. 2. To carve grooves, slashes or other decorative markings into vegetables and fruits. *n.* 1. A stemmed glass with an elongated, V-shaped bowl; used for sparkling wines. 2. A thin, slightly sweet, flute-shaped cookie served with ice cream, pudding or the like. 3. A long, thin loaf of French bread.

fluting knife A small knife with a wedge-shaped blade; used for making shallow decorative grooves, notches or cuts in various foods, especially produce.

fluting knife

FMP Foodservice Management Professional; it is the highest level of certification offered by the National Restaurant Association.

foam The mass that forms when eggs and sugar are beaten together (e.g., in a sponge cake), before the flour is added.

foamed milk Milk that is heated with steam to approximately 150°F (65°C); air is incorporated while heating to create a light foam; it is used for cappuccino and other coffee drinks.

foam frosting *See* seven-minute frosting.

foaming The process of whipping eggs to incorporate air.

focaccia (foh-CAH-chee-ah) Italian flat bread leavened with yeast and flavored with olive oil and herbs; traditionally made with potato flour.

foie gras (fwah grah) The enlarged liver of a duck or goose (the birds are methodically fattened through force-feeding of a corn-based diet); it has two smooth, rounded lobes with a putty color and an extremely high fat content.

fold *v.* To incorporate light, airy ingredients into heavier ingredients by gently moving them from the bottom up over the top in a circular motion. *n.* A measurement of the strength of vanilla extract.

fond (fahn) 1. French for stock. 2. French for bottom and used to describe the concentrated juices, drippings and bits of food left in pans after foods are roasted or sautéed; they are used to flavor sauces made directly in the pans in which the foods were cooked.

fondant (FAHN-dant) A sweet, thick, opaque sugar paste commonly used for glazing pastries (e.g., napoleons) or making candies. *See* rolled fondant.

fond lié (fahn lee-ay) *See* jus lié.

fondu (FON-du) A cheese that has been melted and blended with liquid or powdered milk, cream, butter, casein or whey and sometimes flavorings.

fondue (fahn-DOO) 1. Traditionally, a hot dish of melted cheeses (usually Emmental style) into which diners dip pieces of bread or other foods to be coated and consumed. 2. A hot preparation of other melted foods, such as chocolate, into which diners dip pieces of food to be coated and consumed. 3. A preparation of thinly sliced vegetables cooked slowly in butter over very low heat until reduced to a pulp; used as an ingredient or accompaniment.

Fontina Val d'Aosta (fahn-TEE-nah val DAY-ohs-TA) A cooked, semisoft to firm cheese made in Italy's Piedmont region from whole ewe's milk; it has a dark golden brown rind stamped with purple, a pale yellow interior, and a mild, nutty flavor; when partly aged, it is used as a table cheese, and when fully aged, it is hard and used for grating.

food 1. Any plant or animal product that provides nourishment when ingested. 2. Any raw, cooked or processed edible substance.

food additive Any one of several thousand organic and inorganic, natural and synthetic substances not normally consumed as a food by itself and usually found (intentionally or incidentally) in processed (as opposed to whole) foods either as a component of the food or as an agent affecting a characteristic of the food such as flavor, texture, color or freshness; regulated by the U.S. Food and Drug Administration (FDA), an additive must be safe, effective and measurable in the final product; some additives are available for home use, and others are generally used only for commercial processing purposes.

food and beverage manager The person responsible for all aspects of an establishment's food and beverage operation; known as the F and B.

Food and Drug Administration Part of the U.S. Department of Health and Human Services, its activities are directed at protecting the nation's health against impure and unsafe foods, drugs, cosmetics, medical devices and other products; it approves and regulates food additives, sets standards for food-labeling language, and carries out many of the provisions of The Food, Drug and Cosmetic Act of 1936, as amended.

food danger zone The temperature range of 41–135°F (5–57°C), which is most favorable for bacterial growth; also known as the temperature danger zone.

food mill A tool used to strain and purée foods simultaneously; it consists of a hopper with a hand-crank mechanism that forces the food through a perforated disk; most models have interchangeable disks with various-sized holes.

food mill

food poisoning 1. An illness resulting from the ingestion of foods containing poisonous substances (e.g., certain mushrooms) or foods contaminated with certain insecticides. 2. A term used imprecisely to describe an illness resulting from the ingestion of rancid or partially decomposed (putrefied) foods or foods containing pathogenic bacteria.

food processor An appliance used to purée, chop, grate, slice and shred foods; it consists of a bowl that sits atop a motorized driveshaft; an S-shaped blade on the bottom of the bowl processes food that can be fed into the bowl through an opening or tube on top; some models can be fitted as a juicer and/or pasta maker.

food processor

food rasp A long file with raised points; used for grating nutmeg, cheese, citrus peel, ginger, bread crumbs and so on.

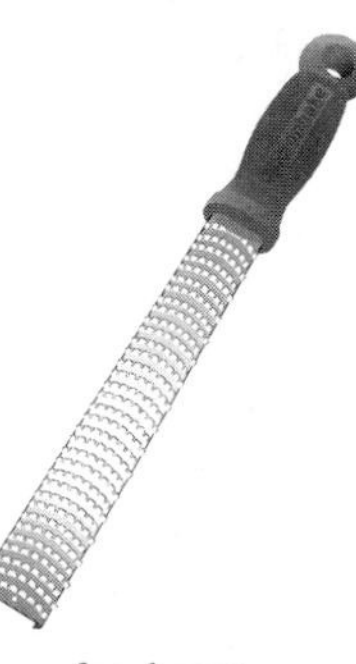
food rasp

fool A British dessert made by folding puréed fruit (traditionally gooseberries) into whipped cream.

forcemeat A mixture of ground cooked or raw meats, fish, shellfish, poultry, vegetables and/or fruits combined with a binder, seasoned and emulsified with fat; it is the primary ingredient in charcuterie items such as pâtés, terrines, galantines and sausages; there are three principal styles: basic, countrystyle and mousseline.

forcemeat, basic A moderately fine forcemeat that is well seasoned, especially with pâté spice; most pâtés and terrines are made with a basic forcemeat.

forcemeat, countrystyle A coarsely ground forcemeat heavily seasoned with onions, garlic, pepper, juniper berries and bay leaves.

forcemeat, mousseline A light, delicate and airy forcemeat, usually made with fish or shellfish; egg whites and cream are often added to lighten and enrich the mixture. *See* mousse.

Fordhook lima bean A plump bean with a slight kidney shape; it has a pale green color and is meatier and more flavorful than a lima bean.

forequarter 1. Either bilateral half of the front section of a beef carcass; it includes the entire rib, chuck, short plate, and brisket and shank primals. 2. Either bilateral half of the foresaddle of a veal carcass; it contains half of the shoulder, rib, and foreshank and breast primals. 3. Either bilateral half of the foresaddle of a lamb carcass; it contains half of the shoulder, breast and rack primals. 4. *See* hindquarter.

foresaddle 1. The undivided forequarters (the front half) of a veal carcass; it includes the shoulder, rib and foreshank and breast primals. 2. The undivided forequarters (the front half) of a lamb carcass; it includes the shoulder, rack and breast primals. 3. *See* hindsaddle.

foreshank 1. A portion of the lower forelimb (below the knee) of a quadruped. 2. A fabricated cut of the beef primal brisket and foreshank; it is tough and flavorful and contains a large amount of connective tissue. 3. A fabricated cut of the veal primal foreshank and breast; it is similar to the beef cut. 4. A subprimal cut of the lamb primal breast; it is similar to the beef cut.

foreshank and breast A primal section of the veal carcass; it is beneath the shoulder and rib primals and consists of cartilaginous tissue, rib bones, breast bones and shank bones, many of which are more cartilaginous than boney; the meat is generally flavorful but somewhat tough; significant fabricated cuts include the veal breast roast, foreshank and cubed and ground products.

forestière, à la (foh-reh-styehr, ah lah) A French preparation for small cuts of meat or vegetables; they are garnished with mushrooms, bacon and diced potatoes.

Formosa Oolong An expensive Taiwanese oolong tea; the beverage has a pale yellow color and light peachy flavor and is best served without milk.

Formosa Pouchong A Taiwanese oolong tea; the leaves are scented with jasmine, gardenia or yulan blossoms; the beverage has a pale yellow color and delicate floral aroma and is best served without milk.

formula The bakeshop term for a recipe.

formula-fed veal *See* veal, milk-fed.

forno, al (FOR-no, ahl) Italian term used to describe an item baked in the oven.

fortified Refers to products such as milk, salt, sports drinks or other beverages to which, subject to U.S. Food and Drug Administration (FDA) regulations, vitamins (e.g., vitamins A and D in milk and vitamin C in sports drinks) and/or minerals (e.g., iodine in salt) have been added during processing to replace nutrients lost during processing, supplement naturally occurring nutrients or add nutrients not normally present in the food. *See* enriched.

fougasse (foo-gahss) A rectangular, ladder-shaped bread from southern France, usually made with baguette dough and flavored with anchovies, olives, herbs or nuts.

fowl Any edible wild or domesticated bird. *See* poultry.

fox grape A North American grape variety; the spherical fruit have a purplish-black skin and a musky flavor; also known as a plum grape or skunk grape.

fraisage (fray-sawgh) A French technique of kneading dough by smearing it across the board with the heel of the hand, then reforming it into a ball.

fraises des bois (frehz duh bwah) Small, elongated wild strawberries grown in France; they have a light red skin, a juicy red flesh and a rich, sweet flavor.

Fraisier; le Fraisier (fray-zee-aihr) A French strawberry layer cake made with rectangular layers of genoise filled with a mousseline cream and sliced fresh strawberries; usually topped with a thin layer of pale pink or green marzipan; also known as bagatelle.

frambozen (frahm-BO-zuh) A Belgian raspberry lambic beer; it should be served chilled in champagne flutes; also known in French as framboise.

Francaise, sauce; French sauce (frahn-saze) A French compound sauce made from beárnaise flavored with a fish glaze and tomato purée.

Francois I, sauce (franz-wahz) A French white wine sauce finished with butter and garnished with diced tomatoes and mushrooms.

frangipane (fran-juh-pahn-ee) 1. An almond-flavored pastry cream used in the preparation of various desserts and cakes; also known as frangipane cream. 2. In classic French cookery, a pastry dough similar to pâte à choux.

frankfurter; frank A smoked, seasoned, precooked sausage made from beef, pork, chicken and/or turkey, with or without a casing; it can contain up to 30% fat and 10% added water; the most common size is 6 in. (15.2 cm) in length; also known as a hot dog or a wiener.

frappé (fra-PAY) 1. Fruit juice or other flavored liquid frozen to a slushy consistency; it can be sweet or savory and served as a drink, appetizer or dessert. 2. French for very cold when used as a wine term. 3. A liqueur served over shaved ice. 4. Italian for milk shake.

free The food-labeling term approved by the U.S. Food and Drug Administration (FDA) and used to describe a food containing no or only physiologically inconsequential amounts of fat, saturated fat, cholesterol, sodium, sugar or calories.

freestone A general description for a fruit that has flesh that does not adhere to its pit. *See* clingstone.

freeze To subject food to a temperature below 32°F (0°C) so that the moisture in the food solidifies; used as a preservation method.

freeze-dried coffee granules or crystals Granules or crystals made from freshly brewed coffee that has been frozen into a slush before the water is evaporated; considered to produce a reconstituted beverage superior in flavor to instant coffee. *See* instant coffee.

freezer An insulated cabinet (reach-in) or room (walk-in) used to store foods at very low (below freezing) temperatures created by mechanical or chemical refrigeration. *See* refrigerator.

freezer burn The surface dehydration and discoloration of food that results from moisture loss at below freezing temperatures.

french, to 1. To cut meat or vegetables into long, slender strips. 2. To remove the meat from the end of a chop or rib, thereby exposing the bone; also known as frenched.

French bread A crusty white yeast bread made with only flour, water, yeast and salt, usually shaped in a long, slender loaf.

French buttercream A rich, creamy frosting made by whipping whole eggs or egg yolks into a thick foam with hot sugar syrup, then beating in softened butter and flavorings.

French doughnuts Doughnuts made from pâte à choux.

French dressing 1. A mixture of oil and vinegar, usually seasoned with salt and pepper and various herbs and garlic; also known as vinaigrette. 2. An American dressing that is creamy, tartly sweet and red-orange in color.

French drip pot A three-tiered coffeemaker; the upper container is filled with water, which drips through a middle container holding the coffee grounds; the coffee is then collected in the bottom container.

frenched A roast, rack or chop of meat, especially lamb, from which the excess fat has been removed, leaving the eye muscle intact, and all meat and connective tissue have been removed from the rib bone.

frenched green bean A green bean cut lengthwise into very narrow strips.

French fries Potatoes cut into matchstick shapes, soaked in cold water, dried, and deep-fried until crisp and golden brown. *See* shoestring potatoes, steak fries *and* straw potatoes.

French fry cutter A tool used to cut a potato into sticks; the potato is forced through a metal cutting grid.

French fry cutter

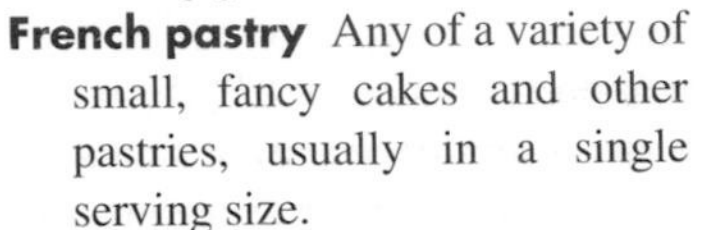

French pastry Any of a variety of small, fancy cakes and other pastries, usually in a single serving size.

French service 1. Restaurant service in which one waiter (a captain) takes the order, does the table-side cooking, and brings the food and beverages while the back waiter serves bread and butter, crumbs the table, serves coffee and the like. 2. Restaurant service in which each item is separately served and placed on a customer's plate (as opposed to all items being plated in the kitchen).

French stick An English term for a long, thin loaf of French bread, commonly known as a baguette.

French toast A breakfast dish of bread dipped in egg and milk, sautéed in butter, sometimes garnished with fruit, and served with syrup or confectioners' sugar.

fresh 1. A food that has not been frozen. 2. A food that has been recently produced, such as a loaf of bread. 3. A food as grown or harvested; not canned, dried or processed and containing no preservatives.

fresh-frozen A food that was frozen while still fresh.

fresh ham A primal section of the pork carcass; it is the hog's hind leg and contains the aitch, leg and hind shank bones and large muscles. *See* ham.

fresh yeast *See* compressed yeast.

Fresno chile A short, conical fresh chile with a green color (that reddens when ripe), a thick flesh, and a sweet, hot flavor; named for the California city where it was first grown commercially; also known as chile caribe and chile cera.

friandises (free-yawn-DEEZ) French for confections served after a meal (e.g., truffles, mints or petit fours).

fricassée (FRIHK-uh-see) A French white stew in which the meat (usually chicken or veal) is cooked in fat but not browned before the liquid is added.

frico (FREE-koh) Thin, lacy, crisp wafers 3 to 4 in. in diameter made by sprinkling grated cheese (usually Asiago, Cheddar and Parmesan) onto a heated skillet and cooking until golden.

fried pies *See* hand pies.

fried rice A Chinese and Chinese–American dish of cold cooked rice seasoned with soy sauce and fried; egg, meat, shellfish, poultry and/or vegetable garnishes are usually added.

fries 1. The intestines of a pig or lamb. 2. The testicles of a pig, lamb, calf or bull. 3. Slang for French fries. 4. *See* fry.

frijoles (free-HOH-lehs) Spanish (particularly in Mexico) for beans, including pink, black, kidney and pinto beans.

frijoles refritos (free-HOH-lehs reh-FREE-tohs) Spanish for well-fried beans (often improperly translated as refried beans).

frisée (free-zay) A variety of endive with yellowish-green curly leaves; also known as chicorée frisée.

frittata (free-tah-ta) An open-faced omelet of Spanish–Italian heritage.

fritter A small, sweet or savory, deep-fried cake made by either combining chopped foods with a thick batter or dipping the food into the batter.

fritto misto (FREET-toh MEES-toh) Italian for mixed fry or mixed fried and used to describe small pieces of meat or vegetables dipped in batter and deep-fried.

friturier (free-too-ree-ay) At a food services operation following the brigade system, the person responsible for all fried items; also known as the fry station chef.

frizzes (FRIHZ-ihs) Dry Italian sausages made from pork or beef, seasoned with garlic and anise; they have a squiggly shape and are available highly spiced (corded with a red string) or mild (corded with a blue string).

frog An amphibian; its legs have an average market weight of 2–8 oz. (57–230 g) and a tender, lean flesh with an ivory-white color and a delicate flavor; significant varieties include the wild common frog and the farm-raised bullfrog.

frog-eye gravy *See* redeye gravy.

Frogmore stew A dish from the American South consisting of crab, shrimp, corn on the cob, potatoes and sausage cooked in a spicy broth; also known as Low Country boil.

Fromage à la Crème (froh-MAJH ah lah krem) A soft, simple French cheese made from cow's milk or a mixture of milk and cream; it has a rich, mild, slightly sweet flavor and should be eaten fresh.

from scratch; scratch To make an item, usually baked goods, from the raw ingredients, without using a mix or processed convenience products (other than items such as baking powder).

front of the house The areas of a restaurant, hotel or the like open to the public or within public view, such as a lobby, bar, dining room or other public space. *See* back of the house.

frost To coat or cover an item with frosting or icing.

frost grape A North American grape variety; the fruit have a dark purple skin and, after a frost, are generally used for home wine making; also known as a chicken grape or winter grape.

frosting 1. A sweet decorative coating used as a filling between the layers or as a coating over the top and sides of a cake; also known as icing. 2. Chilling a mug or glass in the freezer, with or without first wetting it; usually done for serving beer or straight-up cocktails.

fructose 1. A monosaccharide occurring naturally in fruits and honey that is sweeter than table sugar; also known as levulose and fruit sugar. 2. A food additive used as a nutritive sweetener in processed foods such as beverages and candies.

fruitarian One whose diet includes fruits, seeds and nuts but no vegetables, grains or animal products. *See* vegetarian.

fruit butter A sweet spread of fresh fruit flavored with sugar and spices and cooked until thick and smooth.

fruitcake A Christmas cake made with candied fruit, dried fruit and nuts bound with a relatively small amount of a dense, spicy batter.

fruit cocktail A chilled mix of various chopped fruits served as an appetizer; spices or liqueurs are sometimes added.

fruit leather Puréed fruit, sometimes with sugar or honey added, spread in a thin layer and dried; usually rolled and eaten as a snack.

fruits The edible organs that develop from the ovary of flowering plants; they contain one or more seeds and are usually sweet and eaten as is or used as ingredients. *See* vegetable.

fruits de mer (frwee duh MAIR) French for fruits of the sea and used to describe almost any combination of fish and/or shellfish.

fruit-vegetables Foods such as avocados, eggplants, chiles and tomatoes that are botanically fruits but are most often prepared and served like vegetables.

fruit vinegar A flavored vinegar made by steeping whole or crushed fruit in a wine vinegar (the fruit is usually removed before use); typical fruits include raspberries, pears, black currants and strawberries.

frumenty (FROU-men-tee) Hulled wheat cooked in milk and sweetened.

frutti de mare (FROOT-tee dee MA-ray) Italian for fruits of the sea and used to describe almost any combination of fish and/or shellfish.

fry *v. See* frying. *n.*1. An imprecisely used term for almost any fish when it is still young and not more than a few inches long. 2. A single French fry. 3. A social gathering at which foods are fried and eaten (e.g., a fish fry). 4. *See* fries.

fry bread A Native American (especially Navajo and Hopi) bread; it consists of thin rounds of plain dough that are deep-fried and served hot with sweet or savory toppings.

frying A dry-heat cooking method in which foods are cooked in hot fat; includes sautéing, stir-frying, pan-frying and deep-frying.

frying pan A round pan with a single long handle and low, sloping sides and used to pan-fry foods; available with a nonstick surface and in 8-, 10- and 12-in. diameters; also known as a skillet.

frying pan

fudge A semisoft candy made by cooking butter, sugar, cream and flavorings, especially chocolate, together to the soft-ball stage; nuts or other garnishes are often added.

full-cut round A fabricated cut of the beef primal round; it is a very lean, somewhat tough steak cut perpendicular to the bone and includes all of the muscles.

ful medames; ful imdammas (fool MAY-da-mez) 1. Small, plump broad beans (*Lathyrus sativus*) native to the Middle East; they have a light brown skin and nutty flavor; used in Egyptian and other Middle Eastern cuisines. 2. An Egyptian dish of these beans drizzled with olive oil and lemon.

fumet (fyoo-maht) A concentrated stock usually made from fish bones and/or shellfish shells and vegetables; used for sauces and soups.

fun gau (foon gah-oo) A Chinese crescent-shaped dumpling of shrimp, pork, mushrooms and bamboo shoots in a wheat starch wrapper.

fungus *pl.* fungi. A division of plantlike organisms that lack chlorophyll and range in size from single-celled organisms to giant mushrooms; fungi, some of which are pathogenic, are found in the air, soil and water. *See* mold *and* yeast.

funnel A conical-shaped tool with a short, straight tube at the tip; used to transfer liquids into a narrow-mouthed container; some are equipped with strainers in the bottom to clear the liquid of small particles.

funnel cake A deep-fried Pennsylvania Dutch pastry made by pouring batter through a funnel into hot fat with a spiral motion; the fried dough is served with confectioners' sugar or honey.

fusion cuisine A style of cooking that draws on elements from European and Asian cuisines; generally, the application of Asian preparation techniques to European or American ingredients; also known as East meets West.

fuzzy squash; fuzzy melon A large cylindrical squash native to China; it has a medium green skin covered with a hairlike fuzz, a cream-colored flesh, a moderately firm texture, and a bland flavor that absorbs flavors from other ingredients; also known as a hairy melon.

g *See* gram.

gadeed (gah-dad) Thin slices of sun-dried meat, usually lamb or camel, used in North African and Middle Eastern cuisines; also known as gargoosh.

gado gado; gado-gado (GAH-doh GAH-doh) 1. An Indonesian dish consisting of raw and slightly cooked vegetables served with a spicy peanut sauce made with hot chiles and coconut milk. 2. The sauce itself.

Gaelic steak An Irish dish consisting of beefsteak cooked in butter in an iron skillet; shots of Irish whiskey and cream are added to the meat juices to form a sauce; it is traditionally served with cooked potatoes, fried onion rings, mushrooms and green vegetables.

gai choy; gai choi A leafy Chinese vegetable with long, green leaves, a long, pale green stalk and a strong mustard flavor; also known as Chinese mustard cabbage and swatow mustard.

galanga; galangal; galingale root (gah-LAHN-gah) The rhizome of a plant (*Alpina officinarum*) native to Southeast Asia; the rhizome has a reddish skin, an orange or whitish flesh, and a peppery, gingerlike flavor; used dried or fresh as a spice in Thai and Indonesian cuisines.

galantine (GAL-uhn-teen; gal-ahn-TEEN) A forcemeat of poultry, game, fish, shellfish or suckling pig, wrapped in the skin of the bird or animal, if available, and poached in an appropriate stock; usually served cold in aspic.

galantine mold A rectangular porcelain mold with slightly sloping sides and lug handles; the contents are served from the mold.

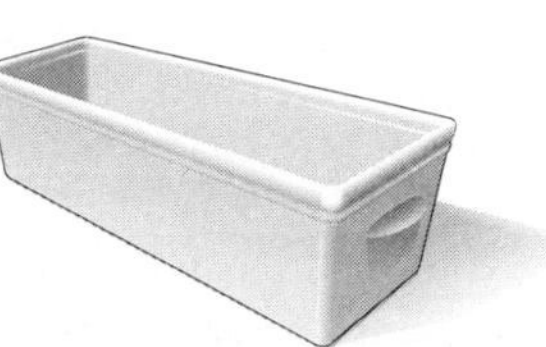

galantine mold

galette (gah-leht) 1. A round, flat, thin French cake made with puff pastry or a yeast-leavened dough, usually sprinkled with sugar before baking. 2. A thin, round cake made from potatoes or cereal grains; also known as a buckwheat crêpe in Normandy. 3. A small shortbread cookie.

galia melon A spherical melon with a netted skin, a brownish color and a moderately dark green flesh.

gallon 1. An American unit of measurement equal to 128 fl. oz.; contains 8 pt. (16 fl. oz. each). 2. An English unit of measurement equal to 1.2 U.S. gallons, 10 lb., or 160 fl. oz.; contains 8 pt. (20 fl. oz. each); also known as the imperial gallon.

galushkes (gal-oosh-keys) A Jewish dish consisting of a water, egg and flour dough that is forced through a colander or special sieve directly into boiling water.

game Wild mammals, birds or fish hunted for sport or food as well as the flesh of these animals; common game include deer, rabbit, hare, bear, boar, duck, goose, pheasant, quail and pigeon, many of which are also ranch raised and available commercially.

game chips British for potato chips that are served with game and poultry; when served with drinks or cocktails, they are called crisps.

game hen A young or immature progeny of Cornish chickens or of a Cornish chicken and White Rock chicken; slaughtered when 4–6 weeks old, it has an average market weight of 2 lb. (900 g), relatively little fat, and a fine flavor. *See* Rock Cornish game hen.

gammon (GAHM-muhn) 1. A British dish of a cured hog's foreleg. 2. A British cut of the pork carcass; it is a thick slice taken from the top of the ham and sometimes smoked; also known as a ham steak.

gamy A tasting term for a food with a penetrating, musky aroma.

ganache (ga-nosh) A rich blend of chocolate and heavy cream and, optionally, flavorings, used as a pastry or candy filling or as a frosting.

gandaria A small, mangolike tropical fruit (genus *Bouea*); it has a thin, yellow- or apricot-colored skin and yellow or orange flesh.

gar; garfish Any of a variety of freshwater fish found in North America with a long beak and large teeth; often smoked; also known as needlefish.

garam masala (gah-RAHM mah-SAH-lah) A flavorful and aromatic blend of roasted and ground spices used in Indian cuisines (usually added toward the end of cooking or sprinkled on the food just before service); the blend usually contains peppercorns, cardamom, cinnamon, cloves, coriander, nutmeg, turmeric and/or fennel seeds; also known as a gorum moshla and masala.

garbanzo bean (gar-BAHN-zoh) *See* chickpea.

garbure (gahr-bewr) A dish from France's Bearn region consisting of a soup made from carrots, potatoes, garlic, cabbage and green beans cooked with pork and preserved goose; the pork and goose are removed before service and browned with a topping of bread crumbs, cheese and butter and served after the soup.

garbure (gar-BOOR) A dish from Spain's Basque region consisting of a thick soup made from potatoes, cabbage, beans and pork, bacon or preserved goose.

garde manger (gahr mohn-zahj) 1. At a food services operation following the brigade system, the person responsible for the cold food preparations, including salads and salad dressings, cold appetizers, charcuterie items and similar dishes; also known as the pantry chef. 2. This category of foods. 3. The area in a kitchen where these foods are prepared; also known as the pantry.

garde-manger section One of the principal work sections of a food services facility; it typically contains a salad station, cold foods station, sandwich station and charcuterie station.

garden relish A relish made from tomatoes, celery, cucumber, green pepper and onion and dressed with olive oil and vinegar.

gari; garri (GAH-ree) 1. A West African term for a coarse cassava powder made from grated, roasted cassava. 2. A stiff porridge made from this powder. 3. Sushi-shop slang for vinegared ginger; also known as béni shoga.

Garibaldi, sauce (gar-ree-BALL-dee) A French compound sauce made from a demi-glaze seasoned with mustard, cayenne pepper and garlic and finished with anchovy butter.

garlic A member of the lily family (*Allium sativum*); the highly aromatic and strongly flavored edible bulb (called a head) is covered in a papery layer and is composed of several sections (called cloves), each of which is also covered with a papery membrane; used as a distinctive flavoring in cuisines around the world.

garlic

garlic bread Slices of French or Italian bread that are spread with garlic butter and toasted, broiled or grilled.

garlic butter Softened butter mixed with minced or crushed garlic; used as a cooking medium, flavoring or spread.

garlic chives *See* chives, garlic.

garlic flakes Bits or slices of dehydrated garlic; used as a seasoning, either dried or rehydrated; also known as instant garlic.

garlic juice; garlic extract The juice of pressed garlic cloves; used as a seasoning.

garlic powder Finely ground dehydrated garlic; used as a seasoning; also known as powdered garlic.

garlic press A tool used to press garlic cloves through a perforated grid to make a paste.

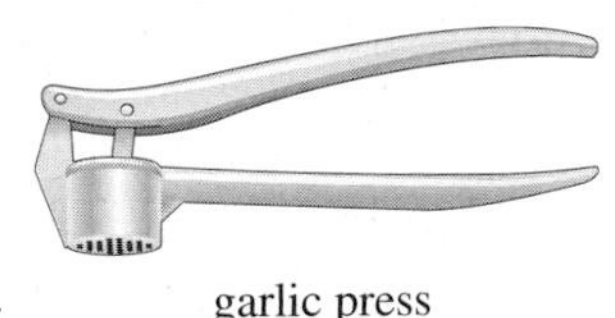

garlic press

garlic salt A blend of garlic powder, salt and an anticaking agent or humectant; used as a seasoning.

garni (gahr-nee) French for garnished and used to describe a dish that includes vegetables and potato.

garnish *v.* To use food as an attractive decoration. *n.* 1. Food used as an attractive decoration. 2. A subsidiary food used to add flavor or character to the main ingredient in a dish (e.g., noodles in chicken noodle soup).

garniture (gahr-nih-TEUR) French for garnish and used to describe the various ingredients that blend with the foods and flavors of the main dish.

garum (GAR-uhm) A condiment popular in ancient Rome; it was made by fermenting fish in brine with aromatic herbs and then mixing the resulting paste with pepper and oil or wine.

Gascogne, sauce (gas-kon-ya) A French compound sauce made from a velouté flavored with a reduction of white wine and herbs and finished with a small amount of anchovy butter.

gastrique (gas-strek) Caramelized sugar deglazed with vinegar and used in fruit-flavored savory sauces (e.g., duck with orange sauce) and tomato-based sauces.

gastronome (GAS-truh-nohm) 1. An epicure. 2. A Russian food store.

gastronome, sauce (GAS-truh-nohm) A French compound sauce made from a Madeira sauce flavored with a meat glaze, seasoned with cayenne pepper and finished with Champagne.

gastronomy The art and science of eating well.

gâteau (gah-toh) 1. French for cake. 2. In the United States, any cake-type dessert. 3. In France, various pastry items made with puff pastry, éclair paste, short dough or sweet dough.

gâteau l'opera (gah-TOH lo-pay-rah) A French pastry composed of three layers of almond genoise filled with coffee buttercream and ganache.

gâteau St. Honoré (gah-TOH san-tah-naw-RAY) A French pastry composed of a base of puff pastry topped with a ring of small choux puffs, attached to the base with caramelized sugar; the center is filled with Chiboust cream and cream Chantilly.

gaufrette (goh-FREHT) A thin, crisp fan-shaped French wafer, often served with ice cream.

gaufrette potatoes; gaufrette pommes de terre (goh-FREHT pohm duh tehr) A French dish of crisp, fried, latticed or waffle-cut potatoes.

gazpacho (gahz-PAH-choh) A cold Spanish soup made of uncooked tomatoes, cucumbers, sweet peppers, onions, oil and vinegar and traditionally thickened with bread crumbs or slices of bread.

gefilte fish (geh-FIHL-teh) A Jewish dish of ground fish (usually carp, pike and/or whitefish) mixed with eggs, matzo meal and seasonings, shaped into balls and simmered in a vegetable or fish stock.

Gehirnwurst (gay-heer'n-vurst) A German sausage made from hog brains and pork meat and fat, seasoned with mace, salt and pepper.

gelatin; gelatine A colorless, odorless and flavorless mixture of proteins from animal bones, connective tissues and other parts as well as from certain algae (agar-agar); when dissolved in a hot liquid and then cooled, it forms a jellylike substance that is used as a thickener and stabilizer in molded desserts, cold soups, chaud-froid creations and the like and as a fining agent in beer and wine.

gelatin, granulated A granular form of unflavored, unsweetened gelatin.

gelatin, leaf Paper-thin sheets of unflavored gelatin; also known as sheet gelatin.

gelatinization The process by which starch granules are cooked; they absorb moisture when placed in a liquid and heated; as the moisture is absorbed, the product swells, softens and clarifies slightly.

gelato (jah-laht-to) An Italian-style ice cream that is denser than American-style ice cream.

gem pan A pan designed to make miniature muffins.

genetically engineered foods *See* bioengineered foods.

genevoise sauce (zhehn-VWAHZ) A French sauce made of fish fumet, mirepoix and red wine, thickened with butter and served with fish dishes.

genip; ginup (heh-NEEP) A cherry-sized tropical fruit (*Melicoccus bijugatus*); it has a slightly ovoid shape, a thick green skin, a gummy yellowish or orange-pink flesh, a single seed or two seeds flattened together, and a flavor reminiscent of grapes; also known as akee (especially in the Barbados), honeyberry, limoncillo, Spanish lime and mamoncillo and imprecisely known as genipa or genipap.

Genoa salami A large sausage from Genoa, Italy, made from pork and beef, highly seasoned with garlic, white peppercorns and other spices; it is cured and air-dried.

genoise (zhen-waahz) 1. A form of whipped-egg cake that uses whole eggs whipped with sugar. 2. A French sponge cake.

Genovese, salsa An Italian pasta sauce made from onions, carrots, tomatoes, dried mushrooms, celery and veal simmered in stock and white wine; sometimes strained.

gentian A plant (*Gentiana lutea*) with a thick rhizome, elliptical blue-green leaves, and showy, stalked, golden yellow flowers; the rhizome is used to make gentian brandy and bitter liqueurs and as a bitter flavoring agent; also known as great yellow gentian.

geoduck clam; gweduck clam (GOO-ee-duhk) A variety of Pacific clam with a soft shell; it can weigh as much as 10 lb. (4.5 kg) and has a large siphon; the tender meat has a rich, briny flavor and is used in Asian cuisines.

geranium, scented Geranium (genera *Geranium* and *Pelargonium*) leaves that have scents reminiscent of fruits and other flavorings, such as oranges, lemons and roses; a syrup or liquid infused with the leaves is used to flavor custards, sugars, preserves and sorbets.

germ 1. An imprecise term used to describe any microorganism, especially pathogenic ones. 2. The smallest portion of a cereal kernel and the only portion containing fat.

German chocolate; German's sweet chocolate Baking chocolate with sugar, milk and vanilla added.

German chocolate cake A rich, American-style layer cake made with sweet chocolate and filled with a cooked coconut-pecan frosting.

German potato salad A salad made with cooked potatoes, bacon, onions, celery and green pepper bound with a dressing of bacon fat, vinegar, seasonings and sometimes sugar; served hot, room temperature or cold.

German sauce *See* allemande, sauce.

germicide An agent capable of killing some kinds of microorganisms; used to protect crops or to sterilize food service areas, it can become an incidental food additive.

germination The process during which a seed, spore, bulb or the like begins to grow and develop into a plant; sprouting.

ghee (gee) 1. Hindi for fat or buttermilk. 2. A form of clarified butter (after the moisture has evaporated, the milk solids are allowed to brown) originating in India but now mass-produced worldwide and used as an ingredient and cooking medium; it has a long shelf life, high smoke point and a nutty, caramel-like flavor; ghee flavored with ginger, peppercorns or cumin is available.

gherkin (gerr-ken) A small, dark green pickling cucumber; usually harvested before it ripens and pickled in vinegar.

gianduja (gyan-doo-hah) A blend of chocolate, usually milk chocolate, and hazelnuts; used for flavoring many Spanish and Mexican pastries.

giant clam A variety of clam found in the tropical waters of the western Pacific Ocean, particularly the South Sea; it can weigh as much as 110 lb. (49.8 kg) and has a large shell with prominent flutes.

giant sea bass A member of the grouper family; it has a lean white flesh, a firm texture, and a mild to sweet flavor and can weigh as much as 550 lb. (249.4 kg); sometimes mistakenly called a sea bass or black sea bass; also known as a jewfish.

giardiniera, alla (jahr-dee-N'YEHR-ah, AH-la) Italian for garden style and used to describe dishes served with vegetables.

gibier (jhee-byay) French for game and used to refer to all wild animals or birds that are hunted for food.

giblets The edible internal organs of a bird; in the United States, these include the heart, liver and gizzard as well as the neck; in France, they also include the cockscomb and kidneys (testes).

Gibson A martini garnished with a small white onion.

gigot d'agneau (jhee-GOH dan-yoh) French for the shank end of the leg of lamb that is suitable for roasting.

gild To brush pastry or other foods with egg yolk so that the brushed surface will brown when cooked.

gill 1. A unit of measurement in the imperial system; it is 0.25 pt. (5 fl. oz.). 2. In England, an informal unit of measurement equal to 0.5 pt. 3. A unit of measurement in the U.S. system; it is 0.25 pt. (4 fl. oz.). 4. A small medieval English glass.

gills 1. The organs on fish and shellfish used to obtain oxygen. *See* beard. 2. Thin curtains of membranes radially arranged under the caps of certain mushrooms and the area that usually bears spores; also known as lammellae.

gilthead; gilt-poll A saltwater fish related to the porgy and found in the Mediterranean Sea and temperate areas of the Atlantic Ocean; it has a bright gold crescent between the eyes and a delicate flavor; also known as a golden eyebrow fish.

ginger; gingerroot The gnarled, bumpy rhizome (called a hand) of a tall flowering tropical plant (*Zingerber officinale*) native to China; it has a tan skin, an ivory to greenish-yellow flesh, a peppery, fiery, slightly sweet flavor with notes of lemon and rosemary and a spicy, pungent aroma; used to flavor beverages and in sweet and savory dishes in Asian and Indian cuisines; available fresh, powdered, preserved in sugar, crystallized, candied or pickled.

ginger, pickled Ginger preserved in rice vinegar, brine or red wine; it has a pinkish color and a slightly spicy, sweet flavor; used in Asian cuisines.

ginger ale A sweetened carbonated beverage flavored with a ginger extract.

ginger beer A carbonated beverage with a strong ginger flavor; can be nonalcoholic or alcoholic.

gingerbread A sweet cake or cookie flavored with ginger and other spices.

ginger bud The fragrant, pink, edible buds of several types of ginger plants (*Phaeomeria sepciosa* and *Nicloaia atropurpurea*) used in Southeast Asian cuisines.

ginger grater A flat ceramic grater with rows of ceramic teeth used for grating ginger.

ginger grater

ginger powder Dried ground ginger; it has a yellow color and a flavor that is spicier and not as sweet as fresh ginger; used in baked goods.

gingersnap A thin, crisp cookie flavored with ginger and molasses.

ginkgo nut The nut of a spherical, plum-sized, brown fruit of the Asian ginkgo tree (*Ginkgo biloba*); the olive-sized kernel turns pale green when cooked and is used in Asian cuisines; also known as maidenhair nut.

ginseng (JIHN-sing) A plant of the ivy family (*Panax ginseng*) native to China; the forked root is highly aromatic, with a flavor reminiscent of fennel, and is used in tisanes, as a flavoring for soups, and as a tonic believed by some to be an aphrodisiac and restorative.

giorno, del (johr-no, del) Italian menu term for speciality of the day.

giouvarlakia (yeh-oo-vah-reh-lah-kha) Greek meatballs; usually lamb or mutton, simmered in stock thickened with avgolémono.

Gipfels (gayp-fels) A type of croissant popular in Germany and Switzerland consisting of a triangle of dough rolled and stretched into a circular crescent; the dough has more and thinner layers than French-style croissants.

gizzard A bird's second stomach; it has a thick muscle used to grind food after it has been mixed with the gastric juices in the first stomach.

glace (glahs) 1. French for ice and ice cream. 2. French for the icing used on a cake.

glacé (glahs-say) French for glazed and used to describe both a fruit dipped in a syrup that hardens when cold and a cake with a shiny, sweet surface (icing).

glace de poisson (glahs duh pwah-sawng) A syrupy glaze made by reducing a fish stock; used to flavor sauces.

glace de viande (glahs duh vee-AHND) A dark brown, syrupy glaze made by reducing a brown stock; used to color and flavor sauces.

glace de volaille (glahs duh vo-lahy) A light brown, syrupy glaze made by reducing a chicken stock; used to color and flavor sauces.

glacier (glahs-ee-yay) At a food services operation following the brigade system, the person responsible for all chilled and frozen desserts.

glassful A traditional measure of volume (especially in Creole cuisine); it refers to the volume of a shot glass, approximately 1/4 cup.

glaze *v.* To apply a shiny coating to a food. *n.* 1. Any shiny coating applied to a food or created by browning. 2. The dramatic reduction and concentration of a stock. 3. A thin, flavored coating poured or dripped onto a cake or pastry.

glazed 1. Food that has been dipped in water and then frozen; the ice forms a glaze that protects the item from freezer burn. 2. Food that has been coated with a glaze (e.g., glazed doughnut).

gliaden *See* gluten.

glister pudding A British steamed pudding made with marmalade and flavored with ginger.

globe artichoke *See* artichoke, common.

globe carrot A carrot with a light orange color and a squat conical to spherical shape.

glögg (gloog) A Swedish drink made of brandy or aquavit, wine, spices and other ingredients served warm with a cinnamon stick and garnished with almonds, raisins and orange peel.

Gloucester, Double A Gloucester made with twice the milk and aged for a longer period than Single Gloucester; it has a creamy interior and a more mellow flavor.

Gloucester; Single Gloucester (GLOSS-tuhr) A very firm cheese made in Gloucester, England, from cow's milk; it has a yellow color, a smooth, waxy texture, a red or brown surface, and a rich, mild flavor.

glucose 1. A monosaccharide occurring naturally in fruits, some vegetables and honey with about half the sweetness of table sugar; used as the principal source of energy for most body functions; also known as dextrose, blood sugar, corn sugar and grape sugar. 2. A food additive used as a nutritive sweetener in processed foods such as confections and candies.

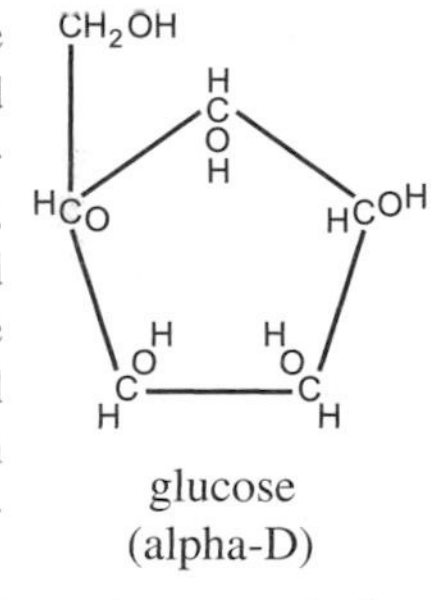

glucose (alpha-D)

gluten An elastic-like network of proteins created when glutenin and gliadin (proteins found in wheat flour) are moistened and kneaded; it is this network that traps gases inside the batter or dough, causing it to rise.

gluten flour A flour made from hard wheat flour from which a large percentage of the starch has been removed; usually used for making bread for diabetic individuals and others who abstain from starch or to add protein to flours, such as rye, that do not produce gluten naturally.

glutenin *See* gluten.

glutinous rice Short- or medium-grain rice with a high starch content available in black (unpolished) and white varieties; used in Japanese and Chinese cuisines for sweet and savory dishes, in part because the rice, which has a slightly sweet flavor, sticks together when cooked, making it easier to eat with chopsticks; also known as sticky rice and sweet rice.

glutinous rice flour A fine white flour made from ground glutinous white rice; it is used in Asian cuisines to make the soft, chewy dough used for sweets, buns and dumplings.

glycerol 1. An organic alcohol that combines with three fatty acids to produce a triglyceride; also known as glycerin or glycerine. 2. A sweet, clear, syruplike liquid that is a by-product of the fermentation of wine; its presence enhances the wine's fattiness and softness. 3. A food additive derived from fats that is used as a sweetener, solvent and/or humectant in processed foods such as confections and candies.

gnocchi (NYOH-kee) Italian for dumplings and used to describe irregularly shaped balls or small concave oval disks made from a dough of potatoes, flour, semolina flour, cornmeal and/or rice flour, with or without eggs; they are boiled or baked.

gnocchi alla romana (NYOH-kee al-lah roh-mah-nah) Italian gnocchi made with semolina, sprinkled with Parmesan and baked.

goat Any of several varieties of horn-rimmed ruminants closely related to sheep and used for their flesh and milk; the meat is generally tough and strongly flavored. *See* kid.

goatfish A family of saltwater fish named for their two long chin barbels (long, slender feelers), which resemble goat whiskers; their skin ranges in color from brilliant yellow to rose red; their flesh is firm and lean, and they are found off the U.S. East Coast, Florida Keys and Hawaii.

goat's milk cheeses Cheeses made from goat's milk; usually pure white with an assertive, tangy, tart flavor; their texture can range from soft, moist and creamy to dry, firm and crumbly and their shape from small- to medium-sized cones, cylinders, disks or pyramids; they are left ungarnished or covered with black ash, leaves, herbs or pepper.

goblet 1. A stemmed drinking vessel with a base and bowl, usually made of glass or precious metal. 2. A method of pruning grapevines so that they take on the shape of a goblet.

goblet

gobstopper A hard sweet English candy.

gold beet A beet with a golden-yellow color and a flavor that is sweeter than that of a red beet; it can be eaten raw or cooked.

golden apple A small, yellow, egg-shaped fruit (*Spondias cytheria*) with a single seed; native to Polynesia, it has a sweet and slightly acidic flavor and is used for preserves and as an ingredient in savory dishes.

golden buck A British dish of Welsh rarebit served with a poached egg on top. *See* Welsh rarebit.

golden raisins Small seedless raisins with a pale gold color made from sultana grapes and used in confectionery and for table use; also known as white raisins and sultanas.

golden syrup A light, sweet syrup with an amber color and a butterscotch flavor; it is a refined by-product of the sugar-refining process. *See* treacle.

golden whitefish caviar Roe harvested from whitefish native to the northern U.S. Great Lakes; the small, golden eggs are very crisp.

gold leaf The pure metal beaten into a gossamer-thin square and sold in packages interleaved with tissue paper; edible in small quantities, it is used to decorate rice dishes in Indian cuisines, and desserts, confections and candies; also known as vark and varak. *See* skewings.

gold powder 22- to 24-karat gold that is ground to dust and used to decorate desserts, pastries and confections.

Golfin, sauce (goal-fahn) A French compound sauce made from a white wine sauce garnished with a julienne of gherkins and pickled tongue.

goma (GOH-mah) Japanese for sesame seeds (used for seasoning and garnishing); white seeds are known as shiro goma, and black seeds are kuro goma.

gombo *See* okra.

good A midlevel U.S. Department of Agriculture (USDA) quality grade for veal and lamb; this meat lacks the flavor and tenderness of the higher grades of prime and choice.

goodwill The value of an established business based on its name or reputation.

goose One of the principal kinds of poultry recognized by the U.S. Department of Agriculture (USDA); domesticated geese have very fatty skin and dark meat with a rich, buttery flavor.

gooseberry A large berry (*Ribes grossularia*) originally grown in northern Europe; it has a smooth or furry green, yellow, red or white skin and a tart flavor;

available dried or fresh and used in preserves and baked goods.

goosefish *See* monkfish.

goose liver *See* foie gras.

goose skirt A British cut of the beef carcass; it is the inner muscle of the belly wall attached to the rump.

gordita (gohr-DEE-tah) Spanish for little fat one and used to describe a thick tortilla made of masa, lard and water, fried and then filled with ground pork or chorizo; it is topped with cheese, lettuce and the like.

goreng bawang (GO-rang bah-wang) Crisp fried onions used as a garnish in Indonesian and Thai cuisines.

Gorgonzola (gohr-guhn-ZOH-lah) An Italian cheese made from cow's milk; it has an ivory interior streaked with blue-green veins and a slightly pungent flavor when young that grows stronger as it ages (it also becomes drier and more crumbly as it ages).

Gorgonzola Bianco (gohr-guhn-ZOH-lah BEE-ahn-coh) A fast-ripening Gorgonzola without the blue mold but with the same flavor and other characteristics of Gorgonzola; also known as White Gorgonzola, Gorgonzola Dolce and Pannerone.

Gorgonzola knife A knife with a rigid, medium-length, broad, blunt-edged 6-in.-long blade; used to dig into a blue-veined cheese, splitting it apart along the veins.

gorp *v.* To eat noisily or greedily. *n.* A mix of nuts, raisins, seeds, dried fruit and oats used as an energy source by athletes; also known as glop and goop.

Gouda (GOO-dah) A semisoft to firm Dutch sweet curd cheese made from cow's milk; it has a yellow interior and a mild, nutty flavor (it is sometimes flavored with cumin or other herbs and spices); marketed in large wheels with a yellow wax coating.

gouge à jambon (gough ah jahm-bohn) A tool with a strong backwardly arched metal trough and a wooden handle used to separate the flesh of the ham from the bone so that the bone can be extracted.

gouge à jambon

gougère (goo-ZHAIR) A savory round or ring-shaped choux pastry flavored with cheese (e.g., Gruyère, Comté or Emmental); it is a traditional accompaniment to wine tastings in France's Burgundy region.

goulash (GOO-lahsh) A Hungarian stew made with beef and vegetables and flavored with paprika; also known as Hungarian goulash.

gourd 1. The nonedible fruit of various plants of the gourd family (*Cucurbitaceae*); generally, they have a tough, hard shell that can be used as a utensil or storage unit once the flesh is removed and the shell is dried. *See* squash. 2. British for several edible squashes.

gourmand (goor-mahnd) A connoisseur of fine food and drink, often to excess.

gourmet (goor-may) A connoisseur of fine food and drink.

gourmet, sauce A French compound sauce made from a demi-glaze, red wine and fish stock; it is flavored with lobster butter and garnished with diced lobster and truffles.

gourmet foods A term used imprecisely to denote foods of the highest quality, perfectly prepared and beautifully presented.

goûter (goo-tay) 1. French for to taste. 2. French for a snack, similar to afternoon tea.

grades *See* USDA quality grades *and* USDA yield grades.

grading A series of voluntary programs offered by the U.S. Department of Agriculture (USDA) to designate a food's overall quality.

graham cracker A sweetened whole wheat cracker.

graham flour Coarsely milled whole wheat flour; named for Dr. Sylvester Graham (1794–1851), an American dietary reformer.

grain alcohol *See* ethyl alcohol.

grains 1. Grasses that bear edible seeds, including corn, rice and wheat. 2. The fruit (i.e., seed or kernel) of such grasses.

grains of paradise The small, reddish-brown seeds of this plant (*Aframomum melegueta*) are used as a spice in many West African cuisines; they have a pungent, peppery flavor; also known as melegueta pepper.

grain whiskey Whiskey made from unmalted grain and distilled in a patent still.

grainy A tasting term for a food with a gritty or mealy texture.

gram (g) The basic measure of weight in the metric system; 28.35 g equal 1 oz., and 1000 g (1 kg) equal 2.2 lb. (U.S.).

gram Hindi for any of a large variety of dried, whole pulses used in Indian cuisines. *See* dhal.

granadilla (gran-ah-DEE-yuh) The fruit of a member of the passion fruit family (genus *Passiflora*); it has a large, spherical shape, a smooth, brittle orange skin that is speckled with tiny white dots, a grayish flesh and seeds and a mildly sweet flavor.

grande cuisine The rich, intricate and elaborate cuisine of the 18th- and 19th-century French aristocracy and upper classes; it was based on the rational identification, development and adoption of strict (and often very elaborate) culinary principles.

grand mère, à la (grahn mer, ah lah) French for in the grandmother's style and used to describe a dish, particularly a chicken casserole, served with pieces of bacon, glazed onions, sautéed mushrooms and fried potatoes.

grand reserve A French labeling term for Armagnac or Cognac; it indicates that the youngest brandy used in the blend was at least 5.5 years old.

granita (grah-nee-TAH) An Italian frozen mixture made with water, sugar and a flavoring such as fruit juice or wine; stirred frequently while freezing, it has a grainy texture.

granité (grah-nee-TAY) A French frozen mixture made with water, sugar and a flavoring such as fruit juice or wine; stirred frequently while freezing, it has a grainy texture.

granola A mix of grains, nuts and dried fruits, sometimes coated with oil and honey, eaten for breakfast or as a snack. *See* musli.

granulated sugar Fine, white sucrose crystals, a general-purpose sweetener; also known as table sugar.

grapefruit A tropical citrus fruit (*Citrus paradisi*) that is an 18th-century hybrid of the orange and pomelo; the relatively thin skin is yellow, and the juicy pulp has a distinctive flavor; available with seeds or seedless.

grapefruit, ruby A grapefruit with yellow-pink to brilliant ruby pulp; it has a sweeter flavor than the white grapefruit.

grapefruit, white A grapefruit with yellow-white pulp; it has a tarter flavor than the ruby grapefruit and is better for juicing.

grapefruit knife A small knife with a curved double-edged serrated blade used to section citrus fruit.

grape juice The liquid constituent of the grape; accounts for more than 85% of the fruit.

grape leaves The large dark green leaves of the grapevine; used in Mediterranean and Middle Eastern cuisines to wrap foods for cooking or as a garnish; available fresh or packed in brine; also known as vine leaves.

grape pie A dessert from the American South consisting of Concord grapes cooked with sugar and thickened with cornstarch and lemon juice and poured into a baked pie shell; when cool, it is garnished with whipped cream and fresh seeded grapes; also known as a jelly pie (especially in North Carolina).

grapes Smooth-skinned, juicy berries (with or without seeds) that grow in clusters; members of the genus *Vitis*, they are used for wine making, raisins and eating out of hand.

grapes, black Grapes with skin colors ranging from light red to purple-black; also known as red grapes.

grapes, red *See* grapes, black.

grapes, red wine Grapes generally used for making red wines; principal varietals grown in the United States include Cabernet Sauvignon, Merlot, Pinot Noir, Zinfandel, Gamay, Petite Sirah, Cabernet Franc, Maréchal Foch, Barbera and Syrah.

grapes, rosé Grapes generally used for making rosé wines; principal varietals grown in the United States include Cabernet, Grenache, Pinot Noir and Zinfandel.

grapes, white Grapes with skin colors ranging from pale yellow-green to light green.

grapes, white wine Grapes generally used for making white wines; principal varietals grown in the United States include Chardonnay, Riesling, Sauvignon Blanc, Chenin Blanc, Sémillon, Seyvel Blanc, Gewürztraminer, Pinot Blanc and French Colombard.

grape scissors A pair of scissors with long handles and 1- to 2-in.-long, snub-tipped blades, one of which is concave and the other straight; used to snip bunches of grapes from a cluster.

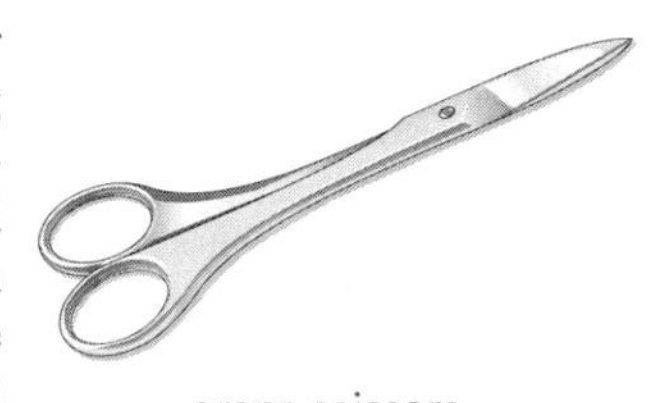
grape scissors

grape seed oil An oil obtained from grape seeds; it has a pale color, a delicate, neutral flavor and high smoke point and is used for frying and other culinary purposes.

grape stones Grape seeds.

grape tomato A very small, ovoid tomato with a bright red or golden yellow color and a very sweet flavor.

grasshopper pie A light, creamy pie flavored with green crème de menthe and white crème de cacao.

grate To reduce food to small pieces by scraping it on a rough surface.

grater A tool used to reduce hard foods to small pieces or long thin strips by passing the food over the sharp raised edges of various-sized holes or slits. *See* box grater, cheese grater, ginger grater, lemon grater, nutmeg grater *and* rotary grater.

gratin, au (GRAW-ten, oh) A dish that is topped with cheese or bread crumbs and baked until browned; usually served in the baking dish.

gratin dish (GRAW-ten) A shallow oval or round metal or ceramic dish, generally with twin handles or a rim that extends on either side to form handles; it is used for preparing dishes that are usually topped with cheese or bread crumbs and cooked in a hot oven; the food is served from the dish.

gratin dish

gratinée (grah-teen-nay) French for a dish that is topped with cheese, bread crumbs or sauce and browned in the oven or under a broiler.

gratuity Money given voluntarily in return for or anticipation of service. *See* tips.

gravlax (GRAHV-lahks) A Swedish dish of salmon cured in a sugar, salt and dill mixture, sliced thin and served on dark bread with a dill and mustard sauce.

gravy A sauce made from meat or poultry juices combined with a liquid (e.g., milk, broth or wine) and a thickening agent (e.g., flour or cornstarch).

gravy boat An elongated, boat-shaped pitcher used to serve gravy; it usually sits on a plate, which is sometimes attached, and has a ladle; also known as a sauceboat.

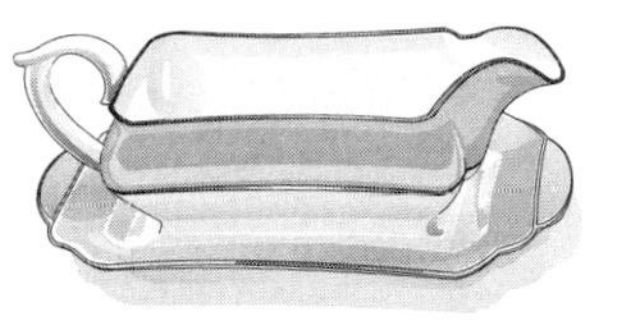
gravy boat

gravy browning A coloring agent used to darken sauces and gravies; usually made with caramelized sugar, salt and water.

gravy separator A clear plastic cup with a long spout set low in the cup; pan drippings are poured into the cup, the fat rises to the top, and the desirable underlying liquid can be poured off through the spout; generally available in 1.5- to 4-cup capacities.

gravy separator

gray sole A member of the flounder family found in the Atlantic Ocean; it has a gray striped skin on top, an average market length of 25 in. (63.5 cm), and a white flesh with a fine flavor; also known as witch flounder.

grazing The practice of snacking or eating small portions of several foods or dishes, usually at a restaurant; also known as modular eating.

grease *v.* To rub fat or a fat substitute on the surface of a cooking utensil or item of cookware. *n.* Rendered animal fat, such as bacon, beef or chicken fat.

great Northern bean A large, flat, kidney-shaped white bean; it has a delicate flavor and is generally available dried. *See* white beans.

great scallop A variety of scallops found in the Atlantic Ocean from Norway to Africa; it has a red to reddish-brown shell with a violet luster, an average diameter of 5–6 in. (12.7–15.2 cm), and a tender, sweet white meat.

grebenes; gribenes; gregen (greh-bah-nehz) A Jewish dish of the chicken fat and skin of the neck, thigh and rear fried with onions; the rendered fat is schmaltz, and the cracklings are eaten as a snack on toast or used for stuffing.

grecque, à la (greh-kew, ah lah) A French preparation method associated with Greek cuisine; the dishes are characterized by vegetables cooked in olive oil and lemon juice, served cold, or by a fish topped with a white wine sauce flavored with celery, fennel and coriander seeds.

green back rashers Unsmoked bacon from the hog's back; it lacks the meaty streak found in belly bacon and is used in British cuisine.

green bean A long, slender green pod that contains several small seeds; the entire crisp pod is edible; also known as a string bean (because of the fibrous string that runs down the side; modern varieties do not have this fiber), fresh bean and snap bean. *See* wax bean.

green chile stew A Native American dish of lamb cooked with onions, tomatoes, garlic, roasted green chiles and pinto beans and flavored with oregano and cumin; generally served on fry bread and topped with chopped onions and grated cheese.

green crab A variety of crab found in the Atlantic Ocean from New Jersey to Maine; it has a dark green or yellow-mottled green shell and an average width of 3 in. (7 cm); more popular in Europe than in the United States, where they are often used as bait.

greengage 1. A small, spherical plumlike fruit (*Prunus italica*) with a greenish-yellow skin and flesh and a tangy–sweet flavor; also known as Reine Claude. 2. An imprecisely used term for any of a variety of yellow- or green-skinned plums.

green garden peas Common small green peas; also known as English peas.

green garlic A young garlic plant that has not yet formed a well-defined bulb; it has long green leaves and a small, soft bulb that is white, sometimes tinged with pink; the immature bulb has a subtle, mild garlicky flavor.

green goddess dressing A salad dressing made from mayonnaise, tarragon vinegar and anchovies, seasoned with parsley, chives, tarragon, scallions and garlic; also used as a sauce for fish or shellfish.

green leaf lettuce A variety of leaf lettuce with bright green, ruffled-edge leaves, a tender texture and a mild flavor.

greenlip mussel; greenshell mussel A variety of large mussels found off New Zealand and Southeast Asia (especially Thailand); it has an elongated ovoid, gray-blue shell with a distinctive green edge, a plump orangish-yellow meat with a firm texture and a sweet flavor.

green mango An unripe mango; it has a high pectin content and a sour flavor and is the basis for chutneys and pickles, especially in India.

green meat Freshly slaughtered meat that has not had sufficient time to age and develop tenderness and a full flavor.

green onions *See* scallions.

green pepper; green bell pepper *See* bell pepper.

greens 1. A general term for the green, leafy parts of various plants that are eaten raw or cooked. 2. Members of the cabbage family, such as kale, spinach and chard, that have edible leaves.

green salad A salad consisting of a variety of salad greens (e.g., lettuce, spinach, endive, chicory and arugula) often combined with garnishes such as croutons, cheese and bacon and dressed with a vinaigrette or mayonnaise-based dressing.

green sauce A mayonnaise-based sauce flavored with finely minced herbs (e.g., parsley, chives, tarragon and watercress) or spinach; also known as mayonnaise verte.

green tea One of the three principal types of tea; the leaves are steamed and dried but not fermented; the beverage is generally a greenish-yellow color with a slightly bitter flavor suggestive of the fresh leaf. *See* black tea *and* oolong tea.

gremolada; gremolata (greh-moa-LAH-dah; greh-moa-LAH-tah) 1. An aromatic garnish of chopped parsley, garlic and lemon zest commonly used for osso buco. 2. A term for a granular ice similar to granita.

grenadin (greh-nah-dihn) A French cut of the veal carcass; it is a small thick steak cut from the leg.

grenadine (GREN-a-deen) A sweet, thick red syrup made from pomegranates; used in cocktails or consumed diluted with water.

grenouilles provençale (gruh-noo-ee pro-vahn-sahl) A French dish of frog legs sautéed in olive oil with garlic and parsley.

gribiche, sauce (gree-beesh) A cold French sauce based on a mayonnaise made with hard-cooked egg yolks instead of raw egg yolks and garnished with capers, herbs and julienne of hard-cooked egg whites; served with calf's head or fish.

griddle 1. A cooking surface similar to a flat top but made of thinner metal; foods are usually cooked directly on its surface. 2. A pan, usually made of cast aluminum or cast iron and sometimes with a nonstick coating, used to fry foods and available with a long handle or two hand grips.

griddle cake Any of a variety of breadlike products cooked on a flat griddle (e.g., pancakes).

griddle scraper A metal tool with a trapezoidal, beveled blade used to remove grease and food debris from a griddle.

grill *v.* To cook on a grill. *n.* 1. Cooking equipment in which the heat source (gas, charcoal, hardwood or electric) is located beneath the rack on which the food is placed; it is generally not enclosed, although it can be covered. 2. A restaurant or room, where, in theory, only grilled foods are served. 3. A restaurant or room, usually in a large hotel, where the service is faster and the meals less elaborate than in the main dining room. 4. *See* mixed grill.

grillade (gree-YAHD) 1. A Creole dish of pounded round steak cooked with tomatoes and other vegetables, seasoned with thyme, parsley and cayenne pepper, and usually served with grits. 2. French for grilled foods, especially meats.

grillardin (gree-yar-dahn) At a food services operation following the brigade system, it is the person responsible for all grilled items; also known as the grill station chef.

grilling A dry-heat cooking method in which foods are cooked by heat radiating from a source located below the cooking surface; the heat can be generated by electricity or by burning gas, hardwood or hardwood charcoals. *See* broiling.

grill pan A round or rectangular pan with a ridged bottom, usually made of cast iron or anodized aluminum, and used to grill meats on a stove top.

grill pan

grill spatula A large offset metal spatula, sometimes perforated, used for turning or removing foods from a grill or other cooking surface.

grill spatula

grilse The young salmon when it first leaves the sea to spawn in fresh water. *See* smolt.

grimslich (greems-lick) A Jewish dish of fritters made from matzo meal.

grind *v.* To reduce an object to small particles, usually by pounding, crushing or milling. *n.* The size, texture or other characteristic of a ground object.

grinder 1. Any of a variety of manual or electrical devices used to reduce food to small particles of varying degrees by the action of rotating blades; also known as a mill. 2. *See* hero.

grissini (gruh-SEE-nee) Thin, crisp Italian breadsticks.

grits Ground dried hominy; they have a bland flavor and a gritty texture; these tiny white granules are available in three grinds: fine, medium and coarse; also known as hominy grits.

groat 1. A grain kernel (e.g., oat and barley) that has had its husk removed. 2. The whole buckwheat kernel.

gross A dozen dozen (144).

gros sel (groh sell) French for crystalline unrefined sea salt; it is grayish in color and has a rich flavor.

gross margin; gross profit Revenue less the immediate (as opposed to overhead) costs associated with the production of the goods sold; in the food services industry, the difference between the costs of food served and the dollars collected for food sales.

ground-cherry 1. A cherry-sized fruit (*Physalis pruinosa*) with a yellow skin and a sweet, tart flavor reminiscent of pineapple; also known as a cossack pineapple and strawberry tomato. 2. An imprecisely used name for the closely related cape gooseberry.

ground lamb *See* lamb, ground.

grounds 1. Small particles of roasted coffee beans used to make coffee; the smaller the grounds, the greater the amount of surface area exposed to the water during the coffee-making process. *See* grind. 2. The sediment at or from the bottom of a liquid.

grouper A family of saltwater fish found in temperate waters worldwide; generally, they have a lean, white flesh, a firm texture, a mild to sweet flavor and an average market weight of 5–20 lb. (2.2–8.8 kg), although some can be much larger.

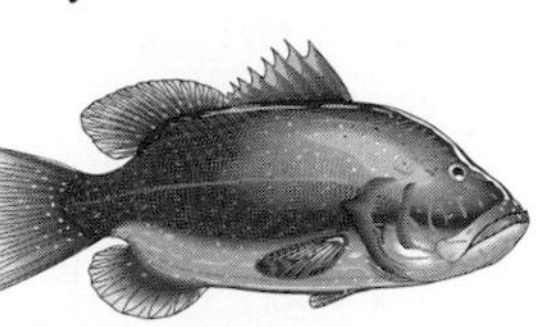
grouper

grouse (grauhs) Any of a variety of game birds found in Europe, especially Great Britain, and similar to the quail, with an average weight of 1.5 lb. (700 g); the flesh is dark red with a rich, gamey flavor.

growlers Containers, usually with a capacity of 1 to 1 $^1/_2$ gallons, used to buy and transport beer from a pub or microbrewery.

gruel A cereal, usually oatmeal, cooked with water or milk; it is usually thin and has little flavor.

grunion (GRUHN-yuhn) A fish found along the southern California coast; it has a silvery skin, an average market weight of 3–6 oz. (85–170 g), a moderately fatty flesh and a rich flavor.

grunt 1. A fish found off Florida; it has a rich, sweet flesh. 2. A colonial American dessert made with fresh fruit topped with biscuit dough and steamed in a closed container; also known as slump.

Gruyère (groo-YAIR) 1. A Swiss cheese, now also produced in France, made from cow's milk; it has a golden brown rind, a pale yellow interior, well-spaced very large holes, and a rich, sweet, nutty flavor. 2. A term used imprecisely, especially in France, for almost any cooked, compressed cheese sold in large rounds, including Emmental, Beaufort and Comté.

guacamole (gwah-kah-MOH-lee; gwah-kah-MOH-leh) A Mexican dip, sauce or side dish made from mashed avocado flavored with lemon or lime juice and chiles; sometimes chopped tomatoes, green onion and cilantro are added.

guajillo (gwah-HEE-yoh) An elongated, tapering dried chile with a deep orange-red color and a brown tinge, a thin flesh, and a sweet, hot flavor with undertones of green tea.

guava (GWAH-vah) A medium-sized tropical fruit (*Psidium guajave*); it has a spherical to plump pear shape, a smooth or rough greenish-white, yellow or red skin, a pale yellow to bright red flesh, small gritty seeds and an acidic, sweet flavor; eaten raw or used for preserves.

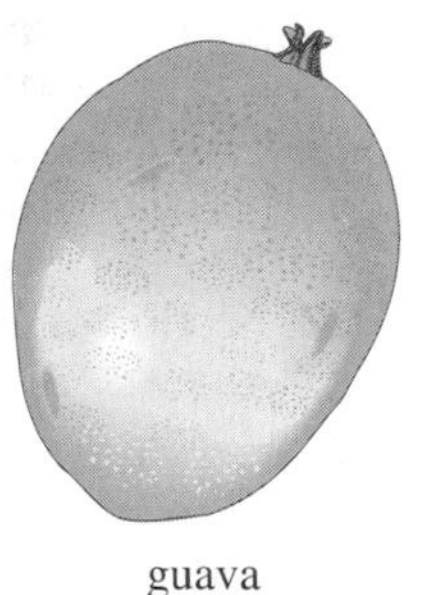
guava

guéridon (gha-ree-dawn) French for a pedestal table and used to describe a rolling cart used for preparing foods table side at a restaurant. *See* flambé trolley.

güero (GWEH-roh) A general name for any of a variety of fresh yellow chiles; usually those with a pale yellow color, an elongated, tapering shape and a medium to hot, slightly sweet flavor.

guest check 1. A form used by a food services facility to record all the food and/or beverages (with their prices) that a customer orders; it is tabulated and, with taxes and sometimes a gratuity added, presented to the customer for payment; also known as a check. 2. A form used by a hotel or the like to record the length of a guest's stay as well as all food, beverages and/or services charged to the room (i.e., account, with their prices) by the guest; it is tabulated and, with taxes added, presented to the guest for payment; also known as a check.

guindilla (gheen-dehl-yah) A sweet, medium-hot Spanish chile.

guinea; guinea fowl One of the principal kinds of poultry recognized by the U.S. Department of Agriculture (USDA) and the domesticated descendant of a game bird; it has light and dark meat, very little fat, a tender texture and a strong flavor.

guisado (ghee-SAH-doh) A Spanish stew of hare, rabbit, goose or pheasant flavored with bacon, herbs and wine; the cooking liquids are thickened with blood from the animal.

gum 1. Any of various thick, sticky, glutinous discharges from plants that harden on exposure to air and are soluble in water or will form a viscous mass with water. 2. *See* chewing gum. 3. Food additives used as emulsifiers, thickeners, binders, stabilizers and/or bodying agents in processed foods.

gumbo A Louisianan stewlike dish of meat, poultry and/or shellfish, okra, tomatoes and onions flavored with bay leaves, Worcestershire sauce and cayenne. *See* okra.

gurnard A fish found in the warmer Atlantic Ocean waters and in the Mediterranean Sea; there are two principal varieties: a red gurnard (also known as a sea cuckoo and sometimes mistakenly sold as a red mullet) and the inferior yellow gurnard.

gut To remove the viscera from animals.

gyoza (gee-OH-zah) Japanese-style Chinese meat-filled dumpling.

gyro (JEER-oh; ZHEER-oh; YEE-roh) A Greek dish consisting of spiced minced lamb molded around a spit and roasted vertically; it is sliced, folded in a pita, and topped with grilled onions, sweet peppers, tomatoes and a cucumber–yogurt sauce; marinated chicken is sometimes used instead of lamb.

H

habañero (ah-bah-NEH-roh) A squat, cylindrical chile with a dark green to orange skin that becomes red when mature and an exceptionally hot flavor; also available dried.

hachée, sauce (ah-schay) A classic French sauce of chopped shallots and onions reduced in vinegar, mixed with demi-glace and tomato purée, and flavored with duxelles, capers, ham and parsley; it is usually served with roasted red meat or venison.

haddock A fish related to the cod, found in the north Atlantic Ocean from Cape Cod to Newfoundland; it has a dark lateral line and a black patch on the shoulder known as the Devil's thumbprint or St. Peter's mark, a very lean, white flesh, a more delicate texture and stronger flavor than Atlantic cod, and an average market weight of 2–5 lb. (1–2.3 kg).

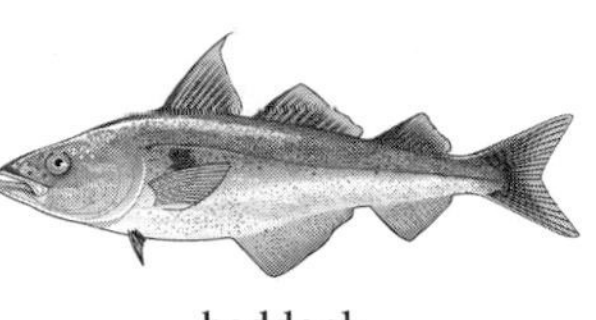

haddock

haejangkook (hey-jong-cook) A Korean beef soup made with abundant bones, marrow and blood pudding that is thought to cure hangovers; some call it Korean menudo.

haggis (HAG-ihs) A Scottish dish consisting of a stomach lining (usually from a sheep) stuffed with a mixture of liver, heart, lungs, onions, suet and oatmeal, seasoned with nutmeg and cayenne pepper, and then simmered. *See* paunch and pluck.

haiga-mai (hah-i-gah-mah-i) A Japanese rice with a nutty flavor; its grains are incompletely polished, leaving the germ intact.

hairy basil A type of basil with long, narrow, pale green leaves and sprigs that culminate in a red-tinged cluster of seed pods that, when dried, are soaked and used to add a lemony aroma and peppery flavor to beverages.

hake A variety of fish related to cod found in the Atlantic Ocean from southern Canada to North Carolina and in the Pacific Ocean along the U.S. West Coast; generally, they have an average market weight of 1–8 lb. (0.5–3.6 kg) and lean white flesh; significant varieties include the black hake, Boston hake, king hake, ling, mud hake and white hake.

half-and-half 1. A mixture of equal parts light cream (with an 18% milkfat content) and milk (with a 3.5% milkfat content); it does not contain enough fat to whip into a foam. 2. An English drink of equal parts stout and ale.

halibut A variety of flatfish found in the Pacific and Atlantic Oceans off North America; it has an average market weight of 10–60 lb. (4.5–27.2 kg) and tender, lean, white flesh with a mild flavor; significant varieties include Atlantic and Pacific halibut.

halvah; halva (hahl-VAH; HAHL-val) A Middle Eastern confection made from ground sesame seeds and honey, sometimes flavored with nuts or chocolate.

ham 1. A subprimal or fabricated cut of the pork primal fresh ham, with or without bones; available fresh, cured or smoked. 2. A term imprecisely applied to certain subprimal cuts of the pork Boston butt or shoulder primals. *See* fresh ham.

ham, country A bone-in ham produced in rural areas of the Southeastern United States; dry-cured in salt, sodium nitrate, sugar and other seasonings, then smoked over hardwood and aged for up to 12 months; it has a salty, well-seasoned flavor and a firm texture.

ham, country-style; ham, country-cured A bone-in ham produced outside of rural areas of the Southeastern United States but in the same manner as a country ham.

ham, sectioned and formed; ham, chunked and formed A boneless ham; the muscles are torn apart, tenderized (and usually defatted), and then reassembled in a casing or mold.

ham, smoked A ham that is smoked or has a smoky flavor imparted by liquid smoke.

ham, water-added A ham with up to 10% of its weight the result of water injected during the curing process; usually available with a smoke flavor.

Haman's ears Deep-fried, ear-shaped Jewish pastries served with sugar or honey at Purim.

hamantaschen (HAH-mahn-tah-shuhn) Small triangular Jewish pastries with a sweet filling of honey and poppy seeds, puréed prunes, apricots or nuts, usually served during Purim.

hamburger A patty made of ground beef; typically served on a bun and garnished with one or more condiments or foods, such as mustard, ketchup, cheese, bacon, and so on, and often identified by the items added (e.g., cheeseburger or bacon burger); also known as burger, beefburger and hamburger steak. *See* beef, ground.

hamburger bun A soft, round yeast roll, 3.5 to 4 in. in diameter; it may be made with regular or whole wheat flour and topped with sesame seeds, poppy seeds or toasted, chopped onions; usually used for hamburgers.

hamburger press A utensil used to form a round, flat ground meat patty; the bottom is a round mold of the appropriate height and depth and holds the meat; a plunger then presses the meat into the mold.

ham hock The lower portion of a hog's hind leg, consisting of bone, flesh and connective tissue and usually available in 2- to 3-in. (5.08- to 7.6-cm) lengths, smoked, cured or fresh; used to flavor soups and cooked vegetables.

hammer oyster An oyster found in the western Pacific Ocean and Indian Ocean; the shell has a hammer or ice pick shape and is 4–8 in. (10–20 cm) across.

ham with water and by-products A ham with water and bits of less desirable cuts of the pork carcass, pressed and formed; the percentage of by-products present must be stated on the label.

hand 1. A cluster of bananas. 2. A multipronged root or rhizome (e.g., ginger). 3. A bunch or bundle of leaves. 4. A British cut of the pork carcass; it is the foreleg and part of the shoulder and the equivalent of the picnic ham.

hand-formed cookies Cookies formed by hand into balls, logs, crescents or other shapes.

handful A traditional measure of weight or volume; it is approximately 1 oz. or 1 fl. oz.

hand pies Small, hand-sized pies made with a biscuit or pie dough crust enclosing a filling of stewed dried fruit; they can be baked or fried; also known as fried pies.

hanging tenderloin A fabricated cut of the beef primal flank not part of the tenderloin, it is somewhat tough but flavorful.

hanging weight The weight of a carcass or portion of a carcass before it is trimmed of any fat or bone.

Hangtown fry An omeletlike dish with oysters and bacon.

hard-ball stage A test for the density of sugar syrup: the point at which a drop of boiling sugar forms a rigid ball when dropped in ice water; this is equivalent to 250–265°F (121–130°C) on a candy thermometer.

hard-boiled egg; hard-cooked egg An egg simmered in its shell until it reaches a hard consistency, usually 12–15 minutes. *See* soft-boiled egg.

hard cheese knife A knife used to cut hard cheeses; the blade ranges in length from 4.5 to 12 in. and has a coped tip, flat cutting edge and etched sides (to prevent the cheese from sticking); its handle is usually offset.

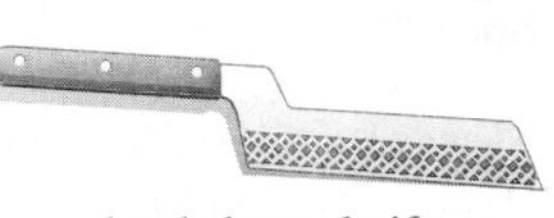
hard cheese knife

hard cider Pressed apple juice fermented without additional sugar; it usually has a relatively low alcohol content and a limited shelf life.

hard-crack stage A test for the density of sugar syrup: the point at which a drop of boiling sugar will separate into brittle threads when placed in ice water; equivalent to 300–310°F (148–153°C) on a candy thermometer.

hard cure A preservation method for meat; the meat is packed in salt, and the salt slowly displaces the meat's moisture content.

hard sauce A dessert sauce made from sugar and butter creamed until fluffy, then flavored with vanilla or a liquor such as brandy or rum; traditionally served with plum pudding; also known as brandy butter.

hard sausages *See* sausages, dried.

hardtack Hard, coarse unleavened bread traditionally used as army or navy rations because of its long shelf life; also known as a sailor's biscuit or sea biscuit.

hare Any of a variety of larger rabbits, usually not domesticated; generally, they have a lean, darkish flesh with a chewy texture and an earthy flavor.

haricot bean (ahr-ee-ko) A general term for several beans native to North America and cultivated in Europe; includes the flageolet, red kidney bean and navy bean.

haricot vert (ahr-ee-ko ver) French for green bean and used to describe a young, very slender green bean with a dull green, tender pod and very small seeds; also known as a French green bean and French bean.

harina enraizada (ah-REE-nah ehn-RAY-zah-dah) Flour made from sprouted wheat; because some of the starch is converted into sugar, it typically imparts a slight sweetness to products made from it.

harina para bollitos (ah-REE-nah pah-rah boh-lee-tohs) Cooked black-eyed peas, ground into a flour used to make fritters that are served as snacks and appetizers in South American and Caribbean cuisines.

harissa (hah-REE-suh) A hot, spicy North African condiment made from oil, chiles, garlic, cumin, coriander, caraway seeds and sometimes dried mint or verbena; served with couscous, soups and dried meat.

Harvard beets A dish of beets cooked in a sauce of vinegar, sugar and butter thickened with cornstarch.

harvest *v.* To gather crops. *n.* 1. The time when ripened crops are gathered. 2. The crops so gathered. 3. *See* crush.

Harvey sauce One of the oldest English bottled sauces; made from anchovies, cayenne pepper, mushrooms, ketchup, juice from pickled walnuts, shallots, garlic and vinegar.

Hasenpfeffer (HAH-zuhn-fehf-uhr) A thick German stew of rabbit flavored with peppers, wine and vinegar, served with noodles and dumplings, and garnished with sour cream.

hash *v.* To cut food into very small, irregularly shaped pieces. *n.* A dish of chopped meat (usually roast beef and/or corned beef), potatoes, and sometimes green pepper, celery and onions; pan-fried and often served with a poached or fried egg on top.

hash browns; hash-browned potatoes Chopped or grated cooked potatoes (green peppers and onions are sometimes added), fried in fat, traditionally bacon fat, pressed into a cake, and fried on the other side.

Hass avocado; Haas avocado An avocado with a dark green, almost black, pebbly skin.

hasty pudding A dish of cornmeal mush made with water or milk and sweetened with honey, maple syrup or molasses; it is served hot with milk or cream as a breakfast dish or dessert; also known as Indian pudding.

haunch The hindquarter of a game animal such as a deer; it consists of the leg and loin.

haupia A Hawaiian pudding of coconut milk, sugar and arrowroot, chilled until firm and cut into squares; it is often served at a luau.

haute cuisine (OHT kwih-ZEEN; kwee-ZEEN) French for high cooking style and used to describe fine foods professionally and elegantly prepared in an appropriate manner.

Havarti (hah-VAHR-tee) A semisoft Danish cheese made from cow's milk; it has a pale yellow interior with small irregular holes and a mild, tangy flavor that intensifies as it ages; also known as Danish Tilsit and Dofino.

Havre, sauce (ahrve) A French white wine sauce flavored with mussel stock and garnished with mussels and shrimp.

haw; hawberry A small berry of a member of the hawthorn family (genus *Crataegus*); it has a dark red color and a tart flavor and is usually used with crab apples for preserves.

Hawaiian salt A sea salt with a mild flavor, coarse texture and reddish tint; also known as alae salt.

hazard, biological In the food safety context, a danger to the safety of food due to disease-causing microorganisms such as bacteria, molds, yeasts, viruses or fungi.

hazard, chemical In the food safety context, a danger to the safety of food caused by chemical substances, especially cleaning agents, pesticides, herbicides, fungicides and toxic metals.

hazard, physical In the food safety context, a danger to the safety of food caused by particles such as glass chips, metal shavings, bits of wood or other foreign matter.

Hazard Analysis Critical Control Points (HACCP) (hass-up) A rigorous system of self-inspection intended to increase food safety by focusing on the flow of food through a food services facility; a critical control point is any step during the processing of food when a mistake can result in the transmission, growth or survival of a contaminant (usually pathogenic bacteria); the HACCP system evaluates the type and severity of the risk at each critical control point and identifies actions that can be taken to prevent or reduce each identified risk.

hazelnut The nut of the wild hazel tree (genus *Corylus*) found in the northern United States; shaped like a smooth brown marble, the nut has a rich, sweetish, distinctive flavor and is used (after the bitter brown skin is removed) in a variety of dishes, especially in baked goods and desserts containing chocolate or coffee flavors. *See* filbert.

hazelnut oil An oil obtained by pressing hazelnuts; it has a nutty-brown color, a full, nutty flavor, and a fragrant aroma; used principally in baked goods and salad dressings.

headcheese A seasoned sausage made from meat picked from a calf's or hog's head; it is cooked in a gelatinous broth, molded, and served cold and thinly sliced.

headwaiter The person responsible for service throughout a restaurant or a section of a restaurant; in smaller operations, this role may be assumed by the maître d' or a captain; also known as a chef de salle.

heart 1. A variety meat; generally tough, chewy and flavorful; lamb and calf hearts are often stuffed and braised; poultry hearts are used for stocks and stuffing. 2. The dense center of a leafy, stalky vegetable such as cabbage. 3. *See* artichoke, common.

hearth The heated floor or baking surface of an oven.

hearth bread Any bread baked directly on the floor of the oven instead of in a pan.

hearts of palm The inner part of the stem of the tropical cabbage palm (family Palmaceae); it has an ivory color, many concentric layers, and a delicate flavor reminiscent of an artichoke; usually available canned (packed in water) and used in salads; also known as chou coco, chou glouglou, chou palmiste, palm hearts and swamp cabbage.

heat diffuser A metal grid, approximately 1 in. tall, placed on a stove top to raise a pot farther from the heat source to help maintain a very slow simmer.

heat diffuser

heather honey A reddish-brown honey with a creamy texture similar to that of soft butter and a strong, distinctive flavor; it is principally made from heather blossoms.

heat lamp A specialized piece of equipment used (especially at banquets or off-premises events) to keep food warm and to maintain the temperature of foods that might become soggy in a chafing dish (e.g., pizza or fried foods).

heat lamp

heavenly hash 1. A dessert made with whipped cream and vanilla wafer cookies. 2. A candy made with marshmallows and nuts and coated with chocolate.

heavy cream; heavy whipping cream *See* cream, heavy whipping.

heavy syrup A mixture of two parts sugar dissolved in one part water; used in beverages and sorbets and for moistening and flavoring sponge cakes.

hedgehog mushroom A wild, creamy yellow mushroom (*Hydnum repandum*) with firm flesh and a succulent, tangy flavor; also known as a wood hedgehog mushroom.

hedgehog pudding Any of several boiled or baked puddings whose upper surface is stuck with slivered almonds.

heel The rear edge of a knife blade; it extends below the bottom line of the handle.

heel; heel of round 1. A subprimal cut from the beef primal round; it is composed of the small muscle groups located in the lower round and adjacent to the femur; also known as horseshoe. 2. A subprimal cut from the veal primal leg.

heel end A subprimal cut of the beef primal round; it is a group of small muscles located in the lower portion of the outside round.

heifers Young cows or cows before their first calving; their flesh is darker, more flavorful and slightly tougher than veal.

heiko (hi-koe) A smooth, thick, dark brown shrimp paste used in Thai and Malaysian cuisines as a flavoring; also known as kapi leaw (Thai).

Heimlich maneuver A first-aid procedure for choking victims; a sudden upward pressure is applied to the upper abdomen to force any foreign object from the windpipe.

hen 1. The female of domesticated fowl, especially the chicken. 2. The female lobster.

hen, stewing A mature hen slaughtered when older than 10 months; it has a good flavor, a slightly tough flesh, a nonflexible breastbone, and an average market weight of 2.5–8 lb. (1–3.5 kg).

hen of the wood mushroom A large wild mushroom (*Grifola frondosa*) with a reddish-orange cap; it has a somewhat chewy texture and mild flavor; also known as ram's head mushroom.

Henry IV A classic French dish consisting of tournedos or kidneys, garnished with pont-neuf potatoes and béarnaise sauce.

herbes de Provence (AIRBS duh proh-VAWNS) Traditionally associated with France's Provence region, it is a blend of dried herbs such as basil, thyme, sage, rosemary, summer savory, marjoram, fennel seeds and lavender.

herbivore An animal that, by nature, eats only plant foods. *See* vegetarian.

herb mill A utensil used to mince herbs; it consists of a hopper with rotating blades that are turned by a crank.

herb mill

herbs Any of a large group of annual and perennial plants whose leaves, stems or flowers are used as a flavoring; usually available fresh and dried. *See* spices.

herb vinegar A flavored vinegar made by steeping herbs in wine vinegar.

Hereford A breed of beef cattle descended from 18th-century English stock; it efficiently converts grass to meat.

Herman Midwestern colloquialism for a sweet sourdough starter made with sugar or honey; used for making sweet breads and coffee cakes.

hermit A colonial New England cookie made with spices, chopped fruit, nuts and brown sugar or molasses.

hero; hero sandwich 1. A large sandwich consisting of a small loaf of French or Italian bread filled with cold cuts and garnished with tomatoes, lettuce, pickles and peppers; also known as grinder, hoagie, po'boy, and submarine sandwich. 2. Any large sandwich built on a small loaf of French or Italian bread and filled with hot or cold foods such as meatballs or tuna salad.

herring A very large family of saltwater fish most often found in the northern Atlantic and Pacific Oceans; generally, they have a long body, a silvery-blue skin, a moderate-to-high fat content, a soft texture, a strong flavor, and an average weight of 8 oz. (226.8 g); usually available smoked, pickled or cured in brine. *See* sardine.

hibachi (hih-BAH-chee) Japanese for fire pot and used to describe a small square, round or oblong container, usually of cast iron, made to hold fuel (usually charcoal); it has a grill that sits on top.

hibachi

hickory nut The nut of any of several trees of the genus *Carya*, including the pecan; the common hickory nut has a very hard shell and a rich, buttery flavor and can be used instead of the thinner-shelled pecan.

high A tasting term for a fully ripened (aged) or overly ripened (aged), strong-smelling cheese or meat (especially game).

high-carbon stainless steel An alloy of carbon and stainless steel that will not rust or corrode; when used for a knife blade, it is easily sharpened and holds its edge. *See* carbon steel *and* stainless steel.

high-gluten flour A term used imprecisely for wheat flour with a high protein content; this results in high gluten-forming potential. *See* gluten.

highlanders British shortbread cookies shaped into small, thick rounds. *See* shortbread.

high ratio 1. A type of cake batter containing a large amount of sugar and liquid as well as an emulsified shortening and mixed using a special method. 2. A mixing method for such cakes (the liquid is added in two stages); also known as the two-stage method.

high-ratio cakes A form of creamed-fat cake that uses emulsified shortening and has a two-stage mixing method.

Himmel und Erbe (him-mel oond her-bae) German for heaven and earth and used to describe a casserole of apples, potatoes, onions and sausage.

hind loin A British cut of the pork carcass; it contains the kidney and tenderloin.

hindquarter 1. Either bilateral half of the back section of a beef carcass; it includes the entire round, short loin, sirloin and flank primals as well as the kidneys. 2. Either bilateral half of the hindsaddle of a veal carcass; it contains half of the loin and leg primals. 3. Either bilateral half of the hindsaddle of a lamb carcass; it contains half of the loin and leg primals. 4. *See* forequarter.

hindsaddle 1. The undivided hindquarters (the rear half) of a veal carcass; it contains the loin and leg primals. 2. The undivided hindquarters of a lamb carcass; it contains the loin and leg primals and both kidneys. 3. *See* foresaddle.

hindshank A portion of the lower hindlimb (below the knee) of a quadruped. *See* shank.

hip bone steak A fabricated cut of the beef primal sirloin; it is a steak cut from the center of the sirloin.

Hippen paste; Hippen masse (hip-in MAHSS) A sweet wafer dough, often flavored with almonds; the batter is spread on a baking sheet, baked, then shaped while still hot to form decorations for pastries or containers for ice cream, custards or fruit.

hob A cooking surface built into the work surface of a kitchen and fitted with two to four gas or electric burners.

hobo egg A dish made from a piece of bread with a hole in its center; an egg is placed in the opening and the entire concoction is fried; also known as ace in the hole.

hochepot (osh-eh-poh) A French and Belgian stewlike dish consisting of layers of vegetables and meats, including pig's ears and feet.

hock 1. The lower portion of a mammal's leg, usually corresponding to the human ankle. 2. British term for German white wines, specifically those produced in the Rhine River region as opposed to the Moselle River region.

hoecake A cornmeal pancake cooked on a griddle; also known as a johnnycake.

hogfish A saltwater variety of catfish.

hog jowl; hog's jowl A hog's cheek, usually cut into squares and then cured and smoked; fattier than bacon, it is used in much the same manner; also known as jowl bacon.

hog plum A small, plumlike fruit (*Spondias mombin*) native to the Southern United States and Caribbean region; it has a thin yellow-orange skin, a yellow-orange flesh and a single large seed; used for preserves.

hogs 1. The collective name for all domesticated swine (family Suidae), including pigs, sows and boars. 2. Domesticated swine weighing more than 120 lb. (54.4 kg) and raised for their flesh.

hoisin (HOY-sihn) A thick, reddish-brown, sweet-and-spicy sauce made from soybeans, garlic, chiles and various spices and used as a condiment and flavoring in Chinese cuisines; also known as Peking sauce, red vegetable sauce and ten-flavored sauce.

hoja santa (OH-hah sahn-tah) A sassafras- or anise-flavored herb (*Piper auritum sanctum*) with large, heart-shaped, dark green leaves and long, thin, creamy-colored flowers; used with fish and in tamales and green moles in Mexican cuisines.

hollandaise; hollandaise, sauce (ohl-lahn-dez) A French leading sauce made from an emulsification of butter, egg yolks and flavorings (especially lemon juice); also known as Dutch sauce.

hollow molding A chocolate or candy molding technique using a two-part hinged mold; the mold is opened and the inside of the entire mold is coated with the candy mixture or melted chocolate; after it sets, the candy or chocolate is removed and the halves are joined, forming a single, hollow unit. *See* solid molding.

Holstein (hol-steen) 1. A French preparation method for a veal escalope; it is breaded, pan-fried, and garnished with poached or fried egg, gherkins, beetroot, olives, capers, anchovies and lemon wedges. 2. A breed of large black and white dairy cattle that produce large quantities of relatively lowfat milk.

Holstein, sauce A French compound sauce made from a béchamel flavored with white wine and fish glaze, seasoned with nutmeg and bound with a liaison of egg yolks.

Holsteiner Schnitzel (HOL-shtigh-nerr SHNIT-serl) A German veal cutlet that is breaded and fried and garnished with a fried egg and anchovy; also known as veal Holstein.

holy trinity The combination of chopped green peppers, onions and celery used in Creole cooking.

homard à l'Américaine (oh-mahr-da la-may-ree-ken) A French dish consisting of a lobster sautéed in olive oil, then cooked in a sauce of tomatoes, garlic, onion, shallots, white wine, brandy, tarragon and parsley.

homard à la nage (oh-MAHR ah lah najg) A French dish consisting of a whole small lobster cooked in white wine stock.

home fries; home-fried potatoes Slices of raw or boiled potatoes that are pan-fried, sometimes with onions and green peppers; also known as cottage fries.

hominy Dried corn kernels from which the hull and germ have been removed by either mechanical methods or soaking the grains in hydrated lime or lye; the white or yellow kernels resemble popcorn and have a soft, chewy texture and a smoky–sour flavor. *See* grits.

homogenization The process by which milk is spun at very high speeds to break down the fat globules and produce a stable, uniform dispersion.

honey A sweet, usually viscous, liquid made by bees from flower nectar and stored in the cells of the hive for food; generally contains 17–20% water and 76–80% sucrose; consumed fresh or after processing, it is usually used as a nutritive sweetener.

honeybun A flat, spiral-shaped yeast breakfast roll glazed with honey.

honeycomb A structure composed of rows of hexagon-shaped wax cells formed by bees in their hives to store honey, pollen and eggs.

honeydew melon A slightly ovoid, large muskmelon; it has a smooth, creamy-yellow rind with a pale green, juicy flesh and a sweet flavor.

honey mushroom A long-stemmed, yellow mushroom (*Armillaria mellea*) that grows wild in large clusters on tree trunks; it has a robust, meaty, slightly astringent flavor and should always be cooked.

hongroise, à la (ohng-wahz, ah lah) French for Hungarian style and used to describe a dish served with onions, sour cream, paprika and perhaps sweet bell pepper, cabbage or leeks.

Hongroise, sauce (ohng-wahz) A French compound sauce made from a velouté or tomato concentrate flavored with onions, paprika and white wine and finished with a Mornay sauce (if used with eggs), a fumet with butter (if for fish), a demi-glaze (if for meat), or additional velouté or suprême sauce (if for poultry).

hood; hood vent *See* vent.

Hoosier cake A coarse-textured gingerbread cake, popular in Kentucky and Indiana during the mid-19th century.

hopping john; hoppin' john A dish from the American South consisting of black-eyed peas cooked with a ham hock and served over white rice.

horchata (oar-CHAH-tay) A Spanish and Mexican beverage made from almonds or pumpkin seeds; alcoholic and nonalcoholic versions are available.

horehound A downy-leaved member of the mint family (*Marrubium vulgare*); the juice extracted from its leaves has a slightly bitter flavor and is used to make horehound candy, cough syrup and lozenges.

horn of plenty mushroom A funnel-shaped wild mushroom (*Craterellus cornucopioides*) found throughout Europe; it has a fluted edge, deep gills, a dark brown-gray to black color, a delicate texture and a rich, buttery flavor (especially if dried and then reconstituted); also known as false truffle and trumpet of death mushroom.

hors d'oeuvre (ohr durv) *sing.* and *pl.*; Americanized *pl.* also hors d'oeuvres. A very small portion of a hot or cold food served before a meal to stimulate the appetite or at a social gathering in lieu of a meal.

horse mushroom A large, white mushroom (*Agaricus arvensis*) that grows in open spaces during the fall and is similar to the common field mushroom but with a more concentrated, slight aniselike flavor.

horseradish A plant (*Armoracia rusticana*) with a large, white root that has a sharp, biting, spicy flavor; the root is peeled and grated and used as a condiment.

horseradish sauce An English sauce made from horseradish, vinegar, sugar, dry mustard, cream, salt and pepper; usually served with roast beef or fish.

horseshoe A subprimal cut of the beef primal round; the primal's heel end, it is somewhat tough and flavorful.

hot and sour A Chinese term for food that is served with a spicy sauce made with chiles, chile oil, ginger, garlic and scallions.

hot black bean sauce A paste of fermented soybeans and ground hot chiles used as a flavoring in Chinese cuisines; also known as chile bean sauce.

hotchpotch; hodgepodge Any of several American dishes based on European stewlike dishes made with layers of various meats and vegetables (particularly onions and potatoes).

hot cross buns Round, sweet yeast rolls containing candied fruit or raisins and marked on top with a cross of white confectioners' sugar icing; traditionally served on Good Friday.

hot dog *See* frankfurter.

hotel pan A rectangular stainless steel pan with a lip; it is designed to rest in a steam table or rack and is used to cook, drain, ice, store or serve foods; a full-sized pan is 12 × 20 in. with pans one-half, one-third, and so on of this size available; depth is standardized at 2-in. intervals (a 2-in.-deep pan is known as a 200 pan); also known as a steam table pan.

hotel pan

hotel steak A fabricated cut of the beef primal loin; it is a bone-in shell steak or boneless strip steak from the top of the loin.

hot-foods section One of the principal work sections of a food services facility; it typically contains a broiler station, fry station, griddle station, sauté/sauce station and a holding area.

hot fudge A thick, rich sauce made with chocolate, butter, sugar and cream; served warm as an ice cream or dessert topping.

hothouse cucumber *See* English cucumber.

hot oven An oven set to a temperature of 400–450°F (204.4–232°C). *See* moderate oven *and* slow oven.

hot plate 1. An electrically heated lidded pan for cooking or warming food. 2. A tabletop cooking device with one or two electric or gas burners.

hotpot A British stewlike dish consisting of layers of vegetables, mutton, sheep's kidneys and sometimes oysters, topped with potatoes.

hot sauce A seasoning sauce, usually commercially made, containing chile peppers, salt and vinegar.

hot smoker, indoor A metal smoke box with a sliding cover; 15 × 11 × 3 in.; it sits on a single burner that heats a small amount of wood shavings in the bottom of the box whose fumes waft up and around a drip-pan insert with an inset rack holding the food.

hot smoking A method of curing, preserving and/or flavoring certain foods by exposing them to smoke at temperatures of 200–250°F (93–121°C); such foods are usually fully cooked after smoking; many hot-smoked meats, fish, shellfish and poultry are first salt-dried or brined. *See* cold smoking.

house The management or ownership of a commercial establishment, as in "house rules" and "on the house."

Hubbard squash A large winter squash with a very thick, bumpy shell, a green to orange color, a grainy, yellow-orange flesh, and a bland, mild flavor; also known as Ohio squash.

huckleberry A wild berry (*Vaccinium myrtillus*) native to North America; it has a thick dark blue skin, a blue flesh, 10 hard seeds in the center, and a mildly sweet flavor and is eaten raw or used in preserves and baked goods; it is sometimes confused with the blueberry, which has a thinner skin and many tiny seeds; also known as bilberry and whortleberry.

huevos rancheros (WEH-vohs rahn-CHER-ohs) A Mexican dish of fried eggs set on a tortilla and covered with a tomato and chile salsa.

Huguenot torte (hue-gah-knot tort) A dessert popular in Charleston, South Carolina, consisting of a baked apple and nut mixture; when cool, it is garnished with whipped cream and sprinkled with chopped nuts.

hui (who-he) Chinese for blending or cooking small bits of food together in a covered pot; the mixture is usually thickened before service.

Huitlacoche (hweet-la-KO-chay) *See* corn smut.

hull *v*. 1. To remove the hull (husk) from grains. 2. To remove the leafy portion of a strawberry found at the base of its stem and often adhering to the fruit. *n*. The general term for the outermost protective covering of a grain kernel or nut; its texture can range from hard and brittle to thin and papery. *See* husk.

hulling A milling process in which the hull (husk) is removed from grains.

humble pie A 17th-century British dish of deer organs (e.g., liver, heart and kidney) cooked as a pie and fed to the servants.

hummingbird cake A moist layer cake made with pineapple and bananas and filled with a cream cheese frosting.

hummus (HOOM-uhs) A Middle Eastern sauce made from mashed chickpeas seasoned with lemon juice, garlic and olive or sesame oil; usually served as a dip.

hundreds and thousands Small, brightly colored sugar candies used as decoration on cakes, trifle and cookies; also known as sprinkles. *See* jimmies.

hundred-year-old eggs Chinese preserved eggs; they are covered with lime, ashes and salt, buried in shallow holes for 100 days, and then eaten uncooked accompanied by soy sauce and minced ginger; also known as Ming Dynasty eggs, fermented eggs, ancient eggs and century eggs.

Hungarian cherry pepper; Hungarian cherry chile A small, almost spherical chile with a deep red color, a thick flesh and mild to medium hot flavor; available fresh or dried.

Hungarian sweet pepper; Hungarian sweet chile An elongated, tapering pepper with a rounded end, a deep red color, a thick flesh and a sweet flavor. *See* paprika.

hunger The sensation resulting from a lack of food and the compelling need to eat; generally experienced as weakness and an unpleasant sensation or even pain in the lower part of the chest. *See* appetite.

hunter's sauce A sauce that contains tomatoes, garlic, onions and mushrooms.

hure (uhr) Meat, fish or vegetables presented in aspic in a terrine; served sliced or in an individual mold; sometimes called an aspic.

hush puppy A deep-fried cornmeal dumpling flavored with onions, traditionally served with fried fish, especially in the American South.

husk The outermost protective covering found on most grains; usually a dry, thin, papery wrapper. *See* hull.

hybrid The offspring of plants or animals of different breeds, varieties, species or genera. *See* variety.

hydrogenated fat Generally, a bland, white semisolid saturated fat (e.g., hard margarine) made from an unsaturated liquid oil.

hydrogenation The process of hardening (solidifying or semisolidifying) an unsaturated fat by adding hydrogen at one or more points of unsaturation.

hydrometer An instrument consisting of a sealed cylinder and weighted bulb that when placed in a liquid indicates its specific gravity by a comparison of the surface of the liquid with gradations on the instrument's emerging stem.

hydroponics The science of growing plants in a liquid nutrient solution rather than soil.

hygroscopic Having the property or characteristic of absorbing or attracting moisture from the air.

hyssop An herb (*Hyssopus officinales*) with dark green leaves and deep blue or pink flowers; the leaves have a strong mint and licorice flavor and aroma and are used in salads and with fatty meats and fish.

Iago (E-ah-go) A small British pastry or petit four named for the villain in Shakespeare's Othello; composed of layers of sponge cake sandwiched with coffee buttercream and topped with coffee fondant.

ibrik (I-brik) A small, long-handled Turkish pot with a bulbous bottom, narrow waist and flared top; used for Turkish coffee.

ice *v.* 1. To chill a glass or serving dish so that a coat of frost forms on its surface. 2. To spread frosting (icing) over the surface of a cake or cookie. *n.* 1. Frozen water; water freezes at 32°F (0°C). 2. A frozen mixture of water, sugar and a flavoring such as fruit juice or wine; stirred frequently while freezing; it has a grainy texture.

ice bath A mixture of ice and water used to chill a food or beverage rapidly.

iceberg lettuce A variety of crisp head lettuce with a compact spherical head of pale green leaves that become whitish-yellow toward the center; developed in the United States at the end of the 19th century.

icebox cookie A type of cookie in which the dough is formed into a log and chilled, then sliced into rounds for baking; also known as a refrigerator cookie.

icebox pie A pie with a cookie-crumb crust and a creamy filling that is chilled or frozen until firm.

ice bucket 1. A bucket, usually plastic, metal or glass, often with a lid and sometimes insulated; used to hold ice needed for drinks. 2. A container in which wine is chilled and/or kept, usually at the table; also known as a wine bucket or wine cooler.

ice chest An insulated box used to keep foods cold. *See* cooler.

ice chipper A metal ice-carving tool resembling a small rake; it has a 2-in.-wide band with six 1-in.-long spikes.

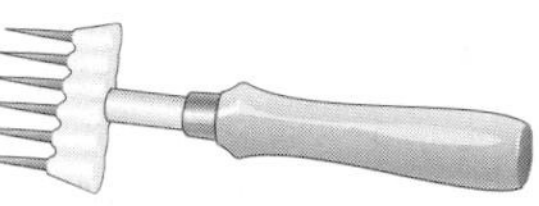

ice chipper

ice cream A rich, frozen dessert made with dairy products, sugar, eggs and various flavorings; the U.S. Department of Agriculture (USDA) requires products labeled ice cream to contain at least 10% milkfat and 20% milk solids.

ice cream cone 1. A wafer rolled into a cone and used to hold ice cream for eating; sometimes dipped in chocolate or other syrup and coated with nuts or the like. 2. A wafer cylinder used to hold ice cream. 3. The cone and ice cream.

ice cream freezer 1. An appliance used to make ice cream; the ingredients are sealed in a metal container equipped with a paddle, the container is placed in a tub of ice and salt, and the paddle is turned by hand or a motor until the mixture is set. 2. An ice cream maker with a layered container; the ingredients are placed in the cavity with a paddle that is turned by hand; there is a refrigerant between the layers, which, when chilled before using, sets the ingredients. 3. An electrical appliance that chills and churns the ice cream mixture.

ice cream salt *See* rock salt.

ice cream scoop A utensil used to remove ice cream from its container; it can be a simple trowel-like tool or have a bowl with a lever-operated blade to remove the bowl's contents; available in various sizes.

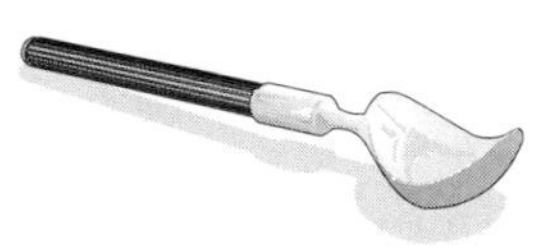

ice cream scoop

ice cream soda A beverage made from soda water, flavored syrup and ice cream, sometimes topped with whipped cream.

iced coffee A beverage of coffee, a sweetener and milk or cream; served chilled with ice in a glass.

iced tea Freshly brewed tea chilled and served with ice and sometimes flavored with a sweetener and/or lemon juice.

iced tea spoon A long-handled spoon used for stirring iced tea.

Iceland scallop A variety of scallops found off Greenland and Iceland through the Arctic Ocean to Japan; the brownish-green shell has an average diameter of 4 in. (10.1 cm); the meat is tender, sweet and white.

ice milk A frozen dessert made with dairy products, sugar, eggs and flavoring; similar to ice cream but made with less milkfat (3–6%), sugar (12–15%) and milk solids (11–14%).

ice pick An awl-like tool with a weighted handle and a strong, thin 5-in. shaft with a sharp point; it is used for chopping large blocks of ice.

ice tongs Small tongs often with claw-shaped tips used to remove ice from an ice bucket.

icing A sweet covering or filling such as buttercream or ganache; used for cakes and pastries; also known as frosting.

icing comb *See* cake comb.

icing stencil A flat plastic disk with words and/or designs cut out of it; it is pressed onto the cake top, leaving an indention that provides a pattern to be followed when squeezing icing from a pastry bag.

icing sugar British for confectioners' sugar.

ikura (ee-koo-ra) Japanese for the orange-red roe of salmon, which, when eaten, release a creamy textured, rich, concentrated, fish-flavored oil; often used as a sushi topping.

ilama A fruit (*Annona diversifolia*) native to Mexico; it has an elongated shape and a smooth or rough skin; there are two principal varieties: pink (has a magenta pink skin with a white bloom, a pink flesh and a flavor similar to a cherimoya) and green (has a green skin with a white bloom, a greenish flesh and a sweeter flavor reminiscent of a sugar apple).

il diplomatico (eel dep-loh-mah-tee-koh) An Italian pastry made by lining a loaf pan with slices of sponge cake soaked in rum and espresso, then filling the pan with chocolate mousse; the loaf is unmolded and coated with melted chocolate or chocolate ganache.

île flottante (eel floh-tahng) 1. French for floating island and used to describe a dessert composed of a single large mound of meringue floating in a pool of vanilla custard sauce. *See* floating island. 2. A French dessert composed of a liqueur-soaked sponge cake topped with jam, nuts and whipped cream that is served in a pool of custard sauce.

imam bayildi (AH-mahn by-yahl-deh) Turkish for the Imam fainted and used to describe a dish of roasted eggplant stuffed with tomatoes, garlic, onions, peppers and pine nuts; served cold.

imitation food A labeling term approved by the U.S. Food and Drug Administration (FDA) to describe a processed food that is intended to substitute for another food and is nutritionally inferior to the food being imitated (e.g., cheese and imitation cheese); although it may have fewer essential nutrients and often less flavor than the food it is intended to imitate, it usually has improved shelf life, cooking properties or other characteristics.

immersion blender A small, narrow, handheld blender with a rotary blade at one end; portable, it has variable speeds and can be immersed directly into a pot; whisk attachments are available.

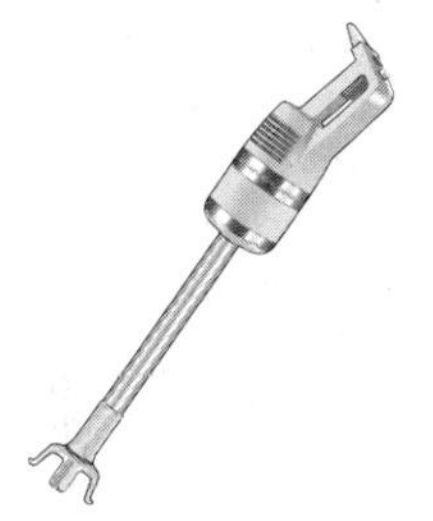

immersion blender

impératrice, à l' (ahn-pair-ah-TREES, ahl) French for empress and used to describe a variety of rich sweet or savory dishes with a rice base; the name is most commonly applied to a dessert made with rice, candied fruits and a Bavarian cream mixture.

impératrice, sauce; empress sauce (ahm-pair-ah-TRESS) A French compound sauce made from an allemande sauce flavored with truffle essence and chicken glaze and finished with unsweetened whipped cream.

impériale, á l' (eem-pay-ree-ahl, ahl) A French garnish for fowl consisting of truffles, foie gras, mushrooms and cockscombs.

imperial system A measurement system used in Great Britain, Canada and other countries associated with the former British Empire; it uses pounds and ounces for weight and pints and fluid ounces for volume. *See* metric system *and* U.S. system.

impossible pie A dessert made with a mixture of eggs, milk, sugar, butter, coconut and a packaged biscuit mix that is baked in a pie tin; the mix settles to the bottom during baking, forming the crust.

IMPS/NAMP *See* NAMP/IMPS.

inaka-miso (ee-nah-kah-mee-so) A rich, red miso made with barley mold; it can be sweet or salty and is used in soups or braised dishes; also known as red miso and sendai-miso.

inamona A Hawaiian condiment of crushed kukui mixed with chiles and salt.

Indian fig; Indian pear *See* prickly pear.

Indian meal Another name for cornmeal.

Indian pudding *See* hasty pudding.

indienne, à l' (een-DYEHN, ahl) A French preparation method associated with Indian cuisines; the dishes are usually prepared with curry powder and served over rice.

individually quick frozen (IQF) A preservation method in which each individual item of food (e.g., a slice of fruit, berry or fish) is rapidly frozen before packaging; IQF foods are not packaged with syrup or sauce.

Indonesian relish A pickle made from vegetables such as cabbage, onions, leeks, carrots and cucumbers; it has a mild flavor and is usually served with smoked fish.

induction cooking A cooking method that uses a special coil placed below the stove top's surface in combination with specially designed cookware to generate heat rapidly with an alternating magnetic field.

infection 1. The condition produced when pathogenic microorganisms (including viruses) invade tissues and multiply there, causing injurious effects. 2. In the food safety context, a type of bacterial illness caused by ingesting pathogenic bacteria (called infectants); the infectants, which cause the illness, can usually be destroyed by cooking foods containing the bacteria to a sufficiently high temperature, generally 165°F (74°C).

infuse To steep a seasoning or food in a hot liquid until the liquid absorbs the item's flavor.

injected meat A cut of meat that has had a curing solution introduced throughout it by injection or pumping; also known as pumped meat.

injera; aenjera (in-jah-raw) An Ethiopian pancakelike bread, often made from teff.

inky cap; ink cap A bell-shaped mushroom (*Coprinus atramentarius*) with a pale gray color.

insecticide A synthetic or naturally occurring substance used to kill insects; used to protect a human or animal food crop, it can become an incidental food additive.

inside chuck roll A subprimal cut of the beef primal chuck; it is a rolled center-cut chuck roast that is flavorful but tough.

inside round; inside top round *See* top round.

instant A processed food or a food from which water has been removed; it is ready to use or consume once rehydrated with the appropriate amount of hot or cold water or other liquid.

instant coffee 1. A powdered soluble extract made by heat-drying freshly brewed coffee. *See* freeze-dried coffee granules or crystals. 2. The reconstituted beverage, usually hot, made from the extract.

instant rice Fully cooked and flash-frozen rice; when rehydrated, it can lack flavor and be gritty; also known as quick-cooking rice.

instant tea 1. Soluble powder or granules made by heat-drying freshly brewed tea; sometimes flavored with sweeteners, lemon and/or other flavorings. 2. The reconstituted beverage, either hot or iced, made from the powder or granules.

institutional cook A cook who generally works with large quantities of prepackaged or prepared foods for a captive market such as a school or prison.

insulated carriers Equipment used to hold food at a constant temperature for a limited period of time by use of various insulating materials; they are often designed to hold hotel pans or sheet pans and are used when preparing for buffets or off-premise catering events; some are equipped with wheels and/or spigots for serving hot or cold beverages.

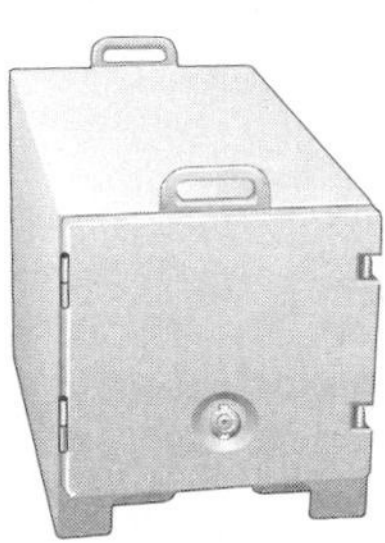
insulated carrier

intermezzo A course served before the entrée, usually sorbet, as a palate cleanser.

intestines A variety meat, generally from cows, calves, lambs and hogs; long tubes of slightly translucentd, somewhat elastic flesh with a bland flavor; used for casings or deep-fried as chittlings.

intoxication 1. A type of bacterial illness caused by ingesting toxin-producing bacteria; although the bacteria are themselves harmless, the toxins produced as a by-product of their life processes can be poisonous, and the toxins are usually not destroyed by cooking foods that contain them (although the bacteria will be destroyed). 2. The condition of being intoxicated.

invert sugar Sucrose that has been broken down (i.e., inverted) into its two components, glucose and fructose, with the use of heat and acid; this inversion prevents crystallization and makes for smoother candies, frostings and confections.

iodized salt Table salt (sodium chloride) containing potassium iodide, a source of the essential nutrient iodine.

Ipswich clams An Atlantic soft-shell clam.

IQF *See* individually quick frozen.

Irish breakfast A hearty breakfast consisting of eggs, meat (sausage, blood sausage, bacon, ham and/or fish), baked goods, jam, juice and tea or coffee.

Irish breakfast tea A blend of Indian Assam teas; the beverage is strong and robust.

Irish Coffee A drink made of Irish whiskey, hot black coffee and sugar with a layer of cream floated on top.

Irish pease pudding An Irish dish of dried green or yellow peas cooked, mashed and mixed with egg and butter and sometimes flavored with Worcestershire sauce; often used as an accompaniment to pickled pork.

Irish soda bread A round, free-form bread made with baking soda and buttermilk, often flavored with currants and caraway seeds.

Irish stew An Irish stewlike dish of mutton layered with potatoes and onions, simmered, and served with pickled red cabbage.

iron A trace mineral principally used for forming hemoglobin and myoglobin and to assist energy utilization; significant sources include red meat, fish, shellfish, eggs, legumes and dried fruits as well as foods to which iron has been added as a nutrient supplement.

ironware Heavy, brittle cookware and utensils made from iron or cast iron, usually preseasoned or coated with enamel; the iron or cast iron distributes heat evenly and retains high temperatures well.

irradiation A preservation method used for certain fruits, vegetables, plant products and grains in which ionizing radiation sterilizes the food, slows ripening and prevents sprouting; irradiation has little effect on the food's texture, flavor or appearance.

Ischl tart (ISH-lehr) An Austrian pastry made with two buttery nut cookies sandwiched together with berry jam; the top cookie has a cut-out center so that the jam shows through; also known as a linzer cookie.

isinglass A very pure form of gelatin made from a sturgeon's swimbladder and used principally as a fining agent.

isleta bread (ees-LEH-tah) Pueblo Indian bread shaped like a bear's claw.

Italian bread An American term for a variety of chewy, hard-crusted yeast breads made with flour, water, yeast and salt.

Italian buttercream A creamy frosting made by beating softened butter into cooled Italian meringue; also known as meringue buttercream.

Italian dressing A salad dressing consisting of olive oil and wine vinegar or lemon juice and seasoned with oregano, basil, dill, garlic and fennel.

Italian garlic A garlic with a mauve-colored outer layer and a milder flavor than American garlic; also known as Mexican garlic.

Italian meringue A fluffy, shiny meringue made by slowly beating hot sugar syrup into whipped egg whites; when used as a cake frosting, known as boiled icing.

Italian parsley A variety of parsley (*Petroselinum neopolitanum*) with flat, darker green leaves and a stronger, coarser flavor than curly parsley; generally used fresh as a flavoring; also known as flat-leaf parsley. *See* parsley.

Italian parsley

Italian sausage A style of pork sausages seasoned with garlic and fennel seeds; available in medium-sized links, there are two principal types: hot (flavored with red chiles) and sweet (without the chiles).

Italian tomato *See* plum tomato.

Italienne, sauce (ee-tahl-lee-een) 1. A French compound sauce made from a velouté flavored with shallots, parsley and mushrooms cooked in white wine. 2. A cold French sauce made from mayonnaise garnished with a purée of calf's brains and chopped fine herbs.

IU International Unit, a measure of quantity used for fat-soluble vitamins (A, D and E) and certain hormones, enzymes and biologics; the measurement is based on potency, not weight.

ivoire, sauce (eve-vwahr) A French compound sauce made from a suprême flavored with a white veal or chicken glaze; usually served with eggs, offal and poached or sautéed chicken; also known as Wladimir sauce.

jackfruit; jakfruit A huge tree-borne fruit (*Artocarpus heterophyllus*) related to the breadfruit and grown in India and Asia; it has an ovoid shape with a spiny skin, a firm, thick flesh, and a flavor reminiscent of pineapple and banana; when green, it is used as a starchy vegetable, with both the flesh and the seeds being eaten; when ripened and sweeter, generally used as a dessert.

jackknife clams *See* razor shell clams.

jack mackerel A fish found in the Pacific Ocean from Canada to Chile and a member of the jack family; it has a dark green back that becomes silvery below and an average market weight of 1–2.5 lb. (0.5–1.14 kg); it is generally used for canning or smoking; also known as horse mackerel and California horse mackerel.

Jacob's cattle An heirloom variety of bean; it is white and maroon with a somewhat sweet flavor.

Jaffa orange A particularly large, flavorful, pulpy variety of navel orange; generally grown in Israel.

jaggery A coarse brown sugar made from the sap of the Palmyra palm (*Borassus flabellifer*) and used in Indian and Southeast Asian cuisines; also known as palm sugar.

jagging wheel A type of pastry wheel with a fluted cutting edge; also known as a pie jagger.

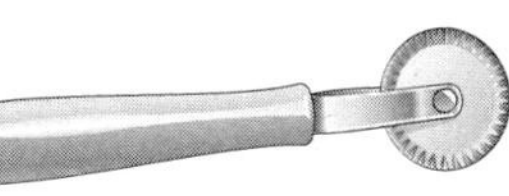

jagging wheel (crimper/cutter)

jalapeño (hah-lah-PEH-nyoh) A short, tapering chile with a thick flesh, a moderately hot, green vegetal flavor and a dark green color (a red version is also available; it is a green chile that has been allowed to ripen); available fresh or canned and named for the Mexican city of Jalapa. *See* chipotle *and* mora.

jallab (jah-lahb) A Middle Eastern sweet purple beverage made from berries and garnished with pine nuts.

jalouise (ZAH-luh-zee) A rectangular French pastry with a lattice top that allows the jam or fruit filling to show through.

jam A fruit gel made from fruit pulp and sugar.

Jamaican hot chile A short, tapering fresh chile with a thin flesh, a red color and a sweet, hot flavor.

Jamaican mango A dark, almost black, mango with a sweet, orange-yellow flesh grown in the Caribbean region.

Jamaican pepper *See* allspice.

jambalaya (juhm-buh-LI-yah) A Creole dish of ham, shrimp, crayfish and/or sausage (usually chaurice) cooked with rice, tomatoes, green peppers, onions and seasonings.

jambon (zham-BOHN) 1. French for ham. 2. A French cut of the pork carcass; it consists of the muscles of the hind leg, usually with the bone in.

jambon de Bayonne (zham-BOHN duh bay-YOHN) A ham from Bayonne, France; it is rubbed with salt, saltpeter, sugar, pepper and aromatic herbs and dried for 4–6 months and then mildly smoked.

Japanese eggplant *See* eggplant, Asian.

Japanese medlar *See* loquat.

Japanese pickled radish Daikon radish pickled in soy sauce and sugar; used as a condiment, especially with fish, in Japanese cuisine; available in chunks, slices and shreds.

Japanese radish *See* daikon.

Japanese rice A short-grain, grayish-white variety of rice with oval, translucent grains; when cooked, it is moist, firm and sticky.

japonaise (zhah-pawng-ayz) A French baked meringue containing ground hazelnuts or almonds.

jardinière, à la (jahr-duh-NIHR) A French term for dishes garnished with vegetables.

Jarlsberg (YAHRLZ-behrg) A Norwegian Emmental-style cheese made from cow's milk; it has a pale yellow interior with large holes and a delicate, sweet, nutty flavor.

jars, Mason Glass containers with threaded necks made especially for home canning, pickling and preserving; they range in size from 4 oz. (1/2 cup) to 1/2 gallon; most brands use two-part self-sealing lids; tapered Mason jars, larger at the mouth than at the base, can be used for freezing and canning.

jasmine flowers The aromatic white to pale yellow flowers of several jasmine shrubs or vines (genus *Jasminum*) that can be used in fruit salads or as a flavoring for ice creams, sorbets and tisanes.

jasmine rice A young, tender rice with a strong flower-like aroma and a delicate flavor; used in Thai and Vietnamese cuisines.

jasmine tea A blend of Chinese black and green teas scented with jasmine petals; the beverage is light and fragrant and best served without milk or lemon.

Java (JAH-va) 1. Arabica coffee beans grown on the main island of Indonesia; the beverage is full bodied, with a strong, peppery flavor. 2. Slang for coffee.

java olive 1. An imprecisely used name for a type of pili nut. 2. A tree grown in Africa and Asia (*Sterculia foetida*); its dark brown, olive-sized seeds are roasted (the seeds are contained in a large, red, lobed pod).

Jefferson, Thomas (Am., 1743–1826) America's third president, author of the Declaration of Independence, and America's first serious gourmet; he introduced America to the waffle iron, pasta maker, dumbwaiter, Parmesan, figs, anchovies, Dijon mustard, tarragon vinegar, vanilla, olive oil, pomegranates, Italian peaches and Italian rice, and his cultivation of native grapevines gave rise to Virginia's wine industry.

jell To congeal.

jelly 1. A clear, shiny mixture of cooked fruit juice and sugar thickened with pectin; its texture is soft but firm enough to hold its shape when unmolded; used as a spread for bread or a glaze on pastries. 2. British for any gelatin dessert.

jelly glass A footed trumpet-shaped glass used to hold sweetened, jelled fruit juice; typically, it has two handles, although it can have one or none.

jelly roll cake A thin sheet of sponge cake spread with jam, jelly or other fillings, then rolled up; the cake is cut crosswise into pinwheel slices.

jelly roll pan A rectangular baking sheet with 1-in.-deep sides; used for baking a thin cake.

jelly roll pan

Jenny Lind A French consommé made from game and garnished with strips of quail and mushrooms.

jerk *v.* 1. To cut meat into long strips and preserve them by sun-drying, oven-drying or smoke curing. 2. To make and serve ice cream and related products at a soda fountain. *n.* A Jamaican preparation method in which meats and poultry are marinated in herbs and spices, then cooked over a pimento (allspice) wood fire; commercial blends of jerk spices are available.

jerky Thin strips of meat, usually beef or turkey, dried in the sun or an oven; they typically have a salty flavor and a tough, chewy texture.

Jerusalem artichoke Not related to the artichoke, this member of the sunflower family (*Helianthus tuberosus*) has a lumpy, multipronged, brown-skinned tuber that has a crunchy texture and a nutty, sweet flavor; it can be eaten raw, cooked or pickled; also known as a girasol and sunchoke.

jícama (HEE-kah-mah) A legume that grows underground as a tuber; this large, bulbous root vegetable has a brown skin, a white flesh, a crisp, crunchy texture, and a sweet, nutty flavor; peeled, it is eaten raw or cooked; also known as ahipa, Mexican potato and yam bean.

jiffy A fabricated cut of the beef primal flank; it is a thinly cut and/or cubed steak.

jigger 1. A standard 1.5-fl. oz. measure used for mixed drink recipes, usually for the amount of liquor; also known as a shot. 2. The glass, metal, plastic or ceramic vessel used to measure this amount. 3. A whiskey glass of this size.

jimmies Tiny chocolate or sugar candies sprinkled on desserts, ice cream or confections. *See* hundreds and thousands.

jira The small seed from a sweet herb; it has a spicy flavor and is used in West Indies cuisine.

Joe's special A popular breakfast or brunch dish from San Francisco; it consists of eggs scrambled with cooked, crumbled ground beef, onions, garlic, mushrooms and spinach.

John Dory A saltwater fish found off Europe; it has a distinctive round black spot outlined in yellow on each side of its body, a firm, flaky white flesh, and a delicate, mild flavor; also known as St. Peter's fish.

John Dory

johnnycake 1. A griddle cake made of cornmeal, salt and boiling water or cold milk; also known as a hoecake. 2. A Caribbean breakfast food made from flour, water, salt and baking powder, shaped into balls and fried.

join To make a seam, as in pinching dough together.

joint *v.* To sever a piece of meat at the joint; also disjoint. *n.* 1. In Great Britain, a large piece of meat for roasting. 2. Anatomically, the fixed or movable place or part where two bones or elements of a skeleton join.

Joinville, sauce (zhwen-veel) A French compound sauce made from a Normandy sauce with a coulis of crayfish, shrimps and sometimes truffles; served with fish, especially sole.

Jolie-fille, sauce (zhow-lee-fill) A French compound sauce made from a suprême garnished with hard-boiled egg yolks and parsley.

Jordan almond A large, plump almond sold plain or coated with a hard pastel candy coating.

joule A unit of work or energy used in the metric system instead of calories; 1 Calorie (kilocalorie) equals 4185.5 joules; 1 calorie equals 4.1855 joules.

jugged A stew made from game, especially hare, cooked in a deep stoneware jug or casserole; sometimes some of the animal's blood is added to the cooking liquid.

juice *v.* To extract the juice of a fruit or vegetable. *n.* 1. The liquid released or squeezed from any raw food, whether animal or vegetable, but particularly fruit. 2. The blood and other liquids that run from meat or poultry during cooking. 3. The liquid surrounding the flesh of certain shellfish, such as an oyster, when first opened; also known as liquor.

juicer An electric or manual device used to extract juice from certain fruits and vegetables; a half fruit is placed onto its ridged cone and pressure is applied. *See* reamer.

juicer

jujubes (JOO-joo-bees) Small fruit-flavored candies with a chewy, gelatinous texture; also known as gummi candies.

Jules Verne, à la A French garnish for meat consisting of potatoes and turnips filled with any of a variety of stuffings and then braised with mushrooms in butter.

Juliana tart A round, shallow French pastry made with a sweet dough topped with apricot marmalade or raspberry jam and almond paste or frangipane; the top is decorated with a lattice of puff pastry.

julienne (ju-lee-en) *v.* To cut a food into a julienne shape. *n.* 1. Foods cut into a matchstick shape of approximately 1/8 × 1/8 × 1/2 in. (0.3 × 0.3 × 2.5–5 cm). 2. A garnish of foods cut in such a shape.

jumble A colonial American cookie; it is a delicate, crisp, ring-shaped sugar cookie made with sour cream and flavored with rosewater.

jumbo A marketing term for a lobster weighing more than 2 1/2 lb. (1.2 kg).

juniper berry The dried, aromatic, blue-black berry of an evergreen bush (*Juniperus communis*); used to flavor gin and savory dishes (especially ones with game); also known as a box huckleberry.

junket A type of British pudding made with milk, sugar and flavorings and set with rennet; it has a soft texture and is usually served well chilled with fresh fruit.

jus lié (zhoo lee-ay) A sauce made by thickening brown stock with cornstarch or similar starch and often used like a demi-glaze, especially to produce small sauces; also known as fond lié.

kaak (kack) 1. A Middle Eastern bread baked to a crunchy hardness and flavored with mahleb and coated with sesame seeds; it is dunked in tea or milk and eaten for breakfast. 2. A Lebanese pastry of yeast-risen dough rolled into ropes, formed into rings, and baked; it is then dipped into a glaze of milk and sugar and often topped with sesame seeds. 3. *See* kaick.

kabob *See* kebab.

kabocha (kah-BOH-chah) 1. A medium to large winter squash; it has a dark green shell with lighter green streaks, a smooth, tender orange flesh, and a sweet flavor. 2. Japanese for pumpkin.

kadayif (kah-dah-eef) 1. Thin pastalike strands of a Middle Eastern dough made with flour and water. 2. A pastry made with buttered layers of this dough filled with either chopped nuts or a creamy rice pudding and topped with a sweet syrup.

kadhai (kah-dhah-ee) An Indian cooking utensil similar to a Chinese wok; it is used for frying food.

kadota fig A small, thick-skinned fig with a yellow-green skin.

kaffir lime A citrus fruit (*Citrus hystrix*); the medium-sized fruit has a knobby dark green skin; the leaves look like a figure eight, with two leaves joined together base to tip; the sharply aromatic, citrus-flavored leaves and the fruit's rind are used as flavorings in Thai cuisine, and the leaves are used in Indonesian cuisine.

Kahlúa (kah-LOO-ah) A dark brown, coffee-flavored Mexican liqueur.

kaick (kah'ck) 1. A Middle Eastern bread flavored with anise; often served as a snack with a sweet syrup flavored with orange blossom water. 2. *See* kaak.

kaiser roll A large, round yeast roll with a crisp crust, used for making sandwiches or served as a breakfast roll; also known as a hard roll or Vienna roll.

kaki (kah-KEE) *See* persimmon.

kalamata; calamata (kahl-uh-MAH-tuh) A large blue-black olive native to Greece; usually packed in olive oil or vinegar and slit to better absorb the marinade.

kale A member of the cabbage family (var. *acephala*) with curly leaves arranged in a loose bunch; the leaf colors, which depend on the variety, range from pale to deep green tinged with lavender, blue or purple to white shaded with pink, purple or green; although all are edible, the green varieties are better for cooking, and the more colorful varieties are better used for garnish.

kale, ornamental The more colorful varieties of kale that are used principally for garnish and decoration; also known as flowering kale and savoy.

kamut (kah-MOOT) A natural variety of high-protein wheat with very large kernels that have a nutty flavor; generally available only in processed foods (e.g., pasta and crackers).

kanafa (kah-naw-faw) A Middle Eastern sweet dough similar to a finely shredded phyllo and used for a pastry of the same name; the pastry can be filled with a thickened cream, nuts or cheese.

Kansas City broil A fabricated cut of the beef primal chuck; it is a bone-in or boneless center-cut steak.

Kansas City steak A fabricated cut of the beef primal short loin; it is a well-trimmed porterhouse or T-bone steak.

kantola A small squash with a bright green shell, a slightly sweet flesh, and edible seeds used in Indian, Chinese and Southeast Asian cuisines.

kao mao (ka-oh me-o) A Thai rice harvested when still slightly immature; with its husk intact, it is flattened and roasted and often used as a coating for fried foods.

kasha (KAH-sha) The hulled, roasted buckwheat groat; it has a reddish-brown color with a strong, nutty, almost scorched flavor and a slightly sticky, chewy texture.

kasha varnishkes (kah-sha var-nish-keys) A Jewish dish of kasha garnished with egg noodles (in the United States, farfalle is used) and sautéed onions.

Kasseri (kuh-SAIR-ee) A Greek cheese made from ewe's or goat's milk; it has a hard texture, a white interior and a salty flavor; grated or used for saganaki.

kati A traditional Chinese measurement of weight approximately 1 1/2 lb. (625 g), used today in vegetable markets.

katsuobushi; katsuo-bushi (KAH-tzu-oh-boo-shi) Pink flakes of bonito tuna that are boiled, smoked and then sun-dried; used in Japanese cuisine as a garnish or in dashi.

Katzenjammer (KAHT-sehn-jahmm-ehr) A German and Austrian dish consisting of thin slices of cold beef marinated in olive oil, vinegar and mustard, then mixed with mayonnaise, gherkins and potatoes; considered a cure for hangovers.

kebab; kabob (kah-BEHB; kuh-BOB) Minced meat or cubes of meat on a skewer, usually marinated before cooking and typically grilled. *See* shish kebab.

kebsa (kab-saw) A North African and Middle Eastern spice mixture, traditionally made with cardamom, cinnamon, cumin and red and black pepper.

kecap manis (ket-chup mah-nees) A dark, thick Indonesian soy sauce flavored with palm sugar, garlic, star anise and other spices.

kedgeree; kegeree (kehj-uh-REE) 1. An Indian dish of rice, lentils and onions. 2. An English variation of the dish in which smoked fish, hard-boiled eggs and a cream sauce flavored with curry are added.

kefta (KEHF-tah) A central European dish consisting of patties of chopped beef, veal, poultry or game mixed with bacon and spices and sometimes bound with egg; the patties are floured and sautéed.

keftedes; keftethes; kephtethakia (kaf-ta-dess; kaf-ta-des; kaf-ta-tah-key-ya) Meatballs or rissoles popular throughout the Balkans and Middle East; made from meat, bread crumbs, onions, eggs and grated cheese and flavored with ouzo or lemon juice.

keg A metal, plastic or wooden container, usually used for beer, with a capacity of 15.5 U.S. gallons or half of a barrel; also known as a half barrel.

Kellogg, John Harvey (Am., 1852–1943) While the superintendent of a sanatorium for dyspepsia (indigestion), he developed a precooked cereal product known as "granola." Later, he and his brother Will perfected a method of flaking, which they tried with wheat and then corn; cornflakes soon became the world's most well known breakfast cereal.

kelp Any large, brown to grayish-black seaweed of the family Laminariceae; often dried and used in Japanese and other Asian and Pacific Island cuisines.

Kentucky Hot Brown An open-face turkey sandwich covered with hot brown gravy and garnished with crisply fried bacon.

Kentucky jam cake A spice cake made with jam, usually blackberry, added to the batter and frosted with caramel icing; also known as a Tennessee jam cake.

Kentucky Wonder Bean The American name for runner bean.

Kenyan 1. Arabica coffee beans grown in Kenya; the beverage is straightforward, with an appealing, rich flavor slightly reminiscent of black currants. 2. A black Kenyan tea; the beverage has a reddish color and a strong flavor.

kernel 1. The softer, usually edible part, contained within the shell of a nut or a stone of a fruit; also known as the meat. 2. The body of a seed within its husk or other outer covering. 3. A whole seed grain (e.g., wheat and corn).

kernel paste A mixture of ground apricot kernels and sugar used as a filling for baked goods.

ketchup; catchup; catsup A spicy sauce or condiment; it is usually made with the juice of cooked fruits or vegetables such as tomatoes, walnuts and mangos as well as vinegar, sugar and spices; the name may be derived from the Chinese kê-tsiap, which means brine of pickled fish.

ketogenic diet A reduction diet high in proteins and low in carbohydrates; the diet causes the body to increase production of ketones, which can lead to ketosis and even death.

ketone; ketone body The substance resulting from the incomplete breakdown of fat for energy (fat is used when carbohydrates are unavailable).

Key lime A small lime with a greenish-yellow skin and a very tart flavor; also known as the Mexican lime, West Indies lime and true lime.

Key lime pie A cream pie made with tart Key limes, usually in a graham cracker– or cookie-crumb crust and topped with whipped cream.

kg *See* kilogram.

kha (khaa) A large gingerroot native to Thailand; it has a whiter color than the common gingerroot; also known as galanga.

khao phoune (ka-oo poon) A Laotian breakfast dish consisting of rice vermicelli in a thick, creamy sauce of coconut milk with meat or fish.

khoob (coob) A large melon grown in Iran; it has a netted orange skin, an orange flesh, and an aroma and flavor reminiscent of pineapple.

kibbeh; kibbi; kibbe (KIHB-beh; KIHB-bee) A Middle Eastern dish of ground meat (usually lamb) with bulgur wheat and seasonings, usually baked.

kibble 1. To grind coarsely. 2. Coarsely ground meal or grain.

kibbled wheat Wheat whose grains have been coarsely ground; it is used in muesli and sprinkled on top of bread and rolls.

kid A goat slaughtered when approximately 6 months old; the lean flesh has a tender texture and delicate flavor similar to that of lamb.

kidney 1. An organ that filters blood to remove waste material and forwards it to the bladder for excretion. 2. A variety meat; generally small with a reddish-brown color, a tender texture, and a strong flavor; beef and veal kidneys are multilobed; lamb and pork kidneys are single lobed.

kidney bean A medium-sized, kidney-shaped bean with a dark red skin, cream-colored firm flesh, and bland flavor; available fresh, dried and canned; also known as red kidney bean. *See* white kidney bean.

kielbasa; kielbasy (kihl-BAH-sah) 1. A general term used for most Polish sausages. 2. A Polish sausage made from pork (with beef sometimes added) flavored with garlic; smoked, usually precooked, and sold in medium to large links; also known as Polish sausage.

kilo- *See* metric system.

kilocalorie *See* Calorie.

kilogram (kg) A measure of weight in the metric system; 1 kg equals 1000 g or 2.2 lb.

kim chee; kimchi (gim-chee) A very spicy Korean pickled cabbage, usually napa cabbage; seasoned with garlic, chiles, green onions, ginger and other spices; also known as Korean cabbage pickle.

King cake A briochelike cake topped with purple, green and yellow icing; a red bean or a small figurine is baked in the cake, promising good luck to the finder; popular in Louisiana during the carnival season before Mardi Gras.

king crab A variety of very large crab found off Alaska that can grow to 10 lb. (24.8 kg); it has an average market weight of 7 lb. (3.2 kg), a flesh that is white with red edges, and a sweet flavor and coarse texture; also known as Alaskan king crab.

king mackerel A member of the mackerel family found in the Atlantic Ocean from Florida to Massachusetts; it has a high fat content, a finely textured and flavorful flesh, and an average market weight of 5–25 lb. (2.3–11.3 kg); also known as a kingfish.

king orange A large orange grown in Florida; it has a somewhat flattened shape with a loose, rough, orange-colored skin, a juicy, pale orange flesh and a sweet–tart flavor.

kipper *v.* To cure, usually fish, by cleaning, salting and drying or smoking. *n.* A male salmon during or shortly after the spawning season.

kippered herring A herring that is butterflied, cured in brine, and cold smoked; it has a smoky, salty flavor and is usually given an artificial golden color.

kippered salmon 1. In the United States, a chunk, steak or fillet of salmon (usually chinook) soaked in brine, hot smoked, and dyed red. 2. In Europe, a split salmon soaked in brine and cold smoked. 3. *See* lox *and* smoked salmon.

Kir (keer) An aperitif of crème de cassis and dry white wine.

kirby cucumber A small cucumber with a dull green skin that can be bumpy or ridged; used for pickling.

Kir Royale (keer roy-al) An aperitif of crème de cassis and Champagne or other sparkling wine.

Kirsch (kersch) A clear cherry brandy; double distilled from small semisweet cherries gathered in Germany's Black Forest, France's Vosges region and areas of Switzerland; it has a characteristic bitter almond flavor that comes from the oils derived from the cherries' crushed stones; also known as Kirschwasser in Germany.

Kirschtorte (kersch-tohr-ta) A Swiss cake composed of two hazelnut meringue layers and two layers of genoise that are alternated with a Kirsch-flavored buttercream; the sides are spread with buttercream and coated with toasted ground hazelnuts, and the top is heavily dusted with confectioners' sugar and decorated with green marzipan leaves and candied cherries; also known as Zugor Kirschtorte.

kishke; kishka (KIHSH-keh) A Jewish sausage made with beef, matzo meal, fat and onions, stuffed into a beef casing, steamed and roasted.

kissel (kee-SUHL) A Russian dessert made with a starch-thickened fruit purée (usually cranberries or another red berry); served warm or cold with custard sauce, cream or yogurt.

kitchen The room or area containing cooking facilities or the area where food is prepared.

kitchen garden A small garden intended to supply produce for the kitchen.

kitchen shears A pair of strong scissors (one blade with a serrated edge) used to cut fish, poultry, meat and produce, crack nuts and remove packaging materials such as bottle caps; sometimes it has tabs to be used as a screwdriver or lever. *See* fish shears *and* poultry shears.

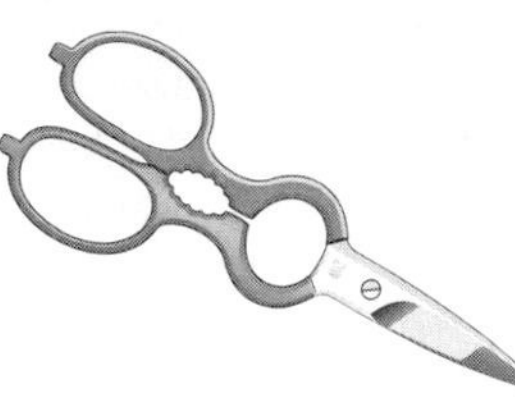
all-purpose kitchen shears

kited fillet A fish cut along the backbone and filleted but left attached at the belly.

kiwano (kee-WAHN-noh) A fruit and member of the cucumber family (*Cucumis metuliferus*) native to New Zealand; it has a bright orange skin studded with little horns, many edible black seeds, and a bright green flesh that has a flavor reminiscent of mango and pineapple; also known as cucumber-horned melon.

kiwi; kiwi fruit; kiwifruit (KEE-wee) A small, barrel-shaped fruit (*Actinidia sinensis*) native to New Zealand; it has a greenish-brown skin covered with fuzz, a brilliant green flesh that becomes yellower toward the center, many small, edible black seeds, and a sweet–tart flavor; named for the flightless bird of New Zealand; also known as the Chinese gooseberry.

klip; klipfish (kleep) A Norwegian dish of salted cod smoked in the open air, cooked and served with butter sometimes flavored with parsley.

knäckebröd (kneh-keh-brurd) A Swedish crispbread made from rye flour and rye meal.

Knackwurst (KNAAK-voost) A plump German sausage made from beef and pork and seasoned with garlic; the casing makes a cracking sound at first bite; also known as Knockwurst.

knafa; knafeh; knafee (kuh-nah-hah) A soft, uncooked wheat dough, similar to shredded wheat, used for pastries in Middle Eastern cuisines; also known as konafa, kadaifa, katafi and kataifi.

knaidel (knayd-dhul) *pl.* knaidlach. A Jewish dumpling sometimes flavored with schmaltz and usually served in beef or chicken soup garnished with carrots, onions and celery.

knead 1. To work a dough by hand or in a mixer to distribute ingredients and develop gluten. 2. To press, rub or squeeze with the hands.

knife A sharp-edged instrument used to cut or spread food; it generally consists of a blade and handle.

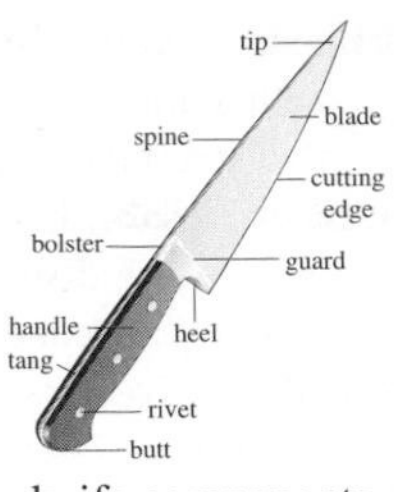

knife components

knife blade The part of a knife used to cut or spread; it is generally made of carbon steel, stainless steel or high-carbon stainless steel and consists of a tip (point), spine (back), cutting edge, bolster, heel, butt and tang.

knife blade, forged A knife blade that is made from metal heated and hammered into shape, creating a heavier, more front-weighted blade with a distinct bolster; this produces a knife with good balance, flexibility and handling quality.

knife blade, stamped A knife blade that is die cut in a press; it is lighter and less expensive than a forged blade and is back-heavy in the hand, requiring more forward pressure to cut.

knife handle The part of the knife gripped by the user and that holds the blade's tang; it can be made of wood, horn, bone, metal, plastic-impregnated wood, plastic or other synthetic substances and can be two pieces attached to the tang by rivets or adhesives or a single piece in which the tang is embedded.

knife point The tip of a knife; it can be a spear, round spatula, sheep's foot (an outward arc from spine to flat cutting edge), cope (an abrupt forward angle from spine to flat cutting edge) or clip (a slightly concave arc from the midspine to the point; the secondary edge can be sharpened and called a swedge or left unsharpened and called a false edge).

knish (KAH-nish) A Jewish dish consisting of a dough made from mashed potatoes, egg, schmaltz and flour stuffed with a savory (e.g., potatoes and ground meats) or sweet (e.g., nuts and rasins) filling and baked.

Knödel (KNUR-derl) Very light German and Austrian dumplings made from flour, potatoes, eggs and sometimes bread crumbs and often stuffed with meat, liver or a sweet filling; also known as Klösse.

knuckle 1. Anatomically, a joint where two bones meet or articulate. 2. A subprimal cut of the beef primal round; it usually contains the leg bone and is fairly tender and flavorful; it is sometimes fabricated into knuckle steaks. 3. On a veal or pork carcass, the lower part of the hind leg. 4. On a lamb carcass, the knee of the hind leg.

Kobe beef (KOH-bay) Beef from cattle raised in Kobe, Japan; the cattle, massaged with sake and fed a diet that includes large amounts of beer, produce meat that is tender and full flavored.

Köche A light, steamed or baked sweet or savory German pudding.

kofta kebab (koff-tah ka-bobb) A Middle Eastern dish consisting of finely minced lamb flavored with onions, baharat, mint, parsley and pepper, skewered and grilled.

kofte (kaff-tee) A Turkish dish of ground or minced meat (usually lamb) flavored with spices and herbs and mixed with rice, bulgar or bread crumbs, shaped into balls (and sometimes threaded onto skewers), and fried, grilled or simmered.

kohlrabi (koal-RAH-bee) A vegetable created by crossbreeding cabbages and turnips (*Brassica oleracea* var. *gongylodes*); it has a pale green or pale purple bulbous stem and dark green leaves; the bulbous stem has a mild, sweet, turniplike flavor and is cooked like a root vegetable; also known as a cabbage turnip.

kolacky; kolachke (koh-LAH-chee) A small, sweet, flaky Polish pastry made with either a yeast dough or cream cheese dough, filled with poppy seeds, jam, nuts or crushed fruit.

kombu; konbu (KOME-boo) Dark brown to grayish-black kelp that is sun-dried and folded into sheets; it is used in Japanese cuisine as a flavoring, stock base and for sushi.

kori dofu (koh-reh doo-foo) Japanese tofu that has been dehydrated by natural freezing and drying; also known as snow-dried tofu.

korma (kor-mah) 1. Hindi for braising, braised and to braise. 2. A spicy Indian and Pakistani dish of curried mutton, lamb or chicken cooked with onions and other vegetables.

kosher 1. The Jewish dietary laws, as found in the Torah (the first five books of the Old Testament) and subsequent interpretations; these laws (1) identify kosher foods and ingredients and (2) define basic dietary principles; also known as kashrus (Yiddish). *See* fleischig, milchig, *and* pareve. 2. A menu or labeling term indicating that the product has been prepared or processed in accordance with Jewish dietary laws. 3. A food prepared in accordance with Jewish dietary laws.

kosher dietary principles Simply stated, meat (fleischig) and dairy (milchig) cannot be cooked or eaten together; fruit, vegetables and grain (pareve or neutral foods) can be eaten with either meat or dairy.

kosher foods Those who keep kosher can only eat (1) meat from animals with hooves and that chew their cud (cattle, goats and some game; no hogs); (2) poultry that is not a bird of prey; (3) fish with gills and scales (no shellfish); (4) dairy products, provided the animal from which the milk comes is kosher; and (5) all fruits, vegetables and grains, provided animal fat is not used in processing.

kosher salt Purified coarse rock salt; approved for use on kosher meats.

kosher style 1. A menu or labeling term indicating that the product has been prepared or seasoned in a particular manner, usually one associated with Jewish cuisines from eastern Europe; the term has no religious significance. 2. A description of pure-beef sausage and corned beef that is seasoned with garlic and spices, imparting a flavor similar to comparable kosher products; the term is prohibited in several states.

kotlety; kotletki (koe-tla-tea) A Russian dish of salmon or chicken patties served with sour cream.

koumiss; kumiss (KOO-mihs) A beverage made from fermented mare's, camel's or cow's milk by the nomadic tribes of central Asia; also known as kefir.

kourabiedes (koo-rah-bee-YAY-dehs) Crescent-shaped Greek cookies made with ground nuts and butter; they are rolled in confectioners' sugar after baking.

K-ration Lightweight packaged foods developed for the U.S. Army in World War II.

kreplach (KREHP-luhkh) Small Jewish noodle squares stuffed with chopped meat or cheese and usually used in soups.

kriek; krieken-lambic (kreek, KREEK-in-lam-bick) A lambic beer flavored with cherries.

kringle 1. A multilayered Christmas pastry filled with fruit or nuts; it is flat, wide and very flaky. 2. A buttery, lemon-flavored Christmas cookie.

Kroc, Ray (Am., 1902–1984) The founder of the McDonald's corporation; before McDonald's, most fast-food stands were found in big cities; Kroc was the first to target small towns.

krumkake (kroom-kah-ka) A Norwegian Christmas cookie flavored with cardamom and made on a special iron; while warm, it is rolled into a cigarette or cone shape and often filled with whipped cream.

krumkake iron A utensil that consists of two 5-in.-diameter round engraved plates that are hinged; batter is placed in the center of one plate and the two are brought together and placed on a ring that sits over a stove burner; used to make krumkakes.

krumkake iron

krupuk (ke-roo-pook) Hard, thin, dried wafers, often flavored with shrimp or fish, that are deep-fried and served as a snack or used as a garnish in Indonesian and Malaysian cuisines.

k'sra (k'shrah) A Moroccan round loaf bread made with a sourdough-type starter and a mix of whole wheat, barley and unbleached flours and garnished with caraway seeds.

kuchen (koo-chen) Yiddish for something baked and used to describe a yeast dough pastry studded with nuts and raisins and topped with streusel.

Küchen (KOO-khehn) 1. German for cake or pastry. 2. A yeast-leavened coffee cake topped with nuts or crumbs.

kudzu A vine (*Pueraria lobata*) with a starchy, irregularly shaped root with white flesh and a mild, sweet flavor; a thin paste made from the ground root and a liquid is used in Japanese cuisine as a thickener or to coat foods before frying.

kugel (koo-gle; koo-gul) A Jewish puddinglike dish made from potatoes, noodles or a grain, eggs and flavorings (e.g., fresh or dried fruit, grebenes, soft cheeses or sautéed onions) and baked.

kugelhopf; gugelhopf (KOO-guhl-hof) A light yeast cake filled with raisins, nuts and candied fruit and baked in a special fluted mold; popular in Alsace, Germany, Poland and Austria, it is often served for breakfast or with afternoon tea.

kugelhopf mold A tall, round baking mold with deeply fluted sides and a narrow center tube; used for baking kugelhopf.

kugelhopf mold

kukui A native Hawaiian nut with an ivory or gray color and an extremely high oil content.

kulcha (kool-cha) An Indian bread made from leavened white flour dough shaped into rounds and baked in a tandoor.

kulebiaka; koulibiaka (koo-lee-BYAH-kah) *See* coulibiac.

kulich (koo-LIHCH) A tall, cylindrical yeast-leavened Russian cake filled with candied fruit, raisins and spices; traditionally prepared for Easter celebrations.

kulolo (koo-loh-loh) A Hawaiian pudding of taro, brown sugar, honey and coconut milk; it is often served at a luau and is also known as taro pudding.

kummelweck A German–American caraway seed bun encrusted with coarse salt.

kumquat A small ovoid to spherical citrus fruit (*Fortunella margarita*) with a soft, thin, golden orange rind, an orange flesh with small seeds, and a tart flavor; the entire fruit is eaten fresh or used for preserves and pickles.

kung pao (gong bao) A Chinese stir-fry dish traditionally made with chicken (shrimp and vegetables are now also used) and great quantities of garlic, ginger, whole dried chiles and fried peanuts (formerly, corn kernels were used).

kuro-su (koo-roh-soo) A Japanese brown rice vinegar with a mellow flavor.

kushi-age (koo-shee-AH-gue) Japanese for morsels of food coated with Japanese-style bread crumbs (panko), skewered, and deep-fried.

kushi-yaki (koo-shee-YAH-kee) Japanese for assorted skewered and grilled foods prepared the same way as yakitori.

kvass; quass (KBAH-ssoo) A weak Russian home-brewed beer made by pouring hot water over dark rye bread and allowing the mix to ferment.

Kyoto cucumber A variety of slicing cucumber developed in Japan; it is longer than typical and not always of a uniform shape.

l *See* liter.

lactase-treated milk Milk treated with the enzyme lactase, which breaks down the lactose into glucose and galactose; used by people who are lactose intolerant.

lactic acid 1. Naturally occurring in several foods, a food additive used as an antimicrobial agent, flavor enhancer, flavoring agent, flavoring adjuvant and/or pH control agent in processed foods such as dairy products and frozen desserts; also known as 2-hydroxypropanoic acid. 2. An acid formed when lactose is fermented with *Streptococci lactis* bacteria, it occurs naturally when milk is soured and is partly responsible for the tart flavor of yogurt and cheese; also used as a preservative.

lactose 1. A disaccharide occurring naturally in mammalian milk; it is the least sweet of the natural sugars, and many people cannot tolerate it in varying quantities; during digestion it is hydrolyzed into its component single sugars: glucose and galactose; also known as milk sugar. 2. A food additive used as a surface-finishing agent in processed foods such as baked goods. 3. Subject to FDA regulations, a filler in pharmaceutical products.

lactovegetarian A vegetarian who does not eat meat, poultry, fish or eggs but does eat dairy products. *See* ovolactovegetarian *and* vegan.

la cuite (lah kweet) A thick, dark sugar syrup cooked until just before it burns and turns bitter; it is used in the American South as a candy, a topping for bread or in baked goods.

laderes (lah-the-rees) Greek for foods braised in olive oil until done; they are usually served cold or lukewarm.

ladle *v.* To move portions of a food using a ladle. *n.* A utensil with a cuplike bowl and a long hooked or pierced handle and available in various sizes (the capacity is often stamped on the handle); used to pour sauces and liquids (e.g., soups) and to push sauces and other foods through a sieve.

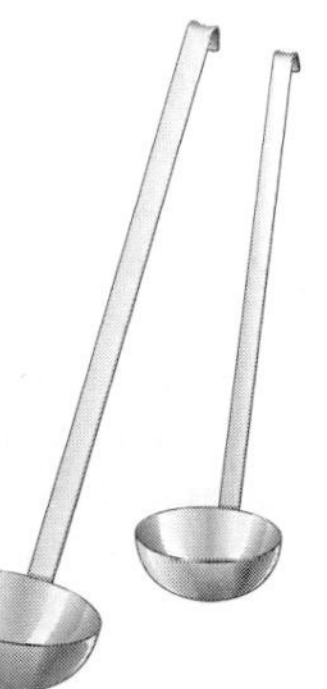

ladles

Lady Baltimore cake A three-layer white cake made with egg whites, filled with raisins, nuts and dried fruit and covered with a fluffy white frosting such as boiled icing. *See* Lord Baltimore cake.

ladyfinger; lady finger A flat, finger-shaped cookie made from a light, sponge cake batter; used as a petit four or to line a pan or mold for desserts.

lag phase A rest period (of 1–4 hours) for bacteria in a culture or colony during which little growth occurs; it usually follows the movement of the bacteria from one place to another and is the period during which the bacteria adjust to their new location. *See* log phase *and* decline phase.

lahvosh; lavash (LAH-vohsh) An Armenian cracker bread leavened with yeast and baked in round sheets that are thin, flat and crisp; they are used like other mildly flavored crackers or can be softened with water and rolled around sandwich fillings. *See* aram sandwich.

lake herring A fish found in the Great Lakes; it has an iridescent silvery skin, an average market weight of 0.5–1 lb. (225–450 g) and a high fat content and is often smoked; sometimes sold as whitefish and is also known as blueback and cisco.

lake sturgeon A fish found in the Columbia River as well as parts of the American Southeast; it has a grayish-green skin, a long pointed snout, an average market weight of 8–10 lb. (3.6–4.5 kg), and a firm flesh with a delicate flavor; also known as common sturgeon and shortnose sturgeon.

lake trout Any of several wild freshwater trout found in North American waters; skin colors vary, with shades of gray and olive predominating; the flesh ranges from pale ivory to deep pink and has a high fat content, a firm texture and a delicate flavor; average market weight is 2–4 lb. (0.9–1.8 kg); significant varieties include the Great Lakes trout and mackinaw; also known as char.

laksa (luck-sa) 1. Filipino for 10,000 and used to describe a dish that contains various vegetables, shrimp, pork and bean flour vermicelli. 2. A Malaysian and Indonesian noodle dish with fish, shrimp or chicken in a creamy curry or tamarind sauce.

lamb The meat of a sheep slaughtered when less than 1 year old; it is generally tender and has a mild flavor; also known as a yearling. *See* baby lamb, spring lamb *and* mutton.

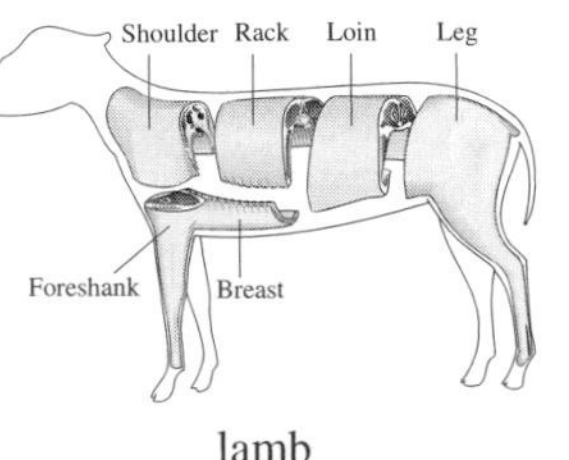

lamb
(American primals)

lamb, ground Lamb ground from muscles found in various primals but principally the shoulder and shank end of the leg.

lamb arm chops *See* lamb shoulder chop.

lamb breast A subprimal cut of the lamb primal breast; it is neither particularly meaty nor flavorful and is available with or without bones.

lamb chop A fabricated cut of the lamb primal rack; it usually contains one rib (called a single chop) or two ribs (a double chop) and the flavorful, tender rib eye muscle.

lamb cushion shoulder roast A subprimal cut of the lamb primal shoulder; it is flavorful but somewhat tough.

Lambert cherry A large sweet cherry with a deep ruby red color, a firm, meaty flesh and a sweet flavor.

lambic (lahm-bic) A style of Belgian beer brewed with wild yeast and beer-souring bacteria.

lamb leg A subprimal cut of the lamb primal leg; available fully or partially deboned, it is quite tender and flavorful and is sometimes further fabricated into steaks.

lamb leg chop A fabricated cut of the lamb primal leg; it is somewhat tough.

lamb loin chop A fabricated cut of the lamb primal loin; it is a tender, flavorful chop.

lamb loin roast A subprimal cut of the lamb primal loin.

lamb medallions A fabricated cut of the lamb primal loin; the medallions are cut from the very tender and flavorful loin eye muscle.

lamb noisettes (nwah-ZET) A fabricated cut of the lamb primal loin; the noisettes are cut from the very tender and flavorful loin eye muscle.

lamb primals The five principal sections of the lamb carcass: the shoulder, rack, breast, loin and leg; each primal contains both bilateral halves.

lamb quality grades *See* USDA quality grades, prime, choice, good, utility *and* cull.

lamb riblets; lamb rib tips A fabricated cut of the lamb primal breast; they are the tips of the ribs (which are part of the primal rack); also known as Denver ribs.

lamb rib roast A subprimal cut of the lamb primal rack; it is one-half of the entire rack kept intact for roasting.

lamb shoulder chop A fabricated cut of the lamb primal shoulder; it contains pieces of several muscles and is sometimes tough.

lamb's lettuce *See* mâche.

lamb square cut shoulder A subprimal cut of the lamb primal shoulder; it is an untrimmed roast.

lamb's quarters A wild, spinachlike green (*Chenopodium albam*) with a mild flavor.

lamellate venus clam A variety of venus clam found in the western Pacific Ocean and Indian Ocean; it has a beige and violet shell that measures 1.5–2 in. (3.8–5.08 cm) across and a sweet meat.

laminated dough *See* rolled-in dough.

lamination The technique of layering fat and dough through a process of rolling and folding; this procedure is used to make puff pastry, croissant dough and Danish pastry dough. *See* rolled-in dough.

lamington An Australian dessert consisting of a square of sponge cake coated in chocolate and dried coconut; named for Lord Lamington, a governor of Queensland.

lamprey A long eel-shaped fish found in freshwater and saltwater of North America and Europe; it has black skin, very fatty flesh and a delicate flavor.

land cress A plant (*Barbarea verna*) with small, slightly cupped dark green leaves and a mild peppery flavor similar to that of watercress; also known as American cress and winter cress.

Lane cake A white or yellow layer cake filled with a mixture of coconut, dried fruit and nuts and covered with a fluffy white frosting such as boiled icing; created by Alabama resident Emma Lane.

langoustine (lahn-goo-STEEN) 1. A variety of small lobster found in the North Atlantic; it has a yellowish-pink shell, no claws, and a lean white flesh with a sweet flavor. 2. French for prawn.

languedocienne, à la (lan-guh-doss-YEN, ah lah) A French preparation method associated with the cuisine of the Languedoc region; the dishes are characterized by a sauce flavored with garlic or a garnish of stuffed eggplants, minced cépes sautéed in oil, tomatoes and parsley and accompanied by pommes château.

langues de chat (lahngg duh sha) French for cat's tongue and used to describe a thin, finger-shaped biscuit or cookie.

lao (lah-oh) Chinese for pan-frying with little to no fat (e.g., cooking wheat flour cakes in a skillet without oil).

lard *v.* To insert long, thin strips of fat into a dry cut of meat to increase its moistness and tenderness after cooking; also known as interlard. *n.* Rendered, clarified and purified pork fat; used as an ingredient and cooking medium; it is very rich. *See* leaf lard.

larding needle A tool used for larding meat; it has a sharp, pointed tip with a hollow body that is used to hold the larding material.

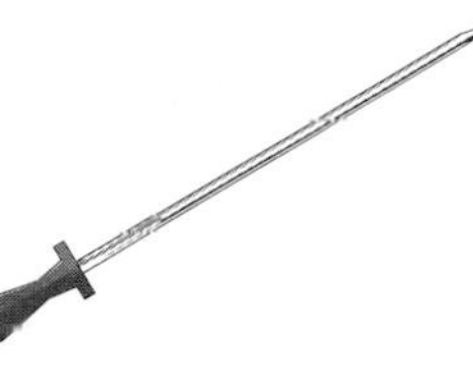

larding needle

lardon; lardoon (LAHR-don; lar-DOON) 1. A long thin strip of fat used to lard meat. 2. Diced, blanched and fried bacon used in French cuisine.

lasagne (luh-ZAH n'yeh) 1. Wide, flat Italian pasta sheets with ruffled or smooth edges. 2. An Italian dish made with boiled lasagna layered with cheese (usually ricotta and mozzarella) and meats and/or vegetables and topped with a tomato, meat and/or béchamel and baked.

lassi (lah-see) An Indian cold beverage made of yogurt thinned with water, sweetened and flavored with rose essence or rosewater.

latke (LAHT-kuh) A Jewish potato pancake usually made from grated potatoes mixed with eggs, onions, matzo meal and seasonings; it is fried and served hot with applesauce.

lattice Strips of pastry dough arranged in a crisscross pattern, usually laid on top of a pie or tart.

lattice cutter 1. A plastic or metal stencil used to cut a diamond-shaped lattice pattern into rolled-out dough. 2. A rolling cutter with a 6-in.-wide axle holding several notched cutting wheels; used to cut a uniform lattice pattern in rolled-out dough; also known as lattice dough roller.

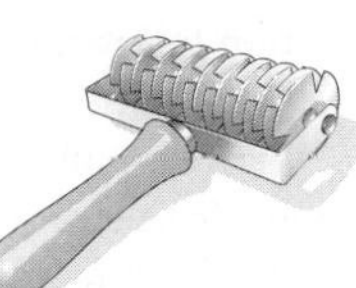

lattice cutter

lau lau; laulau 1. A Hawaiian cooking method in which pork, chicken or fish is steamed in taro leaves tied with ti leaves. 2. A Hawaiian dish of such foods.

laurel leaves Bay leaves from the laurel tree; those from the California laurel (*Umbellularia californica*) are edible and are used as a flavoring.

Lavallière, sauce (lah-vah-lee-yair) A French compound sauce made from a demi-glaze flavored with game essence (extract), thickened with sour cream, and garnished with tarragon and truffles.

La Varenne, François Pierre (Fr., 1618–1678) Considered to be one of the founding fathers of French cuisine, his treatises, especially *Le Cuisinier Français* (1651), detail the early development, methods and manners of French cuisine; his analysis and recipes mark a departure from medieval cookery and a French cuisine heavily influenced by Italian traditions; as a chef he introduced the use of roux and bouquets garni.

lavender An herb (*Lavendula angustifolia*) with spikes of aromatic purple flowers and gray-green leaves, principally used for the strong fragrance of its essential oils; the flowers have a sweet, lemony flavor and are also used fresh in Middle Eastern and French cuisines or crystallized and used as a garnish, especially for baked goods.

lavender honey A thick, deep golden–colored honey with a strong, perfumed flavor; principally made from lavender blossoms in France's Provence region.

layer *v.* 1. To stack one or more items, often with different items interleaved (e.g., a stack of crêpes separated by different fillings or two sheets of phyllo dough separated by melted butter). 2. To arrange items in an overlapping pattern (e.g., carrot slices laid out so that the top of one rests on the bottom half of the previous one). *n.* The single item being layered (e.g., a cake layer). *See* tiers.

layer cake Any cake with two or more layers of cake product joined with an icing or filling; the layers may be baked separately or as one large layer that is sliced horizontally into thinner layers after baking.

lazy-daisy cake A single-layer American yellow cake that is baked, topped with a brown sugar, butter and coconut mixture and finished under a hot broiler.

lazy Susan A rotating tray or platform placed in the center of a dining table from which diners can help themselves to food.

lazy tongs Tongs with a jointed extension framework operated by scissorlike handles; they are used for grasping an object at a distance.

lb. *See* pound.

leading sauces The foundation for the entire classic French repertoire of hot sauces; the five leading sauces (béchamel, velouté, espagnole [also known as brown], tomato and hollandaise) are distinguished by the liquids and thickeners used to make them; they can be seasoned and garnished to create a wide variety of small or compound sauces; also known as mother sauces. *See* small sauces.

leaf lard A high-quality lard made from the fat found around the hog's kidneys.

leaf vegetable; leafy vegetable A general term for any vegetable whose leaves are used for food, either cooked or raw.

lean dough A yeast dough that is low in fat and sugar (e.g., French bread and Cuban bread). *See* rich dough.

leather 1. An animal skin prepared for use by tanning or other process. 2. A description of a very tough, chewy food (usually unexpected or undesired). 3. Thin sheet of dried fruit purée. *See* fruit leather.

leaven *v.* To increase the volume of a dough or batter by adding air or other gas. *n.* A leavening agent.

leavening agent; leavener; leaven 1. A substance used to leaven a dough or batter; it may be natural (e.g., air or steam), chemical (e.g., baking powder or baking soda) or biological (e.g., yeast). 2. A type of food additive used to produce or stimulate production of carbon dioxide in baked goods to impart a light texture.

Leberwurst (LAY-beer-voost) A German sausage made with pork liver and fat and seasoned with pepper and allspice.

Lebkuchen (LAYB-koo-kuhn) 1. A thick, cakelike German cookie made with honey, spices and ground nuts; the dough is usually cut into shapes or pressed into decorative molds; the baked cookies are decorated with a sugar glaze. 2. A Pennsylvania German Christmas pastry flavored with citrus and honey and leavened with yeast.

leche frita (LEH-cheh free-tah) A Spanish custard flavored with lemon zest and cinnamon, baked, deep-fried and dusted with a mixture of cinnamon and confectioners' sugar; it has a crunchy exterior and a creamy interior.

lecithin 1. A fatty substance naturally occurring in animal tissue (especially liver and egg yolks) and plant tissue (especially legumes); it is both water soluble and fat soluble and is often used as an emulsifying agent. 2. A food additive used as a stabilizer, thickener, antioxidant and/or emulsifier in processed foods such as candies, mayonnaise, margarine and baked goods.

leckerle; leckerli (LEH-kehr-lee) 1. A Swiss cookie made with honey, spices, candied citrus peel and ground almonds and covered with a sugar glaze after baking. 2. A Swiss cookie made with a mixture of egg whites, almonds and sugar that is dried, then baked briefly; also known as Zurich leckerli.

le concorde (luh kohn-cord) A French pastry composed of three layers of baked chocolate meringue filled and coated with chocolate mousse and covered with small sticks of baked chocolate meringue.

Lee cake A white layer cake flavored with lemon and orange; named for General Robert E. Lee (Am., 1807–1870) and popular in the American South.

leek A member of the lily family (*Allium porrum*); it has a thick, cylindrical, white stalk with a slightly bulbous root end and many flat, dull dark green leaves; the tender white stalk has a flavor that is sweeter and stronger than that of a scallion but milder than that of an onion and is used in salads and as a flavoring.

leeks

lefse (LEFF-suh) Norwegian flatbread.

leg 1. A primal section of the veal carcass; it is the posterior portion of the carcass, containing both the legs and the sirloin; it contains portions of the backbone, hind shank and tail, hip, aitch and round bones and muscles such as top round, eye round, knuckle, sirloin, bottom round (which includes the sirloin) and butt tenderloin; used as is or fabricated into scallops and cutlets. 2. A primal section of the lamb carcass; it contains both legs and the sirloin; usually separated into the two legs, which are then partially or fully deboned and sometimes further fabricated into steaks.

legumes A large group of plants that have double-seamed pods containing a single row of seeds; depending on the variety, the seeds, the pod and seeds together or the dried seeds are eaten. *See* beans, lentils, peas *and* pulses.

légumier (lay-goo-mee-ay) At a food services operation following the brigade system, the person responsible for all vegetable and starch items; also known as the vegetable station chef.

leguminous plants Plants belonging to the family Leguminosae; they are generally flowering plants that have pods (legumes) as fruits (beans, peas and soybeans); there are three principal subgroups: *Caesalpiniaceae,*

Fabaceae and *Mimosaceae;* they are imprecisely known as the pea family.

lemon A citrus fruit (*Citrus limon*) with a bright yellow skin, an ovoid shape with a bulge at the blossom end, a juicy yellow flesh and a very tart, distinctive flavor.

lemon balm A small perennial herb (*Melissa officinalis*) with slightly hairy, serrated leaves and a strong lemon flavor and fragrance; used in sweet and savory dishes and for tisanes.

lemon butter sauce An English butter sauce flavored with lemon juice and thickened with cornstarch; it is usually served with boiled pike.

lemon cucumber A slicing cucumber with a yellow skin and an ivory flesh.

lemon curd A soft, thick custard made from lemon juice, sugar, eggs and butter; used to fill tarts and cakes and as a spread for sweet breads and scones.

lemongrass A tropical grass (*Cymbopogon citratus*) with long, greenish stalks and serrated leaves; the white to pale green inner stalks have a strong lemon-like flavor and aroma and are used fresh in Southeast Asian cuisines; also known as citronella grass.

lemon grater A grater with a flat or slightly convex grating surface with fine teeth; used to remove the zest from citrus fruit.

lemon grater

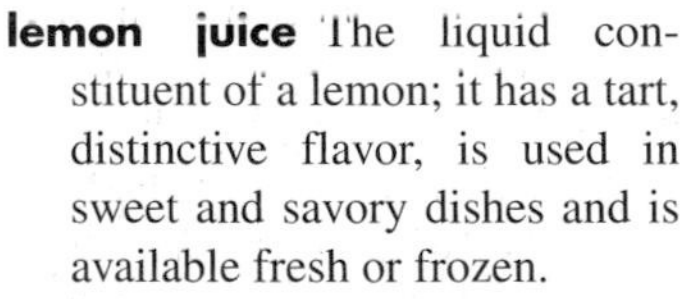

lemon juice The liquid constituent of a lemon; it has a tart, distinctive flavor, is used in sweet and savory dishes and is available fresh or frozen.

lemon meringue pie A dessert composed of a flaky pastry shell filled with a rich lemon custard and topped with a thick layer of soft meringue.

lemon oil The oil obtained from the lemon; it is used as a flavoring agent, especially in reconstituted lemon juice.

lemon sole A member of the flounder family found off the U.S. East Coast; it has a finely textured, white flesh, a sweet flavor and an average market weight of 2 lb. (900 g); also known as blackback flounder and winter flounder. *See* English sole.

lemon verbena An herb (*Lippia citriodora*) with light green pointed leaves and white or lilac blossoms; it has a strong lemonlike flavor and aroma and is used in tisanes and desserts; also known as verbena.

lentils The small flat seeds of a variety of legumes (*Lens esculenta* or *L. culinaris*); sold shelled, dried or cooked.

lentils, Egyptian A smaller, rounder variety of lentils sold without the seed's outer covering; they have a reddish-orange color.

lentils, French A variety of lentils sold with the seed's outer covering intact; they have a grayish-brown exterior and a creamy yellow interior; also known as European lentils.

lettuce Any of a variety of plants of the genus *Lactuca,* probably native to the Mediterranean and now grown worldwide; their leaves are generally consumed fresh in salads or used as a garnish; there are three principal types of lettuces: butterhead, crisp head and leaf.

lettuce, butterhead Any variety of lettuce (*Lactuca sativa*) with a small, spherical, loosely formed head of slightly cup-shaped leaves that have a sweet, buttery flavor and a soft, buttery texture; the outer leaves are pale to medium green and the inner ones tend to be yellow-green (e.g., Boston lettuce); red varieties (especially for baby lettuces) are also available; also known as butter lettuce and butter-crunch lettuce.

lettuce, crisp head Any variety of lettuce with a large, spherical head of densely packed, crisp, pale green, cup-shaped leaves that tend to be paler or a whitish-yellow toward the center; they have a rather bland flavor (e.g., iceberg).

lettuce, head A general name for any lettuce with leaves that grow in a moderately loose to dense rosette; the two principal categories of head lettuce are butterhead and crisp head.

lettuce, leaf Any variety of lettuce whose ruffle-edged leaves are loose rather than bunched in a head and have a mild flavor (e.g., green leaf lettuce and red leaf lettuce); also known as looseleaf lettuce.

levain (le-VAN) A ripened, uncooked sourdough starter.

liaison (lee-yeh-zon) A mixture of egg yolks and heavy cream used to thicken and enrich sauces.

lichee; lichi *See* litchi.

licorice; liquorice 1. A feathery-leafed plant (*Glycyrrhiza glabra*) grown in Europe and Asia; its dried root and an extract taken from the root have a distinctive, sweet flavor similar to that of anise or fennel; used as a flavoring in candies, confections, baked goods and beverages. 2. A candy flavored with licorice extract, usually colored red or black.

lima bean (LY-muh) A flat, kidney-shaped bean native to Peru; it has a pale green color that becomes creamy yellow as it matures and a waxy texture; available fresh, dried, canned or frozen; the mature bean is also known as the butter bean and calico bean.

lime An ovoid citrus fruit (*Citrus aurantifolia*) with a thin, green skin; smaller than a lemon, it has a juicy, pale green pulp and a very tart flavor.

limequat A hybrid of the lime and kumquat; a small citrus fruit with a pale yellow-green rind, a yellowish flesh and a sharp, fragrant flavor; the entire fruit is eaten or used in preserves.

Limerick ham An Irish ham smoked over oak shavings and juniper berries; usually boiled and served hot or cold with a parsley sauce.

limoncillo (lee-mohn-CHEH-loh) 1. An Italian liqueur made by steeping lemon peels in alcohol and adding a sugar syrup. 2. *See* genip.

limpa; limpa bread (LIHM-puh) A moist Swedish rye bread flavored with anise and orange peel.

limpet Any of several varieties of gastropod mollusks found on rocks lining the coasts of temperate to tropical saltwaters; generally, they have a conical, hat-shaped shell and a tough, flavorful flesh; significant varieties include the common Mexican and tortoise-shell limpets.

Lincoln, Mrs. A. D. (Am., 1844–1921) The founder and original principal of the Boston Cooking School, secretary of her own baking powder company and culinary editor of the *American Kitchen* magazine. In 1884, she published *The Boston Cookbook,* the first of its kind to tabulate the ingredients at the start of each recipe and to offer a detailed table of weights and measures.

lingcod Not a true cod but a member of the greenling family found in the Pacific Ocean along the North American coast; this saltwater fish has a mottled brown to bluish-green skin with a cream-colored belly and brown, green or tan spots outlined in orange or light blue; it has very lean, green to bluish-green flesh that whitens when cooked, a delicate flavor, and an average market weight of 5–20 lb. (2.3–9 kg); also known as blue cod, buffalo cod, cultus cod and greenling.

lingonberry (LING-on-bear-ree) A member of the cranberry family (genus *Vaccinium*) grown in North America; it has a red skin and a tart flavor and is used for preserves and sauces.

linguica (lihng-GWEE-suh) A Portuguese and Brazilian sausage made from pork and seasoned with garlic.

Linzer cookie *See* Ischl tart.

Linzertorte (LIHN-zuhr-tort) A thin Austrian tart made with a rich, cookielike dough containing ground hazelnuts and spices, filled with raspberry jam and topped with a dough lattice.

liqueur (lih-kuer) A strong sweet drink made from a distilled spirit base sweetened, flavored and sometimes colored with fruits and aromatics; it generally has a high alcohol content, is viscous and sticky and is sometimes aged; often consumed after a meal or used as an ingredient in a cocktail; also known as a cordial (especially in the United States).

liquor 1. A potable liquid containing ethyl alcohol; generally used to refer only to distilled spirits. 2. In brewing beer, the liquid at any stage of the process. 3. The liquid or juice found in oysters. *See* juice.

Lisbon lemon A variety of lemon; they have a smooth, thin skin and a slightly sweet flavor.

lisci (lee-show) Italian for smooth and used to describe any pasta with a smooth (not grooved or ridged) surface. *See* rigati.

litchi; lychee; lichi; lichee (LEE-chee) A small tropical fruit (*Litchi sinensis*) native to China and Southeast Asia; it has a tough, knobby red skin (that often turns brown during shipping and is not used), a delicate white flesh, a single, large brown seed and a flavor reminiscent of muscat grapes; available fresh or canned.

liter (l) The measure for volume (capacity) in the metric system; 1 l equals 1000 cubic centimeters of water at 20°C or 33.8 U.S. fl. oz. (1.06 qt.) at 68°F.

little A food-labeling term approved by the FDA to describe a food that can be eaten frequently without exceeding dietary guidelines for fat, saturated fat, cholesterol, sodium or calories.

littleneck clam; littleneck quahog An Atlantic hard-shell clam that is under 2 in. (5.08 cm) across the shell; the shells are tannish-gray and the chewy meat has a mild flavor; often served on the half shell.

liver 1. A large, multilobed organ that filters blood to remove and process the nutrients the blood absorbed from the intestines; it also manufactures proteins, secretes bile and destroys or stores toxins. 2. A variety meat; the livers of many varieties of birds (e.g., chicken and goose), fish (e.g., turbot and lote) and mammals (e.g., calf and hog) are edible; an oil extracted from cod and shark livers is used for home remedies.

liverwurst (LIHV-uhr-wurst; LIHV-uhr-vursht) Any of several varieties of seasoned sausages made from pork meat and pork liver; the texture can be semifirm to soft; available smoked or cooked in links, loaves and slices.

loaf 1. A shaped mass of bread (typically a yeast bread) baked in one piece. 2. A shaped, usually rounded or oblong, mass of food (e.g., a veal loaf), cooked or otherwise prepared in one piece. 3. A mass of otherwise shapeless or loosely shaped food cooked in a loaf pan (e.g., a quick bread).

loaf cake Any cake baked in a loaf pan; usually they are pound cakes or fruitcakes.

loaf pan A rectangular baking pan available in a variety of sizes; used for baking breads, cakes and meat loaves.

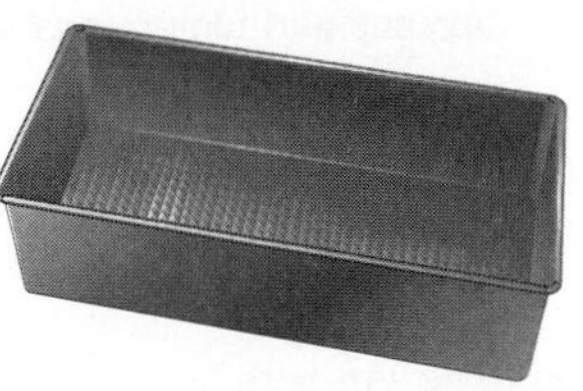

loaf pan

loaf sugar A traditional manner of keeping sugar; refined, crystallized sugar was moistened and compressed into hard cones called loaves; pieces were broken off or grated for table use.

lobster Any of several varieties of crustaceans found in saltwater areas worldwide; generally, they have a jointed body and limbs encased in a reddish-brown to blue-black shell, a large tail, large front claws, and a firm white flesh with a rich, sweet flavor; significant varieties include the Maine lobster, Norway lobster and spiny lobster.

lobster butter A compound butter made by heating ground lobster shells together with butter and straining the mixture into ice water to harden; used as a flavoring for sauces and soups and as a spread.

lobster Newburg A dish of lobster meat heated in a sauce of cream, egg yolks and sherry or Madeira.

lobster Thermidor (THUHR-mih-dohr) A dish of lobster meat bound with a béchamel flavored with white wine, shallots, tarragon and mustard and returned to the shells; it is sprinkled with Parmesan and broiled or covered with a Mornay sauce and glazed under the broiler.

loco moco A Hawaiian breakfast dish consisting of two scoops of rice and a hamburger patty topped with a thick brown gravy and a fried egg.

locro (loh-croh) A stewlike dish made throughout South America from meat, fish and/or shellfish, a grain and other ingredients.

loganberry A berry (*Rubus loganobaccus*) that is a hybrid of the raspberry and blackberry; shaped like an elongated raspberry, it turns purple-red when ripe and has a juicy flesh and a sweetly tart flavor; eaten fresh or used in preserves and baked goods.

log phase A period during which bacteria in a culture or colony experience accelerated growth, usually following a lag phase and continuing until the bacteria begin to crowd others within their colony, creating competition for food, space and moisture. *See* lag phase *and* decline phase.

loin 1. A primal section of the veal carcass; it is posterior to the primal rib and contains two ribs and the very tender and flavorful loin eye muscle and tenderloin. 2. A primal section of the lamb carcass; located between the primal rack and leg, it contains one rib and the very tender and flavorful loin eye muscle and tenderloin and the less tender flank. 3. A primal section of the pork carcass; it is located above the belly and includes the entire rib section and loin and a portion of the sirloin and contains the very tender eye muscle and tenderloin; it is the only pork primal not typically smoked or cured.

loin pork chop A fabricated cut of the pork primal loin; a chop from the rear end of the loin that contains a section of the tenderloin.

loin tip A subprimal cut of the beef primal round; it is a lean, boneless cut from the top round and is further fabricated into a loin tip roast and loin tip steak; also known as a sirloin tip, triangle and top sirloin.

lokma (lo-gh-mah) A Turkish pastry composed of small, sweet balls of deep-fried yeast dough dipped in sugar syrup flavored with honey or lemon; they are crisp on the outside with a hollow interior; known in Greece as loukoumáthes.

lokshen (lock-shen) Yiddish for noodles; usually made with white bread flour and eggs.

lokshen kugel (lock-shen koo-gle) A noodle kugel; it can be sweet (made with cheese, apples and raisins) or savory (made with onions and schmaltz).

lollo rosso A variety of head lettuce with curly, red-tipped, reddish-green leaves.

lombard, sauce (lohm-bar) A French compound sauce made from a hollandaise finished with mushrooms and parsley.

lo mein 1. Fresh Chinese egg noodles. 2. A Chinese–American dish of poultry, shrimp and/or meat with vegetables such as bean sprouts, mushrooms, water chestnuts, bamboo shoots and green onions served over soft noodles.

lomi lomi; lomi lomi salmon A Hawaiian luau dish of salted shredded salmon mixed with tomatoes and onions.

lon (lon) Thai for cooked sauces; they are usually made with coconut milk and served with roasted or fried fish and raw vegetables.

London broil A fabricated cut of the beef primal flank; it is a flank steak that is lean and somewhat tough; sometimes lean slabs of meat from the beef round and chuck primals are imprecisely called London broil.

longan (LONG-uhn) A plum-sized tropical fruit (*Euphoria longana*) native to India and China; it has an ovoid shape, a pink, red or yellow skin and a silvery white flesh surrounding a large black seed with a white eye-shaped marking; it has a very sweet flavor similar to that of a litchi but subtler; also known as a dragon's eye.

long green chile *See* Anaheim chile *and* New Mexico green chile, fresh.

Long Island duck A variety of domesticated duck with white feathers; it has a large, rounded body and a dark flesh with a very rich flavor.

Long John *See* bismarck.

longneck clam An Atlantic soft-shell clam; the ovoid dark blue shell measures 2–5 in. (5.08–12.7 cm) and the meat is tender and sweet.

lop chong; lop cheeng; lop cheong (lah-choong) A highly seasoned, smoked Chinese sausage made from pork and fat; it is slightly sweet, dry and rather hard; also known as Chinese sausage.

loquat (LOH-kwaht) A small- to medium-sized, slightly pear-shaped fruit (*Eriobotya japonica*) native to Japan and China; it has a slightly downy, yellowish-orange skin, a juicy, crisp flesh that can be white, yellow or orange, one to three large, hard seeds and a mildly acidic flavor reminiscent of a slightly sour cherry; also known as Japanese medlar and Japanese plum.

Lord Baltimore cake A three-layer yellow cake made with egg yolks, filled with a mixture of chopped nuts, candied cherries and crushed macaroons, and covered with a fluffy, white frosting such as boiled icing. *See* Lady Baltimore cake.

lorette (low-reht) 1. A French garnish consisting of chicken croquettes, asparagus tips and slices of truffles. 2. Chicken consommé with paprika, garnished with asparagus tips, truffle strips and chervil, with tiny balls of pommes lorette served separately. 3. Corn salad (mâche) accompanied by thin slices of cooked beetroot and thin slices of raw celery. 4. A French method of serving potatoes. *See* pommes lorette.

lotus root The long fleshy rhizome of a water lily (*Nelumbo nucifera*); it has a reddish-brown skin that must be peeled before use, a crisp, white flesh and a flavor reminiscent of coconut; used in Asian cuisines; also known as bhain, hasu, leen ngau and renkon.

Louie sauce An American mayonnaise sauce made with heavy cream and a chile sauce, seasoned with cayenne and lemon juice and garnished with minced onions and green pepper.

Louisane, à la (lou-ee-san, ah lah) A French garnish for fowl or meat consisting of sweet corn fritters and rice darioles on sautéed sweet potatoes and rounds of fried banana.

lovage An herb (*Levisticum officinale*) with tall stalks and large, dark green, celerylike leaves; the leaves, stalks and seeds (which are commonly known as celery seeds) have a strong celery flavor; the leaves and stalks are used in salads and stews, and the seeds are used for flavoring; also known as celeri bâtard (French for false celery), sea parsley, smallage, smellage and wild parsley.

lox Salmon that is brine cured and then typically cold smoked. *See* Nova *and* smoked salmon.

luau (LOO-ow) 1. Hawaiian for taro leaves. 2. A traditional Hawaiian feast, usually featuring a whole roasted pig.

Lucullus, à la (loo-kuhl-us, ah lah) 1. A French garnish consisting of truffles cooked whole in Madeira and filled with quenelles of chicken forcemeat and chopped truffle centers; named for the Roman General Lucullus (106–56 B.C.). 2. A French velouté soup of chicken blended with purée of calves' brains, flavored with sherry and garnished with diced cucumber. 3. A French consommé of beef, garnished with diced carrots and turnips, cauliflowerets and quenelles.

lug A box, crate or basket in which produce is shipped to market; it usually holds 25–40 lb.

lug handle A handle that protrudes like an ear from a vessel.

lumpfish A large fish found in the northern Atlantic Ocean; it has a lumplike dorsal fin and is sought principally for its roe.

lumpfish caviar Roe harvested from the lumpfish; the small and very crisp pinkish eggs are generally dyed black, red or gold; also known as Danish caviar and German caviar and imprecisely known as caviar.

lumpia wrappers Thin round or square sheets of dough made from cornstarch and/or wheat flour and used to wrap foods in Filipino cuisine; also known as egg roll skins.

lutefisk (LOO-teh-feeske) A Scandinavian dish of dried cod soaked in lye before cooking and traditionally served with a cream sauce or pork drippings at Christmas.

lyonnaise, à la (ly-uh-NAYZ, ah lah; lee-oh-NEHZ) A French preparation method associated with the cuisine of Lyon, France; the dishes are garnished or prepared with onions.

lyonnaise, sauce A French compound sauce made from a demi-glaze flavored with white wine and sautéed onions; usually strained and served with meats and poultry.

m *See* meter.

macadamia (mak-uh-DAY-mee-uh) The nut of an Australian evergreen tree (*Macadamia intergrifolia* and *M. tetraphylla*); shaped like a small marble, the nut has a very rich, buttery, slightly sweet flavor and a high fat content; because of the extremely hard shell, it is usually available shelled and raw or roasted; also known as Queensland nut.

macaroni 1. Dried pasta made from a dough of wheat flour and water. 2. In the United States, short, elbow-shaped tubes of pasta.

macaroon 1. A chewy cookie made with sugar, egg whites and almond paste or ground almonds; a variation is made with coconut. 2. A French confection made from two small almond or meringue cookies sandwiched together with jam or chocolate.

macaroon paste A mixture of almond and kernel pastes used to make macaroons.

mace The lacy, reddish-orange outer covering (aril) of the nutmeg seed; it is used ground as a spice; it has a flavor and an aroma similar to those of nutmeg but is milder and more refined. *See* nutmeg.

macédoine (ma-say-DWAHN) A French term for a mixture of fruit or vegetables cut into small dice, cooked or raw, and served hot or cold.

macerate (MAS-uh-rayt) To soak foods in a liquid, usually alcoholic, to soften them.

machaca (mah-cha-kah) A Mexican and Latin American dish of shredded meat usually flavored with chiles and onions.

mâche (MAH-chee) A plant (*Valerianella olitoria*) with small, cupped, tender, dark green leaves and a delicate, slightly nutty flavor; used in salads or cooked like a green; also known as corn salad, field salad and lamb's lettuce.

mâchon (mah-shon) A small meal in southwestern France consisting of a charcuterie item and a salad of potatoes, lentils or dandelion leaves and bacon.

mackerel A family of saltwater fish found worldwide; significant members include tuna, ono, Atlantic mackerel, king mackerel and Spanish mackerel.

mackerel (cero)

mâconnaise, à la (mah-cawn-naiz, ah lah) A French preparation method associated with the cuisine of Mâcon, France; the dishes are cooked with Mâcon wine and garnished with brown glazed onions, fried mushrooms, croutons and shrimps.

macque choux; mocque chou (mock choh) A Cajun dish of corn cut from the cob, cooked with tomatoes, onions and cream and flavored with cayenne and white pepper.

macrobiotic diet A diet that is weighted toward cereals, grains, fish and vegetables (especially those grown with limited or no pesticides, herbicides and so forth); although fish may be eaten, animal proteins are generally avoided.

madeleine (mad-ah-lynn) A French sponge cake baked in a small, shell-shaped mold and eaten as a cookie, especially with tea or coffee.

madeleine pan A flat rectangular plaque with several shallow, shell-shaped indentations for baking madeleines.

madeleine pan

Madère, sauce; Madeira sauce A French compound sauce made from a demi-glaze flavored with sautéed shallots and Madeira and finished with butter; served as is or used as a base for other sauces.

madrilène (MAD-ruh-lehn) A clear Spanish consommé flavored with tomatoes and served hot, cold or jellied.

madrilène, à la (MAD-ruh-lehn, ah lah) French for in the style of Madrid and used to refer to foods cooked in or flavored with tomatoes or tomato juice.

magnolia fig A large fig with an amber-colored skin and pinkish-yellow flesh; also known as a Brunswick fig.

magret (ma-gray) A duck breast, usually taken from the fattened ducks that produce foie gras; it includes the skin but is usually boneless.

mahi mahi (mah-hee mah-hee) *See* dolphinfish.

mahleb; mahaleb (MAAH-lahb) 1. A cherry with a dark red, almost black skin; also known as St. Lucy's cherry. 2. The highly fragrant, golden brown, lentil-sized seeds or pit of this cherry; used ground as a flavoring in Middle Eastern pastries, baked goods and savory dishes.

maidenhair ferns Any of various ferns (genus *Adiantum*) with feathery fronds and edible, fan-shaped leaflets.

maid of honor An individual tartlet filled with almond custard; usually served for afternoon tea in Great Britain.

Maillard reaction (may-YARD ree-AEK-shen) A series of nonenzymatic reactions that occur between some carbohydrates and amino acids in foods; this reaction can occur at room temperature or during cooking and results in browning and the creation of caramel-like flavors.

Maillot, sauce (may-e-yoh) A French compound sauce made from a Madeira sauce seasoned with shallots and white wine and garnished with diced hard-cooked egg whites.

Maine lobster A variety of lobster found off New England; it has a brown to blue-black shell, large claws, and a firm white flesh with an exceptionally rich, sweet flavor; marketed as jumbo (more than 2 lb. [900 g]), large (1.5–2 lb. [680–900 g]), quarter (1.25–1.5 lb. [562–680 g]), chicken (1 lb. [450 g]) and chix (less than 1 lb. [450 g]); also known as American lobster and clawed lobster.

Maintenon, sauce (mahn-tuh-NON) A French compound sauce made from a béchamel flavored with white onions, garlic and grated Parmesan and seasoned with cayenne.

maison, à la (may-ZOHN, ah lah) French for of the house and used to describe a special dish or preparation method associated with the restaurant or its chef.

Mai Tai (my ty) Tahitian for out of this world and used to describe a cocktail made of light and dark rums, lime juice, curaçao, orgeat syrup and grenadine.

mâitre d' (may-truh DEE) *See* dining room manager.

mâitre d'hotel *See* dining room manager.

mâitre d'hôtel, beurre (MAY-truh doh-TELL, burr) Butter mixed with lemon juice and chopped parsley; served with grilled meats, either melted or in rounds or slices.

maki-zushi (mah-key-zoo-shee) Japanese for rolled sushi and used to describe a type of sushi made by rolling zushi and other ingredients (e.g., raw or cooked fish, shellfish and vegetables) in nori; also known as wrapped sushi.

makowiec (mah-koh-ve-eck) A Polish poppy cake; it is a flat layer of dough filled with a mixture of poppy seeds, walnuts, honey, sugar and brandy and rolled into a cylinder before baking.

Málaga raisins Large, very sweet white raisins made from the Muscat grape.

mallard A variety of wild duck found in North America; it has a greenish-black head and neck, a white collar, a chestnut breast and a brown back; it is fatty, with a flavorful flesh, especially if slaughtered during the autumn.

mallow, common A biennial or perennial herb (*Malva sylvestris*) with a tall, straight stem, roundish, toothed and lobed leaves and purplish-rose flowers; the flowers and leaves are used medicinally, and fresh young leaves and shoots are used in salads and soups or cooked as a vegetable.

malossol; malosol (MAHL-oh-sahl) Russian for little salt and used to describe caviar that has had minimal salt added during processing; it has a truer, more delicate flavor.

Malpeque oyster An Atlantic oyster found in Malpeque Bay off Prince Edward Island, Canada; it has a narrow, curved shell.

maltaise, à la (mahl-TEEZ, ah lah) A French preparation method for both sweet and savory dishes; characterized by the use of orange juice, particularly from the Maltese blood orange.

maltaise, sauce (mahl-TEEZ) A French compound sauce made from a hollandaise blended with Maltese orange juice and grated Maltese orange rind; used with vegetables, especially asparagus and green beans.

malted 1. A soda fountain drink made by combining malted milk powder, milk, ice cream and a flavoring such as chocolate or vanilla. 2. A description of barley or other grains that have been soaked, sprouted and dried.

Maltese orange (mahl-TEEZ) A tart variety of medium-sized blood orange grown principally on the Island of

Malta; used in the hollandaise sauce known as sauce maltaise.

malt vinegar A vinegar made from unhopped beer; naturally pale, it is sometimes labeled light malt vinegar; if caramel is added, it is labeled brown malt vinegar. *See* pickling vinegar.

mamey; mamey apple; mamee apple; mamey plum; mamwe plum (ma-MAY) A fruit (*Mammea americana*) native to the West Indies; the size of a large orange, it is spherical with slight points at the top and bottom and has a tough, matte-brown, bitter-flavored skin; the firm, golden flesh has a flavor reminiscent of an apricot.

ma'mool; maamoul (mah'mool) Small Middle Eastern cakes flavored with orange flower water and stuffed with nuts.

mancha (mahn-t'shah) The highest grade of Spanish saffron.

manche à gigot (mansh ah zhee-GOH) A tool used to hold a leg of lamb while carving; it has a flared cap with six internal teeth; the cap is placed over the shank end of the bone and tightened.

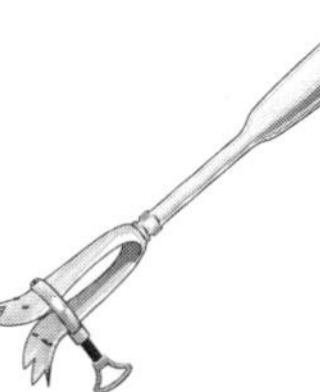

manche à gigot

Manchego (mahn-CHAY-goh) A firm Spanish cheese made from ewe's milk; it has a golden color and a full, mellow flavor; two versions are generally available: Manchego Curado, which is aged for 3–4 months, and the longer-aged Manchego Viejo.

manchette (mansh-ayt) The French paper frill or crown used to decorate the end of a chop or cutlet bone.

mandarin (MAN-duh-rihn) 1. Any of several varieties of a small citrus fruit (*Citrus reticulata*) native to China, including the mandarin, dancy, tangerine, clementine and satsuma. 2. A citrus fruit; it generally has a somewhat flattened spherical shape, a loose yellow to reddish-orange rind, an orange flesh and a sweet flavor that is less acidic than that of an orange.

mandelbrot; mandelbroit (MAHN-duhl-broht) A crisp, twice-baked Jewish almond bread that is eaten as a cookie.

mandoline (MAHN-duh-lihn) A manually operated slicer with adjustable blades; it has a narrow, rectangular body holding a blade and sits at a 45-degree angle; the food is passed and pressed against the blade to obtain uniform slices, matchstick shapes or waffle cuts.

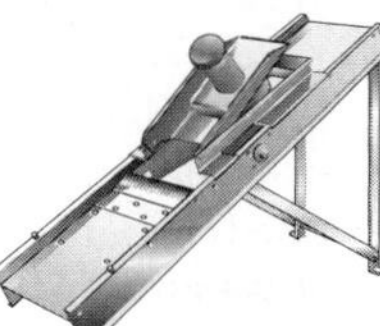

mandoline

mandu (mann-due) Korean meat- or vegetable-filled dumplings, similar to Chinese dumplings, served in soup, boiled, steamed or pan-fried.

manestra (mah-nes-trah) A Greek pasta with a small, grainlike shape.

mange-tout (monj-too) French for eat all and used to describe beans in which both the peas and the pods are eaten (e.g., snow peas and sugar peas).

mango (mann-go) A medium- to large-sized tropical fruit (*Mangifera indica*) native to India; it has a spherical to ovoid shape with a slight ridge on one side and a point at one end; the skin can be yellow or orange with a red blush, greenish-yellow, or golden yellow; the flesh, which is golden orange, encases a large, flat seed and has a sweet, resinous flavor.

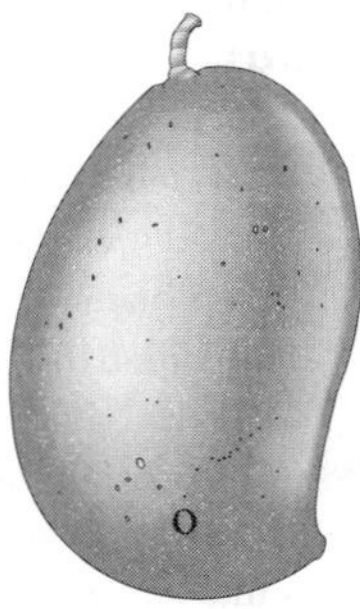

mango

mangosteen (MANG-uh-steen) A small tropical fruit (*Garcinia mangostana*) native to Malaysia and Indonesia; it has a slightly flattened spherical shape, a tough, thick, purple-red rind, an ivory-colored segmented flesh and a sweet–tart flavor.

Manhattan A cocktail made of bourbon or blended whiskey, sweet vermouth and bitters, garnished with a maraschino cherry and served chilled in a cocktail glass; a perfect Manhattan contains equal parts dry and sweet vermouth; a dry Manhattan contains only dry vermouth.

manier (mahn-yay) French term for working a mixture by hand, such as kneading or mixing a fat with flour.

Manila clam A variety of Pacific clam with a brown and white shell that is less than 2 in. (5.08 cm) across; also known as a baby clam and Japanese littleneck clam.

mano (mah-noh) A rectangular stone used to crush corn in a metate. *See* metate.

mansef (mahn-seif) A Middle Eastern meal consisting of a communal platter lined with bread, on top of which is mounded rice and chunks of cooked lamb flavored with allspice, cardamom and pepper; it is garnished with a yogurt sauce and pine nuts.

mantle 1. The membrane embracing a mollusk and lining its shell; it secretes the shell-building materials. 2. A squid's body tube.

Manx broth A thick soup from Great Britain's Isle of Man made with beef brisket, ham knuckle bone, barley, cabbage, turnip, carrots and leeks and flavored with thyme and parsley.

manzana (mahn-ZAH-nak) A medium-sized, bell-shaped fresh chile with a thick yellow-orange skin, black seeds and a medium to very hot, fruity flavor.

maple sugar A sweetener obtained by further concentrating the sap of the maple tree; it has a granular texture and is sweeter and denser than maple syrup.

maple syrup A reddish-brown, viscous liquid with a sweet distinctive flavor, it is made by reducing the sap of the North American maple tree.

marasca A variety of sour cherry grown in Italy; it has a sharp, bitter flavor.

Maraschino (mar-uh-SKEE-noh) An Italian marasca cherry–flavored liqueur.

maraschino cherry (mar-uh-SHEE-noh) 1. A cherry marinated in Maraschino liqueur and used for garnishing cocktails, desserts and baked goods. 2. A pitted cherry macerated in a flavored sugar syrup and dyed red or green; it is used for the same purposes as a maraschino cherry marinated in Maraschino liqueur.

marazine filling A filling made with almond paste, eggs, butter and flour; used in many European pastries. *See* frangipane.

marble cake A moist, buttery cake made by swirling vanilla and chocolate batters together to create a marblelike pattern.

marbling The whitish streaks of inter- and intramuscular fat found in muscles; it adds to the meat's flavor and tenderness and is a principal factor in determining its quality grade.

marc (mar) 1. French for pomace. 2. A clear, brandylike beverage with a high alcohol content distilled from the fermented juice of the pomace; also known as eau-de-vie de marc (French) and grappa (Italian).

marchand de vin, sauce (mah-shon duh vang) A French compound sauce made from a demi-glaze with shallots, red wine, butter, parsley and lemon juice; usually served with steak.

marchpane The traditional name for a paste of sugar and almonds or other nuts made into flat cakes or cookies or molded into ornamental forms; now usually referred to as marzipan.

maréchale, sauce (maahr-ay-shal) A French compound sauce made from an allemande garnished with diced mushrooms.

marengo, à la (mah-rehn-go, ah lah) A French dish of chicken braised with garlic, tomatoes, olives and white wine or brandy; garnished with crayfish and sometimes fried eggs.

margarine A butter substitute made from animal or vegetable fats or a combination of such fats mixed with flavorings, colorings, emulsifiers, preservatives and vitamins and firmed through hydrogenation; like butter, it is approximately 80% fat and 16% water; also known as oleo.

Margarita (mahr-gah-REE-tah) A cocktail made of tequila, lime juice and an orange-flavored liqueur (e.g., Triple Sec or Cointreau); traditionally served in a glass that has had its rim dipped in lime juice and then coated with salt.

Margherita An Italian pizza that is topped with tomatoes, mozzarella and fresh basil.

margosa A slightly cylindrical, bumpy-skinned fruit (*Momordica balsamina*); it has a pale green skin (that turns yellow when ripe), a red flesh and a bitter flavor; used like a vegetable, it is cooked for use in salads or stuffed in Asian cuisines, especially Chinese; also known as a balsam apple.

Marguery, à la (mahr-gew-rey, ah lah) A French garnish for tournedos consisting of artichoke hearts filled with a salpicon of truffles, sautéed morels, cockscombs, and cocks' kidneys; the pan juices are boiled and reduced with port and cream.

Marguery, sauce (mahr-gew-rey) A French compound sauce made from a hollandaise flavored with oyster liqueur and diced poached oysters.

Marie-Jeanne, à la A French garnish for tournedos and noisettes consisting of small tarts filled with peas and tiny balls of carrot and turnip.

Marigny, sauce (mah-rehn-yay) A French compound sauce made from a demi-glaze, flavored with tomatoes and mushroom essence and garnished with sliced mushrooms and black olives.

marinade A seasoned liquid, usually containing an acid, herbs and/or spices, in which raw foods (typically meat, poultry, fish, shellfish or vegetables) are soaked or coated to absorb flavors and become tender before cooking or serving. *See* meat tenderizer.

marinara (mah-ree-NAIR-uh) An Italian pasta sauce made from tomatoes, garlic, onions and oregano.

marinata (mah-ree-nah-tah) A Greek preparation method in which fish are marinated in lemon juice, olive oil and herbs.

marinate To soak or coat a food in a marinade.

mariné (mah-reh-nay) French for marinated or pickled.

marinière, à la (mah-reen-YAIR, ah lah) French for mariner's style and used to describe seafood cooked in white wine and herbs and often garnished with mussels.

marinière, sauce; mariner's sauce A French compound sauce made from a sauce Bercy and mussel stock and garnished with poached mussels.

Marionberry A hybrid berry similar to the blackberry but with a more intense flavor.

marjolaine (mahr-juh-layn) 1. A French pastry composed of rectangular layers of crisp almond or hazelnut meringue sandwiched together with chocolate, coffee and/or praline buttercream. 2. French for sweet marjoram.

marjoram (MAHR-juhr-uhm) An herb and member of the mint family (*Origanum marjorana*) native to the Mediterranean region; it has short, oval, pale green leaves, a sweet flavor reminiscent of thyme and oregano and a strong aroma; also known as sweet marjoram and knotted marjoram. *See* oregano *and* pot marjoram.

market *v.* 1. To attract a specific buyer population. 2. To purchase goods at a grocery or other store. *n.* 1. The number of people who have the ability and desire to purchase a business's goods or services. 2. A geographic area that includes a specific buyer population. 3. A grocery or similar store that sells foods and related items.

market basket competition A culinary contest in which participants are given various foods (unknown to them before the contest) and asked to create a dish or meal; the finished product is judged on flavor, skill and creativity.

marmalade (MAHR-mah-laid) A citrus jelly that also contains unpeeled slices of citrus fruit.

marmalade (mahr-mer-lahd) French for a jellylike purée of fruit or onions.

marmite (mahr-MEET) A tall, straight-sided French metal or earthenware covered pot with a capacity of up to 14 gallons (51 l) used for cooking large quantities of foods, such as soups, cassoulet and pot-au-feu; larger ones are available with a spigot at the bottom.

marquise (mahr-keyz) 1. A French dessert consisting of a fruit ice into which whipped cream is folded. 2. A soft, mousselike chocolate cake. 3. A general term for any semisoft, still-frozen dessert that is molded.

Marquise, sauce (mahr-keyz) A French compound sauce made from a hollandaise blended with caviar just before service.

marron glacé (ma-ROHN glah-SAY) French for chestnuts that are preserved or candied in a sweet syrup.

marrow The soft, fatty vascular substance found in the central cavity of a bone, particularly the shin and leg bones; it has an ivory color after it is cooked and a rich flavor; also known as bone marrow or marrowbone. *See* marrow bone.

marrow bean The largest and roundest of the white bean varieties; available fresh and dried. *See* white beans.

marrow bone A bone, usually from the thigh and upper legs of the beef primal round, with a high marrow content; it is usually cut into 2- to 3-in. (5.08- to 7.6-cm) lengths.

marrow squash 1. An elongated cylindrical summer squash with a green skin and flesh and a bland flavor; it is often stuffed with a meat mixture; also called a vegetable marrow squash. 2. In Great Britain, a general term for summer squash.

marshmallow 1. A perennial herb (*Althaea officinalis*) with a yellow, branched root, a leafy stem with toothed leaves and white or pinkish flowers; the leaves and flowers are used for medicinal, ornamental and culinary purposes; the root has a slightly sweet flavor and is cooked like a root vegetable; the mucilage from the roots was used to make the spongy sweets known as marshmallows. 2. A light, spongy confection made with egg whites, corn syrup and gum arabic or gelatin and formed into a small pillow-shaped candy.

marshmallow crème A thick whipped mixture made from the same ingredients as marshmallows and used in fudges, icings, cakes and candies.

marshmallow icing A boiled icing with a stabilizer, usually gelatin or confectioners' sugar.

marsh samphire (SAM-fy-uhr) A wild perennial herb (*Salicornia europaea*) with small succulent leaves used in salads or cooked like a vegetable; also known as glasswort and sea salicornia. *See* rock samphire.

Martini A cocktail made of gin and dry vermouth, served straight-up or on the rocks, garnished with an olive or lemon twist; when made with vodka, it is known as a Vodka Martini.

maryann pan A round, shallow tart pan with fluted sides and a deep indentation around the circumference that causes the center of the pan's bottom to be raised; sponge cakes and tart shells are baked in the pan, then inverted and the indented center filled with cream or fruit; also known as an Obsttortenform.

Maryland stuffed ham A boiled ham stuffed with cabbage (or other greens) and onions, seasoned with mustard, chiles and other seasonings and served cold.

marzipan (MAHR-zih-pan) A sweet, pliable paste made of ground almonds, sugar and egg whites; often colored and shaped into three-dimensional decorations or used as a candy filling or cake coating. *See* marchpane.

masa (MAH-sah) A Mexican dough made of dried corn kernels that have been soaked and cooked in lime water.

masa harina (MAH-sah ah-REE-nah) 1. Spanish for dough flour. 2. Flour made by grinding dried masa dough; used in Mexican and U.S. cuisines for breads, tortillas, tamales and other foods.

masala (ma-SAH-la) Hindi for spice, spices, spice blend and blend of seasonings. *See* garam masala.

Mascarpone (mas-cahr-POHN-ay) A soft, double or triple cream cheese made in Switzerland and Italy's Lombardy and Tuscany regions from cow's milk; it has an ivory color and a sweet, slightly acidic flavor and is often blended with either sweet or savory flavorings.

mastic A natural resin or gum with a faint licorice flavor; produced in Greece from the Acacia tree, it is used as a flavoring in the Middle East.

maté (MAH-tay) A South American beverage with a low alcohol content made from the fermented dried leaves and shoots of an evergreen tree (*Ilex paraguayenis*) of the holly family; also known as Paraguay tea and yerba maté.

matelote (mah-tuh-lot) A French stew made with freshwater fish, especially eels, flavored with red or white wine and aromatics.

Matelote, sauce (mah-tuh-lot) A French compound sauce made from a demi-glaze flavored with red or white wine, fish stock or trimmings and cayenne and finished with butter.

matignon (mah-tee-yawng) 1. A vegetable fondue with or without bacon, used as a flavoring in various braised or fried dishes. 2. A French garnish for various cuts of meat, consisting of artichoke hearts stuffed with vegetable fondue, sprinkled with bread crumbs and browned. 3. An archaic term used to designate a coarsely chopped mirepoix containing ham.

matsutake (maht-soo-TAH-kee) A large mushroom (*Tricholoma matsutake*) that grows wild on pine trees in Japan; it has a reddish-brown color, a dense, meaty texture and a nutty flavor; usually available dried in the United States; also known as a pine mushroom.

matzo; matzoh (MAHT-suh) A thin, brittle, unleavened bread made with only water and flour and traditionally eaten during the Jewish Passover holiday; it can be ground into meal and used for matzo balls, pancakes and other dishes.

matzo ball *See* matzoh knaidel.

matzo brei (br-eye) A Jewish dish of matzo soaked in water, squeezed dry, dipped in beaten egg and fried; it is usually served with cinnamon sugar, maple syrup, honey or ketchup.

matzoh knaidel (mah-t'zoh knayd-dhul) A Jewish dumpling made from matzo meal and sometimes flavored schmaltz; it can range from light and fluffy to heavy and dense; also known as a matzo ball.

Maui onion A large onion with a golden yellow outer layer, a moist white flesh and a mild, sweet flavor; grown in the delimited area of Maui, Hawaii.

Maximilian, sauce A French compound sauce made from a hollandaise blended with anchovy essence.

mayhaw A hawthorn tree (*Crataegus aestivalis*) that grows in the American South; the acidic, juicy, red berry is used for making jellies and preserves.

mayhaw jelly *See* mayhaw.

mayonnaise (may-o-nayz) A cold, thick, creamy sauce consisting of oil and vinegar emulsified with egg yolks; used as a spread or base for a salad dressing or dip. *Note*: French mayonnaise sauces are listed alphabetically by their principal modifier (e.g., mayonnaise cressonière is listed cressonière, mayonnaise).

mazzard A wild sweet cherry native to Europe; the black-skinned fruit have a rich flavor and are often used for flavoring liqueurs in central Europe; the mazzard is a particularly hardy species and it is often used as a grafting stock; also known as a bird cherry or gean.

mead A drink made from a fermented mixture of honey and water; also known as honey wine.

measuring cups, dry Vessels, usually made of plastic or metal, with a handle and a rim that is level with the top measurement specified; they are used to measure the volume of dry substances and are generally available in a set of 1/4-, 1/3-, 1/2-, and 1-cup capacities; metric measures are also available.

measuring cups, liquid Vessels, usually made of glass, plastic or metal, with a handle and a spout that is above the top line of measurement; specifically used to measure the volume of a liquid and generally available in 1-, 2- and 4-cup to 1-gallon capacities; metric measures are also available; also known as glass cup measures.

measuring spoons Plastic or metal spoons with a round or oval bowl and used to measure volume; they usually come in sets of four to measure 1/4, 1/2, and 1 teaspoon and 1 tablespoon.

meat 1. The flesh (muscles, fat and related tissues) of animals used for food. 2. The edible part of nuts. 3. The fleshy part of fruits and vegetables.

meat and potatoes 1. Slang for a hearty meal, usually something plain and basic; also known as steak and potatoes. 2. Slang for someone who is not an adventurous eater.

meatballs; meat balls Small balls shaped from a mixture of minced or ground meats, usually flavored with onions, herbs and spices and bound with bread crumbs and/or egg; they are poached, pan-fried, threaded on skewers and grilled or broiled; served with or without a sauce in various cuisines worldwide.

meat by-products The edible and wholesome parts of a beef, veal, lamb or pork carcass other than skeletal meat. *See* variety meats.

meat grinder; meat mincer A tool used to grind meat; the meat is placed in a hopper and forced through a rotating blade, then through a perforated disk (various sizes are available) and extruded; manual or electric, it can be fitted with attachments (e.g., one to hold sausage casings).

meatloaf; meat loaf A loaf-shaped mixture of ground meat (beef, veal, lamb or pork) or poultry, seasonings and usually onions, bound with bread crumbs and/or eggs and baked; served hot or cold.

meat pounder; meat bat A metal tool used for flattening and tenderizing meat; it has a flat, broad face with a 5- × 4-in. striking surface and weighs 1.5–7 lb.

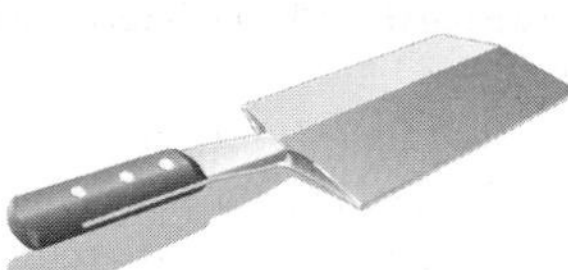
meat pounder

meat product; meat food product A labeling term recognized by the USDA for any food product containing more than 3% cattle, sheep, swine or goat meat.

meat tenderizer 1. A preparation of enzymes (principally the protease papain) applied to meat before cooking to help break down connective tissues; unlike a marinade, which can contain a meat tenderizer, it is not intended to add flavor. *See* marinade. 2. A metal or wooden hammerlike tool used to tenderize meat; one striking face has a fine-toothed surface, and the other has a coarse-toothed surface; also known as a meat hammer.

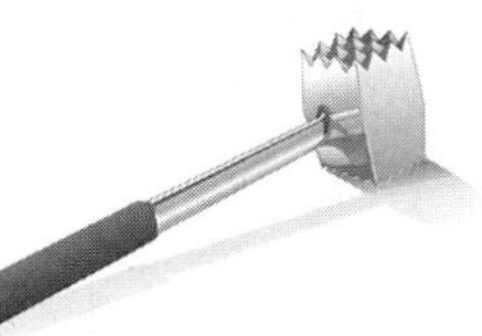
meat tenderizer

medallion A small, round or oval piece of meat (especially from the rib or loin of beef, veal, lamb or pork) or fish.

Médici, sauce A French compound sauce made from a béarnaise flavored with tomato purée and red wine.

medium A degree of doneness for meat; the meat should have a rosy pink to red center and be slightly firm and springy when pressed. *See* very rare, rare, medium rare, medium well *and* well done.

medium rare A degree of doneness for meat; the meat should have a bright red center and be slightly springy when pressed. *See* very rare, rare, medium, medium well *and* well done.

medium well A degree of doneness for meat; the meat should have very little pink at the center (almost brown throughout) and be firm and springy when pressed. *See* very rare, rare, medium rare, medium *and* well done.

medlar (MEHD-lehr) A medium-sized fruit (*Mespilus germanica*) native to Iran; it has a yellowish-brown color and is picked when ripe and stored in moist bran or sawdust until it browns and softens; it has a slightly acidic, winy flavor.

mein (Cantonese); mian (Mandarin) (main) Chinese for noodles and often used to describe thin noodles made from wheat flour; usually preceded by another word or phrase indicating a type of noodle or noodle dish.

melba (MEHL-bah) A French garnish for small cuts of meat consisting of small tomatoes filled with a salpicon of chicken, truffles and mushrooms mixed with a velouté, sprinkled with bread crumbs and browned; it is often accompanied by braised lettuce.

Melba, sauce A French dessert sauce made with puréed raspberries, sugar, red currant jelly and cornstarch. *See* Peach Melba.

melba toast Very thin slices of white bread baked in a low oven until golden brown and very crisp.

melegueta pepper The berry of a plant (*Aframomum melegueta*) native to Africa; it has a spicy, peppery flavor.

melon A member of the gourd family Cucurbitaceae; grown on vines worldwide, these fruits generally have a thick, hard rind, many seeds and a sweet, juicy flesh; there are two principal types: muskmelons and watermelons. *See* muskmelon *and* watermelon.

melon ball cutter A tool used to scoop smooth or fluted spheres or ovoids from melons, cucumbers or other foods; available with a single scoop on a handle or a handle with a scoop at either end, one larger than the other. *See* Parisian scoop.

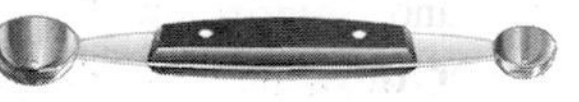
melon ball cutter

melt The process by which certain foods, especially those high in fat, gradually soften and then liquefy when heated. *See* patty melt.

melting moments A British confection made of sweet dough shaped into balls, rolled in crushed cornflakes or dried, sweetened coconut and topped with a candied cherry or angelica before baking.

ménagère, sauce (meh-nah-zher) A French compound sauce made from a demi-glaze flavored with onions, finished with lemon juice and garnished with chopped anchovies and parsley.

menudo (meh-NOO-doh; meh-NOO-thoh) A spicy Mexican soup made from tripe, calf's feet, green chiles, hominy and seasonings and garnished with lime wedges, chopped chiles and onions.

merguez; mirqaz (mayr-GEZ) A North African and Spanish sausage made from beef and mutton, seasoned and colored with red chiles; sometimes used to garnish couscous.

meringue (muh-RANG) A mixture of stiffly beaten egg whites and sugar; depending on the ratio of sugar to egg whites, a meringue may be soft (used as a fluffy topping for pies or cakes) or hard (baked into crisp cookies, disks or shells for use in pastries and desserts). *See* common meringue, Italian meringue *and* Swiss meringue.

meringue powder A fine, white powder made with dried egg whites, sugar and gum; used to replace fresh egg whites when making icings and meringues.

mesclun (MEHS-kluhn; MEHS-klahn) A mixture of several kinds of salad greens, especially baby lettuces; although there is no set standard, the mixture usually includes baby red romaine, endive, mâche, oak leaf, radicchio and rocket, among others.

mesquite (meh-SKEET) A hardwood tree (genus *Prosopis*) native to the American Southwest and Mexico; when burned for cooking or smoking foods, it imparts a distinctive aroma and a slightly sweet flavor.

mess 1. Slang for an amount of food (e.g., he cooked up a mess of fish). 2. Archaic term for a serving of a soft, semiliquid food such as porridge. 3. A military term that refers to group dining.

metate (meh-TAH-teh) A concave stone used by Native Americans and others living in the American Southwest or Mexico to grind corn into cornmeal using a mano. *See* mano.

meter (m) The basic measure of length in the metric system; 1 m equals 39.37 in.

méthode champenoise (meh-toh'd shahm-peh-n'wahz) The French term for the classic method of making Champagne or other sparkling wine; the process consists of (1) bottling a blend of still wines with sugar and yeast to create a second fermentation within the bottle; (2) the second fermentation creates carbon dioxide, which is trapped in the bottle and dissolved in the wine, thus producing the effervescence; (3) sediment is formed, however, which must be disgorged. *See* Charmat process *and* vinification.

méthode rurale A rarely used method of making a sparkling wine; the still wine is bottled before fermentation is complete; the trapped carbon dioxide creates a slight sparkle.

metric system A measurement system developed by the French and used worldwide; a decimal system in which the gram, liter and meter are the basic units of weight, volume and length, respectively; larger or smaller units are formed by adding a prefix such as *centi-* (0.01, a centigram is 0.01 g), *deca-* (10, a decameter is 10 m), *deci-* (0.10), *hecto-* (100), *kilo-* (1000), *milli-* (0.001) and *quintal-* (100,000). *See* imperial system *and* U.S. system.

Mettwurst (MEHT-wurst; MEHT-vursht) A soft, fatty German sausage made from pork, seasoned with coriander and white pepper, cured and smoked; it has a bright red color; also known as Schmierwurst.

meunière (muhn-YAIR) French for miller's wife and used to describe a style of cooking in which the food (e.g., fish) is seasoned, lightly dusted with flour and sautéed in butter.

Mexican chocolate A sweetened chocolate flavored with almonds, cinnamon and vanilla; used in hot beverages.

Mexican coffee A cocktail made of tequila, Kahlua or sugar syrup and strong hot black coffee; served in a large mug and garnished with whipped cream.

Mexican wedding cookies; Mexican wedding cakes Small, round, buttery cookies made with ground nuts and rolled in confectioners' sugar after baking; also known as Russian tea cakes.

meza; mezza; maza (mehz-zah) Arabic for hors d'oeuvre; it can be any of a wide variety of hot or cold salads, dips, fritters, pickles, savory pastries and the like.

meze (meh-ZAY) Greek and Turkish for hors d'oeuvre and used to describe both the social occasion preceding a meal during which they are served and the foods (e.g., feta cheese, olives, nuts and shellfish).

mezzaluna (mehz-zuh-LOO-nuh) A two-handled knife with one

mezzaluna

or more thick, crescent-shaped blades used to chop or mince vegetables; also known as a mincing knife.

mg *See* milligram.

microwave cooking A heating method that uses radiation generated by a special oven to penetrate the food; the radiation agitates water molecules, creating friction and heat; this energy then spreads throughout the food by conduction (and by convection in liquids).

microwave oven An oven that cooks with microwaves; available with a revolving platform so that foods can cook more evenly.

middlings Coarse particles of wheat that contain the endosperm, bran and germ; a by-product of flour milling.

mie (mee) 1. French for the soft interior part of a loaf of bread. 2. French for fresh bread crumbs made from crustless white bread.

migas (MEE-gahs) 1. A Spanish dish consisting of small squares of bread soaked in milk and fried in oil. 2. A Mexican dish of scrambled eggs, onions, jalapeños and stale tortilla strips, garnished with cheese.

mignonette (mee-nyohn-EHT) 1. A small, coin-shaped filet of meat; a medallion. 2. French for coarsely ground white pepper.

Mignonette, sauce A French sauce of red wine, white pepper and minced shallots; usually served cold with oysters on the half shell.

milanaise, à la (mee-lah-NEEZ, ah lah) 1. A French preparation method associated with the cuisine of Milan, Italy; the principal foods are dipped in egg and bread crumbs mixed with Parmesan cheese and then fried in clarified butter. 2. A method of preparing macaroni; it is served in a sauce of butter with grated cheese and a tomato sauce. 3. A garnish for cuts of meat consisting of macaroni with cheese, coarsely shredded ham, pickled tongue, mushrooms and truffles all blended in a tomato sauce. 4. Dishes cooked au gratin with Parmesan. 5. A method of preparing risotto; it is scented with saffron.

milanaise, sauce A French compound sauce made from a demi-glaze flavored with tomatoes and garlic and garnished with mushrooms.

milchig (mill-chigg) Yiddish for dairy and dairy products; one of the three categories under Jewish dietary laws (kosher). *See* fleischig, kosher *and* pareve.

mile-high cake; mile-high pie A tall, multilayer cake or a tall pie topped with several inches of ice cream or meringue.

milk *v.* To extract milk from a mammal. *n.* 1. The white or ivory liquid produced by adult, female mammals and used to nurture their young; it is composed of water, milkfat and milk solids; some milks are used for human consumption, either as is or processed into products such as cheese. 2. Whole cow's milk. 3. Any liquid resembling milk, such as the liquid in a coconut or the juice or sap of various plants.

milk, evaporated A nonsweetened milk product made from whole milk from which 60% of the water has been evaporated; it is then sterilized and canned, resulting in a cooked flavor and darker color; it must contain at least 7.25% milkfat and 25.5% milk solids.

milk, raw Unpasteurized milk; used principally for cheese making.

milk, sweetened condensed A thick, sweet, slightly caramel-flavored milk product made from sweetened whole milk from which 60% of the water has been evaporated; usually sold canned, it cannot generally be substituted for whole or evaporated milk because of the sugar; also known as condensed milk.

milk bread A white wheat bread in which either all of the liquid is milk or it contains not less than 8.8 parts (by weight) of milk solids for each 100 parts of flour (by weight).

milk chocolate Sweetened chocolate containing not less than 12% milk solids and not less than 10% chocolate liquor; used for candies, creams and confections. *See* chocolate-making process.

milkfat The fat found in milk; a significant component in dairy products such as butter, cream and cheeses; the higher the milkfat content, the richer and creamier the product; also known as butterfat.

milk solids The proteins, milk sugar (lactose) and minerals (but not the milkfat) present in milk.

milk toast Buttered toast, sometimes sprinkled with sugar and cinnamon, over which milk is poured; traditionally served to children and the infirm.

milkweed A wild plant (*Asclepias suriaca*) that yields a milky substance when cut; used by Native Americans as a flavoring and thickener.

milky cap mushroom A wild mushroom (*Lactarius deliciosus*) that exudes a milk when the flesh is broken; it has a firm texture, a reddish color and a pleasant flavor.

mill *v.* 1. To grind, pulverize or break down into smaller particles. *See* milling. 2. To agitate or stir until foamy. *n.* 1. A building equipped with machinery for grinding grain into flour or meal; the device that does so. 2. A device that reduces a solid or coarse substance into pulp or minute grains by crushing, grinding or pressing (e.g., a pepper mill). *See* grinder. 3. A device that releases the juice of fruits and vegetables by pressing or grinding (e.g., cider mill).

mille-feuille (meel-FWEE) 1. French for thousand leaves and used to describe any sweet or savory dish made with puff pastry. *See* feuilletage. 2. A French pastry composed of rectangular pieces of puff pastry layered with pastry cream, whipped cream and fruit or ganache; also known as a napoleon.

millet A cereal grain (*Panicum milaiceum*) with a bland flavor and a white color; in the United States, it is used principally for animal feed, and in Asia, North Africa and southern Europe, it is usually ground into flour; also available as flakes.

milligram (mg) A metric measure of weight; 1000 mg equal 1 g; 1 g equals 0.0353 oz.

milliliter (ml) A metric measure of volume; 1000 ml equal 1 l.

milling The mechanical process of changing the shape of grains or separating certain portions of the grains, such as the hull from the bran.

mimosa (mih-MOH-suh) A garnish of finely chopped hard-cooked egg yolk; so named because of its resemblance to the yellow mimosa flower.

mince To cut or chop a food finely.

mincemeat A rich, finely chopped mixture of dried fruit, nuts, beef suet, spices and rum or brandy; used as a filling for pies, tarts and cookies; traditionally, lean meat was included in the mixture.

miner's lettuce A salad green with small, slightly cupped, triangular leaves with tiny flowers in the center and a fresh, mild spinach flavor; also known as claytonia.

minestrone (mee-ness-TROH-nay) Italian for big soup and used to describe a vegetable soup flavored with herbs and sometimes garnished with pasta; there are variations made with rice, bacon, tomatoes, sage and cheese (in northern Italy), with navy beans (in Tuscany) and with beans, sauerkraut, potatoes, cumin seeds and garlic (in northeastern Italy).

Minneola (mehn-nee-oh-lah) A tangelo with a knob at the stem end, a dark orange rind and a rich, sharp flavor.

mint 1. A large family of herbs (genus *Mentha*) known for their aromatic foliage, many of which have flavors and/or aromas reminiscent of fruits (e.g., lemon) and other flavorings (e.g., chocolate). 2. A candy flavored with mint, often used as a breath freshener; it can be a hard candy or a soft patty with a hard candy or chocolate coating.

mint

mint sauce A sauce made from vinegar, water, sugar and salt mixed with finely chopped mint leaves, marinated for several hours and strained before service.

minute steak A fabricated cut of the beef flank, chuck or round primals; it is a small, very thin, cubed steak.

Mirabeau, à la (meer-ah-bo, ah lah) A French garnish for grilled meats, consisting of anchovy fillets, stoned olives, chopped tarragon and anchovy butter.

Mirabeau, sauce A compound sauce made from allemande flavored with garlic and beaten with beurre maître d'hôtel.

mirabelle (mihr-uh-BEHL) 1. A small, round greengage grown in Great Britain and parts of continental Europe; its skin color ranges from golden yellow to red, and it is used principally for tarts and preserves; also known in Great Britain as a cherry plum. 2. A French eau-de-vie made from the mirabelle.

mirepoix (meer-pwa) A mixture of coarsely chopped onions, carrots and celery used to flavor stocks, stews and other foods; generally, a mixture of 50% onions, 25% carrots and 25% celery, by weight, is used.

mirin (mee-REEN) A Japanese low-alcohol, sweet, syrupy, thin, golden-colored rice wine used to add sweetness and flavor to glazes, sauces and a variety of dishes.

mirliton (MIHR-lih-ton) 1. A puff pastry tart filled with almond cream and decorated with three almond halves arranged in a star pattern. 2. A crisp almond cookie flavored with orange flower water. 3. American name for the chayote.

mise en place (meez ahn plahs) French for putting in place and used to describe the preparation and assembly of all necessary ingredients and equipment for cooking. *See* batterie de cuisine.

miso (ME-so) A thick paste made by salting and fermenting soybeans and rice or barley and then inoculating the mixture with yeast; it is used in Japanese cuisines as a flavoring and thickener; the lighter the color, the sweeter the flavor.

Mission fig A fig with a purple-black skin; it was brought to California by Franciscan missionaries from Spain; also known as a black Mission fig.

Mission olive A ripe medium-sized green olive that has obtained its characteristic black color and flavor from lye curing and oxygenization.

Mitzithra (me-zeeth-rah) A Greek cheese made from the whey remaining after feta has been made; it has a white color, a soft texture and a mild flavor.

mix *v.* 1. To combine ingredients in such a way that they are evenly dispersed throughout the mixture. 2. To create or form something by combining ingredients (e.g., a cocktail). *n.* 1. A mixture of ingredients that usually requires only the addition of water and/or yeast to produce a batter or dough. 2. A commercially packaged mixture of ingredients that usually requires only the addition of a liquid and/or a fresh product such as eggs, meat or fish and heating to produce a completed dish.

mixed grill 1. A British dish consisting of assorted grilled or broiled meats (e.g., lamb chops, beefsteak, sausages, kidneys and liver) served with grilled tomatoes, watercress and mushrooms. 2. A dish consisting of assorted grilled or broiled meats, fish and/or poultry.

mixer 1. A kitchen appliance equipped with various beaters, dough hooks and other attachments and used for mixing, beating, kneading, whipping or creaming foods; it can be portable or stationary. 2. A nonalcoholic beverage such as a soft drink that is combined with an alcoholic beverage to make a cocktail.

mizuna (mih-ZOO-nuh) A feathery Japanese salad green with a delicate flavor.

mocha (moh-kah) A flavor created by combining coffee and chocolate, widely used in pastries and confections.

mochi (MOH-chee) A short-grain, sweet, gelatinous rice with a high starch content; used in Japanese cuisine to make rice cakes and confections.

mock apple pie A pie made with Ritz crackers and spices; popular during the Depression.

mock duck A fabricated cut from the lamb shoulder; it is partly boned, with the shank bone turned up and outward, and the whole roast is tied and decorated to resemble a duck.

mock turtle soup An English soup prepared by cooking a calf's head in water; the meat is served in the clear, brownish broth, which is usually spiced and thickened.

mocque chou *See* macque choux.

modeling chocolate A stiff dough made with melted chocolate and glucose or corn syrup; it is used for creating pastry decorations or garnishes.

moderate oven An oven set to a temperature of approximately 350°F (177°C). *See* hot oven *and* slow oven.

moderne, à la (mo-darin, ah lah) A French garnish for small cuts of meat consisting of individual dariole molds of layered carrot, turnip, green beans and peas, sealed with forcemeat, cooked in a bain marie and unmolded for service.

Moelle, sauce (mwahl) A French compound sauce made from a bordelaise based on white wine instead of red wine, garnished with poached beef bone marrow.

moisten A baking term meaning to add enough liquid to the dry ingredients to make them damp or moist, but not wet.

moist-heat cooking methods Cooking methods, principally simmering, poaching, boiling and steaming, that use water or steam to transfer heat through convection; moist-heat cooking methods are used to emphasize the natural flavors of foods. *See* dry-heat cooking methods.

Mojito (moh-hee-toh) A cocktail made of light rum, lime juice, sugar and club soda; garnished with a mint sprig.

mokhalafat (moe-kah-law-faht) Pickles, relishes, condiments, plates of fresh herbs, vegetables, cheese and yogurt and other side dishes served with an Iranian meal.

molasses 1. A thick, sweet, brownish-black liquid that is a by-product of sugar refining; used in breads, cookies and pastries for its distinctive, slightly bitter flavor and dark color. 2. A syrup made from boiling down sweet vegetable or fruit juices.

molasses, blackstrap A molasses removed after the third boiling of the sugarcane in the sugar-refining process; it is thick and dark and has a strong, distinctive flavor.

molasses, dark A molasses removed after the second boiling of the sugarcane in the sugar-refining process; darker, thicker and less sweet than light molasses, it is generally used as a flavoring.

molasses, light A molasses removed after the first boiling of the sugarcane in the sugar-refining process; it has a lighter body, color and flavor (although it is sweeter) than dark molasses and is usually used as a syrup.

mold *v.* To shape a food by using a vessel. *n.* 1. A vessel into which foods are placed to take on the container's shape; molds are available in a wide range of shapes and sizes, many of which are associated with a particular dish. *See* timbale. 2. A food shaped by such a vessel. 3. Any of a large group of fungi that form long filaments or strands that sometimes extend into the air and appear as fuzzy masses; molds can grow at almost any temperature, moisture or pH level; a few that grow on food are desirable (e.g., those used in cheese making); most are not dangerous and merely affect the appearance of food, but some, called mycotoxicoses, produce toxins. 4. The fungi or their spores that contribute to the character of a cheese; they are generally absorbed during the ripening process either as a surface mold (which helps ripen the cheese from the surface inward) or internal mold (which helps ripen from the interior outward, such as those for blue cheeses).

molded cookie A type of cookie formed by pressing the dough into a decorative mold before baking.

molding 1. The process of shaping gelatin-thickened foods in a decorative container. 2. The process of shaping foods, particularly grains and vegetables bound by sauces, into attractive, hard-edged shapes by using metal rings, circular cutters or other forms.

mole; mole poblano de Guajolote (MOE-lay poe-BLAH-noh day goo-ah-hoe-loh-tay) A Mexican sauce usually served with poultry; it consists of onions, garlic, chiles, ground pumpkin or sesame seeds and Mexican chocolate.

molinet (mo-li-NAY) A long-handled wooden tool with deep grooves and several loose wooden rings at one end; created in 16th-century Spain for blending chocolate beverages.

mollusks One of the principal classes of shellfish; they are characterized by a soft, unsegmented body with no internal skeleton (many have hard outer shells); includes univalves (e.g., abalone), bivalves (e.g., clams) and cephalopods (e.g., octopus). *See* crustaceans.

Mongolian hot pot An Asian (northern Chinese) cooking method in which each diner dips his or her own food into a pot of simmering stock to cook it; there are usually several condiments and sauces available.

monkey bread A sweet yeast bread made by piling small balls of dough in a tube pan; raisins, nuts, sugar and cinnamon are usually added, and then the dough is allowed to rise; after baking, the mounds can be pulled apart for service. *See* baobab.

monkfish A fish found in the Atlantic Ocean and Mediterranean Sea; only the tail flesh is edible and it is usually available as fillets; it is lean, with a pearly white color, a very firm texture and a rich, sweet flavor; also known as angler fish, bellyfish, devilfish, frogfish, goosefish, poor man's lobster, rapé and sea devil.

monosodium glutamate (MSG) A food additive derived from glutamic acid, an amino acid found in seaweed and certain vegetable proteins, and used as a flavor enhancer; widely used in Chinese and Japanese cuisines; also known as aji-no-moto and sold under the brand name Ac'cent. *See* Chinese restaurant syndrome.

monounsaturated fat A triglyceride composed of monounsaturated fatty acids; generally, it comes from plants (olive, peanut and cottonseed oils are high in monounsaturated fats) and is liquid (an oil) at room temperature.

monstera (mon-STAIR-uh) A tropical fruit (*Monstera deliciosa*) native to Central America; it has a thick, green skin covered in hexagonal scales that separate and loosen as the fruit ripens and a creamy, smooth, ivory flesh with a flavor reminiscent of pineapple, banana and mango; also known as ceriman, fruit salad fruit, Mexican breadfruit and Swiss cheese plant fruit.

Mont Blanc (mohn blon) A French dessert made with whipped cream and sweetened chestnut purée; the chestnut mixture is passed through a ricer to create small strands, which are piled into a fluffy mound.

Monte Cristo sandwich A sandwich of bread, ham, chicken and Emmental or Emmental-style cheese dipped in beaten egg and fried.

monter au beurre (mohn-tay ah burr) To finish a sauce by swirling or whisking in butter (raw or compound) until it is melted; it is used to give sauces shine, flavor and richness. *See* mount, to.

Monterey Jack A cooked and pressed cheese traditionally made in Monterey, California, from whole, skimmed or partly skimmed cow's milk; it has an ivory color, a semisoft texture and a rather bland flavor (varieties flavored with peppercorns, spices, herbs or jalapeños are available); it is high in moisture and melts easily; also known as Jack or California Jack, especially if not produced near Monterey.

Montmorency, à la (mon-moh-REHN-see, ah lah) French for made or served with cherries and used to describe both sweet and savory dishes.

Montmorency cherry (mon-moh-REHN-see) A sour cherry with a red skin, a creamy beige flesh and a mildly tart flavor.

Montrachet (mohn-truh-SHAY) A soft cheese made in France's Burgundy region from goat's milk; it has a creamy texture and a mild, tangy flavor; usually sold in white logs, sometimes covered with a gray, salted ash.

monzù (mohn-ZOO) An 18th-century term for a chef or cook in a well-to-do household of southern Italy; these chefs were often trained in France.

moonshine Illegally distilled whiskey, usually made from corn mash; also known as white lightning.

moo-shu; moo-shoo A Chinese stir-fried dish containing shredded pork, chicken or beef, scallions, tiger lily buds, wood ears, scrambled eggs and various seasonings; the mixture is rolled in a small, thin pancake, usually spread with plum sauce or hoisin sauce.

mopping sauce Liquids brushed on meat during barbecuing to add flavor and moisture; the sauce is usually applied with a small, moplike cotton utensil.

mora A dried jalapeño smoked over mesquite wood; it has a reddish-brown color and a moderately hot, smoky, mesquite wood flavor with strong tobacco and plum undertones.

morcilla blanca (mohr-SEE-yah blahn-kah) 1. A Spanish sausage made from chicken, hard-boiled egg and bacon and seasoned with black pepper and parsley. 2. A Spanish sausage made from pig's lights and tripe, fat and cereal.

morcilla negra (mohr-SEE-yah nay-graw) A Spanish black pudding made with pig's blood and pork fat, seasoned with onions, cayenne, black pepper and marjoram, stuffed into a pig's bladder and boiled.

morel (muh-REHL) A wild mushroom (*Morchella esculenta* and *M. vulgaris*) that grows during the spring in Europe, North America and Southeast Asia; it has a cream to buff-colored conical cap covered in irregular indentations, giving it a spongy, honeycombed appearance, a creamy white hollow stem and a smoky, earthy, nutty flavor; usually purchased dried; also known as sponge mushroom and spongie.

Morello cherry (muh-REHL-oh) 1. A sour cherry with a dark red skin and flesh and a sharp, tart flavor; often used to flavor liqueurs and brandies; also known as an English Morello cherry. 2. An imprecisely used term for any of a variety of sour cherries.

Mornay, sauce (mor-nay) A French sauce made by adding grated cheese (Parmesan, Gruyère and/or Emmental) to a basic white sauce; served with fish, shellfish, vegetables and chicken.

Moroccan olive A large, round, black olive; it is usually salt brine cured and packed with herbs.

moros y christianos (moh-rohs e chres-teh-ah-nos) A Cuban dish of black beans and rice usually served with meat and fried plantains.

mortadela (mohr-tah-DEH-lah) A Spanish sausage made from lean pork, seasoned with brown sugar, saltpeter, garlic, herbs and brandy or other liquor.

mortadella (mohr-tuh-DELL-uh) 1. An Italian smoked sausage made with ground beef, pork and pork fat and flavored with coriander and white wine; it is air-dried and has a smooth, delicate flavor. 2. An American sausage made from bologna with pork fat and flavored with garlic.

mortar and pestle A tool, usually made of stone, wood or ceramic, used for grinding foods; the bat-shaped pestle presses and rotates the food against the sides of the bowl-shaped mortar.

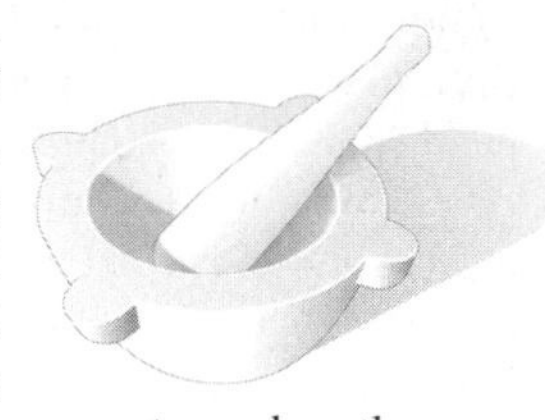

mortar and pestle

moscovite, sauce (mahs-koh-veet) A French compound sauce made from a demi-glaze flavored with pepper and juniper berries or an infusion of juniper berries, garnished with sultanas and pine nuts and finished with Marsala or Málaga; served with game.

mother of vinegar A slimy, gummy substance consisting of various bacteria (especially *Mycoderma aceti*) that cause fermentation in a wine or cider, turning it into vinegar (it is removed once the vinegar-making process is completed).

mother sauces *See* leading sauces.

mount, to A cooking method in which small pieces of cold, unsalted butter are whisked into a sauce just before service to give it texture, flavor and a glossy appearance. *See* monter au beurre.

mountain oysters The testicles of an animal such as a lamb, calf or boar; they have little flavor and usually a coarse texture; also known as Rocky Mountain oysters and prairie oysters.

Mourteau (moor-toh) A lightly smoked French pork sausage; it is eaten cold or hot, usually served with beans, cabbage or sauerkraut.

moussaka; mousaka (moo-SOCK-kah) A Greek dish consisting of layers of eggplant and ground lamb or beef covered with a béchamel or cheese and baked; variations contain onions, artichokes, tomatoes and/or potatoes.

mousse (moos) 1. French for foam. 2. French for the head that forms on sparkling wine or beer. 3. A soft, creamy food, either sweet or savory, lightened by adding whipped cream, beaten egg whites or both.

mousse cake A dessert made by molding mousse on top of or between layers of sponge cake.

mousseline (moos-uh-leen) 1. A delicately flavored forcemeat based on white meat, fish or shellfish lightened with cream and egg whites. 2. A sauce or cream lightened by folding in whipped cream. 3. A tall cylinder of brioche bread, usually baked in a coffee can or similar mold.

Mousseline, sauce A French compound sauce made from a hollandaise mixed with stiffly whipped cream.

mouth feel The sensation, other than flavor, that a food or beverage has in the mouth; a function of the item's body, texture and, to a lesser extent, temperature.

Mozzarella (maht-suh-REHL-lah) 1. A southern Italian pasta filata cheese, originally made from water buffalo's milk but now also from cow's milk; it has a white color and a mild, delicate flavor; used mostly for cooking. 2. An American version usually made from cow's milk; it is drier and stringier than the fresh water buffalo's milk variety and becomes very elastic when melted; also known as pizza cheese.

MSG *See* monosodium glutamate.

muajeenot (moo-ah-ja-not) Arabic for savory pastries; generally, they are made from a thin, flaky and crunchy crust and are filled with meat and nut mixtures, creamed chicken, cheese, cooked vegetables, zaatar paste or the like; they can be crescent shaped, triangular, round, oval or rectangular, with the filling open or enclosed.

muddle *v.* To crush and mix ingredients in the bottom of a bowl or glass (e.g., crushing and mixing sugar and mint leaves with a spoon when making a Mint Julep); to mix something up. *n.* An American southern fish stew made with potatoes, tomatoes and onions and flavored with thyme, bay leaves and cloves.

mud pie A dessert that consists of a chocolate cookie crust filled with chocolate, vanilla and coffee ice cream and drizzled with chocolate sauce.

muffin 1. A tender quick bread baked in small, cup-shaped pans; the batter is often flavored with nuts or fruit. 2. An English muffin. 3. In Great Britain, a small yeast-leavened product baked on a griddle.

muffin method A mixing method used to make quick bread batters; it involves combining liquid fat with other liquid ingredients before adding them to the dry ingredients.

muffin pan; muffin tin A rectangular baking pan with cup-shaped depressions for holding muffin batter.

muffin pan

muffin ring A small ring, usually of tinned iron, used to make muffins such as English muffins.

muffuletta; muffaletta (muhf-fuh-LEHT-tuh) A New Orleans hero-style sandwich consisting of a round loaf of Italian bread that is split and filled with layers of provolone, salami and ham and topped with a mixture of chopped green olives, pimientos, celery, garlic, capers, oregano, olive oil and red wine vinegar.

mug A flat-bottomed vessel, usually glass or ceramic, with a single handle and generally ranging in size from 8 to 14 fl. oz.; often used to serve hot beverages or beer.

mulato (moo-LAH-toh) A long, tapering dried poblano chile with a dark chocolate brown color and a mild to medium hot flavor.

mulberry A berry (genus *Morus*) similar to a blackberry in size and shape with a rather bland, sweet–sour flavor; there are three principal varieties: black, red and white; eaten raw or used for preserves, baked goods or mulberry wine.

mulberry, black A variety of mulberry native to western Asia; it is similar to a loganberry and has a dark red to purplish-black skin and a good flavor.

muligapuri (moo-lee-ga-poo-ree) An Indian condiment mix of fenugreek seeds and powdered roasted red chiles; usually served with breads.

mull To heat a beverage such as wine, cider or beer with herbs, spices, fruit and sugar and serve it hot.

mullet A variety of fish found in the Atlantic Ocean off the southern U.S. East Coast, the Gulf of Mexico and the Pacific Ocean off California; generally, it has a dark-bluish striped skin on top that becomes silvery on the sides, an average market weight of 2–3 lb. (0.9 g–1.36 kg), a moderate to high fat content, and a firm, tender flesh with a mild, nutlike flavor; significant varieties include black mullet, Florida mullet, silver mullet and striped mullet; also known as gray mullet.

mullet

mulligan stew (MUHL-ee-gahn) A stew of various meats, potatoes and vegetables.

mulligatawny soup (muhl-ih-guh-TAW-nee) A spicy soup from southern India consisting of meat or vegetable broth flavored with curry and garnished with chicken, meats, rice, eggs, coconut shreds and cream.

mung bean A small dried bean (*Phaseolus lunatus*) with a green or sometimes yellow or black skin, a tender yellow flesh and a slightly sweet flavor; used to grow bean sprouts and in Chinese and Indian cuisines as a bean and ground for flour; also known as green gram and moong.

Muscadine (MUHS-kah-dine) 1. A grape variety native to the southern United States; it has a thick purple skin and a strong musky flavor; used principally for eating out of hand and for jams and jellies; also known as southern fox grape. 2. A red wine, generally sweet, made from this grape; similar to a light cordial.

muscles Animal tissue consisting of bundles of cells or fibers that can contract and expand; they are the portions of a carcass usually consumed.

muscovado sugar (muhs-coh-vah-doh) A raw, unrefined sugar that is dark or light and has a strong molasses flavor.

muscovy duck; musk duck (mus-kove-ee) A domesticated duck; young birds have a rich flavor and tender texture; older ones have a tougher texture and a strong aroma.

mush A thick porridge or cereal made by cooking cornmeal with water or milk; served for breakfast with milk or maple syrup or cooled, cut into squares, fried and served with gravy as a side dish.

mushi-ki (moo-shee-ki) Japanese wood steamers with bamboo latticework bases; they are used in tiers over simmering water.

mushroom Any of many species of cultivated or wild fleshy fungus (class Basidiomycota; edible ones are generally members of the genus *Agaricus*), usually consisting of a stem, cap (which may have gills) and mycelium; available fresh or dried and eaten raw, reconstituted or cooked.

muskellunge; muskie A freshwater fish of the pike family found in the northern United States and Canada; it has a light skin with dark patterning, an average market weight of 10–30 lb. (4.5–13.5 kg), a low fat content and a firm flesh with many small bones.

muskmelon A category of melons (*Cucumis melo*) characterized by a dense, fragrant flesh, a central fibrous seed cavity, a hard rind that can be netted (e.g., cantaloupe and Persian) or smooth (e.g., casaba and honeydew), rind colors that include ivory, yellow, orange and green, and flesh colors that include ivory, yellow, lime green and salmon; also known as sweet melon. *See* watermelon.

musli; muesli (MYOOS-lee) A breakfast cereal made from raw or toasted cereals (e.g., oats, wheat, barley and millet), dried fruits, nuts, bran, wheat germ, sugar and dried milk solids and usually eaten with milk or yogurt; sometimes imprecisely known as granola.

mussels Any of several varieties of bivalve mollusks found in the shallow waters of the Atlantic and Pacific Oceans and Mediterranean Sea; they generally have a dark blue shell with a violet interior, an average length of 2–3 in. (5.08–7.6 cm) and tough meat with a slightly sweet flavor; significant varieties include blue mussels and greenshell mussels.

mustard Any of several species of a plant that is a member of the cabbage family (*Brassica nigra* and *B. juncea*); the seeds are used for a spice and the leaves are eaten as vegetables.

mustard, ground A blend of finely ground mustard seeds; it has a bright yellow color; also known as powdered mustard and dry mustard.

mustard, prepared A condiment made from one or more kinds of powdered mustard seeds mixed with flavorings, a liquid such as water, wine or vinegar and sometimes a thickener such as wheat flour.

mustard, whole grain A coarse prepared mustard made from ground and slightly crushed whole mustard seeds (the husks are not removed); it has a hot, earthy, nutty flavor.

mustard greens The large, dark green leaves of the mustard plant; they have a peppery, pungent flavor.

mustard greens, salted A bitter mustard plant preserved in brine, sometimes with wine added; it has a salty, sour, tangy flavor and is used in Chinese cuisines.

mustard oil 1. A cooking oil infused with mustard flavor and aroma. 2. An oil obtained by pressing mustard seeds; it is used as a flavoring and in certain cosmetics and soaps.

mustard seeds The seeds of three different varieties of mustard plants; all are small, hard spheres with a bitter flavor and no aroma; white and yellow seeds have the mildest flavor, and black seeds have the strongest flavor; brown seeds are moderately hot and generally have their husks attached; fine to coarsely ground mustard seeds are used for the condiment prepared mustard or as a spice.

mutton The meat of a sheep slaughtered after its first year; the meat is generally tougher and more strongly flavored than lamb. *See* baby lamb, lamb *and* spring lamb.

mycelium (mi-SEE-lee-um) The fine, threadlike structures at the base of a fungus that act like roots to gather nutrients.

myrtle (meer-teyl) A shrub (*Myrtus communis*) native to the Mediterranean region; its blue berries have a sweet, acidic flavor and its leaves have a flavor reminiscent of juniper and rosemary.

naan (nah'-han) An Indian flatbread made with white wheat flour and sourdough starter, traditionally baked on the wall of a tandoor oven; it is slightly puffy with a chewy texture and is often flavored with garlic, onions and other seasonings.

nabemono (nah-beh-MOH-noh) Japanese for communal one-pot meals that are served family style or cooked by the individual diner at the table; they are accompanied by various condiments and sauces.

nachos (NAH-choh) A Mexican and American Southwest snack of a crisp tortilla or tortilla chips topped with melted cheese and chiles, sometimes with salsa, sour cream, refried beans or other garnishes.

nage, à la (nahj, ah lah) A French preparation method, especially for shellfish; the principal items are cooked in a court bouillon flavored with herbs and are then served with the bouillon, either hot or cold.

naked frying A cooking method in which foods, usually small items, without any flour or batter coating are deep-fried in moderately hot oil.

nakiri-bōtchō (nah-KEE-ree-BOH-cho) A Japanese knife used to cut produce; it has an elongated rectangular blade with a blunt tip and a straight 8-in.-long cutting edge.

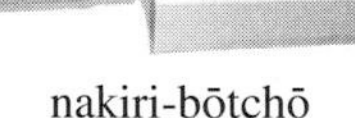

nakiri-bōtchō

NAMP/IMPS The Institutional Meat Purchasing Specifications (IMPS) published by the USDA; the IMPS are illustrated and described in *The Meat Buyer's Guide* published by the National Association of Meat Purveyors (NAMP).

nam pla (num PLAH) A salty condiment made from fermented fish and used in Southeast Asian cuisines.

nam prik (num preek) A spicy Thai sauce made by pounding together salted fish, garlic, chiles, nam pla, fresh lime juice, light soy sauce and palm sugar.

Nanaimo bar (nah-naa-moh) A Canadian multicolored pastry with three layers; the bottom layer is made of chocolate, butter, sugar, dried coconut, graham crackers and walnuts, the middle layer is buttercream flavored with vanilla or Grand Marnier, and the top layer is dark chocolate; the pastry is chilled and cut into bars or squares for serving.

Nantua, sauce (nan-TOO-uh) A French compound sauce made from a béchamel flavored with cream and crayfish butter and garnished with crayfish tails; it is served with fish, shellfish and egg dishes.

napa cabbage A member of the cabbage family with a stout, elongated head of relatively tightly packed, firm, crinkly, pale yellow-green leaves with a thick white center vein and a mild, delicate flavor; also known as chard cabbage, Chinese cabbage and snow cabbage.

napoleon (nuh-POH-lee-uhn) A French pastry made with rectangular sheets of puff pastry layered with pastry cream, whipped cream and fruit or chocolate ganache; the top is then dusted with powdered sugar or coated with fondant glaze; also known as mille-feuille.

napoletana, alla (nah-poa-lay-TAA-nah, al-ah) An Italian method of preparing and garnishing foods associated with Naples, Italy; the foods (e.g., pasta, grilled dishes and pizza) are often topped with a pizzaiola sauce.

nappe (nap) *v.* To coat a food with sauce. *n.* 1. The consistency of a liquid, usually a sauce, that will coat the back of a spoon. 2. French for tablecloth.

naranjilla (nah-RAHN-hee-lah) A small fruit (*Solanum quitoense*) native to South America; it has an orange skin, a yellowish-green segmented flesh, many tiny, flat seeds and a sweet–sour flavor reminiscent of a pineapple and lemon.

nasi goreng; nassi goreng (nahg-SEE goh-REHNG) An Indonesian dish consisting of rice cooked with foods such as shrimp or other shellfish, meat, chicken, eggs, onions, chiles, garlic, cucumber, peanuts and seasonings.

nasturtium An annual or perennial herb (genus *Tropaeolum*); the leaves have a peppery flavor and can be used like watercress; the yellow- to rust-colored flowers also have a peppery flavor and can be used in salads, as a flavoring or garnish, and the immature flower buds can be pickled and used like capers; also known as Indian cress.

natto (NAH-toh) Steamed, fermented, and mashed soybeans used as a condiment and flavoring in Japanese cuisine; the resulting product has a strong cheeselike flavor and a glutinous texture.

natural food 1. A food altered as little as possible from its original farm-grown or ranch-raised state. *See* processed food. 2. A popular and often misleading label term not approved by the FDA and used for a food that does not contain any additives and/or has been minimally processed; its use is intended to suggest that consuming such food will promote health.

navarin (nah-veh-rahng) A French stew made from lamb or mutton, onions, turnips, potatoes and other vegetables and flavored with a bouquet garni and garlic.

navel orange A variety of large orange with a thick, bright orange rind, an orange meaty flesh, a sweet, citrusy flavor and few if any seeds.

navy bean A variety of kidney bean; small and ovoid with a white skin and flesh; a staple of the U.S. Navy since the 1880s, it is also known as the beautiful bean, Boston bean and Yankee bean. *See* white beans.

Neapolitan ice cream Three layers of ice cream, usually chocolate, vanilla and strawberry, molded together, then sliced for service.

neck A British cut of beef, veal, lamb and pork carcasses; it extends from the neck, through the shoulder, and into the rib cage

nectar 1. In Greek and Roman mythology, the drink of the gods. 2. A sugary liquid secreted by many flowers and attractive to bees. 3. In the United States, undiluted fruit juice or a mixture of fruit juices. 4. In France, the diluted, sweetened juice of peaches, apricots, guavas, black currants or other fruits, the juice of which would be too thick or too tart to drink straight.

nectarine A medium-sized stone fruit (*Prunus persica*) with a smooth red and yellow skin, a firm yellowish-pink flesh and a peachy flavor with undertones of almond; available as freestone and clingstone.

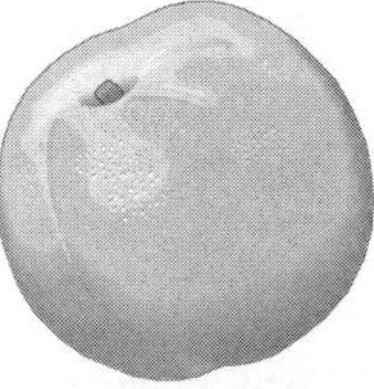

nectarine

needling A process used to tenderize meat; the meat is penetrated by closely spaced, thin blades with sharp points, the muscle fibers are thus cut into shorter lengths; also known as pinning.

negimaki (NAH-ghee-MAH-kee) A Japanese–American dish of sliced beef wrapped around a scallion, broiled with a soy-based sauce and served with a thicker soy-based sauce.

neige (nehzh) 1. French for snow and used to describe egg whites whisked until they form stiff peaks. 2. A type of sorbet or grated ice used in the presentation of certain French dishes.

Nemours, à la (nuh-moor, ah lah) 1. A French garnish for entrées consisting of green peas, carrots and pommes duchesse. 2. A French garnish for meats consisting of sautéed mushrooms and tournée potatoes. 3. A French dish of poached fillet of sole coated with shrimp sauce, topped with a sliced truffle and garnished with quenelles and small mushrooms in a sauce normande.

néroli bigarade (neh-row-li be-gahr-rahd) A bitter orange tree (*Citrus aurantium* var. *bergamia*); its fruit and flowers yield a highly aromatic oil.

neroli oil The aromatic oil produced from the néroli bigarade; it is used to flavor soft drinks and desserts.

Nesselrode pudding A pudding mixed with chestnut purée, candied fruit, raisins and Maraschino liqueur and then topped with whipped cream; often frozen or used to fill a pie shell.

netted melon A type of muskmelon with a raised, weblike surface pattern; there are two principal varieties: cantaloupes and Persian melons.

nettle, common A perennial herb (*Urtica dioica*) with long, pointed, coarsely serrated leaves; the young shoots are added to salads, cooked as a vegetable or used to make nettle beer; also known as a stinging nettle.

net weight The weight of a package's contents; the container and packaging (tare) are not included.

Neufchâtel (noo-shuh-TELL) 1. A soft, unripened cheese made in France's Normandy region from cow's milk (the milkfat content varies); it has a white color and a slightly salty flavor that becomes more pungent as it ages; sold as small cylinders, rectangles or hearts. 2. An American cheese made from pasteurized milk or a mixture of pasteurized milk and cream; similar to cream cheese and smoother than its French inspiration.

New Brunswick stew A Canadian casserole of roasted lamb or beef, smoked ham, string beans, wax beans, new potatoes, onions, green peas and carrots cooked in the oven.

Newburg A dish consisting of cooked shellfish (lobster, shrimp or crab) in a rich sauce of cream and egg yolks flavored with sherry; usually served over toast points.

New Mexico green chile, dried A dried New Mexico green chile; it has an olive to dark green color and a sweet, light, smoky flavor with hints of citrus and dried apple; also known as the dried California chile.

New Mexico green chile, fresh A very long, thin, tapering chile with a pale to medium green color, a moderately thick flesh, and a medium to hot, sweet, earthy flavor; also known as the long green chile.

New Mexico red chile, dried A dried New Mexico red chile; it has a dark red to brown color and a medium hot to hot flavor; available as crushed flakes or powder; also known as chile Colorado and dried California chile.

New Mexico red chile, fresh A ripened New Mexico green chile; it has a dark red color, a thick flesh and a medium to medium hot, sweet flavor.

new potato 1. A small, immature red potato. 2. An imprecisely used term for any variety of small young potato.

New York chowder A clam chowder that contains aromatic vegetables and clams in a tomato broth.

New York steak; New York strip steak *See* strip loin steak.

Niagara grape A spherical to ovoid table grape grown in the eastern United States; it has a pale greenish-white color and a sweet, foxy flavor.

nibs Cleaned, roasted cocoa kernels that are ready for processing. *See* chocolate-making process.

niçoise (nee-SWAHZ) A tiny black olive native to the Mediterranean region.

niçoise, à la (nee-SWAHZ, ah lah) A French preparation method associated with the cuisine of Nice, France; the dishes are characterized by the use of tomatoes, garlic, black olives, green beans and anchovies.

niçoise, salad (nee-SWAHZ) A salad from Nice, France, consisting of tomatoes, green beans, black olives, tuna, hard-cooked eggs and herbs, dressed with olive oil and garlic.

niçoise galette (nee-SWAHZ gah-lyet) A round, thin French pastry made with a base of sablée dough and a filling of rum frangipane and topped with shortbread cookie dough.

nigella; nigella seeds (nee-gell-a) A spice that is the seeds of an annual herb (*Nigella sativa*); the black seeds have a mild peppery flavor and are used in Indian and Middle Eastern cuisines in baked goods and sweet dishes; also known as black cumin (no relationship) and fennel flower (no relationship).

nightshade Any plant of the Solanaceae family (e.g., tomato, pepino and eggplant).

nigiri-zushi (nee-gui-ree-zoo-shi) Japanese for squeezed sushi and used to describe a type of sushi made by placing tane (the topping, which can be raw, marinated or cooked fish or shellfish or other food) on a bed of pressed zushi; also known as Edomae-zushi.

nikiri (nee-key-ree) A Japanese condiment; it is a reduction of soy sauce and mirin.

nimono (nee-MOH-noh) Japanese for foods such as meat, fish and vegetables that are simmered in a seasoned broth.

nitter kibbeh; nit'r k'ibé (nitter key-bah) A golden yellow, clarified butter flavored with onions, garlic, ginger, turmeric, cardamom seeds, cinnamon, cloves and nutmeg and used as a flavoring in Ethiopian cuisine.

noble rot The desirable deterioration of ripened white wine grapes affected by the mold *Botrytis cinerea;* the mold forms on the grape's skin, reducing liquid content and concentrating sugars; this is responsible for the characteristic sweetness of wines such as Sauternes, Beerenauslese and Tokay Aszú.

noble scallop A variety of scallops found in Japanese waters; it has a violet, salmon and yellow symmetrical shell and a tender, sweet, white meat.

nohu A variety of rock cod fish found off Hawaii; it has a lean, large-flaked, white flesh and an average weight of 2–3 lb. (0.907–1.35 kg).

noisette (nwah-ZEHT) A small, tender, round slice of meat taken from the rib or loin of lamb, veal or beef.

noix (nwah) 1. A French cut of the veal carcass; a lengthwise cut from the upper part of the filet end of a veal leg. 2. A French cut of the veal carcass; it is the eye muscle of a cutlet. *See* cuisseau.

nondairy creamer A product used to lighten and dilute coffee and tea; made from a hydrogenated oil or saturated fat such as coconut or palm oil, sweeteners, preservatives and emulsifiers; it is available in powdered, liquid or frozen form; also known as coffee whitener.

nonna, della (NOH-nah, DEH-lah) Italian for grandmother's style and used to describe a homestyle or traditional dish.

nonpareille, sauce (nuhn-pah-reel) A French compound sauce made from a hollandaise flavored with crayfish butter and garnished with diced crayfish tails, mushrooms and truffles.

nonpareils (non-puh-REHLZ) 1. Tiny sugar pellets used to decorate cakes and confections. 2. Small chocolate disks coated with these pellets. 3. French for without equal and used to describe small capers from France's Provence region.

nonperishable Foods and beverages that do not quickly spoil or deteriorate, especially if stored under appropriate conditions.

nonreactive A term used to describe cooking and serving utensils made of materials that do not react with acids and brine (a salt and water solution) to discolor foods or form toxic substances; nonreactive saucepans and pots include all of those with undamaged nonstick interiors, plus pots and pans made from flameproof glass, glass ceramic, stainless steel, enameled steel and enameled iron; uncoated iron and copper form toxic substances when used for cooking high-acid foods; uncoated aluminum darkens some fruits and may become pitted if salty mixtures are left standing in them.

nonstick plastic; nonstick coating; nonstick finish A polymer such as polytetrafluoroethylene (PTFE) that is applied to the surface of some cookware; it provides a slippery, nonreactive finish that prevents foods from sticking and allows the use of less fat; easily scratched.

noodles 1. Ribbons of various lengths, widths and thicknesses made from a dough of wheat flour, water and eggs (or egg yolks) and generally boiled; also known as egg noodles. *See* pasta. 2. A generic term for ribbons of boiled dough (whether made with eggs or wheat flour) of various lengths, widths and thicknesses; used principally to describe Asian products. 3. British for fettuccini and similar pasta shapes.

nopales (noh-PAH-lays) The pads of the nopal cactus (genus *Nopalea*) native to Mexico; they have a flat, irregular oval shape, short stinging needles, a pale to dark green color and a delicate, tart flavor reminiscent of green beans.

nori (NOH-ree) Dark green, purple or black paper-thin sheets of dried seaweed with a sweet, salty ocean flavor; used in Japanese cuisine to wrap sushi or as a garnish or flavoring. *See* yakinori *and* afifsuke-nori.

nori-maki (NOH-ree-mah-kee) A category of Japanese sushi; a core of principal ingredients (e.g., raw fish and sprouts) are rolled in zushi and the whole is wrapped in nori; the roll is then cut into bite-sized slices.

normande, à la (nohr-MAHND, ah lah) A French preparation method associated with the cuisine of Normandy; the dishes are characterized by the use of typical Norman products such as butter, fresh cream, seafood, apples, cider and Calvados.

normande, sauce A French compound sauce made from a fish velouté with mushroom stock and oyster liquor, thickened with a liasion, and finished with butter.

no roll A beef carcass or cut that has not been officially graded.

northern pike A freshwater fish found in North America; it has a dark skin with light spots, an average market weight of 0.5–1.5 lb. (225–680 g) and a lean, firm, flaky flesh; also known as a grass pike and lake pickerel.

northern pike

northern red snapper *See* red snapper.

Norway lobster A variety of lobster found in the northern Atlantic Ocean; it has an elongated tail and claws, a brick to salmon red shell, a maximum length of 9 in. (22.5 cm), a tender flesh and a sweet, delicate flavor; also known as Icelandic lobster and lobsterette.

nostrale; nostrano (noh-STRA-lee; noh-STRAH-noh) Italian for homemade and used to describe local products, such as cheeses, wines or sausages.

no-time dough A bread dough made with a large quantity of yeast; except for a short rest after mixing, no time is set aside for fermentation.

nouet (noo-ay) A muslin bag containing herbs, spices or other flavorings and tied with a string; used in French cuisine to impart flavors to a liquid without leaving solid particles behind. *See* bouquet garni *and* sachet.

nougat (noo-guht) A French confection made with a cooked sugar or honey syrup mixed with roasted nuts and candied fruit; sometimes the confection is made with egg whites, which produce a white, chewy, taffy-like candy.

nougatine (noo-gah-teen) A crisp French nut brittle made with caramelized sugar and almonds or hazelnuts; before it cools, nougatine can be cut into pieces or shaped into cups or containers for creams or other pastries; once it hardens, nougatine can be crushed and used to flavor ice cream, pastries or other confections.

nouvelle cuisine (noo-vehl kwee-zeen) French for new cooking and used to describe a mid-20th-century movement away from many classic cuisine principles and toward a lighter cuisine based on natural flavors, shortened cooking times and innovative combinations.

Nova Salmon that is brine cured and then typically cold smoked; it is less salty than lox. *See* smoked salmon.

nuoc cham (noo-AHK CHAHM) An all-purpose Vietnamese condiment made of chiles, nuoc mam, sugar and lime juice.

nuoc mam (noo-AHK MAHM) Vietnamese for a salty condiment made from fermented fish.

nut 1. The edible single-seed kernel (the meat) of a fruit surrounded by a hard shell (e.g., hazelnut); it has high protein and fat contents and is used for snacking or to provide flavor and texture to foods. 2. A term used imprecisely to describe any edible seed or fruit with an edible kernel surrounded by a hard shell (e.g., walnut).

nutcracker A utensil used to crack nuts; it consists of two pivoted 7-in. (17.8-cm) lengths with small and large arc inserts with ridges to grip the nut.

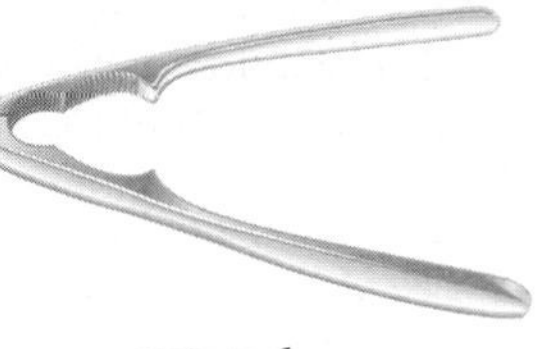
nutcracker

Nutella The proprietary name for a paste made from hazelnuts, cocoa and sugar; it is used as a spread for bread or toast and as a flavoring for pastries and confections.

nut flour A flour made of finely ground nuts and used in certain cakes and other pastries.

nut meat; nutmeat The edible kernel of a nut.

nutmeg The hard seed of a yellow fruit from a tree (*Myristica fragrans*) native to the East Indies; it has an oval shape, a smooth texture and a strong, sweet aroma and flavor; used ground (grated) in sweet and savory dishes. *See* mace.

nutmeg grater A grater used for reducing a whole nutmeg to a powder; the grating surface can be flat or convex.

nutmeg grater

nut mill A tool used to produce a nut flour; shelled nuts are put into the hopper and pressed against the grating drum by a rotating hand crank.

nut oil Any oil extracted from a nut; typically labeled as pure, it generally has the strong aroma and flavor of the nut from which it was processed.

nutrients The components of food (i.e., carbohydrates, lipids [fats], proteins, vitamins, minerals and water) that provide the energy and raw materials for the growth, maintenance and repair of the body.

nutritionist A person who has specialized in the study of nutrition or related fields and, generally, has an advanced degree; a nutritionist may also be a registered dietitian. *See* dietitian.

oak leaf lettuce A leaf lettuce with red-tinged green leaves similar in shape to an oak tree's leaves.

oat bran The oat kernel's bran; used as a high-fiber nutrient supplement.

oatcake A large, round disk of dough made of oatmeal, salt, bacon fat and warm water; cut into segments, it is sprinkled with oatmeal and cooked in an iron skillet until the edges curl upward; it is served hot or cold with unsalted butter or cottage cheese.

oat groat The oat kernel with the husk removed; it is the portion most often consumed as a cereal or in baked goods.

oatmeal Coarsely ground oats that are cooked as a hot cereal and used in baking.

oats A cereal grass (*Avena sativa*) with a highly nutritious grain kernel.

oblique cuts Small pieces of food, usually vegetables, with two angle-cut sides; also known as roll cuts.

O'Brien potatoes A dish of diced potatoes (sometimes precooked) fried with onions and red and green sweet peppers.

Obsttorte (ohbst-tor-ta) A fruit tart made with a maryann pan.

ocean perch A member of the rockfish family found in the Atlantic Ocean from New England to Labrador and in the Pacific Ocean from California to Alaska; it usually has an orange to bright red skin (brownish-red varieties are available), a firm, lean, white flesh and an average market weight of 0.5–2 lb. (225–900 g); also known as deep-sea perch, longjaw rockfish, red perch, redfish and rosefish.

octopus Any of several varieties of cephalopod mollusks found in the Atlantic and Pacific Oceans and the Mediterranean Sea; generally, they have a large head and tentacles but no cuttlebone; the skin is gray when raw and turns purple when cooked and the lean, white flesh has a firm, somewhat rubbery texture and a mild flavor; also known as devilfish.

oeuf en gelée (ouf ahn ghee-leh) A French dish consisting of a poached or boiled egg in aspic.

oeufs à la neige (OUF ah lah nehzh) French for snow eggs and used to describe the dessert known in the United States as floating island.

offset spatula A tool with a flat, unsharpened stainless steel blade with a bend or step near the handle, forming a Z shape; the end of the blade is rounded and blunt; available in a variety of lengths and widths; used for spreading batter, filling and frosting cakes and pastries and moving items from one place to another; depending on the size of the blade, an offset spatula may also be referred to as a grill spatula or a cake spatula.

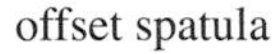

offset spatula

ogen A variety of small cantaloupe grown in Israel; it has a rough yellow skin with green stripes and a green flesh.

oignon brûlée (ohn-nawng brew-lay) French for burned onion and used to describe charred onion halves that are used to flavor and color stocks and sauces.

oignon pique (ohn-nawng pee-k) French for pricked onion and used to describe a peeled onion with a bay leaf tacked with a clove to its side; used to flavor sauces and soups.

oils Fats (generally derived from plants) that are liquid at room temperature.

okra The seed pod of a tropical plant (*Abelmoschus esculentus*) of the hollyhock family native to Africa; the oblong, tapering pod has ridged green skin and a flavor reminiscent of asparagus and is used like a vegetable in African and southern U.S. cuisines; because it develops a gelatinous texture if cooked for long periods, it is also used as a thickener; also known as gombo, gumbo and ladies' fingers.

olallieberry; olallie berry A berry that is a hybrid of a youngberry and a loganberry; it resembles an elongated blackberry in shape and color and has a sweet, distinctive flavor.

oleo *See* margarine.

Olestra (OH-less-trah) A molecularly restructured fat (a sucrose polyester) that passes through the human body without being absorbed, thus adding no calories or cholesterol to the food in which it is used; available for use only in commercial food processing.

olivada (oh-lee-VAH-dah) An Italian spread that consists of black olives, olive oil and black pepper.

olive The small fruit of a tree (*Olea europaea*) native to the Mediterranean region; it has a single pit, a high oil content, a green color before ripening and a green or black color after ripening and an inedibly bitter flavor when raw; it is eaten on its own after washing, soaking and pickling or pressed for oil; available in a range of sizes, including (from smallest to largest) medium, colossal, supercolossal and jumbo.

olive oil An oil obtained by pressing tree-ripened olives; it has a distinctive fruity, olive flavor and is graded according to its degree of acidity; used as a cooking medium, flavoring and ingredient.

olive oil, extra virgin Olive oil produced from the first cold pressing, the finest and fruitiest; it has a pale straw to bright green color and not more than 1% acid.

olive oil, pure An olive oil that has been cleaned, filtered and stripped of much of its flavor and color by using heat and mechanical devices during the refining process; it has up to 3% acid.

olla (ohl-lah) A round earthenware pot with a globular body, a wide mouth and handles; it is used to heat or hold water and to cook stews in Spain and South and Central America.

Olympia oyster; Olympia flat oyster A small Pacific flat oyster native to the northwest U.S. coast; it has a grayish-white shell and an extremely delicate flavor.

omelet; omelette (AHM-leht) A dish made from beaten eggs, seasonings and sometimes milk or water, cooked in butter until firm; it can be plain or filled with sweet or savory fillings and served flat or folded.

omelet pan

omelet pan A shallow pan with gently curved sides, a flat bottom and a single long handle; available with a nonstick surface and in 6- to 10-in. diameters.

one mix A cake-mixing method in which all of the ingredients are combined and beaten at one time.

one-stage method A cookie-mixing method in which all of the ingredients are added to the bowl at once.

one-two-three-four cake A simple American yellow cake with a recipe that is easy to remember: 1 cup shortening, 2 cups sugar, 3 cups flour and 4 eggs plus flavoring and leavening.

onglet (on-GLAY) A French cut of the beef carcass; it consists of two small muscles joined by the elastic membrane that supports the diaphragm.

onion 1. Any of a variety of strongly aromatic and flavored bulbous vegetables of the lily family (genus *Allium*) and native to central Asia; flavors range from relatively sweet to strongly pungent, the color of the outer papery layer ranges from white to yellow to red, the shape ranges from spherical to ovoid and sizes vary depending on the variety (larger onions tend to be sweeter and milder); an onion can be eaten raw, cooked like a vegetable or used as a flavoring. 2. Commonly, a medium-sized to large spherical to slightly ovoid onion (*Allium cepa*) with a bright golden yellow outer layer, crisp white flesh and strong, pungent flavor; also known as a yellow onion.

onion sauce An English sauce made from onions cooked in butter and cream; it is usually served with shoulder of lamb.

ono A saltwater fish of the mackerel family found off Hawaii; it has flaky, firm, lean flesh that whitens when cooked, a mild flavor and an average market weight of 20–40 lb. (9–18 kg); it is used for sashimi; also known as wahoo.

on the half shell Raw shellfish served in their bottom shell, usually on a bed of crushed ice with lemon juice, cocktail sauce, horseradish, ketchup or other condiments.

oolong tea One of the three principal types of tea; the leaves are partially fermented to combine characteristics of black and green teas; particularly popular in China and Japan, the beverage is generally a pale color with a mild, fragrant flavor. *See* black tea *and* green tea.

opah A saltwater fish found off Hawaii; it has a large-flaked, fatty, pinkish flesh and a market weight of 60–200 lb. (27.1–90.0 kg); also known as a moonfish.

opakapaka; opaka-paka (oh-pah-kah-pah-kah) A variety of snapper found off Hawaii; it has pink skin, a moist, light pink flesh that whitens when cooked, a delicate flavor and a market weight of 1–12 lb. (0.45–5.4 kg).

opal basil A variety of basil with purple crinkled leaves and a slightly milder flavor than sweet basil; available fresh and dried.

open-faced sandwich A slice of bread topped with foods such as cheese, cucumbers, sliced meats and so on; served cold or hot (it is usually heated by pouring hot gravy over it).

open pit A barbecue cooking pit or style of cooking in which the meat is placed directly over hardwood coals. *See* closed pit.

open side The left side of a beef carcass; also known as the loose side. *See* closed side.

opihi A small mollusk found along the Hawaiian coast; it has a black shell, a flavor similar to that of an oyster, and a chewy, snail-like texture.

orange Any of a variety of citrus (*Citrus sinensis*) with juicy, orange-colored segmented flesh, a thin to moderately thick orange-colored rind and a flavor ranging from bitter to tart to sweet; depending on the variety, an orange can be eaten fresh, cooked in sweet or savory dishes, juiced or used as a flavoring or aromatic.

orange and port wine sauce An English sauce made from orange juice and port, thickened with cornstarch; it is usually served with fried or grilled poultry.

orange blossom honey A clear liquid honey with a pale reddish-gold color and a delicate flavor; made principally from orange blossoms in Florida and California.

orange fannings Relatively large particles of broken tea leaves. *See* fannings *and* dust.

orange flower water A clear, fragrant liquid distilled from bitter orange flowers; used to flavor baked goods, confections (especially in Middle Eastern cuisine) and beverages.

orange oil The oil expressed from the fruit's fresh peel.

orange pekoe (PEE-koh) The smallest size grade of whole black tea leaves, generally the ones picked from the top of the plant.

orangequat An orange and kumquat citrus hybrid.

orange rockfish A member of the rockfish family found off the U.S. West Coast; it has a light olive-gray skin with prominent orange-red colorations, three yellow-orange stripes across the head, reddish-orange streaks along its body, an average market length of 30 in. (76 cm), firm, white flesh and a mild flavor.

orange roughy A fish found off New Zealand and Australia; it has a bright orange skin, a firm, pearly white flesh, a low fat content, a bland flavor and an average market weight of 3.5 lb. (1.6 kg).

oregano (oh-REHG-uh-noh) An herb (*Origanum vulgare*) and the wild form of marjoram; it has a woody stalk with clumps of tiny, dark green leaves that have a pungent, peppery flavor and are used, fresh or dried, principally in Italian and Greek cuisines; also known as wild marjoram. *See* marjoram.

oregano

Oregon grape *See* barberry.

organic farming A method of farming that does not rely on synthetic pesticides, fungicides, herbicides or fertilizers.

organic food 1. A food grown without the use of chemical fertilizers, pesticides or other such substances. 2. A labeling term approved by the FDA for a processed food product, 95% of which (exclusive of water and salt) is grown according to federal organic farming standards.

orgeat (OHR-zhat) 1. A sweet syrup made from almonds, sugar and rosewater or orange flower water; its strong almond flavor is used as a flavoring for cocktails and baked goods. 2. A barley–almond mixture, similar to English barley water. *See* almond syrup.

oriental sesame oil An oil obtained from roasted sesame seeds; it is darker and more strongly flavored than sesame oil and is used as an accent oil.

Orléans, sauce A French compound sauce made from a fish velouté flavored with white wine and mushrooms, seasoned with cayenne and finished with crayfish butter.

Oscar; Oskar (OS-kuhr) A dish that consists of the main ingredient (e.g., veal cutlets) sautéed, topped with crab or crayfish meat and béarnaise and garnished with spears of asparagus.

osetra A very flavorful caviar; the medium-sized crispy eggs are golden yellow to brown and quite oily.

ostrich A large flightless bird native to Africa; its meat is lean and purple, turning brown when cooked, and has a flavor similar to that of lean beef. *See* emu *and* rhea.

Othello A British pastry named for the Moor in Shakespeare's *Othello;* made with two round cookies or biscuits sandwiched together with chocolate buttercream, then coated completely with chocolate fondant.

oven An enclosed space used for baking and roasting.

oven frying A method of frying without turning; the food, usually meat, is dredged in flour, rolled in melted fat, placed on a baking sheet and baked in a hot oven; also known as ovenizing.

over egg An egg that is flipped once during frying; the yolk is often broken during the process. *See* sunny-side-up egg.

overproof *v.* To allow a yeast dough to rise (ferment) too long. *n.* Alcoholic beverages with an alcohol content greater than 50% or 100 proof.

ovolactovegetarian A vegetarian who does not eat meat, poultry or fish but does eat eggs and dairy products. *See* lactovegetarian *and* vegan.

oxalic acid An acid found in certain plants (e.g., rhubarb, spinach and sorrel); it inhibits the absorption of calcium and iron and is poisonous in large amounts.

Oxford pudding A British dessert consisting of an apricot tart topped with meringue.

Oxford sauce A British sauce of red currant jelly dissolved with port and flavored with shallots, orange zest and mustard; usually served with game.

oxidation 1. A chemical reaction between a substance and oxygen; it changes the nature of the substance, usually to its detriment. 2. An energy-releasing metabolic process during which a nutrient breaks down and its components combine with oxygen.

oxtail A fabricated cut of the beef primal round or veal primal leg; it is a portion of the tail and contains many bones but is quite flavorful.

oyster A member of a large family of bivalve mollusks found in saltwater regions worldwide; generally, they have a rough gray shell (the top shell is flat and the bottom is somewhat convex) and a grayish tan flesh with a soft texture and briny flavor; they are eaten raw or cooked; there are four principal types of domestic oysters: Atlantic oysters, European flat oysters, Olympia oysters and Pacific oysters.

oyster cracker A small, round, slightly hard cracker; it is traditionally served with oyster stew.

oyster knife A knife used to pry open oyster shells; it has a fat, 3-in.-long, pointed, arrow-shaped blade and usually a protective flange for the hand; also known as a shucking knife.

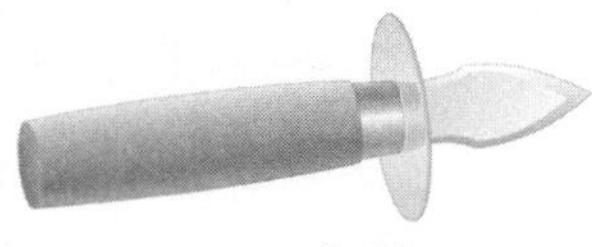
oyster knife

oyster meat In poultry, it consists of the two succulent ovals of meat along either side of the backbone, level with the thigh.

oyster mushroom A wild, fan-shaped mushroom (*Pleurotus ostreatus*) that grows in clusters on dead logs and tree stumps and is now cultivated in limited quantities; it has a gray to dark-brownish-gray cap, a grayish-white stem and a slightly peppery, oysterlike flavor that becomes milder when cooked; also known as a tree oyster mushroom, phoenix mushroom and sovereign mushroom.

oyster sauce A thick brown concentrated sauce made from oysters, brine and soy sauce; used as a flavoring in Asian cuisines.

oysters Bienville (bee-en-vell) An American dish of oysters covered with a béchamel, green peppers, onions, cheese and bread crumbs and baked.

oysters Rockefeller (OEHY-stur rock-ee-fehl-lehr) An American dish of oysters served hot on the half shell with a topping of spinach, bread crumbs and seasonings.

Ozark pudding A baked pudding made with chopped apples, walnuts and vanilla and served with rum-flavored whipped cream.

paan (pahn) Hindi for leaves of the betel pepper plant; also the digestive preparation made with betel leaf, lime paste and betel nut.

Pacific barracuda A fish found in the tropical waters of the Pacific Ocean; it has a silvery skin, an average market weight of 4–8 lb. (1.8–3.6 kg), a white flesh with a firm texture, a moderately high fat content and a slightly sweet flavor.

Pacific clams Any of several varieties of clams found along the U.S. West Coast; they generally have hard shells; significant varieties include the butter clam, geoduck clam, Manila clam and pismo clam.

Pacific halibut A variety of halibut found in the Pacific Ocean from California to Canada; it has lean white flesh with a sweet, mild flavor and firm texture; also known as Alaskan halibut, northern Pacific halibut and western halibut.

Pacific oysters; Pacific cupped oysters; Pacific king oysters Any of several varieties of oysters native to the China Sea, the waters off Japan and other areas of the Pacific Rim and now aquafarmed along the U.S. West Coast; they generally have a high domed, compact shell that can grow as large as 1 ft. (30.4 cm) in diameter and silvery-gray to gold to almost white flesh; also known as Japanese oysters.

Pacific venus clam, large A variety of venus clam found in tropical waters of the Pacific Ocean; it has an ivory to brown shell that measures 3 in. (7.6 cm) in diameter.

packed under federal inspection The voluntary inspection program of the USDC for fish and shellfish; it signifies that fish and shellfish are safe and wholesome, properly labeled, have reasonably good flavor and odor and have been produced under inspection in an official establishment; also known as PUFI (puffy).

paella (pah-AY-lyah) A rustic Spanish dish of rice, vegetables, sausages, poultry, fish and shellfish seasoned with saffron.

paella pan A wide, shallow pan with slightly sloping sides and two handles; often made of metal or earthenware, it is used for cooking paella. *See* sarten.

paella pan

paillard (pahy-lahrd) A scallop of meat or poultry pounded until thin; usually grilled.

pain au chocolat (pahn oh shok-kol-lah) A French pastry consisting of a rectangle of croissant dough rolled around dark chocolate.

pain au fromage blanc (pahn oh froh-MAJH blahn) French for bread with farmer cheese and used to describe wheat bread dough enriched with farmer cheese.

pain complet (pahn kohm-pleh) French for whole wheat bread.

pain de mie (pahn duh me) French for white wheat sandwich bread.

pain d'épice (pahn d'eh-spehs) A rich, spicy, breadlike French cake, similar to gingerbread.

pain ordinaire (pahn or-dinn-AIR) French for an ordinary or daily bread and used to describe a bread made with only white wheat flour, yeast, water and salt.

pain perdu (pahn pehr-DOO) French for lost bread and used to describe French toast.

painted pony A small brown bean with a white eye.

paiolo (pye-OH-loh) An Italian deep, rounded copper pan used for making polenta.

pakoras (pah-KO-rah) Indian fritters of vegetables, meat, fish or nuts held together with besan and deep-fried; also known as bhajias.

palermitaine, sauce (pah-lehr-me-tain) A French compound sauce made from a demi-glaze flavored with shallots and a hearty Italian red wine, finished with shallot butter and garnished with orange zest.

palmier (pahlm-YAY) A thin, crisp French cookie made with puff pastry dough rolled in granulated sugar; also known as an elephant ear.

palm-kernel oil An oil obtained from the nut (kernel) of various palms; it has a yellowish-white color, a mild flavor and a high saturated fat content; it is used in margarine and cosmetics and interchangeably with coconut oil.

palm oil An oil obtained from the pulp of the African palm's fruit (*Elaeis guineensis*); it has a red-orange color and a very high saturated fat content; used in West African and Brazilian cooking or decolored and deodorized and used for generic processed fat and oil products.

palm sugar *See* jaggery.

palm syrup A very dark, sticky syrup made from the concentrated sap of various species of palm tree; used in Middle Eastern, Indian and Asian cuisines.

Paloise, sauce (pahl-wahz) A French compound sauce made from a hollandaise flavored with fresh mint; it is served with lamb or mutton; also known as sauce pau.

pampano A small dolphinfish with an average market weight of 5 lb. (2.7 kg).

pan 1. Any of various metal vessels of different sizes and shapes in which foods are cooked or stored; generally, they have flat bottoms and low straight or sloped sides. 2. A pot with a single long handle and low straight or sloped sides.

panada; panade (pah-nahd) 1. Something other than fat added to a forcemeat to enhance smoothness, aid emulsification or both; it is often béchamel, rice or crustless white bread soaked in milk. 2. A mixture for binding stuffings and dumplings, notably quenelles; it is often choux pastry, bread crumbs, fangipane, puréed potatoes or rice.

panaeng (pah-nang) A dry red Thai curry paste, usually used with beef and always cooked with coconut milk.

panage (pah-nahj) French for coating a food with bread crumbs before frying or grilling.

pan bagnat (pan ban-YAH) A sandwich that consists of a large loaf of bread that is brushed with olive oil and filled with green pepper slices, onion slices, black olives, anchovies, tomato slices and hard-cooked egg slices drizzled with vinaigrette.

pan-broiling A dry-heat cooking method that uses conduction to transfer heat to food resting directly on a cooking surface; no fat is used and the food remains uncovered.

pancake A flat, round, leavened bread cooked on a griddle and served with butter and sweet syrup, especially for breakfast; also known as griddle cake, hot cake and flapjack.

pancake syrup A sweet sauce made from corn syrup and flavored with maple; used as a topping for pancakes and waffles.

pancetta (pan-CHEH-tuh) An Italian pork belly bacon cured with salt, pepper and other spices (it is not smoked); available rolled into a cylinder and used to flavor items such as pasta dishes, sauces and forcemeats.

pandoro (pahn-DOH-roh) An Italian Christmas bread from Verona; similar to panettone and baked in a star-shaped mold; the eggs and butter give it a golden color.

pandoro mold A star-shaped mold used for baking pandoro.

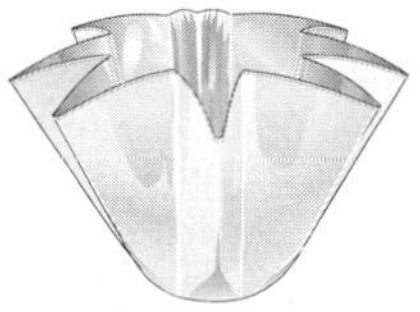
pandoro mold

pandowdy A deep-dish dessert made with apples or other fruit mixed with molasses or brown sugar, spices and butter, then topped with a biscuitlike dough and baked.

pan-dressed A market form for fish in which the viscera, gills and scales are removed and the fins and tail are trimmed.

pan dulces (pahn dool-chays) Mexican and Latin American sweet breads eaten for breakfast.

pané (pah-nay) French for to coat in bread crumbs.

panela An unrefined dark brown cane sugar sold in cakes or cones and eaten plain as candies or used to make syrups for desserts in Latin American cuisines.

pané station A kitchen area that is organized and set aside for breading foods.

panetière, à la (pan-eh-tyayr, ah lah) A French cooking method in which foods are put into round scooped-out loaves of bread and finished in the oven.

panettone (PAH-neh-TOH-nay) A sweet Italian yeast bread filled with raisins, candied citrus peel and pine nuts; traditionally baked in a rounded cylindrical mold and served as a breakfast bread or dessert.

panfish Refers to almost any small freshwater fish big enough to eat and usually pan-fried.

panforte (pahn-FOHR-tay) A dense, rich Italian fruitcakelike pastry made with honey, nuts, candied fruit and spices, baked in a flat round or square shape, then heavily dusted with confectioners' sugar; also known as a Siena cake.

pan-frying A dry-heat cooking method in which the food is placed in a moderate amount of hot fat.

pan gravy A sauce made by deglazing pan drippings from roasted meat or poultry.

panino; panini pl. (pah-NEE-noa) Italian for roll, biscuit or sandwich.

panko (PONG-ko) Large-flaked, unseasoned Japanese bread crumbs.

panna cotta (PAHN-nah COTT-ta) An Italian dessert consisting of a simple molded custard made with gelatin, usually served with fresh fruit or chocolate sauce.

panocha (pah-NOO-chah) 1. Dark brown raw sugar, usually sold in cone-shaped pieces. 2. A fudgelike Mexican candy made with brown sugar, milk, butter and sometimes nuts; also known as penuche. 3. A U.S. southwestern pudding made with harina enraizada, brown sugar or molasses, vanilla and cream.

pan sciocco (pahn SHOH-koh) Unsalted bread from Italy's Tuscany region.

panzanella alla marinna (pahn-tsah-NAYL-lah ah-la may-reh-neh) An Italian salad made from bread cubes mixed with capers, anchovies, tomatoes, cucumbers and other ingredients dressed with olive oil.

papain (pah-PAI-un) 1. A protein-splitting enzyme. 2. A food additive enzyme derived from papaya and used as a texturizer and/or tenderizer in processed foods such as meat products and meat tenderizer preparations; also known as papaya enzyme. 3. An enzyme obtained from the juice of a papaya; it breaks down the protein in meat and is used as a natural tenderizer.

pa-pao-fan (pah-pao-phahn) A traditional Chinese dessert of rice pudding decorated with eight different dried or candied fruits or nuts; also known as eight treasures and eight-precious pudding.

papaw (PA-paw) A slightly elongated and curved medium-sized fruit (*Asimina triloba*) native to North America; it has a smooth yellowish skin, a pale yellow flesh, a custardlike texture, many seeds and a flavor and aroma reminiscent of a banana and pear.

papaya A large pear-shaped tropical fruit (*Carica papaya*); it has a yellowish skin, a juicy orange flesh (that contains papain) and a central mass of black seeds encased in a gelatinous coating; the peppery seeds are edible, and the flesh has a sweet, astringent flavor; also known as a pawpaw.

paper bread *See* piki bread.

paper cases Accordion-pleated paper cups used to present sweets or line muffin tins.

paper pastry cone A triangular piece of parchment paper rolled into a cone and used instead of a pastry bag for decorating, especially when piping chocolate or royal icing.

papillote, en (pa-pee-yoht, ahn) A food (e.g., fish with a vegetable garnish) enclosed in parchment paper or a greased paper wrapper and baked; the paper envelope is usually slit open table side so that the diner can enjoy the escaping aroma.

papio A small white ulua; it has an average market weight of 10 lb. (4.5 kg).

pappadam (PAH-pah-duhm) A wafer-thin Indian flatbread made with lentil flour; it may be grilled or deep-fried and flavored with various herbs and spices; it is eaten before or after a meal.

paprika (pa-PREE-kuh; PAP-ree-kuh) A blend of dried red-skinned chiles; the flavor can range from slightly sweet and mild to pungent and moderately hot and the color can range from bright red-orange to deep blood red; used in central European and Spanish cuisines as a spice and garnish; also known as Hungarian sweet pepper.

paprikás csirke (PAH-pree-kash CHEER-kah) A Hungarian dish of chicken (meat or fish is sometimes used) and onions braised in chicken stock and flavored with bacon drippings, paprika and other seasonings; the braising liquid is mixed with sour cream for a sauce.

paraath (pa-RAHDH) A large high-rimmed Indian platter used for mixing and kneading dough, cleaning dal or basmati rice and preparing and cutting vegetables.

paraffin The wax coating applied to the rinds of some cheeses to protect the cheeses during transport and increase shelf life; generally the paraffin is red, black, yellow or clear.

parasites Any of numerous organisms that live within, on or at the expense of another organism (known as the host); parasites include the protozoa and worms living within the host's body, especially in the digestive tract and body cavities.

parasol mushroom A large wild mushroom (*Lepiota procrera*) that grows during the summer and autumn; it has a distinctive musky flavor.

paratha (pah-RAH-tah) A flat, unleavened Indian bread made with whole wheat flour and fried on a griddle.

parboiled rice *See* converted rice.

parboiling Partially cooking a food in a boiling or simmering liquid; similar to blanching, but the cooking time is longer.

parch A term meaning to dry or roast a food, usually grain or coffee, over an open fire or on the stove top.

parchment paper Heavy grease-resistant paper used to line cake pans or baking sheets, to wrap foods for baking en papillote and to make disposable piping bags.

parcooking Partially cooking a food by any cooking method.

pare To remove the thin outer layer of foods such as fruits (e.g., apple) and vegetables (e.g., potato) with a small, short-bladed knife known as a paring knife or with a vegetable peeler.

pareve; parve (PAHR-vuh) One of the principal categories of food under the Jewish dietary laws (kosher); referred to as neutral foods, they include fruits, vegetables and grains, and, provided they are not processed with animal products, they can be eaten with either meat or dairy; they are sometimes designated with *U* in a circle or *K* in a circle. *See* fleischig, kosher *and* milchig.

parfait (pahr-FAY) 1. A dessert composed of layers of ice cream, sauce and whipped cream served in a tall, narrow glass. 2. A French frozen custard or water ice usually flavored with fruit.

paring knife A small knife used for trimming and peeling produce or detail work; it has a 2- to 4-in.-long rigid blade. *See* bird's beak knife.

paring knife

paring knife, sheep's foot

paring knife, sheep's foot A small paring knife with a semi-flexible blade and a curved tip.

Paris-Brest (pah-ree-BREHST) A French pastry made with pâte à choux shaped into a ring and sprinkled with sliced almonds; after baking it is split and filled with pastry cream or buttercream (traditionally praline flavored); the dessert takes its name from a bicycle race run between the cities of Paris and Brest in 1891.

Parisian scoop The smaller scoop on a two-scoop melon cutter.

Parisienne, sauce; Parisian sauce A French sauce made by blending cream cheese, olive oil, lemon juice, chervil and sometimes paprika; used to top cold asparagus.

Paris sticks Soft, finger-shaped shortbread cookies with one or both ends dipped in chocolate.

Parker House rolls A white flour yeast roll shaped by folding each individual round of dough in half along an off-center crease before baking; named for the Parker House Hotel in Boston.

Parma ham (PAHR-muh) Ham from Parma, Italy; it is seasoned, salt cured and air-dried but not smoked and has a rosy-brown color and a firm, dense texture; known as prosciutto in the United States.

Parmentier (pahr-mahng-tee) A French term generally used to describe dishes that include potatoes in some form.

Parmesan (PAHR-muh-zahn) 1. A Parmigiano-Reggiano–style cheese made from cow's milk in places other than Italy. 2. An imprecisely used term to describe any grana or grana-style grating cheese. 3. A dish whose main ingredient (e.g., veal cutlet) is dipped in an egg mixture and then bread crumbs, Parmesan and seasonings, sautéed, and covered with a tomato sauce; sometimes a slice of mozzarella is melted on top before adding the tomato sauce.

Parmesan knife A knife with a leaf-shaped 5-in.-long blade and a sharp or somewhat rounded tip; after piercing the cheese, the blade is twisted, causing the cheese to come apart.

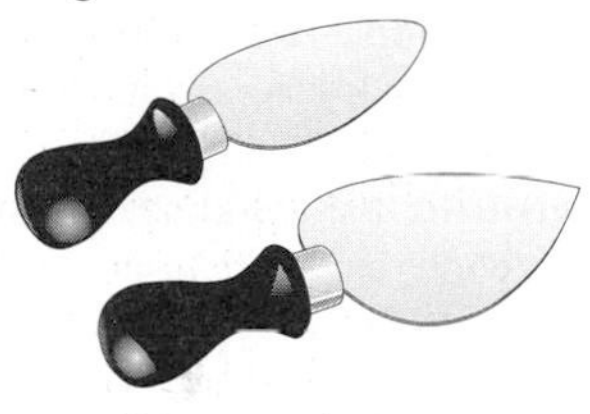

Parmesan knives

parmigiana, alla (parh-mee-J'YAH-nah, AH-lah) A dish made in the style of Parma, usually with large amounts of parmigiano and prosciutto. In the United States, it means something coated in bread crumbs, fried, topped with tomato sauce, mozzarella and parmigiano and baked.

Parmigiano-Reggiano (pahr-muh-ZHAH-noh-reh zhee-AH-noh) A hard grana cheese made in Italy's Parma region from cow's milk; it has a golden yellow interior, a hard, oily rind and a spicy, rich, sharp flavor; aged for 2–3 years, it is used for grating; also known as Genuine Parmigiano and Parmigiano.

parsley An herb (*Petroselium crispum*) with long, slender stalks, small, curly, dark green leaves and a slightly peppery, tangy fresh flavor (the flavor is stronger in the stalks, which are used in a bouquet garni); generally used fresh as a flavoring or garnish; also known as curly parsley. *See* Italian parsley.

parsley

parsley root A member of the parsley family; its beige, carrotlike root has a flavor reminiscent of a carrot and celery; also known as Hamburg parsley and turnip-rooted parsley.

parsnip A root vegetable (*Pastinaca sativa*) with bright green, feathery leaves; the long, tapering root has a creamy-white skin and flesh and a slightly sweet flavor reminiscent of a carrot.

partridge Any of several varieties of game birds; generally, the bird has an average weight of 1 lb. (450 g), a dark flesh, a somewhat tough texture and an earthy flavor; significant varieties include the Hungarian partridge and chukar partridge.

parts 1. Traditional cooking term for a nonspecific unit of measure (e.g., two parts water to one part sugar). 2. A portion of a whole; any of several equal units into which something can be divided or separated (e.g., "take three parts beef").

pasilla (pah-SEE-yah) A name used incorrectly for the fresh poblano and its dried forms, the ancho and mulato. *See* chilaca.

paskha (PAHS-khuh) A Russian Easter dessert made with pot cheese or cottage cheese, sugar, sour cream, almonds and candied fruit; it is molded into a four-sided pyramid and decorated with almonds to form the letters *XB* (Christ is risen).

passion fruit A small ovoid tropical fruit (*Passiflora edulis*); it has a wrinkled, purple skin, a soft, golden flesh with tiny edible seeds and a tropical sweet–tart flavor; often used as a flavoring for sauces and beverages; also imprecisely known as granadilla.

pasta (PAHS-tah) 1. Italian for dough or pastry. 2. An unleavened dough formed from a liquid (eggs and/or water) mixed with a flour (wheat, buckwheat, rice or other grains or a combination of grains) and cut or extruded into tubes, ribbons and other shapes; flavorings such as herbs, spices and vegetables (e.g., tomatoes and spinach) can be added to the dough; pasta is usually boiled and served with a sauce. *See* noodles. 3. The second course of an Italian meal, served after the antipasto.

pasta e fagioli (PAHS-tah ay fah-JOA-lee) Italian for pasta and beans and used to describe a thick soup of pasta and red or white beans.

pasta fazool (PAHS-tah fah-zool) American slang for the Italian dish pasta e fagioli.

pasta filata (fe-LAH-toa) 1. An Italian term describing the curds resulting from a special cheese-making process during which the fermented curds are heated until they are plastic, allowing them to be stretched into ropes, kneaded and shaped; the resulting cheeses are free of holes and whey and can be eaten fresh or, after aging, used for cooking; also known as plastic curds or spun curds. 2. A description of the cheeses (e.g., Mozzarella and Provolone) made by this process.

pasta fork A long, scooplike fork with 1-in.-long blunt-tipped prongs with slots between; used to lift and drain pasta and portion single servings of already sauced pasta; also known as a spaghetti fork or spaghetti rake.

pasta fork

pasta primavera (PAHS-tah pree-mah-VEH-rah) An American dish of pasta with a sauce of sautéed vegetables.

paste 1. The interior portion of a cheese, especially a surface-ripened one. 2. A smooth mixture of a starch (such as flour) and a liquid.

pastel (pahs-TAYL) 1. A South American method of garnishing a casserole with a crust of eggs and puréed corn. 2. Spanish for a pie, pastry, cupcakes or filled roll.

Pasteur, Louis (Fr., 1822–1895) A chemist and bacteriologist who discovered the sterilization method known as pasteurization and is credited with conducting the first scientific study of fermentation.

pasteurization The process of heating milk to a high temperature (usually 161°F [72°C]) for approximately 15 seconds to kill pathogenic bacteria and destroy enzymes that cause spoilage, thus increasing shelf life; by law, all grade A milk must be pasteurized before sale.

pasteurization, ultrahigh-temperature (UHT) A form of ultrapasteurization in which milk is held at a temperature of 280–300°F (138–150°C) for 2–6 seconds; packed in sterile containers and aseptically sealed to prevent bacteria from entering; the product can be stored (unopened) without refrigeration for at least 3 months; also known as ultrahigh-temperature processing.

pasteurize To sterilize a food, especially milk, by heating it to a temperature of 140–180°F (60–82.2°C) for a short period to kill bacteria.

pastilla *See* b'steeya.

pastillage (phast-tee-ahz) A paste made of sugar, cornstarch and gelatin; it may be cut or molded into decorative shapes.

pastis (pas-TEES) 1. A category of anise-based, licorice-flavored French aperitifs, including Pernod and Ricard; when mixed with water, the aperitif turns white and cloudy. 2. A variety of yeast-leavened pastries found in southwestern France and flavored with brandy and orange flower water.

pastitsio (pah-STEE-tshis-oh) A Greek casserole dish consisting of pasta, ground beef or lamb, grated cheese, tomatoes and béchamel flavored with cinnamon.

pastrami (puh-STRAH-mee) A cut of beef (usually from the plate, brisket or round), rubbed with salt and a seasoning paste containing garlic, peppercorns, red pepper flakes, cinnamon, cloves and coriander seeds, then dry cured, smoked and cooked.

pastry 1. A dough made with flour and shortening and used for the crust of pies, tarts and the like. 2. A food made with such a dough. 3. A term used broadly and imprecisely for all fancy sweet baked goods, including cakes, sweet rolls and cookies.

pastry bag A cone-shaped bag with two open ends, the smaller of which can be fitted with a plastic or metal tip; the bag is filled with icing, cream, dough or batter, which is squeezed through the tip in decorative patterns or designs; available in a range of sizes and variety of materials; also known as a piping bag.

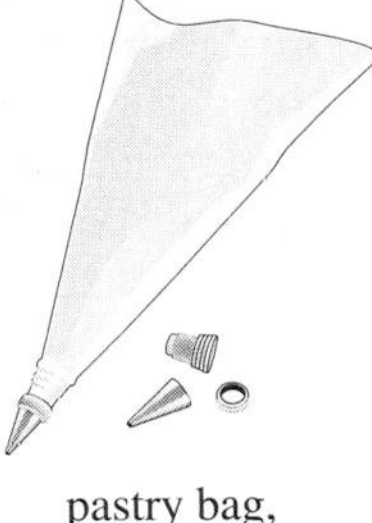
pastry bag, couplers, & tip

pastry blender A tool with several U-shaped metal wires attached to a wooden or plastic handle; used to cut cold fat into flour.

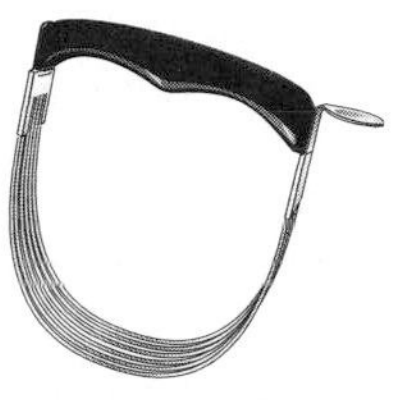
pastry blender

pastry brush A small brush used for applying glaze, egg wash and the like to doughs, buttering pans and brushing excess flour from dough; available in a variety of sizes, with either a round or flat head and natural or nylon bristles.

pastry cloth A large piece of canvas or plastic-coated cotton used as a nonstick surface for rolling out dough.

pastry cream A rich, thick custard made with milk, eggs, sugar and flour or cornstarch, and cooked on the stove top; used to fill éclairs, tarts, cakes and other pastries; also known as crème pâtissière.

pastry cutters A nested set of tinned steel cutters; one edge is rolled and the other is sharp for cutting through doughs; they can be plain or fluted and are available in various shapes (e.g., rounds, hearts and stars). *See* dough cutter.

pastry flour A weak flour made primarily from low-gluten soft wheat with a high starch content and used to produce tender, crumbly baked goods such as pastries.

pastry tip A small cone-shaped metal or plastic insert for a pastry bag; the small end of each tip is cut, bent or perforated so that the mixture forced through it will form various designs or patterns; used for piping creams, fillings, frostings and other soft mixtures into decorative shapes and patterns.

pastry tips

pastry wheel A small tool with a thin, sharp wheel (plain or fluted) attached to a short handle; used for cutting doughs. *See* jagging wheel.

pastry wheel (straight-edged)

pasty (PAS-tee) A British short crust pastry filled with a meat (beef, lamb, veal or pork) and potato mixture; traditionally, this savory filling was at one end and a sweet filling at the other; also known as a Cornish pasty.

pâte (paht) French for dough, paste or batter.

pâté (pah-TAY) 1. French for pie. 2. Traditionally, a fine savory meat filling wrapped in pastry, baked and served hot or cold. 3. A pork, veal, lamb, beef, game, fish, shellfish, poultry and/or vegetable forcemeat that is seasoned and baked; it is served hot or cold.

pâte à choux (paht uh SHOO) French for cream puff dough or choux pastry.

pâte au pâté (paht oh pah-tay) A specifically formulated pastry dough used for wrapping pâté when making pâté en croûte.

pâte brisée (paht bree-ZAY) French for a rich, flaky short dough used as a crust for sweet or savory dishes.

pâté de campagne (pah-tay duh cam-pah-gnae) French for country pâté; it is made with pig's liver, pork shoulder and fat bacon and usually flavored with herbs, shallots, garlic, salt, pepper and Armagnac.

pâté de foie gras (pah-tay duh fwah gwah) A pâté made with 80% goose liver (foie gras) and usually flavored with truffles.

pâté en croûte (pah-tay awn croot) A pâté baked in a pastry dough such as pâte au pâté.

pâté en croûte mold, oval fluted An oval metal mold with hinged sides embossed with a fluted pattern; the sides lock in place along the rim of the bottom plate

pâté en croûte mold

and are easily removed when the pâté is finished; traditionally used for meat and game pâtés en croûte.

pâté en croûte mold, rectangular A metal mold with two L-shaped side pieces that are connected by pins and fit into a rim on the bottom; the sides are often embossed with a herringbone design that imprints on the sides of the pâté; available in 1- to 2-qt. capacity and 10–14 in. long.

pâte feuilletée (paht fuh-yuh-tay) A rolled-in dough used for pastries, cookies and savory products; it produces a rich and buttery but not sweet baked product with hundreds of light, flaky layers; also known as puff pastry.

patent flour A fine grade of wheat flour milled from the interior of the wheat kernel.

pâte sablée (paht SOB-lee) French for a delicate, sweet, short dough used for tarts, tartlets and cookies; also known as sandy dough.

pâté spice A blend of herbs and spices used to season forcemeats; generally includes cloves, dried ginger, nutmeg, paprika, dried basil, black pepper, white pepper, bay leaf, dried thyme, dried marjoram and salt.

pâte sucrée (paht soo-CRAY) French for a sturdy, rich, sweet dough made with butter and egg yolks; used for pies, tarts and as a base for other pastries; also known as sweet dough.

pathogenic bacteria In the food safety context, bacteria that are harmful when consumed by humans. *See* infection *and* intoxication.

pâtisserie (pah-tees-uh-ree) 1. French for the general category of all sweet baked goods and confections. 2. French for the art of pastry making. 3. French for a shop where pastries are made and sold.

pâtissier; pâtissiére (pah-tes-SYAY) 1. French (masculine and feminine, respectively) for pastry cook or pastry chef. 2. At a food services operation following the brigade system, the person responsible for all baked goods, including breads, pastries and desserts; also known as a pastry chef.

Patna rice An Indian rice with a very long grain.

patty 1. A small thin round of ground or finely chopped foods such as meat, fish or vegetables. 2. A round flat piece of candy (e.g., peppermint patty). 3. A West Indies crescent-shaped pie with a flaky pastry shell and a highly spiced minced meat filling; also known as a pastechi and pastelilo.

patty melt A dish that consists of a ground beef patty on a slice of bread, garnished with grilled onions and cheese, topped with another slice of bread and grilled until the cheese melts.

pattypan squash A medium-sized spherical, somewhat flat summer squash with a deeply fluted shell, a pale green, smooth to slightly bumpy shell and a pale green flesh; also known as a cymling squash, custard squash and scalloped squash.

patty shell A small, baked, cup-shaped shell, usually made of puff pastry, used to hold individual servings of creamed preparations.

patum peperium A Victorian English spread for toast consisting of pounded anchovies, butter, cereal, spices and salt; also known as Gentleman's Relish.

paunch and pluck The principal ingredients for haggis: the paunch is the lamb or sheep's stomach used as the casing, and the pluck is the heart, liver and lungs used for the filling.

paupiette (poh-PYEHT) A thin slice of meat, usually beef or veal, rolled around a filling of finely ground meat or vegetables and then fried, baked or braised in wine or stock; also known as a roulade.

pavé (pah-VAY) French for paving stone and used to describe any square or rectangular cake or pastry, especially one made with multiple layers of sponge cake and buttercream.

Pavlova (pav-LOH-vuh) An Australian dessert named for the Russian ballerina Anna Pavlova; it consists of a crisp meringue shell filled with whipped cream and fresh fruit, usually passion fruit, kiwi and pineapple.

paysanne (pahy-sahn) 1. Foods cut into flat squares of approximately 0.5 × 0.5 in. and 0.25 in. thick (12 × 12 × 6 mm). *See* brunoise. 2. Foods garnished with vegetables cut to this size.

paysanne, à la (pahy-sahn, ah lah) 1. French for peasant style and used to describe dishes prepared with a mixture of vegetables, especially potatoes, carrots and turnips, cut into small squares and used for soups or to garnish meat, fish or omelets. 2. Various braised dishes cooked with softened vegetables. 3. Potatoes cut into rounds and simmered in an herb-flavored stock.

payusnaya (pah-yah-oos-nah-yah) A coarse, pressed form of caviar.

pea bean The smallest of the dried white beans. *See* white beans.

peach A medium-sized stone fruit (*Prunus persica*) native to China; it has a fuzzy, yellow-red skin, a pale orange, yellow or white juicy flesh surrounding a hard stone and a sweet flavor; available as clingstone and freestone. *See* Persian apple.

Peach Melba A dessert made with poached peach halves, vanilla ice cream and raspberry sauce; created by the French chef Auguste Escoffier for the opera singer Nellie Melba. *See* Melba sauce.

peanut A legume and not a true nut (*Arachis hypogea*); it is the plant's nutlike seed that grows underground; the hard seed has a papery brown skin and is encased in a thin, netted tan pod; the seed is used for snacking and for making peanut butter and oil; also known as a groundnut, earthnut, goober (from the African word nguba) and goober pea.

peanut butter A paste made of ground peanuts, vegetable oil (usually hydrogenated) and salt; available in smooth and chunky styles.

peanut butter pie A baked dessert from the American South consisting of a flaky pie crust and filling made by folding beaten egg whites and whipped cream in a mixture of peanut butter, butter and cream.

peanut oil A clear oil obtained by pressing peanuts; it has a delicate flavor and a high smoke point and is used as an all-purpose culinary oil.

peanut sauce A Southeast Asian (particularly Indonesian) sauce made from peanut oil, garlic, onions, chiles, soy sauce and peanut butter.

pear A spherical to bell-shaped pome fruit (*Pyrus communis*), generally with a juicy, tender, crisp, off-white flesh, a moderately thin skin that can range in color from celadon green to golden yellow to tawny red and a flavor that can be sweet to spicy; pears can be eaten out of hand or cooked and are grown in temperate regions worldwide.

pearl onion A small onion with a white to yellow outer layer, a white flesh and a mild flavor; it is usually cooked like a vegetable or used in stews and soups.

pearl sugar A coarse granulated sugar used for decorating pastries and confections; also known as sanding sugar and crystal sugar.

peas 1. The edible seeds contained within the pods of various vines of the family Leguminosae (Fabaceae); the seeds are generally shelled and the pod discarded; although available fresh, peas are usually marketed canned or frozen. *See* beans. 2. A term used imprecisely as synonymous with beans.

pease pudding A British dish of dried, soaked, cooked and puréed split peas.

pea shoot; pea tendril The growing tip of the pea plant; it has soft, tender green leaves and is used in Hong Kong cuisine; also known as dao minu.

pecan (pih-KAHN; PEE-kan) The nut of a tree of the hickory family (*Carya oliviformis*) native to North America; it has a smooth, thin, hard, tan shell enclosing a bilobed, golden brown kernel with a beige flesh and a high fat content. *See* hickory nut.

pecan pie A dessert from the American South made with a single flaky crust filled with a very sweet, rich mixture of butter, eggs, brown sugar and pecans, then baked until firm.

peck A unit of volume measurement equal to 1/4 bushel; in the U.S. system, it is equal to approximately 538 cu. in. or 8 dry quarts; in the imperial system, it is equal to approximately 555 cu. in.

pectin 1. A polysaccharide present in plant cell walls. 2. A gummy, water-soluble dietary fiber that can lower blood cholesterol levels by modest amounts. 3. A food additive used as a thickener in foods such as jams and jellies.

peel *v.* To remove rind or skin. *n.* 1. A wooden or metal tool with a long handle and large blade used to transfer pizzas and yeast breads to and from a baking stone or baking sheet in the oven; also known as a baker's peel or pizza paddle. 2. The rind or skin of a fruit or vegetable.

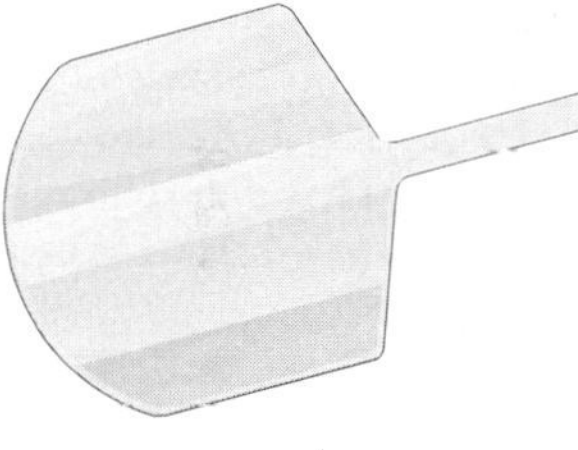

peel

peeled A fruit or vegetable from which the skin or rind has been removed.

peeler crab A hard-shell blue crab that has a fully formed soft shell beneath its hard outer shell. *See* buckram *and* crab, soft-shell.

Peking duck A Mandarin Chinese dish consisting of a duck whose skin is separated from the meat by means of an air pump; the duck cavity is stuffed with a mixture of soy sauce, garlic, leeks, brown sugar and ginger, trussed and hung, coated with flour and honey and then roasted.

pekoe (PEE-koh) The medium-size grade of whole black tea leaves; generally coarse.

pemmican (PEM-eh-kan) A mixture of buffalo or venison, melted fat, berries and sometimes marrow; it is compressed into a small cake and dried; used in Native American cuisine.

peperonata (pehp-uh-roh-NAH-tah) An Italian dish of sweet peppers, tomatoes, onions and garlic cooked in olive oil; served as an antipasto or a condiment.

peperoncini (peh-peh-rohn-CHEE-neh) Italian small, sweet, green or red peppers, usually pickled.

peperoni (peh-peh-ROH-nee) Italian for sweet peppers.

Pépin, Jacques (Fr., 1935–) Former chef to three French heads of state, including Charles de Gaulle; now a well-known cooking teacher, newspaper columnist and author of numerous English-language cookbooks, including *La Technique, La Methode* and *The Art of Cooking,* Volumes 1 and 2.

pepino (puh-PEE-noh) A medium- to large-sized subtropical fruit (*Solanum muricatum*) native to Peru; it has a smooth, glossy, violet-streaked golden skin, a juicy flesh, a fragrant aroma and a flavor reminiscent of a pear with undertones of vanilla; also known as a melon pear.

pepitas (peh-PEE-tah) Hulled and roasted pumpkinseeds; used in Mexican cuisine as a snack and thickener.

pepper 1. The fruit of various members of the *Capsicum* genus; native to the Western Hemisphere, a pepper has a hollow body with placental ribs (internal white veins) to which tiny seeds are attached (seeds are also attached to the stem end of the interior); a pepper can be white, yellow, green, brown, purple or red and can have a flavor ranging from delicately sweet to fiery hot; the genus includes sweet peppers and hot peppers. *See* chile *and* sweet pepper. 2. Peppercorns, whole or ground.

peppercorn The berry of the pepper plant (*Piper nigrum*), a climbing vine native to India and Indonesia; it has a brown color when fully ripened and is available in three principal varieties: black, green and white. *See* pink peppercorn.

peppercorn, black A peppercorn picked when green and dried in the sun until it turns black; it has a slightly hot flavor with a hint of sweetness; whole or ground, it is the most commonly available peppercorn.

peppercorn, decorticated A black peppercorn that has had its skin removed by a mechanical process so that it has the appearance of a white peppercorn.

peppercorn, green An unripened peppercorn that is either freeze-dried or pickled in brine or vinegar; it has a soft texture and a fresh, sour flavor similar to that of capers.

peppercorn, Tellicherry A fine black peppercorn from southwest India.

peppercorn, white A peppercorn allowed to ripen on the vine; the berry is then fermented and its red-brown skin removed; it has a light white-tan color and milder flavor and aroma than those of a black peppercorn; available whole or ground.

peppermint An herb and member of the mint family (*Mentha piperita*); it has thin, stiff, pointed, bright green, purple-tinged leaves and a pungent, menthol flavor; used as a flavoring and garnish.

pepperoncini (pehp-per-awn-CHEE-nee) 1. A short, tapered dried chile with an orange-red color, thin flesh and a medium hot, slightly sweet flavor. 2. Small, short pickled green peppers used as a garnish and salad ingredient.

pepperoni (pehp-puh-ROH-nee) A slender, firm, air-dried Italian sausage made from beef or pork, seasoned with chiles and red and black pepper.

pepperpot; pepper pot 1. A West Indian stew made with poultry, game or other meats, chiles and vegetables and thickened and flavored with cassareep. 2. A colonial American soup of tripe, meat, vegetables, black peppercorns and other seasonings; also known as Philadelphia pepperpot.

pepper steak 1. Beef steak coated with coarsely ground black peppercorns; it is sautéed in butter and served with a sauce made from the drippings, stock, wine and cream; sometimes flamed with brandy or Cognac. 2. A Chinese stir-fry dish consisting of beef, green pepper and onions cooked with soy sauce and other seasonings.

pequín; piquin (pee-kihn) A small, conical dried chile with an orange-red color, a thin flesh and a sweet, smoky flavor.

perch Any of various freshwater fish found in North America and Europe; they generally have an olive skin that becomes yellow on the sides, dark vertical bands, red-orange fins, and firm flesh with a delicate, mild flavor; the most significant variety in the United States is the yellow perch, and in Europe it is the pike perch.

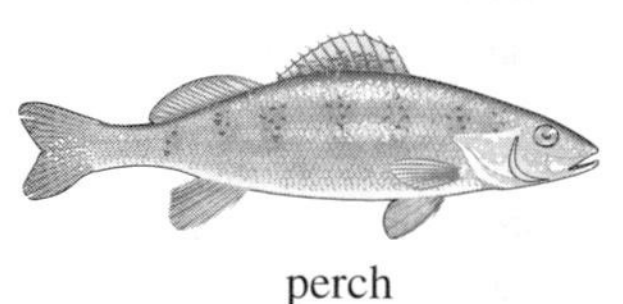
perch

percolation (per-koh-lay-shun) A method of obtaining a liquid extract of a food such as coffee; a liquid is heated in the bottom of a container and then pumped to the top, where it is sprayed over the material to be extracted, dripping back to the bottom to be repercolated repeatedly until the desired flavor has been extracted.

percolator An electric coffeepot in which boiling water rising through a tube is deflected downward through a perforated basket containing coffee grounds.

périgourdine, à la (pay-ree-gour-DEEN, ah lah) A French preparation method associated with Perigord, a region in France famous for black truffles; dishes are garnished or flavored with truffles and sometimes foie gras.

Périgueux, sauce (pay-ree-GOUH) A French compound sauce made from a demi-glaze flavored with Madeira and truffles.

perishable Foods and beverages that can spoil or deteriorate rapidly, even under appropriate storage conditions.

periwinkle A univalve mollusk found in freshwater and saltwater; it has a small, conical, spiral-shaped shell with a gray to dark olive surface and reddish-brown bands; it is eaten in various European cuisines after being boiled in its shell and has a chewy texture and yellow-ivory color; also known as a winkle or sea snail.

Pernod (pair-noh) A French licorice-flavored pastis; similar to absinthe but made without oil of wormwood.

Persian apple A traditional name for the peach; native to China, the fruit originally came to Europe and the Western Hemisphere via Persia.

Persian lime The most common market variety of lime (*Citrus latifolia*).

Persian melon A melon with a subtly netted yellowish-green skin and a dense, fragrant flesh.

persillade (payr-se-yad) 1. A food served with or containing parsley. 2. A mixture of bread crumbs, parsley and garlic used to coat meats, usually lamb.

persimmon A spherical fruit with a glossy yellow to bright red skin, an orange-red flesh, a jellylike texture and a sweet flavor when ripe; also imprecisely known as kaki and Sharon fruit.

persimmon

pescatora, alla (peh-skah-TOH-rah, AH-lah) Italian for the fisherman's style and used to describe a dish containing fish or shellfish.

pesto (PEH-stoh) 1. An Italian pasta sauce made from basil, garlic, olive oil, pine nuts and Parmesan or Pecorino. 2. In the United States, a term imprecisely used to describe a sauce or spread made principally from one herb (e.g., basil or cilantro) mixed with olive oil and a sharp, hard cheese, with pine nuts sometimes added.

petite marmite (peh-tee mar-meet) 1. French for a rich consommé garnished with beef and vegetables and served in the small earthenware pot in which it is cooked. 2. A miniature marmite used for serving single portions of soups, stews and the like.

petit four (peh-tee FOOR) 1. A French term for any bite-sized cake, pastry, cookie or confection served after a meal or with coffee or tea. 2. A French confection consisting of a small piece of filled sponge cake coated with fondant icing and elaborately decorated.

petit four glacé (peh-tee FOOR glahs-say) An iced or cream-filled petit four.

petit fours sec (peh-tee FOOR seck) French term for small, dry, crisp cookies often served with coffee or tea or as an accompaniment to ice cream or sorbet.

petits pois (peh-tee PWAH) French for green garden peas.

petrale sole (peh-TRAH-lee) A member of the flounder family found off the U.S. West Coast; it has an olive brown skin, a lean, white flesh, a fine texture, an excellent flavor and an average weight of 2.5 lb. (1.14 kg); also known as a brill sole.

pe-tsai (pa-tza-ee) A form of cabbage native to China; similar in appearance to romaine lettuce but with yellow-green leaves; it is eaten raw or cooked.

petticoat tail British for a pie-shaped wedge of shortbread cut from a large round; said to resemble a 12th-century woman's petticoat.

Pfeffernüesse (FEF-ferr-noos) A hard, round, spicy German Christmas cookie flavored with honey and black pepper.

pheasant A game bird with a light to medium dark flesh, a tender texture, a sweet flavor and an average dressed market weight of 1.5–2.2 lb. (0.3–1 kg); also farm raised.

pho (fo) A northern Vietnamese beef noodle soup; when made with chicken it is known as pho ga.

phyllo; filo Pastry dough made with very thin sheets of a flour-and-water mixture; several sheets are often layered with melted butter and used in sweet or savory preparations.

phytochemical A chemical found in plants believed to help prevent some cancers and promote others.

pibil (pee-bill) A Mexican and Latin American method of pit cooking foods; replaced today by wrapping food in a banana leaf and steaming it.

pica (PIE-ka) An appetite for nonfood substances, such as clay, ashes, plaster and laundry starch.

picadillo (pee-kah-DEE-yoh) Spanish for hash and used to describe a Central American and Caribbean dish of ground pork and beef or veal, onions, garlic and tomatoes used as a stuffing (in Mexico) or sauce (for beans in Cuba).

piccalilli (PIHK-uh-lih-lee) An English relish of pickled tomatoes, sweet peppers, onions, zucchini, cucumber, cauliflower and cabbage, flavored with brown sugar, allspice and cider vinegar.

piccata (pih-CAH-tuh) An Italian dish of thinly sliced chicken or veal, lightly floured, sautéed in butter and sprinkled with lemon juice.

picholine (pee-show-leen) A large green olive grown in France.

pickerel A freshwater fish and member of the pike family; it has an average market weight of 2–3 lb. (0.09–1.35 kg), a low fat content and a finely textured flesh with a moderately strong flavor.

pickle *v.* To preserve food in a brine or vinegar solution. *n.* Food that has been preserved in a seasoned brine or vinegar.

pickled eggs Shelled hard-boiled eggs immersed in vinegar and peppercorns; often served as bar food.

pickled herring Herring marinated in vinegar and spices and then bottled in either a sour cream or wine sauce.

pickled walnuts Green (young) walnuts pickled in vinegar, caramel, black pepper and other spices; they turn black and are eaten with cold cuts and cheese.

pickling lime A fine white powder (calcium hydroxide) that reacts with acidic ingredients such as cucumbers, tomatoes and melons to make them crisp.

pickling spices A spice blend used to flavor the solution used to pickle foods or as a seasoning; generally the blend contains whole or coarsely broken allspice, red chile flakes, bay leaves, peppercorns, mustard seeds, cardamom seeds, coriander seeds, cloves and ginger.

pickling vinegar A malt vinegar flavored with black and white peppercorns, allspice, cloves and small hot chiles.

picnic 1. Traditionally, a meal eaten inside or outside to which each guest brought a dish. 2. A meal, usually midday, eaten outside; although hot and cold foods can be served, if foods are cooked, it is usually referred to as a barbecue.

picnic ham; picnic shoulder A subprimal cut of the pork primal shoulder; cut from the foreleg, it is usually deboned and smoked; also known as a California ham, cala and pork shoulder.

pico de gallo (PEE-koh day GI-yoh) Spanish for rooster's beak and used to describe a relish of finely chopped jicama, onions, bell pepper, oranges, jalapeños and cucumbers.

pie 1. A pastry consisting of a sweet filling in a pastry crust baked in a slope-sided pan, it may have a bottom crust only or a top and bottom crust. 2. A savory meat- or vegetable-filled turnover or pastry. 3. A sweet fruit mixture baked in a deep dish with only a top crust (e.g., cobbler).

pièce de résistance (pee-ace duh rae-see-stans) A French term traditionally reserved for the most important or impressive dish served at a meal and now also used for the main course.

piémontaise, à la (pyay-mohn-tez, ah lah) A French garnish for poultry and meat consisting of risotto with shredded truffles; prepared in a timbale or as a border around the dish.

piémontaise, sauce à la; piédmont sauce (pyay-mohn-tez, sos ah lah) A French compound sauce made from a cream sauce flavored with chicken glaze, lemon juice, onions and garlic, garnished with truffles and pine nuts and finished with garlic butter.

pie pan; pie plate A round, 1- to 2-in.-deep glass or metal pan with sloped sides used for baking pies.

pierogi (peer-OH-gee) A Polish dish consisting of dumplings or noodles stuffed with mixtures such as pork, onions and cottage cheese or cabbage, mushrooms, potatoes and rice and boiled, baked or fried.

pie weights Ceramic or aluminum pellets used to weigh down a pie crust that is baked without a filling. *See* bake blind.

pig The young swine of either sex weighing less than 120 lb. (54 kg). *See* boar *and* sow.

pig, suckling A pig slaughtered when it is 6–8 weeks old; the meat has a light-colored flesh with a succulent flavor and a tender texture.

pigeon 1. One of the principal kinds of poultry recognized by the USDA; domesticated pigeon has dark meat and an earthy, gamy flavor. 2. A mature pigeon slaughtered when older than 4 weeks has a coarse skin, a moderately tough flesh and an average market weight of 1–2 lb. (0.45–1 kg). 3. French for squab.

pigeon pea A small, slightly flattened pea (*Cajanus cajan*) native to Africa; it grows in a long, twisted, fuzzy pod, has a grayish-yellow color and is usually available dried and split into two disks and used in African and Caribbean cuisines; also known as arhar dhal, channa dhal, goongoo, congo pea, gungo pea, red gram, cajan, no-eyed pea and tropical green pea.

pigment A substance that contributes color to a food or processed food; either naturally occurring (e.g., the yellow-orange beta-carotene pigment found in carrots) or a chemical additive. *See* coloring agent.

pig pickin' American southern (especially North Carolina) slang for a social gathering at which pulled pork is cooked and served.

pig's feet A pig's ankles and feet; available fresh, pickled or smoked, they contain many small bones and connective tissue and are rich in pectin; also known as trotters (especially in Great Britain).

pigs in blankets 1. Sausages (usually small cocktail sausages) wrapped in pie or bread dough. 2. Breakfast sausages wrapped in pancakes.

pig's knuckles A fabricated cut of the pork carcass; part of the pig's feet and available fresh and pickled.

pike Any of various freshwater fish found worldwide; they generally have a greenish skin that becomes white on the belly, red fins, an average market weight of 4–10 lb. (1.8–4.5 kg), a low fat content and a firm flesh with a mild flavor and many small bones; significant varieties include the muskellunge and pickerel.

piki bread (pee-kee) A traditional Hopi bread made with blue cornmeal and ashes; the batter is baked in very thin sheets on a hot stone, then rolled into a cylinder; also known as paper bread.

pilaf (PEE-lahf) A cooking method for grains; the grains are lightly sautéed in hot fat and then a hot liquid (usually stock) is added; the mixture is simmered without stirring until the liquid is absorbed.

pilau; purloo (pi-loe; puhr-loo) A rice dish from the Low Country of the American South consisting of long-grain rice cooked in an aromatic broth until almost dry; meat, fish or shellfish is usually added and the whole is garnished with minced parsley.

pilchard (PIHL-chuhrd) A small fish found in the Atlantic Ocean from Scandinavia to Portugal; it is similar to a sardine and has a high fat content.

pili pili A West African condiment; the basic sauce consists of tomatoes, onions, garlic, chiles and horseradish, with other ingredients added to complement the dish with which it will be served.

piloncillo (pee-loan-che-yoh) Mexican brown sugar packaged in pyramid-shaped pieces.

pilot cracker A form of hardtack, but usually sweetened.

pimento (pee-MEHN-toh) Another name for allspice, the dried aromatic berry of the tree *Pimenta officinalis;* also known as Jamaican pepper and pimenta.

pimiento A large, heart-shaped pepper with a red skin and a sweet flavor; used in paprika and to stuff olives.

pimiento cheese Any cheese to which chopped pimientos have been added.

pinch A traditional measure of volume; refers to the amount of a seasoning or other food one can hold between the thumb and forefinger, approximately 1/16 teaspoon.

pineapple 1. A tropical fruit (*Ananas comosus*) with a spiny, diamond-patterned, greenish-brown skin and swordlike leaves; the juicy yellow flesh surrounds a hard core and has a sweet–tart flavor. 2. *See* bromelin.

pineapple corer A tall tool with two concentric rings with serrated teeth; as the corer is pressed down over the pineapple, one ring separates the flesh from the skin and the other separates the core from the flesh.

pineapple guava *See* feijoa.

pine nut The nut of various pine trees (genus *Pinus*); it has a shell that covers ivory-colored meat, a rich distinctive flavor and a high fat content; also known as a pine kernel and Indian nut.

pink bean A smooth reddish-brown dried bean, similar to the pinto bean.

pink peppercorn The dried berry of a South American rose plant; it has a rose color and a bitter, pinelike flavor and is available dried or pickled in vinegar. *See* peppercorn.

pink salmon A variety of salmon found in the Pacific Ocean from California to Alaska; it has a bluish-green skin with numerous black blotches, a lean, soft, pink flesh and a mild flavor and is generally used for canning; also known as a humpback salmon.

pink snapper *See* opakapaka.

pint 1. A unit of volume measurement; in the U.S. system, it is equal to 16 fl. oz., and in the imperial system, it is equal to 20 fl. oz. 2. British slang for a beer.

pinto bean A medium-sized pale pink bean with reddish-brown streaks; available dried; also known as a crabeye bean and a red Mexican bean.

pip A seed of a fleshy fruit that has many seeds, such as an orange, apple or pear; also known as a carpel.

pipérade (pee-pay-RAHD) A Basque stewlike dish of tomatoes and sweet peppers seasoned with onions and garlic and cooked in olive oil or goose fat and then mixed with beaten eggs.

pipikaula; pipi kaula (PEE-pee-kah-OO-lah) A Hawaiian dish of sun-dried beef jerky sometimes brushed with teriyaki sauce before drying; it is usually eaten as is or in salads.

piping Forcing a material, such as icing, chocolate, buttercream or choux pastry, from a pastry bag in a steady and even manner to form specific shapes or decorative designs.

piping chocolate Melted chocolate mixed with water, a simple syrup or other liquid to make it fluid enough for piping.

piping gel A sweet but flavorless, colored transparent substance made from sugar, corn syrup and vegetable gum; used for decorating cakes and pastries.

piquant (pee-kant) 1. French for spicy. 2. An agreeably pungent, sharp or tart aroma or flavor.

piquante, sauce A French compound sauce made from a demi-glaze flavored with shallots, wine and vinegar and garnished with herbs and gherkins.

piri-piri (pee-ree-pee-ree) Portuguese for small, very hot, red chiles.

piroshki; pirozhki; pirogi (pih-ROSH-kee) Russian or Polish turnovers made of choux pastry, puff pastry or a yeast dough filled with a savory mixture of meat, fish, cheese or mushrooms, baked or deep-fried; usually served as an hors d'oeuvre or with soups or salads. Pirogi are larger versions and are served as an entrée.

pirouettes (pir-oh-ET) Thin wafer cookies that are curled tightly around a dowel while still hot; the ends are often dipped in melted chocolate.

pissaladiere (pee-sah-lah-DYAIR) A savory southern French tart consisting of a crust topped with onions, anchovies, black olives and sometimes tomatoes.

pistachio (pih-STASH-ee-oh) A pale green nut (*Pistacia vera*) encased in a hard, tan shell that is sometimes dyed red with food coloring or blanched until white; it has a delicate, subtle flavor.

pistou (pees-TOO) 1. A condiment from France's Provence region made from fresh basil crushed with garlic and olive oil; sometimes Parmesan and tomatoes are added. 2. A French soup made with white beans, green beans, onions and tomatoes and seasoned with pistou.

pit *v*. To remove the pit or stone from a fruit. *n*. The seed or stone of a fruit, such as a cherry, peach or apricot.

pita; pita bread; pitta; pitah (PEE-tah brehd) An oval- or round-shaped, hollow Middle Eastern flatbread leavened with yeast; it is often split open or cut crosswise to form a pocket, then filled with a stuffing; also known as pocket bread.

pitanga; petanga (pee-than-gah; pae-than-gaw) A cherry-sized fruit of a tree (*Eugenia uniflora*) native to Central America; it has a bright red skin marked by deep furrows, one or more seeds and a pleasant, slightly sour flavor and is usually made into jams; also known as Surinam cherry.

pith The bitter, white membrane found in citrus fruit between the rind (zest) and the pulp.

Pithiviers (pee-tee-vee-a) A round, thin French pastry made with two circles of puff pastry dough enclosing a frangipane (almond) filling; a spiral or rosette pattern is etched on the top before baking; a speciality of the town of Pithiviers in France's Loire region.

pitmaster A cook responsible for turning meat into barbecue.

pi t'si (pe tsi) The small, horseshoe-shaped tuber of an aquatic herb; it has a crunchy texture and a coconut-like flavor and is used in Chinese cuisines; sometimes imprecisely called a water chestnut.

pitter A tool used to remove stones from cherries and olives; it has two handles: the top one has a metal shaft and the bottom one is ring shaped and holds the fruit; when squeezed together, the shaft pushes the pit through the fruit and out the hole; also known as a stoner.

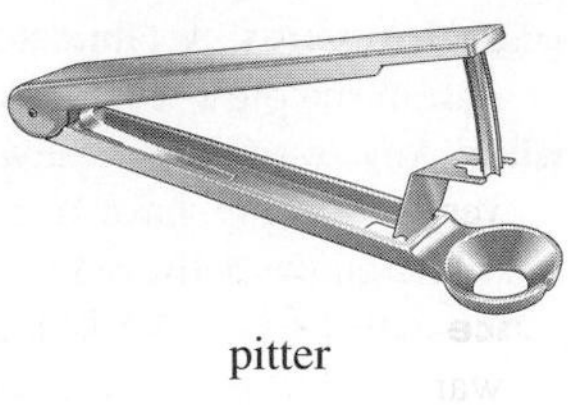
pitter

pizza (PEET-tzah) An Italian dish consisting of a flat pie or tart made from bread dough topped with any of a variety of foods, but principally tomato sauce and cheese (often Mozzarella) and baked.

pizza, New York–style An American pizza style that uses a thin, moderately soft (as opposed to crispy) dough.

pizza, thin crust An American pizza style that uses a thin, usually crispy dough.

pizza, white An American variation on a pizza; made without any tomato sauce.

pizza cheese A pasta filata cheese made in the United States from pasteurized milk; similar to Mozzarella, it is used to make pizzas.

pizza dough A yeast dough used as the crust for pizzas; it may be thick and bready or thin and crisp.

pizzaiola, alla (peat-zee-OHL-ah, ah-lah) An Italian method of garnishing a dish with a sauce of tomatoes, garlic and oregano.

pizza pan A large round metal pan with a shallow, rounded, raised rim used to bake pizza; available with a perforated bottom that allows steam to escape and helps brown the crust.

pizza wheel; pizza cutter A tool with a sharp-edged revolving wheel; the wheel is dragged across the pizza to cut it.

pizzelle (peets-TSEH-leh) A large, crisp, round Italian cookie made from a rich batter of butter, eggs, sugar, flour and vanilla; the batter is cooked on a pizzelle iron.

pizzelle iron Similar to a waffle iron, it is a tool with two embossed or intricately carved 5-in.-wide disks hinged together and attached to a long handle and used to make pizzelle; the iron is heated on the stove top, the batter is poured in and it is

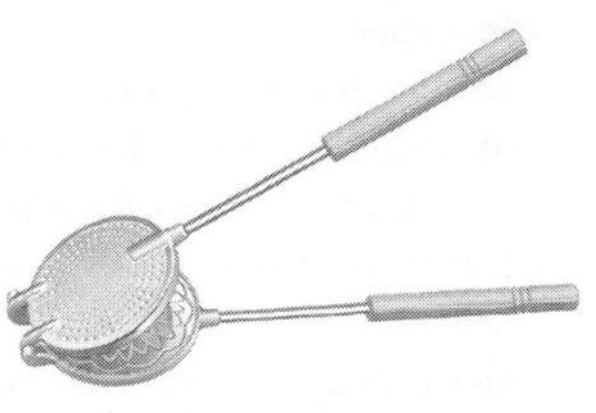
pizzelle iron

all returned to the stove to bake; the pattern imprints onto the cookies.

pizzette (peet-zay-tay) A miniature pizza made with very thin dough.

pla Thai for fish.

place setting 1. The selection of china, glasses, flatware and napery necessary for the meal. 2. A set of various pieces of china and flatware necessary for one person for any meal (e.g., a five-piece place setting).

plaice, American (plas) A member of the flounder family found in the northern Atlantic Ocean; it has a reddish to gray-brown skin, a lean, pearly white flesh, a sweet flavor and an average market weight of 2–3 lb. (0.9–1.4 kg); also known as a dab or sanddab.

plank; planked A method of cooking and serving meat or fish on a seasoned board; some of the wood flavor is imparted to the food.

plantain; plantain banana (plahn-TAYNE) A starchy banana (*Musa paradisiaca*) with a green skin, a fairly firm, pinkish flesh, a fatter, longer shape than an eating banana and a squashlike flavor; used for cooking much like a squash; also known as a cooking banana.

plat de côtes (plah duh COAT) 1. A French cut of the beef carcass; it is the equivalent of American short ribs. 2. A French cut of the pork carcass; it is a whole forequarter flank.

plat du jour (pla duh zjur) French menu term for the speciality of the day.

plate *v.* To place foods on a plate; it can be done with extreme care to create an appealing visual impression. *n.* 1. A smooth, thin, relatively flat dish, usually china or pottery, on which food is served to each individual. 2. The contents of a dish (e.g., a plate of sausages). 3. Service and food for one person at a meal. 4. Serviceware, dinnerware, flatware and the like covered with a thin coating of a precious metal, such as gold or silver. 5. A cut of the beef carcass that combines the beef short plate and brisket (without the shank) primals.

plate lunch 1. A Hawaiian meal consisting of two scoops of rice, a mayonnaise-bound macaroni or potato salad and an entrée such as beef stew, fried fish, teriyaki chicken, meatloaf or barbecued short ribs; it is often sold from a plate lunch wagon. 2. *See* blue plate special.

plättar (PLAH-tar) Small Swedish pancakes, traditionally served with lingonberries.

plett pan A flat cast-iron pan with seven round, shallow, 3-in.-wide indentions; used to make plättar.

plett pan

plov (plahv) A Russian and central Asian pilaf; it can be sweet but is usually savory and flavored with lamb and garnished with carrots, chickpeas and raisins.

pluck *v.* To remove the feathers from poultry and gamebirds. *n.* The lungs, heart and other entrails of a mammal.

plum A small- to medium-sized ovoid or spherical stone fruit (genus *Prunus*) that grows in clusters; it has a smooth skin that can be yellow, green, red, purple or indigo blue, a juicy flesh, a large pit and a sweet flavor. *See* prune.

plum

plum duff A traditional English boiled suet pudding flavored with raisins or currants.

plump, to A cooking technique in which dried fruit is soaked in a liquid until the fruit softens and swells slightly from absorbing the liquid.

plum pudding A steamed breadlike British dessert containing spices, prunes and other dried fruit; usually served warm, flamed with rum or brandy and accompanied by hard sauce.

plum sauce A spicy, fruity sauce made from plums, chiles, vinegar and sugar; used in Chinese cuisine as a dip and flavoring; also known as duck sauce.

plum tomato A medium-sized ovoid tomato with a meaty flesh and a red skin (a yellow variety is also available); also known as an Italian tomato or Roma tomato.

plunger coffeepot A coffeemaker consisting of a glass pot fitted with a plunger covered with a fine mesh; coffee grounds and hot water are added to the pot, allowed to brew and then the plunger is pushed down, trapping the grounds; the coffee then rises through the mesh; also known as an infusion coffeepot.

plunger coffepot

pluot An apricot and plum hybrid; it has a smooth, yellow-spotted russet skin with a juicy flesh.

poaching A moist-heat cooking method that uses convection to transfer heat from a hot (approximately 160–180°F [71–82°C]) liquid to the food submerged in it.

poblano (poh-BLAH-noh) A long, tapering fresh chile with thick flesh, a medium to hot flavor and a dark green color tinged with purple or black; sometimes known imprecisely as pasilla. *See* ancho *and* mulato.

po'boy; poor boy *See* hero.

pocket bread *See* pita.

pod The outer covering of certain seeds such as peas and beans.

poêler (pweh-lay) French for to roast in a covered pot with butter and sometimes aromatic vegetables; the closest English translation of this very specific French culinary term is pot-roasting. *See* casserole braising.

poi (POH-ee) A Hawaiian dish consisting of fermented pounded taro root; eaten mixed with milk or used as a condiment for meat or fish.

Point, Fernand (Fr., 1897–1955) The chef-owner of La Pyramide, located near Lyon, France; his cuisine was based on high-quality foods enhanced by preparation; he disdained dominating sauces and distracting accompaniments and garnishes and believed that each dish should have a single dominant ingredient, flavor or theme; he refined and modernized the classic cuisine of Escoffier and is credited with laying the foundation for nouvelle cuisine.

pointe de filet (pwan't duh fee-lay) A French cut of the pork carcass; it is cut from the posterior of the pork loin.

poire Belle-Helene (pwahr bel-ay-LEN) A French dessert consisting of a pear poached in vanilla syrup served on top of vanilla ice cream with warm chocolate sauce.

poissonier (pwah-sawng-yay) At a food services operation following the brigade system, the person responsible for all fish and shellfish items and their sauces; also known as the fish station chef.

poivrade, sauce (pwahv-rahd) Any of various French sauces in which peppercorns provide the dominant or characteristic flavor.

pojarski (pah-jar-skee) 1. A Russian dish of veal chopped and mixed with butter, bread soaked in milk, seasoned, reformed on the bone and fried in butter. 2. A cutlet of chicken or salmon, covered with flour or bread crumbs and sautéed in butter.

poke (poh-kay) A Hawaiian dish consisting of bite-sized bits of raw fish traditionally seasoned with salt, limu and inamona; today soy sauce, ginger, garlic, sesame oil, sesame seeds, green onion and chile peppers are also used.

poke; pokeweed A wild field green (*Phytolacca americana*) native to North America; the young shoots are cooked like asparagus, and the leaves are used in salads.

pole bean A variety of bean that is cultivated on poles rather than allowed to grow freely on the ground.

polenta (poh-LEHN-tah) 1. Italian for cornmeal. 2. An Italian dish made by cooking cornmeal with a liquid until it forms a soft mass; it is eaten hot or cooled, cut into squares and grilled or fried.

Polignac, sauce (poh-lee-nyak) A French white wine sauce finished with heavy cream and garnished with julienne of mushrooms.

Polish ham A boneless ham covered with a layer of fat and skin; smoked and then cooked.

pollock, Alaskan A fish similar to the American pollock and found off Alaska; it has a light gray, flaky flesh, a mild flavor and an average market weight of 2 lb. (900 g); it is used principally to make imitation shellfish products; also known as Pacific pollock, snow cod and walleye pollock.

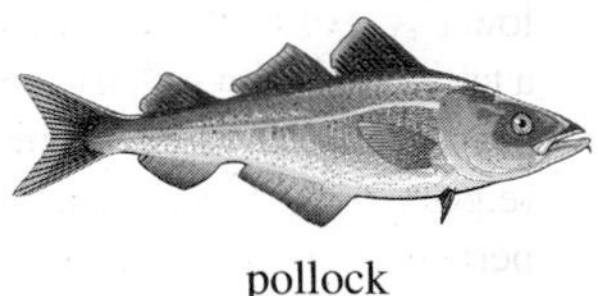

pollock

pollock, American A fish related to cod and found in the Atlantic Ocean from Nova Scotia to Virginia; it has a deep olive skin on top that pales to a yellow or smoky gray, a lean flesh, a slightly sweet flavor and an average market weight of 4–12 lb. (1.8–5.4 kg); used in gefilte fish, salted, smoked or to make imitation shellfish products; also known as Boston bluefish and blue cod.

polonaise, à la (pohl-loh-NEHZ, ah lah) A French preparation method associated with the cuisine of Poland; the dishes, especially cauliflower and asparagus, are boiled, then sprinkled with chopped hard-boiled egg yolk, parsley, bread crumbs and melted butter.

Polonaise, sauce (pohl-loh-NEHZ) 1. A French compound sauce made with veal velouté mixed with sour cream, horseradish and chopped fennel. 2. A French compound sauce made with a demi-glaze flavored with reduced red wine, sugar and vinegar and garnished with raisins and sliced almonds.

polyunsaturated fat A triglyceride composed of polyunsaturated fatty acids; generally, it comes from plants (cottonseed, safflower, soybean, corn and sesame oils are high in polyunsaturated fats) and is liquid (an oil) at room temperature.

pomegranate (POM-uh-gran-uht) A medium-sized fruit (*Punica granatum*) with a thin, red to pink-blushed yellow, leathery skin and many seeds encased in a pinkish, translucent flesh separated by an ivory-colored, bitter membrane; the flesh has a sweet–tart flavor and the seeds are crunchy.

pomegranate syrup A thick sweet–sour syrup made by boiling the juice of sour pomegranates; also known as grenadine molasses.

pomelit A fruit grown in Israel that is a hybrid of a grapefruit and pomelo; it has a yellowish-green to green rind, juicy segmented flesh and a flavor similar to that of a grapefruit but sweeter.

pomelo; pommelo; pummelo (pom-EH-loh) The largest citrus (*Citrus maxima*); it has a thick, coarse, yellow to pink rind and yellow to pink segmented flesh with a tart grapefruitlike flavor; also known as shaddock.

pomes Members of the family Rosaceae; these fruits (e.g., apples, pears and quince) grow on trees in temperate and cooler climates worldwide; they generally have a thin skin and moderately firm to firm juicy flesh surrounding a central core containing many small seeds (called pips) and a tart to sweet flavor.

pomfret (POHM-freht) 1. A fish found in the north Atlantic Ocean, Pacific Ocean and Mediterranean Sea; it has a brown-gray skin and a lean, delicate flesh. 2. A term used imprecisely in Europe for members of the butterfish family.

pommes à la bordelaise (pomz ah lah bore-day-laze) A French dish consisting of cubed potatoes sautéed in butter with a little garlic.

pommes Anna (pomz ahn-nah) A French dish of thinly sliced potatoes that are layered with butter, cooked in a lidded dish and then inverted and cut into wedges for service.

pommes Anna pan A round, tin-lined copper pan used to make pommes Anna; it has a 6.5- to 9.5-in. diameter, a 3-in. depth and a lid that cuffs nearly 1.5 in. over the pan's sides to compact the potatoes.

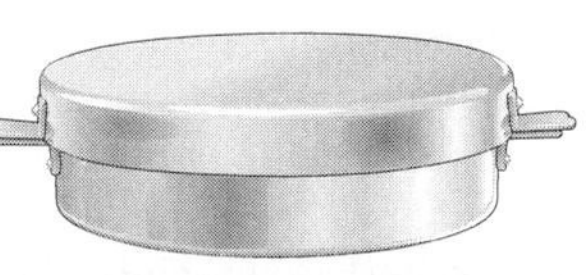

pommes Anna pan

pommes bonne femme (pomz bun fam) A French dish consisting of potatoes cooked in stock with small whole braised onions.

pommes château (pomz sha-toe) A French dish of potatoes cut into 1.5-in.-long pieces, tournéed and sautéed in butter until browned; traditionally used as a garnish for châteaubriand.

pommes dauphine (pomz doa-fawng) A French dish of potatoes mashed with butter and egg yolk, blended with choux pastry, shaped into balls and fried; served with grilled or roasted meat or game.

pommes dauphinoise (pomz doa-feen-wahz) A French dish of potatoes cut in thick round slices and layered with cream in a gratin dish rubbed with garlic and butter (or a mixture of eggs, milk and cream is poured over the potatoes), sprinkled with grated cheese and baked.

pommes duchesse (pomz doo-shess) A French garnish or dish of mashed potatoes mixed with raw eggs, piped (especially if a garnish) or shaped into patties and oven browned.

pommes fondantes (pomz fohn-dant) A French dish of tournéed potatoes (larger than château) cooked in butter in a covered pan.

pommes frites (pomz FREET) French for French-fried potatoes.

pommes lorette (pomz low-reht) A French dish of pommes dauphine shaped into small crescents and deep-fried.

pommes Lyonnaise (pomz lee-oh-nez) A French dish of sliced boiled potatoes browned in butter with onions and sprinkled with parsley.

pommes noisette (pomz nwah-ZEHT) Potatoes cut into small hazelnut-shaped balls and sautéed in butter.

pommes rissolées (pomz ree-soh-lay) A French dish of pommes château cooked until dark brown.

pommes soufflées (pomz soo-flay) A French dish of thinly sliced potatoes puffed into little pillows through a double-frying process.

pommes vapeur A utensil with a bulbous bottom and a V-shaped top used to steam potatoes; the bottom is filled with water and the potatoes are placed on a perforated insert; the condensation collects on the domed lid and is directed to the sides and falls to the bottom, thus preventing sogginess; also known as a potato steamer.

pommes vapeur

Pompadour, sauce (poam-pah-dohr) A French white wine sauce finished with crayfish butter and garnished with sliced truffles, diced crayfish tails, tarragon and chervil.

pompano (pahm-pah-noh) A fish found off Florida; it has a metallic blue skin on top that becomes silvery on the belly, an average market weight of 1.5–4 lb. (0.68–1.8 kg) and a firm, white flesh with a moderate amount of fat; also known as cobblerfish and palmenta.

ponentine A small, slender, purple-black olive from Italy; it is salt brine cured and packed in vinegar.

Pont l'Évêque (pon lay-VEHK) A surface-ripened French cheese made from cow's milk; it has a creamy, pale yellow interior, a golden brown skin, a sharp, tangy flavor and a strong odor.

pont neuf (pon nuf) French for a cut of potato that is 1/2 × 1/2 × 3 in. (1.27 × 1.27 × 7.6 cm); also known as steak fries.

pont-neuf batter (pon-nuf) A French pastry dough made with equal parts of pastry cream and pâte à choux flavored with Kirsch.

ponzu (PON-zoo) A Japanese dipping sauce made with lemon juice or rice vinegar, soy sauce, mirin or sake, kombu and dried bonito flakes.

poolish (poo-LEESH) A semiliquid starter dough, usually yeast leavened, that has fermented for at least 6 hours before being used to make bread.

popcorn 1. A variety of corn that explodes when it is exposed to dry heat (the moisture and air inside the kernel expands, forms steam, splits the hull and turns the kernel inside out); available as unpopped seeds and fully popped, plain or flavored. 2. Small pieces of battered and deep-fried shrimp, chicken, clams and the like.

popover A batter quick bread baked in a muffin shape; the crust is crisp and brown and the interior moist and almost hollow.

popover pan A heavy baking pan used for making popovers and Yorkshire pudding; similar to a muffin pan but with deeper, tapered indentions that are spaced farther apart.

popover pan

poppy, common An annual herb (*Papaver rhoeas*) with a slender, branched stem, toothed, lobed leaves and a single red flower; the flower petals are used medicinally and the leaves are eaten as a vegetable; also known as corn poppy.

poppy seed The tiny, round, hard, blue-gray seed of the poppy (genus *Papaver*); it has a sweet, nutty flavor and is used in baked goods or processed for oil.

porcini (poar-CHEE-nee) Italian for bolete.

porgy (POHR-gee) A saltwater fish and member of the perch family native to the Atlantic Ocean from New England to the Carolinas; it has a dull silver skin with dusky spots that becomes white with dusky spots on the belly, an average market weight of 1–2 lb. (450–900 g), a tender texture, a low fat content and a delicate, mild flavor; also known as bream, scup and sea bream.

pork The flesh of hogs, usually slaughtered under the age of 1 year.

pork belly *See* belly.

pork cutlet A fabricated cut of the pork primal fresh ham; a small boneless cut from the shank.

pork loin roast, full A subprimal cut of the pork primal loin; it is a roast taken from either end of the loin or can be the entire trimmed loin.

pork loin roast, rolled A subprimal cut of the pork primal loin; it is a tender, boned, rolled roast.

pork primals The five principal sections of the pork carcass: the Boston butt, shoulder, loin, belly and fresh ham; each side of pork contains one of each primal.

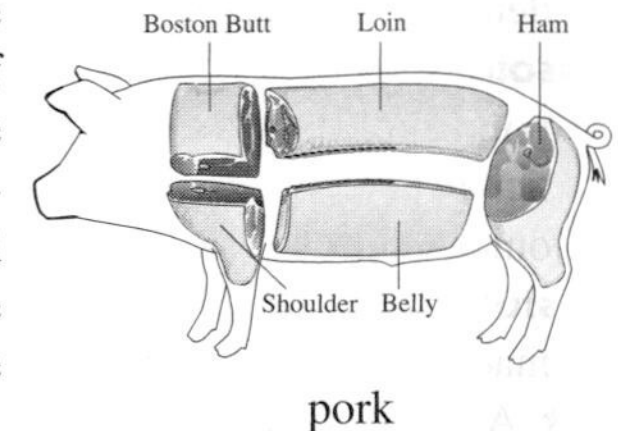

pork
(American primals)

pork quality grades The USDA quality grades for pork are no. 1 (the highest quality), no. 2, no. 3 and utility. *See* USDA quality grades *and* utility.

pork sausage Any of several varieties of fresh sausage made from ground pork and pork fat, typically seasoned with pepper and sage; sold as links, patties or in bulk and also available smoked.

pork tenderloin A subprimal cut of the pork primal loin; it is the tender, lean tenderloin muscle and can be used as is or further fabricated into medallions.

porridge A thick, puddinglike dish made from any of various cereals or grains cooked in water or milk; usually eaten hot for breakfast with sugar and cream or milk.

portabella (pohr-tah-bel-lah) A very large crimini; the mushroom has a dense texture and a rich, meaty flavor.

porterhouse steak A fabricated cut of the beef primal short loin; this tender cut contains a distinctive T-shaped portion of the backbone and large portions (on either side of the center bone) of the loin eye muscle and tenderloin; also known as a king steak. *See* club steak *and* T-bone steak.

portion scale Small spring scale used to measure the weight of an ingredient or portion. *See* electronic scale *and* spring scale.

portion scoop A utensil similar to an ice cream scoop with a lever-operated blade for releasing contents held in its bowl; used for portioning soft foods such as salads and batters, it is available in several standardized sizes (the number stamped on it indicates the number of level scoopfuls per quart); also known as a disher.

portugaise, à la (pohr-tay-gaez, ah lah) A French garnish for meat consisting of small stuffed tomatoes and pommes château with sauce Portugaise.

Portugaise, sauce (pohr-tay-gaez) A French compound sauce made from a demi-glaze flavored with tomato purée, onion and garlic.

port wine sauce 1. A sauce made from the drippings of roasted mutton or venison, red currant jelly, port and lemon juice. 2. A compound sauce made with demi-glaze flavored with port.

posole; pozole (poh-SOH-leh) A Mexican soup of pork and broth, hominy and onions, flavored with garlic, chiles and cilantro and garnished with lettuce, onions, cheese and cilantro.

Postum The proprietary name for a coffee substitute made of cereal.

pot A cylindrical vessel with straight sides, two loop handles and usually a flat or fitted lid; used for steaming, simmering and boiling foods.

potable (POH-tuh-bil) Any liquid suitable for drinking; used principally to describe water.

potage (poh-TAHZH) French for soup and used to describe a puréed soup that can be thickened with cream or egg yolks. *See* consommé.

potager (poh-tah-zaj) At a food services operation following the brigade system, the person responsible for all stocks and soups; also known as the soup station chef.

potato The starchy tuber of a succulent, nonwoody annual plant (*Solanum tuberosum*) native to the Andes Mountains; it is cooked liked a vegetable, made into flour, processed for chips and used for distillation mash.

potato, mealy Any of a variety of potatoes (e.g., russet) with a high starch content, low sugar content, low moisture content and thick skin; used principally for baking, deep-frying and making into whipped or puréed potato dishes; also known as a baker or starchy potato.

potato, waxy Any of a variety of potatoes (e.g., red potato) with a low starch content, high moisture content, high sugar content and thin skin; used principally for boiling; also known as a boiling potato.

potato chips Very thinly sliced, deep-fried potatoes, usually salted; also called Saratoga chips because they were first made in Saratoga Springs, New York; also known as potato crisps.

potato flour An ultrafine, soft, white powder that is the pure starch obtained by either soaking grated potatoes in water or grinding cooked, dried potatoes; used as a thickener or for baking (alone or blended with wheat flour); also called potato starch.

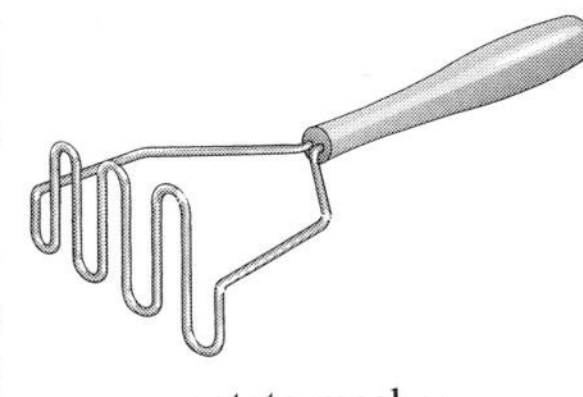
potato masher

potato masher A utensil with an inflexible zigzag wire and a wooden or metal handle; it is used to reduce high-starch vegetables such as potatoes or parsnips to a soft, fluffy mass.

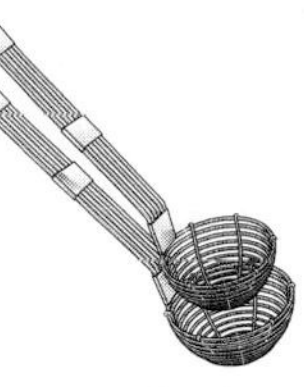
potato nest basket

potato nest basket An assemblage of two wire baskets, one smaller than the other; shredded potatoes are placed in the larger basket, and the smaller basket is placed on top of the potatoes; the assemblage is submerged in hot fat and cooked; available in various sizes.

potato salad A dish of cooked, sliced or diced potatoes bound with mayonnaise and flavored with ingredients such as onions, green peppers, cooked eggs, herbs and spices; usually served chilled.

potato salad, German A dish of cooked, sliced or diced potatoes bound with a vinegar dressing, flavored with bacon, bacon fat and onions and served warm.

pot au feu (poa toh fuh) French for pot on the fire and used to describe a thick French soup of meat and vegetables; the broth is often served separately before the meat and vegetables.

pot de crème (poa duh kreme) 1. A French dessert consisting of a rich, baked custard, usually chocolate. 2. A small porcelain pot with a lid, one or two handles, a capacity of 2.5–8 oz. and used for serving pot de crème.

potentially hazardous foods Foods on which bacteria thrive and that should be handled with care to avoid transmitting an infection, intoxication or toxin-mediated infection; includes foods high in protein, such as meat, fish, shellfish, grains and some vegetables as well as dairy products, eggs and products containing eggs, such as custards.

potherb 1. A term used from the 16th to the 19th century for any plant with stalks and leaves that could be boiled as greens. 2. Culinary herbs, as opposed to medicinal herbs.

pot liquor; potlikker The liquid remaining after cooking greens or other vegetables; served in the American South with cornbread.

potluck; potluck supper A meal offered to a guest without the host having made any special preparations; sometimes consisting of dishes brought by the guests or foods delivered from restaurants.

pot marjoram A species of marjoram with a stronger (and slightly more bitter) flavor than sweet marjoram, which is also slightly bitter.

potpie; pot pie A casserole dish of meat or poultry and vegetables in a rich sauce topped with a crust and baked.

pot roast *v.* To cook a piece of meat by first browning it in hot fat and then braising it in a covered pot. *n.* 1. A subprimal cut of the beef chuck or round primals; it is usually tough and flavorful. 2. *See* Yankee pot roast.

pot stickers Small Chinese dumplings made of won ton wrappers with a meat, fish, shellfish and/or vegetable filling, either fried or browned and then cooked in a broth or steamed; usually served with dipping sauces; also generally known as Chinese dumplings.

potted A preservation method in which foods (particularly meat and shrimp) are seasoned, cooked, stored in a container with a layer of fat on top and chilled.

poularde (poo-LAHRD) French for a neutered, fattened hen.

poule (pull) French for boiling fowl.

poulet (poo-LAY) French for a young, tender spring chicken.

Poulette, sauce (poo-let) A French compound sauce made from an allemande flavored with mushroom essence and lemon juice and garnished with parsley.

poultry Any domesticated bird used for food; the USDA recognizes six kinds of poultry: chicken, duck, goose, guinea, pigeon and turkey; each includes various classes. *See* fowl.

poultry lacer A large needle used to pierce the skin of fowl and lace the cavity closed with twine.

poultry product; poultry food product A labeling term recognized by the USDA for any food product containing more than 2% poultry flesh.

poultry quality grades USDA quality grades; grade A poultry has thick flesh and a well-developed fat layer and is free of pinfeathers, deformities, tears, broken bones and discoloration; if frozen, it is free from storage and freezing defects; grades B and C are of lesser quality and used in processed poultry products.

poultry seasoning A commercial blend of herbs and spices, usually sage, parsley, majoram and thyme, used to season poultry stuffing.

poultry shears A pair of strong scissors with slightly curved blades (one blade has a notched and serrated edge) used to cut through poultry flesh and bones. *See* kitchen shears.

poultry shears

pound *v.* To beat a food with a heavy object to break down its texture and make it tender. *n.* A basic measure of weight in the U.S. system; 16 oz. equal 1 lb. and 1 lb. equals 453.6 g, or 0.4536 kg.

pound cake A dense, rich cake originally made with 1 lb. each of butter, flour, sugar and eggs.

pound of eggs A traditional measure of eggs; approximately 1 dozen large eggs.

pound of flour A traditional measure of weight for flour; depending on the type of flour, it can have a volume of 3–4½ cups.

poured sugar Sugar cooked to the hard-crack stage and poured into a shallow template; when hard, pieces can be glued together with royal icing or hard-crack sugar to form three-dimensional shapes.

poussin (poo-SAHN) French for a squab chicken; also known as petit poussin.

poutine (poo-TEN) A French-Canadian snack of french fries topped with cheese curds and smothered in gravy; eaten while hot with a fork.

powdered eggs Dehydrated whole eggs; used in commercial food production.

prahok; prahoc (prah-hock) A paste made from fish pressed under banana leaves, mixed with coarse salt, sun-dried and then pounded to a paste and left to ferment; it is used as a condiment and sauce in Cambodian cuisine.

praline (PRAY-leen) A rich, fudgelike candy made with cream, brown sugar and pecans, shaped into small flat patties; popular in Louisiana and Texas.

praline (prah-leen) 1. French hard candy made with caramelized sugar and nuts, usually almonds or hazelnuts; eaten as a candy or crushed and used as a flavoring, filling or decoration for pastries and confections. 2. A 17th-century French term for roasted almonds.

praliné (pra-lee-NAY) Food that is garnished, coated or made with praline or almonds.

praline paste A thick, bittersweet paste similar to peanut butter made by grinding caramelized almonds or hazelnuts; used to flavor pastries, creams and candies.

prawn 1. An anadromous shrimplike crustacean with a narrower body and longer legs than a shrimp; it has an average market length of 3–4 in. (7.6–10.1 cm), firm, pearly white flesh and a sweet, delicate flavor. *See* shrimp. 2. A term used imprecisely to describe any large shrimp (i.e., a shrimp that weighs more than 1 oz. [15 or fewer per pound]). 3. A term used imprecisely to describe a small lobster that has an average market length of 6–8 in. (15.2–19.3 cm); also known as a Caribbean lobsterette, Danish lobster, Dublin Bay prawn and Florida lobsterette.

Prazská sunka (prash-kah soon-kah) Prague ham; a very delicately smoked ham from the Czech Republic; first salted, placed in a mild brine, smoked over beechwood ashes and then aged.

precook To cook a food partially or completely before using it to complete a dish.

pregelatinized starch Starch that has been processed to permit swelling in cold water; used as a base or food additive for instant puddings, cake mixes and soup mixes; also known as gelatinized wheat starch.

preheat To bring an oven, broiler or pan to the desired temperature before putting in the food.

prep and schlep Slang for supplying catered food to an off-site location.

prepared pan A pan thinly coated with fat and perhaps dusted with flour so that foods baked in it will not stick to the insides.

preportioned foods Foods divided into portions before or during their preparation as opposed to after preparation and right before service.

preprepared foods Foods for which some or all of the preparation is done before the foods are needed for further preparation or service; it can be done by the purveyor or on-site by the food services facility.

preservative A food additive used to increase the shelf life of processed foods by retarding decomposition, fermentation, microbial growth, oxidation and/or other processes that spoil food.

preserve *v.* To extend the shelf life of a food by subjecting it to a process such as irradiation, canning, vacuum packing, drying or freezing and/or by adding preservatives. *n.* A fruit gel that contains large pieces of whole fruits.

preserved lemons Lemon slices or chunks cured in a salt–lemon juice mixture; used as an ingredient or flavoring, especially in Moroccan cuisine.

presifted flour Flour that is sifted before packaging.

pressed beef A cut of beef, usually from the primal flank, cooked with calves' feet, onions and seasonings, then pressed flat and served cold.

pressed cookies Small, dainty cookies formed by pressing dough through a cookie press or pastry bag fitted with a decorative tip.

pressed duck 1. A Chinese dish consisting of a steamed, boned duck that is pressed and steamed and flattened again; quartered and fried. 2. *See* canard à la presse.

pressure cooker A pot with a locking lid and a valve for escaping steam, usually available in 4- to 10-qt. capacities and sometimes with a wire basket insert; food is quickly cooked and tenderized under the high heat of steam pressure.

pressure cooker

pressure cooking A method of cooking food in a pressure cooker at specific levels of pressure; the higher the pressure, the higher the temperature at which water boils; by cooking food in a liquid under pressure, the trapped steam cooks the food in less time than conventional methods of steaming.

presunto (pray-ZOON-toh) A Portuguese cured and smoked ham, often sliced thin and eaten raw.

pretzel A hard, crisp snack food made from a slender rope of leavened dough that is coated with salt and baked into a loose knot or stick.

prick To make small holes in the surface of a food, especially an unfilled pie crust.

prickly pear The small barrel or somewhat pear-shaped fruit of a species of cactus *(Opuntia ficus-indica);* studded with small sharp pins and stinging fibers, it has a green to purplish-red skin, a soft yellow-green to deep pink flesh with numerous black seeds, a melonlike aroma and a sweet, bland flavor; also known as barbary fig, barbary pear, cactus pear, Indian fig, Indian pear and tuna fig.

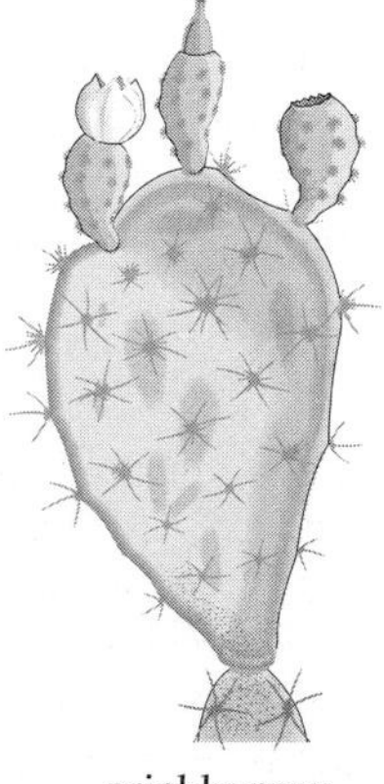

prickly pear

prik dong (preek dong) A Thai bottled chile sauce made from chiles, onions, apricots, lemon, garlic and vinegar.

prik yuak (phrik you-ak) Medium to large, light green to red Thai chiles; they are usually stuffed and fried.

primal; primal cut The primary divisions of muscle, bone and connective tissue produced by the initial butchering of a mammal's carcass; primals are further broken down into smaller, more manageable cuts that are called subprimals or fabricated cuts; also known as a wholesale cut.

primavera, alla (pree-mah-VAY-rah, ah-lah) Italian for springtime and used to describe dishes garnished with fresh vegetables.

prime The highest USDA quality grade for beef, lamb and veal; the meat is well aged, is well marbled, with thick external fat, has a rich flavor and is produced in limited quantities.

princesse, à la (pran-ses, ah lah) 1. A French garnish for poultry, salmon and vol-au-vents characterized by sliced truffles and asparagus tips in a cream sauce. 2. A French garnish of asparagus tips stuffed in artichoke bottoms.

princesse, sauce (pran-ses) A French compound sauce made from a béchamel blended with chicken glaze and mushroom essence.

printaniére, sauce (prin-tan-yey) A French compound sauce made from a velouté finished with herb butter and garnished with diced spring vegetables (e.g., asparagus, carrots and green peas); also known as sauce Spring.

private label A marketing term for a line of foods, beverages or sundries that carry the name of the retailer on the label.

processed cheese A cheese made from one or more cheeses of the same or different varieties; the cheeses are finely ground, mixed together with an emulsifying agent and sometimes flavoring ingredients (e.g., spices or liquid smoke), heated and molded. *See* cold-pack cheese.

processed cheese food A processed cheese made from cheese and other dairy products such as cream, milk, skim milk and cheese whey; oils or milk solids are often added to make it soft and spreadable; at least 51% of the final weight must be cheese.

processed cheese spread Processed cheese food with additional moisture and less fat; it must be spreadable at 70°F (21.1°C); herbs, spices, fruits, vegetables, meats, fish or other flavorings can be added.

processed food Food that has been subjected to any artificial form of modification, such as enriching, bleaching, milling or cooking. *See* natural food.

produce Agricultural products such as fruits and vegetables but usually not herbs or grains.

professional cooking 1. A system of cooking based on a knowledge of and appreciation for ingredients and procedures. 2. To engage in cooking as an occupation for pay.

profiterole (pro-FEHT-uh-rohl) 1. A miniature cream puff filled with either a sweet or savory cream or custard. 2. A French dessert consisting of small cream puffs filled with pastry cream, ice cream or Chantilly cream, usually mounded into a low pyramid and topped with chocolate sauce.

proof To allow shaped yeast dough products to rise a final time before baking. *See* fermentation.

proof box A cabinet or room in which heat and humidity are controlled to create the correct environment for proofing yeast doughs.

proofing The rise given shaped yeast products just before baking.

prosciutto (proh-SHOO-toh) Italian for ham and used to describe a seasoned, salt cured, air-dried product that is not smoked. *See* Parma ham.

prosciutto crudo (proh-SHOO-toh KROO-doa) Cured, uncooked prosciutto; it can be eaten without cooking because it is fully cured.

proteins A class of nutrients containing hydrogen, oxygen, carbon and nitrogen arranged as strands of amino acids (some amino acids also contain sulfur); they occur naturally in animals and plants (significantly in grains) and are essential for the growth and repair of animal tissue.

provençale, à la (pro-vohn-sahl, ah lah) 1. French for dishes cooked in the style of Provence, France, usually with garlic and olive oil. 2. French for entrées that are garnished with small grilled tomatoes, stuffed mushroom caps and sauce Provençale.

Provençale, sauce (proh-vohn-SAHL) A French compound sauce made with demi-glaze and flavored with garlic, tomatoes, olive oil, onions, olives, anchovies and eggplant.

Provolone (proh-voh-LOH-nee) An Italian pasta filata cheese traditionally made from water buffalo's milk but now also cow's milk; it has a light ivory color, a mild, mellow flavor and a smooth texture that cuts without crumbling; shapes include a sausage, squat pear and piglet.

prune 1. A dried red or purple plum. 2. A variety of plum grown in Italy. 3. French for plum.

pudding 1. A soft, creamy cooked dessert made with eggs, milk, sugar and flavorings and thickened with flour or another starch. 2. The dessert course of a British meal.

pudding mold, steamed A bucket-shaped mold with plain or fluted sides and a central tube; the lid is clamped in place and has a handle on top; used for steaming puddings.

pudding mold

pudim de leite (poo-dim day la-eta) A Portuguese dessert of a rich egg custard with caramelized sugar; it is sometimes flavored with lemon.

puffball mushroom A round white mushroom (genus *Lycoperdales*) found in various sizes; it has a mild, blandly nutty flavor and a firm texture.

puff pastry A rich flaky pastry made by enclosing fat, usually butter, in a sheet of dough, rolling the dough out, and continuing to fold and roll the dough until many thin layers of fat and dough are created; as it bakes, the layers rise and separate slightly, due to the steam released by the fat; it is used in many preparations, both sweet and savory (e.g., napoleons, palmiers, tart shells, vol-au-vents and fleurons); also known as pasta sfogliata and pâte feuilletée. *See* feuilletage *and* mille-feuille.

PUFI (puffy) *See* packed under federal inspection.

pull date A date stamped on a product by the manufacturer, distributor or retailer indicating the date by which the product should be removed from the shelf; after that date, the product will begin to deteriorate.

pulled meat Shredded cooked meat, usually barbecued or roasted beef or pork, torn from a larger cooked cut such as a shoulder; it is typically used for sandwiches.

pulled sugar Sugar cooked to the hard-crack stage, then kneaded and pulled by hand until it is soft and pliable enough to shape into flowers, ribbons, fruits and other decorative shapes; these decorations are assembled into elaborate centerpieces or displays or used to garnish pastries, especially fancy cakes.

pullet A young hen, less than 1 year old (more particularly, one between the age of the first laying of eggs and the first molting); it has a tender texture.

pulling sauces The practice of pulling a knife or toothpick through one or more differently colored sauces, usually dessert sauces, to create an interesting pattern.

pullman loaf A yeast bread that is proofed and baked in a lidded rectangular pan; this keeps the loaf flat and even textured.

pullman pan A lidded rectangular loaf pan used to proof and bake yeast bread into an even rectangular loaf.

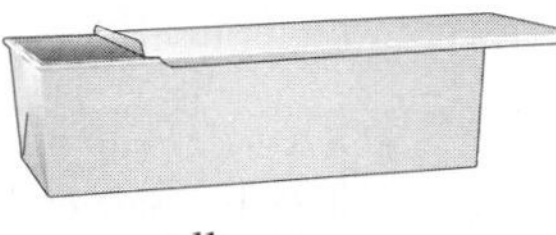
pullman pan

pulp The flesh of a fruit.

pulses The dried edible seeds of any of a variety of legumes, such as beans, peas and lentils.

pumpernickel (PUHM-puhr-nik-uhl) 1. Coarsely ground rye flour. 2. A coarse, dark German-style bread with a slightly sour flavor; it is made with dark rye flour and molasses; also known as Westphalian rye bread.

pumpkin A spherical winter squash with a flattened top and base; can range in size from small to very large and has a fluted orange shell (yellow, green and white varieties are also available), a yellow to orange flesh with a mild sweet flavor and numerous flat, edible seeds.

pumpkin pie A baked custard dessert made with a single flaky crust and a smooth filling of puréed pumpkin, sugar, eggs, milk and spices; traditionally served at Thanksgiving dinner.

punch A hot or cold drink blended from various ingredients, usually with a fruit or fruit juice base and often with sparkling wine or one or more liquors (although it does not have to contain any alcohol); punch is derived from the Hindi panch (five), referring to the original recipe's five ingredients: lime, sugar, spices, water and arak; made in a large bowl and served to a number of people; individually made punches are called cups.

punch down A folding and pressing technique used to deflate fermented yeast dough to expel and redistribute pockets of carbon dioxide and to relax the gluten. *See* bread-making process.

Punschtorte An Austrian dessert composed of a genoise split into three layers and soaked in a rum-flavored syrup, then filled with apricot jam and frosted with pink fondant icing.

pupu; pu pu (POO-poo) Hawaiian for any hot or cold hors d'oeuvre.

purée (pur-ray) *v.* To process food to achieve a smooth pulp. *n.* A food that has been processed by mashing, straining or fine chopping to achieve a smooth pulp.

purée soup A soup usually made from starchy vegetables or legumes; after the main ingredient is simmered in a liquid, the mixture, or a portion of it, is puréed.

purslane (PURSC-leen) A small plant (*Portulaca oleracea*) with stiff, reddish stems and fleshy, rounded leaves with a mild flavor and crisp texture; it can be eaten raw or cooked.

purveyor A vendor supplying goods or services to a buyer at the wholesale or retail level.

putrefaction (pyoo-trah-FAK-shun) The decomposition, rotting or breakdown of organic matter; this decay, often accompanied by an obnoxious odor and poisonous by-products such as ptomaines, mercaptans and hydrogen sulfide, is caused by certain kinds of bacteria and fungi.

puttanesca (poot-tah-NEHS-kah) An Italian sauce that consists of tomatoes, onions, capers, black olives, anchovies, oregano and garlic cooked in olive oil and is usually served with pasta; the name is a derivation of puttana, which is Italian for whore.

qt. *See* quart.

quail, American A small nonmigratory game bird related to the partridge family; it has 1–2 oz. (30–60 g) of breast flesh, a light, lean flesh, a delicate texture and a sweet, nutty flavor; varieties include the bobwhite, blue quail and Gambel.

quail, European A small migratory game bird related to the partridge family; it has 1–2 oz. (30–60 g) of breast flesh, a medium-dark, lean flesh, a tender texture and a sweet, nutty flavor.

quaking custard A soft New England cream custard dessert, usually garnished with meringue.

quality control A system for ensuring the maintenance of proper production standards; it is often achieved by inspection or testing.

quart (qt.) A measure of volume in the U.S. system; 32 fl. oz. equal 1 qt., and 4 qt. equal 1 gallon.

quarter *v.* To cut into four equal pieces. *n.* 1. A one-fourth portion of something (e.g., a quarter of a pound). 2. One leg plus attached parts of a four-legged animal (e.g., a hind quarter). 3. A marketing term for a 1 1/8- to 1 1/4-lb. (510- to 567-g) lobster.

quatre-épices (KAH-tray-PEES) French for four spices and used to describe a blend of black pepper corns with lesser amounts of nutmeg, cloves and dried ginger (and sometimes cinnamon or allspice).

quatre-quarts (ka-truh-kar) A French pound cake, originally made with 1 lb. each of butter, flour, sugar and eggs.

Queen cake 1. A round white loaf cake usually iced with hard white icing; it was popular during the 18th century. 2. A small diamond- or heart-shaped currant cake; it is sometimes iced.

queen of puddings A British dessert made with custard and bread crumbs layered with strawberry jam, topped with meringue and lightly browned.

queen olive A large edible variety of green olive not used for oil.

Queen's biscuit A small diamond- or heart-shaped currant cake; it is sometimes iced. *See* Queen cake.

queen scallop A variety of scallops found in the Atlantic Ocean from Norway to North Africa and in the Mediterranean Sea; it has a reddish-brown shell with a slightly marbled surface, an average diameter of 3 in. (7.6 cm) and tender, sweet, white meat.

Queensware Light-bodied earthenware with lead glaze introduced by Josiah Wedgewood in Staffordshire, England, in 1750 and named in honor of Queen Charlotte, wife of George III.

quenelle (kuh-NEHL) A small ovoid dumpling made of seasoned ground fish, chicken, veal or game, bound with panada or egg and poached in stock; usually served with a rich sauce or in a soup.

quesadilla (keh-sah-DEE-yah) A Mexican and American Southwestern dish of a flour tortilla filled with cheese and sometimes meat, chicken, refried beans or the like, folded in half and grilled; usually served with salsa and sour cream.

queso de tuna (KEH-soh day too-nah) A paste formed from fermented prickly pear juice; it has a sweet flavor and is used in Mexican confections.

queso fundido (KEH-soh fuhn-DEE-doh) Spanish for melted cheese and usually served as an appetizer; it may sometimes contain jalapeños, cooked pork, chicken or beef.

quiche (keesh) A French dish consisting of a pastry crust filled with a savory custard made with eggs and cream and garnished with ingredients such as cheese, bacon, ham, onions, broccoli, mushrooms and/or shellfish.

quiche dish A fluted porcelain dish that is 1.5 in. high and 5–12 in. in diameter.

quiche dish

quick breads A general category of breads and other baked goods made with quick-acting chemical leavening agents, such as baking powder and baking soda; these products are tender and require no kneading or fermentation (e.g., biscuits, scones, muffins and coffee cakes). *See* yeast breads.

quick frozen (QF) A general term to describe a product that was rapidly frozen by any of several processes in an attempt to retain flavors, nutritional values and/or other properties.

quince (kwenc) A spherical or pear-shaped fruit (*Cydonia vulgaris* or *C. oblonga*) with a downy yellow skin, hard, yellowish-white flesh and astringent, tart flavor reminiscent of a pear and apple; always used cooked.

quinoa (KEEN-wah) A grain that was a staple of the ancient Incas; it has a high protein content (contains all essential amino acids), a small beadlike shape, an ivory color and a delicate, almost bland flavor; it is now prepared like rice.

quintal; quintale (KWINT-l) A measure of weight in the metric system; 1 quintal equals 100 kg, or 220.46 lb.

rabadi (RA-bhree) An East Indian beverage of thickened or reduced milk.

rabbit, domesticated Any of a variety of small burrowing mammals with long ears; farm raised, it has a lean flesh with an ivory color, a relatively tender texture and a mild, delicate flavor; the average market weight for a young rabbit is 2.2 lb. (1 kg), and for a mature rabbit it is 3–5 lb. (1.4–2.3 kg).

rabbit, wild Any of several varieties of rabbits that have not been domesticated; generally, it has a lean flesh with a tannish color and a tougher texture and gamier flavor than that of a domesticated rabbit. *See* hare.

Rachel, sauce (rah-shell) A French compound sauce made from a béarnaise flavored with a demi-glaze and garnished with diced tomatoes.

rack A primal section of the lamb carcass; it contains both bilateral portions of eight ribs along with the tender, flavorful rib eye muscle and is usually split in half along the backbone and used as is or further fabricated into chops; also known as a hotel rack and, when split into bilateral halves, as a split rack.

Râclette (rah-KLEHT) 1. A firm Emmental-style cheese or group of cheeses made in Switzerland from cow's milk; it has a mellow, nutty flavor. 2. A dish of Râclette heated, usually by an open fire, and scraped off as it melts; served with boiled potatoes, dark bread and cornichons.

radiation cooking A heating process that does not require physical contact between the heat source and the food being cooked; instead, energy is transferred by waves of heat or light striking the food; two kinds of radiant heat used in the kitchen are infrared and microwave.

radicchio (rah-DEE-kee-oh) A variety of chicory native to Italy; the purple and white cup-shaped leaves have a bitter flavor and can be used in salads, as garnish or cooked like a vegetable; also known as red-leaf chicory.

radicchio di Treviso (ra-DEE-key-oh dee trae-VEE-soh) A variety of radicchio that has a tight, tapered head of narrow pointed leaves with a pink to dark red color.

radicchio di Verona A variety of radicchio that has a small, looseleaf head of burgundy red leaves with white ribs.

radish A member of the mustard family grown for its root (*Raphanus sativus*); generally, the crisp white flesh has a mild to peppery flavor and is usually eaten raw.

radish, white A medium-sized conical radish with a dull white-tan skin, a white flesh and a peppery flavor. *See* daikon.

raft A clump of clearmeat and impurities from the stock formed during clarification; it rises to the top of the simmering stock and releases additional flavors.

ragoût (rah-goo) 1. Traditionally, a well-seasoned, rich French stew containing meat and vegetables and flavored with wine. 2. Any stewlike dish, whether containing meats, poultry, vegetables and/or fruits.

raidir (ray-deer) French term for sealing or searing foods quickly in butter.

rainbow trout A freshwater trout found throughout North America; some are anadromous; it has a broad reddish band or rainbow along its side that blends into its dark olive skin, which becomes silvery on the belly, a pink to red flaky flesh, a delicate flavor and an average market weight of 5–10 oz. (140–280 g). *See* steelhead trout.

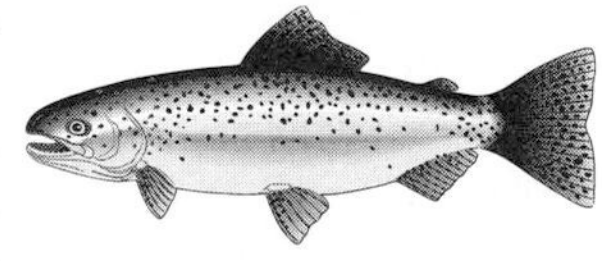

rainbow trout

Rainier cherry (ray-NER) A heart-shaped sweet cherry with a light red-blushed yellow skin, a yellowish-pink flesh and a sweet flavor.

raised In the United States, refers to a cake, muffin or other baked good made with yeast or other leavening agent added to the dough.

raised pie A British double-crusted savory pie; the crust rises during baking and aspic is poured into it.

raisin 1. A sweet dried grape. 2. French for grape.

raita (RI-tah) An eastern Indian yogurt salad that consists of yogurt and various chopped vegetables (e.g., cucumbers, eggplant, potatoes or spinach) or fruits (e.g., bananas) and flavored variously with garam masala, black mustard seeds and herbs.

Raki (ray-KEE) 1. A Turkish liqueur made from fermented raisins, figs or dates and flavored with aniseed; it resembles Pernod and turns milky when mixed with water. 2. A generic term for spirits in the Balkans.

rambutan (ram-BOO-ten) A variety of litchi (*Nephelium lappaceum*) native to Malaysia; it has a thick red shell covered with hooked hairs, a large stone with a flavor reminiscent of almonds and a pale aromatic flesh with a more acidic flavor than that of the common litchi.

ramekin; ramequin (RAM-ih-kihn) 1. A small ceramic soufflé dish with a 4-oz. capacity. 2. A small baked pastry filled with a creamy cheese filling.

ramekin

ramen (RAH-mehn) 1. A Japanese dish of noodles in broth garnished with small pieces of meat and vegetables. 2. Packets of such instant noodles and dehydrated broth.

ramp A wild onion that resembles a scallion with broad leaves; also known as a wild leek.

ranch beans A dish of dry pinto beans cooked in water and flavored with onions, garlic and bacon.

ranchero (rahn-cheh-roh) A Spanish term for a dish prepared country style, usually containing tomatoes, peppers, onions and garlic.

rancid A tasting term to describe a product with a fetid or tainted character.

range An appliance with surface burners on which foods are cooked.

Rangoon sauce A sauce, popular in Florida, made from tropical fruits, butter, parsley and lemon juice and served over fish.

Ranhofer, Charles (Am., 1836–1899) The first internationally renowned chef of an American restaurant, Delmonico's in New York City; in 1893 he published his Franco-American encyclopedia of cooking, *The Epicurean,* which contains more than 3500 recipes.

rape (rayp) A vegetable (*Brassica napus*) related to the cabbage and turnip families; it has a tall, leafy, green stalk with scattered clusters of tiny broccoli-like florets and a pungent, bitter flavor; also known as broccoli raab, brocoletti di rape and rapini.

rapeseeds Seeds of the rape; they are used to make a cooking oil marketed as canola oil. *See* canola oil.

rare A degree of doneness for meat; the meat should have a large, deep red center and provide a slight resistance and be spongy when pressed. *See* very rare, medium rare, medium, medium well *and* well done.

ras al-hanout (rass al-ha-noot) A spice blend generally including cloves, cinnamon and black pepper and used in North African (especially Moroccan and Tunisian) cuisines.

rasher (RAH-sher) 1. A thin slice of bacon. 2. A serving of two or three thin slices of bacon or ham.

raspberry A small ovoid or conical berry (*Rubus idaeus*) composed of many connecting drupelets (tiny individual sections of fruit, each with its own seed) surrounding a central core; it has a sweet, slightly acidic flavor; the three principal varieties are black, golden and red.

raspings Bread crumbs made from dried bread crusts.

ratatouille (ra-tuh-TOO-ee; ra-tuh-TWEE) A vegetable ragoût made in France's Provence region from tomatoes, eggplant, zucchini, onions, garlic, sweet peppers and herbs simmered in olive oil.

rattail tang *See* tang.

rattlesnake bean A medium-sized, oblong dried bean with a light brown skin streaked with mahogany; it has a strong, tangy flavor.

rau ram (row ram) An herb (*Polygonum* sp.) with purple-tinged stems, long, slender, deep green leaves and a flavor similar to that of basil and mint; used in Vietnamese fish and noodle dishes.

Ravigote, sauce (rah-vee-GOT) 1. A cold French sauce made from a vinaigrette garnished with capers, chopped onions and herbs. 2. A French compound sauce made from a velouté flavored with white wine, vinegar and shallots and finished with herbs; usually served with calf's head, brains and boiled fowl.

ravioli mold A metal tray with fluted-edge indentions; the pasta dough is laid on the tray, filled, and another sheet of dough is placed on top; a rolling pin is then used to seal and cut the layered pasta.

raw sugar Sugar in the initial stages of refining; according to the U.S. Department of Agriculture (USDA), true raw sugar is unfit for direct use as a food ingredient.

razor shell clams Any of several varieties of clams found in tropical saltwaters; they have long, narrow, straight or slightly curved shells; also known as jackknife clams.

reach-in A refrigerator or freezer in which foods are stored on shelves and are accessible by opening a door and reaching in; it can be a freestanding unit or located under or above a counter. *See* walk-in.

ready to cook (RTC) A processed food product that is ready to cook (usually heat); all of the preparation has been done by the manufacturer or on-site at the food services facility.

ready to eat (RTE) A processed food product that is fully prepared and ready for service to the customer; the preparation can be done by a manufacturer or on-site at the food services facility.

reamer A cone-shaped wooden utensil with a ridged surface; used for extracting juice from fruit, particularly citrus. *See* juicer.

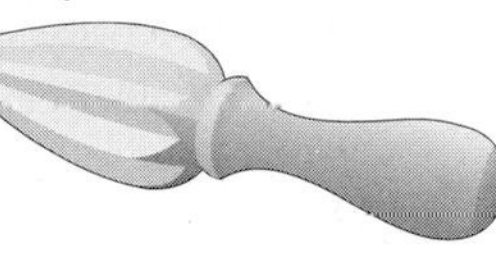
reamer

recado (reh-cah-doh) Mexican and Latin American seasoning pastes made of ground chiles and/or other spices.

recipe A set of written instructions for producing a specific food or beverage; also known as a formula (especially with regards to baked goods). *See* standardized recipe.

recipe costing Calculating the exact cost of every ingredient in a recipe to determine total recipe cost and portion cost.

recommended daily allowance (RDA) Published by the Food and Nutrition Board; it identifies the amount of protein and several vitamins and minerals that should be consumed on a daily basis to avoid clinical nutrient deficiencies; the recommendations are tailored by gender, age, size and other factors.

recommended daily intake (RDI) A Nutrition Facts term approved by the U.S. Food and Drug Administration (FDA) that represents the percentage of the daily recommended intake of vitamin A, vitamin C, calcium and iron per serving based on the balanced diet of a standard adult; formerly known as the U.S. RDA.

reconstitute To build up again by adding back the part or parts that have been subtracted, such as adding back the appropriate amount of water to dry milk solids.

recovery time The length of time it takes hot fat to return to the desired cooking temperature after food is submerged in it.

red banana A short, squat banana; it has a red skin, sometimes with a green stripe, pink-tinged creamy white flesh and a sweeter flavor than that of a common yellow banana.

red bass *See* redfish.

red bean A medium-sized, kidney-shaped bean (*Phaseolus vulgaris*) with a dark red skin and flesh; available dried.

red beans and rice An American Southern dish of red beans cooked with ham and served over white rice.

red beet eggs A Pennsylvania Dutch dish consisting of eggs steeped in the liquid remaining from beets pickled in vinegar, water and brown sugar.

redbreast sunfish A member of the sunfish family found in eastern North American lakes and rivers; it has a long black ear flap, a bright orange-red belly, an average market weight of 0.5–2 lb. (225–900 g) and a mild flavor; also known as robin, sun perch and yellow belly sunfish.

red chile pepper paste A spicy purée of hot chiles, blended with oil and used as a condiment or flavoring.

red clover A perennial herb (*Trifolium pratense*) with dark green leaves and reddish-purple flowers; the leaves are used fresh in a salad or cooked like a vegetable, and the flowers are used in tisanes.

red cooking A Chinese cooking method in which the food is browned in soy sauce, changing its color to a deep red.

red currant syrup A sweetened syrup made from red currants and used as a flavoring agent in beverages and desserts; also known as sirop de groseilles.

red durum wheat Wheat obtained from the durum wheat kernel; it is used for processed pastas.

redeye gravy; red-eye gravy; red ham gravy A thin gravy made from ham drippings and water, often flavored with coffee; also known as frog-eye gravy.

redfin A small freshwater fish of the carp family found in lakes throughout the United States; it has distinctive red fins; also known as a shiner.

redfish A member of the drum family found in the southern Atlantic Ocean and Gulf of Mexico; it has a reddish-bronze skin with a black-spotted tail, an average market weight of 2–8 lb. (0.9–3.6 kg) and a firm, ivory flesh with a mild flavor; also known as channel bass, red drum and red bass. *See* ocean perch.

red flame seedless grapes *See* flame seedless grapes.

red flannel hash A dish from the New England region of the United States; it consists of fried beets, potatoes, onions and bacon; usually served with cornbread.

red leaf lettuce A variety of leaf lettuce with dark red-tinged green leaves that have ruffled edges, a tender texture and a mild flavor.

red mayonnaise An English and American mayonnaise sauce blended with lobster coral and beetroot juice; usually served with lobster salad.

red mullet A fish found in the Mediterranean Sea; not a true mullet, it is a member of the goatfish family; it has a reddish-pink skin, an average market weight of 0.5–2 lb. (225–900 g) and a lean, firm flesh.

red onion A medium to large onion with a maroon-colored outer layer, a light pinkish-white flesh and a slightly sweet, mild flavor; also known as a purple onion.

red pepper 1. A generic name for any of various red chiles with a hot flavor; generally dried and available whole, flaked or powdered. 2. *See* cayenne; cayenne pepper.

red porgy A fish found in the Atlantic Ocean from New York to Argentina and in the Mediterranean Sea; it has a reddish-silver skin with many tiny yellow spots that create a striped pattern on the upper half of the body, an average market weight of 2.5 lb. (1.2 kg) and a mild flavor.

red rice 1. An American Southern dish of rice cooked with tomatoes; often served with shrimp. 2. A glutinous variety of rice grown in China and the Camargue region of France; it has a dull, pale red color and a flavor similar to that of brown rice.

red rockfish; red rock A member of the rockfish family found in the Pacific Ocean from California to Alaska; it has a deep red skin that becomes lighter at the belly, whitish streaks along its side and black spots around its head and an average market length of 3 ft. (90 cm); sometimes marketed as red snapper even though it is unrelated to the Atlantic red snapper; also known as rasphead.

red sauce In the United States, any of several varieties of Italian-style tomato sauces, some with meat.

red snapper A fish found along the U.S. East Coast and in the Gulf of Mexico; it has red eyes, a rosy skin fading to pink and then white at the belly, a lean, flaky, pink flesh that whitens when cooked, a delicate, sweet flavor and an average market weight of 2–8 lb. (0.9–3.6 kg); also known as the American snapper, American red snapper, Mexican snapper and northern red snapper.

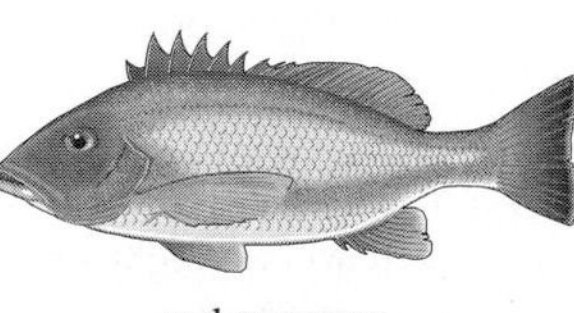

red snapper

reduce To cook a liquid mixture, often a sauce, until the quantity decreases through evaporation; typically done to concentrate flavors and thicken liquids.

reduction A sauce or other liquid that has been reduced.

red velvet cake An American cake composed of three or four layers of a rich chocolate cake dyed bright red with food coloring and filled and frosted with white cream cheese icing.

red vinegar A clear, pale red liquid with a delicate, tart, slightly salty flavor; used in northern Chinese cuisine as a condiment.

red wine sauce A sauce made from a reduction of red wine flavored with shallots, garlic and bay leaves and beaten with butter until incorporated. *See* marchand de vin, sauce.

refined A food freed of inedible or undesirable components through processing (e.g., refined cereals consist of the starchy endosperm after the chaff, bran and germ are removed).

réforme, sauce; reform sauce A French and English pepper sauce garnished with julienne of hard-cooked egg whites, mushrooms, ox tongue and gherkins and served with lamb or venison cutlets; it was created by Alexis Soyer.

refreshing 1. The process of adding a newer wine, distilled spirit or other beverage to the existing one to give the old product a new liveliness. 2. Submerging a food (usually a vegetable) in cold water to cool it quickly and prevent further cooking; also known as shocking. 3. The pleasantly fresh flavor of a food or beverage.

refried beans A Mexican–American dish of cooked and mashed pinto beans; served as a side dish or filling. *See* frijoles refritos.

refrigerator An insulated cabinet (reach-in) or room (walk-in) used to store foods at low temperatures created by mechanical or chemical refrigeration. *See* freezer.

Régence, sauce; Regency sauce (ray-ZHANSS) 1. A French compound sauce made from a demi-glaze flavored with a Rhine wine, mirepoix and truffle peelings. 2. A French compound sauce made from a suprême flavored with mushrooms, truffle peelings and a Rhine wine.

regional cuisine A set of recipes based on local ingredients, traditions and practices; within a larger geographic, political, cultural or social unit, regional cuisines are often variations of each other that blend together to create a national cuisine.

Rehrücken (RAY-rew-kern) 1. German for saddle of venison. 2. An Austrian pastry composed of a chocolate–almond cake baked in a saddleback pan, then glazed with chocolate and studded with almond slivers; the cake's shape represents a saddle of venison, and the riblike pattern is used as a cutting guide.

rehydrate To restore the water lost during a drying process (usually by cooking, storing or freeze-drying).

reine, sauce (ren) A French compound sauce made from a suprême blended with whipped cream and garnished with strips of poached chicken breast.

Reine de Saba (rehn da SAW-bah) A dense, rich, single-layer French cake made with almonds and chocolate and topped with a poured chocolate glaze; also known as a Queen of Sheba cake.

religieuse (reh-leh-geh-oose) French for nun and used to describe a pastry or large cake resembling a nun in her habit; it is composed of two choux pastry puffs filled with chocolate, vanilla or coffee pastry cream and frosted with chocolate or coffee icing.

relish A cooked or pickled sauce usually made with vegetables or fruits and often used as a condiment; it can be smooth or chunky, sweet or savory and hot or mild.

relish tray; relish plate A small dish of olives, pickles, carrot sticks, cherry tomatoes, celery stalks and the like served as an appetizer; there is usually one dish per table and diners help themselves, usually while waiting for and enjoying their drinks.

relleno (rreh-YEH-noh) 1. Spanish for stuffing or forcemeat. 2. Any of several Mexican dishes consisting of an item such as a chile stuffed with cheese and usually dipped in batter and fried.

remouillage (rhur-moo-yahj) French for rewetting and used to describe a stock produced by reusing the bones from another stock.

rémoulade (ray-muh-LAHD) A French mayonnaise-based sauce flavored with mustard, capers, chopped gherkins, herbs and anchovies; usually served with cold shellfish, fish or meat.

rempah (r'm-pah) A flavoring paste made from ingredients such as lemongrass, fresh or dried chiles, onions, garlic, coriander, ginger and shrimp paste; used in Malaysian and Indonesian curry dishes and to season meat for satays.

render 1. To melt and clarify fat. 2. To cook meats and poultry to remove the fat.

rennet 1. A substance found in the mucous membranes of a calf's stomach; it contains rennin, an acid-producing enzyme that aids in coagulating milk and is used in cheese making. 2. A term imprecisely used to describe any substance used to facilitate the separation of curds and whey during cheese making.

rest The period during which a food (e.g., bread or a roasted turkey) is allowed to lay undisturbed immediately after cooking and before slicing or carving.

restaurant A food services operation offering customers foods and beverages from a menu, usually for consumption on the premises.

retard To refrigerate a yeast dough to slow fermentation.

Reuben; Reuben sandwich A sandwich of corned beef, an Emmental-style cheese and sauerkraut on rye bread and sometimes fried in butter.

reverse osmosis A water filtration method that uses pressure to force water through a fine membrane to remove inorganic contaminants.

rex sole A small member of the flounder family found off the U.S. West Coast; it has a white flesh and a mild flavor.

rhea A large flightless bird native to South America; smaller than an ostrich, its meat is similar: lean and purple, turning brown when cooked, and with a flavor similar to that of lean beef. *See* emu *and* ostrich.

rhizome A creeping, usually horizontal, underground storage system (a branch or stem) that sends up leafy shoots each year.

rhubarb A perennial plant (*Rheum rhaponticum*) with long, pink to red, celerylike stalks and large green leaves that are toxic; the stalks have an extremely tart flavor and are used in baked goods; also known as pie plant.

rhubarb chard A variety of chard with bright ruby red stalks and leaf veins and dark green-purple leaves; it has a stronger flavor than chard.

rib 1. A primal section of the beef carcass; it consists of ribs 6–12 and a portion of the backbone; it includes such subprimal or fabricated cuts as the blade, rib roast, short ribs, rib eye roast and rib eye steaks. 2. A primal section of the veal carcass; it consists of both bilateral portions of seven ribs and includes such subprimal or fabricated cuts as a veal hotel rack and chops; also known as a double rack. 3. A single stalk of a vegetable such as celery.

ribbon 1. A term used to describe the consistency of a batter or mixture, especially a mixture of beaten eggs and sugar; when the beater or whisk is lifted, the mixture will fall slowly back onto its surface in a ribbon-like pattern. 2. A long strip or strand of pasta.

rib eye roast A subprimal cut of the tender eye muscle of the beef primal rib; boneless, it is sometimes known erroneously as a prime rib roast.

rib eye roll A lean subprimal cut of the rib eye muscle from the beef primal rib.

rib eye steak A fabricated cut of the tender eye muscle of the beef primal rib.

Ribier grape A large grape with a tough blue-black skin, a juicy flesh and few seeds; used for eating and generally not for wine.

riboflavin *See* vitamin B_2.

ribollita (ree-boh-LEE-tah) Italian for reboiled and used to describe a hearty Tuscan soup made with beans, olive oil, vegetables, bread and cheese, left to stand and reheated.

rib roast A large subprimal of the beef primal rib containing the tender eye and other muscles, a large amount of marbling and available with or without the bones; also known as prime rib roast and prime rib of beef. *See* rolled rib roast *and* standing rib roast.

rib roast, full A subprimal cut of the pork primal loin; the entire trimmed rib section.

rib steak A fabricated cut of the beef primal rib; it has eye muscle meat attached to a portion of a rib bone; also available boneless.

ricci (REE-chee) Italian for curly and used to describe various widths of otherwise flat pasta strips that have one or both edges wavy or rippled.

rice The starchy seed of a semiaquatic grass (*Oryza sativa*), probably originating in Southeast Asia and now part of most cuisines; there are three classifications based on seed size—long grain, medium grain and short grain—each of which is available in different processed forms such as white rice and brown rice.

rice, long-grain Rice with a length four to five times its width; when cooked, it produces firm, fluffy grains that separate easily.

rice, medium-grain Rice that is shorter than long-grain rice and less starchy than short-grain rice; when cooked, it produces relatively moist, tender grains that begin to stick together as the rice cools.

rice, short-grain Rice with a fat, almost round, grain and a high starch content; when cooked, it produces moist, tender grains that tend to stick together.

rice cooker An electric utensil, usually round with a lid, used for steaming rice; when the rice is done, it shuts off automatically; it can also be used to steam vegetables.

rice flour Finely ground white or brown rice; used as a thickener for baking and in cosmetics.

rice noodles Very thin noodles made from finely ground rice and water and used in many Asian cuisines; when deep-fried they expand greatly in size and become crispy, when stir-fried they remain soft; also known as rice flour noodles and rice vermicelli.

rice paper 1. An edible paper made from water and the pithy root of the rice paper plant, an Asian shrub (sometimes rice flour is also used). 2. A thin, dry, almost translucent sheet made from a dough of rice flour and water and used as wrappers in Vietnamese and Thai spring rolls.

rice powder Long-grain rice, pan roasted until golden brown and ground to a powder; used in Vietnamese cuisine as a garnish for salads and plain rice and as a binder in fillings.

rice pudding A creamy, custardlike dessert made with milk, sugar, eggs and rice, often flavored with spices and garnished with raisins or currants.

ricer A tool used to reduce a cooked food, such as a potato, into ricelike pieces; the food is placed in a hopper and pushed through a die by a plunger; also known as a potato ricer.

ricer

rice sticks Generally broad, ribbonlike Asian noodles made from a rice flour dough; they are brittle, dry and hard when made and white, somewhat opaque, shiny and smooth when cooked and are available dried and fresh; also known as thin sticks.

rice vermicelli (ver-mih-chehl-ee) A fine, creamy-white noodle made from a dough of finely ground rice and water. *See* rice noodles.

rice vinegar; rice wine vinegar A type of vinegar made from rice wine; it is generally clear with a straw color; Chinese rice vinegars are sharp and sour, whereas Japanese ones are mellow and almost sweet.

rich dough A yeast dough that contains a high ratio of fat, eggs or sugar (e.g., challah, brioche and Danish pastry dough). *See* lean dough.

Riche, sauce (reesh) A French compound sauce made from a sauce normande flavored with lobster butter and garnished with diced lobster and truffles; also known as sauce diplomat.

Richelieu, à la (reesh-ul-LOU, ah lah) 1. A French garnish for meat, consisting of stuffed tomatoes and mushrooms, braised lettuce and pommes château. 2. A French dish of fish dipped in melted butter and white bread crumbs, fried, then topped with mâitre d'hôtel butter.

Richelieu, sauce (reesh-ul-LOU) 1. A French compound sauce made from a tomato sauce flavored with a meat glaze. 2. A French compound sauce made from a demi-glaze flavored with white wine, chicken stock and truffle essence and finished with Madeira wine. 3. A French compound sauce made from an allemande flavored with onions and chicken stock, finished with chicken glaze and butter and garnished with chervil.

Ricotta (rih-COH-tah) 1. A rich fresh Italian cheese made from the whey remaining after other cow's milk cheeses have been made; it has a white color, a moist, somewhat grainy texture and a slightly sweet flavor and is used in both savory and sweet dishes; sometimes allowed to age until firm enough for grating; also known as Brocotta. 2. In the United States, the whey is usually mixed with whole or skimmed cow's milk and the cheese is similar to cottage cheese; also known as whey cheese and albumin cheese.

Ricotta Salata (ree-COH-tah sah-LAH-tah) An Italian ewe's milk whey or whey and whole milk cheese sold in plastic-wrapped wheels; it has a firm, yet tender, smooth texture, a pure white interior and a mild, usually sweet, nutty, milky flavor.

rigati (ree-gah-tee) Italian for grooved and used to describe pasta that has a grooved or ridged (not smooth) surface. *See* lisci.

rijsttafel (RAY-stah-fuhl; RIHS-tah-fuhl) Dutch for rice table and used to describe an Indonesian-inspired dish of spiced rice surrounded by small dishes of foods such as hot curried, steamed or fried fish, shellfish and/or vegetables and served with chutneys.

rillette (rih-YEHT; ree-yeht) A French dish of meat, poultry or fish slowly cooked, mashed and preserved in its own fat, packed in small pots and served cold, usually spread on toast.

rillettes pot A porcelain pot with slightly bowed sides and a raised rim lid; available with an 8- to 12-oz. capacity and used to pack, store and serve pork pâté.

rillettes pot

rillons (ree-yahng) A French dish made by salting pieces of pork belly or pork shoulder and then cooking them in lard; served hot or cold.

rind 1. A relatively thick, firm coat, skin or covering found on certain foods such as fruits, vegetables and cheeses. 2. The outer surface of a cheese, produced naturally or by adding mold during curing; some rinds are edible and all rinds vary in texture, thickness and color.

rioler (re-yoh-lee) A French term meaning to decorate with strips of dough; used principally for decorating tarts with strips of dough placed over the surface in a diagonal pattern.

ripe 1. Fully grown and developed fruit; the fruit's flavor, texture and appearance are at their peak and the fruit is ready to eat. 2. A tasting term for a food (e.g., cheese) or beverage (e.g., wine) that is fully aged; it is mature and has the appropriate flavor. 3. An unpleasant odor indicating that a food, especially meat, poultry, fish or shellfish, may be past its prime.

ripening 1. The period during which the bacteria and mold present in a green cheese change the cheese's texture and flavor; a cheese can ripen from the surface inward by the application of microorganisms to the cheese (called surface-ripened cheese), from the interior outward by the injection of microorganisms into the cheese (used for certain blue-veined cheeses) or all through the cheese by the microorganisms already present; also known imprecisely as aging and curing. 2. The period during which fruits mature.

ripiéno (ree-PYAP-no) Italian for stuffing or forcemeat, especially when used for tomatoes, sweet peppers, poultry and meat.

risi e bisi (REE-see eh BEE-see) An Italian Venetian dish consisting of green peas and rice; served with a bowl of Parmesan.

risotto (rih-zot-toh; ree-ZAW-toh) 1. A cooking method for grains (especially rice) in which the grains are lightly sautéed in butter and then a liquid is gradually added; the mixture is simmered with nearly constant stirring until the still-firm grains merge with the cooking liquid. 2. A Northern Italian rice dish prepared in this fashion.

risotto Milanese (ree-ZAW-toh me-lay-nay-say) An Italian risotto flavored with saffron.

rissole (rih-SOHL; ree-SOHL) 1. A sweet- or savory-filled turnover-shaped pastry; it can be baked or fried. 2. A small, partially cooked potato ball that is browned in butter until crisp.

rissolé (RIHS-uh-lee; ree-saw-LAY) French for a food that has been fried until crisp and brown.

ristras (rees-trass) A Spanish sausage shape; the filled sausage is tied off at intervals and then shaped into large loops. *See* sarta *and* vela.

riverbank grape 1. A North American grape variety; the fruit have an amber or purplish-black skin and a tart flavor. 2. A vine that grows wild in the

United States; it produces a very sour black berry that is used in baked goods and preserves.

riz a l'imperatrice (REE ahl-ahm-pair-ah-tres) A very rich French rice pudding made with vanilla custard, whipped cream and candied fruit.

roast 1. The large joint of meat or game (with or without the bones) that has been roasted or is intended for roasting. *See* roasting. 2. The entrée course served after the sorbet and before the entremets during a French grande cuisine meal. 3. The entrée course, consisting of roasted meats, following the soup, fish and poultry or game courses during a 19th-century British meal.

roast, city The most widely used roasting style for coffee beans in the United States; the beans are medium roasted, resulting in a moderately flavorful, acidic beverage that may lack brilliance or be a bit flat; also known as American roast, brown roast and regular roast.

roasting A dry-heat cooking method that heats food by surrounding it with hot, dry air in a closed environment or on a spit over an open fire; the term is usually applied to meats, poultry, game and vegetables. *See* baking.

roasting pan A deep or shallow, oval or rectangular, metal or ceramic pan with two handles.

roasting rack A slightly raised flat or V-shaped rack used to keep a roast or poultry above the pan during roasting to prevent it from cooking in its drippings. *See* vertical roaster.

Robert, sauce (roh-bare) A French compound sauce made from a demi-glaze flavored with onions, white wine and vinegar and finished with a Dijon-style mustard.

robusta coffee beans (ro-BUS-tah) A species of coffee beans grown around the world in low-altitude tropical and subtropical regions; although they do not produce as flavorful a beverage as that made from arabica beans, they are becoming increasingly important commercially, particularly because the trees are heartier and more fertile than arabica coffee trees. *See* arabica coffee beans.

rocambole (ROK-uhm-bohl) A leeklike plant that grows wild in Europe; the bulb has a mild garlicky flavor and is used as a flavoring; also known as a sand leek, giant garlic and giant leek.

rock bass A member of the sunfish family found in eastern North American lakes and rivers; it has a dark olive skin with brassy brown blotches, bright red eyes, an average market weight of 0.5–4 lb. (0.23–1.8 kg) and a delicate flavor; also known as redeye bass and goggle-eye bass.

rock cake; rock bun British for a small cake or cookie filled with chopped dried and candied fruits and baked in a mound that resembles a rock.

rock candy A hard candy made by crystallizing a concentrated sugar syrup around a small wooden stick or a piece of string.

Rock Cornish game hen; Rock Cornish hen A young or immature progeny of a Cornish chicken and White Rock chicken slaughtered when 4–6 weeks old; it has an average market weight of 2 lb. (900 g), white and dark meat, relatively little fat and a fine flavor.

rocket *See* arugula.

rockfish A large family of fish found in the Pacific Ocean from California to Alaska; generally, their skin ranges from black or olive to bright orange or crimson and is sometimes spotted or striped; they have a firm, white flesh with a mild flavor; significant varieties include bocaccio, ocean perch, orange rockfish, red rockfish and yellowtail rockfish. *See* striped bass.

rock salt A large, coarse salt that is less refined than table salt; it has a grayish cast and is generally not used for consumption but rather as a bed for shellfish or in hand-cranked ice cream makers; also known as bay salt and ice cream salt.

rock samphire A perennial herb (*Crithmum maritimum*) that grows along the cliffs of European seacoasts; the crisp, fleshy leaves have a salty, fishy flavor and are used as a flavoring, cooked like a vegetable or pickled. *See* marsh samphire.

rock shrimp A variety of shrimp found off Florida; it has a tough, ridged exoskeleton, a firm and chewy texture, and a rich, sweet flavor and comes 20–25 per pound.

rocky road A flavoring combination of chocolate, marshmallows and nuts; used as a candy and in ice creams, pies, cakes and other desserts.

rogan josh (row-gan josh) An Indian dish of lamb braised in yogurt, cream and spices; a Kashmiri speciality.

roll A small bread made with yeast dough; it can be variously shaped and flavored. *See* bread-making process.

roll cutting A method of diagonal cutting; a diagonal cut is made about 1 5/8 in. (4 cm) from one end of the vegetable, the vegetable is rolled a quarter of a turn, a second cut is made the same distance along and rolling and cutting are continued to the end; usually used for root vegetables.

rolled A general term for any of several boneless cuts of meat (beef, veal, lamb or pork), usually consisting of more than one set of connected muscles, rolled or folded together and tied; usually used as a roast.

rolled cookie A cookie made by rolling out a firm dough to an even thickness, then cutting it into various shapes with a knife or cookie cutter.

rolled fondant An icing with the consistency of a dough; made from confectioners' sugar, corn syrup, gelatin and glycerin, it is rolled out with a rolling pin and draped over a cake to create a perfectly smooth, plasterlike surface for decorating; naturally pure white, it can be colored with food dyes; also known as Australian icing.

rolled-in dough A dough in which a fat is incorporated in many layers by using a rolling and folding procedure; it is used for flaky baked goods such as croissants, puff pastry and Danish; also known as laminated dough. *See* lamination.

rolled rib roast A rib roast that has been boned and tied.

rolling mincer A tool with five or more circular blades set in a handled housing; used to mince herbs, garlic, onions and the like by rolling the tool back and forth over the foods.

rolling pin A heavy, thick, smooth cylinder of hardwood, marble, glass or other material; used to roll out doughs.

rollmops Fillets of Bismarck herring wrapped around a pickle slice, secured with a wooden pick and preserved in vinegar and spices.

roly-poly A British pudding made with a suet pastry dough covered with jam or dried fruit, rolled up in a spiral, tied in a towel and steamed or boiled.

romaine, sauce à la; Roman sauce (RO-mahn) A French compound sauce made from a demi-glaze flavored with sugar, white wine vinegar and game stock and garnished with sultanas, dried currants and pine nuts; it is usually served with tongue, light meats and game.

romaine lettuce (roh-MAYN) A lettuce with an elongated head of loosely packed crisp leaves that are dark green and become paler toward the center; the leaves have a slightly bitter flavor and a crunchy stem; also known as cos lettuce and Manchester lettuce.

Romanesca cauliflower; Romanesco (roh-mah-NEHS-kah) An Italian cauliflower that is pale lime green with a delicate flavor; it has flowerettes that form a pyramid of pointed, spiraling cones.

Romano (roh-MAH-noh) A hard grana cheese made in southern and central Italy; it has a brittle texture, a pale yellow-white color and a sharp flavor; generally used for grating after aging for 1 year.

Romanoff; Romanov (rho-mahn-off) 1. A French garnish for meat associated with the Imperial family of Russia; it consists of cucumbers stuffed with duxelles and duchesse potato cases filled with a salpicon of celeriac and mushrooms in a velouté seasoned with horseradish. 2. *See* strawberries Romanoff.

romesco (roh-MEHS-koh) A Spanish sauce that consists of a finely ground mixture of tomatoes, red bell peppers, onions, garlic, almonds and olive oil; usually served with grilled fish or poultry.

rondeau (rohn-doh) A shallow, wide, straight-sided pot with loop handles.

rondeau/brazier

rondelles (ron-dells) Disk-shaped slices of cylindrical vegetables or fruits; also known as rounds.

rooster The male of the domestic fowl, especially the chicken; generally too tough to eat but used for stocks; also known as a cock. *See* capon.

root beer 1. Traditionally, a low-alcohol-content, naturally effervescent beverage made by fermenting yeast and sugar with various herbs and roots, such as sassafras, sarsaparilla, ginger and wintergreen. 2. A nonalcoholic sweetened, carbonated beverage flavored with extracts of various roots and herbs.

root vegetables A general category of vegetables that are used principally for their taproots (e.g., carrots, celery roots and parsnips) or tubers (e.g., potatoes).

Roquefort (ROHK-fuhr) A semisoft to hard French cheese made from ewe's milk; it has a creamy white interior with blue veins and a pungent, somewhat salty flavor; considered the prototype of blue cheeses, true Roquefort, produced only in Roquefort, France, is authenticated by a red sheep on the wrapper and contains approximately 45% milkfat.

Roquefort dressing A salad dressing made with Roquefort, heavy cream or sour cream, lemon juice, chives, Worcestershire sauce and Tabasco sauce. *See* blue cheese dressing.

rose apple A tropical fruit (*Syzygium malaccensis*) grown in Thailand, Sri Lanka, Malaysia and Indonesia; it has the size and shape of a small pear, a rosy red, waxy skin, a crisp or mealy flesh and a flavor reminiscent of an apple.

rose geranium A plant (*Pelagonium graveolens*) whose flowers and fragrant leaves are used as a flavoring in tisanes and some baked goods.

rose hip The berrylike portion of the rose (genus *Rosa*) that contains its seeds; it has a red-orange color and a tart flavor; usually available dried and ground and used for syrups, tisanes and preserves.

rosemary An herb (*Rosmarinus officinalis*) with silver-green, needle-shaped leaves, a strong flavor reminiscent of lemon and pine and a strong, sharp, camphorlike aroma; available fresh and dried.

rosemary

rose paprika A piquant and very pungent Hungarian paprika with a medium-fine texture.

rosetta (roh-ZEH-tah) A very crisp hollow roll resembling a rose; a Venetian specialty.

rosette (roh-ZEHT) 1. A flowerlike design made with icing, whipped cream or the like using a piping bag fitted with a star-shaped tip. 2. A deep-fried pastry made by dipping a rosette iron into a thin, rich batter, then into hot fat; when crisp and brown, the rosette is removed from the fat and dusted with confectioners' sugar or cinnamon sugar. 3. A French sausage made from pork; its casing, which is thick and fat, helps keep the meat moist; smoked and eaten raw.

rosette iron A long, L-shaped metal rod with a heatproof handle at one end and various interchangeble decorative metal forms attached to the other end; used for making rosettes.

rosewater An intensely perfumed flavoring distilled from rose petals; widely used in Asian and Middle Eastern pastries and confections.

Rossini, à la (roh-SEE-nee, ah lah) A French garnish for meat named for the Italian operatic composer Gioacchino Rossini; it consists of a fried steak placed on a crouton and topped with a slice of foie gras, truffles and a Madeira sauce made with pan drippings and demi-glaze.

rösti; roesti (RAW-stee; ROOSH-tee) A large cake made from sliced or shredded potatoes fried until golden brown.

rotary egg beater A tool with two flat-bladed beaters connected to a gear-driven wheel with a hand crank located near the handle; used to whip cream, eggs and the like.

rotary grater The food is held in a hopper above a grating cylinder that is rotated by turning a handle.

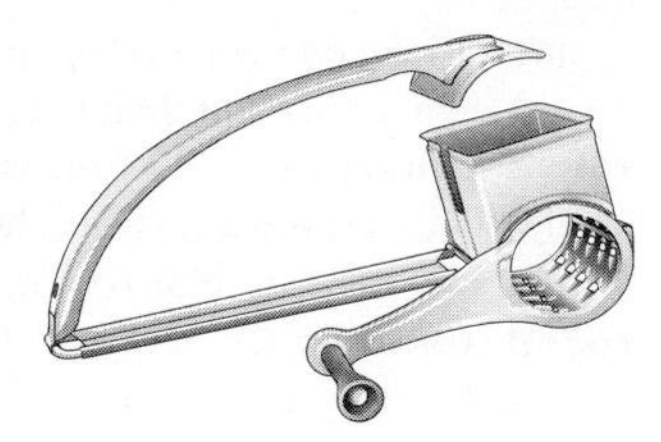
rotary grater

rôti (roe-TEE) French for to roast and used to describe a dish of roasted meat and the course during which it is served.

roti (RO-tee) 1. A Caribbean stew flavored with curry powder, jira and Scotch bonnet pepper. 2. Hindi for the collective name for breads, including chapati (an unleavened whole wheat griddle-baked bread), naan (a yeast-leavened baked flatbread cooked against the walls of the tandoor), paratha (a flaky, unleavened whole wheat flatbread), puri (or poori, a deep-fried whole wheat bread) and kulcha (an oval yeast-leavened tandoor-baked or deep-fried white bread often containing onions).

rotisserie (row-TIS-ahr-ee) 1. Cooking equipment that slowly rotates food (usually meat or poultry) in front of or above a heat source. 2. A restaurant or shop that specializes in roasted meats. 3. The area in a large restaurant kitchen where roasting is done.

rotisseur (roh-tess-uhr) At a food services operation following the brigade system, the person responsible for all roasted items and jus or related sauces; also known as the roast station chef.

rouelle (roo-ell) A French cut of the veal carcass; it is the thick part of the leg between the rump and knuckle and includes the cuisseau or noix.

rouennaise, sauce (roo-an-NEZ) A French compound sauce made from a bordelaise flavored with cayenne, lemon juice and puréed duck livers; usually served with duck.

rouille (roo-EE; roo-YUH) A rust-colored spicy French paste made from hot chiles, garlic, fresh bread crumbs, olive oil and stock; it is served as a sauce or garnish with fish stews.

roulade (roo-lahd) 1. A slice of meat, poultry or fish rolled around a stuffing. 2. A filled and rolled sponge cake. 3. *See* paupiette.

round 1. A primal section of the beef carcass; it is the animal's hind leg and contains the round, aitch, shank and tail bones; it produces fairly tender and flavorful subprimal and fabricated cuts such as the top round, eye round, bottom round, knuckle and shank. 2. A wine-tasting term for a wine that is well balanced and complete without a major defect, but not necessarily a fine wine.

round fish A general category of fish characterized by round, oval or compressed bodies with eyes on either side of their heads; they swim in a vertical position and are found in freshwater and saltwater regions worldwide (e.g., catfish, cod and salmon). *See* flatfish *and* whole fish.

rounding The process of shaping yeast dough into smooth, round balls to stretch the outside layer of gluten into a smooth coating. *See* bread-making process.

round steak A fabricated cut of the beef primal round; it is a steak cut from the top, bottom and/or eye section and is available with or without the bone.

roux (roo) A cooked mixture of equal parts flour and fat, by weight, used as a thickener for sauces, soups and other dishes; cooking the flour in fat coats the starch granules with the fat and prevents them from forming lumps when introduced into a liquid.

rowanberry The small berry of the mountain ash tree or rowan tree (*Sorbus aucuparia*); it has a bright red skin, grows in clusters and has a sour, astringent flavor; used to make syrups, preserves and liqueurs.

Royal Ann cherry A heart-shaped sweet cherry with a golden-pink skin and flesh and a sweet flavor; it is eaten fresh, canned or used to make maraschino cherries; also known as Napoleon cherry.

royale (rwah-yal) A custard cooked in a dariole mold, cut into shapes and used as garnish for clear soups in French cuisine.

royal glaze; glacé royale A French compound sauce made from béchamel, hollandaise and unsweetened whipped cream folded together, spread over various dishes and then glazed under the broiler.

royal icing A decorative icing made with confectioners' sugar, egg whites and lemon juice; pure white and very hard when dry; it is used for fine-line piping and making durable decorations such as flowers.

rubbed A coarsely ground dried herb.

rubs Dry seasonings massaged into meat before it is cooked.

rue (roo) An herb (*Ruta graveolens*) that grows to a small shrub; it has blue-green serrated leaves and greenish-yellow flowers; its extremely bitter leaves are used medicinally and in salads.

rugalach (RUHG-uh-luhkh) Bite-size crescent-shaped Jewish cookies made with a cream cheese dough rolled around various fillings, such as nuts, chocolate, poppy seed paste or fruit jam; also known as kipfel.

rughetta (rou-get-tah) A plant grown in Italy; it is a salad green similar to lamb's lettuce and has a slightly peppery flavor.

rum A spirit distilled from fermented sugarcane juice, sugarcane molasses, sugarcane syrup or other sugarcane by-products; generally made in the Caribbean, it is aged in wooden barrels; its color can range from clear to gold to amber (dark) and its flavor from delicate to heavy.

rumaki (ruh-MAH-kee) 1. A hot hors d'oeuvre consisting of a slice of water chestnut and piece of chicken liver skewered and wrapped in bacon, marinated in soy sauce, ginger and garlic and grilled or broiled. 2. An imprecisely used name for any hors d'oeuvre consisting of a crunchy item (e.g., almond) on a skewer surrounded by a softer, chewier one (e.g., date) and served hot or cold.

rum balls A confection made with a mixture of cake or cookie crumbs, rum and ground nuts shaped into small balls and rolled in melted chocolate or chocolate jimmies.

rumbledethumps A Scottish dish made from boiled potatoes and cabbage mashed with pepper and sometimes onions.

ruminant Any hoofed, cud-chewing quadruped mammal such as cattle, bison and deer; their multiple stomachs can digest cellulose.

rump roast A subprimal cut of the beef primal round; it is the round's upper part, next to the primal sirloin, and is a lean, boned, rolled roast. *See* culotte de boeuf.

rum tum tiddy A New England dish of tomato soup, Cheddar cheese and egg, flavored with dry mustard and served on buttered toast.

runcible (ruhn-see-bl) A utensil that is curved like a spoon and has three broad prongs, one of which has a sharp edge; used for pickles and other condiments.

runner bean A fresh bean with a long green pod containing medium-sized, red-streaked beige-colored seeds, available fresh, dried and canned; also known as scarlet runner bean and stick bean.

rusk A slice of a slightly sweet yeast bread baked until dry, crisp and golden brown; also known as Zwieback.

russe, à la (roose, ah lah) A French preparation of shellfish coated in aspic, covered with chaud-froid or thick mayonnaise and served with a Russian salad.

Russe, sauce (roose) A French compound sauce made from a velouté flavored with tarragon vinegar, finished with sour cream and garnished with grated horseradish.

russet apples Any of a variety of apples ranging in size from tiny to very large and with a crisp flesh, a flavor reminiscent of pears and a rough golden brown skin, often red spotted or with a faint red blush.

russet potato A long, flattened ovoid potato with a rough, thick brown skin, a mealy white flesh, numerous large eyes, a low moisture content and a high starch content; principally used for baking and frying.

Russian dressing A salad dressing made from mayonnaise, chile sauce, pimiento, green peppers and chives.

Russian salad A French salad of a macédoine of vegetables bound with mayonnaise and garnished with capers, beets and hard-boiled eggs.

Russian service A style of service in which a waiter serves the entrée, vegetables and starches from a platter onto the diner's plate.

Russian tea 1. A black tea from the Republic of Georgia in the former Soviet Union; the beverage has a full-bodied flavor and should be served strong with lemon rather than milk or cream; traditionally served in a glass with a separate holder and consumed with a sugar cube held in the teeth. 2. A hot spiced tea punch made with lemon and orange rinds and lemon, orange and pineapple juices.

rutabaga (roo-tuh-BAY-guh) A member of the cabbage family (*Brassica napobrassica*); the medium-sized, somewhat spherical root has a thin, pale yellow skin, sometimes with a purple blush, a firm, pale yellow flesh and a slightly sweet flavor; also known as a swede or Swedish turnip.

rye A cereal grass (*Secale cereale*) similar to wheat; its seed is milled into flour or used to make whiskey in the United States, Holland gin in the Netherlands and kvass in Russia.

rye flour A flour milled from rye seeds; it has a dark color and low gluten-forming potential; it is often combined with wheat flour for baking.

saag (sahng) Hindi for leafy greens (e.g., spinach, mustard, collard, beet and escarole); they are usually cooked.

sabayon (sah-by-on) A foamy, stirred French custard sauce made by whisking eggs, sugar and wine over low heat; known in Italian as zabaglione.

sablée (SAH-blay) A French cookie with a delicate, crumbly texture, often flavored with citrus zest or almonds.

sablefish A fish found in the northern Pacific Ocean; it has a compressed body with a slate black to green skin on top that lightens at the belly, a soft, white flesh, a mild flavor and an average market weight of 8 lb. (3.6 kg); it is often smoked; also known as Alaska cod and black cod, even though it is not a true cod.

sabler (sahb-lay) French for to break up and used to describe the dough preparation technique in which butter and flour are worked together with the fingertips to break the mixture into little beads or chunks.

saccharides The scientific name for sugars.

saccharin 1. Discovered in the late 1800s, it is a nonnutritive (1/8 calorie per teaspoon) artificial sweetener about 300 to 500 times as sweet as sugar; it may leave a bitter aftertaste, especially if heated. 2. A food additive used as a sweetener, especially in processed foods such as beverages and candies; sometimes used as a salt form (e.g., ammonium saccharin, calcium saccharin or sodium saccharin); some believe saccharin may be carcinogenic.

Sachertorte; Sacher torte (ZAH-kuhr-tohrt) A Viennese pastry composed of three layers of a very dense, rich chocolate cake filled with apricot jam and coated with a poured chocolate glaze.

sachet; sachet d'épices (sah-say; sah-say day-pea-sah) A French seasoning blend of aromatic ingredients tied in a cheesecloth bag and used to flavor stocks, sauces, soups and stews; a standard sachet consists of parsley stems, cracked peppercorns, dried thyme, cloves and sometimes garlic. *See* bouquet garni *and* nouet.

sad cake An American Southern dessert made with raisins, coconut and pecans; it sinks in the middle after baking, giving it a sad appearance.

saddle 1. A cut of the lamb, mutton and venison carcasses; it is the unseparated loin (from rib to leg) from both sides of the animal. 2. A cut of the hare or rabbit carcass; it is the main body cavity without the hind legs and forelegs.

saddleback pan A trough-shaped cake pan with deep, curved crosswise ridges; the shape is intended to be a trompe l'oeil representation of a saddle of venison and is used in preparing the Austrian pastry known as Rehrücken; also used for quick breads and cakes; also known as a deerback pan and a rehrücken mold. *See* Rehrücken.

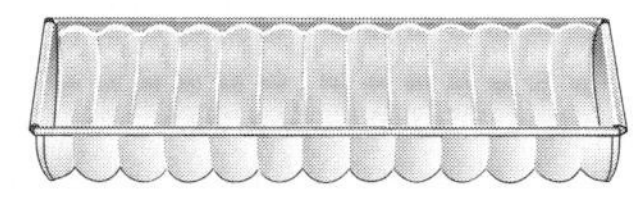

saddleback pan

safflower A plant (*Carthamus tinctorius*) with a flower that looks like a saffron crocus; its flavorless threads have a deep burnt orange color and are used as a food coloring; also known as bastard saffron, false saffron, haspir, Mexican saffron and saffron thistle.

safflower oil A viscous oil obtained from the seeds of the safflower; higher in polyunsaturated fats than any other oil; it has a strong flavor, a rich yellow color and a high smoke point and does not solidify when chilled.

saffron (SAF-ruhn) A spice that is the dried yellow-orange stigma of a crocus's purple flower (*Crocus sativus*); native to the Middle East, it has a slightly bitter, honeylike flavor and a strong, pungent aroma; used as a flavoring and yellow coloring agent.

saganaki (sah-gah-NAH-kee) A Greek appetizer of kasseri fried in butter or oil and sprinkled with lemon juice; it is sometimes soaked in brandy and flamed.

sage An herb (*Salvia officinalis*) native to the Mediterranean region; it has soft, slender, slightly furry, gray-green leaves and a pungent, slightly bitter, musty mint flavor; used for medicinal and culinary purposes; available fresh or dried and chopped, whole or rubbed.

sage

sago (SAY-goh) A starch extracted from the pith of the sago palm (genus *Cycas*) and various other tropical palms; it is processed into flour, meal and sago pearl and is used for baking, desserts and as a thickener.

saignant (sah-nyahng) French for bloody and used to describe meat, game and duck cooked very rare or underdone.

sake; saké (sah-KEE) A clear Japanese wine made from fermented rice and served hot or cold; because of its grain base, it is sometimes categorized as a beer; also known as rice wine.

salad A single food or a mix of different foods accompanied or bound by a dressing; it can be served as an appetizer, a second course after an appetizer, an entrée or a course following the entrée or dessert and can contain almost any food.

salad, composed A salad whose ingredients (greens, garnishes and dressing) are arranged carefully and artfully on the plate.

salad, tossed A salad whose ingredients (greens, garnishes and dressing) are placed in a bowl and tossed to combine.

salad bowl lettuce A general term for a variety of common lettuces used for green salads (e.g., iceberg and romaine).

salad burnet (BUR-niht) *See* burnet.

salad dressing A sauce for a salad; most are cold and are based on a vinaigrette, mayonnaise or other emulsified product.

salad fork A short, broad fork with four tines and used for salads and desserts; also known as a cake fork and dessert fork.

salad greens Any of a variety of leafy green vegetables that are usually eaten raw.

salad oil 1. A highly refined blend of vegetable oils. 2. Any oil used as a cooking medium or ingredient. *See* cooking oil.

salad relish A relish of cabbage and green tomatoes that is flavored with brown sugar, mustard seeds, celery seeds, cloves and cinnamon and cooked in vinegar.

salad spinner A tool used to remove moisture from the surface of salad greens; the produce is held in a perforated bowl sitting inside a container; the inner container is spun, displacing the water through centrifugal forces and through the perforations into the outer container.

salamander 1. A small overhead broiler used primarily to finish or top-brown foods. 2. A tool with a heavy iron head attached to a metal shaft with a wooden handle; heated over a burner and held closely over a dish to brown the food.

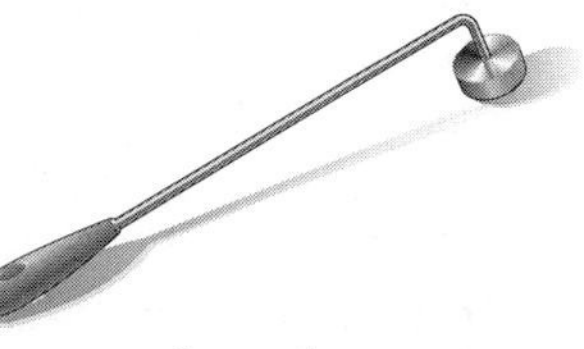

salamander

salamandre (sah-lah-mahndr) 1. French for salamander. 2. A French garnish of bread crumbs fried in butter until golden.

salami (suh-LAH-mee) 1. A style of Italian sausages made from pork and beef, highly seasoned with garlic and spices; rarely smoked, they are cured and air-dried and vary in size, shape and seasonings (e.g., Genoa and cotto). 2. Used in English as the singular; in Italian, the singular is *salame*.

Salisbury steak (SAWLZ-beh-ree) A beef patty seasoned with parsley, broiled or fried with onions and served with a gravy made from the pan drippings.

saliva The mildly alkaline secretion that begins the digestive process by moistening food, assisting mastication, lubricating the mouth and initiating the breakdown of starches.

Sally Lunn A rich, slightly sweet British yeast bread flavored with lemon and nutmeg and served for afternoon tea.

salmagundi; salmagundy (sal-mah-GON-de) A saladlike dish of chopped meat, hard-boiled eggs, anchovies, onions and vinegar; it is usually served over lettuce leaves.

salmon A large family of anadromous fish found in the northern Atlantic and Pacific Oceans; generally, they have a silver to gray skin, a pink-red flesh, a firm texture and a rich flavor; principal

salmon

varieties include the Atlantic salmon, chinook salmon and coho salmon.

Salmonella A genus of bacteria that cause food poisoning (called salmonellosis); the bacteria are commonly transmitted through poultry, eggs, milk, meats and fecal matter.

salpicon (sal-pee-kon) Diced foods bound together by a sauce, syrup or other liquid.

salsa (SAHL-sah) 1. Spanish for sauce. 2. Traditionally, a Mexican cold sauce made from tomatoes flavored with cilantro, chiles and onions. 3. Generally, a cold chunky mixture of fresh herbs, spices, fruits and/or vegetables used as a sauce or dip. 4. In Italian usage, a general term for pasta sauces.

salsify A long, thick root vegetable (*Tragopogon porrigolius*) with a white flesh, numerous offshoots and a delicate flavor reminiscent of oysters; also known as an oyster plant and vegetable oyster.

salt 1. A substance resulting from the chemical interaction of an acid and a base, usually sodium and chloride. 2. A white granular substance (sodium chloride) used to season foods.

salt beef A British dish consisting of salted, spiced beef similar to corned beef.

saltcellar A bowl filled with salt; the bowl, which can be metal, glass, ceramic or wood and range from the simple to the very elaborate, is set on the table and diners take a pinch of salt with their fingers or use a salt spoon; sometimes a second cellar filled with ground black pepper is set beside it.

salt cod Cod that is salted and dried.

salt curing The process of surrounding a food with salt or a mixture of salt, sugar, nitrite-based curing salt, herbs and spices; salt curing dehydrates the food, inhibits bacterial growth and adds flavor.

salted plums Dried, heavily salted Chinese plums with a sweet–sour flavor; served as a confection, appetite stimulant or breath freshener.

saltfish Salted, dried fish, usually cod, used in Caribbean cuisine.

saltimbocca (salt-eem-BOHK-ka) An Italian dish of veal scallops sautéed in butter, topped with thin slices of prosciutto and braised in white wine.

saltine A thin, crisp cracker sprinkled with coarse salt.

saltpeter A common name for potassium nitrate, which is used to preserve food.

salt pork Very fatty pork, usually from the hog's sides and belly, cured in salt and used principally as a cooking fat or flavoring; also known as corned belly bacon and white bacon. *See* fatback.

salt-rising bread A bread leavened with a fermented mixture of flour, cornmeal, water and salt instead of yeast.

saltspoonful A traditional measure of volume; it is approximately 1/4 teaspoon.

saltwater taffy A taffy made with a small amount of saltwater; popular in Atlantic City, New Jersey, during the late 1800s.

salumi (sah-LOO-mee) The general Italian term for cured meats such as salami, prosciutto, coppa and other pork products; they are typically eaten cold and sliced.

Salzburger nockerl (zahlt-BOOR-gehr nokh-rehl) An Austrian dessert consisting of a sweet, lemon soufflé traditionally baked in three mounds in an oblong dish.

sambals; sambols Any of several very spicy mixtures or relishes based on chiles; used in Indian and Southeast Asian cuisines as a flavoring and condiment.

sambar masala (sam-bar ma-saa-laa) A tart spice mixture used in southern India to season a thin vegetable curry that is the traditional accompaniment to dosa.

samosa (sah-MOH-sah) East Indian snacks consisting of triangular pastries filled with meat and/or vegetables and deep-fried; they are often served with a dipping sauce.

samovar (SAM-ah-vahr) A Russian metal urn with a spigot at the base and a central tube for holding charcoal or an alcohol lamp; water is kept heated in the space between the urn's outer surface and the inner metal tube; a small teapot fits on top of the metal tube, and the thick, strong tea brewed in it is diluted with the hot water held in the samovar; used to boil water for tea.

samp Broken or coarsely ground hominy.

sand cherry The small, sweet, purple-black berry of a small tree native to the Midwest.

sanddab *See* dab *and* plaice, American.

sandwich spreader A short, spatula-like tool with one dull and one serrated edge; the dull edge is used to scoop and spread, and the serrated edge is used to cut.

sandwich spreader

Sangria (sahn-GREE-ah) A Spanish punch usually made of red wine, lemon and orange slices, sugar and sometimes soda water.

sanitation 1. The design, implementation and application of practices that will establish conditions favorable to health, especially public health. 2. In the food safety context, the design, implementation and application of practices that will prevent food contamination and food-borne illnesses.

sanitize In a food safety context, to reduce pathogenic organisms on an object or in an environment to a safe level. *See* clean *and* sterilize.

sanitizing solutions Chemical solutions used to sanitize or sterilize food-contact surfaces; they are recognized as indirect food additives.

sansho (SAHN-sho) A Japanese fragrant pepper; the green berry of the prickly ash tree (genus *Zanthoxylum*), crushed to a fine powder to make an aromatic spice.

Santa Claus melon A member of the muskmelon family; it has a long ovoid shape, a splotchy green and yellow skin, a yellow-green flesh and a flavor similar to that of honeydew melon; also known as a Christmas melon, because its peak season is December.

Santa Fe grande A broad-shouldered, long chile with a pale yellow color (which turns orange-red when ripe), a thick flesh and a medium hot flavor with a slightly sweet, melonlike undertone.

santoku A Japanese-style knife with a sheep's foot blade; used for chopping vegetables.

santoku

sap The watery fluid of a plant.

sapodilla A small spherical fruit (*Manilkara zapota*) native to Central America; it has a yellow skin covered by brown fuzz, flat, black seeds and a yellow-brown juicy flesh with a flavor reminiscent of brown sugar; also known as chikkus and naseberry.

sapote (sah-PO-tay) A medium- to large-sized ovoid tropical fruit (*Pouteria sapota*) native to the Caribbean; it has a rough, russet-colored skin, a salmon-colored flesh and a sweet flavor; used for preserves.

Sarah Bernhardt An individual-sized British pastry consisting of an almond macaroon topped with a cone of rich chocolate ganache, then coated with dark chocolate glaze; named for the popular 19th-century actress.

sar bo (sar bo) A Chinese cooking pot made from light, sandy, porous clay usually unglazed on the outside and sometimes glazed on the inside; also known as a sand pot.

sarde, à la (sard, ah lah) A French garnish for meats, especially steak, consisting of grilled or fried tomatoes, stuffed cucumber or zucchini and croquettes of saffron-flavored rice.

sardine 1. A generic name for any of several small, soft-boned, saltwater fish, such as the pilchard, sprat, herring and alewife; generally not available fresh outside the area in which they are caught and usually available smoked, salted, pickled, cured in brine or packed in tomato sauce, mustard sauce or oil. 2. A young herring.

sarsaparilla 1. The dried roots of a number of American woody vines (genus *Smilax*) of the lily family; formerly used for medicinal purposes. 2. A sweetened, carbonated beverage similar to root beer made from an extract of these roots; today, sarsaparilla products generally use artificial flavorings.

sarta (sahr-tah) A horseshoe shape used for raw or cooked Spanish sausages. *See* ristras and vela.

sarten (sahr-tan) A flat, heavy, two-handled Spanish pot used for cooking paella; sometimes the pot itself is known as a paella. *See* paella pan.

sashimi (sah-SHEE-mee) A Japanese dish of sliced raw fish served with condiments such as soy sauce, daikon, wasabi or ginger. *See* sushi.

sassafras An aromatic, native American tree (*Sassafras albidum*) belonging to the laurel family; the bark of the root is dried and used as a flavoring for root beer, and the leaves are pounded to make filé powder.

saté; satay (sah-TAY) A Southeast Asian dish consisting of small cubes or strips of meat, fish or poultry threaded on skewers and grilled or broiled; usually served with a spicy peanut sauce.

satsuma (saht-SOO-mah) A member of the mandarin orange family native to Japan; the fruit has a small, squat shape, an orange rind, a pale orange flesh and a sweet flavor; usually available in the United States as canned mandarin oranges.

saturated fat A triglyceride composed of saturated fatty acids and implicated in raising blood cholesterol levels; generally, it is solid at room temperature and comes from a few plants (e.g., coconut and palm) and most animals, except fish (e.g., butter, lard and suet).

sauce *v.* To add a sauce; to flavor or season a food with a sauce. *n.* 1. A thickened liquid or semiliquid preparation used to flavor and enhance other foods. *See* leading sauces *and* small sauces. 2. Slang for an alcoholic beverage (to hit the sauce).

saucepan A round metal cooking vessel with one long handle and

saucepan

straight or sloped sides; generally smaller and shallower than a pot, it is available in a range of sizes, from 1 pt. to 4 qt., and sometimes with a fitted lid.

saucepan, flare-sided A thick, heavy saucepan with flared sides and a long handle; it has a wide surface area and is used for rapid evaporation; also known as a Windsor saucepan.

saucepot A large saucepan with a lid and two handles; available in sizes from 4 to 14 qt.

sauce whisk An elongated whisk; its nine fairly rigid looped wires create a pear-shaped outline; also known as a piano-wire whisk.

sauce whisk

saucier (saw-see-yay) At a food services operation following the brigade system, the person responsible for all sautéed items and most sauces; also known as a sauté station chef.

saucisse (soh-CEESE) French for a small sausage.

saucisse de Toulouse (soh-CEESE duh too-loos) A fresh French sausage made from pork and used in cassoulet.

saucisson (soh-SEES-sohn) French for a large sausage.

saucisson de porc (soh-SEES-sohn duh por) A French salami-like sausage of finely diced fat and lean pork with a flour coating to prevent the fat from melting.

saucisson sec (soh-SEES-sohn seck) Any of several varieties of regional French dried, salami-like sausages.

Sauerbraten (SOW-er-brah-t'n) German for sour roast and used to describe a beef roast marinated in a sour–sweet marinade and then braised; it is usually served with dumplings, boiled potatoes or noodles.

sauerkraut (SOW-uhr-krowt) A German dish of shredded, salted, fermented green cabbage, sometimes flavored with juniper berries.

sausage A forcemeat stuffed into a casing; the principal ingredients, seasonings, shape, size, casing type, curing technique and degree of drying vary.

sausages, dried A style of sausages made from cured meats and air-dried; they may or may not be smoked or cooked; also known as hard sausages, summer sausages and seminary sausages.

sautéing (saw-tay-ing) A dry-heat cooking method that uses conduction to transfer heat from a hot pan to food with the aid of a small amount of hot fat; cooking is usually done quickly over high temperatures.

sauteuse (saw-toose) The basic sauté pan with sloping sides and a single long handle.

sauteuse

sautoir (saw-twahr) A sauté pan with straight sides and a single long handle (if very large, it may have a loop handle on the other side); used to fry foods quickly in a limited amount of fat.

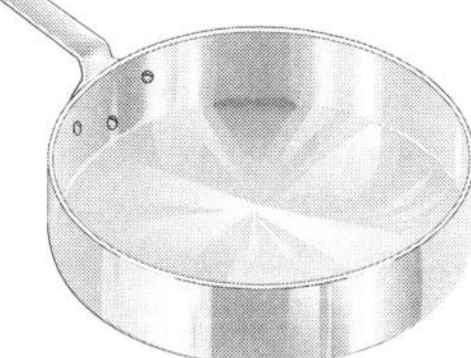
sautoir

savarin (SAV-uh-rahn) A rich French yeast cake baked in a ring mold, soaked with rum syrup and filled with pastry cream, crème Chantilly and fresh fruit. *See* baba.

savarin mold A plain, shallow ring mold, usually metal, used for baking savarins or for molding gelatins, aspics or Bavarians.

savory 1. A food that is not sweet. 2. An herb of the mint family.

savory, summer An herb (*Satureja hortensis*) with small, narrow, gray-green leaves and a similar but milder flavor than that of winter savory; available fresh and dried.

savory, winter An herb (*Satureja montana*) with small, narrow, gray-green leaves and a bitter, pungent flavor reminiscent of thyme and rosemary; available fresh and dried.

savoyarde, à la (sahv-wah-yahd, ah lah) 1. A French dish of gratin potatoes made with milk and cheese. 2. Any of a variety of egg dishes, including omelettes stuffed with potatoes and Gruyère.

savoy cabbage A member of the cabbage family with a spherical, relatively loose head of curly, wrinkled leaves in variegated shades of green and purple; it has a milder flavor than that of red or green cabbage.

savoyed A description for any leaf vegetable with bumpy, wavy, crinkly and/or wrinkly leaves.

scald To heat a liquid, usually milk, to just below the boiling point.

scale *v.* 1. To remove the scales from a fish, usually by scraping. 2. To measure ingredients by weight. *n.* One of the many small hard plates, either flat or with small, teethlike projections, that form the covering of a fish.

scales Equipment used to measure the weight of an object. *See* balance scale, beam balance scale, electronic scale, portion scale *and* spring scale.

scaling The act of measuring ingredients, especially those for a bread formula. *See* bread-making process.

scallions 1. The immature green stalks of a bulb onion. 2. A variety of onion with a small white bulb and long, straight, hollow green leaves. 3. A bulbless onion with these green stalks; also known as green onions, spring onions and bunch onions.

scallop *v.* 1. To cook a food (e.g., potatoes) by layering it with cream or a sauce and usually topping it with crumbs before baking. 2. To form a raised, decorative rim on a pie crust. *n.* A thin, boneless round or oval slice of meat or fish.

scallop roe The orange or red egg sacs next to the adductor muscle found in some scallops; the eggs have a crunchy texture and salty flavor.

scallops A family of bivalve mollusks found in saltwater regions worldwide; they have rounded, fan-shaped shells with small ears or wings at the hinge; the adductor muscle generally has an ivory or pinkish-beige color that becomes white when cooked, a tender texture and a sweet flavor; most scallops are shucked aboard ship; significant domestic varieties include the bay scallop, calico scallop, Pacific pink scallop and sea scallop.

scaloppina (skah-luh-PEE-nah) An Italian term for a thin scallop of meat, usually veal; often dredged in flour and sautéed.

scampi (SKAHM-pee) 1. Italian for a small lobster. *See* prawn. 2. An American dish of large shrimp cooked in butter, seasoned with lemon juice, garlic and white wine; also known as shrimp scampi.

scant A traditional measuring term for just barely (e.g., 1 scant teaspoon).

scent A tasting term for the pleasant odor or smell of a food (particularly fresh fruits, vegetables and cheeses) or beverage (e.g., wine, beer or distilled spirit).

Schaum torte; Schaumtorten (SHOWM tohrt) An Austrian dessert composed of baked meringue filled or topped with whipped cream and fresh fruit.

schmaltz Yiddish for rendered fat, usually chicken fat, used in Jewish cuisines as a cooking medium, ingredient and spread.

schnitz and knepp (shneetz and kae-nep) A Pennsylvania Dutch dish of dried apples simmered with ham; spoonfuls of batter are added to the cooking liquid to make dumplings.

Schnitzel (SHNIHT-suhl) German for cutlet and used to describe a thin slice of meat, typically veal, that is dipped in egg, breaded and fried.

scimitar (SIM-ah-tahr) *See* butcher knife.

scimitar

scone (skohn; scahn) 1. A traditional Scottish quick bread originally made with oats and cooked on a griddle. 2. A rich, delicate quick bread similar to a biscuit; it is sometimes studded with raisins or other dried or fresh fruit and is usually served with jam, butter or clotted cream.

score To make shallow cuts in meat or fish, usually in a diamond pattern; done for decorative purposes, to assist in absorbing flavors and to tenderize the product.

Scotch; Scotch whisky A whisky distilled in Scotland from a mash made from sprouted barley that has been dried over a peat fire (which gives the spirit its distinctive flavor); aged for at least 3 years in casks of American oak or used sherry casks.

Scotch bonnet chile A short, conical, fresh chile with a pale yellow-green, orange or red color and a very hot, smoky flavor with a fruity undertone.

Scotch broth A Scottish soup made with lamb or mutton, barley and various vegetables; also known as barley broth.

Scotch egg A British dish of a hard-cooked egg coated with sausage, dipped into beaten egg, rolled in bread crumbs and deep-fried; served halved, hot or cold.

Scoville heat units A subjective rating for measuring a chile's heat.

scramble To mix a food or foods until well blended.

scrape down To remove batter or dough from the sides of a mixing bowl with a spatula; the material gathered is typically added to the bulk of dough or batter in the bowl.

scrapple A Pennsylvania Dutch dish of boneless pork simmered with cornmeal flavored with sage, packed in a loaf pan and chilled, then sliced and fried in bacon fat; usually served at breakfast.

scripture cake A colonial American cake made with ingredients mentioned in certain verses of the Bible.

scrod A marketing term for Atlantic cod or haddock weighing less than 2.5 lb. (1.1 kg); it has a very mild flavor.

scullery 1. Traditionally, the part of a household in charge of the dishes and cooking utensils. 2. A room near the kitchen for cleaning and storing utensils, cleaning vegetables and similar work.

scum The froth that forms on the top of boiling liquids; it usually contains impurities and other undesirable items and is removed with a skimmer.

Scuppernong (SKUHO-pehr-nong) 1. A native American grape, cultivated in the southeastern United States. 2. A white wine made from this grape since colonial times; it is pungent, aromatic and sweet (sugar is usually added to assist fermentation).

sea anemone A flowerlike saltwater invertebrate of various bright colors; its tentacles are generally not consumed, but its somewhat chewy body cavity is sliced, battered and fried.

sea bream An imprecisely used term to describe various members of the perch family native to waters off Southeast Asia; they generally have a market weight of 1–2 lb. (450–900 g), a lean flesh, a coarse texture and a delicate flavor. *See* bream *and* porgy.

sea cucumber An invertebrate saltwater animal; it has an elongated cylindrical shape with a leathery, velvety or slimy body tube and a mouth surrounded by short tentacles; the body is generally boiled, sun-dried and then smoked and used in Japanese and Chinese cuisines as a flavoring; also known as a sea slug.

seafood 1. Shellfish. 2. Shellfish and other small, edible marine creatures. 3. Saltwater shellfish. 4. Saltwater shellfish and fish. 5. All shellfish and fish, saltwater and freshwater.

sear To brown a food quickly over high heat; usually done as a preparatory step for combination cooking methods.

sea salt Salt recovered through the evaporation of seawaters; it is available in fine and coarse crystals and is used for cooking and preserving.

sea scallop A variety of scallop found off the east coasts of the United States and Canada; it has a light brown shell and a tender, sweet meat with an average diameter of 1.5 in. (3.8 cm) and a pale beige to creamy-pink color; also known as the Atlantic deep sea scallop, giant scallop and smooth scallop.

season 1. Traditionally, to enhance a food's flavor by adding salt. 2. More commonly, to enhance a food's flavor by adding salt and/or ground pepper as well as herbs and other spices; other than adding salt and pepper, seasoning is usually done by the chef and not by the diner. 3. To mature and bring a food (usually beef or game) to a proper condition by aging or special preparation. 4. To prepare a pot, pan or other cooking surface to reduce or to prevent sticking.

seasoned salt A seasoning blend; its primary ingredient is salt, with flavorings such as celery, garlic or onion added.

seasoning; seasoner 1. Traditionally, an item added to enhance the natural flavors of a food without changing its flavor dramatically; salt is the most common seasoning. 2. More commonly, salt as well as all herbs and spices; other than salt and ground black pepper, seasonings are usually added to the dish by the chef. *See* condiment.

sea trout A fish of the drum family found along the U.S. East Coast; it has an iridescent dark olive skin with black, dark green or bronze spots, an average market weight of 0.5–3.5 lb. (0.25–1.6 kg) and a tender flesh with a mild flavor; also known as a gray sea trout, speckled trout, squeteagues, summer trout and weakfish.

sea urchin An invertebrate saltwater animal; its ovaries and gonads are used in Japanese cuisine.

seaweed A general name for a large group of primitive sea plants belonging to the algae family; seaweed can be flat, stringy or green bean shaped and dark green, brown or bluish and generally has a salty, earthy flavor; it is used as a flavoring, stabilizer and thickener.

sectioned and formed A meat product consisting of entire muscles or muscle systems that are closely trimmed, massaged and formed into the desired shape.

seize A culinary word applied to melted chocolate when it becomes a thick, lumpy mass; usually caused by steam or a minute amount of liquid.

select 1. A marketing term indicating that an item has certain qualities or attributes setting it apart from others; the term has no legal significance. 2. A midlevel U.S. Department of Agriculture (USDA) quality grade for beef; the meat lacks the flavor and marbling of the higher grades. 3. A marketing term for a 1 ¼- to 1 ¾ lb. (567 to 793 g) lobster.

self-rising flour An all-purpose white wheat flour to which salt and baking powder have been added.

seltzer; seltzer water 1. A mineral water from the town of Nieder Selters in Germany's Weisbaden region. 2. A flavorless water with induced carbonation consumed plain or used as a mixer for alcoholic drinks and soda fountain confections; also known as club soda and soda water.

semi à la carte menu A menu on which some foods (typically appetizers and desserts) and beverages are priced and ordered separately, while the entrée is accompanied by and priced to include other items, such as a salad, starch or vegetable.

semifreddo (seh-mee-FRAYD-doh) A chilled dessert made with frozen mousse, custard or cream into which large amounts of whipped cream or meringue are folded to incorporate air; layers of sponge cake and/or fruit may be added for flavor and texture (e.g., frozen soufflées, marquis, mousses and neapolitans); also known as a still-frozen dessert.

semisweet chocolate A type of chocolate containing moderate amounts of sugar and from 15 to 35% chocolate liquor; usually sold in bars or chips and eaten as a candy or used for baking. *See* chocolate-making process.

semmel (ZEH-merl) A Pennsylvania Dutch yeast roll, usually served for breakfast.

semolina (seh-muh-LEE-nuh) A grainy, pale yellow flour coarsely ground from wheat (usually durum or other hard wheats) with a high protein content and gluten-forming potential; used principally for pasta dough.

Senate bean soup A soup served in the U.S. Senate dining room; made from white beans cooked with smoked ham hocks, mashed potatoes, onions and garlic.

Sencha (SEHN-cha) A Japanese green tea; the beverage has a yellow color and vegetal flavor and is often consumed with meals.

serrano (seh-RRAH-noh) A short, tapered fresh chile with a green or orange-red color, a thick flesh and a very hot flavor.

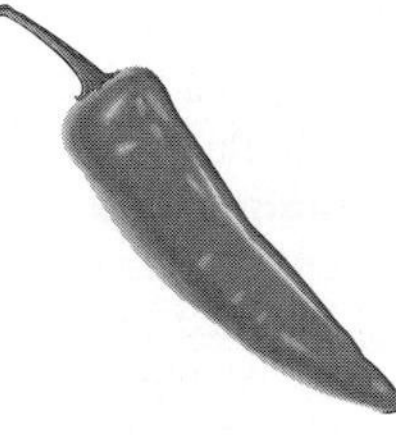

serrano pepper

serrated edge The cutting edge of a knife; generally used for slicing items with a hard exterior and a soft interior (e.g., crusty bread or tomato); the blade has a series of tiny, sharp V-shaped teeth that saw the food.

service 1. The act or style of providing beverages and/or food to customers as requested. 2. A place setting. 3. A set of dishes, serviceware and/or utensils used for serving and consuming a particular food or course (e.g., tea service).

serviceware The china, flatware, glassware, trays, tools and other items used to serve food.

serving size A Nutrition Facts term approved by the U.S. Food and Drug Administration (FDA) to identify the FDA-defined serving size for a food; reflecting the amount that people generally consume, it is intended to make it easier for consumers to compare the nutritional contents of different brands.

sesame balls A Chinese dessert or pastry made with a dough of glutinous rice powder and water, shaped into a ball, filled with sweet bean paste, rolled in sesame seeds and deep-fried.

sesame oil; sesame seed oil An oil obtained from sesame seeds; it has a light brown color and a rich, nutty flavor and is used for dressings and cooking. *See* oriental sesame oil.

sesame paste A thick, somewhat dry paste made from toasted white sesame seeds and used as a flavoring in many Southeast Asian cuisines.

sesame seeds The tiny, flat seeds of a plant (*Sesamum indicum*) native to India; they have a nutty, slightly sweet flavor and are available with a red, brown, black or grayish-ivory color; also known as benne seeds.

set 1. To allow a mixture to thicken or congeal, usually by chilling (e.g., gelatin). 2. To place on a table the napery, flatware, glassware and dinnerware necessary for dining.

seven-minute frosting A fluffy meringue frosting made by beating egg whites, sugar and corn syrup together in a double boiler until stiff peaks form; also known as seafoam frosting and foam frosting.

seven-spice powder A spice blend generally consisting of ground anise pepper, sesame seeds, flax seeds, rapeseeds, poppy seeds, nori and dried tangerine (or orange) peel; used in Japanese cuisine.

seviche; ceviche; cebiche (seh-VEE-chee; seh-VEESH) A Latin American dish of raw fish marinated in citrus juice, onions, tomatoes and chiles and sometimes flavored with cilantro.

Seville orange An orange (*Citrus aurantium*) grown principally in Spain with a thick, rough orange skin, a bitter, tart flesh and many seeds; used for marmalades and flavoring liqueurs; also known as bitter orange and sour orange.

sevruga (sehv-ROO-guh) Caviar harvested from a small species of sturgeon; the tiny eggs are a light to dark gray color and tend to clump together.

sfoglia (sfo-glee-ah) Italian for a thin, flat sheet of pasta dough that can be cut into ribbons, circles, squares or other shapes.

shabu-shabu (SHAH-boo-SHAH-boo) A Japanese dish consisting of raw meat and vegetables cooked in a pot of hot broth by each diner and served with various sauces; noodles are added to the broth and served as soup.

shad roe The roe of the American shad; the eggs are large and bright red.

shaggy mane mushroom A small wild mushroom (*Coprinus comatus*) with a thin-edged cap; it has a crunchy, firm texture and a delicate flavor.

shallot (SHAL-uht; shuh-LOT) A member of the onion family (*Allium ascalonicum*) native to the Middle East and formed like garlic, with a head composed of several cloves covered in a thin papery skin; the outer covering can be pale brown, bronze, pale gray or rose; it has a pink-tinged ivory-colored flesh and a flavor that is more subtle than that of onion and less harsh than that of garlic.

shallow poaching A moist-heat cooking method that combines poaching and steaming; the food (usually fish) is placed on a vegetable bed and partially covered with a liquid (cuisson) and simmered.

shandy; shandygaff A British drink made of beer and lemonade or ginger beer; also known as Alsterwasser and Panaché.

shank 1. The lower portion (below the knee) of a quadruped's limb. *See* foreshank *and* hindshank. 2. A subprimal cut of the beef primal round; it has a large amount of connective tissue and flavorful meat; also known as the hindshank.

shao-mai (shah-mae) Canton Chinese steamed pork dumplings consisting of won ton wrappers filled with ground pork, celery and bamboo shoots and flavored with rice wine and soy sauce.

sharbat A thick, sweet beverage from India flavored with fruit juice or flower petals and sometimes eaten with a spoon.

shark Any of a variety of marine invertebrates found in tropical to temperate saltwater areas worldwide; they generally have a lean red- or pink-tinged white flesh that becomes off-white when cooked, a firm texture and a mild flavor; usually available as wheels, loins or smaller cuts; varieties with culinary significance include the mako (which is often sold as swordfish), sand shark (also known as the dogfish), dusky shark, sharpnose shark, bonnethead shark, blacktip shark, angel shark and thresher shark.

shark's fin The fins and cartilaginous segments of the tail of the dogfish; believed by some to be an aphrodisiac, it provides a protein-rich gelatin used in Chinese cuisine, especially shark's fin soup.

sharpening stone *See* whetstone.

shawarma (shaw-whar-mah) A Middle Eastern cooking method for lamb or chicken; a large amount of thinly sliced lamb or chicken (usually flavored with baharat, garlic, vinegar and herbs) is placed on a vertical skewer that rotates before a flame running along a vertical shaft; bits of meat are sliced vertically from the mass and served on flatbread and garnished with yogurt, cucumbers, tomatoes and the like.

shea A tropical tree (*Butyrospermum parkii*) native to Africa; its fruit contains oily seeds that are crushed to form a butterlike fat called shea butter, which is used for cooking in several African countries.

she-crab soup An American Southern soup made with fresh crabmeat and roe, flavored with sherry.

sheepshead 1. A saltwater fish found in the Gulf of Mexico and the Atlantic Ocean off the southeast U.S. coast; it has several dark vertical stripes on the side, an average market weight of 0.75–8 lb. (0.34–3.6 kg) and a tender white flesh with a flaky texture and a mild flavor. 2. A freshwater fish found in the Great Lakes and midwestern rivers; it has a silvery skin, an average market weight of 0.25–5 lb. (0.11–2.3 kg) and a lean white flesh; also known as a gasperou, gray bass, freshwater drum and white perch.

sheeter A machine used in professional kitchens for rolling out large pieces of dough, especially puff pastry and Danish pastry doughs.

sheet pan extender A 2- to 4-in.-high semiflexible rectangular frame that is placed inside a sheet pan to extend the height of the pan's sides; it is used for baking cake batter and assembling and molding multilayer pastries.

shelf life The period that a product such as a processed food or medicine remains suitable or useful for consumption.

shelf stable Pertaining to a product that can be stored at room temperature for an extended period; used especially with regard to canned goods.

shell *v.* To remove the edible part of a food from its natural container (e.g., clam meat from its shell, a pea from its pod or a corn kernel from its ear). *n.* 1. A glass shaped like a tall, tapered, plain cylinder; it is used for beer or cocktails. 2. The hard outer covering of a mollusk, crustacean, tortoise, egg, nut or the like. 3. The lower pastry crust of a pie, tart or the like, usually baked before the filling is added. 4. A small, delicate pastry or chocolate container used to hold a sweet preparation; it can be shaped like a shell or other object. 5. A pasta shaped like an open clamshell.

shell beans Any of various beans cultivated for their edible seeds rather than their pods.

shellfish Any of many species of aquatic invertebrates with shells or carapaces found in saltwater and freshwater regions worldwide; most are edible; shellfish are categorized as crustaceans and mollusks. *See* crustacean, mollusks *and* fish.

shellfish quality grades U.S. Department of Commerce (USDC) grades for common shellfish packed under federal inspection; each species has its own grading criteria; grade A products are top quality with good flavor and odor and practically free of blemishes, grade B products are good quality and grade C products are fairly good quality and usually canned or processed.

shell steak A fabricated cut of the beef primal short loin; it is a club steak without the tail ends.

shepherd's pie An old English dish of ground meat, usually lamb or mutton, and sometimes vegetables such as corn or peas, bound with a gravy, topped with mashed potatoes and baked.

sherbet A frozen dessert made with fruit juice, sugar and water; it can also contain milk, cream and egg whites. *See* sorbet.

sherry A fortified wine made principally from the Palomino grape in a delimited district in southern Spain centering around the city of Jerez de la Frontera; a sherry can range from pale gold and bone dry to dark brown and very sweet; its distinctive flavor and aroma are partly the result of a flor forming during the solera.

sherry vinegar A nutty brown–colored vinegar with a full, round flavor made from sherry and aged in wooden barrels in a process similar to that used to make sherry.

shiitake (shee-TAH-kay) A mushroom (*Lentinus edodes*) native to Japan and now cultivated in the United States; it has a tough stem that is usually not eaten and a dark brown cap that has a velvety texture and a meaty, smoky flavor; available fresh and dried; also known as black forest mushroom, flower mushroom, winter mushroom, doubloon and golden oak.

shin of beef A British cut of the beef carcass; it is the foreshank.

Shirley Temple A child's mocktail made of lemon–lime soda and grenadine syrup; garnished with a maraschino cherry.

shiro miso (SHEE-roh MEE-soh) A white or light-colored Japanese bean paste.

shirred eggs Eggs covered with milk or cream and sometimes bread crumbs and baked in a small dish until the whites are firm.

shish kebab (SHIHSH kuh-bob) 1. A Mediterranean dish of marinated meats (usually lamb or beef) and vegetables threaded on a skewer and grilled or broiled; also known as shashlik. 2. A term used imprecisely to describe a grilled or broiled skewer of meats, poultry, shellfish, firm fish, vegetables and/or fruits; the foods are often marinated.

shmear A Yiddish word used in delicatessens to describe a dab of something, usually a condiment such as cream cheese, to be spread on a bagel or bread.

shoestring potatoes Very slender French fries.

shoofly pie A Pennsylvania German dessert consisting of a flaky pastry shell filled with a spicy molasses and brown sugar custard.

shortbread A rich, crumbly British butter cookie; the dough is traditionally formed into a circle and cut into pie-shaped wedges called petticoat tails. *See* highlanders.

shortcake A dessert made with a sweet biscuit split in half and filled with fresh fruit, especially strawberries, and whipped cream; angel food cake or sponge cake is sometimes used instead of a biscuit.

short crust; short pastry A dough made with a high fat content, such as a pie crust.

shortening 1. A white, flavorless, solid fat formulated for baking or deep-frying. 2. Any fat used in baking to tenderize the product by shortening gluten strands.

short loin A primal section of the beef carcass; the front portion of the beef loin, just behind the rib; it contains one rib and a portion of the backbone, the very tender loin eye muscle (a continuation from the rib eye muscle) and the short tenderloin and produces fabricated cuts such as club steaks, T-bone steaks and porterhouse steaks. *See* tenderloin.

short-order cook At a food services operation, the person responsible for preparing foods quickly; he or she works the grill, griddles and deep-fryer and makes sandwiches and some sautéed items.

short-order section One of the principal work sections of a food services facility; it typically contains a griddle station, fry station and broiler station.

short plate A primal section of the beef carcass; it is under the primal rib and contains a large amount of connective tissue; includes such meaty subprimal or fabricated cuts as short ribs and skirt steak.

short ribs 1. A fabricated cut of the beef primal short plate consisting of not more than five ribs (numbers 6–10); it is meaty and has a high percentage of connective tissue; also known as plate short ribs and beef ribs. 2. A fabricated cut of the beef primal chuck; they are rectangular chunks of meat, typically 2–3 in. (5.08–7.6 cm) long, with layers of fat, meat, bone and connective tissue.

short tenderloin The smaller portion of the tenderloin found in the beef primal short loin; it is used to fabricate filet mignon, tournedos and tenderloin tips. *See* butt tenderloin.

shoulder 1. A primal section of the veal carcass; it consists of the animal's shoulder and contains the often tough muscles along a portion of the backbone, four rib bones and the bladebone and arm bones and a large amount of connective tissue; its meat is usually ground, cubed or fabricated into shoulder chops and steaks. 2. A primal section of the lamb carcass; it consists of the animal's shoulder, four ribs and many small, tough muscles; it is usually diced, ground or fabricated into chops or boned for roasts. 3. A subprimal cut of the beef primal chuck; somewhat tough but flavorful, it is often fabricated into steaks and roasts. 4. A primal section of the pork carcass; it consists of the hog's lower foreleg and contains the arm and shank bones; relatively tough, lean and flavorful, it is often fabricated into steaks or diced. 5. *See* bolster.

shraab (sah-ruhb) A Middle Eastern beverage of reduced, sweetened fruit juices.

shraak (shrah-hack) A thin, crispy unleavened Middle Eastern bread; it is typically used for layering foods or torn into shreds and used for eating chicken or lamb dishes.

shred To shave, grate, cut or otherwise reduce a food to relatively long, narrow pieces.

Shrewsbury cake A flat, round, crisp sugar cookie flavored with cinnamon, nutmeg or cardamom and caraway seeds.

shrimp Any of several varieties of crustaceans found worldwide, particularly in the Atlantic and Pacific Oceans and Gulf of Mexico; generally, they have 10 legs, a shell that can be light brown, pink, red, grayish-white, yellow, gray-green or dark green, a lean, white flesh and a rich, sweet flavor; usually sold according to count (number per pound) and categorized as colossal (10 or less per pound) jumbo (11–15), extra large (16–20), large (21–30), medium (31–35), small (36–45), miniature (about 100) and titi (about 400); significant varieties, which are generally distinguished by shell color, include brown, pink, white, Caribbean white, sea bob and royal red shrimps. *See* prawn *and* rock shrimp.

shrimp, dried Small, pinkish-orange, dried shrimp, usually rehydrated before being used as a flavoring in many Asian and Latin American dishes.

shrimp and grits An American Southeastern dish of shrimp sautéed with onions and green pepper, simmered in chicken or shrimp broth and served over grits; usually served at breakfast.

shrimp chips Dried wafers of shrimp and tapioca; deep-fried and eaten as snacks in China and Southeast Asia; also known as prawn crackers.

shrimps de Jonghe An American dish of shrimps flavored with garlic, sherry, parsley, cayenne and paprika, topped with buttered bread crumbs and baked.

shrimp deveiner A tool with a handle and a curved blade with a serrated tip; the tool follows the arc of the shrimp's shell; as it is pushed from the head to the tail, the ridged edge removes the intestinal vein while the upper edge cuts the shell.

shrinkage 1. Loss of weight or volume during storage or preparation of a food; it is usually caused by a loss of moisture. 2. Loss of merchandise or supplies because of theft.

shrink wrap *v.* To use a plastic, self-adhering wrapping material to cover a food; the wrap conforms to the shape of the food or its container and helps prevent contamination and moisture loss. *n.* The self-adhering wrapping.

shuck *v.* To remove the edible part of a food (e.g., clam meat, a pea or ear of corn) from its shell, pod or husk. *n.* A shell, pod or husk.

shutome A broadbill swordfish found off Hawaii; it has a pinkish flesh, a high fat content and a mild flavor and weighs 10–600 lb. (4.5–27.5 kg).

Siamese gourd A variety of squash with a striped, white-spotted green skin and a stringy, cinnamon-flavored flesh; often used to make jam; also known as angel's hair squash.

sicilienne, sauce (see-see-l'yehn) A French compound sauce made from a demi-glaze flavored with game glaze or game stock, finished with Marsala and garnished with fried onion rings.

sideboard A serving table in a dining room, sometimes with a marble top and often having one or two narrow drawers in the apron.

side dish The name given to a dish such as a starch or vegetable that accompanies the main dish or entrée; usually served in a separate dish.

side masking The technique of coating only the sides of a cake with garnish.

side order An à la carte menu item intended to be ordered as part of or an accompaniment to an entrée or main dish.

sieve *v.* 1. To strain a liquid from a food through the fine mesh or perforated holes of a strainer. 2. To rub or press food through strainer with a utensil such as the back of a spoon. *n.* A utensil with perforated holes or fine mesh wire used for straining a liquid from a food. *See* wire mesh strainer.

sift To pass dry ingredients, such as flour and baking powder, through a sieve or sifter to remove lumps and blend and aerate the ingredients.

sifter A handheld utensil used to sift dry ingredients, especially flour; it consists of a cylinder with four curved rods connected to a hand crank; the rods brush the contents through a fine mesh screen; battery-powered models are available; also known as a flour sifter.

flour sifter

signature item A unique or typical food or beverage item prepared in an atypical fashion for which an establishment or person is known (e.g., a signature drink or signature dessert); also known as a speciality item.

silicone baking mat A thin, flexible sheet of reusable siliconized plastic with a nonstick surface; it is heat resistant and used to line sheet pans.

silicone paper Paper coated on both sides with a nonstick surface of silicone able to withstand very high temperatures; it is used for lining baking pans.

silver leaf The pure metal beaten into a gossamer-thin square and sold in packages interleaved with tissue paper; it is edible in small quantities and is used to decorate rice dishes in East Indian cuisines as well as desserts, confections and candies; also known as vark.

simmering 1. A moist-heat cooking method that uses convection to transfer heat from a hot (approximately 185–205°F [85–96°C]) liquid to the food submerged in it. 2. Maintaining the temperature of a liquid just below the boiling point.

simnel cake (SEHM-nul) 1. A rich, lavishly decorated British spice cake made with dried and candied fruit and layers of almond paste. 2. A light biscuitlike bread made from flour that was boiled and then baked; popular during the Middle Ages.

Simplesse The proprietary name of a fat substitute made from egg and milk proteins and used in processed foods.

simple syrup A syrup made by mixing equal parts of sugar and water and then boiling until the sugar dissolves; it is used for glazing and moistening cakes and pastries and in beverages and sorbets; also known as bar syrup. *See* sugar syrup.

singing hinny A northern English griddle cake made with flour, ground rice, lard, currants and milk.

siphon A thick fleshy tube found in certain varieties of clams (especially Pacific clams) that cannot be retracted and through which the clam takes in and expels water.

sippets; sipets (SEHP-pehtz) 1. Traditionally, toasted bread soaked in gravy, sauce or wine; also known as sops. 2. A soup containing such bread. 3. Triangular pieces of toast served with melted cheese or minced beef dishes in 19th-century England.

sirloin A primal section of the beef carcass; it is located between the short loin and round and contains a portion of the backbone and hip bone and a portion of the tenderloin muscle; other than the tenderloin, the meat is less tender than that of the strip loin; it is used to produce fabricated cuts such as the sirloin butt and strip loin steak.

sirloin butt A subprimal cut of the beef primal sirloin; this moderately tough cut consists of several muscles from the posterior end of the backbone and is used to fabricate roasts and steaks.

siroper (see-rho'p) French for to soak in syrup and used to describe the addition of a flavored syrup to an item such as a genoise to moisten or flavor it.

sizzling platter A Chinese–American presentation method in which cooked foods are placed on a heated metal platter at table side; when the moist foods come in contact with the hot metal, they sizzle.

sizzling rice soup A Chinese broth with chicken or pork and vegetables served in bowls over deep-fried rice cakes; the cakes sizzle and pop when the broth is added.

skate A kite-shaped saltwater fish found worldwide; the winglike pectoral fins have a firm, white flesh with a mild, sweet flavor; also known as a ray.

skewer *v.* To impale small pieces of meat or other food on a skewer. *n.* 1. A long, narrow, sharp-pointed metal or wooden pin that is put through the center of a large piece of food (particularly meat) or several small pieces of meat in order for them to be cooked together. 2. A small, slender metal pin that is used to hold meat together when it is stuffed. 3. A spit.

skewings Confetti-like pieces of pure gold leaf that can be sprinkled onto pastries and confections.

skim To remove the upper part of a liquid while leaving the rest intact (e.g., removing fat from a liquid or scum from a soup or stew).

skimmer A long-handled tool with a shallow mesh or perforated bowl; used for skimming stocks and removing food from a liquid.

skimmer

skim milk Whole milk with its milkfat content reduced to 0.5%; also known as nonfat milk.

skin *v.* To remove the skin, peel or outer layer from a food, such as poultry, fish, fruits or vegetables, before or after cooking. *n.* 1. The membranous tissue forming the outer covering of an animal; in vertebrates, it consists of the epidermis and dermis. 2. An animal pelt. 3. A usually thin outer covering of a whole food (particularly produce and cheese) or a prepared food (e.g., sausage skin). 4. A container for liquids, often wine, made of animal skin.

skipjack tuna A variety of tuna found in the Pacific Ocean from Chile to California; it has a dark blue skin that becomes silvery on the belly and black to dusky stripes on the lower sides, an ivory-pink flesh and an average market weight of 4–24 lb. (1.8–10.8 kg); often used for canning; also known as a striped tuna.

skirt steak 1. A fabricated cut of the beef primal short plate; the lean flat cut has a tough, stringy texture and a good flavor. 2. A British cut of the beef carcass; it is cut from the flank.

slab bacon Unsliced bacon, usually cut from the hog's belly.

slack dough A yeast dough that contains more water than it should; the excess water impairs handling.

slake To mix cornstarch or arrowroot with water so that it can be used as a thickener.

slice *v.* To cut a food into relatively broad, thin pieces. *n.* 1. The cut pieces of the food. 2. A triangular spatula used for lifting, especially cakes and fish.

slicer A knife with a long, thin flexible or rigid blade used primarily for slicing cooked meats; the tip can be round or pointed.

slicer

slicer, serrated A knife with a long, thin flexible or rigid blade used primarily for slicing bread or pastry items; the blade has a serrated edge and its tip is round or pointed.

slider A small, sometimes square, hamburger topped with chopped, grilled onions; popular in the American Midwest.

slipper lobster A variety of small lobster found off Hawaii; it has a relatively large tail and small claws, a brownish shell and a white flesh with a rich, sweet flavor.

sliver *v.* To cut into long, narrow strips. *n.* A long, thin piece of food such as cheese or meat or a small piece of pie.

sloeberry; sloe The wild plum that is the fruit of the blackthorn (*Prunus spinosa*); it is purple skinned and has a tart, yellow flesh; also known as blackthorn plum.

sloppy Joe A dish of ground beef, onions and green peppers, flavored with ketchup and other seasonings and served on a hamburger bun; also known as loose meat sandwich and tavern.

slow food A movement begun in Italy to use traditional preparation and cooking methods as well as quality ingredients.

slow oven An oven set to a temperature of 300–325°F (148.8–162.8°C). *See* hot oven *and* moderate oven.

slumgullion (sluhm-GUHL-yuhn) Slang from California's Gold Rush days for a weak alcoholic beverage or a meat stew made from leftovers.

slump A baked cobbler-type dessert made with fresh fruit and a biscuit or dumpling dough topping.

slurry A mixture of raw starch and a cold liquid used for thickening.

small sauces Any of a large variety of French sauces made by adding one or more ingredients to a leading sauce; they are grouped together into families based on their leading sauce; some small sauces have a variety of uses, and others are traditional accompaniments to specific foods; also known as compound sauces. *See* leading sauces.

small sugar pumpkin A pumpkin variety used principally for pie filling.

smell *v.* To perceive an odor through the nose by means of the olfactory nerves. *n.* An odor or scent.

smelt A variety of anadromous fish; they generally have a slender body, a silvery skin, large, fanglike teeth, an average market length of 4–7 in. (10–17.5 cm), a high fat content and a rich, mild flavor; significant varieties include the eulachon, rainbow smelt and whitebait.

Smithfield ham A country-cured ham from the Smithfield, Virginia, area; it comes from hogs raised on hickory nuts, peanuts and acorns and is processed by dry curing, seasoning, hickory smoking and aging for 6–12 months; the lean flesh has a dark color and a rich, salty flavor.

smoked butt A subprimal cut of the pork primal Boston butt; it is a smoked roast.

smoked salmon Salmon cured by either hot smoking or cold smoking; often, the origin of the salmon is added to the name (e.g., Irish smoked salmon). *See* lox *and* Nova.

smoke point The temperature at which a fat begins to break down, releasing an acrid blue gas and giving a burned flavor to foods.

smoking A method of preserving and flavoring foods by exposing them to smoke; this includes (1) cold smoking, in which the foods are not fully cooked, and (2) hot smoking, in which the foods are cooked; also known as smoke curing. *See* cold smoking *and* hot smoking.

smolt A salmon that is 2 years old and leaving the freshwater spawning grounds for the sea. *See* grilse.

smoothie A beverage made by puréeing fruits or vegetables with juice, yogurt, milk and/or ice cream to a thick consistency; nutrient supplements are sometimes added; served chilled.

smørbrød (SMURR-brur) Norwegian for open-faced sandwich.

s'mores Confections made by sandwiching milk chocolate and marshmallows between graham crackers and heating the sandwich, often over an open fire, until the chocolate melts.

smörgåsbord (SMOHR-guhs-bohrd) Swedish for bread-and-butter table and used to describe a Swedish buffet of salads, open-faced sandwiches, cooked vegetables, pickled or marinated fish, sliced meats and cheeses.

smorgasbord (smore-gas-bord) In the United States, a buffet of various hot and cold dishes.

smørrebrød (smoe-rae-bored) 1. A Danish buffet table of salads, open-faced sandwiches, cheeses and marinated fish. 2. An imprecisely used term for Danish open-faced sandwiches.

smother A cooking method in which one food is completely covered with another food or sauce while baking or braising in a covered container.

snack A small amount of food that is served or eaten informally, usually between meals.

snails Univalve land animals found in warm to temperate climates worldwide; significant varieties include escargot de Bourgogne and escargot petit-gris.

snickerdoodle A cookie with a crackly surface; usually flavored with cinnamon and nutmeg and coated in sugar before baking.

snip *v.* 1. To cut foods (e.g., chives) into uniform lengths using kitchen shears. 2. To remove a leaf, bud, sprig or the like from a plant (often an herb) using a small pair of scissors. *n.* The item so cut.

snipe A large family of small game birds found worldwide; they generally have an average dressed weight of 2–10 oz. (56.7–283.5 g) and an excellent flavor; significant varieties include the common snipe, dowitcher, great snipe, jack snipe and red-breasted snipe.

snow ball A dessert consisting of a scoop of ice cream rolled in shredded coconut and topped with chocolate syrup.

snow crab A variety of crab found in the Pacific Ocean from Alaska to Oregon; it has long, slender legs, a white flesh with vivid red markings, a delicate, succulent flavor and a tender texture; also known as queen crab, spider crab and tanner crab.

snow pea A bean (*Pisum sativum* var. *macrocarpon*) with a bright green pod and small, paler green seeds; the thin, crisp pod and the tender, sweet seeds are eaten cooked or raw; also known as the Chinese snow pea and sugar pea.

soba; soba noodles (so-BAH) Japanese noodles made from buckwheat and wheat flour; they are thin, flat and grayish-brown in color.

sockeye salmon A variety of salmon found in the Pacific Ocean from Washington to Alaska; it has a greenish-blue skin with silvery sides and belly, no spots, a deep red flesh, a high fat content, a rich flavor and an average market weight of 3–12 lb. (1.4–5.4 kg); generally used for canning; also known as blueback salmon and red salmon.

soda 1. Slang for any nonalcoholic, flavored and/or colored, carbonated drink; used principally in the American Northeast; also known as soft drink and soda pop. 2. Another name for baking soda. 3. A fountain drink made with scoops of ice cream topped with a flavored soft drink or soda water and a flavored syrup.

sofrito; sofritto (so-FREE-toe) 1. Spanish for fried. 2. A Caribbean and Central American sauce made from salt pork, annatto oil, onions, garlic, green peppers and tomatoes cooked in oil and flavored with cilantro and oregano. 3. A Greek dish of a steak cooked in a garlic sauce. 4. *See* battuto.

soft-ball stage A test for the density of sugar syrup: the point at which a drop of boiling sugar will form a soft, sticky ball when dropped in cold water; equivalent to approximately 234–240°F (112–115°C) on a candy thermometer.

soft-boiled egg; soft-cooked egg An egg simmered in its shell, at least until some of the white has solidified, usually 3–5 minutes. *See* hard-boiled egg.

soft-crack stage A test for the density of sugar syrup: the point at which a drop of boiling sugar will separate into firm but bendable strands when dropped in cold water; equivalent to approximately 270–290°F (132–143°C) on a candy thermometer.

soft drink A beverage that does not contain alcohol; it is usually carbonated, flavored, sweetened and/or colored.

soften To prepare a food, usually butter, by leaving it at room temperature until it becomes pliable but not runny.

soft peak A mixture of eggs and sugar whipped to the point at which it forms a peak that is wet and has a tendency to fold over; also known as wet peak.

sole A family of saltwater flatfish related to the flounder family; they generally have a white belly, a brown to gray skin on top, a finely textured, pearly white flesh and a sweet, distinctive flavor; the most significant variety is Dover sole; many flounder harvested in American waters are also marketed as sole (e.g., petrale sole and English sole). *See* flounder.

sole, Dover 1. A flatfish found in the English Channel and North Sea; it has an average market weight of 1–2 lb. (450–900 g), a firm, white flesh and a pleasant flavor; also known as black sole (especially in Ireland) and true Dover sole. 2. A flatfish found in the Pacific Ocean from California to Alaska; it has a slender body covered with a heavy slime, an average market weight of 2–6 lb. (0.9–2.7 kg), a white flesh and a flavor inferior to that of true Dover sole.

sole bonne femme (bohn FEHM) A French dish of poached sole served with a white wine sauce and lemon juice and garnished with small onions and mushrooms.

sole Marguery (mar-geh-ree) A French dish of sole poached in white wine and fish stock, garnished with mussels, shrimps and a white sauce and browned.

sole Véronique (vay-roh-neek) A French dish of baked sole topped with a cream sauce, garnished with seedless white grapes and browned.

solid molding A chocolate or candy molding technique using a two-part hinged mold; the mold is closed and filled with the candy mixture or melted chocolate; after it sets, the mold is opened, yielding a single, solid unit. *See* hollow molding.

solid pack Canned fruits, vegetables, fish or other products with little or no water added.

solid shortening Shortening that remains firm at room temperature. *See* shortening.

somen (SO-mehn) Fine, glossy, white, Japanese noodles made from wheat flour; usually sold dried; various colors and flavors are available, including yellow (made with egg yolk), pink (flavored with strawberries), green (flavored with green tea) and gold (flavored with citrus).

sommelier (suhm-uhl-YAY) The person at a restaurant in charge of the wine cellar (and sometimes all other beverages, alcoholic or not); he or she generally assists patrons in selecting wine and then serves it; also known as the wine steward or wine captain.

songaya (sang-kha-yaa) A traditional Thai dessert consisting of egg custard flavored with jasmine or orange flower water; it is baked inside the shell of a young coconut.

sopaipilla (soh-pah-PEE-yuh) A crisp deep-fried Mexican pastry or bread that is puffy with a hollow center; usually served with honey or a cinnamon-flavored syrup.

soppresso (sop-PRESS-soh) A northern Italian pork and beef salami.

sops; soppets *See* sippets.

sorbet (sor-BEY) A soft, smooth frozen dish made with puréed fruit or fruit juice and sugar and sometimes flavored with liqueur, wine or coffee; served as a dessert or a palate cleanser between courses. *See* sherbet.

sorghum A grass (*Holcus sorghum*) cultivated as a grain and forage; a relative of millet; it is used for flour in parts of the Middle East, Africa and Northern China; also known as juwar.

sorrel Any of a variety of members of the buckwheat family (genus *Rumex*); they have spear-shaped, dull, gray-green leaves with a tart, sour flavor and are eaten raw or cooked; also known as sour dock, sour grass, spinach dock and herb patience dock.

soubise (soo-BEEZ) 1. An onion purée, usually thickened with rice and served as an accompaniment to meats. 2. Dishes (e.g., oeufs à la soubise) that are topped or accompanied by a creamy onion sauce.

soubise, sauce (soo-BEEZ) A French compound sauce made by adding puréed cooked onions to béchamel sauce.

souchong (soo-chohng) The largest size grade of whole black tea leaves.

soufflé (soo-FLAY) A sweet or savory French dish made with a custard base lightened with whipped egg whites and then baked; the whipped egg whites cause the dish to puff.

soufflé mold A round, porcelain mold with a ridged exterior and a straight, smooth interior; available in 2- to 3.5-qt. capacities.

soufflé mold

soufflé potatoes *See* pommes soufflées.

soul food Traditional African-American cuisine, especially as developed in the American South; characterized by such foods as sweet potatoes, collard greens, black-eyed peas, corn bread, chitterlings and ham hocks.

soup A combination of meats, poultry, fish, shellfish, vegetables and/or fruits cooked in a liquid; it can be garnished with any of an extremely wide range of garnishes, can be hot or cold, sweet or savory, thin or thick and served as a first course or main dish.

soup bones Bones from the foreshanks and/or hindshanks of a beef or veal carcass; rich with marrow, they are used for stocks and soups.

soup bowl A deep bowl, usually without a rim, used for soups, stews or other foods with a liquid component.

soup spoon A spoon with a large rounded or slightly pointed bowl used for eating soup.

soup spoon

sour *v.* 1. To ferment. 2. To spoil or become rancid. *n.* 1. An acidic, tart, possibly unpleasant flavor. 2. A wine-tasting term for a wine that has spoiled and become vinegary. 3. A cocktail made of liquor, sugar and citrus juice shaken with cracked ice and served in a sour glass with a maraschino cherry and orange slice.

sour cream Pasteurized, homogenized light cream (containing not less than 18% milkfat) fermented by the bacteria *Streptococcus lactis;* it has a tangy flavor, a gel-like body and a white color; used as a condiment and for baking and cooking.

sourdough A bread dough leavened with a fermented starter; this gives the bread a tangy, slightly sour flavor. *See* starter.

soursop A very large fruit of a tree (*Annona muricata*) native to the Caribbean and northern South America; it has an irregular ovoid shape, a thin, tender, leathery skin with soft spines and a yellow color when ripe, a white, soft, juicy, segmented flesh with few seeds and an aroma and flavor reminiscent of a pineapple; also known as guanabana.

sous-chef (SOO-chef) 1. French for underchef. 2. At a food services operation following the brigade system, the chef's principal assistant and the one responsible for scheduling personnel, acting as the aboyeur and replacing the chef and station chefs as necessary; also known as the second chef.

souse (sahus) *v.* To pickle a food in brine or vinegar. *n.* Sour pork in aspic, now sold commercially as luncheon meat.

sous-vide (soo-VEED) A food-packaging technique; fresh ingredients are combined into various dishes, vacuum-packed in individual-portion pouches, cooked under a vacuum and chilled for storage.

souvlaki; souvlakia (soo-VLAH-kee; soo-VLAH-kee-uh) A Greek dish consisting of lamb chunks marinated in olive oil, lemon juice, oregano and other seasonings, then skewered (sometimes with vegetables such as green peppers and onions) and grilled.

Souwaroff, sauce (soo-wha-roff) A French compound sauce made from a béarnaise flavored with meat glaze and garnished with julienne of truffles.

sow The adult female swine.

soybean; soyabean; soy pea A versatile legume (*Glycine max*) whose beans are used to make a variety of products, including curds, milk and soy sauce; the pods are tan to black with a tawny to gray fuzz, and the beans, which range from pea to cherry sized, can be red, yellow, green, brown or black and have a bland flavor; also known as soi and soya.

Soyer, Alexis (Fr., 1809–1858) A French chef who spent most of his career in England; he was a restaurant owner (introducing the cocktail bar to England), a chef at the Reform Club, an inventor (e.g., a portable stove for the military), an entrepreneur (he bottled and sold his own sauce and condiments), a social activist and the author of *The Modern Housewife* (1849) and *A Schilling Cookery for the People* (1855).

soy flour; soybean flour A fine, light beige flour made from soybeans; although it does not have glutenin and gliaden, it is high in other proteins and is usually added to wheat flour for baking.

soy milk A pale yellow liquid made by pressing ground, cooked soybeans; it has a slightly bitter flavor and is used for people with milk allergies and in infant formulas and cooking; available plain or flavored with honey or carob.

soy protein A product made from processed soybeans; it has a very high protein content and is used as a nutrient supplement and meat extender; also known as vegetable protein.

soy sauce A sauce made from fermented boiled soybeans and roasted wheat or barley; its color ranges from light to dark brown and its flavor is generally rich and salty (a low-sodium version is available); used extensively in Asian cuisines (especially Chinese and Japanese) as a flavoring, condiment and sometimes a cooking medium.

spa cuisine An American preparation method for foods; it emphasizes fresh, low-fat, low-sodium ingredients prepared without added fat.

Spaetzle; Spätzle (SHPEHT-slee) Irregular-shaped Austrian and German noodles made from a dough of flour, water and sometimes eggs and formed by rubbing the dough through a colander or special sieve directly into boiling water or broth.

Spa Food The trademarked name of dishes created at New York's Four Seasons Restaurant by chef Seppi Renggli; they are low in calories, fat, cholesterol and sodium.

spaghetti con carne (kon KAHR-nee) Italian for spaghetti with meat sauce.

spaghetti squash A large watermelon-shaped winter squash (*Cucurbita pepo*) with a creamy yellow shell and a slightly nutty-flavored flesh that separates into yellow-gold spaghetti-like strands when cooked; also known as noodle squash and vegetable spaghetti.

spanakopita (span-uh-KOH-pih-tuh) A Greek dish consisting of phyllo dough baked with a stuffing of feta cheese and spinach bound with an egg.

Spanish cream An American dessert made with milk, egg yolks and sugar, thickened with gelatin and lightened with whipped egg whites; it is shaped in a decorative mold and garnished with fresh fruit and whipped cream.

Spanish mackerel A member of the mackerel family found in the Atlantic Ocean from Brazil to New England and in the Pacific Ocean from California to the Galápagos Islands; it has a dark blue skin that pales to silver on the belly and many small yellow or olive spots, a high fat content, a firm, flavorful flesh and an average market weight of 1.5–4 lb. (0.68–1.8 kg).

Spanish melon A large ovoid member of the muskmelon family; it has a ribbed, green skin, a pale green flesh and a sweet, succulent flavor.

Spanish olive A green olive that is picked young, soaked in lye and then fermented for 6–12 months; packed in a weak brine and sold with the pit, pitted or stuffed with other flavorings such as a pimiento, almond or pearl onion.

Spanish onion A white- or yellow-skinned onion with a mild flavor.

Spanish potato A large, reddish-brown variety of sweet potato used in Spain for both sweet and savory dishes.

Spanish wind torte An Austrian confection of a meringue shell decorated with piped shell shapes, rosettes and crystallized violets, filled with fresh berries and whipped cream and topped with a decorated meringue disk; in Austria a meringue is called Spanish wind.

spareribs A fabricated cut of the pork primal belly; it is a long, narrow cut containing the lower portion of the ribs and breastbone.

spat An oyster younger than 1 year.

spatula A utensil with a handle and a broad or narrow, long or short, flexible or rigid flat blade.

spatula

spatula, metal 1. A spatula with a narrow flexible metal blade; used to spread foods such as icings. 2. A spatula with a broader, less flexible metal blade; used to turn foods while cooking or to remove them from a heat source or cookware; also known as a grill spatula.

spatula, rubber A spatula with a beveled and slightly curved rectangular rubber blade; available with blades ranging from 1 × 2 to 3 × 5 in.; used to press and smooth foods, remove foods from bowls and fold and stir ingredients.

spatula, silicone A spatula with a flexible, heat-resistant silicon blade; used like a metal or rubber spatula.

spatula, wooden A spatula with a wooden blade; used to mix foods when high heats are present or to turn food or remove it from a heat source or cookware.

spearmint An herb (*Menta spicata*) and member of the mint family; it has soft, bright green leaves and a tart menthol flavor and aroma that is milder than that of peppermint; used as a flavoring, garnish and tisane.

speckled butter bean A fresh baby lima bean that is mottled with purple. *See* lima bean.

speculaa (spac-coo-la-ah) A crisp, spicy Dutch gingerbread cookie traditionally made by pressing the dough into elaborately carved wooden molds.

speculaus (spay-que-low) A Belgian cookie containing rock candy, cinnamon, cloves, nutmeg, ginger and other spices; available in various shapes and sizes, it is particularly popular in the shape of St. Nicholas.

speed rack 1. A stainless steel trough below the bar and directly in front of the bartender, usually at the cocktail station, holding bottles of frequently ordered distilled spirits, mixes or wines sold by the glass. 2. Slang for a baker's rack.

spek (speck) Cured pig fat; it has a hard texture and a rich, strong flavor and is used in Dutch cuisine for larding meats or as a flavoring in stews.

spelt A hard wheat kernel with the husk attached; used as a thickener in soups or served as a side dish.

spice cake A cake flavored with cinnamon and nutmeg and studded with dried and candied fruits.

spice mill A tool similar to a meat grinder with a clamp to fix it to the work surface; electric grinders are also available.

Spice Parisienne (pa-ree-ZYEHN) A spice and herb blend that includes white pepper, allspice, mace, nutmeg, rosemary, sage, bay leaves, cloves, cinnamon and marjoram.

spices Any of a large group of aromatic plants whose bark, roots, seeds, buds or berries are used as a flavoring; usually available dried, either whole or ground. *See* herbs.

spicy 1. A tasting term for a food with a predominant flavor from one or more spices; although the flavors can range from very mild to very hot, the term is more often used to describe hot, pungent foods. 2. A wine-tasting term for a wine with a bouquet and/or flavor reminiscent of black peppercorns, cinnamon and other spices. 3. A cheese-tasting term for a flavor reminiscent of pepper or other spice; usually not applied to cheeses that are flavored with spices or herbs. 4. A coffee-tasting term used to describe an aroma or flavor reminiscent of a particular spice or group of spices.

spider 1. A hand tool with a long handle attached to a mesh disk used for skimming stocks or removing foods from liquids, especially hot fat. 2. A cast-iron frying pan with a long handle and three legs that stands over a bed of coals in the hearth.

spigot (spee-gut) A metal or wooden tap used to drain liquids from a barrel or tank.

spinach A vegetable (*Spinacea oleracea*) with dark green, spear-shaped leaves that can be curled or smooth and are attached to thin stems; the leaves have a slightly bitter flavor and are eaten raw or cooked; also known as Persian herb.

spinach beet; spinach green A beet whose leaves resemble a coarse form of spinach and are used like spinach; also known as beetgreen.

spinach dock *See* sorrel.

spine The thick, unsharpened (top) edge of a knife blade; also known as the back.

spiny lobster A variety of lobster found in temperate and tropical saltwater areas worldwide; it has a mottled brown, orange and blue shell, small claws, a large meaty tail, a lean, snow-white flesh with a sweet flavor and an average market weight of 2–5 lb. (0.9–2.3 kg); usually sold as a frozen tail; also known as rock lobster, sea crawfish and sea crayfish. *See* cold-water tails *and* warm-water tails.

spit A thin metal bar on which meat, poultry or game is placed to be roasted before an open fire. *See* skewer.

splash 1. An imprecise measure of volume for a liquid; usually a small amount. 2. A small amount of a liquid ingredient added to a drink or other food item.

splatter screen A disk with small perforations and a handle placed over a frying pan to reduce grease splatters while allowing vapors to escape.

spleen A variety meat, especially from cows; it has a brown color and a spongy texture and is used in mixed offal dishes; also known as melts.

Splenda The proprietary name of a sweetener made from sugar (sucrose); it is 600 times as sweet as sugar, but is unable to be metabolized; available granular and in packets.

sponge 1. A soupy mixture of flour, liquid and yeast used as the first stage in making certain breads; the sponge is allowed to ferment, then the remaining ingredients are incorporated and the bread is finished; a sponge gives the bread a slightly tangy flavor and a denser texture. 2. A light dessert made with whipped gelatin, beaten egg whites and whipped cream.

sponge cake; spongecake A light, airy cake leavened primarily by air whipped into egg whites, which are then folded into the remaining batter ingredients; it can be flavored and shaped in a wide variety of ways. *See* genoise.

spoom A type of French sherbet made with fruit juice or wine; when partially frozen, an Italian meringue is folded in, making the mixture frothy or foamy.

spoon bread; spoonbread A puddinglike cornbread baked in a casserole and served as a side dish; also known as egg bread.

spot A member of the drum family found off the U.S. East Coast and in the Gulf of Mexico; it has 12–15 yellowish bars above the lateral line, a yellowish-black spot behind the gills and a lean, flaky flesh; also known as a goody and Lafayette.

spotted cabrilla (cah-bree-yay) A variety of Pacific grouper.

spotted dick; spotted dog A British steamed pudding made with suet and raisins.

sprat (spraht) A small saltwater fish, similar to a herring, found in the Atlantic Ocean off Europe; it has a fatty flesh and an average length of 6 in. (15.2 cm).

spread *v.* 1. To distribute a food (e.g., a condiment or icing) evenly over the surface of another. 2. To prepare a table for dining or to arrange platters of food on it. *n.* 1. The butter, cream cheese, mayonnaise or the like used on bread, crackers, canapé bases or similar items, often before one or more garnishes or sandwich fillings are added. 2. An abundant meal laid out on a table. 3. A tablecloth or other fabric used on a table.

spreader Any of several utensils used to distribute a soft food over the surface of another food (e.g., a butter knife or spatula).

sprig A small branch of a leafy substance such as thyme or rosemary.

Springerle (SPRING-uhr-lee) German Christmas cookies flavored with anise; the dough is molded or imprinted with a decorative design before baking.

springform pan A circular baking pan with a separate bottom

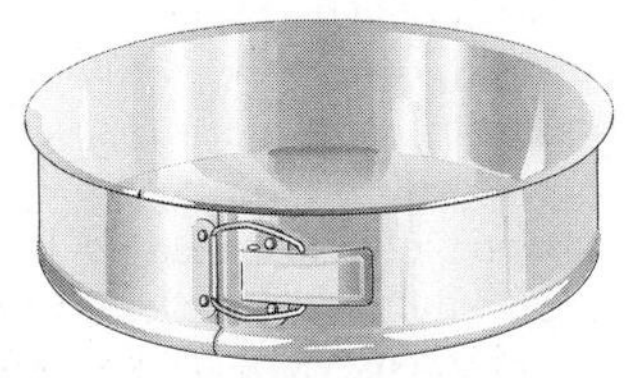

springform pan

and a side wall held together with a clamp that is released to free the baked product; used primarily for baking cheesecakes.

spring lamb The meat of a sheep slaughtered when it is 3–5 months old and between March and early October; the pink meat is quite tender and has a mild flavor. *See* baby lamb, lamb *and* mutton.

spring roll A smaller, more delicate version of the egg roll; it is wrapped in rice paper and traditionally eaten on the first day of spring.

spring scale A scale that weighs objects according to the degree that an internal spring is depressed when the object is placed on a tray above the spring; the weight is indicated by a needle on a dial that can be calibrated in the metric, U.S. or imperial system; a spring scale is often used as a portion scale. *See* electronic scale.

sprinkle To scatter small amounts of a dry substance or drops of liquid over the surface of a food.

sprouts The very young shoots emerging from germinated seeds; generally, they have a soft texture, a white or yellow stem, a green leaf bud and a delicate, sometimes nutty flavor.

spumoni; spumone (spuh-MOH-nee) An Italian dessert made with variously flavored layers of ice cream and whipped cream, often containing candied fruit.

spun sugar A sugar syrup cooked to the hard-crack stage (310°F [153°C]), then drawn out into fine, golden threads with a fork or whisk; these threads are used to decorate desserts and pastries.

squab An immature pigeon, slaughtered when 4 weeks old or younger; it has a tender flesh, a small amount of fat, an average market weight of 0.75–1.5 lb. (0.3–0.7 kg) and an earthy, gamy flavor.

squash 1. The edible fleshy fruit of various members of the gourd (*Cucurbitaceae*) family; generally divided into two categories based on peak season and skin type: summer and winter. 2. A British beverage made by diluting a sweetened citrus concentrate, usually with soda water.

squash, summer Any of several varieties of squashes with edible thin skins, soft seeds, a moist flesh and a mild flavor; they have a peak season of April through September and can be eaten raw or grilled, sautéed, steamed or baked. *See* marrow squash.

squash, turban A category of winter squash characterized by a hard bumpy shell and a turbanlike formation at the blossom end; they have an elongated, plump, pearlike shape, with a yellow, orange or green shell, and a firm, dry, sweet flesh that is a deep orange color; they are often used as decorations.

squash, winter Any of several varieties of squashes with hard skins (called shells) and hard seeds, neither of which are generally eaten; the flesh, which is usually not eaten raw, tends to be sweeter and more strongly flavored than the flesh of summer squashes; winter squashes have a peak season between October and March and can be baked, steamed, sautéed or puréed for soups and pie fillings.

squash blossoms The edible blossoms of both winter and summer squashes; usually stuffed and fried, they have a slight squash flavor.

squid Any of several varieties of cephalopod mollusks found in the Atlantic and Pacific Oceans; generally, they have a long, slender body, an elongated head and tentacles, an ivory-white flesh, a firm, tender texture and a mild, sweet flavor; they vary greatly in size and are available whole or in steaks; also known as inkfish.

sriacha (sree-ah-chah) A Thai sauce made from chiles, salt, sugar and vinegar.

stabilizers; stabilizing agents A type of food additive used to produce viscous solutions or dispersions, impart body, improve consistency, improve texture and/or stabilize emulsions; it includes thickeners, suspending agents, bodying agents, setting agents, jellying agents and bulking agents.

stack cake A cake consisting of seven thin layers of baked cake batter; each layer is spread with a spiced dried apple filling and the top layer is garnished with confectioners' sugar.

stainless steel An alloy of steel, usually with chromium; it is strong and will not rust or corrode; when used for a knife blade, it is difficult to sharpen but holds its edge; when used for cookware, it does not react with acids but is a poor heat conductor, so it is sometimes sandwiched with cooper. *See* carbon steel, high-carbon stainless steel *and* tinned steel.

stale 1. A tasting term for a food or beverage that has lost its freshness because of age, moisture loss or improper storage. 2. A beer- and wine-tasting term for a product that has lost its lively, fresh, youthful character and has become flat, dull, musty and flavorless; often the result of a beverage being kept too long.

staling A change in the distribution and location of water molecules within baked products; stale products are firmer, drier and more crumbly than fresh baked goods; also known as starch retrogradation.

stamp and go A Caribbean fritter made from a heavy batter and salty cod, flavored with annatto, onions and chiles.

standard 1. A midlevel U.S. Department of Agriculture (USDA) quality grade for beef and the second-lowest quality grade for veal; the meat lacks the flavor and marbling of the higher grades. 2. A norm of quantity and/or quality against which comparisons are made.

standard breading procedure The procedure for coating foods with crumbs or meal by passing the food through flour, then an egg wash and then the crumbs; this process gives food a relatively thick, crisp coating when deep-fried or pan-fried.

standardized recipe A set of written instructions for producing a known quantity and quality of a specific food or beverage for a specific food services operation. *See* recipe.

standards of identity Standards mandated by the U.S. Food and Drug Administration (FDA) for processed food recipes that manufacturers must follow if they want to use the common name for the product (e.g., ketchup); these standards encompass approximately 300 foods, and adherence to the standard allows the manufacturer to omit listing the ingredients on the label.

standing rib roast A rib roast that includes the last three ribs and is roasted resting on the rack of rib bones.

staples 1. Certain foods regularly used throughout the kitchen (e.g., cooking oil, flour and salt). 2. Certain foods, usually starches, that help form the basis for a regional or national cuisine and are principal components in a diet.

star anise The dried, dark brown, star-shaped fruit of the Chinese magnolia (*Illicium verum*); its seeds have a pungent, bitter licorice flavor and are available whole or ground; the fruit is used in Chinese cuisine and as an ingredient in Chinese five-spice powder; also known as badian and Chinese anise.

star apple A fruit (*Chrysophyllum cainito*) native to South America and the Caribbean region; it has a purple skin, a flesh that changes from purple near the skin to white toward the center, a mild, sweet flavor and, when cut open, transparent seeds in a star pattern; also known as a cainito.

starch 1. A polysaccharide hydrolyzed into glucose for energy; it has little or no flavor and occurs naturally as a minute, white granule in seeds, tubers and other parts of plants, especially vegetables. 2. A rice, grain, pasta or potato accompaniment to a meal.

star fruit *See* carambola.

starry flounder A member of the flounder family; it has an alternating pattern of orange, white and black bars on the fins, a dark brown to black mottled skin on top, a pearly white flesh, a good flavor and an average market weight of 5–10 lb. (2.3–5.4 kg).

starter 1. A foamy, pungent mixture of flour, liquid and yeast (either commercial or wild) that is allowed to ferment; a portion of the starter is used to leaven bread dough, and the starter is then replenished with additional flour and liquid and reserved for later use. *See* sourdough. 2. Fermenting yeast started in a small amount of sterile wort and, after growth, added to the wort to activate fermentation for the beer-brewing process. 3. The first course or appetizer of a meal.

station 1. An area of a buffet dedicated to a particular type of food (e.g., carved meats or desserts) or preparation (e.g., omelettes). 2. *See* workstations.

station chefs At a food services operation following the brigade system, the individuals who produce the menu items and are under the supervision of the chef and sous-chef; generally, each station chef is assigned a specific task based on either cooking method and equipment (e.g., fry station chef) or category of items to be produced (e.g., garde-manger); also known as chefs de partie.

steak 1. A cross-sectional slice of a round fish with a small section of the bone attached. 2. A fabricated cut of meat, with or without the bone.

steak and kidney pie A British dish of chopped beef, kidneys, mushrooms, onions and beef stock (potatoes, hard-cooked eggs and/or oysters are sometimes added), topped with a pastry crust and baked.

steak au poivre (oh PWAHV-rh) A French dish consisting of a steak covered with crushed peppercorns before being broiled or sautéed.

steak fries Large flat or wedge-shaped French fries.

steak knife 1. A small, slender, slightly bowed knife with a very sharp blade used in place settings. 2. A large, broad-bladed knife with a large handle used in place settings.

steamed bread A moist, tender bread leavened with baking powder or baking soda; it is placed in a covered container and steamed for several hours.

steamed buns Soft, round yeast rolls cooked in a bamboo steamer; created in regions of China where wheat was plentiful and now a standard dim sum dish.

steamed milk Milk that is heated with steam to approximately 150–170°F (65–76°C); used in coffee drinks.

steamed pudding A sweet, dense, breadlike dessert made by steaming batter in a covered container; the batter is often made with bread crumbs, spices and dried fruit (e.g., plum pudding).

steamer 1. An appliance used to steam foods in a closed compartment; the steam is generated by a built-in heat source. 2. An assemblage of two pots and a lid used on a stove top to steam foods; the bottom pot holds the water, and the upper pot, which rests on or in the bottom pot and has a perforated bottom, holds the food; also known as a vegetable steamer. *See* asparagus steamer *and* bamboo steamer. 3. A perforated metal or bamboo insert placed in a pot and used to steam foods. 4. A type of soft-shell clam from the U.S. East Coast.

steamer clam A small Atlantic soft-shell clam; it has a sweet, tender meat.

steaming A moist-heat cooking method in which heat is transferred by direct contact from steam to the food being cooked; the food to be steamed is placed in a basket or rack above a boiling liquid in a covered pan.

steam kettle; steam-jacketed kettle An appliance similar to a stockpot except that it is heated from the bottom and sides by steam (generated internally or from an outside source) circulating between layers of stainless steel; available in sizes from a 2-gallon table model to a 100-gallon floor model.

steamship round A subprimal cut of the beef primal round; it is a round rump with the shank partially removed.

steam table A large hollow table with a heat source and a grid top that accommodates various-sized hotel pans; water is added to the table and the steam that is created keeps the food warm for service.

steel 1. Any of various artificially produced modified forms of the element iron; strength, hardness and elasticity vary depending on its exact composition. 2. A textured rod of steel or ceramic used to hone or straighten a knife blade immediately after and between sharpenings; also known as a butcher's steel and a straightening steel. *See* whetstone.

steelhead trout An anadromous rainbow trout found off the U.S. West Coast; after it returns to the saltwater from spawning, it acquires a grayish skin and loses its rainbow-striped olive to silver skin color; it has a pink to red flaky flesh and a mild flavor; also known as a salmon trout.

steep To soak a food or seasoning in a hot liquid to extract flavors or impurities or to soften the item's texture.

steers Male cattle castrated before they mature and principally raised for beef.

sterilize In a food safety context, to destroy all living microorganisms on an object or in an environment. *See* clean *and* sanitize.

Sterno The proprietary name for canned solid fuel often used with chafing dishes or other serviceware to keep foods warm.

stew *v.* To cook by stewing. *n.* Any dish prepared by stewing, usually containing meat and vegetables.

steward The person in charge of the storeroom where food, beverages, supplies, etc., are kept.

stewing A combination cooking method similar to braising but generally involving smaller pieces of meat that are first blanched and then served with a sauce and various garnishes.

St. Honoré (san-toh-naw-RAY) *See* gâteau St. Honoré.

sticky bun A sweet yeast roll flavored with cinnamon and brown sugar; usually shaped into a pinwheel and baked atop a layer of butter and sugar, which caramelizes and becomes sticky.

sticky rice *See* glutinous rice.

stiff but not dry A culinary term for egg whites that are beaten until they hold firm peaks and are still glossy; they are moist and not too finely grained.

still frozen A term used to refer to creamy or liquid items that are frozen without churning (e.g., marquise).

Stilton (STIHL-tn) A hard cheese made in England's Leicester, Derbyshire and Nottinghamshire areas from cow's milk; it has a pale yellow interior with blue-green veins, a wrinkled, melonlike rind, a rich, creamy, yet crumbly texture and a pungent, tangy flavor.

stiphado; stefado (stee-fah-doh; sta-pha-doh) A thick Greek stew of beef or lamb, tomatoes and pearl onions, flavored with garlic, cinnamon, oregano and red or white wine.

stir-fry 1. A dry-heat cooking method similar to sautéing in which foods are cooked over very high heat with little fat while stirring constantly and briskly; usually done in a wok. 2. Any dish that is prepared by the stir-fry method.

stirring A mixing method in which ingredients are gently mixed until blended using a spoon, whisk or rubber spatula.

St. Lawrence dressing A Canadian dressing made from olive oil, green olives, lemon juice, orange juice, paprika, onions, Worcestershire sauce, parsley and mustard.

stock 1. A clear, unthickened liquid flavored by soluble substances extracted from meat, poultry or fish and their bones as well as from a mirepoix, other vegetables and seasonings; used for soups and sauces. 2. A plant or stem onto which a graft is made. 3. Total merchandise on hand.

stockpot A large pot that is taller than it is wide, with two handles, a flat lid, a capacity of 8–20 qt. and sometimes a spigot at the bottom to release liquid contents; used for making stocks or soups or boiling large amounts of water for pasta.

stockpot (with spigot)

stollen (STOH-luhn) A sweet German yeast bread filled with dried fruit, shaped like a folded oval and topped with a confectioners' sugar icing and candied cherries.

stomach A saclike distensible enlargement of the alimentary canal located between the esophagus and small intestine; it stores food, adds gastric juices, begins the breakdown of proteins and churns food into a liquid mass.

stone boiling A method of cooking used by Native Americans such as the Pueblos; foods are placed in a basket and hot stones are added.

stone crab A variety of crab found in the Atlantic Ocean from the Carolinas to Florida; it has a purple or reddish-brown mottled shell, large claws with black tips and firm, white claw meat with a sweet flavor similar to that of lobster; only the claws can be marketed; they have an average weight of 2.5–5.5 oz. (75–155 g).

stoneground A method of preparing cornmeal or whole wheat flour by grinding the grist between two slowly moving stone wheels; the end product is generally coarse and contains all of the components of the grain.

stove-top grill A cast-iron grill with a ridged cooking surface (similar to both a frying pan and a griddle), often coated with a nonstick finish; it uses the stove top as a heat source.

St. Peter's fish *See* John Dory.

Stragotte, sauce (stra-gut) A French compound sauce made from a demi-glaze flavored with a game stock and trimmings, herbs, tomato purée and red or white wine, finished with butter and Madeira wine and garnished with mushrooms.

straight cut A cutting method in which the food is cut perpendicular to the cutting surface with one smooth downward stroke; also known as guillotine cut.

straight dough method A technique for mixing yeast breads in which all ingredients are combined at once.

straight flour Wheat flour milled from all parts of the wheat kernel except the bran and germ.

strawberries Romanoff; Romanov (roh-mahn-off) A dessert consisting of strawberries soaked in orange-flavored liqueur, then topped with whipped cream.

strawberry A low-growing plant (genus *Fragaria*) with a conical berry that has tiny seeds on the outside of its red skin; the berry has a red to white juicy flesh and a sweet flavor.

strawberry guava A variety of small, particularly sweet guava.

strawberry huller A pair of tweezers with gripping surfaces on each rounded end used to grasp a picked strawberry's leaves; the leaves are twisted and pulled, removing them and the berry's core.

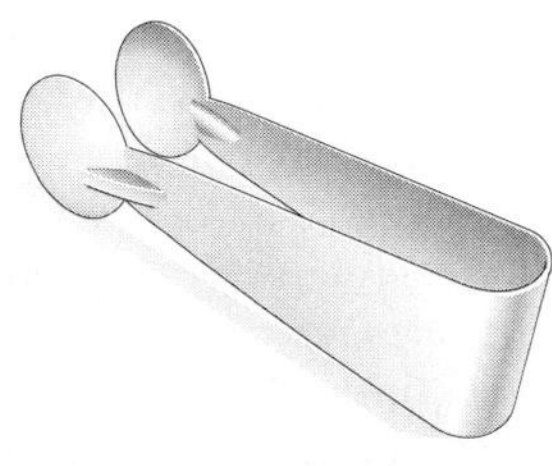

strawberry huller

straw mushroom A mushroom (*Volvariella volvacea*) with a long, conical cap over a bulbous stem; it has a gray-brown color, a silky texture and a mild flavor and is usually available canned; also known as a paddy-straw mushroom.

straw potatoes Long, thin French fries.

streaky bacon Smoked bacon from the hog's belly.

street food Hot and cold snacks prepared and sold by street vendors.

Streptococcus lactis Bacteria found in some buttermilk and that helps digest lactose.

streusel (STROO-zuhl) A crumbly mixture of fat, flour, sugar and sometimes nuts and spices; used to top baked goods.

string cheese A mozzarella-style cheese made in the United States from cow's milk; the cheese is formed into ropes that can be pulled apart and eaten.

striped bass 1. A true bass, this anadromous fish is rarely available commercially. 2. A hybrid of the striped bass and white bass or white perch aquafarmed along both coasts of the United States and marketed as striped bass; it has a silvery skin with horizontal dark gray stripes, a firm, slightly fatty, flaky white flesh, a rich, sweet flavor and an average market weight of 1–15 lb. (0.5–6.8 kg); mistakenly known as rockfish.

strip loin steak; strip streak A fabricated cut of the beef primal short loin; it is the flavorful, tender, usually boneless top loin or eye muscle; also known as a Delmonico steak, Kansas City strip steak and New York steak.

stripper A tool with a short flat blade with a U-shaped indention used to cut thin strips of citrus zest or to peel vegetables in a decorative pattern; also known as canelle knife and citrus stripper.

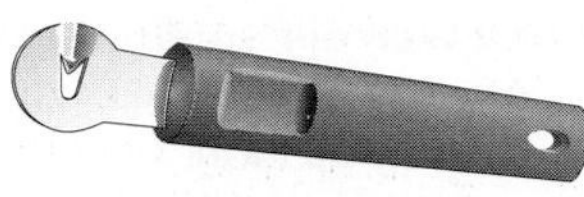
stripper

stroganoff (STROH-guh-noff) A Russian dish of beef, onions and mushrooms in a sour cream sauce; usually served over noodles.

stromboli (strohm-bow-lee) A Philadelphia speciality sandwich of pizza dough wrapped over fillings such as mozzarella and pepperoni and baked. *See* calzone.

strudel (STROO-duhl) A long rectangular German pastry made with many layers of a very thin dough rolled around a sweet or savory filling and baked until crisp and golden.

stud To insert a decoration or flavor-enhancing edible substance into the surface of food (e.g., cloves into a ham).

stuff To fill a cavity in a food with another food.

stuffing 1. A seasoned mixture of foods used to fill a natural or created cavity in poultry, meats, fish and vegetables or around which a strip of poultry, meat, shellfish, fish or vegetables may be rolled. 2. *See* dressing.

sturgeon An anadromous fish found in the Black Sea, Caspian Sea, the Pacific Ocean off the northwest U.S. coast and in the southern Atlantic Ocean; it has a pale gray skin, an average market weight of 60 lb. (27 kg), a high fat content and a firm flesh with a rich, delicate flavor. *See* caviar *and* isinglass.

style 1. A particular, distinctive or characteristic mode of cooking, garnishing and/or presenting foods and/or beverages. 2. The sum of flavors and other sensory characteristics used to compare foods and beverages; foods and beverages of the same style tend to have the same general flavor profile.

su-age (sue-ah-guh) A Japanese cooking method in which foods, usually small items without any flour or batter coating, are deep-fried in moderately hot oil.

subcutaneous fat The fat layer between the hide and muscles of a carcass; it appears on the outer edges of certain fabricated cuts; also known as exterior fat.

submersion poaching A poaching method in which the food is completely covered with the poaching liquid.

subprimal cuts The basic cuts of meat (with or without bones) produced from each primal; relatively large, they are sometimes further reduced into fabricated cuts.

subtle A tasting term for a food or beverage that has delicate flavor nuances not easily detected.

succory (SOOK-ko-ree) A variety of chicory; its root is roasted and ground and used as a coffee substitute or blended with coffee to add aroma and body. *See* Creole coffee.

succotash (SUHK-uh-tash) An American Southern dish of corn, lima beans and sometimes red and green peppers.

sucrine 1. A small, firm-headed lettuce with a sweet flavor; grown in France. 2. A variety of medium-sized, pear-shaped squash with a dark green skin.

sucrose A disaccharide derived from sugarcane, sugar beet, sorghum and other sources; available as white or brown sugar, molasses or powdered sugar; sweeter than glucose but not as sweet as fructose; during digestion it is hydrolyzed into its component single sugars: glucose and fructose; also known as table sugar and sugar.

sucrose polyester (SPE) An artificial fat used instead of oil or butter; indigestible, it contributes no calories to the diet.

suédoise, mayonnaise; Swedish mayonnaise (soo-dwahz) A French mayonnaise sauce blended with apple purée that has been cooked with white wine; it is garnished with horseradish.

suet The hard, crisp, white fat found around the kidneys of cattle, sheep and other animals; used as an ingredient, flavoring and cooking medium.

sugar 1. A group of carbohydrates containing one (monosaccharide) or two (disaccharide) sugar units; occurring naturally principally in fruits and honey, it is sweet, soluble and readily absorbed to be used as an energy source. 2. A sweet, water-soluble crystalline carbohydrate; used as a sweetener and preservative for foods. *See* confectioners' sugar, crystal sugar, molasses, raw sugar, sucrose, sugar beet, sugarcane, superfine sugar *and* turbinado sugar.

sugar, raw A natural sugar that has been washed to remove the impurities; it has a light golden color and a large crystal.

sugar beet A variety of beet (*Beta vulgaris*) with a white flesh and a white, yellow or black skin; it has an extremely high sugar content and is used to produce table sugar.

sugar bloom A white crust of sugar crystals that forms on the surface of chocolate or other candies; sugar is drawn out of the candies and dissolves in the surface moisture; when the moisture evaporates, the sugar crystals remain.

sugarcane; sugar cane A very thick, tall, perennial grass (*Saccoharum officinarum*) grown in tropical and subtropical areas; its sap has an extremely high sugar content and is used to produce table sugar.

sugar dredger A container with a perforated lid used for coating a food with sugar.

sugarplum A small sugary candy made with dried fruits and fondant.

sugar snap pea A sweet pea that is a hybrid of the English pea and snow pea; the bright green, crisp pod and the paler green, tender seeds are both edible.

sugar syrup 1. A syrup made from sugar and water heated gently until the sugar is dissolved; also known as a simple syrup. 2. Melted sugar cooked until it reaches a specific temperature.

sui maai (soo-ee mah-ha-ee) Chinese wrappers similar to won tons.

sukiyaki (soo-kee-YAH-kee) A Japanese dish of sliced beef or chicken cooked with soy sauce and often garnished with bamboo shoots, soybean curd, onions and other vegetables.

sulfites Sulfur-containing agents used as preservatives for fresh and frozen fruits and vegetables; they can cause allergy symptoms in sensitive individuals.

sultanas *See* golden raisins.

sumac; sumaq (soo-mak) A shrub (genus *Rhus*) native to Turkey; its fleshy petals and berries are dried and reduced to a purple powder that has an acidic flavor, and its leaves are steeped in water and have a sour, slightly peppery flavor; both are used as flavorings in Middle Eastern cuisines.

summer coating A mixture of sugar, vegetable fat, flavorings and colorings used as a candy coating (it does not contain cocoa butter); also known as confectionery coating.

summer pudding A British dessert consisting of slices of white bread and sweetened fresh berries, usually red currants, molded in a casserole dish and served with whipped cream.

sundae A dessert made with one or more scoops of ice cream topped with one or more sweet sauces and garnished with whipped cream and chopped nuts.

sun-dried tomato A tomato that has been dried in the sun; it has a dark, ruby red color, a chewy texture and an intense flavor; available dried or packed in oil (including flavored oils).

sunfish A large family of small to moderately large freshwater fish; generally known for vivid skin colors and a subtle, sweet flavor; significant varieties include the bluegill, crappie, rock bass and warmouth.

sunflower oil; sunflower seed oil An oil obtained from sunflower seeds; it has a pale yellow color and virtually no flavor and is high in polyunsaturated fats and low in saturated fats; used for cooking and in dressings.

sunflower seeds The seeds of the sunflower plant; they have a hard black-and-white-striped shell that is removed before eating; usually eaten dried or roasted, with or without salt.

sunny-side-up egg An egg that is not flipped during frying; its yolk should remain intact. *See* over egg.

sunomono (SOO-noh-moh-noh) Japanese for vinegared foods, used to describe salads of raw or cooked vegetables that are coated with vinegar, sometimes sweetened with sugar and flavored with various seasonings.

superfine sugar A finely granulated form of refined sugar; used in beverages and frostings because of the speed with which it will dissolve; also known as castor (caster) sugar.

super-Tuscans High-quality red and white wines produced in Italy's Tuscany region using methods, varietals or compositions not approved by the DOC/DOCG.

supper 1. Traditionally, a light meal served in the evening. *See* dinner. 2. Now, the main meal of the day in the United States, served in the evening; also known as dinner.

suprême A boneless, skinless chicken breast with the first wing segment attached.

suprême, sauce (soo-prem) A French sauce made by adding cream to a velouté made from chicken stock; it is used to make several compound sauces of the velouté family.

suprême de volaille (soo-prem duh vo-lye) A French dish consisting of a chicken breast served with a cream sauce.

surf clam Any of several clams found in deep waters off the east coasts of the United States and Canada; they have white, ovoid shells and a somewhat chewy, pinkish-tan flesh; often used for canning; also known as bar, beach, hen, sea and skimmer clams.

surf-n-turf Meat and seafood served on the same plate (usually a steak and lobster).

surimi (soo-REE-mee) A Japanese processed food made from a mild white-fleshed fish such as Alaskan pollock, shaped, flavored and colored to resemble various types of shellfish, such as crab and shrimp.

sushi (SOO-shee) 1. A Japanese dish of cooked seasoned rice (zushi) garnished with a variety of cooked or raw ingredients such as fish, shellfish and vegetables; there are four principal types of sushi: chirashi-zushi, maki-zushi, nigiri-zushi and oshi-zushi. 2. An imprecisely used term for nigiri-zushi. 3. An incorrectly used term for sashimi. *See* sashimi.

sushi, squeezed *See* nigiri-zushi.

sushi bar A restaurant or an area within a restaurant featuring sushi and sashimi (although other Japanese foods are often available); typically, diners are seated at a counter so that they can watch the chefs prepare the food.

sushi meshi (SOO-shee MEH-shee) Japanese for the vinegared rice used in sushi dishes.

sushi su (SOO-shee soo) Japanese for seasoned vinegar.

sweating Cooking a food (typically vegetables) in a small amount of fat, usually covered, over low heat without browning until the food softens and releases moisture; sweating allows the food to release its flavor more quickly when it is later cooked with other foods.

Swedish meatballs A dish of ground beef mixed with onions, bread crumbs soaked in milk, eggs and seasonings, shaped into small balls and fried or broiled and then served in a brown gravy made from the pan drippings and cream.

sweet 1. One of the basic taste sensations. 2. Something having a flavor of or like sugar. 3. A candy or other small sweetly flavored treat. 4. A wine-tasting term for a wine that retains some detectable amount of sugar after fermentation; it is generally quite noticeable on the palate (e.g., Sauternes). 5. A coffee-tasting term used to describe a smooth and palatable coffee.

sweet-and-sour Any of a variety of dishes that combines sweet and sour flavors, usually sugar and a vinegar-based ingredient.

sweetbreads The thymus gland of a calf, lamb or young hog; it consists of two principal parts, the elongated throat bread and the more spherical heart bread; both have a mild, delicate flavor.

sweet cicely An herb from a bushy perennial plant (*Myrrhis odorata*) with hairy, thin, fernlike leaves that have a sweet scent and a flavor reminiscent of anise.

sweet cider Freshly pressed apple juice that has not been fermented.

sweet dough *See* pâte sucrée.

sweetened condensed milk *See* milk, sweetened condensed.

sweetener Anything used to add a sweet flavor to foods (e.g., sugar, molasses, saccharin and honey).

sweetmeat Any small piece of sweet candy or pastry, especially candied fruit.

sweet pepper 1. The fruit of various plants of the genus *Capsicum;* it has a mild, sweet flavor with undertones of various fruits and spices; a fresh sweet pepper can be white, yellow, orange, green, red, brown or purple, and its shape is generally conical to nearly spherical; sweet peppers are rarely used dried. *See* bell pepper, chile *and* pepper. 2. A term used imprecisely for a bell pepper.

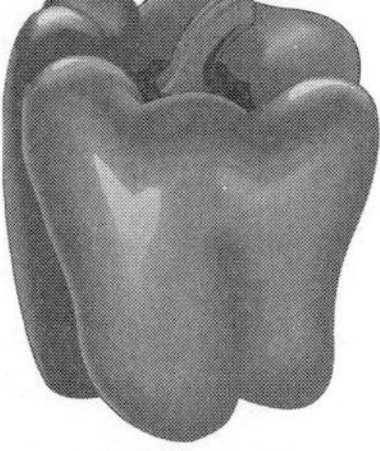
sweet pepper

sweet potato The starchy tuber of a morning glory plant (*Ipomoea batatas*) native to South America; it is unrelated to the potato plant and yam and has a sweet flavor.

sweet potato, red A variety of sweet potato with a thick, dark orange skin and an orange flesh that remains moist when cooked; sometimes erroneously called a yam.

sweet potato, white A variety of sweet potato with a thick, light yellow skin, a pale yellow, mealy flesh that becomes dry and fluffy when cooked and a flavor that is less sweet than that of a sweet potato; also known as a batata dulce, boniato, camote and Cuban sweet potato.

sweet potato pie A baked custard dessert made with a single flaky crust and a smooth filling of puréed sweet potatoes, sugar, eggs, milk and spices.

sweetsop A medium-sized, irregularly shaped fruit (*Annona squamosa*) grown in Central America; it has a bumpy, scaly, yellowish-green skin, a white flesh, a clovelike flavor and large black seeds; eaten fresh or used for beverages and sherbets; also known as a sugar apple. *See* cherimoya.

sweet tea Tea that has been sweetened before service; popular in the American South.

Swiss meringue A mixture of stiffly beaten egg whites and sugar made by combining the ingredients, heating them over simmering water to approximately 140°F (60°C), then whipping until light, fluffy and cool.

Swiss roll A thin sponge cake spread with jam and rolled in a spiral so that slices resemble a pinwheel.

Swiss steak A thick piece of beef, usually round or chuck, coated with flour and browned, then braised, baked or simmered with tomatoes, onions, carrots, celery, beef broth and seasonings; also known as smothered steak (especially in England).

Swiss water method A chemical-free method of removing caffeine from coffee beans by first steaming the beans and then mechanically scraping away the outer layer of caffeine; the process can weaken the flavor of the beverage made from such beans. *See* direct contact method.

swordfish A fish found in the tropical oceans off the Americas; it has a long upper jaw and snout that forms a flat, sharp, double-edged sword, a dark, purplish skin that fades to white on the sides and belly, a moderately lean, gray, off-white or pink flesh that whitens when cooked, a very firm texture, a sweet, mild flavor and an average market weight of 100–200 lb. (45–90 kg); usually sold as wheels or smaller cuts.

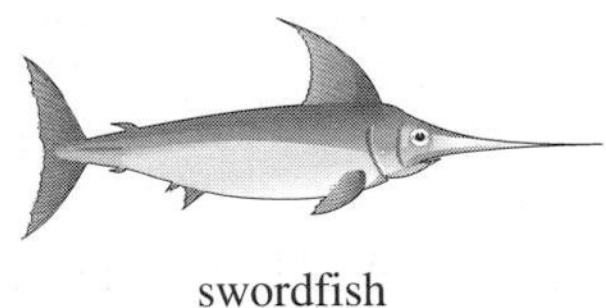

swordfish

syllabub (SIHL-uh-buhb) An old English thick, frothy drink made of milk and wine.

synthetic sweetener *See* artificial sweetener.

syrup 1. A thick, sweet, sticky liquid consisting of sugar dissolved in a liquid, usually water; it is often flavored with spices or citrus zest. 2. The juice of a fruit or plant boiled with sugar until thick and sticky; it is usually used as a topping or sweetener.

Szechwan pepper; Szechuan pepper The dried berry and husk of a type of ash tree (*Xasthoxylum piperitum*); it has a hot, peppery, spicy flavor and is used as an ingredient in Chinese five-spice powder and in the cuisines of China's Szechwan and Hunan provinces; also known as anise pepper and Chinese pepper.

T. *See* tablespoon.

t. *See* teaspoon.

Tabasco (tah-BAHS-koh) A small, tapering chile with an orange-red color, a thin flesh and a very hot flavor with celery and onion undertones; named for the Mexican state of Tabasco, it is used principally to make Tabasco Sauce.

tabbouli (tah-BOO-lee) A fine grind of bulgur.

table In the culinary context, a term often used to describe a product (e.g., wine or cheese) of modest quality, served routinely with a meal or a product (e.g., fruit) served without any further preparation.

table cream *See* cream, light.

table d'hôte (tah-buhl DOHT) A menu offering a complete meal for a set price; also known as prix fixe.

table grapes Any variety of grape eaten out of hand (as opposed to being used principally for wine making).

tablering A commonly used method for tempering chocolate by hand; melted chocolate is spread out and stirred on a marble slab to cool it to the proper temperature. *See* tempered chocolate.

table salt Finely ground and refined rock salt; it usually contains anticaking agents and other additives.

tablespoon 1. A spoon with a large, slightly pointed bowl used to serve foods at the table. 2. A measure of volume in the U.S. system; 1 tablespoon (T.) equals 3 teaspoons or 0.05 fl. oz.

table sugar *See* sucrose *and* granulated sugar.

tabouli; tabbouleh; tabuli (tuh-BOO-luh) A Middle Eastern dish consisting of bulgur wheat mixed with tomatoes and onions, flavored with parsley, mint, olive oil and lemon juice; served cold; also known as suf.

taco (tah-COH) A Mexican dish consisting of a small folded corn or flour tortilla filled with beef, pork, chicken, chorizo and/or refried beans and garnished with tomatoes, lettuce, cheese, onions, guacamole, sour cream and/or salsa; it can be crisp (deep-fried into a U-shaped holder) or soft.

taffy A soft, chewy candy made with cooked sugar, butter and flavorings; the mixture is pulled repeatedly into long ropes and twisted as it cools; this incorporates air and creates a shiny, opaque color; the ropes of taffy are then cut into bite-sized pieces. *See* saltwater taffy.

tahini (tah-HEE-nee) A thick, oily paste made from crushed sesame seeds and used in Middle Eastern cuisines as a flavoring.

tail 1. The largest edible part of shellfish such as shrimp, prawns, crayfish and lobsters. 2. The rear appendage of certain mammals; it is bony, and its tough, flavorful meat is generally used for stocks and stews.

Taillevent (Fr., c. 1312–1395) Born Guillaume Tirel, Taillevent was the master chef for Charles V of France; sometime around 1375 he wrote *Le Viandier*, the oldest known French cookbook, which describes a cooking style that relies on pounding, puréeing, saucing and spicing most foods so that the finished dish bears little resemblance in shape, texture or flavor to the original principal ingredients.

tajine; tajin (TAH-jin) *pl.* touajen. 1. A deep, earthenware dish with a tight-fitting conical lid that fits flush with the dish; used in North African cuisines. 2. Any of several meat and vegetable stews made in such a dish.

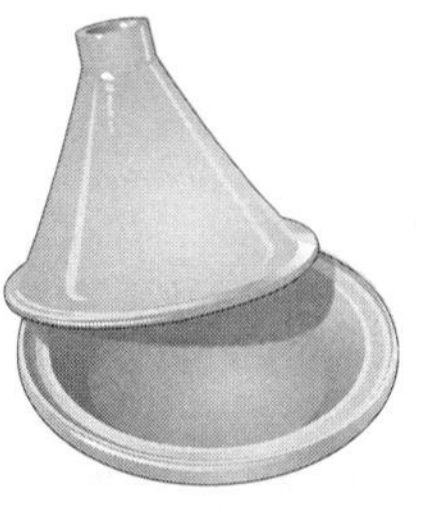

tajine

tallow An animal fat (principally mutton and beef) used as a source of fat in cake mixes, shortening and cooking oils.

Tallyrand, sauce (tal-lee-rahn) A French compound sauce made from a chicken velouté flavored with white wine and shallots, finished with cream and Madeira wine and garnished with brunoise of celery, carrot, onion, truffle and pickled tongue; usually served with braised poultry, sautéed and fried meat, and large roasted or braised joints.

Tallyrand-Perigord, Charles Maurice (Fr., 1745–1838) A French statesman who was a celebrated host and connoisseur of fine food, in part because he employed the great chef Carême; Tallyrand's dinner menus regularly consisted of two soups, two removes (a change of dishes during the meal), one of which was fish, two roasts, four sweets and dessert; this menu became the rule for all the best tables; his name is associated with numerous food preparations.

taloa (tah-loh-ah) A Basque corn bread leavened with yeast and shaped like an English muffin; used for sandwiches.

tamago yaki (TAH-mah-goh YAH-kee) A Japanese-style omelet cooked in a thin sheet and rolled to form a loaf; it is served in sushi bars.

tamale (tuh-MAH-lee) A Mexican dish consisting of chopped meat or vegetables coated with a masa dough, wrapped in a softened corn husk and steamed (the husk is not eaten); sweet tamales are filled with fruit.

tamale pie A casserole dish made of ground beef, cheese, cornmeal batter and seasonings; the ingredients are layered and baked.

tamari (tuh-MAH-ree) A Japanese sauce made from soybeans; it is usually aged, making it thicker, darker and more mellow than soy sauce; used as a condiment, sauce and baster.

tamarillo (tam-uh-RIHL-oh; tam-uh-REE-oh) A small- to medium-sized ovoid fruit (*Cyphomandra betacea*) native to South America; it has a tough, smooth skin that can be red, purple, amber or yellow, a red or yellow flesh, black seeds and a rich, sweet, slightly tart flavor; also known as a tree tomato.

tamarind (TAM-uh-rihnd) The fruit of a tree (*Tamarindus indica*) native to Asia and northern Africa; the long pods contain small seeds and a sweet–sour pulp that is dried and used as a flavoring agent in Indian and Middle Eastern cuisines as well as in Worcestershire sauce; also known as an Indian date.

tamis (TAM-ee) *See* drum sieve.

tandoor; tandoor oven An Indian barrel-shaped clay oven fueled by hot coals whose temperatures reach up to 800°F (425°C); the tandoor sears meat in seconds and bakes flatbread in minutes.

tandoori A menu term for foods cooked in a tandoor oven; correctly spelled tandur.

tane (tah-nay) Japanese for the ingredients used to top nigiri-zushi. *See* zushi.

tang The unsharpened rear extension of a knife blade that is attached to or embedded in the handle; a full tang runs the entire length of the handle; a three-quarter tang extends partially into the handle, and a rattail tang is a rod that runs down the handle's length.

tangelo (tan-JEHL-oh) A small- to medium-sized citrus; a hybrid of a mandarin orange or tangerine and pomelo; it has a loose, yellow-orange to dark orange, smooth or rough rind, few seeds, a juicy, orange flesh and a sweet flavor.

tangerine A small- to medium-sized citrus (*Citrus reticulata*); it has a thick, loose, orange rind, a dark orange, juicy flesh and a sweet flavor; named after the city of Tangier, Morocco.

tant pour tant (TPT) (tahn poor tahn) French for as much as and used in pastry making to refer to a mixture containing equal amounts of powdered nuts, usually blanched almonds, and confectioners' sugar.

tapas (tah-pahs) Spanish appetizers that can be hot or cold, simple or complex.

tapenade (TA-puh-nahd; ta-pen-AHD) A thick paste made from capers, anchovies, olives, olive oil, lemon juice and seasonings in France's Provence region; used as a condiment, garnish and sauce.

tapioca 1. A starch extracted from the root of the cassava plant and used for thickening. 2. A milk pudding made with processed pellets of tapioca, known as pearl tapioca.

taproot The single root of a plant (e.g., carrot); it extends deep into the soil to supply the aboveground plant with nutrients; also known as a root.

tarama (tah-rah-mah) Greek and Turkish for pale orange carp roe.

taramasalata (tah-rah-mah-sah-LAH-tah) A Greek dish consisting of tarama, lemon juice, milk-soaked bread crumbs, olive oil and seasonings; served as a creamy dip.

Tarla A hardwood rolling pin with short knob handles and a thin sheet of copper covering the cylinder; used for rolling out doughs with a high fat content or hot sugar mixtures such as nougatine.

taro The large tuber of the tropical taro plant (*Colocasia esculenta*); it has a brown skin, a starchy, gray-white flesh and an acidic flavor when raw that becomes somewhat nutty when cooked; also known as Caribbean cabbage, colasse and old cocoyam.

tarragon An herb (*Artemisia dracunculus*) native to Siberia with narrow, pointed, dark green leaves, tiny gray flowers, a distinctive aniselike flavor with undertones of sage and a strong aroma; available fresh and dried.

tarragon vinegar A red or white wine vinegar in which tarragon has been steeped.

tart *n.* A shallow-sided pastry dough crust filled with a sweet or savory mixture; the tart may or may not have a top crust. *adj.* A sharp, piquant, often acidic or sometimes sour flavor.

tartare An imprecisely used term for any dish featuring a raw ingredient (e.g., salmon tartare).

Tartarian cherry (tar-TAIR-ee-uhn) A large sweet cherry with a dark purple, almost black skin and a juicy flesh.

tartar sauce; tartare, sauce A mayonnaise-based sauce made with dill pickles, capers, onions, lemon juice or vinegar and traditionally served with fried fish.

tarte au suif (tahrt-tah oh soo-if) A Canadian tart or pie consisting of a suet crust filled with chopped nuts, beaten eggs and maple syrup; it is baked and served cold.

tarte Tatin (tahrt tah-TAN) A French apple tart in which layers of butter, sugar and sliced apples are placed in a sauté pan and topped with puff pastry or sweet dough; after baking, the dish is inverted so that the caramelized apples become the topping for service.

tartlet A small, single-serving tart.

tartlet pan A small pan, 2 to 4 in. in diameter and 0.75 to 1.5 in. high, available in many shapes including round, oval, rectangular and square, with plain or fluted straight or sloping sides; it is used for baking tartlets and usually made of tinned or black steel and generally without a removable bottom.

tart pan A pan, 4.5 to 12.5 in. in diameter and 0.75 to 1.25 in. high, usually round, square or rectangular, with fluted, slightly sloping sides; it is used for baking tarts and usually made of tinned or black steel with a removable bottom.

tasso; tasso ham (TAH-soh; TA-soh) A Cajun sausage made from cured pork or beef, seasoned with red pepper, garlic, filé powder and various herbs and spices and then smoked; principally used as a flavoring ingredient.

taste *v.* 1. To test the flavor of something by placing it in the mouth or on the tongue. 2. To sample a food or beverage. *See* flavor. *n.* One of the five senses; concerned with perceiving and distinguishing the flavors (e.g., sweet, sour, umami, salty and bitter) of foods and beverages.

tatsoi A salad green with thick, dark green, rounded leaves and a rich mustard flavor; also known as rosette bok choy.

tayberry A large berry developed in Scotland that is a hybrid of the blackberry and raspberry; it has a bright purple color, an elongated conical shape and a flavor similar to that of a ripe blackberry.

T-bone steak A fabricated cut of the beef primal short loin; this tender cut contains a distinctive T-shaped portion of the backbone and on either side of the center bone, a large portion of the loin eye muscle and a smaller portion of the tenderloin. *See* club steak *and* porterhouse steak.

tea 1. An aromatic beverage made by infusing water with the cured leaves of the shrub *Camellia sinensis*; a mild stimulant due to caffeine, a tea is generally named for its leaf type and size or region of origin. 2. The leaves used to make the beverage. *See* black tea, green tea, oolong tea *and* white tea. 3. An imprecisely used term for a beverage made from steeping the leaves of shrubs, herbs or other plants in water. *See* tisane. 4. An imprecisely used term for a very thin, runny sauce, usually one flavored with vegetables, herbs or spices.

tea, afternoon 1. A light British meal or refreshment of bread and butter, cucumber or other delicate sandwiches, cookies, scones and Devonshire cream and the like served with a pot of tea during the late afternoon. 2. A formal social occasion or reception at which tea and other refreshments are served.

tea, high A late afternoon or early evening British meal, usually quite substantial and consisting of meat and/or fish dishes, biscuits and jam, an array of cakes and pastries and a pot of tea.

tea biscuit British expression for any of a variety of cookies or crackers served with afternoon tea; also known as a tea cake.

teacupful A traditional measure of volume; approximately 3/4 cup.

tea egg A hard-cooked egg; its shell is cracked and the egg is simmered in strong tea, creating a marblelike effect; an appetizer in Chinese cuisine.

teal A small wild duck with dark blue-green coloring and a very flavorful flesh; often grilled or roasted and served with a port sauce.

tea leaves *See* Camellia sinensis.

tea melon A small cucumber-shaped fruit with a yellow skin, crisp texture and mild flavor; also known as a Chinese cucumber, Chinese melon and sweet cucumber.

tear (taher) To pull a food apart and into pieces, usually of different, uneven shapes and sizes.

teaspoon 1. A small spoon with a slightly pointed bowl used to stir tea or coffee. 2. A measure of volume in the U.S. system; 1 teaspoon equals 1/3 or 0.17 fl. oz.

tea strainer A small perforated bowl placed over a cup to strain the leaves when the tea is poured into the cup.

teff A North African high-protein, high-carbohydrate grain with a mild nutty flavor; sometimes spelled t'ef.

Teflon The proprietary name of a synthetic coating used on cooking utensils to prevent food from sticking.

tefteli; teftely (tyef-tel-ee) Russian meatballs, usually served with boiled rice, kasha or potatoes.

tempe; tempeh (TEHM-pay) A fermented soybean cake with a yeasty, nutty flavor used in Asian and vegetarian cuisines.

temper To bring something to the proper temperature or texture by mixing, stirring, heating or cooling (e.g., to temper eggs by slowly whisking in hot milk to avoid curdling).

temperature danger zone The broad range of temperatures between 41 and 135°F (5 and 57°C) in which bacteria thrive and reproduce; by keeping foods out of this temperature range, the chances of an infection, intoxication or toxin-mediated infection are decreased. *See* time-and-temperature principle.

tempered chocolate Chocolate treated with a heating and cooling process to stablize the cocoa butter crystals; tempered chocolate is shiny, smooth and unblemished by bloom.

tempering 1. Heating gently and gradually. 2. The process of slowly adding a hot liquid to eggs or other foods to raise their temperature without causing them to curdle.

tempering machine An electric machine designed for melting and tempering chocolate, then holding it at the correct temperature for use in making candy or decorations.

temple orange A medium-sized ovoid orange that is a hybrid of an orange and a tangerine; it has a rough, thick, deep orange rind, a dark orange flesh, many seeds and a sweet–tart flavor.

tempura (TEM-poo-ra) A Japanese dish of battered and deep-fried pieces of fish and vegetables, usually accompanied by a sauce.

tender 1. A fabricated cut of the beef primal sirloin; it is a trimmed, boneless steak. 2. A strip of flesh found on the inside of the chicken breast next to the bone.

tenderize To soften and/or break down tough muscle fibers in meat by cubing, needling, pounding, marinating in acidic ingredients, adding enzymes and/or cooking in moist heat.

tenderized steak *See* cubed steak.

tenderizer An additive or substance used to soften and/or break down tough meat fibers; includes enzymes (e.g., papain) and acidic marinades (e.g., a red wine marinade).

tenderloin A flavorful and very tender muscle that runs through the beef short loin and sirloin primals; it is part of T-bone and porterhouse steaks or can be cut into châteaubriand, filet mignon and tournedos. *See* butt tenderloin *and* short tenderloin.

tenderloin tips A fabricated cut of the beef primal short loin; they are small pieces of the short tenderloin.

10 X sugar *See* confectioners' sugar

tepary bean (the-PAHR-ray) A bean grown in the hot, arid conditions of the American Southwest; it is similar to a pinto bean.

tepín A small ovoid or spherical fresh chile with a thin flesh and a very hot flavor; also known as chíltepin or chíltecpin.

teppan-yaki (tep-PAHN-YAH-kee) A Japanese style of cooking done on a large grill in front of diners.

tequila (tuh-KEE-luh) A spirit made in Mexico from the fermented and distilled sap and pulp of the maguey plant (it must contain at least 51% maguey sugars); it has a high alcohol content, colorless to straw color and somewhat herbaceous flavor; it is often sold as either blanco (white) or plata (silver).

teriyaki (tayr-ee-YAH-kee) 1. A Japanese dish of beef, chicken or pork marinated in soy sauce, ginger, sugar and seasonings, skewered and grilled or broiled. 2. A Japanese marinade or sauce made from soy sauce, ginger, sugar and seasonings.

terrine 1. Traditionally, coarsely ground and highly seasoned meats baked without a crust in an earthenware mold and served cold. 2. A coarsely or finely ground and highly seasoned meat, fish, shellfish, poultry and/or vegetable forcemeat baked without a crust in an earthenware mold, usually lined with pork fat, and served hot or cold. *See* pâté. 3. The earthenware, metal or glass mold used for such preparations; usually a long, narrow rectangular loaf pan with a flared edge to hold the cover.

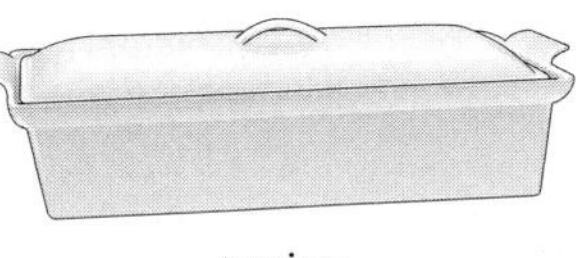

terrine

Texas sheet cake A large, rich single-layer chocolate cake.

Texas toast A very thick slice of white bread that is toasted and brushed with butter; often served with steaks.

Texmati rice An aromatic U.S. white or brown rice that is a cross between long-grain rice and basmati.

Tex-Mex A term used for food that is based on the combined cultures of Texas and Mexico; these foods include burritos, nachos and tacos, and the principal flavorings include tomatoes and chiles.

texture A tasting term for the fabric or feel of a food or beverage as it enters the mouth and is sensed on the palate; it can be smooth, grainy, creamy, flaky, dense, crumbly, brittle, hard, soft, firm, springy and so on.

textured plant protein; textured vegetable protein Isolated, flavored and processed proteins from plants such as soybeans, peanuts and wheat; used to create high-protein, nutritious ersatz foods or to extend other food products nutritiously; also known as meat extender and meat replacements.

Thai chile A short, thin, elongated and pointed chile with a green to red color, a thick flesh and a very hot flavor.

Thai curry paste A paste of aromatic herbs, spices and vegetables used in Thai cuisine as a flavoring; yellow paste is the mildest, red can vary in heat and green is the hottest.

thermidor (THERM-ee-dohr) A dish prepared by poaching or roasting the main ingredient (e.g., lobster or fish) and making a sauce by reducing the juices, white wine and fish fumet and adding this concentrate to a béchamel sauce seasoned with mustard.

thermometer A device designed to measure temperatures; it can be calibrated in Fahrenheit and/or Celsius and can be a column of mercury with temperatures indicated on a glass tube or a stem-type thermometer in which temperatures are noted by an arrow on a dial or a digital readout.

thermometer, instant-read A thermometer used to measure the internal temperature of foods; the stem is inserted into the food, producing an instant temperature readout.

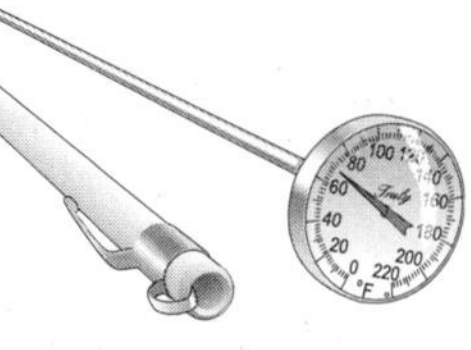

thermometer, instant-read

thermometer, internal A stem-type thermometer inserted into a food for 1–2 minutes while it is being cooked; generally it is more accurate than an instant-read thermometer and registers temperatures of 0–220°F (−18 to 104°C); also known as a quick-read thermometer.

thermometer, meat A thermometer inserted into the meat to read the internal temperature; the top of the thermometer usually has a scale indicating the temperatures of doneness for certain meats.

thicken The process of making a liquid substance dense by adding a thickening agent (e.g., flour or gelatin) or by cooking to evaporate some of the liquid.

thickening agents; thickeners 1. Ingredients used to thicken sauces, including starches (flour, cornstarch and arrowroot), gelatin and liaisons. 2. A type of food additive used to produce viscous solutions or dispersions, impart body and/or improve texture or consistency; includes stabilizers, suspending agents, bodying agents, setting agents, jellying agents and bulking agents.

thimbleberry Any of a variety of thimble-shaped raspberries, especially the black raspberry, grown in the United States.

thin *v.* To dilute mixtures by adding more liquid. *adj.* A tasting term for a product that is watery or lacks body.

thinh (think) Toasted, ground rice used in Vietnamese cuisine (especially in ground pork dishes) for its distinctive aroma, flavor and texture.

Thompson Seedless The most widely planted grape in California; used for raisins, table grapes or to make a neutral wine used in blends of inexpensive jug white wines.

Thousand Island dressing A salad dressing or sandwich spread made from mayonnaise, cream and chile sauce garnished with pickles, green peppers, olives and hard-cooked eggs.

thread stage A test for the density of sugar syrup; the point at which a drop of boiling sugar will form a thin thread when dropped in cold water; equivalent to approximately 230–234°F (110–112°C) on a candy thermometer.

three-compartment sink An assembly of three adjacent sinks used for sanitizing dishes and equipment; the item to be sanitized is first scraped and sprayed and then washed in the first sink, rinsed in the second, sanitized in the third and left to air-dry.

Thuringer (THOOR-ihn-juhr) A style of German sausages made from chopped pork and/or beef, seasoned with herbs, spices and other flavorings such as garlic, coriander or mustard; they are preserved by curing, drying and smoking and have a semidry to moist, soft texture.

thyme (time) A low-growing herb (*Thymus vulgaris*) with small purple flowers and tiny, gray-green leaves; the leaves have a strong, slightly lemony flavor and aroma; used fresh and dried.

tian (tyahn) A square or rectangular earthenware dish with slightly raised edges and used in France's Provence region to prepare gratin dishes, which are also called tians.

tiers The different levels in an assemblage of items, one stacked on top of another (e.g., a wedding cake). *See* layer.

tiffin (ti-fen) An Indian lunch or midmorning snack, usually consisting of rice or bread, curry and dal, delivered in tiered aluminum or enameled containers.

tiger lily bud The dried bud of the tiger lily (*Lilium lancifolium*); it has an elongated shape, a golden color and a delicate and musky-sweet flavor and is used as a garnish and in stir-fry dishes in Chinese and other Asian cuisines; also known as golden needle and lily bud.

tiger nut A small wrinkled tuber of a plant (*Cyerus esculentus* var. *sativus*); it has a crisp white flesh and a sweet, nutty flavor somewhat similar to that of an almond; also known as chufa and earth almond.

tilapia (tuh-LAH-pee-uh) 1. A generic name for several species of freshwater fish aquafarmed worldwide; they generally have a gray skin, a lean white flesh, a firm texture, a sweet, mild flavor and an average market weight of 3 lb. (1.3 kg); sometimes marketed as cherry snapper or sunshine snapper, even though not members of the snapper family; also known as mudfish. 2. One such fish, native to Africa and aquafarmed in the United States, with an average market weight of 1–1.5 lb. (450–700 g).

ti leaves (tee) The long, narrow leaves of the ti plant (*Cordyline terminalis*); they are used to wrap foods for cooking in Pacific Island cuisines.

tilefish A fish found in the Atlantic Ocean from the mid-Atlantic states to New England; it has a multicolored skin with distinctive yellow dots, a lean flesh, a firm texture and an average market weight of 4–7 lb. (1.8–3.2 kg).

tilting kettle A large, flat-bottomed, freestanding pan about 6 in. deep with an internal heating element below the pan's bottom; used as a stockpot, fry pan, griddle or steam table; it usually has a hand-crank mechanism to turn or tilt the pan to pour out the contents.

timbale 1. A dish, usually a custard base mixed with vegetables, meats or fish, baked in this mold. 2. A pastry shell made with a timbale iron; it can be filled with a sweet or savory mixture.

timbale mold A $1\frac{1}{2}$ in. (3.8 cm) deep, flair-sided, round, stainless steel mold with a capacity of 4 oz. (113.4 g); it is used for single servings of foods such as eggs in aspic. *See* aspic mold.

timbale mold

time-and-temperature principle Keep hot foods hot and cold foods cold; by keeping potentially hazardous foods outside the temperature danger zone, the chances of an infection, intoxication or toxin-mediated infection are decreased.

tin 1. A soft silver-white, malleable metal used as an alloy and in making tinfoil, utensils and the like. 2. A pan used for baking (e.g., pie tin, loaf tin and flan tin). 3. A can or comparable metal container, especially in Great Britain.

tinned steel Steel coated with tin and used for baking tins and molds; it is tough, durable and does not warp over high heat but does rust.

tips An acronym for To Insure Prompt Service and used to describe gratuities given to someone for performing a service; also known as gratuity.

tipsy pudding; tipsy parson A British dessert similar to trifle made with several layers of whipped cream, custard and wine-soaked sponge cake.

Tiramisù; tirami sù (tih-ruh-mee-SOO) Italian for pick me up and used to describe a dessert made with layers of liqueur-soaked ladyfingers or sponge cake, sweetened mascarpone cheese and zabaglione, usually garnished with whipped cream and shaved chocolate.

tirópita (tee-rop-PEE-tah) A Greek dish made with phyllo dough, cheese and eggs, baked as a pie or folded into rolls or small triangles and served as a meze.

tisane (teh-ZAHN) An infusion of herbs, flowers, spices and other plant matter, usually consumed hot for refreshment, medicinal, calming or rejuvenating purposes; also known as herb tea or herbal tea and known imprecisely as tea.

toad-in-the-hole A British dish of Yorkshire pudding baked with small link sausages.

toast *v.* To make an item (usually baked goods) crisp and hot. *n.* 1. A piece of bread grilled or broiled on both sides. 2. A speech made or a phrase stated before drinking a beverage in a person's or thing's honor. 3. The beverage consumed in honor of someone or something. 4. Slang for an item that has been greatly overcooked.

toaster oven A small electrical appliance used on the countertop for toasting, baking or broiling foods.

toast points Triangular pieces of toast, usually without the crusts, used as a base for cream sauce dishes or canapés.

toffee; toffy 1. A firm but chewy candy made with brown sugar or molasses and butter; Danish and English versions are hard and brittle instead of chewy. 2. The British spelling of taffy.

tofu (TOH-foo) A custardlike product made from curdled soy milk from which some of the water has been removed by pressure; it has a white color and a slightly nutty, bland flavor that absorbs other flavors; available dried and fresh (usually packed in water) and used in Asian cuisines in soups or cooked; also known as soybean curd and bean curd. *See* bean curd.

tofu, cotton A common variety of tofu; it has a firm texture, an irregular surface pattern (caused by the weave of the cotton fabric used during pressing) and a low moisture content.

tofu, silk A common variety of tofu; it has a smooth, soft texture, a smooth surface pattern (the silk fabric used during the pressing does not leave any patterns) and a high moisture content.

tofu pudding Soft curds of soy milk, generally unpressed or lightly pressed; also known as soybean pudding and soft soybean curds.

togarashi (to-gah-RAH-shee) Japanese for dried chiles used as a seasoning or garnish.

Toll House cookie A drop cookie made with brown sugar and chocolate chips; sometimes nuts are added.

tom 1. A male turkey. 2. Thai for to boil.

tomalley (TOM-al-ee; toh-MAL-ee) 1. The olive green liver of a lobster; it is often used to flavor sauces and other items. 2. The rich, yellow, fatty yolk of crab eggs.

tomatillo (tohm-ah-TEE-oh) A plant (*Physalis ixocarpa*) native to Mexico whose fruit resembles a small tomato with a papery tannish-green husk; the fruit has a thin, bright green skin (yellow and purple varieties are also available) and a firm, crisp, pale yellow flesh with a tart, lemony–herb flavor; used like a vegetable in American Southwestern and Mexican cuisines; also known as jamberry, Mexican green tomato, Mexican husk tomato and husk tomato.

tomato The fleshy fruit of the *Lycopersicon esculentum*, a vine native to South America and a member of the nightshade family; used like a vegetable, tomatoes are available in a range of sizes, from tiny spheres (currant tomatoes) to large squat ones (beefsteak tomatoes), and colors from green (unripe) to golden yellow to ruby red.

tomato aspic An aspic made with tomato juice and gelatin.

tomato juice The thick liquid produced by blending the pulp and juice of a tomato.

tomato knife A knife used to slice tomatoes, sausages and hard cheeses; it has a 5-in.-long, ridged, wave cut blade with two prongs on the end for transferring slices to a plate; also known as a European tomato knife.

tomato knife

tomato paste A thick, slightly coarse paste made from tomatoes that have been cooked for several hours, strained and reduced to form a richly flavored concentrate used as a flavoring and thickener; also known as tomato concentrate.

tomato purée A thick liquid made from cooked and strained tomatoes; often used as a thickener for sauces.

tomato sauce 1. A French mother or leading sauce made by sautéing mirepoix and tomatoes; white stock is added, and the sauce is then thickened with a roux; also known as sauce tomate. 2. A pasta sauce made from skinned, cooked, deseeded tomatoes; it can be thick or thin, seasoned with a variety of herbs and spices and garnished with meat, mushrooms, onions or the like. 3. A slightly thinned tomato purée, often seasoned, used as a base for sauces or as a flavoring or topping ingredient.

tongs A utensil with two long handles attached at the top; there are two types: those with a heavy wire scissor action and those with a spring; both are made in either stainless steel or chromed steel and are used as a retrieval tool.

tongue A variety meat (typically from a cow, although tongues from other animals are also available); generally it is skinned before service; it has a pink color and a tough, chewy texture and is available fresh, pickled, salted, smoked and corned.

tongue press A hinged metal plate and bowl used for pressing tongue; it keeps the meat flat as it cools.

tonic; tonic water Quinine-flavored water infused with carbon dioxide to create effervescence; also known as quinine water.

tonnato (tohn-NAH-toh) An Italian dish that contains or is accompanied by tuna.

top-brown To brown a food (often one with a bread crumb, grated cheese or other topping) under an overhead heat source.

topneck clam; topneck quahog An Atlantic hard-shell clam that is under 4 in. (10.1 cm) across the shell; the shells are a dark tannish-gray, and the chewy meat has a mild flavor.

top round A subprimal cut of the beef primal round; it is the muscle along the leg bone on the inside portion of the animal's leg; it is fairly tender and flavorful and sometimes fabricated into round steaks; also known as the inside round.

top sirloin *See* loin tip.

toque (toke) The tall, white, pleated hat worn by a chef.

toro (toh-roh) Japanese for tuna belly; it is the fatty cut of raw prime tuna used for sashimi.

torrone (tor-ROHN-nay) An Italian nougat of honey and nuts.

Torte (TOR-ta) 1. German for cake. 2. German for a cake made with ground nuts or bread crumbs instead of flour; some versions are single layered, and others are multilayered and filled with whipped cream, jam or buttercream.

tortilha (tor-TEE-lya) Portuguese for an open-faced (unfolded) omelette; also known as omellatta.

tortilla (tohr-TEE-yuh) A round, thin, unleavened Mexican bread made from masa or wheat flour and lard and baked on a griddle (depending on its use, it could then be deep-fried), it is eaten plain or wrapped around or garnished with various fillings.

tortilla chips Corn or flour tortillas cut into wedges and deep-fried or baked; eaten as a snack, usually with a dip or salsa.

tortilla press A metal utensil used to flatten tortilla dough; it consists of two hinged disks: the top disk has a handle and is lowered over the ball of dough resting on the lower disk.

tortoni (tohr-TOH-nee) A rich frozen Italian dessert made with whipped cream or ice cream, flavored with rum and coated with macaroon crumbs or ground almonds.

tortue, sauce à la (tor-too, saus ah lah) A French compound sauce made from a demi-glaze flavored with white wine, turtle herbs, truffle essence, cayenne and Madeira.

tostada (toh-STAH-duh) A Mexican dish of a crisp-fried tortilla topped with refried beans and garnished with meat, cheese, lettuce, tomatoes, sour cream, guacamole and/or salsa.

tostones (tohs-TOH-nays) A Caribbean dish of green plantain slices that are soaked in adobo-flavored water before being deep-fried; after cooling, they are flattened and refried.

touffe (touf) French for a bundle of herbs and/or vegetables with their stalks, tied in a bundle.

toulousaine, sauce (too-loo-zhan) A French compound sauce made from an allemande flavored with mushroom and truffle essences.

Toulouse sausage (too-loos) A small French sausage made from pork, seasoned with garlic and wine.

touraine A variety of medium-sized, spherical squash with a pale green flesh covered with darker green spots and streaks.

tournant (toor-nahn) At a food services operation following the brigade system, the person who works wherever needed; also known as the roundsman or swing cook.

tournedo (tour-nah-doe) A fabricated cut of the beef primal short loin; cut from the short tenderloin, it is very lean, tender and flavorful and smaller than a filet mignon.

tournedos Rossini (toor-nuh-dohs roas-see-nee) A French dish of tournedos sautéed in butter, placed on a crouton, garnished with foie gras and truffles and served with a brown sauce flavored with Madeira.

tournéed An English version of the French verb used to describe a vegetable that is cut into a football shape with seven equal sides and blunt ends.

tourner (toor-nay) French for to trim or to turn and used to describe the act of cutting foods, usually vegetables, into football-shaped pieces with seven equal sides and blunt ends.

tourte (toor-teh) A French open-faced savory pastry tart.

tourtière (tour-tea-yay) 1. French for the pie dish used to make a tourte. 2. A Canadian pie made with pork, veal and onions, flavored with allspice and baked in a pastry shell; it is eaten hot or cold.

trail The intestines of a game bird.

tranche (tranch) 1. French for a slice. 2. A slice (usually of fish) that is cut on the diagonal to increase the apparent size of the item.

trattoria (trah-toh-REE-ah) A causal, local eating place in Italy.

treacle (TRE-kehl) 1. British for molasses. 2. A sweet syrup or ingredient made from molasses and corn syrup; also known as golden syrup.

trifle (TRI-fuhl) A deep-dish British layered dessert made with sponge cake, sherry, custard, jam or fruit and whipped cream.

trim loss The amount of a product removed when preparing it for consumption.

trimmed whisk A utensil made by cutting the wires of a whisk so that only a few inches remain attached to the handle; used for spun sugar.

tripe The first and second stomachs of ruminants such as cattle, oxen and sheep; it has a tender texture and a subtle flavor.

triticale (triht-ih-KAY-lee) A cereal grain that is a hybrid of wheat and rye; it contains more protein and has less gluten-forming potential than wheat and has a nutty, sweet flavor; available in whole berries, as flour and in flakes.

trivet 1. A three-legged stand used to hold a kettle near a fire. 2. An ornamental stand (either flat or with short feet) placed under a hot dish at the table.

trout Any of various fish belonging to the salmon family, some of which are anadromous and many of which are aquafarmed; they generally have a firm, white, orange or pink, flaky flesh, a low to moderate fat content and an average market weight of 8–10 oz. (225–280 g); important varieties include lake trout, rainbow trout, brook trout, brown trout and steelhead trout.

truffle 1. A fungus (genus *Tuber*) that grows underground near the roots of certain trees, usually oaks; generally spherical and of various small sizes, with a thick, rough, wrinkled skin; there are two principal varieties: black and white. 2. A rich, creamy chocolate candy made with chocolate, butter, cream and flavorings, formed into small rough balls and coated with cocoa powder or melted chocolate.

truffle slicer A small tool used to shave slivers or slices from a truffle; it consists of an adjustable blade mounted at a 45-degree angle on a frame; the truffle is pressed down and across the blade.

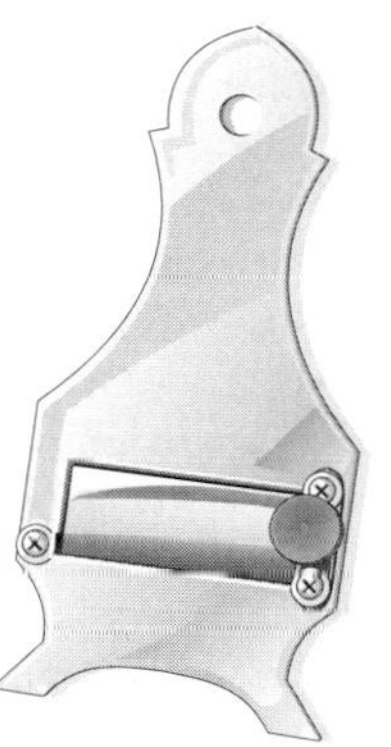
truffle slicer

truite au bleu (tre-wee toh bluh) A French dish of freshly killed trout poached in court bouillon and served with hollandaise or melted butter and garnished with parsley.

truss To secure poultry or other food with string, skewers or pins so that it maintains its shape during cooking.

tsatsiki; tzatziki (tzah-tzee-key) A Greek salad consisting of cucumber dressed with goat's milk yogurt and garnished with mint leaves and paprika.

tsp. *See* teaspoon.

tsukémono (tzu-ke-mow-no) The pickles that accompany most Japanese meals.

tube pan A deep round pan with a hollow tube in the center; used for baking cakes, especially angel food, chiffon and pound cakes. *See* Bundt pan.

tube pan

tuber The swollen, fleshy part of a plant's underground stem.

tuile (twee) French for tile and used to describe a thin, crisp wafer cookie traditionally shaped while still hot around a curved object such as a rolling pin.

tulipe (too-LEEP) A thin, crisp French wafer cookie that is formed into a ruffled, cuplike shape while still hot and used as an edible container for ice cream, fruit, mousse and other desserts.

tumblerful A traditional measure of volume; it is approximately 2 cups.

tuna Any of several varieties of saltwater fish of the mackerel family found in tropical and subtropical waters worldwide; they generally are available as loins or smaller cuts and have a low to moderate fat content, a dark pink, flaky flesh that becomes light gray when cooked, a firm texture and a distinctive rich flavor; significant varieties include albacore tuna, bluefin tuna, bonito, skipjack tuna and yellowfin tuna.

tuna salad A salad of tuna (usually canned) typically garnished with celery and onions, bound with mayonnaise and often flavored with celery salt.

tunneling A condition in quick breads caused by overmixing and characterized by elongated holes.

tuong (too-ong) A thick, strongly flavored Vietnamese sauce made of fermented soybeans, sugar and salt and used in dips and marinades for roasted meats.

turban (thur-bahn) 1. A French preparation method for certain foods, especially forcemeats, cooked in a circular border mold. 2. A French presentation method for foods arranged in a circular pattern on a plate.

turbinado sugar Raw sugar that has been cleaned with steam to make it edible; it is light brown and coarse, with a molasses flavor.

turbot (thur-bow) 1. A diamond-shaped flatfish found in the Atlantic Ocean off Europe and in the Mediterranean Sea; it has a silvery-brown skin, a firm, white flesh, a delicate flavor and weighs up to 30 lb. (13.5 kg). 2. A marketing name given to several Pacific Ocean flatfish of no culinary significance.

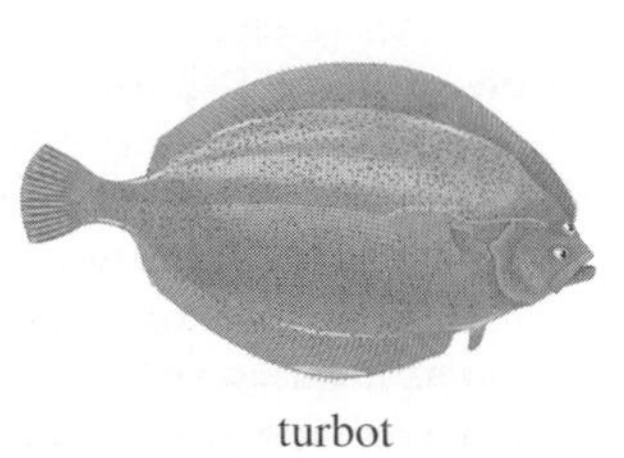
turbot

turbot poacher A large diamond-shaped pan designed to poach a whole turbot; it is 25 in. long and 6 in. deep, with an inset rack.

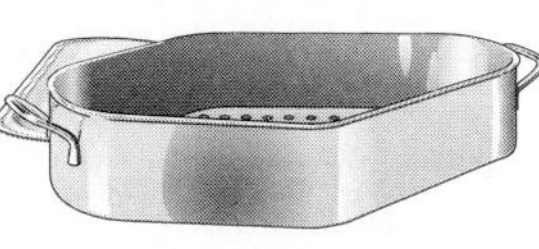
turbot poacher

tureen A deep dish, usually with two handles and a notch in the lid for a ladle; used to serve soups, stews and the like.

turkey One of the principal kinds of poultry recognized by the U.S. Department of Agriculture (USDA); it has light and dark meat and a relatively small amount of fat.

Turkish coffee A very strong coffee made by boiling finely ground coffee, sugar and water three times, cooling the mixture briefly between boilings; made in an ibrik and served in small cups immediately following the third boil; also known as Greek coffee.

Turkish delight A chewy, rubbery Middle Eastern candy made with cornstarch or gelatin, honey and fruit juice, often flavored with nuts; the candy is cut into small squares and coated with powdered sugar.

turmeric (tehr-MEHR-rik) A dried, powdery spice produced from the rhizome of a tropical plant related to ginger (*Curcuma longa*); it has a strong, spicy flavor and yellow color and is used in Indian and Middle Eastern cuisines and as a yellow coloring agent; also known as Indian saffron.

turn To shape a vegetable or fruit with a paring knife. *See* tourner.

turner (offset) A utensil used to turn food or transfer food from cookware; it has a handle and a broad, flat metal blade that can be solid or perforated (to help drain liquids) with a round or straight edge; available in sizes from 2.5 × 2.5 in. (6.3 × 6.3 cm) to 5 × 3 in. (12.7 × 7.6 cm).

turner (offset)

turnip The rounded, conical root of the turnip plant (*Brassica rapa*); it has a white skin with a purple-tinged top, a delicate, slightly sweet flavor that becomes stronger as it ages and a coarse texture.

turnip greens The crinkly green leaves of the turnip plant; they have a sweet, peppery flavor when young that becomes more bitter with age.

turnover 1. A square piece of pastry dough folded in half over a sweet or savory filling to create a triangle. 2. The frequency with which stock is sold and replenished during a given period.

turtle 1. Any of several varieties of land, freshwater or saltwater reptiles; they generally have a domed shell on top (called a carapace) and a flat shell below (called a plastron); the most significant variety for culinary purposes is the green turtle. 2. A round, flat, caramel and pecan candy coated with chocolate.

turtle herbs A spice blend consisting of basil, thyme and marjoram; used to flavor soups, such as mock turtle soup.

Tutové (too-tohv) A French rolling pin with deep, horizontal ridges in the cylinder; used to distribute fat evenly in layers of dough, as when making puff pastry or croissant dough.

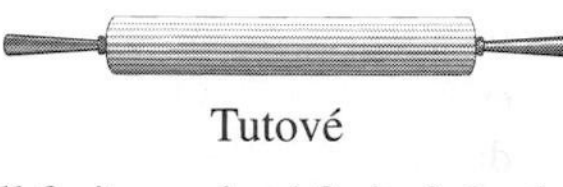
Tutové

tutti-frutti 1. Italian for all fruit or mixed fruit. 2. In the United States, a sweet fruity flavoring used for gum, candy, ice cream and the like.

Twelfth-Night cake A rich British spice cake made with candied fruits, almonds and almond paste; traditionally served on January 6, the twelfth day after Christmas.

twice-baked An expression used to refer to a product that is baked, then reworked and baked a second time (e.g., twice-baked potatoes or biscotti).

two-pronged fork A fork with two long tines; used to turn large pieces of meat or to hold meat or poultry while carving. *See* carving fork.

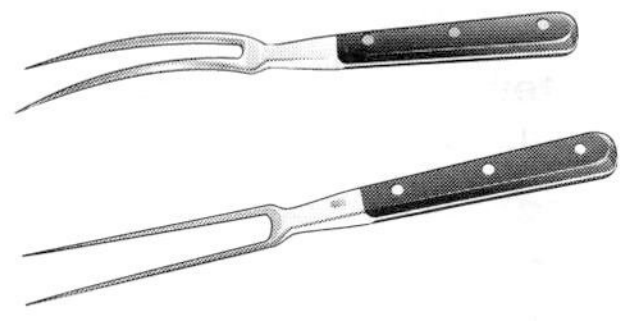
two-pronged forks

Tyler pie; Tyler pudding pie A pie named for President John Tyler and popular throughout the American South; it is made with brown sugar, butter, cream and eggs and topped with grated coconut.

tyrolienne, à la (tee-roll-YEN, ah lah) 1. A French preparation for fish; it is fried, served on tomato concassée and garnished with fried onion rings. 2. A French preparation for meat; it is pan-fried, served on tomatoes, garnished with onion rings and topped with a sauce Tyrolienne.

Tyrolienne, sauce (tee-roll-YEN) A French compound sauce made from a sauce béarnaise prepared with olive oil instead of butter.

tzimmes (TSIHM-ihs) A Jewish dish of root vegetables (e.g., sweet potatoes, potatoes or carrots), dried fruit (e.g., raisins) or fresh fruit (e.g., apples) and sometimes meat, such as beef brisket, flavored with honey and cinnamon.

udon; udong (oo-DOHN) Wide, flat, ribbonlike Japanese noodles made from wheat flour (or sometimes corn flour); available in a variety of widths, either dried, fresh or precooked.

ugli; usli (OO-gli) A large hybrid citrus fruit that is a cross between a grapefruit, orange and tangerine; it is grown in Jamaica and has a very thick, yellow-green, loose skin, a yellow-orange flesh and a flavor reminiscent of a mandarin with overtones of honey and pineapple.

uku A fish with a pale pink flesh, a firm texture, a delicate flavor and an average weight of 4–18 lb. (1.8–8.1 kg); also known as a gray snapper and jobfish.

ultrahigh-temperature pasteurization; ultrahigh-temperature processing *See* pasteurization, ultrahigh temperature.

ultrapasteurization *See* pasteurization, ultra.

ulua (oo-lu-ah) A fish found off Hawaii; a member of the jack family; it has an average market weight of 10–40 lb. (4.5–18 kg), a firm flesh with minimal red muscle and a mild flavor; there are two principal varieties: black ulua and white ulua; also known as jackfish. *See* papio.

umami (u-MOM-ee) One of the five primary sensations comprising the sense of taste; it refers to the savory taste of protein.

ume-boshi (OO-meh-boh-shee) Japanese pickled plums; they have a dusty pink color and a tart, salty flavor.

unbleached flour Wheat flour that has not been treated with a whitening agent.

univalves A general category of mollusks characterized by a single shell and a single muscle; significant varieties include abalone, limpet, periwinkle, snails and whelks; also known as gastropods.

unmold To remove food from the container (usually a decorative dish) in which it was prepared; it is usually done by inverting it over a serving plate.

unsaturated fat A triglyceride composed of monounsaturated or polyunsaturated fatty acids and believed to help reduce the amount of cholesterol in the blood; generally, it comes from plants and is liquid (an oil) at room temperature. *See* monounsaturated fat *and* polyunsaturated fat.

unsweetened chocolate Chocolate liquor or mass, without added sugar or flavorings; used in baking. *See* chocolate-making process.

upside-down cake A dessert made by lining the bottom of a baking pan with butter, sugar and fruit (typically pineapple), then adding a light cake batter; after baking, the cake is inverted so that the glazed fruit becomes the top surface.

USDA (U.S. Department of Agriculture) A cabinet-level department of the executive branch of the federal government; one of its principal responsibilities is to make sure that individual foods are safe, wholesome and accurately labeled, and it attempts to meet these responsibilities through inspection and grading procedures; it also provides services for food producers and publishes nutrition information.

USDA quality grades 1. A voluntary U.S. Department of Agriculture (USDA) system of grading beef, lamb, pork and veal based on the animal's age and the meat's color, texture and degree of marbling; grading is intended to provide a guide to the meat's tenderness, juiciness and flavor. *See* beef quality grades, lamb quality grades, pork quality grades *and* veal quality grades. 2. The USDA's voluntary system of grading poultry based on overall quality; it has little bearing on the product's tenderness or flavor. *See* poultry quality grades.

USDA yield grades A voluntary U.S. Department of Agriculture (USDA) system based on conformation and finish and used to measure the amount of usable meat (as opposed to fat and bone) on a beef or lamb carcass and providing a uniform method of identifying cutability differences among carcasses; the grades run from 1 to 5, with 1 representing the greatest yield.

U.S. system A measurement system used principally in the United States; it uses ounces and pounds for weight and cups for volume. *See* imperial system *and* metric system.

utility The lowest U.S. Department of Agriculture (USDA) quality grade for pork and one of the lowest for beef, lamb and veal; the meat is usually used for ground, canned or otherwise processed products.

utility knife An all-purpose knife used for cutting produce and carving poultry; it has a rigid 6- to 8-in.-long blade shaped like a chef's knife but narrower.

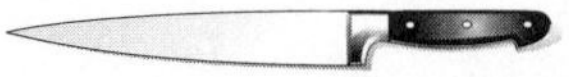

utility knife

Uzès, sauce (eu-zehz) A French compound sauce made from hollandaise flavored with anchovy paste and Madeira wine.

V

vacherin (vasher-ANN) A French dessert consisting of a crisp baked meringue container filled with ice cream or Chantilly cream and fruit.

vacuum packaging A food preservation method in which fresh or cooked food is placed in an airtight container (usually plastic); virtually all air is removed through a vacuum process, thus sealing the container and eliminating the environment necessary to sustain the growth of certain microorganisms that would otherwise spoil the food.

Valencia orange A sweet, juicy, almost seedless orange; it is spherical and has a thin skin.

Valencia rice A short- to medium-grain rice that does not become creamy when cooked; it has a nutlike flavor and is used principally for paella.

vanilla bean; vanilla pod The dried, cured podlike fruit of an orchid plant (*Vanilla planifolia*) grown in tropical regions; the pod contains numerous tiny black seeds; both the pod and the seeds are used for flavoring.

vanilla custard sauce A stirred custard made with egg yolks, sugar and milk or half-and-half and flavored with vanilla; served with or used in dessert preparations; also known as crème anglaise.

vanilla extract A vanilla-flavored product made by macerating chopped vanilla beans in a water–alcohol solution to extract the flavor; its strength is measured in folds.

vanilla sugar Granulated sugar infused with the flavor of vanilla and made by burying vanilla beans in a container of sugar for a brief time; used in baked goods, creams and with fruit.

vanilla wafers Small, round, golden-colored crisp cookies with a strong vanilla flavor.

vanillin (vah-NIL-lahn) 1. A fragrant, crystalline substance produced by vanilla beans or made synthetically; used for flavoring and in perfumes. 2. Synthetic vanilla flavoring.

variegated scallop A variety of scallops found in the Atlantic Ocean from Norway to West Africa and in the western Mediterranean Sea; it has a domed shell in a variety of colors with an average diameter of 2.5 in. (6.3 cm) and a tender, sweet, white meat.

variety 1. A plant produced by the fertilization of one member of a species by another; the two plants are similar genetically but have different qualities or characteristics, and the resulting plant has features of both. *See* hybrid. 2. A term imprecisely used to describe a commercial variant or market name of a particular whole food. 3. In the nutrition context, the consumption, over the course of a day and at each meal, of foods from various sections of the food pyramid as well as different foods within each section.

variety meats The edible organs and other portions of a mammal; includes the brain, heart, kidneys, liver, pancreas, thymus (sweetbreads), tongue, stomach wall (tripe), hog intestines (chitterlings), testicles (fries), spleen, oxtail and pig's feet; also known as offal (especially in Great Britain). *See* meat by-products.

vark Indian gold and silver foil.

veal Meat from calves slaughtered when younger than 9 months (usually at 8–16 weeks); it has a lean, light pink flesh, a delicate flavor and a tender, firm texture.

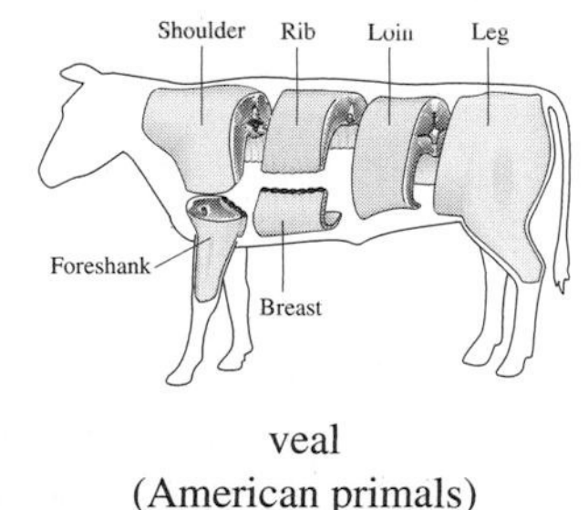

veal
(American primals)

veal, free-range The meat of calves that are allowed to roam freely and eat grasses and other natural foods; the meat is pinker and more strongly flavored than that of milk-fed calves.

veal, milk-fed The meat of calves that are kept in pens and fed milk-based formulas; the meat is pale pink and very delicately flavored; also known as formula-fed veal.

veal Orloff A dish of braised loin of veal carved into even horizontal slices, each spread with a thin layer of puréed sautéed mushrooms and onions, stacked back in place and tied to reform the loin; this is covered with additional mushroom mixture, topped with béchamel sauce and grated Parmesan and browned in the oven.

veal Oscar Sautéed veal cutlets served with béarnaise and garnished with asparagus tips and crab.

veal primals The five principal bilateral sections of the veal carcass: the shoulder, foreshank and breast, rib, loin and leg.

veal rib chop A fabricated cut of the veal primal rib; it usually contains one rib and the flavorful, tender rib eye muscle.

vegan (VEE-gun; VAY-gun) A vegetarian who does not eat any animal products. *See* lactovegetarian *and* ovolactovegetarian.

Vegemite A salty, dense vegetable paste made in Great Britain; popular in Australia.

vegetable coloring Commercial dye preparations derived from vegetable sources and used to color foodstuffs such as Easter eggs and icings.

vegetable oil 1. A category of specific oils obtained from plants. 2. A general term describing blends of different vegetable oils such as corn, safflower, rapeseed, cottonseed and/or soybean oils; these blends are generally intended to have little flavor and aroma and to be used as all-purpose oils.

vegetable peeler A knifelike utensil whose stationary or swiveling blade has two slits; used for thinly stripping the peel from produce.

vegetables The edible parts of plants, including the leaves, stalks, roots, tubers and flowers (and in certain cases the fruit); they are generally savory rather than sweet and often salted or otherwise dressed; some are always consumed cooked, others always raw (fresh) and some can be consumed either cooked or raw; sometimes associated with meat, fish, shellfish and poultry as part of a meal or ingredient; vegetables are mostly water (approximately 80%) and usually contain vitamins, minerals, carbohydrates, protein and fats. *See* fruits.

vegetarian A person who eats primarily or exclusively plant foods. *See* lactovegetarian, ovolactovegetarian, vegan *and* fruitarian.

vein steak A fabricated cut of the beef sirloin or strip loin primals; it contains a distinctive crescent-shaped piece of connective tissue.

vela (veh-lah) A Spanish sausage shape; the straight sausage usually contains large pieces of meat and is sliced thin and served raw as tapas. *See* ristras *and* sarta.

velouté, sauce (veh-loo-TAY) A French leading sauce made by thickening a veal stock, chicken stock or fish fumet with a white or golden roux; also known as a blond sauce.

velveting A Chinese preparation method for fish; the fish is marinated in egg white, cornstarch and rice wine and fried.

venison The flesh of any member of the deer family, including the antelope, caribou, elk, moose, reindeer, red-tailed deer, white-tailed deer and mule deer; it typically has a dark red color with very little intramuscular fat or marbling, a firm, dense, velvety texture, a mild aroma and a sweet, herbal, nutty flavor; significant cuts include the loin, leg, rack and saddle.

vent *v.* 1. To allow the circulation or escape of a liquid or gas. 2. To cool a pot of hot liquid by setting the pot on blocks in a cold water bath and allowing cold water to circulate around it. *n.* An exhaust fan, usually vented outdoors, that is mounted above or near a stove; used to eliminate odors while cooking; also known as a hood and hood vent.

venus shell clams Any of several varieties of clams with an elongated, compressed, smooth, thin, glossy shell that ranges from dull pink to bluish purple; they have an average length of 5–7 in. (12.5–17.5 cm) and a very sweet, relatively tender meat.

Veracruz (ver-ah-KROOZ) A Mexican preparation method associated with the state of Veracruz; the principal ingredient, usually fish or shellfish, is cooked in a sauce of tomatoes, chiles, onion and garlic, flavored with oregano and lime juice and usually served over rice.

Verdi, sauce; Verdi mayonnaise (verh-dee) A French mayonnaise sauce made with chopped spinach, gherkins, chives and sour cream.

verjus; verjuice (vair-jue) The unfermented juice of unripened grapes; it has a very high acid content and is sometimes used as a substitute for vinegar.

vermouth A neutral white wine flavored with various herbs, spices and fruits and fortified to a minimum of 16% alcohol; used as an aperitif and cocktail ingredient.

Véronique (vay-roh-NEEK) A French term describing dishes garnished with seedless white grapes.

verte, mayonnaise (vehrt) A French mayonnaise sauce flavored with tarragon, parsley, watercress and basil.

vertical cutter/mixer (VCM) An appliance that operates like a very large, powerful blender; usually floor mounted and with a capacity of 15–80 qt.

vertical roaster A towerlike cross-braced metal stand used for roasting poultry; generally 9.5 in. high with a 6-in. base, it prevents the poultry from cooking in its drippings. *See* roasting rack.

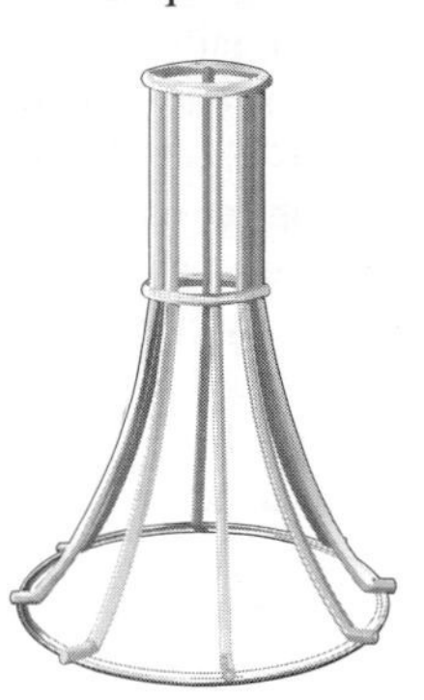
vertical roaster

vervain (VUR-van) An herb (*Verbena officinalis*) and member of the same family as lemon verbena; used to flavor liqueurs and infusions.

very rare A degree of doneness for meat; the meat should have a very red, raw-looking center, the center should be cool to the touch and the meat should provide almost no resistance when pressed; also known as bleu. *See* rare, medium rare, medium, medium well *and* well done.

Vichy (VEE-shee) A French mineral water from the town of Vichy.

Vichy, carottes à la (VEE-shee, kah-rote ah lah) A French dish of carrots cooked in Vichy water.

vichyssoise (vee-shee-swahz) A French soup made from puréed onions or leeks, potatoes, cream, chicken stock and seasonings, garnished with chives and usually served cold.

Victoria, sauce A French white wine sauce seasoned with cayenne, finished with lobster butter and garnished with truffles and diced lobster.

Victoria sandwich; Victoria sponge A British dessert consisting of two layers of sponge cake filled with raspberry jam and whipped cream or buttercream; usually served for afternoon tea; also known as sandwich cake.

Vidalia onion A large onion with a pale yellow outer layer and a sweet, juicy white flesh; grown in a delimited area around Vidalia, Georgia.

Vienna sausage 1. An Austrian sausage similar to a frankfurter. 2. A small sausage with a mild flavor; often available canned with gelatin.

Viennese coffee Strong, hot coffee sweetened to taste and topped with whipped cream; served in a tall glass.

viennoise, à la (veen-NWAHZ, ah lah) 1. A French preparation and presentation method for escallops of veal, chicken or fish; they are rolled in egg and bread crumbs, pan-fried and garnished with hard-boiled eggs, capers, olives, parsley, beurre noir and lemon slices. 2. A Viennese preparation in which the meat, fish or poultry is breaded, pan-fried and garnished only with lemon slices.

Vierge, sauce (vee-erge) A French compound sauce made from a béchamel blended with artichoke purée and finished with whipped unsweetened cream.

villeroi, sauce; villeroy sauce (vee-loh-wah) A French compound sauce made from an allemande flavored with ham and truffle peelings or essence.

vinaigrette (vihn-uh-GREHT) A temporary emulsion of oil and vinegar (usually three parts oil to one part vinegar) seasoned with herbs, spices, salt and pepper; used as a salad dressing or sauce. *See* French dressing.

vindaloo (VEN-deh-loo) A spicy Indian dish consisting of meat or chicken flavored with tamarind juice, lemon juice and a masala of cayenne pepper, cumin, ginger, turmeric, cinnamon and oil, usually served over rice.

vinegar From the French vin aigre (sour wine); a weak solution of acetic acid made from a fermented liquid such as cider, wine or beer, subjected to certain bacterial activity; generally clear, the liquid can be tinted various shades depending on the base liquid and can reflect the flavor of the base liquid or be flavored by the introduction of other ingredients.

vinegar pie A sweet dessert made with a mixture of eggs, sugar, flour, vinegar and nutmeg baked in a flaky pie shell.

vinification The process of transforming grape juice into a still wine: generally (1) grapes are gently crushed to release their juice; (2) the crushed grapes and juice (collectively, the must) are put in a vat to ferment (if the wine will be a white one, the grape skins are removed and only the juice is allowed to ferment); (3) the juice is removed and the residue is pressed to extract more juice (for red wines only); (4) the fermented product, now called wine, is transferred to containers (often barrels) for aging (a process called racking); (5) after this preliminary aging, the wine is transferred to bottles for further aging and distribution; also known as the wine-making process.

virus The smallest known form of life; although it can survive on its own, a virus is parasitic in that it is completely dependent on nutrients inside a host's cells for its metabolic and reproductive needs; some viruses are food-borne and can cause an illness or disease.

viscera Internal organs.

vitamin A class of nutrients composed of noncaloric complex organic substances necessary for proper body functions and health maintenance; with the exceptions of vitamins A, D and K, they are essential nutrients occurring naturally in animals and plants and can be categorized as fat soluble (vitamins A, D, E and K) or water soluble (the B vitamins and vitamin C).

vitamin B_2 A water-soluble vitamin essential for forming cells and enzymes and maintaining vision and tissues; not destroyed during ordinary cooking; significant sources include dairy products, eggs, leafy green vegetables, brewer's yeast, liver and whole grain or enriched breads and cereals; also known as riboflavin, lactoflavin and vitamin G.

vitello tonnato (vee-TEL-loa toan-NAA-toa) An Italian dish consisting of veal served with sauce flavored with tuna fish.

vodka (VAHD-kah) A distilled spirit made from potatoes and various grains, principally corn, with some wheat added; it is distilled at proofs ranging from 80 to 100 and is sometimes flavored.

vol-au-vent (vawl-oh-VAHN) A large, deep puff pastry shell often filled with a savory mixture and topped with a pastry lid.

vol-au-vent cutter A tinned steel tool for cutting vol-au-vents from puff pastry; it looks like a double cookie cutter with an inside cutter about 1 in. smaller and slightly shorter than the other.

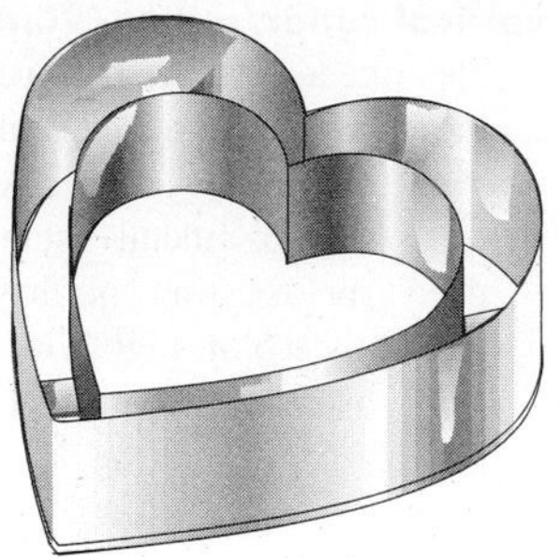

vol-au-vent cutter

volume 1. The space occupied by a substance. 2. The measurement typically used to measure liquids; volume measurements are commonly expressed as liters, teaspoons, tablespoons, cups, pints, gallons, fluid ounces and bushels. 3. A quantity of something, either tangible or intangible (e.g., a volume of goods or business).

W

wafer A very thin, crisp cookie or cracker; it can be sweet or savory.

waffle A thin, crisp, light cake with a honeycomb surface; it is baked in a waffle iron and served with sweet or savory toppings.

waffle iron An appliance used for making waffles; there are two types: a stove-top waffle iron, which consists of two hinged honeycomb-patterned forms with handles (the forms are heated on the stove, the batter is poured in and cooked on one side then turned to cook the other side), and an electric waffle iron with a built-in heat source.

wagashi (wah-gah-shee) Japanese confections, cakes, cookies and candies; design is often more important than flavor; there are three principal classifications: namagashi, han namagashi and higashi.

waiter's wine opener A tool with a coiled wire worm, perpendicular handle, hinged arm, and two small knife blades set at opposite ends; it measures about 4 ½ in. long and 5/16 in. wide; used for removing the cork from a wine bottle or the cap from a beverage.

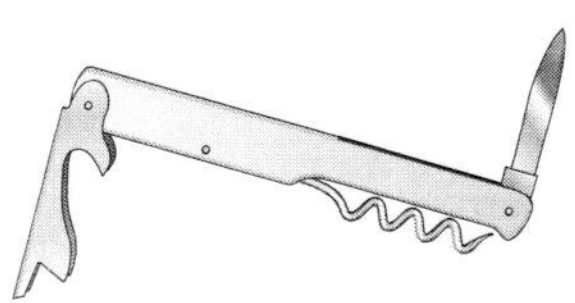

waiter's wine opener

Waldorf salad A salad of apples, celery and sometimes walnuts in a mayonnaise dressing.

Walewska; Waleska (vah-LEF-skah) A French dish in which the main ingredient (e.g., poached sole) is garnished with lobster and truffles, coated with Mornay sauce and browned.

walk-in A large insulated box or room used to store foods on adjustable shelves at appropriately low temperatures; it is large enough to enter; a separate walk-in freezer is sometimes attached. *See* reach-in.

war bread A bread popular in the New England region of the United States for almost 200 years; most of the white wheat flour (which would be scarce in wartime) is replaced with a mixture of oats, cornmeal and whole wheat.

warka (vahr-kah) A round, thin, translucent pastry leaf used in Moroccan cuisine; it is similar to phyllo.

warm To bring a food slowly to a slightly higher temperature.

warming oven An oven used to maintain cooked foods at a proper temperature or to gently warm cooked foods to the proper temperature; it usually has a limited temperature range, with the highest setting at 200–250°F (93–121°C).

warmouth A freshwater fish of the sunfish family found in the eastern United States; it has a dark olive skin with bluish lines radiating from its red eyes and a soft flesh with a muddy flavor; also known as a stump knocker.

warm-water tails Tails harvested from spiny lobsters caught off Florida and Brazil and in the Caribbean Sea; available frozen, their flavor is inferior to that of cold-water tails.

warty venus clam A variety of venus clam found off western Europe and West Africa and in the Mediterranean Sea; it has a brownish-red, slightly ovoid bumpy shell measuring 1–3 in. (2.54–7.6 cm) and sweet meat.

wasabi; wasabe (wah-SAH-bee) The root of an Asian plant (genus *Armoracia*) similar to horseradish; it is ground and, when mixed with water, becomes a green-colored condiment with a sharp, pungent, fiery flavor used in Japanese cuisines.

wash *v.* 1. To apply a liquid to the surface of an object to remove dirt; a cleansing agent is often added to the liquid; the process may not kill microorganisms. 2. To apply a liquid to the surface of a food. *n.*1. A liquid such as water, milk or eggs applied to the surface of a food, usually before baking. 2. A solution of thickening agent (such as flour) in a cool liquid. 3. The liquid obtained from fermenting wort with yeast; the raw material for the first distillation in the pot still and the only distillation in the patent still. 4. A Caribbean beverage made of brown sugar, water and lime juice or sour orange juice.

Wassail Bowl A punch made of brown sugar, Cognac or gold rum, nutmeg, ginger, mace, allspice, cloves, eggs, cinnamon, baked apples and Madeira, sherry, port or Marsala and served in a large wassil bowl (similar to a punch bowl) garnished with small roasted apples.

water 1. A tasteless, odorless, colorless liquid; each water molecule consists of two hydrogen atoms and one oxygen atom (H_2O). 2. The principal chemical constituent of the body; essential for life, it provides the medium in which metabolic activities take place and also acts as a transportation medium, lubricant and body-temperature regulator. 3. A beverage.

water, acidulated A mildly acidic solution of water and lemon juice or vinegar that is used to prevent cut fruits and vegetables from darkening.

water, carbonated Water that has absorbed carbon dioxide; the carbon dioxide produces an effervescence and increases mouth feel.

water, distilled Water that has had all the minerals and impurities removed through distillation; generally used for pharmaceutical purposes.

water, drinking Water that comes from a government-approved source and has undergone some treatment and filtration; it can be bottled or available on tap and is used for drinking and general culinary purposes.

water, mineral Drinking water that comes from a protected underground water source and contains at least 250 parts per million of total dissolved solids such as calcium.

water, sparkling Water that has absorbed carbon dioxide, either naturally or artificially; the carbon dioxide produces effervescence and increases mouth feel.

water, spring Water obtained from an underground source that flows naturally to the earth's surface.

water, still Water without carbonation.

water activity A measure of the amount of moisture bacteria need to grow; often written as Aw; water has an Aw of 1.0, and any food with an Aw of 0.85 or greater is considered potentially hazardous.

water added The U.S. Department of Agriculture (USDA) labeling term indicating that a processed meat product has been injected with a curing solution in excess of the amount of natural fluids lost during curing and smoking.

water biscuit A bland, thin, crisp cracker, often served with cheese and wine.

water caltrop A two-horned nut (*Trapis bicornis*) with a shiny black skin, a crisp, white flesh and a flavor similar to that of a water chestnut; used in Chinese and Indian cuisines.

water chestnut The fruit of a water plant (genus *Trapa*) native to Southeast Asia; it has a brownish-black skin, an ivory to tan flesh, a crisp texture and a slightly sweet, nutty flavor; used in various Asian cuisines; also known as water caltrop.

watercress A plant (*Nasturtium aquaticum*) with small, dark green leaves and a pungent, peppery, slightly bitter flavor; used as an herb, a garnish and in soups, salads and sandwiches.

water ice A frozen dessert of sugar and water flavored with fruit juice, coffee, liquor or another beverage; made without fat or egg whites.

water lemon A short, ovoid fruit (*Passiflora laurifolia*) native to South America with a yellow or orange color and a sweet juicy flesh; also known as yellow granadilla and Jamaican honeysuckle.

watermelon 1. A category of melons (*Citrullus vulgaris*) native to Africa; they are characterized by a very thick rind, a very juicy granular flesh with seeds generally disbursed throughout the flesh and a sweet flavor. *See* muskmelon. 2. A large to very large ovoid to spherical melon with green striped or pale to dark green rind and a pink to red flesh; a seedless variety is available; also known as a red watermelon.

water pack Canned fruits, vegetables or fish with water or other liquid (e.g., juice) added.

waterzooi (VAH-tuhr-zoh-ee) A Belgian (Flemish) dish of freshwater fish and eel (chicken is sometimes substituted) cooked in a court bouillon with herbs; after vegetables are added, it is finished with butter and cream and sometimes thickened with bread crumbs.

wax bean A yellow version of the green bean; it has a slightly waxier pod.

wax paper; waxed paper Semitransparent paper with a waterproof coating on both sides and used to line baking pans and cover foods for storage; also known as greaseproof paper. *See* silicone paper *and* parchment paper.

waxy starch; waxy maize starch The starch portion of a waxy corn; sometimes used as a food additive to thicken puddings and sauces; also known as amioca.

wedding cake An elaborately tiered and decorated cake that is the centerpiece of a wedding meal or celebration.

Wehani rice An American russet colored aromatic rice that splits slightly when cooked; it has an aroma similar to that of popcorn.

weight The mass or heaviness of a substance; weight measurements are commonly expressed as grams (metric), ounces and pounds (U.S. and imperial).

well-and-tree platter A serving platter with a depressed design of a tree with branches and a trough at the bottom of the tree; these indentations allow meat juices to drain away and collect in the trough.

well done A degree of doneness for meat; the meat should have no red (and be brown throughout), be quite firm and spring back when pressed. *See* very rare, rare, medium rare, medium *and* medium well.

Wellfleet oyster An Atlantic oyster found off Wellfleet, Cape Cod; it has an oval shell and plump flesh with a firm texture and moderately salty flavor.

Welsh rarebit; Welsh rabbit (RARE-beht) A British dish of cheese melted with beer, poured on toast and broiled. *See* golden buck.

Westcott Bay oyster A variety of Pacific oyster found off Westcott Bay, in the U.S. Northwest.

western lettuce A variety of crisp head lettuce similar to iceberg.

western omelet An omelet made with green peppers, onions and diced ham; also known as a Denver omelet.

western oyster An oyster native to the Pacific Ocean off the U.S. West Coast; it has a round shell, grows up to 2 in. (5 cm) across and has an extremely delicate flavor; also known as an Olympia oyster, Olympia flat oyster and native Pacific oyster.

western sandwich A sandwich of eggs scrambled with green peppers, onions and diced ham served on white bread or toast; also known as a Denver sandwich.

Westphalian ham (wehst-FAIL-ee-uhn) A German-style boneless ham that is dry cured (sometimes with juniper berries added to the salt mixture) and smoked over a beechwood fire to which juniper twigs and berries have been added.

wet aging The process of storing vacuum-packaged meats under refrigeration for up to 6 weeks to increase tenderness and flavor. *See* dry aging.

wheat A cereal grass (genus *Triticum,* especially *T. aestivum*) grown worldwide; there are three principal varieties: durum, hard and soft; in many climates, there can be as many as three planting cycles per year; crops are sometimes identified by the planting season as winter, spring or summer wheat.

wheat, hard A wheat berry with a high protein content; flour ground from hard wheat has a high gluten-forming potential and is used for yeast breads.

wheat, soft A wheat with a low protein content; flour ground from soft wheat has a low gluten-forming potential and is used for baking tender products such as cakes.

wheat berry The whole, unprocessed wheat kernel; it consists of the bran, germ and endosperm.

wheat bran The wheat berry's rough outer covering; it is high in fiber and is used as a cereal and nutrient supplement.

wheat bread A bread made from a mixture of white and whole wheat flours.

wheated bourbon A bourbon made with wheat instead of rye grain.

wheat germ The embryo of the wheat berry; it is very oily and rich in vitamins, proteins and minerals, has a nutty flavor and is generally used as a nutritional supplement.

wheel 1. A cut from a large roundfish (e.g., swordfish and tuna); the fish is cut in a thick slice perpendicular to the backbone and then fabricated into steaks; also known as a center cut. 2. A cylindrical cheese. 3. A citrus fruit sliced in the shape of a wheel and used as a garnish.

whelks A group of gastropod mollusks found in saltwater areas worldwide; they have an ovoid, spherical, pear-shaped or spiral shell and a flavorful, lean and very tough adductor muscle; significant varieties include the channeled whelk and knobbed whelk.

whetstone A dense-grained stone used to put an edge on a dull knife; also known as a sharpening stone or oilstone. *See* steel.

whey The liquid portion of coagulated milk (curds are the semisolid portion); used for whey cheese, processed foods (e.g., crackers) and principally livestock feed.

whipping A mixing method in which foods are vigorously beaten to incorporate air; a whisk or an electric mixer with its whip attachment is used.

whipping cream *See* cream, heavy whipping; *and* cream, light whipping.

whisk A utensil consisting of several wire loops joined at a handle; the loops generally create a round or

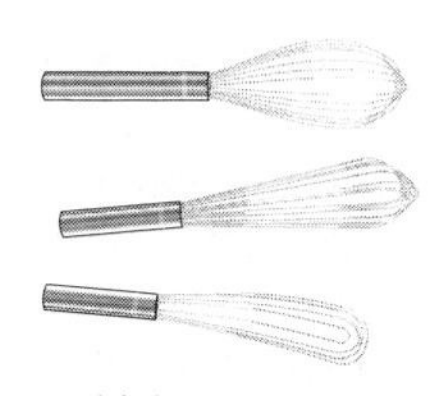

whisks (balloon, sauce and flat)

teardrop-shaped outline and range in sizes from 8 to 18 in. (20.3 to 45.7 cm); used to incorporate air into foods such as eggs, cream or sauces; also known as a whip. *See* balloon whisk, flat whisk, sauce whisk *and* trimmed whisk.

whiskey 1. An alcoholic beverage distilled from a fermented mash of grains such as corn, rye and barley; whiskeys vary depending on factors such as the type and processing of the grain and water as well as the length and type of aging process. *See* Scotch. 2. The American, English and Irish spelling for this spirit; used to identify these countries' products; in Scotland and Canada it is spelled whisky.

whiskey-making process The process for making whiskey: generally, (1) ground grain (corn, rye and/or wheat) is cooked to release starch from the tough cellular coating; (2) malt is added to convert the starches into fermentable sugars; (3) this mix is soaked in water to form the wort; (4) yeast is added to the wort, which goes into fermenting vats to ferment; (5) the fermented mix, now called beer, is distilled and then called whiskey; (6) the whiskey is then aged (usually in charred white oak barrels) and sometimes (7) blended.

whisky 1. Canadian and Scottish spelling of whiskey. 2. In the United States, the spelling approved by the federal government; whiskey, however, is still generally used for all products.

white bacon Salt pork, especially in the U.S. South. *See* salt pork.

white beans A generic term used for a variety of ovoid or kidney-shaped beans with an ivory-white skin and flesh and a delicate to bland flavor; the four principal varieties are the marrow bean, great Northern bean, navy bean and pea bean.

white chocolate 1. A candy made from cocoa butter, sugar, milk solids and flavorings; because it contains no chocolate liquor it is usually labeled white confectionary bar or coating; it can be eaten as a candy or used in confections and pastries. 2. *See* chocolate-making process.

white deadnettle A perennial herb (*Lamium album*) with a creeping rhizome and an erect, leafy stem; its white flowers are used for a tisane, and the tender, thin young leaves are cooked like greens; also known as archangel.

whitefish A member of the salmon family found in North American freshwater lakes and streams; it has a silver skin, a moderately high fat content, a flaky white flesh, a sweet flavor and an average market weight of 2–6 lb. (0.9–2.7 kg); significant varieties include lake whitefish, eastern whitefish and inland whitefish. *See* chub *and* lake herring.

white kidney bean A medium-sized, kidney-shaped bean with a creamy-white skin, cream-colored firm flesh and a flavor similar to that of the red kidney bean but not as robust; also known as cannellini. *See* kidney bean.

white pizza An American pizza topped with roasted garlic, basil, oregano, mozzarella and olive oil.

white rice Rice that has been pearled to remove the husk and bran; it has a mild flavor and aroma; also known as polished rice.

white sausage A type of sausage made with poultry, veal, pork or rabbit, often mixed with bread crumbs.

white sea bass Not a true bass but a member of the drum family found in the Pacific Ocean from Alaska to Chile; it has a gray to blue skin that becomes silvery on the sides and white on the belly, a firm white flesh, a mild flavor and an average market weight of 10 lb. (4.5 kg); also known as a white corvina.

white stew *See* fricassée *and* blanquette.

white stock A light-colored stock made from chicken, veal, beef or fish bones simmered in water with vegetables and seasonings.

white tea A type of tea for which the leaves are simply steamed and dried; the beverage is generally light and fragrant.

white walnut A native American nut (*Juglans cinera*) with a brownish-gray shell and a rich oily meat; generally used for baked goods; also known as a butternut. *See* black walnut.

whitewash A thin mixture or slurry of flour and cold water used like cornstarch for thickening.

white wine sauce 1. A French compound sauce made from a velouté flavored with a fish fumet or chicken stock and white wine and beaten with butter until emulsified. 2. A French sauce made from a fish fumet or chicken stock and white wine reduced to a glaze and beaten with butter; also known as sauce vin blanc.

whiting A fish found in the Atlantic Ocean from New England to Virginia and along the European coast; it has grayish-silver skin and an average market weight of 0.5–5 lb. (0.25–2.3 kg); also known as silver hake and silver perch.

whole fish A market form for fish; the fish is in the condition in which it was caught; intact; also known as round fish.

wholemeal 1. Flour that contains a certain proportion of bran. 2. A flour made from a blend of rye and wheat flours.

whole wheat A flour that is either milled from the entire hulled kernel or has had some of the components restored after milling.

whoopie pie A Pennsylvania German confection similar to a cupcake; usually made with leftover chocolate cake batter and white icing.

wiener *See* frankfurter.

Wiener Schnitzel (VEE-nuhr SHNIHT-shul) German for Viennese cutlet and used to describe veal scallops that are breaded, sautéed and served with lemon slices and sometimes hard-cooked eggs, capers and anchovies.

wild boar A close relative of the domesticated hog found in Europe, North America, Asia and North Africa; the lean, dark red flesh of the mature animal (usually 1–2 years old) has a firm texture and a rich, sweet, nutty flavor that is stronger than that of pork; generally available during the autumn; also known as boar.

wild pecan rice A unique long-grain rice grown only in the bayous of southern Louisiana; it has a strong nutty flavor and an exceptionally rich aroma; also known as pecan rice.

wild rice The grain of a reedlike aquatic plant (*Zizania aquatica*) unrelated to rice; grown in the United States and Canada, the grains are long, slender and black, with a distinctive earthy, nutty flavor; available in three grades: giant (a very long grain and the best quality), fancy (a medium grain and of lesser quality) and select (a short grain).

wild strawberry Any of a variety of strawberries growing wild in Europe and North America; the fruit are generally small, with a tapered, conical shape, a yellowish-red to bright red skin and an intense flavor. *See* Alpine strawberry.

wine The fermented juice of a fruit, typically freshly gathered ripe grapes.

wine-making process *See* vinification.

wine vinegar A vinegar made from any wine; it has an acidity of approximately 6.5%.

winged bean A tropical legume (*Psophocarpus tetrago-nolobus*) with four ruffled wings running the length of the pod; the pod can be green, purple or various shades of red; the bean seeds have a flavor similar to that of cranberry beans and the texture of starchy green beans; also known as asparagus pea, drumstick and goa.

winter cherry 1. A cherry-sized fruit (*Phylsalis alkekengi*) native to Europe; it has a bright red skin and is enclosed in a loose, papery, lantern-shaped red husk; usually cooked with sugar to make a syrup; also known as apple of love, bladder cherry, Chinese lantern, love in a cage and lantern herb. 2. An imprecise name for the closely related cape gooseberry.

wintergreen An evergreen plant (*Gultheria procumbens*) with small red berries that produce a pungent oil used in jellies or to flavor candies and medicines; also known as checkerberry and teaberry.

winter melon A large muskmelon with a pale green rind, a white flesh and a flavor reminiscent of zucchini; used in Asian cuisines in sweet and savory dishes.

wire mesh strainer A tool with a mesh bowl, sometimes reinforced with narrow crossbands and a handle; available in various sizes and thicknesses of mesh; it is used to strain liquids from solids or to sift dry ingredients; also known as a strainer. *See* sieve.

wishbone 1. The forked bone found between the neck and breast of a chicken or turkey. 2. The cut of chicken containing the wishbone.

wok Cookware with a rounded bottom and curved sides that diffuses heat and makes it easy to toss or stir contents; it usually has a domed lid and two handles, although a single long-handled version is available; used originally in Asian cuisines.

wok

wolffish; wolf fish A fish found in the northern Pacific and Atlantic Oceans; it has a bluish-brown skin, weighs up to 40 lb. (18.0 kg) and has a firm, white flesh.

won ton; won-ton (WAHN tahn) A small Chinese dumpling made from a thin dough filled with a mixture of finely minced meats, poultry, fish, shellfish and/or vegetables; it can be steamed, fried or boiled and eaten as dumplings, in soups and as appetizers.

won ton skins Wafer-thin sheets of dough made from flour, eggs and salt and used to wrap fillings; available in squares or circles.

won ton soup A Chinese soup consisting of chicken broth garnished with won tons, green onions, pork or chicken and/or vegetables.

woodcock A small wild game bird related to the snipe; its darkish flesh has a rich flavor, and its trail is a great delicacy.

woodruff An aromatic herb (genus *Asperula*) native to Europe and used as a flavoring in May wine; also called sweet woodruff.

Worcestershire sauce (WOOS-tuhr-shuhr; WOOS-tuhr-sheer) A thin, dark brown sauce developed in India for British colonials and first bottled in Worcester, England; it consists of soy sauce, tamarind, garlic, onions, molasses, lime, anchovies, vinegar and other seasonings.

workstations The various preparation areas within a food services facility's kitchen, usually defined by the equipment used or foods produced.

wormweed *See* epazote.

wormwood A bitter, aromatic herb (*Artemisia mayoris* and *A. vulgaris*), the oil of which is used in distilling absinthe.

wot' (what) Ethiopian for stew; usually one made with meat or vegetables and legumes.

wrap An American sandwich consisting of a filling and spread rolled in a soft flour tortilla (unlike a classic Mexican tortilla, the one used for a wrap can be flavored with herbs, spices or the like). *See* burrito.

Xérès, sauce au (sair-ress) A French compound sauce made from a demi-glaze flavored with dry or medium-dry sherry.

xun (shoon) A Chinese cooking method in which an ingredient, usually raw, is smoked with wood shavings (pine or poplar), tea leaves, sugarcane pulp and brown sugar and then steamed or deep-fried; the ingredient may be steamed or deep-fried before being smoked.

XXX; XXXX Labeling symbols that indicate the fineness of confectioners' sugar: the more Xs, the finer the sugar was pulverized.

Y

yabby; yabbie Australian for crayfish.

yahni (yah-neh) 1. A Greek preparation method; the food is braised with onions in olive oil, then a little water or tomatoes are added and all are simmered. 2. A Turkish stew usually made with mutton, lamb or hare.

yakhni (YAHF-nee) Arabic for stew, especially one with potatoes.

yakinori (YAH-kee-NOH-ree) Toasted sheets of nori.

yakitori (yah-kih-TOH-ree) A Japanese dish of chicken marinated in soy sauce, sugar and sake, placed on skewers and broiled or grilled.

yam The thick, starchy tuber of various tropical vines native to Asia (genus *Dioscorea*) and unrelated to the potato and sweet potato; it has an off-white to dark brown skin and flesh that can range from creamy white to deep red; it is less sweet than a sweet potato.

yampie A small tuber with a white flesh and delicate flavor; often served boiled in Caribbean cuisines.

yanagi-ba-bōtchō (yah-NAH-ghee-bah-BOH-cho) A Japanese knife used to make sushi; it has a 10- to 14-in.-long slender blade ground on one side.

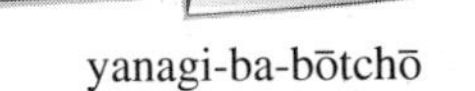

yanagi-ba-bōtchō

Yankee pot roast A pot roast to which vegetables have been added during braising. *See* pot roast.

yard-long bean A very thin, exceptionally long legume; it resembles a green bean with a more pliable pod and a similar but less sweet flavor; also known as long bean and asparagus bean.

yarrow A perennial herb (*Achillea millefolium*) with dark green leaves, downy stems and a compact flower head; the leaves have a slightly bitter, peppery flavor and are used in salads; also known as milfoil.

yeast A microscopic fungus (genus *Saccharomyces,* especially *S. cerevisiae*) that converts its food (carbohydrates) into carbon dioxide and alcohol through a metabolic process known as fermentation; yeast is necessary for making beer, wine, cheese and some breads. *See* compressed yeast *and* active dry yeast.

yeast breads A general category of breads that use yeast as a leavening agent; these breads have a wide variety of textures and shapes but all require kneading to develop gluten (e.g., French bread, sourdough bread, croissant and challah). *See* quick breads.

yellow cake A cake made from a batter containing egg yolks.

yellow-eyed pea The seed of a member of the pea family native to China; it is small and beige with a yellow circular eye on the inside curved edge; used in American southern cuisine. *See* black-eyed pea.

yellowfin tuna A variety of tuna found in the Pacific Ocean from Chile to California; it has a yellowish skin, an ivory-pink flesh and a weight of 30–150 lb. (13.5–68 kg); often used for canning.

yellow granadilla A variety of passion fruit grown in the Caribbean region; it has a yellow skin and an ovoid shape; also known as water lemon.

yellow perch A fish found in North American lakes and streams; it has a dark-banded golden yellow skin that becomes white on the belly, an average market weight of 4–12 oz. (110–340 g) and a lean, white flesh with a firm texture and mild flavor; also known as coon perch, lake perch, ringed perch and striped perch.

yellowtail A game fish related to the pompano and found in the Pacific Ocean; it weighs up to 100 lb. (45 kg) and has a distinctive yellow tail fin, a firm flesh that whitens when cooked and a rich flavor.

yerba maté (yehr-bah MAH-ta) *See* maté.

yield 1. The total amount of a food item created or remaining after trimming or fabrication; the edible portion of the as-purchased unit. 2. The total amount of a product made from a specific recipe.

yield test An analysis conducted during the butchering and fabrication of meat, fish or poultry or during the cleaning and preparation of produce to determine the usable amount of the product (the yield) remaining after preparation.

ylang-ylang (E-lahn-E-lahn) A large tree native to the Philippines (*Cananga odorata*); the oil made from its flowers has a strong, flowerlike aroma and bitter flavor and is used in soft drinks, ice cream, confectionery and baked goods.

yogurt; yoghurt (YOH-gert) A thick, tart, custardlike fermented dairy product to which bacteria cultures (e.g., *Streptococcus thermophilus, Thermobacterium bulgaricum* and *T. jogurt*) have been added; it has the same percentage of milkfat as the milk from which it is made.

yogurt, frozen A soft frozen confection made from a sweetened yogurt base and various natural and/or artificial flavorings; low-fat and nonfat products are available.

yolk The yellow portion of the egg; it contains all of the egg's fat and most of its calories, minerals, vitamins (except riboflavin) and lecithin.

York ham An English ham from Yorkshire pigs; it is cured with salt, saltpeter and brown sugar for at least 3 weeks before being smoked and then cooked.

Yorkshire pudding A British bread made of popover batter (eggs, flour and milk) baked in hot beef drippings; the finished product is puffy, crisp, hollow and golden brown and is traditionally served with roast beef.

youngberry A hybrid blackberry with a dark red color and a sweet, juicy flesh.

young dough Underfermented yeast dough.

yuba A film made from dehydrated soybean milk and used in Japanese cuisine; also known as bean curd sheets.

yuca (jhew-kah) Spanish for cassava root or tapioca; a staple throughout South and Central America and the Caribbean region.

yue bing (ee-who a-bing) Chinese for moon cakes and used to describe a short pastry with a decorative design enclosing various sweet fillings made of bean paste, nuts or fruits surrounding a piece of salted duck egg yolk.

yufka (yoof-kah) Very thin, Turkish pastry dough; similar to phyllo dough and used to make sweet and savory pastries.

yule log English for Bûche de Noël.

yuzu (yoo-zoo) A small citrus fruit (*Citrus aurantium*) native to Tibet and China; it has a thick, bumpy, yellowish-green rind, pale yellowish-green flesh with a slightly acidic flavor and many seeds.

zaatar; zatar (ZAH-tahr) A Middle Eastern flavoring blend consisting of dried thyme, dried wild marjoram (oregano), sumac and toasted sesame seeds; it can be mixed with oil or left dry.

zabaglione (zah-bahl-YOH-nay) An Italian foamy dessert custard made by whipping together egg yolks, sugar and wine (usually Marsala). *See* sabayon.

zabaglione pot (zah-bahl-YOH-nay) A round-bottomed unlined copper pot with a long handle; designed to allow easy whisking while being held over simmering water; used to make zabaglione.

zabaglione pot

Zante grape A small purple grape used as a garnish or dried (and known as a currant).

zebrine (za-bree-na) A variety of eggplant grown in France; it has violet and white stripes.

zephyr A sweet or savory dish served hot or cold and characterized by a light and frothy consistency; used to describe quenelles, mousses and the like.

zest *v.* To remove strips of rind from a citrus fruit. *n.* The colored, outermost layer of citrus rind; used for flavoring creams, custards and baked goods; it can be candied and used as a confection or decoration. *See* albedo.

zester A tool used to cut slivers of zest from citrus; its short, flat blade has five small holes with sharp edges.

zester

zingara, à la (zihn-GAH-rah, ah lah) French for gypsy style and used to describe dishes that are garnished with chopped ham, tongue, mushrooms and truffles combined with tomato sauce, tarragon and sometimes Madeira; usually served with meat, poultry and eggs.

zouave, sauce (zwhav) A French compound sauce made from a demi-glaze mixed with tomato purée, flavored with mustard and garlic and garnished with tarragon.

zucchini (zoo-KEE-nee) A moderately long, cylindrical summer squash with smooth, dark green skin and a slightly bumpy surface, a creamy white-green flesh and a mild flavor; also known as courgette (especially in Europe).

zucchini blossoms The long, pale yellow blossoms of the zucchini; they are sometimes battered and fried.

zucchini corer A utensil with a long, pointed, trough-shaped blade that is inserted into the zucchini and rotated, thus removing the core and leaving a space for stuffing.

zuppa Inglese (ZOO-pah in-GLAY-zay) Italian for English soup and used to describe a refrigerated dessert similar to English trifle; it is made by layering rum-soaked slices of sponge cake in a deep bowl with custard, whipped cream, candied fruit and nuts.

zushi (zhoo-she) The seasoned rice used for sushi; also known as shari.

Zwieback (ZWY-bak) German for twice-baked and used to describe bread that is baked, sliced and returned to the oven and baked until dry and crisp. *See* rusk.

Appendices

COMMON EQUIVALENTS IN THE U.S. SYSTEM

⅛ teaspoon	=	dash
½ teaspoon	=	30 drops
1 teaspoon	=	⅓ tablespoon or 60 drops
3 teaspoons	=	1 tablespoon or ½ fluid ounce
½ tablespoon	=	1½ teaspoons
1 tablespoon	=	3 teaspoons or ½ fluid ounce
2 tablespoons	=	1 fluid ounce
3 tablespoons	=	1½ fluid ounces or 1 jigger
4 tablespoons	=	¼ cup or 2 fluid ounces
5⅓ tablespoons	=	⅓ cup or 5 tablespoons + 1 teaspoon
8 tablespoons	=	½ cup or 4 fluid ounces
10⅔ tablespoons	=	⅔ cup or 10 tablespoons + 2 teaspoons
12 tablespoons	=	¾ cup or 6 fluid ounces
16 tablespoons	=	1 cup or 8 fluid ounces or ½ pint
⅛ cup	=	2 tablespoons or 1 fluid ounce
¼ cup	=	4 tablespoons or 2 fluid ounces
⅓ cup	=	5 tablespoons + 1 teaspoon
⅜ cup	=	¼ cup + 2 tablespoons
½ cup	=	8 tablespoons or 4 fluid ounces or 1 gill
⅝ cup	=	½ cup + 2 tablespoons
¾ cup	=	12 tablespoons or 6 fluid ounces
⅞ cup	=	¾ cup + 2 tablespoons
1 cup	=	16 tablespoons or ½ pint or 8 fluid ounces
2 cups	=	1 pint or 16 fluid ounces
1 pint	=	2 cups or 16 fluid ounces
1 quart	=	2 pints or 4 cups or 32 fluid ounces
1 gallon	=	4 quarts or 8 pints or 16 cups or 128 fluid ounces
2 gallons	=	1 peck
4 pecks	=	1 bushel

TEMPERATURE EQUIVALENTS

FAHRENHEIT	CELSIUS
32°F	0°C (water freezes)
40°	4.4°
50°	10°
60°	15.6°
70°	21.1°
80°	26.7°
90°	32.2°
100°	37.8°
110°	43.3°
120°	48.9°
130°	54.4°
140°	60°
150°	65.6°
160°	71.1°
170°	76.7°
180°	82.2°
190°	87.8°
200°	93.3°
212°	100°(water boils)
250°	121°
300°	149°
350°	177°
400°	205°
450°	233°
500°	260°

CONVERTING TO METRIC

WHEN THIS IS KNOWN	MULTIPLY IT BY	TO GET
teaspoons	4.93	milliliters
tablespoons	14.79	milliliters
fluid ounces	29.57	milliliters
cups	236.59	milliliters
cups	0.236	liters
pints	473.18	milliliters
pints	0.473	liters
quarts	946.36	milliliters
quarts	0.946	liters
gallons	3.785	liters
ounces	28.35	grams
pounds	0.454	kilograms
inches	2.54	centimeters
Fahrenheit	subtract 32 multiply by 5 divide by 9	Celsius (centigrade)

CONVERTING FROM METRIC

WHEN THIS IS KNOWN	DIVIDE IT BY	TO GET
milliliters	4.93	teaspoons
milliliters	14.79	tablespoons
milliliters	29.57	fluid ounces
milliliters	236.59	cups
liters	0.236	cups
milliliters	473.18	pints
liters	0.473	pints
milliliters	946.36	quarts
liters	0.946	quarts
liters	3.785	gallons
grams	28.35	ounces
kilograms	0.454	pounds
centimeters	2.54	inches
Celsius (centigrade)	multiply by 9 divide by 5 add 32	Fahrenheit

STAGES OF COOKED SUGAR

STAGE	TEMPERATURE	WHEN A SMALL AMOUNT OF SUGAR SYRUP IS DROPPED INTO ICE WATER IT:
Thread	230° to 234°F (110° to 112°C)	Spins a soft 2-inch thread
Soft ball	234° to 240°F (112° to 116°C)	Forms a soft, flat ball
Firm ball	244° to 248°F (118° to 120°C)	Forms a firm but pliable ball
Hard ball	250° to 265°F (121° to 129°C)	Forms a hard, compact ball
Soft crack	270° to 290°F (132° to 143°C)	Separates into hard but not brittle threads
Hard crack	300° to 310°F (149° to 154°C)	Forms hard, brittle threads
Caramel	320° to 338°F (160° to 170°C)	Forms hard, brittle threads and the liquid turns brown

CANNED GOOD SIZES

SIZE	NUMBER OF CANS PER CASE	AVERAGE WEIGHT	AVERAGE NUMBER OF CUPS PER CAN
No. 1/2	8	8 oz.	1
No. 1 tall (also known as 303)	2 or 4 dozen	16 oz.	2
No. 2	2 dozen	20 oz.	2½
No. 2½	2 dozen	28 oz.	3½
No. 3	2 dozen	33 oz.	4
No. 3 cylinder	1 dozen	46 oz.	5⅔
No. 5	1 dozen	3 lb. 8 oz.	5½
No. 10	6	6 lb. 10 oz.	13

CONVERSION GUIDELINES

1 gallon	=	4 qt.
		8 pt.
		16 c. (8 oz.)
		128 fl. oz.
1 fifth bottle	=	Approximately 1½ pt. or exactly 26.5 fl. oz.
1 measuring cup	=	8 fl. oz. (a coffee cup is generally 6 fl. oz.)
1 large egg white	=	1 oz. (average)
1 lemon	=	1–1¼ fl. oz. of juice
1 orange	=	3–3½ fl. oz. of juice

OVEN TEMPERATURES

°F	°C	GAS NUMBER	OVEN HEAT
225°F	110°C	1/4	Very cool
250°F	130°C	1/2	Very cool
275°F	140°C	1	Cool
300°F	150°C	2	Slow
325°F	170°C	3	Moderately slow
350°F	180°C	4	Moderate
375°F	190°C	5	Moderately hot
400°F	200°C	6	Moderately hot
425°F	220°C	7	Hot
450°F	230°C	8	Hot
475°F	245°C	9	Very hot
500°F	260°C	10	Very hot

OVERSIZED WINE BOTTLES

NAME	NUMBER OF 750-ml BOTTLES	NUMBER OF LITERS	NUMBER OF FLUID OUNCES
Magnum	2	1.5	50.7
Double magnum	4	3.0	101.4
Jeroboam	4	3.0	101.4
Rehoboam (champagne)	6	4.5	156
Methuselah (champagne)	8	6.0	204.8
Imperial	8	6.0	204.8
Salmanazar	12	9.0	307.2
Balthazar	16	12.0	416
Nebuchadnezzar	20	15.0	570

COMMONLY USED INTERNATIONAL TERMS

ENGLISH	JAPANESE	RUSSIAN	FRENCH	GERMAN	ITALIAN	SPANISH
alcohol	arukoru	spirt	álcool	Alkohol	alcool	alcohol
bacon	bekon	shpik	lard	Speck	pancetta	tocino
banana	banana	banan	banane	Banane	banane	1. plátano 2. banana
beans	mame	1. fasol 2. bobi	haricots	Bohnen	fagioli	frijoles
beef	gyuniku	govyadina	boeuf	Rindfleisch	1. manzo 2. bue	carne de res
beer	biru	pivo	bière	Bier	birra	cerveza
beverage	nomimono	napitok	boisson	Getränk	bevanda	bebida
bread	pan	khleb	pain	Brot	pane	pan
breakfast	1. choshoku 2. asagohan	zavtrak	petit déjeuner	Frühstück	prima colazione	desayuno
butter	bata	maslo	beurre	Butter	burro	mantequilla
cafe	kissaten	kafé	café	Cafe	caffè	café
cake	keki	1. keks 2. tort	gâteau	1. Küchen 2. Torte	torta	1. tarta 2. pastel
candy	kyande	konfeta	confiserie	1. Konfekt 2. Süssigkeit	zucchero candito	caramelo
carrot	ninjin	morkov'	carotte	Karotte	carota	zanahoria
celery	serori	selderey	céleri	Sellerie	sèdano	apio
cheese	chizu	syr	fromage	Käse	formaggio	queso
cherry	sakurambo	chereshnya	cerise	Kirsche	ciliegia	cereza
chicken	1. hiyoko 2. niwatori	tsypljenok	poulet	Geflügel	pollo	pollo
chocolate	chokoreto	shokoladnyj	chocolat	Schokolade	cioccolata	chocolate
coconut		kokos	noix de coco	Kokosnuss	noce di coco	nuez de cocco
coffee, with milk	N/A	kofe s molokom	café au lait	Kaffee mit Milch	caffé latte	café con leche
coffee	kohi	kofe	café	Kaffee	caffè	café
cold	1. samui 2. hirashi	kholodnye	froid	kalt	freddo	frío
cookies	1. bisket-to 2. kukki	1. biskviti 2. pechenè	biscuits	Kekse	biscotti	galletas
corn	tomoro-koshi	kukuruza	mais	Maïs	granturco	maíz
crab	kani	krab	crabe	Krabbe	granchio	1. cangrejo 2. jaiba

ENGLISH	JAPANESE	RUSSIAN	FRENCH	GERMAN	ITALIAN	SPANISH
cream	kurimu	1. krem 2. slivki	crème	Creme	1. crema 2. panna	1. nata (on boiled milk) 2. crema (whipped)
cucumber	kyuri	ogurez	concombre	Gurken	cetriolo	pepino
dessert	dezato	dessert	dessert	Nachtisch	dolci	postre
dinner	bansan	1. obed 2. uzhin	dîner	Abendessen	cena	cena
duck	ahiru	utka	canard	Ente	anitra	pata
egg	tamago	1. yaizo 2. jajtsa	oeuf	Eier	uovo	huevo
fat	shibo	zhir	graisse	Fett	grasso	grasa
fish	sakana	rybá	poisson	Fisch	pesce	pescado
food	1. tabemono 2. shokuryo 3. ryori	eda	nourriture	Speise	cibo	comida
fork	foku	vilka	fourchette	Gabel	forchetta	tenedor
fried	agemono	zharenniy	frit	fritiert	fritto	frito
fruit	kudamono	frukt	fruit	1. Frucht 2. Obst	frutta	fruta
garlic	nin'niku	chesnok	ail	Knoblauch	aglio	ajo
grapes	budo	vinograd	raisins	Trauben	uvas	uvas
ham	hamu	vetchina	jambon	Schinken	prosciutto	jamón
herb	kusa	lechebnie	herbe	Kräuter	erba	hierba
hot	atsui	goryachee	chaud	heiss	caldo	caliente
hotel	hoteru	gostinitza	hôtel	Hotel	albergo	hotel
ice cream	aisu-kur-imu	morozhena	1. glace 2. crème glacée	Eis	gelato	helado
ice	kori	led	glace	Eis	ghiaccio	hielo
jam	jamu	varen'em	confiture	1. Konfitüre 2. Marmelade	marmellata	1. confitura 2. mermelada
juice (n)	1. juse 2. frutsu jus	sok	jus	Saft	succo	1. jugo 2. zumo
kitchen	1. daidokoro 2. kitchin	kuhnya	cuisine	Küche	cucina	cocina
knife	naifu	nozh'	couteau	Messer	coltello	cuchillo
lamb	ko-hitsuji	barashek	agneau	Lamm	agnello	cordero
lemon	remon	limon	citron	Zitrone	limone	limón

(continued)

ENGLISH	JAPANESE	RUSSIAN	FRENCH	GERMAN	ITALIAN	SPANISH
lettuce	retasu	salat	laitue	1. Salat 2. Lattich	lattuga	lechuga
lunch	chushoku	poludennik	déjeuner	Mittagessen	colazione	almuerzo
meat	niku	myaso	viande	Fleisch	carne	carne
melon	meron	dynya	melon	Melone	melone	melón
menu	menyu	menu	carte	Speisekarte	1. lista 2. carta	1. menú 2. lista de platos
milk	miruku	moloko	lait	Milch	latte	leche
mint	hakka	myato	menthe	Minze	mente	hierbabuena
mushroom	mashshurum	gribi	champignon	1. Champigon 2. Pilze	fungo	1. seta 2. champiñon
napkin	napukin	salfetka	serviette	Serviette	tovagliolo	servilleta
nut	nattsu	orekh	noix	Nüss	noce	nuez
oil	abura	1. maslo 2. mazat	huile	Öl	olio	aceite
onion	tamanegi	luk	oignon	Zwiebel	cipolla	cebolla
orange	mikan	apel'sin	orange	Orange	arancia	naranja
peach	momo	persik	pêche	Pfirsich	pesca	1. melocotón 2. durazno
pear	nashi	grusha	poire	Birne	pera	pera
pepper	kosho	perez	poivre	Pfeffer	pépe	pimienta
pineapple	painappuree	ananas	ananas	Ananas	ananas	piña
plate	sara	tarelka	assiette	Platte	piatto	plato
pork	buta	svinina	porc	Schwein	maiale	1. cerdo 2. puerco
potato	jagaimo	kartofel	1. pommes 2. pommes de terre	Kartoffel	patata	1. patata 2. papa
raw	nama no	syroy	cru	roh	crudo	crudo
restaurant	ryoriten	restaran	restaurant	Gaststätte	ristorante	restaurante
rice	kome	ris	riz	Reis	riso	arróz
salad	sarada	salat	salade	Salat	insalata	ensalada
salmon	sake	losos	saumon	Lachssalm	salmóne	salmón
salt	shio	sol	sel	Salz	sale	sal
sandwich	sandoitchi	buterbrod	sandwich	Belegtes	panino	bocadillo
sauce	sosu	sous	sauce	Sosse	salsa	salsa
shrimp	ebi	krevetka	crevettes	Garnele	gambero	1. camarónes 2. gambas

ENGLISH	JAPANESE	RUSSIAN	FRENCH	GERMAN	ITALIAN	SPANISH
soup	1. supu 2. jiru	sup	1. soupe 2. potage	Suppe	zuppa	sopa
spice	yakumi	pryanosti	épice	1. Gewürze 2. Würze	spèzia	especia
spicy	karai	ostriy	piquant	1. würzig 2. pikant	piccante	1. picante (pepper) 2. condementada
spoon	saji	lozhka	cuillère	Löffel	cucchiaio	cuchara
stew	shichu-ryori	sup	ragoût	Schmoren	stufato	estofado
strawberry	ichigo	klubnika	fraise	Erdbeere	fragola	fresas
stuffed	tsumeru	farshirovanniy	farci	gefüllt	farcito	relleno
sweet	amai	sladkiy	sucré	süss	dolce	dulce
table	1. teburu 2. shokutaku	stol	table	Tisch	tavola	mesa
tea	ocha	chai	thé	Tee	tè	té
tomato	tomato	pomidor	tomate	Tomate	pomodoro	tomate
vegetables	yasai	ovoschi	légumes	Gemüse	contorni	verduras
water	mizu	voda	eau	Wasser	acqua	agua
wheat	komugi	zerno	blé	Weizen	grano	trigo
yogurt	yoguruto	prostok-vasha	yaourt	Joghurt	iogurt	yogur

COMMON FOOD ADDITIVES

Food additives are any of several thousand organic and inorganic, natural and synthetic substances not normally consumed as a food by themselves and usually found (intentionally or incidentally) in processed (as opposed to whole) foods either as components of the food or as agents affecting a characteristic of the food such as flavor, texture, color or freshness. They are regulated by the U.S. Food and Drug Administration and must be safe, effective and measurable in the final product.

DEFINITION KEY

■ Processing Aids

Stabilizers, Thickening Agents and Texturizers: produce viscous solutions or dispersions, impart body, improve texture and/or stabilize emulsions.

pH Control Agents: maintain or change acidity or alkalinity.

Emulsifiers: create a uniform dispersion, improve/preserve homogeneity and stability.

Humectants: retain moisture.

Leavening Agents: produce or stimulate production of carbon dioxide.

Anticaking Agents: prevent caking, lumping or agglomeration in finely powdered or crystalline substances.

Maturing and Bleaching Agents, Dough Conditioners: accelerate aging and produce a more stable baked product.

● Nutritional Aids

Nutrients: enrich (add specific vitamins) or fortify (add nutrients not normally present or supplement naturally occurring nutrients) foods.

▲ Product Quality and Freshness Aids

Preservatives: increase shelf life by retarding decomposition, fermentation, microbial growth, oxidation and protect natural color or flavor.

◆ Desirability Aids

Flavoring Agents: heighten or restore flavor.
Coloring Agents: remove, add or maintain colors.
Sweeteners: sweeten foods.
Flavor Enhancers: add, preserve or intensify the flavor of a food without imparting their own (new or additional) flavors.

ADDITIVES COMMONLY ADDED TO SOME FOODS

Additive	Function
Acetic acid	■ pH control
Acetone peroxide	■ dough conditioner
Aconitic acid	◆ flavor
Adipic acid	◆ flavor ■ pH control
Agar agar	■ stabilizer/thickener
Algae, red and brown	◆ flavor
Alginic acid	■ stabilizer/emulsifier
Allyl compounds	◆ flavor
Aluminum ammonium sulfate	■ pH control
Aluminum calcium silicate	■ anticaking
Ammonium alginate	■ stabilizer/thickener
Ammonium carbonate	■ dough conditioner/pH
Ammonium hydroxide	■ leavening agent/pH
Ammonium sulfate	■ dough conditioner/pH
Amyl compounds	◆ flavor
Anisyl compounds	◆ flavor
Annotto extract	◆ color
Anoxomer	▲ preservative
Arabinogalactan	■ emulsifier, stabilizer
Arginine	● nutrient
Bakers' yeast extract	■ emulsifier and thickener
Bakers' yeast glycan	■ emulsifier
Bakers' yeast protein	● nutrient
Bentonite	■ processing aid; fining
Benzaldehyde	◆ flavor
Benzoic acid	▲ preservative
Benzoyl peroxide	■ bleaching agent

Benzyl butyrate	◆ flavor
Benzyl propionate	◆ flavor
Birch	◆ flavor and sweetener
Blue no. 1	◆ color
Borneal	◆ flavor
Brilliant blue FCF	◆ color
Bromated vegetable oil (BVO)	■ stabilizer
Butyl acetate; butyl heptanoate	◆ flavor
Butylated hydroxyanisole (BHA)	▲ antioxidant
Butylated hydroxytoluene (BHT)	▲ antioxidant
Butyl butyryllactate	◆ flavor
Butylparaben	▲ preservative
Butyric acid	■ pH control
Calcium acetate	■ pH control, thickener
Calcium alginate	■ stabilizer, thickener
Calcium ascorbate	▲ preservative
Calcium bromate	■ bleaching agent
Calcium chloride	■ pH control, stabilizer, anticaking, thickener ▲ preservative
Calcium disodium ethylenediaminetetraacetate (EDTA)	◆ color, flavor ▲ preservative
Calcium iodate	■ dough conditioner
Calcium oxide	■ anticaking
Calcium phosphate	■ leavening agent
Calcium propionate	▲ preservative
Calcium stearate	◆ flavor
Camphene flavor	◆ flavor, synthetic
Canaga oil	◆ flavor
Canthaxanthin	◆ color
Caprylic acid	◆ flavor
Carbonated ammonia	■ leavening agent
Carnuba wax	■ anticaking
Carrageenan	■ emulsifier,
Carvacrol	◆ flavor
Caseinate	■ emulsifier
Castor oil	■ antisticking
Chlorine dioxide	■ bleaching agent
Cholic acid	■ emulsifier
Cinnamic acid	◆ flavor
Citral	◆ flavor

Citrus red no.2	◆ color
Cochineal extract	◆ color
Copper gluconate and copper sulfate	● nutrients
Corn endosperm	◆ color
Corn gluten	● nutrient
Crestyl acetate	◆ flavor
Cuminic aldehyde	◆ flavor
Cuprous iodide	● nutrient
Cyclamate	◆ sweetener, artificial
Cyclohexyl compounds	◆ flavor
Cysteine; cystine	● nutrient
Dextrin	◆ sweetener
Diaceytl	◆ flavor
Diacetyl tartaric acid of mono- and diglycerides (DATEM)	■ emulsifiers
Dicalcium phosphate	■ dough conditioner
Diglycerides	■ emulsifiers
Dihydroacetic acid	▲ preservative
Dilaury thiodipropionate	▲ preservative
Dimethyl dicarbonate	▲ preservative
Dimethylpolysiloxane	■ antifoaming
Dipotassium monophosphate and dipotassium phosphate	■ emulsifier, pH
Disodium calcium	
DL-alanine	◆ sweetener
Ethylenediaminetetraacetate (EDTA)	▲ preservative, color
Ethyl formate	◆ flavor
Ethyl sorbate	◆ flavor
Eugenyl compounds	◆ flavor
FD&C colors	◆ color
Blue # 1	◆ color
Blue # 6	◆ color
Green # 3	◆ color
Red # 3	◆ color
Red # 40	◆ color
Yellow # 5	◆ color
Yellow # 6	◆ color
Ferrous compounds	● nutrients
Fish protein isolate	● nutrient
Folic acid	● nutrient
Formic acid	◆ flavor
Fructose corn syrup	◆ sweetener

Gellan gum	■ thickener
Glacial acetic acid	◆ flavor
	▲ preservative
Glycerine	■ humectant
Guar gum	■ thickener
Gum tragacanth	■ thickener
Heptanone compounds	◆ flavoring agents
Heptyl paraban	▲ preservative
Hexyl compounds	◆ flavoring agents
High-fructose corn syrup (HFCS)	◆ sweetener, nutritive
Hydrogen peroxide	■ bleaching agent
Invert sugar syrup	◆ sweetener
Iron-choline citrate complex	● nutrient supplement
Iron oxide	◆ coloring agent
Isobutyl compounds	◆ flavoring agents
Karaya gum	■ emulsifier, stabilizer
Larch gum	■ thickener
Lecithin	■ thickener
Linolenic acid	● nutrient supplement
	◆ flavoring agent
Locust bean gum	■ stabilizer/thickener
Maltodextrin	■ bodying agent
Maltol	◆ flavor enhancer
Manganese compounds	● nutrients
Mannitol	◆ sweetener,
	▲ preservative
Methylcellulose	■ humectant
Methyl compounds	◆ flavoring agents
Modified food starch	■ stabilizer
Monocalcium phosphate	● nutrient
	■ leavening agent
Monosodium glutamate (MSG)	◆ flavor enhancer
Monosodium phosphate	■ pH control
Nerol and nerolidol	◆ flavoring agents
Octyl compounds	◆ flavoring agents
Parabens	▲ preservatives
Pentyl acetate	◆ flavoring agent
Phenylacetaldehyde	◆ flavoring agent
Phosphates	■ pH control
	◆ flavor enhancers
Polysorbates	■ emulsifiers
Potassium bisulfite and metabisulfite	▲ preservatives

Potassium iodide	● nutrient
Potassium nitrite	▲ preservative
Propylene glycol	■ anticaking
Riboflavin	● nutrient
Santalol	◆ flavoring agent
Silicon dioxide	■ anticaking
Sodium aluminum phosphate	■ leavening agent
Sodium benzoate	▲ preservative
	◆ flavoring agent
Sodium citrate	■ pH control
Sodium hydroxide	■ pH control
Sodium nitrate	▲ preservative
	◆ color stabilizer
Sodium propionate	▲ preservative
	◆ flavoring agent
Sodium stearyl lactylate	■ emulsifier
Sorbic acid	▲ preservative
Sorbitol	◆ sweetener
	■ humectant, emulsifier
Stearic acid	◆ flavoring agent
Stearyl monoglyceridyl citrate	■ emulsifier
Succinic acid	◆ flavor enhancer
	■ pH control
Sulfur dioxide	▲ preservative
Tannic acid	◆ flavoring agent
Tertiary butylhydroquinone (TBHQ)	▲ antioxidant
Thiamine hydrochloride	● nutrient
Titanium dioxide	◆ color
Tragacanth	■ thickener
Tricalcium silicate	■ anticaking
Xanthan gum	■ thickener

SELECTED PRODUCE VARIETIES

APPLE

VARIETY	SKIN COLOR	FLAVOR	FLESH	USE
Baldwin	red streaked with yellow	sweet-tart	crisp	all-purpose
Beauty of Bath	pink and green	sharp, sweet		
Belle du bois	yellow with orange	sweet	mealy	
Belle fille d'Indre	yellow with red blush	sweet	juicy	
Braeburn	red blushed green	sweet-tart	crisp, juicy	eating
Cameo®	red stripe over cream	sweet-tart	firm	fresh or cooking
Carel	yellow	intense aroma	crisp	
Claville blanche d'hiver	yellow	aromatic	juicy	
Cortland	red and yellow	acidic	crisp	all-purpose
Cox; Cox orange pippin	brown-green with faint red stripes	sweet-tart	crisp	all-purpose
Crispin/Mutsu	greenish-yellow	slightly sweet	creamy white, firm	all-purpose
Criterion	yellow, blushed with red	sweet	firm, juicy	
Discovery (America)	scarlet	sweet	creamy white	
Discovery (Britian)	bright crimson and green	raspberries	pink-tinged	
Elstar	red blushed yellow	sharp	firm, yellowish	
Empire	red and yellow	sweet-tart	crisp, juicy, white	all-purpose
Fugi	yellow, orange, red streaked	sweet	crisp, white	eating, salad, applesauce
Gala	yellow-red	mild, sweet	creamy yellow	eating, salads, applesauce
Ginger Gold	yellow	sweet, mildly tart	crisp, cream color	eating, salads
Golden Delicious	yellow, yellow-green	bland	juicy, crisp	all-purpose
Granny Smith	emerald green	tart, sweet	firm	all-purpose
Gravenstein	red streaked	acidic	crisp, juicy	pies, applesauce
Gros Locard	brown-spotted yellow	very sweet	white	
Honeycrisp	mottled red and yellow	sweet-tart	crisp, yellow	eating, salads, applesauce
Idared	red and yellow	sweet, mildly acidic		cooking, baking
Irish peach	golden	peach		

VARIETY	SKIN COLOR	FLAVOR	FLESH	USE
Jonagold	yellow with red blush	sweet-tart		all-purpose
Jonathan	bright red	sweet-tart	tender	pies, baking
Lady	red to red-blushed yellow	sweet-tart		garnish
Macoun	deep red	very sweet	crisp, juicy white	eating
McIntosh	red-striped green or yellow	sweet-tart	soft, juicy	eating, applesauce
Mercier	red blushed, mottled brown yellow	slightly sour	crisp	
Mother	golden with red blush	rich, sweet	creamy	
Newton pippin	yellowish-green	slightly tart	crisp, juicy	pies, applesauce
Northern Spy	red and yellow striped	sweet-tart	crisp	all-purpose
Ontario	yellow-green	sweet-tart	delicate, white	
Pepin de Bourgueil	yellow-orange	sweet-tart	white	
Pierre rouge	yellow, red-blushed		juicy, white	
Pink Lady	pink blush over yellow	sweet-tart	fine grained, firm	all-purpose
Pomme Gris	gray to russet		yellowish, crisp	
Porter	yellow marked with red	sweet-tart	juicy, crisp, yellowish	
Ravaillac	red			cider, jellied fruit
Red Astrachan	red	sweet, acidic, full		
Red Delicious	red	sweet	crisp, juicy	eating, salads
Red Star	dark red or burgundy	sweet	firm, yellow	
Reinette blanche de la Creuse	bright yellow-gold	very sweet	juicy	
Reinette bure	tannish gold			dried and used to flavor mulled wine
Reinette de Caux	wrinkly, yellow-orange-red	sweet-tart	crisp	
Reinette du Mans	brown and white spotted yellow	vanilla	white	tarte Tatin
Reinette grise de Saintonge	yellow-spotted brown	aniselike	white	
Rhode Island Greening	pale green	sharp	crisp	cooking

VARIETY	SKIN COLOR	FLAVOR	FLESH	USE
Robillard	orange-blushed yellow-orange	sweet-tart	juicy	
Rome Beauty	deep red	bland, sweet-tart	ivory-white	baking, pies, sauce
Rose de Benauge	yellow, red blushed	sweet-tart		baking
Rose de Touraine	dark red	sweet-tart	pinkish	
Roxbury Russet	green to yellow	flavorful	coarse	
Starkimson	dark red, burgundy with small yellow spots	sweet	moderately firm	
Stayman	dull, red striped	tart	moderately firm	all-purpose
Stayman Winesap	yellow-streaked	tangy	firm, aromatic	all-purpose
Wealthy	yellowish-green red	tart	white to cream colored	all-purpose, cider
White Joaneting	yellow with red flush	good	juicy	
White Transparent	pale, almost transparent	mild		cooking
Winesap	yellow streaked, red	tangy	firm	all-purpose
Worcestar Pearmain	yellow flushed with bright red	strawberry	firm	eating, cooking
Wright	lemon yellow with pinkish red blush	musty, aromatic, vinous	tender white	
York Imperial	yellow streaked red	tartly sweet	off white, moderately firm	cooking

APRICOT

VARIETY	SKIN COLOR	FLESH	FLAVOR	USE
Blenheim	deep golden	yellow	sweet-tart, honeyed	fresh, canning, dried
Early Golden	golden yellow	whitish-yellow	sweet, rich, juicy	fresh, canning, dried
Early Rivers	red-blushed yellow		sweet	
Moorpark	red with yellow	yellow	sweet	canning, dried, fresh
Stark Tilton	yellow-orange	whitish-yellow	sweet	

LEMON

VARIETY	COLOR/SHAPE	PULP	FLAVOR	USE
Eureka	yellow, elliptical, rough	greenish-yellow, tender	very acid	juice, pies
Femminello Ovale	short-elliptic, medium size, blunt nipple	tender, juicy	very acid	juice
Genoa	ovate-oblong, yellow	medium juicy	acid	
Interdonato	oblong, pointed nipple	greenish-yellow	very acid, slightly bitter	juice
Lisbon	elliptical to oblong	pale greenish-yellow, juicy	very acid, few seeds	all-purpose
Meyer (cross of lemon and orange)	obovate, elliptical or oblong, light orange	pale orange-yellow	moderately acidic with medium lemon flavor	concentrate, preserves, used in cooking
Ponderosa	obovate, lumpy, light orange-yellow	pale green	juicy, acid	home use

NECTARINE

VARIETY	SKIN COLOR	FLESH	FLAVOR	USE
Early Rivers	red-blushed yellow		mild	
Goldmine	red-blushed white	white	rich, sweet	
Karla Rose	red	white	mild, sweet	cooking, fresh
Red Gold	red-blushed yellow	white	good	
Sun Gold	orange-red	firm	aromatic	fresh, cooking
Sun Red	red	yellow	sweet	fresh, cooking

PEACH

VARIETY	SKIN COLOR/ SHAPE	FLESH	FLAVOR	USE
Elberta (freestone)	yellow with red	yellow	sweet	fresh, canning, cooking
Elegant Lady (freestone)	red over yellow	yellow, firm	sweet, balanced	fresh

VARIETY	SKIN COLOR/ SHAPE	FLESH	FLAVOR	USE
Giant Babcock (freestone)	red, large	white	sweet, aromatic	fresh
Golden Jubilee (freestone)	yellow brushed with red, oblong	yellow	sweet	fresh, canning
Indian Blood (clingstone)	red	red	rich	canning
Nectar (freestone)	dark pink blush over cream	white tinged with red	sweet	fresh
Peento	squat, spherical	crisp, juicy	honeylike	fresh
Peregrine	orange-flushed golden	yellowish-white	sweet	fresh
Redskin (freestone)	red-blushed yellow	yellowish-white	sweet	
Suncrest (freestone)	large, red over yellow	very firm, yellow	sweet, juicy	fresh
White Heath (clingstone)	creamy white	white, juicy	meltingly rich	canning
White Lady (freestone)	red, medium to large	white, firm	sweet, well-balanced	fresh

PEAR

VARIETY	SKIN COLOR/ SHAPE	TEXTURE	FLAVOR	USE
Abbé	greenish brown with red blush	good	sweet	dessert
Althorp Crasanne	brown-spotted yellow	firm	sweet spicy	eating
Anjou (also known as Beurré d' Anjou)	broad, lopsided shape, russet marked yellowish	firm	sweet succulent	eating or cooking
Bartlett	bell-shaped, red blushed yellow-green	tender	sweet, musky	fresh, canned, baked, poached, salads
Bosc (also known as Beurré Bosc)	long, tapering neck, dark yellow with russet	slightly gritty	sweet, buttery, aromatic	all-purpose
Clapp Favorite	broad based, greenish-yellow, some russeting	granular	sweet	dessert

VARIETY	SKIN COLOR / SHAPE	TEXTURE	FLAVOR	USE
Comice (also known as Doyenné du Comice)	broad, blunt shape, greenish-yellow to red-blushed yellow	smooth, firm	sweet, aromatic	dessert
Conference	russet, long, thin shape	firm	sweet	cooking
Durondeau	rust-blushed green and yellow	ivory flesh	sweet	
Jargonelle		gritty	distinctive aroma	dessert and cooking
Josephine de Malines	pink flesh		hyacinthlike aroma	
Louise Bonne de Jersey	yellow with red blush and red spots	juicy	sweet	
Merton Pride	yellow	soft and juicy	strong flavor	eating
Olivier de Serres	greenish-brown, squat, short neck			dessert
Passe crasanne	dull greenish-brown, big and broad	coarse	well flavored	cooking
Perry pears	small		bitter, astringent	juice
Red Bartlett	yellow flushed with red	juicy	sweet	
Rocha	greenish-yellow with russet or brown spots	firm	sugary	
Seckel	brownish yellow and russeted with red blush	granular	spicy	
Tientsin	spherical, pale yellow, rough	firm, juicy, crisp, grainy	sweet	
Warden	small			cooking
Williams bon Chrétien	dull green with red blush, also clear green and red kinds		pleasantly musky	dessert, cooking, canning
Winter Nelis	roundish, medium-sized, greenish-yellow with cinnamon-brown russeting and rough skin	soft and juicy	sweet and spicy	all-purpose

PLUM

VARIETY	SKIN COLOR	FLESH	FLAVOR	USE
American beach	red, yellow or purple		sweet	preserves
Beach, wild	dark purple	dark purple	tart, slightly bitter grapelike	jams, jellies, condiment for meat
Cherry	red, yellow or purple	juicy	sweet	
Damson	bluish-black, medium ovoid	bluish-red	sweet, spicy	pies, preserves
Gaviota	reddish-yellow, large	ruby-colored, juicy	sweet	
Golden Transparent	yellow		sweet	
Japanese	orange-red or golden, large, conical		mild, sweet	
Laxton's gage; Laxton's supreme	reddish-yellow		very sweet	
Pearl	yellow	yellow	rich, sweet	
Quetsch	mauve	yellow	aromatic	baked goods, preserves, brandy
Red Diamond	reddish-purple	red, juicy	sweet	
Victoria	yellow heavily flushed with scarlet, large, ovoid	golden yellow	sweet	
Washington	reddish-yellow		very sweet	
Wild	red or yellow, very small		tart	

POTATO

VARIETY	SKIN COLOR	FLESH	SHAPE	USE
All Blue	purple	blue	oblong	chips, mashed
Arran Pilot	brown	firm, waxy	medium	boiling
Bintje	golden-brown	yellow	high-yield	
Burbank Russet	brown	white, mealy	long, heavy, smooth	baking
Charlotte	light yellow	yellow	long oval	boiling, salad
Chef's	same as white, round			
Creamers	light brown	white	small, round	steaming, roasting
Estima	light brown	pale yellow, moist, firm		boiling, general purpose
Fingerling	light brown	low starch	finger-shaped	roasting, salad

VARIETY	SKIN COLOR	FLESH	SHAPE	USE
Idaho	Same as Burbank Russet			
Irish	brown	creamy	spherical	boiling, frying, roasting
Kerr's Pink	pink	floury white	round	baking, general purpose
King Edward	white with pink coloration	cream to pale yellow, floury	oval to long oval	baking, chips, roasting, mashing
Maris Piper	pale yellow	creamy white, floury	short oval	chips, roasting, baking, boiling
Négresse	purple-black	purple-white mottled	small, long, thin	boiling
Ozette	yellow	yellow	small, long	
Purple Peruvian	deep purple	purple, mealy	moderately long, slightly spherical	baking
Ratte	creamy	white, nutty taste	long oval	cook in skins, salad
Red skinned	red	white, waxy	round	salad, scalloped, boiling
Rooster	red	pale yellow, floury	round	baking, frying, general purpose
Roseval	carmine	yellow waxy	oval	salad
Sato imo	dark brown, hairy	pale gray		
Satsuma imo	red	golden yellow, slightly sweet		
White, long	gray-brown	waxy white or yellow	long, slightly rounded	boiling, sautéing
White, round	pale gray-brown	tender, waxy yellow or white	spherical	boiling, all-purpose
White rose	gray-brown	waxy white	long, slightly rounded	boiling, sautéing
Yellow Finn or Finnish yellow	golden	creamy yellow, buttery	spherical	all-purpose
Yukon gold	golden	yellow, buttery, almost nutty in flavor	lightly flat and oval	baking, boiling, frying, mashing

STRAWBERRY

VARIETY	SHAPE/SIZE	FLAVOR	JUNEBEARING	USE
Alpine	small, tapered conical	intense		eating
Baron Solemacher	relatively large	mild		eating
Chilean Pine	large	pineapple	yes	eating
Earlyglow	small	sweet	yes	fresh, processing
Little Scarlet	small	intense	yes	preserves
Louisiana	small	sweet		eating
Ozark Beauty	large	sweet	ever-bearing	
Reine des vallées	small	similar to wild berry		
Rugen	small	sweet	yes	eating
Scarlet Virginian	large	sweet	yes	eating
Titan	very large	excellent	yes	eating, processing
Tribune	large	tart	ever-bearing	fresh, processing
Tristar	medium	very sweet	ever-bearing	fresh

TOMATO

VARIETY	COLOR	FLESH	SIZE/SHAPE	USE
Alisa Craig	red	juicy	large, spherical	slicing
Amish paste	bright red	meaty	medium	sauces, canning, slicing
Anna Russian	pink-red	excellent	large, heart-shaped	
Beefmaster	red	meaty	large	slicing
Beefsteak	bright red	juicy with many seeds	slightly squat, elliptical	slicing or cooking
Better Boy	deep red, smooth	meaty	large	all-purpose
Big Beef	red	meaty, firm, juicy	globe-shaped, smooth	salad, slicing, canning
Big Boy	scarlet red	meaty	large, smooth, firm	slicing
Black Krim	maroon	purple-red, earthy taste	medium-large	slicing, salads
Black Plum	deep mahogany to brown	excellent flavor	elongated, cherry	

VARIETY	COLOR	FLESH	SIZE/SHAPE	USE
Black Prince	garnet-red	juicy green, rich flavor	small	salads
Brandywine	dark reddish pink	meaty, flavorable	large, boat-shaped	slicing
Cherokee Purple	dark maroon	low acid	lobed, flat shape	slicing
Costoluto Genovese	red	firm, sweet	deeply ridged	
Currant	red or yellow	flavorable	small	garnish
Early Girl	red	flavorable	medium	slicing
Eva's Purple Ball	pinkish-purple	juicy, sweet flavor	spherical, small	
Evergreen	green	tomato flavor	medium	salad
Golden Jubilee	deep orange	juicy	medium, round	soups, sauces
Golden Sunrise	yellow-orange	yellow-orange, fruity	small, spherical	salads
Ida Gold	orange, yellow-orange	juicy	cherry	salad
Lemon Boy	yellow	yellow, lemony flavor	medium, oblate	salad, slicing, cold soup
Marble Stripe	pink and red	mild acid	medium	salads, cooking
Roma	red or yellow	meaty	medium, ovoid	sauce, slicing
Royal Flush	red		slightly flat	fresh, sauce
Sugar cherry	red	juicy	extremely small (pea-size)	garnish
Sun Gold	orange	sweet	bite-size, spherical	salads
Sweet Million	red	sweet	cherry	salads
Sweet 100	red	sweet	cherry	salads
Washington	red	flavorful	cherry	
Zebra Stripe	amber with dark green stripes	acidic	small to medium	salads

COMMON FOOD LABELING TERMS

THE FOOD AND DRUG ADMINISTRATION regulations use certain terms to describe the level of a nutrient or calories in a food. Serving size refers to the serving size on the product label.

Free: A term used to describe a food that contains no amount or only a trivial amount of certain nutrients or calories. Synonyms for free are "without," "no" and "zero."

calorie-free or **no calories**—less than 5 calories per serving.
cholesterol-free—less than 2 mg per serving and 2 g or less of saturated fat per serving.
fat-free—less than 0.5 g per serving.
saturated-fat free—less than 0.5 g per serving.
sodium-free—less than 5 mg per serving.
sugar-free—less than 0.5 g per serving.

Lean and extra lean: Terms used to describe the fat content of meat, poultry, seafood and game meats.

lean—less than 10 g fat, 4.5 g or less saturated fat and less than 95 mg cholesterol per serving and per 100 g.

extra lean—less than 5 g fat, less than 2 g saturated fat and less than 95 mg cholesterol per serving and per 100 g.

Low: A term used for foods that can be eaten frequently without exceeding dietary guidelines. Synonyms for low include "little," "few," "low source of" and "contains a small amount of."

low-fat—3 g or less per serving.

low-saturated fat—1 g or less per serving.

low-sodium—140 mg or less per serving.

low-cholesterol—20 mg or less and 2 g or less of saturated fat per serving.

low-calorie—less than 40 calories per serving.

Reduced: A term used for a food that has been nutritionally altered to contain less than 25 percent of a nutrient or calories than a reference or regular product.

reduced-calorie—at least 25 percent fewer calories than a product's regular form.

reduced fat—at least 25 percent less fat than found in a product's regular form.

reduced saturated fat—same as reduced fat, but in reference to saturated fat.

reduced cholesterol—at least 25 percent less cholesterol than found in a product's regular form and 2 g or less saturated fat per serving.

reduced sugar—at least 25 percent less sugar than found in a product's regular form.

reduced sodium—at least 25 percent less sodium than found in a product's regular form.

Other Definitions:

added fiber or **more fiber**—2.5 g or more per serving.

enriched or **fortified**—contains 10 percent or more of the per serving Daily Value for protein, vitamins, minerals, dietary fiber or potassium.

fresh—food that is raw, has never been frozen or heated and contains no preservatives.

fresh frozen, flash frozen, frozen fresh, freshl frozen—food that is quickly frozen from it fresh state.

good source of—a food that contains 10 to 19 percent of the Daily Value for a particular nutrient in a serving.

good source of fiber—2.5 to 4.9 g per serving.

high fiber—5 g or more per serving.

high in, rich in, excellent source of—a food that contains 20 percent or more of the Daily Value for a particular nutrient in a serving.

less—a food, altered or not, contains 25 percent or less of a nutrient or calories than the reference food.

light, lite—a nutritionally altered food that contains one-third fewer calories or half the fat of the reference food.

light in sodium—a food in which the sodium content has been reduced by at least 50 percent.

more—a food, altered or not, that contains a nutrient that is at least 10 percent of the Daily Value more than the reference food.

natural—a product that has no artificial ingredients or intentional additives.

natural flavorings—flavorings derived from plant material; may contain hydrolyzed protein and hydrolyzed vegetable protein (HVP) both of which contain monosodium glutamate (MSG).

Percent Daily Value—nutrient reference values (recommended daily amount) that help consumers see how a food fits into an overall daily diet.

percent fat free—a product that must be low-fat or fat-free and accurately reflect the amount of fat present in 100 g of the food (ex., ground beef that is 97% fat-free).

rich in, excellent source of—a food that contains 20 percent or more of the Daily Value per serving.

unsalted or **no salt added**—no salt used during processing.

Health Claims:

calcium and osteoporosis—a food must contain 20 percent or more of the Daily Value for calcium

(200 mg) per serving, have a calcium content that equals or exceeds the food's content of phosphorus and contain a form of calcium that can be readily absorbed and used by the body.

fat and cancer—a food must meet the nutrient content claim requirements for "low-fat" or "extra lean."

fiber-containing grain products, fruits and vegetables and cancer—a food must be or must contain a grain product, fruit or vegetable and meet the nutrient content claim requirements for "low-fat," and, without fortification, be a "good source" of dietary fiber.

fruits, vegetables and grain products that contain fiber and risk of coronary heart disease (CHD)—a food must be or must contain fruits, vegetables and grain products and meet the nutrient content claim for "low-saturated fat," "low-cholesterol," and "low-fat" and contain, without fortification, at least 0.6 g soluble fiber per serving.

fruits and vegetables and cancer—foods must meet the nutrient content claim requirements for "low-fat" and that, without fortification, for "good source" of dietary fiber or vitamins A and C.

saturated fat and cholesterol and coronary heart disease (CHD)—a food must meet the nutrient content claim of "low-saturated fat," "low-cholesterol," and "low-fat," or, if fish or game meats, for "extra lean."

sodium and hypertension (high blood pressure)—a food must meet the nutrient content claim requirements for "low-sodium."

soluble fiber from certain foods, such as whole oats and psyllium seed husk and heart disease—the fiber needs to be part of a diet low in saturated fat and cholesterol, and the food must provide sufficient soluble fiber.

PASTA TERMS

acini di pepe (ah-CHEE-nay dee PAY-pay) "Peppercorns," rice-shaped pasta.

agnolotti (ahn-nyoa-LOT-tee) Crescent-shaped ravioli.

alfabeto (ahl-fah-BEH-toh) Pasta in the shape of letters.

amorini (ah-mah-REE-nee) "Little cupids," small pasta in the shape of cupids.

anelli (ah-NEH-lee) " Rings," used in soups.

anellini (ah-NEH-lee-ni) "Little rings," small pasta rings used in soup.

anellini regati (ah-NEH-lee ni ree-gah-tee) "Gears," grooved rings of pasta.

angel hair *See* capelli d'angelo.

anolini (ah-noh-Lee-nee) Small, half-moon–shaped ravioli with ruffled edges.

astri (as-tree) "Stars," pasta in the shape of small stars.

avena (ha-vae-nah) "Oats," pasta in the shape of small, dimpled disks.

bavattini (bah-ve-tee-nae) Very narrow bavette.

bavette (bah-VEH-the) Oval ribbons of pasta.

bigoli (BEE-goh-lee) Spaghetti-shaped whole wheat pasta.

bucati (boo-CAH-tee) Hollow or pierced pasta.

bucatini (boo-kah-TEE-nee) Thin, straight, tubular dried pasta, slightly thicker than spaghetti.

cannelle (kahn-eh-LEE) "Small reeds," large, hollow pasta.

cannelloni (kahn-eh-LONE ee) "Large reeds," large, hollow rings of pasta, usually boiled, stuffed and baked and served with a sauce and grated cheese.

capelli d'angelo (kah-PEH-lee D'AHN-jeh-loh) "Angel's hair," very thin, long strands of pasta; also known as angel hair pasta.

capellini (kahp-payl-LEE-nee) "Fine hair," extremely fine spaghetti.

capelvenere (cah-pel-va-neh-rae) "Maidenhair fern," very fine strands of pasta used in soups.

cappelletti (kahp-PAYL-et-tee) "Little hats," small dumplings in the shape of a peaked hat.

cappelli di prete (kahp-PAYL-lee de pray-tee) "Priests' hats," pasta in the shape of a priest's hat.

cappelli pagliaccio (kahp-PAYL-lee pah-glee-ACH-chee-oh) "Clowns' hats," pasta in the shape of a clown's hat.

cavatappi (kah-vah-TAH-pee) Corkscrew-shaped pasta.

cavatelli (kah-vah-TEH-lee) Narrow, crinkle-edged shells.

chifferi (KEE-feh-ree) Small (1-inch), moon-shaped macaroni.

chiocciolo (kee-yoh-chee-OH-LOH) "Snail," short, ribbed, snail-shaped pasta.

conchiglie (kon-KEE-l'yeh) "Shells," shell-shaped pasta, usually with ridges.

coralli (ko-rah-lee) "Coral," small smooth or ribbed tubes of pasta, usually used in soups.

crescione (cray-SHOW-nay) Crescent-shaped pasta used to garnish soups.

creste di galli (KRES-teh dee GAH-lee) "Cockscombs," a curved pasta shape with curly edges.

ditali (dee-TAH-lee) "Thimbles," small, short, curved pasta tubes.

ditalini (dee-TAH-lee-nee) Small ditali, usually used in minestrone.

elbow macaroni Small, semicircular tubes of pasta.

farasine (fah-rah-seen) Ribbon-shaped pasta.

farfalle (fah-FAHL-lay) "Butterfly," bow-shaped pasta; also known as pasta bows and bowties.

fedelini (feh-duh-lee-nee) Long, thin pasta strands.

fettucce riccie (feht-tuh-chay ree-tchee-a) "Curly ribbons," narrow pasta ribbons with one ruffled edge.

fettuccine (feht-too-CHEE-nee) Thin, flat ribbons of pasta.

fusilli (foo-SEEL-lee) "Twists," spiral-shaped pasta, usually served with thick sauces.

fusilli bucati (foo-SEEL-lee boo-cah-tee) Spirals of pasta tubes with a hole.

gemilli (ge-mel-lee) "Twins," a pasta shape in which one side is folded and turned to look like two joined strands.

gigantoni (jee-gahn-TOH-nee) " Super giants," very large macaroni, about 2 inches long and 1½ inches wide.

gramigna (grah-MEE-n'yah) "Grass," curly pasta with a hole in the middle.

grattini (grah-TEE-nee) Tiny pasta used in soups; looks like grated cheese.

lancette (lahn-chay-tay) "Spear," spear-shaped pasta used for soup.

lasagna; *pl.* **lasagne** (lah-ZAH-n'yeh) Wide, flat pasta noodles with ruffled or smooth edges.

linguine (leen-GWEE-neh) "Little tongues," long, narrow, slightly flattened ribbons of pasta.

lumache (loo-MAA-chay) "Snails," snail-shaped pasta.

macaroni Elbow-shaped tubes of pasta.

maccheroni (mah-keh-ROH-nee) Italian for macaroni.

mafalde (mah-FAHL-day) Pasta ribbons with ruffled edges, wider than fettuccine and narrower than lasagna.

maglietti (mah-glee-ET-tee) "Link," short, slightly curved rods of pasta.

maltagliato (mahl-tah-L'YAH-tee) Irregularly shaped flat ribbons of pasta with corners cut on the bias.

mandilli de saêa (mahn-DEE-lee deh SAY'ah) "Silk handkerchiefs," thin sheets of pasta dough served with pesto.

manicotti (mah-nee-KOH-tee) Hollow tubes of pasta, 4–5 inches long; usually boiled and stuffed and served with a sauce.

Margherita "Daisy," narrow pasta ribbon with one ruffled edge.

maruzze (mah-rou-tze) "Seashell," conch-shaped pasta available in several sizes; the larger sizes are usually stuffed.

mezzani (medz-DZAHN-nee) "Medium," medium-length maccheroni.

mostaccioli (mos-tah-chee-OH-lee) "Little mustaches," medium-sized pasta shells with ends cut on a diagonal.

nastrini (nas-tree-nee) Small pasta bows with a zigzag edge all around.

occhi di lupo (OH-kee de loo-poh) "Wolf's eyes," large tubes of pasta.

occhi di passeri (OH-kee de PAH-she-reh) "Sparrow eyes," tiny rings of pasta used for soups.

orecchiette (oh-reh-K'YEH-the) "Small ears," pasta that is formed from a twist of the fingertips; tiny disk shapes.

orzo (OHR-zoh) "Barley," rice-shaped pasta.

Paglia e fieno (PAY-ya ee FYE-noh) "Straw and hay," thin, flat ribbons of yellow and green pasta.

pansôti; pansotti (pan-SOHT-tee) "Pot bellied," triangular-shaped stuffed ravioli with zigzag edges.

panzarotti (pahn-zah-ROH-tee) "Little bellies," pasta half-moons that are boiled or fried.

pappardelle (pah-pahr-DEH-leh) "Gulp down," long, flat, broad noodles; usually served with a game sauce.

passatelli (pah-sah-TELL-lee) Very thin pasta ribbons.

pastini (pahs-STEE-nee) Very small pasta usually used for broth-based soups.

penne (PEN-nay) "Pen or quill," short- to medium-length straight tubes (ridged or smooth) of pasta with diagonally cut ends.

perciatelli (pehr-ch'yah-TEH-lee) Thin, straight, hollow pasta.

pizzoccheri (pee-T'ZOH-keh-ree) Thick, dark-colored pasta strips made from buckwheat flour.

pulchini (pool-tchee-knee) "Little chickens," pastini in the shape of small chickens.

quadrettini (kwah-drae-tee-nee) Small, square, flat pasta.

quadrucci (kwah-DROO-chee) Stuffed pasta squares used in soup.

radiatori (rah-dee-ah-TOH-ree) "Radiator," a pasta shape that resembles a radiator heater.

ravioli (rav-ee-OH-lee) "Little wraps," small squares or rounds (sometimes with ridges) of stuffed pasta.

ricci (REE-chee) "Curly," various widths of flat pasta strips that have one or both edges wavy or rippled.

ricciolini (ree-tchee-oh-lee-nee) "Little curls," wavy strips of pasta.

rigati (ree-gah-tee) Pasta that has a grooved or ridged surface.

rigatoni (ree-gah-TOE-nee) Large, grooved, slightly curved pasta tubes.

rotelle (roh-tell-lae) Pasta shaped like a wheel with spokes.

rotini (roh-TEE-nee) Short spirals of pasta.

ruote; ruote di carro (roo-OH-the dee KAH-roh) "Cartwheels," small, spoked wheel-shaped pasta.

seashell pasta *See* conchiglie.

semi di melone (SEH-mee dee meh-LOH-nee) "Melon seeds," small melon seed-shaped pasta used in soup.

spaghetti (spah-GEH-tee) "Little strings," long, thin, round strands of pasta.

spaghettini (spah-geh-TEE-nee) Very thin spaghetti.

stelline (steh-LEE-neh) "Little stars," tiny star-shaped pasta with a hole in the middle; used in soups.

stivaletti (stee-vah-lae-tea) "Little boots," pastini in the shape of boots.

tagliarini (tahl-yah-REE-nee) Long, flat, thin strips of pasta approximately 0.15 in. wide.

tagliatelle (tahl-yuh-TEHL-ee) Long, flat, thin strips of pasta approximately 0.75 in. wide.

tagliolette (tah-yoh-LAY-tay) Long, flat, thin strips of pasta approximately 0.5 in. wide.

tagliolini (tah-yoh-LEE-nee) Long, flat, thin strips of pasta approximately 0.25 in. wide.

tonnarelli (ton-nah-RAL-lee) Very thin pasta ribbons; known as pasta alla chitarra.

tortelli (tohr-TEH-lee) "Little cakes," fat, elongated ravioli.

tortellini (tohr-te-LEEN-ee) "Small twists," small stuffed pasta shaped like a ring.

tortelloni (tohr-te-LONE-ee) Large tortellini.

tortiglioni (tohr-tee-LYOH-nee) Large, spiral-edged tubes of pasta.

trenette (treh-NEH-the) Thin strips of pasta, usually served with pesto.

trenne (TREN-neh) Triangular penne.

tubetti (too-BEH-tee) "Little tubes," tiny, hollow tubes of pasta.

tufoli (too-FOE-lee) Large pasta tubes; used for stuffing.

vermicelli (vehr-mee-CHEH-lee) "Little worms," very thin spaghetti, less than 1/10 in. thick.

ziti (ZEE-tee) "Bridegrooms," thin tubes of pasta ranging from 2 to 12 in. in length.

zitoni (TSEET-toh-neh) Large, grooved ziti.